Ordinary Sisters

The Story of the

Sisters of St. Agnes

1858-1990

ORDINARY SISTERS

THE STORY OF THE

SISTERS OF ST. AGNES

1858-1990

MARGARET LORIMER, CSA

Published by the Congregation of Sisters of St. Agnes
320 County Road K
Fond du Lac, WI 54935
www.csasisters.org

Cover art, "Ordinary Sisters" © by Artist Doris Klein, CSA
Text and page design by Marilyn Ellickson, CSA

Printed in the United States of America
Action Printing
N6637 Rolling Meadows Drive
Fond du Lac, WI 54935
www.actionprinting.com

Library of Congress PCN: 2005927813

ISBN: 978-0-9769983-0-3 (softcover)
         978-0-9769983-1-0 (hardcover)

CONTENTS

Foreword

Ordinary Sisters recounts the congregation's founding by Austrian missionary Father Caspar Rehrl and the early struggles and challenges it faced in schooling immigrant children at the same time it educated and provided spiritual formation to its own members on the Wisconsin frontier. The book both thoroughly reviews historical evidence and explores individual lives, as a reminder that a congregation is much more than the story of its founders, its administrators, or its institutions. It is the story of pioneer women, girls even, who were willing to sacrifice everything they possessed to respond to a call to follow the gospel.

Response to that call is traced from Mother Agnes Hazotte's extending the geographical range and variety of the congregation's missions, increasing membership, and creating institutions to serve local needs, through an era of rapid growth and expansion, to the Second Vatican Council, and the turbulence and questioning of vocations wrought by the 1960's and '70's. The stereotypes of popular culture sometimes obscure what Margaret Lorimer, CSA, recaptures in her narrative: the "entrepreneurial" work of religious in founding institutions for United States and Latin American education, health care, and community well-being. In addition to teaching in parish schools from Wisconsin, Kansas, to Pennsylvania and New York, the congregation established hospitals, served in orphanages, staffed a hostel to aid newly-arrived German immigrants in New York City, high schools, a nursing home, and a college. It also looked beyond United States borders in Nicaraguan missions.

This volume treats the inner life of the congregation, discussing tensions arising from the ordinary conflicts attendant upon the establishment of any idealistic venture. From the great adaptability and flexibility of its early years, the congregation moved to more restricted dress and a lifestyle that limited contact with the laity. Responding to the call of Vatican II, the congregation chose to live as contemporary women. Today, after rapid shifts in norms in the 1970's and '80's, issues have arisen around what constitutes community for members choosing their own missions in a variety of living arrangements away from convents. Throughout, Sister Margaret addresses not only what decisions the congregation made about how to change, but how it made them in communal discernment.

"Few persons in the first half of the twentieth century," Sister Sandra Schneiders reminds us, "possessed as much power over a large group of individuals as the superior general of a religious congregation."[1] In its profiles of each of the congregation's superiors and discussions of the challenges she faced, *Ordinary Sisters* offers an important contribution to the study of women in leadership of an organization that rivals most others in complexity and scope.

Told in the context of world events and Church history, the story of the congregation ranges from controversy over Bingo in Yonkers, New York, to ethical and social issues raised by the revolution in Nicaragua. This retelling, carefully crafted from historical documents and living memory, is a tribute to a legacy and to an institution that continues to live the gospel in new ways.

Henry L. Lindborg, Ph. D.
July 29, 2006

---

1. Sandra M. Schneiders, IHM, *Finding the Treasure: Locating Catholic Religious Life in a New Cultre and Ecclesial Context* (New Jersey: Paulist Press, 2000), 165.

Introduction

Ordinary Sisters is the history of one congregation of women religious and the lives of the women who made such communities possible. Unique in some ways, the story of the Sisters of St. Agnes is also very much that of thousands of other sisters.

In 1790, four Carmelite nuns established the first convent in the United States for prayer and contemplation. In 1860, two years after the Sisters of St. Agnes were founded, there were over five thousand women religious. The majority were not technically nuns as were the Carmelites, but sisters, women who combined prayer and action in the service of the church. They were teachers and nurses, social workers and housekeepers, but they also founded, administered, and staffed charitable institutions. No task was too difficult or too menial if it was God's work.

By the middle of the twentieth century, sisters were experiencing growing tension between the medieval rules under which they lived and the world in which they prayed and worked. Even so, when the Second Vatican Council called religious to renewal and adaptation to this world, sisters were faced with a profound dilemma. The decision of the Sisters of St. Agnes to make a whole-hearted response to that call led to several decades of confusion. It led also to new life as sisters struggled to find ways to be faithful to their heritage as they discovered new ways to serve God in a world torn by injustice and poverty.

The first Sisters of Saint Agnes, although governed by the centuries-old canon law of the church, were still women of the frontier. Almost one hundred and fifty years later they are women formed by the culture of their own time and place but remain devoted to the service of God in the fields of education, health care, and social service. Today they are engaged in promoting systemic change for the quality of life through individual ministries, their sponsored institutions, and collaboration in movements furthering economic justice for the poor and the role of women in church and society.

This history could not have been written without the help of many people. They prayed. They provided documents, letters, and memories. They agreed to interviews, reviewed the manuscript and made suggestions. Some were Sisters of St. Agnes. Some were not. Their interest and belief that this history should be written provided a much-needed spark of motivation. I am most grateful to them all.

Chapter I

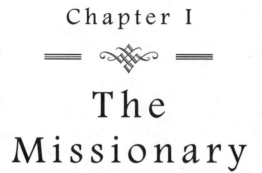

The
Missionary

The Sisters of St. Agnes count as their founders one woman and two men but, at no time did the three plan or work together to form a religious community. The woman, Mother Agnes Hazotte, years later would matter-of-factly comment that "our community sprang up among thorns; and many dark clouds of adversity passed over its head during the short period of its existence."[1] While each one of them would eventually rejoice over the congregation's founding, it was the man with the original dream and vision who paid the greatest price. That man was Caspar Rehrl, who came from Austria to Wisconsin with an early wave of German immigrants.

CASPAR REHRL

Caspar Rehrl was born on December 31, 1809, in Aigen, a little village on the outskirts of Salzburg in the Austrian Empire. It was a time of great political upheavals, felt even in the small hamlets and cottages in the valleys of the Alps. Europe was still in the grip of Napoleon. That very year the Austrians had launched an unsuccessful war against the French, but Phillip and Walburga Rehrl were too busy with their six daughters and five sons to worry much about Austria's ever-changing military and political situation. The Rehrls, known for their piety and honesty, belonged to the artisan class. To support his growing family, Phillip Rehrl was a baker, a miller, and a maker of water jars.[2]

The family was also a loving one.[3] Caspar, the eldest, enjoyed both his studies and the outdoors. He did so well in the local parish school that when he was fourteen, he was able to attend the Royal and Imperial Lyceum in Salzburg as a scholarship student. He lived with his uncle, a priest, and began his studies for the priesthood as a typical impoverished student. One of his contemporaries, Michael Heiss, later Archbishop of Milwaukee, wrote of his school days there, "Bread and the like was furnished to me from home. Only once a day I got some warm food, a scanty dinner costing about six or eight kreuzers (three or four cents). For breakfast I had a piece of bread and the same for supper; and only now and then a glass of beer."[4]

Although the living conditions of the young men inured them to the hardships they would later experience on the frontier, the curriculum at that time was scarcely designed to prepare young men for pastoral work, much less missionary work. Scripture, philosophy, theology, canon law, Hebrew, Latin, Greek, French, and English were part of the seminary's curriculum. Caspar also studied Syriac, Chaldaic, and Arabic. He took his studies seriously, eventually receiving his doctorate in theology.[5] In one of his school compositions he wrote, "The better you apply yourselves to the higher studies the firmer will be your principles in holy religion and the greater your joy afterwards in your priestly life to conduct the children of God to the heavenly fatherland."[6] In spite of the stringent seminary course, he took time to hike around the mountains of Salzburg. He loved to study the plants of the area and was particularly fascinated by medicinal herbs.

Because priests of the time still catechized the children, Caspar obtained a normal school license in 1828. Like other young men at twenty-one, he was liable for military service and in 1830 served a short time in the Austrian army. Back at his studies, he earned another teaching license and progressed uneventfully towards his ordination as a priest on September 20, 1835, at the age of twenty-six. After spending a short time as curate at Henndorf near

Salzburg, he was appointed as assistant in a parish in Nonnenthal, where he served until 1840. Father Rehrl was living the traditional life of the young priest in Central Europe. He was doubly fortunate that in many German-speaking areas the church was recovering from the Napoleonic attacks on Christianity and experiencing a revitalization that would produce Catholics ablaze with love of their faith.

One result of this religious renewal was an enthusiastic interest in the overseas missions. The Leopoldine Society was founded in 1829 and, patronized by affluent and devout Catholics, supported Austrian missionary priests by helping to underwrite their work.[7] The society also published its *Annals* and letters from the priests on the missions. Among the priests the society helped over the years were the first three Archbishops of Milwaukee.

While the religious environment was improving, political and economic upheavals resulting from both the French and Industrial Revolutions were rapidly destroying the centuries-old agricultural society of Central Europe. Peasants and craftsmen were suffering economic distress. Overpopulation, crop failures, loss of land, fear of military conscription, and, in some cases, religious persecution and forced emigration were all factors leading to emigration to new lands. Enthusiastic letters from the United States extolling the cheap and abundant land, lower taxes, political freedom, and social equality gave compelling reasons to the courageous, desperate, or merely adventurous to undertake the dangerous voyage to America.

A CALL TO THE MISSIONS

The young priest was swept up in the general interest in missionary activity. He had spent nine productive, but uneventful, years serving in parishes around Salzburg; but he was an active, vigorous man and a wholehearted priest. To carry the faith to the Americas was a challenge his ardent nature found difficult to resist. One brother, Stephen, was a priest, and the rest of the family was in adequate circumstances; so there was no reason why he could not become a missionary. In the autumn of 1843, he petitioned the Chancery Office for permission to serve in the New York diocese. His prudence, however, cautioned him to seek permission to be re-admitted into the Salzburg diocese if he should desire to return to Europe.

The reference Rehrl submitted to the prefect of the Salzburg vicariate to support his request provides a glimpse into his character. Father Anton Ensmann, his pastor, attested that the young priest conducted himself "as a true priest and showed great zeal in preaching, in catechizing in school, in visiting the sick, and especially in his restless efforts in the confessional, but above all by his true exemplary conduct as a priest."[8] It was over a year before the permissions from the chancery office and the government arrived. By that time Rehrl had rejected New York as his destination and decided to go west into the recently opened territory of Wisconsin.[9] He booked his passage for the port of New Orleans, which allowed entrance to the Mississippi River and access to the frontier. The Leopoldine Society contributed four hundred florins (approximately one hundred and twelve dollars) and undoubtedly he had other funds from gifts and savings.[10]

In October 1844, the new missionary began his long and arduous journey. He left Salzburg by stagecoach for Paris by way of Kufstein, Munich, and Strasbourg, then by train to Rouen, and again by mail coach to Havre de Grace, where he boarded the three-masted packet, the *Tarquin*.

There were not many passengers on the schooner, fifty or sixty Germans and a sprinkling of Italians and French. Rehrl had little to say about his voyage other than recalling the heat he endured when the schooner made its way around Cuba and Santo Domingo. Typically, he spent many of the forty-two days on the schooner studying English with the help of a businessman from New Orleans. When the *Tarquin* arrived at New Orleans early in 1845, the same gentleman introduced his shipmate to Bishop Antoine Blanc, who welcomed him warmly and pointed out the impossibility of traveling on the Mississippi River until the ice had broken in spring.[11]

Bishop Blanc was in desperate need of priests for his rambunctious diocese. From 1837 to 1844 he engaged in a struggle with the French trustees of the cathedral over the appointment of a pastor. The controversy reached such a point that the bishop placed the cathedral under interdict.[12] The Louisiana Supreme Court finally ruled in favor of the bishop. Of the six or eight thousand German Catholics in his charge, many were indifferent and some were openly hostile to the church. The bishop, who was expecting a German priest, invited the missionary to remain and take charge of the

German congregation at the Church of St. Vincent de Paul. Rehrl agreed to stay for a time, and had the satisfaction of preparing twenty young people between the ages of twelve and seventeen for Holy Communion and Confirmation. They received the sacraments on April 28, 1845.[13]

Working with the recalcitrant Germans in New Orleans was not the kind of ministry Rehrl had in mind. He refused the bishop's invitation to remain in New Orleans and journeyed to Mobile, where he worked for a short time among the Germans there. An alms of $1.95 he sent to Father Martin Kundig[14] in Wisconsin brought him a description of the conditions among the poor German immigrants there and an invitation to join Kundig in his missionary work.

CATHOLIC WISCONSIN

Catholic priests followed the German immigrants into Wisconsin in the 1830s, although mission activity in Wisconsin had begun in 1661 when the Jesuit priest, René Menard, said the first Mass there while the territory was still claimed by the French. A few missionaries, Jesuit and Franciscan, penetrated the area but were unable to build a thriving church among the few scattered fur traders and natives. A mission established in Green Bay endured until 1728, leaving the closest Catholic mission 250 miles away in Mackinac. During the next hundred years, the territory had undergone no development although it became one of the spoils of war when England won it, as well as Canada, from France in 1763; and the United States acquired it twenty years later with the defeat of England in the Revolutionary War. After the defeat of the British in 1812, Wisconsin became part of the territory of Michigan. Beginning in 1817, priests again began to visit Wisconsin; and it seems probable that the first Mass was offered in Milwaukee by a Belgian, Florimond Bonduel, in 1835, a year before Wisconsin became a territory.

The territory boasted a terrain of great variety; it had plains, fields and forests, meadows and woods, rivers and lakes. The Fox and Wisconsin Rivers ran diagonally across the territory. Two important waterways afforded the territory unusual accessibility: the Great Lakes on the east linked it with the Northeast; the Mississippi

River on the west connected it with the Ohio Valley to the east and
with St. Louis and New Orleans in the south. The climate was similar to that of northern Europe, even though its summers surpassed
Europe in heat and its winters in bitter cold. The soil was fertile and
the land, cheap and abundant.

The end of the Indian wars, with the defeat of Chief Blackhawk
in 1832 and the subsequent removal of the Indian tribes, opened up
the territory. The first wave of new settlers were Eastern land spec-
ulators followed by farmers from New York and New England.
Emigrants from Germany began to arrive in small numbers as early
as 1831 but came in the thousands by the end of the decade. So
many of these new immigrants were Catholic that in 1843 a new
diocese was carved out of the Michigan diocese, with Milwaukee as
the See city. John Martin Henni, a highly-regarded leader of the
German Catholic community in Cincinnati, was appointed
Milwaukee's first bishop. In 1844, just one year before Rehrl
arrived, Bishop Henni counted twelve Catholic chapels in the diocese and fourteen priests, one of whom was German and the others
were Irish nationals. He noted that Catholics numbered about fifteen thousand, of whom the majority were German, and that immigration was rapidly increasing their number.[15] However, faith among
the German immigrants was not always the strongest; one priest
from Europe complained in a letter that "the few conversions of the
Americans are offset by the apostasy of many Catholics, particularly among our German countrymen."[16]

THE BISHOP AND THE MISSIONARY

Bishop Henni would prove to be a firm friend to Rehrl, and, indeed,
to all of his priests. A Swiss, he was born in 1805 and educated principally in Lucerne and Rome. When he was twenty-three, he came
to the United States at the request of the vicar general of the diocese of Cincinnati and was ordained there by Bishop Edward
Dominic Fenwick, OP.[17] In America he found a church wrestling
with a chronic shortage of priests and a steadily growing Catholic
population of poverty-stricken immigrants. The faith of these people had to be preserved as they entered into a Protestant and predominately secular society which feared and rejected them for a
faith apparently opposed to American democratic ideals. Within the

church itself there was the further challenge of balancing the ethnic and national tensions that quickly developed with the flood of immigrants. Henni was appointed pastor to work with the Germans in the first German parish in Cincinnati. His work led him to found the *Wahrsheit-Freund,* the first German Catholic newspaper in the United States, in 1837. His success there led to his appointment as bishop in the territory of Wisconsin, four years before it was admitted to the Union. Its population at the time, estimated to be between sixty-five thousand and seventy thousand, was concentrated in the southern part of the territory. Catholics, the greater number being German, numbered between eight thousand and ten thousand with the majority located south of the Wisconsin and Fox rivers and along the shore of Lake Michigan.

It was to this territory that Father Rehrl was determined to go. Fortunately, an Alsatian priest arrived who was willing to provide for the Germans in New Orleans. As soon as the Mississippi became navigable, Rehrl boarded a steamboat and set out for Wisconsin. Bishop Blanc had given him twenty dollars toward travel expenses, and for fifteen dollars he was able to get both cabin and board on the steamboat for the thousand-mile journey to St. Louis. Anxious to get to Milwaukee, he stayed only one day with Bishop Peter Kenrick, who invited him to remain in that diocese, then continued on to Peru, Illinois. There he took a stagecoach to Chicago where "a professor of the small seminary... exhausted all his eloquence to gain me for the diocese."[18] The professor's pleas were to no avail; Rehrl left the next day for Milwaukee.

Bishop Henni gladly welcomed the scholarly young priest to Milwaukee and urged him to assume a pastorate among the Germans there, but a city parish, even in a city as raw and unfinished as Milwaukee, was not what Rehrl had in mind. When the bishop invited him to look over territory in the Fox River Valley, meet the people, and decide if he could minister effectively there, he welcomed the offer.

The settlements he visited were in Calumet Township on the east shore of Lake Winnebago, the largest inland lake in Wisconsin. The lake, almost thirty miles long and ten miles wide, was only seventy-four miles from Milwaukee. Low marshy land lay along the shores of the lake with level prairie land and an abundance of fresh spring water at the south end. The area, home of the Indians of the

Winnebago tribe, contained some of the best land in the state, with its deep and rich soil and with fewer stones than on the land further east.[19] The settlements there became known as Calumet Harbor, Calumetville, and Pipe. Pipe, the principal village in the area, contained a store with goods for Indian trading.

Bishop Henni had described the Catholics there as a "good sort of people" from the diocese of Treve and Cologne. "After they have built a few huts to shelter their families and cultivated a little land, their first concern is building a church. They are at present engaged in the erection of frame chapels in four places."[20] Only four years earlier the first families had reached the area from neighboring Sheboygan. Others would come south from Green Bay or up the Fox River. In Germany most of the people were farmers or mechanics. Nearly all had enough money to buy either government land or improved farmlands, although usually all their resources had gone to acquiring the land for their new life. It would be some years before they would attain anything like a comfortable existence.[21] The majority of the newcomers were Catholics and soon began to assemble at the house of John Perord for prayers.

The three days Father Rehrl spent in the area holding divine services and hearing confessions convinced him that he had found God's will for him. Well-pleased with the situation, he returned to Milwaukee, where the bishop gave him charge of a region extending from the eastern shores of Lake Winnebago to the west shore of Lake Michigan, and from Milwaukee to Green Bay.

THE APOSTLE OF CALUMET

With his return to Calumet, Father Rehrl began his life as a missionary. At that time he was thirty-six years old. Of medium stature, his Alpine boyhood and his experiences in the army hardened him to endure the difficulties of field and forest, freezing Wisconsin winters, and sultry mosquito-laden summers. More importantly, "his strong will power which had been perfected through hard study, [and] his developed character ... helped him over many privations, which others would never have been able to bear."[22] If anything, his contemplative spirit seemed to thrive as he tramped the woods. And, doubtless it was these experiences that led him to write, "No step is lost, no drop of sweat is in vain, if one lives in grace and acts through the love of God."[23]

On his first mission trip, Father Rehrl set out with his chalice, crucifix, books, and other necessary paraphernalia on his back. The roads, former Indian trails, were not always clearly marked; some had sinkholes and hidden snags. There are few places darker than a forest, especially when the wolves are howling and bears are nearby. He slept on a layer of twigs or close to some fallen trees. He lost his way, but after three days and two nights, he came upon the cabin of Isaac Verbeck in what is now West Bend. There he spent the night, sleeping on the ground before the fire, and left the next morning. A day later he arrived in Fond du Lac, a trading post at the foot of Lake Winnebago where he said Mass in the home of a French family.[24]

The land he saw on the way to the village was striking; woodlands provided sugar maples, hickory and butternuts, wild fruit trees, wild grapevines, and berries. There were signs of the newcomers as trees were being felled to make room for crops of potatoes, corn, and wheat. The timber could often be sold at the lumber mills as well as provide material for the settlers' dwellings. The poverty that had been promised by Father Kundig was also evident. The migrants who came into the territory usually had no capital, although most had a wagon, a team of oxen, and a few crude implements and utensils.

Instead of the well-built structures of Aigen, Rehrl saw small cabins generally put up by the owners. The cabins ranged from twelve to twenty feet in length and had one or two rooms. They were seldom more than six feet in height at the eaves. Shortage of help in the early years dictated that the diameter of the logs be kept to a minimum so that each one could be lifted into place by two or three people. Floors were rare, and lack of glass kept the cabins windowless. The little dwellings did not always have doors, so during the winter months their narrow entrances were blocked with curtains of sailcloth or animal skins. Tables and stools were usually homemade, as were the rope beds, whose frames were attached to corner walls. The mattresses were ticks filled with straw or cornhusks.

Basic fare included bread made of wheat or rye flour, or even, in case of necessity, of middlings;[25] pancakes made of cornmeal or buckwheat flour, potatoes very often brought to the table with the skins on, sauerkraut, pork, beans, meat, butter, milk, cheese, and coffee. Tea was given only to the sick. In places where the flour mill was too far away, the settlers themselves ground their wheat or rye in small coffee mills at home.[26] Even so, Rehrl saw great potential in the area and the beginnings of a good life for the settlers.[27]

In September 1845, Rehrl reached Johnsburg. The village was small and with "wretched dwellings."[28] But the poverty meant very little to the missionary when he could bring the sacraments to people who were able to attend their first service in years. On one occasion benediction with the Blessed Sacrament was given in a little schoolhouse. The priest intoned the *Tantum Ergo* and the men continued the hymn with robust voices, but the women, hearing this, began to weep and sob to such an extent that it was hard to distinguish the singing from the weeping. It was the first sacramental blessing the people had received in three years.[29]

Father Rehrl had no horse; if he could have had one, providing it with fodder and shelter would have proved an insurmountable challenge.[30] Carrying his knapsack of sacred vessels and walking barefoot in moderate weather to save shoe leather, he went in search of Catholics over the whole vicinity. The areas around Fond du Lac, Chilton, Green Bay, and Sheboygan were known as having some of the worst trails east of the Rockies. Father Corbinian Vieracker added that in winter travelers often suffered frozen legs or caught the flu; in summer they could remain bedridden for a week, blind and lame, because of poison ivy. With no wells to quench their thirst, the newcomers drank strained swamp water and became ill.[31]

No richer than his parishioners, the missionary's clothes soon became ragged; a cassock was out of the question, and his alb reached only to his knees.[32] For a long time his only vestment was the single white one sent to him by his younger brother George; he used it for Easter and Requiem Masses alike. Another brother, Stephen, who was pastor in Aurach in the Tyrol, came to his aid with stipends for Masses, books, and a new vestment that was made from materials supplied by a patroness and that he himself had designed to be sturdy and portable.[33] His salary consisted of the meals he was given; he slept where he could find shelter. If the people didn't invite him, he ate nothing the whole day. When his coat was torn, he would say to the girls in his school, "Girls, please patch these holes again."[34]

As time went on, the lives of the people improved, and for almost all of the next thirty-five years of his life Father Rehrl journeyed from churches to cabins on his mission of preserving and spreading the faith. He traveled in all directions, sometimes making thirty or thirty-five miles in a day. Even though he often had to use an interpreter, he made friends with the Indians he met along the trail and taught them the rudiments of Christianity. He knew almost every Indian trail in Washington, Ozaukee, Sheboygan, Fond du Lac, and Brown Counties.[35]

One young boy never forgot his experience of the missionary:

> We boys had said our rosary and gone to bed. About midnight the cattle in the enclosure near the house had become restless and bellowed; thinking that the bears were doing mischief we arose and took our guns. While making our way through the thicket, I stumbled over something that made me suspect that it might be a human being; I waited for my brother to come with the lantern, when lo and behold! It was Father Rehrl, who had strayed from his road on the way to Sheboygan where he was due the next day. He was wet from head to foot. When we aroused him, he told us how it all happened ... The bridge over the creek had been swept away by the current caused by the melting snow. Then he looked for another crossing and finding none, he waded through the creek where it appeared shallow. Being wet and uncomfortable, he walked for hours carrying his heavy bag which contained everything he needed on his missionary wanderings. He soon grew tired, dropped to the ground, and fell asleep. Then we took him to the house and made him comfortable.[36]

MAKING THE ROUNDS

When Rehrl stopped at homes of contented families, he must often have thought of his own devout parents and brothers and sisters. His home, if he could be said to have had one, was in Johnsburg. The families there had begun to arrive in 1841, mostly from areas of Trier and Koblenz in the Rhine region. By September 1845 there were enough people to start building a log church, which they dedicated to St. John the Baptist. The churches built at that time were simple. A typical church:

> Consisted of rough-hewn trunks, placed one upon another without any attempt at art, in the form of a cross. The right wing had not as yet been completed, while the beams of the nave were caulked both inside and outside with mortar. The left wing was scantily furnished as a pastoral residence. The entire furniture consisted of a little table, a chair and a long box which closely resembled a Swiss 'Schnitztrog' in which the farmers preserved their dried fruit. This melancholy looking box which resembled a coffin more than anything else, had served our predecessor, the venerable Father Rehrl as a bed.[37]

With Father Rehrl's arrival, St. John the Baptist became the Catholic center for the entire region east of Lake Winnebago. A fellow priest wrote, "The persistent and sincere activity of Rev. Rehrl made the people rejoice. He was the spiritual father without fear, the man who mastered his missionary task. At all times he was cheerful and contented."[38] In 1847, the parish was further blessed by the arrival of Rehrl's classmate, Fabian Bermadinger, a Capuchin Franciscan from Vienna. Accompanied by three lay brothers, he came to Johnsburg in response to a letter from Rehrl describing the conditions of the Catholics in the area.[39] Now he was able to make longer and more frequent mission trips to such towns as Chilton, Sheboygan, Fond du Lac, and Green Bay. Some churches he visited twice a year; some, like Holy Name in Sheboygan, every three months. As he walked along the paths across the prairies, he could still see signs of the Indians' abandoned wigwams and sugar houses.

According to Father Vieracker, in 1847 the missionary visited Byron, Ashford, and Green Bay. There he was regular pastor for the Germans, until the people founded St. Mary Parish in 1851. After 1848 he visited the Catholics at Plymouth alternatively with another missionary. Every two months he read Mass at Dotyville at the home of Mathias Engels. Bermadinger became pastor of Marytown in 1849; after him this place was taken care of by Rehrl. In 1849, Father Bonduel built a chapel in honor of St. Louis at Fond du Lac. Shortly thereafter, Father Rehrl took care of the church until 1850 and was also pastor of St. James near Eden for a time.[40]

Father Rehrl's technique in dealing with the settlers could, at the least, be called straightforward. Passing through New Franken in 1847 on the way to Sheboygan, as he did twice a year, he found a satisfactory number of Catholics in the area. When he returned on his next round, the parishioners had managed only to get furnishings for the altar. He called them together and told them that Bishop Henni had instructed him to raise a church wherever he could find enough Catholics. The bishop had also authorized him to select building sites for new churches. He then chose a spot, erected a cross, and instructed parishioner John Peter Schauer to have a suitable church built, saying to him, "I have found a place where I have erected a cross, and there you shall build a church without any contradiction; in the name of God begin your work and He will bless you." The parishioners named the newly erected church for St. Kilian, the patron saint of Würzberg, where the majority of German families in that area had originated.[41]

THE 1847 DIOCESAN SYNOD

In June of 1847, Bishop Henni convoked a diocesan synod.[42] Of the thirty priests in the territory, eighteen were there the first day; three more arrived later, and nine were unable to attend. Maximilian Gaertner, a Premonstratensian priest from Green Bay, kept a diary. In it we learn that he and "Mr. Caspar Rehrl" were assigned to stay at the house of Victor Schulte, a carpenter, during the retreat. The retreat started on June 20 with an 8:00 a.m. Mass for the German

priests and a 9:00 a.m. Mass for the Irish priests. The bishop had
prepared a demanding schedule for the group:

4:45	Rising and Benedicamus
5:30	Morning prayer and meditation
6:30	Mass shortly after
7:00	Breakfast; free time in silence
8:00	Reading of the New Testament
8:15	Little Hours in common
9:00	Spiritual reading in common; free time
10:15	Meditation
11:15	Conference (sermon in English); then visit to the Blessed Sacrament for five minutes
12:00	Examination of conscience; dinner. Relaxation in silence
1:45	Reading of Thomas à Kempis in common
2:00	Discussion on practice of the rubrics of the Mass
2:30	Vespers and Compline in common
3:00	Free time
4:00	Meditation for 45 minutes, then free time
5:00	Matins and Lauds
6:00	Examination of conscience; supper; relaxation in silence
7:00	Benediction of the Blessed Sacrament; then reflection
8:00	Conference, then night prayer
9:00	Litany of the Blessed Virgin Mary

Committees were formed to take care of the business of the diocese. Rehrl's name appeared on two different committee rosters.
One committee discussed the garb of the priests. The members
apparently voted "no" to the requirement that priests wear black,
but the matter was not settled. The second committee dealt with the
power of dispensations for marriages. In spite of his great interest in
education, Rehrl was not a member of the committee formed to discuss the establishment of Catholic schools.

EDUCATION IN EARLY WISCONSIN

When the Catholics in the area were identified and provisions were
made for the building of churches, Rehrl could devote more time to
education. A prudent person surveying the status of education in

early Wisconsin would have blanched at the prospect of starting a school. The least difficult element was providing a schoolhouse because almost any building or shelter would do. About half of the first schools were log cabins. A box stove, usually in the middle of the room, provided heat, but the children often had to chop wood during the school day. It wasn't considered necessary to have desks for all of the pupils. Usually there were a few desks that were used in turn by pupils practicing their penmanship. As for textbooks, each pupil brought along what the family could provide, while blackoards and maps were rare indeed. Cleaning the school and keeping it warm were the responsibility of the teacher.

The difficulty lay in providing teachers. *The Report of the State Superintendent, 1849* provides a vivid picture of teaching in those early days:

> You will there see a teacher surrounded by fifty or sixty scholars, and often more, of all ages, from four to twenty, and with studies ranging from the alphabet to the highest English branches. You will also perceive that the teacher is required to "work off" daily about forty recitations upon an average, in the space of six hours …. To accomplish so much work in so short a time, *speed* is required; and to enable the teacher to 'get round' that no one may have occasion to complain of being slighted or neglected, the briefest space only can be allowed to each recitation, and while the pupils are reciting, if such a term is appropriate, the teacher must at the same time mend pens, set copies, solve problems, correct mistakes, answer questions, and keep order by the exercise of his eyes and ears, hands and feet, and sometimes of rod.[43]

In 1846, the average length of a school term was just short of four months, although it lasted twice as long in some school districts. A Wisconsin territorial law stipulated that a school must be kept open at least three months.[44] Twenty years later there were usually two terms, one in November and one in April, lasting almost three months each. Often in the winter, men who could not find work on a farm would teach, and women would teach in the summer. The men received the same wages as an unskilled laborer; the women received less. Few received special training, and not more than one in ten liked to teach. The average teaching career lasted eighteen months.[45] Enrollments varied wildly, from a very few to an average of forty by 1860. When Father Rehrl found incompetent teachers, alcoholic teachers, and even a few whom he considered dangerous to the young girls in their school, he was even more determined to build his own schools.[46]

REHRL'S SCHOOLS

The importance of Catholic schools for the success of the church in the new republic had been clear from the beginning. John Carroll, the first Roman Catholic bishop in the country, had set the church on a course that had enabled it to expand, absorb new immigrants, and establish parish schools.[47] At the time Rehrl arrived, popular education was in its infancy. An educated man himself, he was keenly aware of the necessity of adapting the church to the needs of the time. A school combined with a church, therefore, was the best means of maintaining the faith. The saying "Build the school first and the school will build the church" was commonplace among the Germans. He also, like most of the German-speaking clergy, agreed with Father Antony Urbanek that the faith and language go together. "German Catholic schools are the crying need in this country, because German children, if anglicized, by some strange fate generally become alienated from Catholic life. On the other hand, Irish children, if well instructed by their priest in any English catechism, generally are saved to the Catholic faith."[48]

Religion had become linked to culture, language, and ethnicity. The Catholic school would insure that the link would not be broken. Furthermore, the public schools had, in fact, a strong Protestant orientation and Bible reading was widely regarded as an indispensable part of the school program. Given the fact that "many were bigoted and even harbored the mental reservation that the Catholic Church was not part of the Christian community,"[49] Catholics were genuinely fearful that their children would be indoctrinated with Protestantism. Consequently, some Catholics would rather see the children uneducated than placed in danger of losing their faith.

For Father Rehrl, providing Catholic schools, open to all children, was the only acceptable option. Because public and private schools were all one in those days, his school house in Johnsburg was the first district public school, and he was its first director and teacher. It is interesting to note that Rehrl soon accepted the American principle of separation of church and state. He came to hold that a majority of the voters in a school district could place control and operation of the public school in religious hands, but could prohibit religious instruction and even prayer before and after school when they were financed by public monies.[50]

At times Rehrl must have wondered which was the more difficult—providing schools or providing teachers. In his manual, *Reflections for Catholic Christians*, he complained about:

> So-called "picnics" held for the benefit of church and school. It seems that there is no other way to build churches and schools but by obligatory drinking and dancing. And so, one postpones the erection of new churches and schools until people are urged by fear of God and the necessary enthusiasm to take the [illegible] steps to proceed with plans and final construction and with the intention of honoring and glorifying God, plus the welfare of human souls.[51]

Father Rehrl also believed in providing for the whole child. In his school the day began with Mass at 8:00 a.m. and ended with a hot lunch at 2:00 p.m. Potatoes were boiled; the women brought bread and a common dinner was served.[52]

FIRST GLIMPSE OF MOUNT CALVARY

Soon after Rehrl had arrived in Wisconsin, he lost his way as he was going from Sheboygan to Fond du Lac. He passed a hill a few miles east of Johnsburg, and feeling a great desire to ascend it, as he later wrote, "Arriving at the summit, I was delighted with the panorama round about. Oh how beautiful, I thought to myself, a church would be up here! But there isn't a sign of a human being for miles around, no house, no hut, as far as I can see from this delightful viewpoint."[53] He then searched for a small knife to mark the place, but couldn't find it. Instead he made a cross of two branches, and went on his way. He came to the home of a Catholic family, the Blonigens, and described the hill and the marker.

Three years later, in 1849, as Catholic settlers began to move into that area, Father Rehrl notified the men to gather at the home of John Blonigen to discuss the founding of a new parish. Meanwhile, Blonigen had purchased the land the priest had desired for a church. Still convinced that the hill was the right place for the new church, Rehrl purchased the land from Blonigen for fifty dollars. The following day the men began to cut the logs.[54]

Meanwhile, with the aid of Dr. Joseph Salzmann, Rehrl was able to buy for fifty dollars an adjoining hill that he named Mount Carmel. While St. Nicholas was being built, he had the men build two cabins on Mount Carmel with the remaining logs. He held services in one house, and in the other he taught school. The dedication of the church on June 24, 1850, was a grand occasion, and perhaps a surprising one, because Bishop Henni renamed the church Holy Cross, and the first hill and village, Mount Calvary. Later, at the little program, one of the school children recited a verse written by Father Rehrl.[55]

Father Corbinian Vieracker gave a vivid description of Sundays at the church:

> St. Nicholas became quite an attraction when a church choir was organized by John Blonigen, and the forte and tremolo in singing were rendered more effectively with the assistance of a hollow hand and cone-shaped paper tubes. No wonder the good people who lived south of the hill could not be detained from church, although a good stretch of the path leading through the woods was under water, and strong men like George Ochs had to carry the women on their backs, while the men and the younger generation took their chances in jumping from log to log.[56]

MOVE TO MOUNT CALVARY

It was not long after when a smoldering controversy in Johnsburg over the placement of a new church building erupted. Parishioners who found their church to be in an unfavorable location decided to build a new and more accessible church. Father Bermadinger left because of the arguments, and Father Rehrl, who still resided in Johnsburg, wanted the church in the old place and consequently resigned over the move. At the end of July 1850, he moved to Mount Calvary. It was a great relief to him when a very pious twenty-six-year-old woman from Luxemburg, Mary Guidinger, offered her services as a teacher free of charge. In addition, she also turned over her possessions, including a deed to land and buildings, to him so that he could pay the debts on the land and furnish the two log cabins as schools. She recruited the children and "even though her methods of teaching and her knowledge were rather defective, nevertheless she knew how to keep good order and uphold their ambitious spirit."[57]

Two other young women from Luxemburg, Johanna and Maria Mose [sic], attempted to teach in Johnsburg for Father Rehrl but, according to Father Corbinian, they "lacked the necessary strength to do supernatural works. One morning with bag in hand they appeared before the log cabin; nothing could move them to remain. They had nothing to eat. The buttered bread which the children had left behind had been their last nourishment."[58]

FATHER REHRL DISAPPOINTED

Back at Mount Carmel, Mary Guidinger learned that she could study English with the School Sisters of Notre Dame who had recently arrived in Milwaukee from Bavaria.[59] Soon after she met the sisters, Mary informed Father Rehrl of her decision to join that community. He was not only supportive of her decision, but hoping eventually to obtain sisters to teach in Mount Carmel from the community, he returned the deed of the land and buildings to her. When almost a year passed, and no sisters arrived, Rehrl wrote repeatedly to their superior, Mother Caroline Freiss, begging for help. Early in the summer of 1851, Mother Caroline responded to his pleas and went to look over the property. Her trip to look over the land provides an unforgettable picture of the priest sitting on a tree stump blackening his boots in preparation for a Corpus Christi procession.[60] "My God!" Mother Caroline said later, "I have never seen such wilderness and such poverty before. A log cabin without chairs, without a floor!"[61] Mother Caroline returned to Milwaukee, impressed with the asceticism of the missionary, but sent no sisters.

Again Rehrl bombarded both Mother Caroline and Bishop Henni with letters asking for sisters. Mary, now Sister Cecilia, was brought into the matter and wrote a desperate letter to him. After explaining that she had hoped that Mother Caroline would send a sister to Carmel, she wrote that Mother Caroline told her that she could not. Then Sister Cecilia continued:

> On Friday the Rt. Rev. Bishop visited us to confer with Reverend Mother regarding your Reverence's letters. Mother said that she would leave it entirely to me and would not endeavor to persuade me to remain here. For this reason she sent me to the reception room without informing me who awaited me there. As soon as I beheld the Rt. Rev. Bishop it seemed to me that some question regarding Carmel awaited consideration ... he informed me that your Reverence had written three times and desired that I return if no other Sister can be sent. He remarked then that should I decide to go, such resolution would imply my withdrawal from the novitiate, ceasing to be a Candidate, and not becoming a sister .... What remained for me to do? Forego completely and hopelessly relinquish the search for that to find which I might have had the grace, or, as I am almost constrained to believe, to find which I have not been found worthy in the sight of God![62]

When the determined candidate informed the bishop that she would not leave the Notre Dames even if she "be permitted to remain as a house sister only" he told her that the decision would simplify matters and such a resolution would remove temptation. Sister Cecilia's calm after her unexpected meeting with Bishop Henni was shattered by the time she had to write to Father Rehrl,

"O God, what shall I do? To remain and to go strive within me and I know not how to be advised. O, Rev. Father, please do not feel offended if I permit myself to ask you whether you cannot give up the school at St. Mary's and take the one at Carmel."[63]

Mother Caroline added a few lines assuring Father Rehrl that she had not dissuaded Cecilia from returning to Carmel. She explained that the venture, in the opinion of the bishop, was premature and that her sisters would be glad to go to Carmel "as it is a special grace to be missionaries."[64] Mother Caroline kept her word and sisters arrived there in 1852. A short time later Sister Cecilia joined them, but lived only to 1855.

A FURTHER SEARCH FOR SISTERS

There were other little country missions needing schools. Recruiting sisters still seemed to be the best way to staff them, but the two teaching orders in Wisconsin at that time, the Sinsinawa Dominicans and the Notre Dames, were recent arrivals with only a few members. Meanwhile, the general crop failures in Europe, particularly the potato crop failures in southwestern Germany in 1846 and 1847, had contributed to the expanding number of immigrants to the Wisconsin Territory. In 1846, there were 155,000 settlers in the area; in 1850, there were 305,000, half of whom had arrived during the previous four years. The need for schools was becoming ever more acute.

Father Rehrl's pleas for help from European convents yielded no results. One reason may have been that teaching was not regarded as work particularly suitable for sisters.[65] Rehrl came to the conclusion that the only solution seemed to be to return to Europe, make personal visits to motherhouses, and make money to finance his plans. Father Rehrl went back to Europe in September 1852. Father Corbinian provides an interesting insight into his decision. "At Calvary the parish had been so well established that it seemed against his nature to remain any longer, 'I should spare myself,' he said, 'and should allow the spark of my powers to slowly die?'"[66] And whether his devotion to duty prevented him from admitting it, even to himself, he must have yearned to see his family and the majestic mountains of his home, as well as to participate again in the magnificent liturgies of Salzburg. Unwilling even to await the

arrival of his successor—his own brother George, recently
ordained—he left the parish and returned to his native Austria.
From his arrival in Wisconsin in 1845 until his departure, Father
Rehrl had either helped found or served in the churches of
Johnsburg, Marytown, Mount Calvary, Sheboygan, St. Anna,
Byron, Dotyville, Eden, Fond du Lac, Green Bay, Appleton,
Manitowoc, Two Rivers, and Eldorado.

Back in his home diocese, the returned missionary spent much
time working on and publishing a two-volume prayer book,
Katholische Christen (*The Catholic Christian*), which he had printed in
Salzburg. The twin volumes contained many devotions for High
Masses, litanies, and instructions for confession and communion.
He was at the disposal of the bishop and helped out wherever he
was sent. However, his major objective remained to procure sisters
to teach in the schools he was so desperately determined to establish. It is all too easy to visualize the gaunt and shabby missionary
visiting the convents and offering the Mother Superior a chance to
send her sisters to live in want on the Wisconsin frontier. Their
reluctance may have been increased as it probably became clear to
the superiors that Father Rehrl had little understanding of religious
life or the needs of sisters.[67] After three years of unsuccessful visits to
convents, he obtained permission to visit Rome but did not arrive
there until the summer of 1855.

AN INSPIRATION FROM ST. AGNES

It is not difficult to picture the scholarly Father Rehrl happily
absorbed in visiting the monuments of the ancient Rome he had
studied about so many years ago. But it was the churches, the basil-
icas, and the catacombs he visited so devoutly that spoke to his
heart, especially one of the most ancient Christian foundations,
Sant'Agnese fuori le Mura (St. Agnes Outside the Walls). It was the
church of the young martyr St. Agnes. St. Ambrose tells us that
Agnes was only thirteen years of age at the time of her death.
Beautiful and wealthy, she had already dedicated herself to God
when she was besieged by the young nobles of Rome for her hand
in matrimony. It was 303 A.D., the time of the last major persecution of the Christians, when the Emperor Diocletian issued edicts
designed to uproot the sect. Legends tell us that Agnes, declaring

that she was espoused to Jesus Christ, enraged the young men, who then accused her to the governor of being a Christian. There are various accounts of her death. One of them tells of abortive attempts to force her to sacrifice to the gods and marry. Upon her continued refusals, she finally was condemned to be beheaded. Ambrose tells us that Agnes "went to the place of execution more cheerfully than others go to their wedding."[68] Her body was buried a short distance from Rome near the Via Nomentana. In the fourth century the Emperor Constantine's daughter, Constantia, erected a basilica over her tomb. The young martyr's universal appeal to Christians is evidenced to this day by the number of churches throughout the world dedicated in her honor and the legends that have grown around her.[69]

When Caspar Rehrl entered the basilica and the catacombs of St. Agnes and knelt by the tomb venerated by Christians for over fourteen hundred years, his thoughts must have turned from the child martyr, Agnes, to the children whom he saw as deprived of both the knowledge of their faith and the education necessary to lead a useful Christian life. Praying before the tomb of the martyr, he asked for her help in founding a teaching sisterhood and promised to name it in her honor. As the story later was told among the sisters, he then had a vision of the saint leading a group of women dressed in black and white. Shaken yet exalted by his experience, the missionary determined to lay his plan for a sisterhood before the pontiff. Years later Sister Genevieve remarked to him, "One should think you have seen St. Agnes." He responded, *"Mann kann es glauben.* (One can believe it.)"[70]

The missionary next had an audience with Pope Pius IX, to whom he poured out his dreams. Blessing him, the Holy Father counseled him never to give up and to submit his plan to Bishop Henni. Then after his society had successfully been in existence for ten years, he should submit its rule to Rome. Contented with his progress, Rehrl set sail for New York as soon as possible and arrived in Wisconsin the fall of 1855. This time there would be no return to Europe; he intended to become an American citizen. When he met with Bishop Henni upon his return to Milwaukee, he found a sympathetic ear and a new assignment: twelve mission parishes and two "woebegone" Catholic schools.[71]

Meanwhile, as Germans moved into Milwaukee, the area directly to the north of the city became more densely populated, and little mission churches rose up along the old Indian trails. Father Rehrl
settled in Barton, where he said the town's first Mass on Christmas
Day, 1857.[72] From his base in Barton, a small village on the
Milwaukee River, he was able to do what he loved best: move about
from church to church, administer the sacraments, hold divine services and, when he could, encourage the establishment of schools.
Although Barton would never fulfill its promise, at that time it was
believed to be on the way to becoming the most important town in
the Milwaukee River Valley.

The village was near West Bend, in an area he found to be lack-
ing the sturdy Catholicity of the Johnsburg area. He found there
"the air full of infidelity, unbelievers, scoffers over wine cups, 48'ers,
free thinkers."[73] Nevertheless, the prospect of evangelizing seemed
to energize the missionary. In one year, one of the early sisters said
later, that he visited as many as thirty-two missions. He started a
school from which no child was turned away, although Protestant
children, if able, were to pay twelve cents a month.[74] In other parishes on his circuit, he tried to arrange for the religious education of
the children by appointing men to hold classes on Sundays.

Father Rehrl organized at least two sodalities for young women
in hopes that some would join him in Barton as members of his projected society. Although the sodalities must have had some degree of
success, as the young ladies of Sts. Peter and Paul were able to
deposit in the local bank $7.50 in June of 1863—no small sum in
those days—he received no candidates from either sodality.[75] His
great desire, to provide a group of dedicated and trained women to
teach in the rural schools, was still unfulfilled.

THE FIRST SISTER OF ST. AGNES

Father Rehrl not only discussed his dream of founding a sisterhood
with his fellow priests but also wrote to them asking them to send
candidates to him. In an old notebook possessed by Archbishop
Sebastian Messmer, the following letter was found:

To give more influence to the Catholic faith by a scientific and moral education of the youth, I established under the authority of Bishop Henni the
Sisterhood of St. Agnes in the village of Barton near
West Bend of Irish and German Sisters to be sent in
every place where they are wished for to teach male
and female children. I heard that the Rt. Rev. Bishop
being with you said that your young people look very
intelligent. Would it not be a shame by such an intelligent people not to find a couple of pious virgins
who would consecrate themselves entirely to God to
serve Him guiding children to Him? No excuse,
Father, you ought to send me *two*.[76]

Whether or not there was any connection with Rehrl's letter, the
first candidate who arrived was sent by Father Joseph Reindl, pastor
of St. Lawrence Church in Washington County. Gertrude went to
the priest and asked for help in following her vocation. The story of
Gertrude Rehberg is both a tribute to her own determination and
an appreciation of Rehrl's dedication to his mission rounds. Because
she had lacked the dowry to enter an order in Europe, she had
decided to come to Wisconsin to join her brother in Hartford and
search for a welcoming congregation in America.[77] Although she
had very little money, her possessions included a bed, a chair, a
trunk, and some clothing; she also had good health and testimonials
of good conduct.[78]

With Father Reindl's recommendation in hand, Gertrude set out
to find the missionary. The date was June 29, 1858. Father Rehrl
was undoubtedly at Nenno, where the parish of Sts. Peter and Paul
was celebrating *kirmes*, the parish festival. On that hot summer day,
she walked from her brother's house in Hartford over a road rutted
with wagon wheels to the village of Addison. Arriving at the church,
she discovered Father Rehrl had already left for Theresa, six miles
further north. Wilted and tired from the heat, she arrived in Theresa
only to be told that the pastor was not there but was expected in
Mayville the next day. With true pioneer hospitality, the farmer
offered to escort her the next morning to Mayville; meanwhile she
could stay with his family overnight. The next morning, the farmer

led the way as Gertrude timidly walked a rod behind him the whole six miles.[79]

It was now the morning of June 30. Father Rehrl had just finished saying Mass in St. Mary Church in Mayville. The congregation was leaving and he was kneeling in prayer at the foot of the altar when Gertrude approached him. Shyly she gave him her name and said that in a few days she would be twenty-seven years old. She was from Proveny, Steinbach Kurhessen, and her dream was to become a religious.

In later years, Gertrude spoke of her first meeting with the priest. She described his worn gray coat, his blue drill shirt, his torn boots, his "cylinder" hat, and his sandy hair.[80] Father Rehrl's welcome was so warm and his desire to establish a society of sisters was so compelling that she agreed to find some companions to join her and meet him in Barton in three days' time. There she would begin her new life.[81]

From Barton, Rehrl sent Gertrude to a Notre Dame convent to make a retreat and become acquainted with religious life.[82] She returned to her brother's parish, St. Lawrence, on August 10, its patronal feast. To Gertrude's joy, Bishop Henni was there and expressed pleasure in meeting her. He blessed her and gave Father Rehrl permission to accept her as his first aspirant after she made a two-day retreat.

Father George Rehrl was also there. When Gertrude met him and excitedly told him of her plans for the future, the young priest's response was anything but encouraging, "It is a weighty venture which you are to undertake. I fear that nothing will come of it. But proceed in God's Name. Should it come to naught, God will open to you another door through which you may enter and find that which you now seek.[83]

By August 12, two more young women arrived to join Gertrude. On that day in 1858, Gertrude Rehberg, Magdalene Hapfer, and Katherine Goetz became the first Sisters of St. Agnes.[84] Canon law prescriptions were not in force at this time, but Bishop Henni was empowered to authorize Father Rehrl to preside over the investing ceremonies. As a sign of his great devotion to Agnes and Mary, the mother of God, each sister was given the name Mary Agnes as well as another saint's name. Gertrude became Sister Mary Agnes Clara; Magdalene, Sister Mary Agnes Gertrudis; and, Katherine, Sister

Mary Agnes Mechtildis.[85] These women made promises for one year of poverty, chastity, and obedience, including the commitment "to devote myself assiduously to my perfection and personal education, and most carefully to instruct and educate the youth entrusted to my care, and even to perform manual labor."[86]

LIFE OF THE FIRST SISTERS

The three young women boarded with neighboring families until Father Rehrl could complete the arrangements for buying a field-stone house, the former home of village founder Barton Salisbury, and property that included forty acres of woodland and twenty acres of farmland.[87] True to his Austrian heritage, Rehrl had chosen a house on a hill near the western end of the village, and the view, overlooking the Milwaukee River, was scenic. There he built a one-story convent of gray fieldstones, with Gothic windows and a steep gabled roof for the sisters.

The convent was sparsely furnished even by the standards of the day. It had no stove. The sisters slept on blankets spread over straw ticks. They chopped their own wood and carried drinking water from a spring more than two blocks away. They had neither proper implements nor the strength and skill needed to cultivate the eleven acres of farmland that was to provide much of their food. As a result, they were often hungry. Days went by when breakfast consisted of pap (flour and water) and a crust of dry bread; dinner, potatoes; and supper, pap again.[88] In the fall, they had pumpkins boiled without sugar to spread on bread.[89] Through it all, Father Rehrl, who often returned to Barton having eaten nothing for two days, was oblivious to their needs.

The sisters wore a plain black dress with a cape, a white collar, and a small black bonnet and a white forehead band. A voluminous black apron covered the dress.[90] Sister Clara yearned for a veil. Rehrl, however, "didn't care for a sister's habit as such; he just wanted a society of ladies to teach children and take care of his missions."[91] When he was in Rome, he had admired the work of the catechists who wore simple little black bonnets instead of a veil. He was determined that the members of his society would do the same. Clara disagreed. She repeatedly begged that the sisters be allowed to wear veils. There was little a man could do when it came to women's clothing, so Father Rehrl gave in. One day, however, while passing through the convent yard, he found a veil that had flown off the clothesline and was being tossed about by the wind. He picked it up, took it into the convent, and insisted that the sisters return to their little bonnets.[92]

Other girls and women soon joined them. Their immediate duty was to prepare the children in their charge for their first Holy Communion. They soon discovered that Father Rehrl, their director, gave them ample opportunity to live out their commitments and his spirituality. In Father Rehrl's original constitutions, he wrote, "Agnes Sisters shall live on school money, on the labor of their hands and on liberal donations, but they shall not ask some [money] of anybody."[93]

If a girl was fourteen and knew a little English, Father Rehrl sent her out to teach.[94] She would be given board and room by one of the parish families while she did her best to share what little knowledge she had. This boarding system had the further result of relieving the pressure on the convent's limited supply of space and food. On Sundays and feast days, Father Rehrl sent the little choirs of sisters he had formed to the mission churches to sing with the parishioners.

FATHER REHRL'S FIRST RULE[95]

Father Rehrl very much wanted his society recognized by Rome. Since 1855 he had treasured his conversation with Pope Pius IX and the encouragement he had been given. Although he had not intended to found a traditional sisterhood, he wanted his community to have the closest possible ties with the universal church. So in spite of the very few sisters and uncertain conditions under which they were living, he spent much time writing a rule for the sisters. In 1858, he submitted his rule to Bishop Henni.

The first rule Father Rehrl wrote visualized the sisters primarily as teachers in rural areas and as servants of the priests. Their motherhouse should be located in the country, or at least on the outskirts of a village. They should have the usual farm animals and gardens, but in addition, they should plant grapes and have honey bees, raise and manufacture flax, spin their own wool, and make their own dresses. They should make candles and church vestments, clean the church, and wash the vestments and linen. If the priest in a parish had no cook, the sisters should cook for him, but he could not eat in their house. "They would," he said, "belong to the altar and service of the priests."[96] Bishop Henni did not find this rule satisfactory.

When the missionary returned from his lengthy trips, he was scarcely in the house when he would call together his little community for instructions. A born teacher, he spent some of his happiest hours instructing the candidates. He would have them sit in the chapel and read the Bible while he would explain it to them. All were taught music, basic Christian doctrine, and the traditional elementary subjects. Because almost all of the sisters spoke German as their first language, learning English correctly became a priority. The curriculum also included Latin because the sisters were to recite the divine office.[97] Those who did not know Latin would pray in their native language "as Agnes sisters shall neither sing nor pray what they do not understand."[98] More advanced students went to Fond du Lac to prepare with the county superintendent to take the biannual exams for teachers' certificates. Needless to say, because the young women's educational background was problematic at best, the lack of textbooks was particularly frustrating. One of Father Rehrl's dreams soon became to procure a printing press to write and publish his own textbooks and prayer books.

A TRAGIC YEAR

On January 17, 1860, Father Rehrl suffered a severe blow. His brother, Father George Rehrl, died at the age of thirty-four.[99] He had been ordained in 1850 and appointed pastor of St. Nicholas Church in Mount Calvary in 1852. Considered to be "of great promise,"[100] he was appointed in 1856 to the faculty of St. Francis de Sales Seminary in Milwaukee as professor of Latin and German. George was Caspar's connection to home, family, and native land. The brothers also shared a love of scholarship, but above all they shared in the priesthood. Father George's death left a place in the missionary's heart that could never be filled.[101]

At the beginning of 1860, the society numbered about eighteen members.[102] Both the little community and the school at Barton were doing reasonably well. Although the two women who had arrived with Gertrude Rehberg left after they had fulfilled their promise of trying their vocation for one year, more arrived and the following summer saw five young women professed as Sisters of St. Agnes. Twelve girls ranging in age from eleven to thirteen became novices, and within a few months a few of the older ones were professed. Father Rehrl, absent most of the time on his mission trips, had appointed Sister Clara superior. It was a choice that was doomed from the beginning. Not only was she from the old country without an understanding of American women, but she did not have the temperament and experience to keep order in a house that had nei-ther an established rule nor sisters seasoned in religious life. Success built upon such a shaky foundation could not last.

Then a catastrophe hit the little group. The school seemed to be under some kind of attack. There were "vexatious occurrences and disturbances of hidden origin" causing distress for the pupils. Filth was thrown onto possessions and dolls were said to be dancing on the tables. The convent burned in four corners, but when the fire engine and apparatus from West Bend came, they found only smoke. Thinking someone was buried there who was not at rest, men opened the floors to investigate. Finally, it was blind Sister Ursula Hofen[103] visiting a friend from West Bend who overheard two schoolgirls plotting their next mischief. With the expulsion of the culprits, all was serene again. In later years, more than one sister continued to believe that the girls had been sent to the school in order to destroy it.[104]

CRISIS OF MEMBERSHIP

More blows came. Early in 1861 when Father Rehrl returned from one of his mission trips, he found only two sisters remaining. One was Sister Clara Rehberg, the first woman to enter the community; the other was Sister Ursula. Then Sister Clara told him that she could no longer remain. She intended to enter a Franciscan convent in Milwaukee. She wanted to live the life of the nuns she had known in Europe, with their rules, traditions, and settled serenity. When she could not be shaken from her decision, Father Rehrl blessed her, but predicted that she would return.

Melancholy as the circumstances were, Father Rehrl had a strong supporter in Bishop Henni who, whatever his reservations, refused to withdraw his support. One sister who had departed, Sister Agnes Maus from Detroit, had visited Bishop Henni to request that he disband the society. As recorded by Sister Julia Dullea, "The Bishop was kind to her and she had dinner, but said, 'No. I don't forbid Father Rehrl. He did too much for the missions. Tell the girls they can all go if they wish. They are free.'"[105]

It is not easy to think of Caspar Rehrl's situation in 1861. By then he was fifty-one years old. His dream of establishing a sisterhood of teachers which had seemed so close to realization just shortly before, had become almost a mockery. His brother had died, depriving him of his dearest friend. It was true that Bishop Henni supported him; it was also true that the bishop's support came from loyalty, not from a conviction that the dream could come true. For his part, Father Rehrl was sustained only by his unwavering faith.

Chapter II

Conflicting Visions

It was not in Father Rehrl's nature to give up. In order to care for his now teacherless schools, he found six young women to fill the posts vacated by the discouraged sisters. Although he hoped they would eventually become sisters, they left as soon as others came. Meanwhile, Sister Clara had not been able to find the peace she craved. She had been gone only one month when she met Father Rehrl by chance one day in Milwaukee. When he asked after her well-being, Clara's reply was: "Oh, Father, my trunk is homesick."[1]

After the first Sister of St. Agnes returned to Barton, she was joined in a remarkably short time by other women. It is difficult not to be impressed by the quality of the faith that propelled the next half dozen young women to throw in their lot with Father Rehrl and his struggling group. Nevertheless, young women did come. For the most part, children of hard-working immigrant parents, they were responsible, energetic, committed. In 1863 Sister Emerentia (Mary) Ryan, whom Rehrl named directress,[2] would "contribute greatly toward the re-establishment of its [the community's] former status."[3] Unfortunately Sister suffered from a mental illness, was institutionalized, and died shortly thereafter. Of the next three directresses, the one most significant for the future growth of the congregation was Melanie Dulso. Although she would leave the community one day, it was through her that Mary Hazotte came to Barton.

Melanie Dulso was born in Lennigenaltorff, Lothringen (Lorraine) on October 5, 1836, but her parents later emigrated to Detroit. She was well-educated and could speak French, German, and English. When she was nineteen, she entered the Notre Dame Convent in Milwaukee. Less than a year later, she returned to her home in Detroit. We next hear of her as a traveling companion to the wife of a United States army officer. It was April 1861. The party had left Detroit and arrived near Cairo, Tennessee, when the first shots of the Civil War were fired.[4] The officer was ordered to return to his home in Washington D.C. Melanie chose not to go with the couple but to travel to a convent in Cincinnati where her aunt was a nun. As Melanie told the story years later, she then secured passage on a boat and sent her trunk on ahead to Cincinnati. As she was standing on the wharf, a messenger brought back her trunk saying it was too late for the boat. She had just made up her mind not to go to Cincinnati, after all, when a young man stepped up to her, handed her an envelope, tipped his hat, and walked away. She opened the envelope to find a letter from Father Rehrl, containing directions and the exact sum of money to get to Barton. He told her of the convent and invited her to join the Sisters of St. Agnes at Barton. She always maintained that she could never explain how the envelope came to be delivered to her.[5]

In any case, in 1861 Melanie arrived in Barton and was welcomed by Sisters Agnes (Maurer), Emerentia Ryan, Ursula Hofen, and Genevieve Popp. Several other sisters were teaching in surrounding villages. Sister Thecla was placed in charge of the boarding school in Barton, which Rehrl had recently established. The convent school attracted boys and girls from miles around. He welcomed "any child, Indian or White, healthy, blind, or crippled .... " At one time there were sixty pupils.[6] "The parents brought us wheat, flour, meat, vegetables, and groceries, sometimes in lieu of tuition, at other times in gratitude for what we did for the children. We suffered no want."[7] Each pupil also was responsible for chores around the property. The school attracted students from both Barton and West Bend. Assisted by Sisters Genevieve and Euphrosine Popp, Sister Thecla would always remember that they were all very happy.

For the society, the arrival of an educated and talented woman was a special blessing.

THE SECOND RULE

During this period, Father Rehrl completed a second rule. The 1862 constitutions are more carefully structured and less detailed although the spirit remains the same.[8] In each diocese where the sisters served, they were to have a motherhouse under the authority of the local bishop who would appoint a chaplain as their guardian and confessor. The parish priest was to oversee their observance of the rules. Although it is not easy for us today to regard these strictures positively, it is clear that Rehrl saw the sisters as closely connected with the life of the local church. It is not as clear if he saw sisters as capable of managing their own lives and their own community, or if the subservience to male authority figures so apparent in the documents was simply an attempt to conform to the requirements of canon law and society's expectations of women and prevailing cultural expectations.

As Father Rehrl traveled from mission to mission, he must have often visualized his future society. The motherhouse would be situated on a quadrangle which would also contain a chapel, chaplain's residence, guest house, and an infirmary for aged priests. There would be fruit and vegetable gardens and a vineyard, domestic animals (including lambs to watch at recreation), and bees. The sisters would make candles, plant flax, make linen, and weave cloth for their own clothes, but they would not make church vestments.[9]

They would wear a full habit and a face veil to cover their faces when they went out or came within the presence of men. They were not allowed to visit anyone in their homes with the exception of dangerously ill parents or pupils. Conversations with lay persons would be strictly limited, and if it were necessary to speak with a male, the sister had to be protected by a grill and converse for fewer than five minutes.

The order of the day was rigorous. From October 1 to March 31 the sisters were to rise at 5:00 a.m., the rest of the year at 4:00 a.m. They would begin their day with a half-hour meditation and morning prayers. They would recite the office at the appropriate hours, gather together for common spiritual reading, meditate again in the evening for fifteen minutes, examine their consciences, say night prayers, and retire at 9:00 p.m.

The rule also included a section on education. Father Rehrl recommended that the sisters take the prescribed examinations and use the textbooks required by the government because he wished them also to teach in the public schools as a source of income. If one sister taught in a public school, another sister should teach in a Catholic school in the same village or town. Rehrl gave hints on classroom management; although he insisted upon strict discipline, he also exhorted the sisters to be kind to the children. The society should own a printing press because Catholic schools needed their own textbooks. Unlike many other religious orders at the time, the Sisters of St. Agnes were to instruct both boys and girls. The Catholic children should pray before and after school but the non-Catholic children were not held to those prayers. Rehrl's views have been praised both as educationally sound and remarkably tolerant because he freed the sisters to teach wherever they were needed and to teach all children in need of an education.[10]

At this juncture Sister Thecla received a letter from her mother in Detroit informing her of the death of Victor, the youngest son of their neighbors, the Hazotte family. Sister Thecla, who had been praying desperately for help for the school, later told how at the time of the consecration in the Mass, she suddenly thought of "little Mary Hazotte" and prayed that she might be given a vocation to the community.[11] Mary had been born in Buffalo on May 7, 1847, the youngest child of Christoph and Mary Ann Potier Hazotte. The child, baptized Anne Marie, was now a talented young woman of fifteen. The Hazotte family had been neighbors, and Thecla, although much older, had enjoyed playing with the little girl who, at three or four, already possessed the charm that was always so evident. The family had emigrated to Buffalo a few years earlier from Nancy, in Lorraine, France, in time to escape the Revolution of 1848. In common with many other French families, they moved westward to Detroit. Instead of replicating the middle-class prosperity the family had enjoyed in France, however, the Hazotte family suffered the severe blows of illness and death. It was a period when childhood diseases, pneumonia, and tuberculosis took their toll. Twenty-one-year-old Theresa had died when Mary was five; five months later her father died. Later that same year the oldest daughter, Appoline, died at the age of twenty-three. The widow was left with six children: John Nicholas, Joseph, Charles, Clementine, Victor, and Mary.[12] She apparently had some means—visible in a photograph of her taken in Paris a few years later with her two youngest children, Victor and Mary.

When Mary was five, she was enrolled in St. Mary's, a parochial school conducted by the School Sisters of Notre Dame who had come to Detroit in 1852 to teach with the Christian Brothers from Montreal. From twelve to fourteen, she attended a school conducted by the religious of the Society of the Sacred Heart.[13] Because she showed musical talent, she was given the further advantage of music lessons. Tragedy struck the family when she was thirteen: her mother died, and two years later her brother Victor. It was a letter reporting Victor's death, which Sister Thecla received in the winter of 1862 that would prove so important to the little band of women in Wisconsin.

Letters were rare, so Sister Thecla shared hers with the other sisters at recreation. As she was sharing her memories of the bright little girl with the sisters, she suddenly realized what an asset Mary could be to the society. The reasons probably had much to do with Sister Thecla's remembrance of Mary's buoyant temperament. She was bright, independent, outgoing, and, from a toddler on, more pious than is usual in small children. Mary was now fifteen. She was the youngest in the family; perhaps she would be free to come to Barton and help, and eventually she might even become a sister. Sister Thecla lost no time writing back to her mother, suggesting that she encourage Mary to come to Barton for a visit. She asked her mother to provide Mary with suitable clothes and the train ticket. (It is worth noting that Sister Thecla apparently gave no thought to inviting Mary's older sister, Clementine.)

Sister Thecla was right. For Mary, the thought of joining the sisters and her old friend in Wisconsin was immensely appealing. Disregarding the tears of Clementine and the objections of her brothers, Mary left Detroit to begin her new life. When she arrived, Sister Thecla and a little group of excited sisters were waiting to meet her. They took her directly to Father Rehrl's little dwelling on the hill. He was waiting to greet her and, placing his hand on her head, he said, "Your name shall be Agnes."[14]

One of Mary's first tasks was to learn to speak German well. Soon she could speak German as well as French and English. Along with the other candidates she was kept busy. The younger ones, two at a time, accompanied the missionary on some of his mission trips to instruct the children for their First Confession and First Communion. The older ones taught at St. Agnes Academy, Barton; St. Anthony; and Sts. Peter and Paul, Nenno.[15]

As Father Rehrl was planning to expand into Fond du Lac County, Mary was sent to study for her teacher's license under the county superintendent in Fond du Lac. Rehrl sometimes borrowed a team of horses and took her himself; at other times he arranged to have her go with a farmer on his way to market.[16] Mary made her first acquaintance with Fond du Lac, the town which would be of such importance in the community's future.

Sister Thecla, aware of Mary's musical ability, also put her in charge of the singing classes in the academy, where she was immediately successful. Rehrl, who had been born and raised in one of the most musically sophisticated cities in the world, now had occasion to purchase the organ for which he had been longing. A little later when the seminarian, J. E. Halbenkann,[17] assisted the priest in the parish, he was drafted to teach Agnes liturgical music. The devotion to church music that Father Rehrl and the young seminarian instilled in the young woman would have a marked impact on the future of the Sisters of St. Agnes.

Agnes suffered only one severe bout of homesickness a few months after her arrival. Sister Thecla was understanding and asked Father Rehrl for fifteen dollars so Agnes could return home. He gave it, but when Sister Thecla offered Agnes the money, she turned impetuously away. From that hour forward, she would later say, she never thought of leaving again.[18]

That summer, on July 2, 1863, Mary Hazotte and four other young women made their first yearly vows in the congregation. Mary would henceforth be known as Sister Mary Agnes. Although the years since the birth of the infant society had been difficult, the years ahead would scarcely be easier. From 1858 until August 1870, ninety-nine names appear in the congregational records. While these records are probably not complete, they do project a sense of constant unrest as women came and went. Looking at the names of those invested during the period, we see three in 1858, twelve in

1859, none in 1860, nine in 1861, two in 1862, three in 1863, one in 1864, three in 1865, eighteen in 1866, six in 1867, five in 1868, twelve in 1869, and thirteen in 1870. In addition, there were candidates aspiring to membership. In spite of the fluctuating membership, in 1864 the "Society of St. Agnes" still was listed as teaching at St. Agnes Boarding School in Barton, St. Anthony, and Sts. Peter and Paul. In 1865-1866 the fifteen members (sisters and aspirants) added three more schools: St. Bridget in Wayne, St. Peter in Farmington, and Holy Trinity in Newburg.

AN AMERICAN SOCIETY

What kind of society did these young women join? It could scarcely have been called a community. Other religious congregations established in Wisconsin during this period had originated in Europe. Their members had a rule, a history, and traditions; their founders had been formed in religious life. They had a clear sense both of congregational identity and their own roles as women religious. The few Agnesians in Barton had no heritage, little structure, and an adequate formation. They were forced to rely on their own resources and sense of personal responsibility, along with the example of dedication they were given by their founder. Father Rehrl was an undeniably holy man, however deficient he may have been in understanding the needs of young women and the complexities of religious life in community. Although at that time they had to overcome many disadvantages, the Sisters of St. Agnes have always regarded the circumstance of being founded on American soil as a gift to be cherished and celebrated.

In the meantime the disadvantages of their origin outweighed the advantages. In 1864, Sister Thecla left for France with her mother.[19] Mrs. Dulso had come to Barton for a visit and a favor: to convince her daughter to accompany her on a trip to an uncle who was a priest. When Sister Thecla and her mother left, it was planting season. Because the schoolchildren were needed at home, they were dismissed until the following October. Rehrl, trying to make the most of an equivocal situation, optimistically believed that Sister Thecla could help him in a new campaign of recruiting young women to the society. His letters published in the *Katholische Blaetter* in April and June of 1864 were addressed to the women of Tyrol.

He pleaded with his readers to "raise the banner of faith all over America," inviting young women to contact Sister Thecla in France.[20]

Father Rehrl had not stopped dreaming. Because Maximilian, brother of the Emperor of Austria, had recently been established on the throne of Mexico, Rehrl held out the prospect of serving in Mexico as a further lure to patriotic Austrians:

> What if a call should come from Mexico to the Agnesians! It is possible! Or should an Austrian prince, marry the Crown Princess of Brazil, as rumor has it, then we would certainly want Agnesian sisters to open a mission field in that country. And finally, should true peace come to the United States of America, where now the fury of war is raging, offer a challenge to the Sisters to aid in the restoration of churches and schools now vacated and devastated by Civil War.[21]

In May, Rehrl wrote another letter to the paper in which he published chapter headings of the rule he had printed in 1862 and again asked for volunteers. Once more he was unsuccessful.

CRITICAL APPOINTMENTS

After Sister Thecla left, Father Rehrl made two important decisions. Agnes was named superior and placed in charge of the school at Barton. Because Rehrl had been purchasing more land from time to time, Sister Genevieve Popp was placed in charge of the farm at Barton.[22] Sister Genevieve had been a solid addition to the group, "motherly and kind" and with her knowledge of running a farm household, she was able to bring some order into the daily life of the sisters."[23]

It was in 1864 that Bishop Henni, who had been keeping an eye on the little convent,[24] advised Father Rehrl to have the sisters elect their own superior.[25] On July 2, 1864, the same day she renewed her vows, Agnes became the first elected superior at the age of seventeen. Out of five sisters eligible to vote, she received four votes. Agnes was superior, but in reality Rehrl retained control of the administration of the community, as well as responsibility for its spiritual and educational guidance. He decided which schools to attempt to staff, and it is hard to imagine him rejecting any offer or leaving to another the decision where each sister should be placed.

The boarding school at Barton was his special joy. He wanted to help out poor children who lived far away. They came with their bedding, food from home, and whatever textbooks the families could provide. He was not concerned with any child's ethnicity or physical condition but placed each one under the care of Sister Genevieve Popp. Like a loving mother, she proudly dressed the little girls on Sundays in figured pink dresses and pink sunbonnets. After her election, Agnes was sent to nearby Schlesingerville (Slinger) where she was both organist and teacher. As for Sister Thecla, on her return in 1865, she was sent as principal to the school in St. Lawrence.[26]

At Barton, young women and girls were still coming and trying out the life, but few stayed. Father Rehrl, too, must have experienced frustrations. In spite of his age, he was still making his mission trips, always on foot and with a knapsack on his back. Over the years, he took care of thirty-two mission churches. Traveling through the icy blasts of Wisconsin winters for more than twenty years, he must have experienced frostbite, suffered severe colds, and developed painful arthritis. On his return, he still taught his classes, but the young women were sent out as soon as they could meet the minimum state requirements.[27] These Agnesian candidates often were frustrated, and the pastors were not always pleased with the results of the young women's labors. There was little hope for a change, however, because nothing in the missionary's rule provided for the education and religious formation of the women.

The candidates were trying to live a life they understood imperfectly and were doing work for which they were unprepared. They had no viable rule, and their director was already overburdened with his own work. Under these conditions, it is difficult to think of the community's survival as anything less than a miracle.

THE CAPUCHINS

It is impossible to write the history of the early days of the Sisters of St. Agnes without understanding their connection with the

Capuchin Franciscans. The Franciscans, founded in the thirteenth century, were inspired by St. Francis of Assisi and his ideals, particularly those regarding poverty and community. The Capuchin branch of the Franciscan Order had resulted from the Reform of 1528, when the Order had sought to recapture its founding spirit. Two young secular priests, Gregory Haas[28] and John Frey—friends since their university days at Freiberg—heard in 1855 that every religious order except the Capuchins was represented in the United States. From that time on they dreamt of establishing a Capuchin monastery there. They wrote of their plans to their fellow Swiss, Bishop Henni, who welcomed them to his diocese in Milwaukee.

In September 1856 when the priests arrived, Bishop Henni offered them a choice between two beautiful sites: Holy Hill, not far from Milwaukee, and the more remote Mount Calvary. They chose Mount Calvary and began the arduous process both of becoming Capuchins themselves and of establishing the order in a new country. One of their members, Fr. Pacificus Berleman, OM, Cap.,[29] became the pastor of Marytown, situated in the eastern portion of Calumet Township and only a few miles from the monastery.

Sister Agnes was sent to this little hamlet in June of 1865. She had passed her examination for a Fond du Lac County teaching certificate and was to open the public school in Marytown. Another sister, Gertrude Laughlin, was teaching in the Catholic school. Gertrude, two years younger than Agnes, had been born Catherine Laughlin in Theresa, Wisconsin, to John and Anna Garrity Laughlin. She had much in common with Agnes besides her age. Both were women of firm character and intelligence, and they also had a love and enjoyment of life that helped them transcend the difficult circumstances in which they were placed.

Hard as the sisters worked, however, they were barely surviving. The economic depression resulting from the Civil War continued. The wars in Europe, rooted in the attempts to unify Germany, dried up the supply of money from Austria to the missions. Poverty was everywhere, food was scarce, and goods were very expensive. Father Rehrl was so hard-pressed for money that in January 1866, he was forced to give Bishop Henni a mortgage for $300.[30] The schools were providing very little from tuition. The sisters were reduced to making short collection tours, either on foot or in wagons drawn by oxen and horses.

FATHER REHRL'S "COLLECTIONS"

Father Rehrl also did his share of collecting. In February of 1866, he visited Marytown to see the sisters. On his return, he visited one of his old friends, Caspar Blum, who welcomed him with the question, "Father, what is it you need today, how much wheat and how much barley?" The farmer's thirteen-year-old daughter was busy washing dishes. "I need her," said Father Rehrl, pointing to Anna. Her father could only say, "Then you've got something," as Anna, well-acquainted with the sisters, announced that she would like to be a sister, too, "just like Sister Mary Agnes and Sister Mechtildis."[31]

Another recruit was twenty-seven-year-old Catherine Recker. Rehrl was visiting another family at Marytown and passed through the kitchen where Catherine was washing the dishes. After greeting her, he said, "I am looking for girls for my convent."[32] As an invitation to consider a religious vocation, it was brief but effective. Catherine, together with Anna Blum and Catherine Groeschel, left for Barton that spring.

Catherine Recker became Sister Rosa that summer. Anna Blum had to wait until she was seventeen to become Sister Hyacintha. "A flower you are and a flower you will remain," Father Rehrl pronounced upon giving the young woman a first name to match her family name, which meant "flower" in German.[33] Catherine Groeschel did not live to make her religious profession. She died as a novice in 1867. Whether or not it was on the same February trip, Rehrl also brought back to Barton four young orphaned sisters from St. Anna. Three of the sisters eventually entered the community— Sisters Eulalia, Dorothea, and Beatrice Kreuder.

CONTINUING HARDSHIPS

Meanwhile, Sister Agnes remained as superior, principal, teacher, and organist in Marytown. She walked five miles a week to St. Anna for lessons from the pastor, an accomplished musician. Even though she was stationed far from the motherhouse in Barton, she was well aware of the problems the sisters were facing there. The 1868 *Catholic Almanac* listed twenty-eight professed sisters and seven novices in the congregation, but nowhere near that many remained. The hardships never seemed to abate, and few could cope with physical deprivation, the demands of ministry, and the uncertainties of their lives. Sister Agnes undoubtedly heard complaints from the chronically discontented, but it was the ones who had good cause for dissatisfaction that caused her the most pain.

Sister Agnes was also suffering from the tensions in her own house. The mission at Marytown, which had begun so happily, had been disturbed by the arrival of Sister Lidwina Hazotte.[34] On October 16, 1865, the same older sister who had objected so strongly to the departure of Agnes from Detroit in 1862, joined her in Barton. In 1866 Clementine had been professed as Sister Lidwina. Agnes, although younger, had a stronger and more attractive personality than her sister. Lidwina was dependent on Agnes, and, it seems, was envious of other relationships in her sibling's life, particularly Agnes' friendship with Gertrude. Agnes was left spending a considerable amount of energy trying to keep the peace between her friend and her sister.

In the midst of the tension and hard work, Sister Agnes found both support and advice from the Capuchins in the parish, Fathers Pacificus Berleman and Cajetan Krauthahn. As members of a religious community themselves, the friars must have been appalled by the situation in which the young women found themselves. Their lack of training in religious life was all too evident, and it was only by the grace of God that they did as well as they did. In spite of discouragement from his superiors, Father Pacificus attempted to remedy the situation as best he could.[35] He gave the sisters in Marytown regular conferences and a daily order that included visits to the Blessed Sacrament and recitation of the office.[36]

In the spring of 1869, Sister Agnes wrote to Father Rehrl to inform him that she had given Sister Gertrude permission to go home to visit her sick parents, who would pay for the trip. She was unsure but believed that this was in accordance with the rule. She requested that Father Rehrl change his plan of sending Sister Gertrude to Little Chute. She also intended to send Sister Rosa to another mission because the people where she was presently located had known her previously and did not give her the respect she deserved. Although it appears that the contents of the rule were neither clear nor familiar to her, Agnes openly asserted her right as superior to make decisions about the sisters.[37]

Always in the background was the reality that the sisters were barely eking out their existence and furthermore were accumulating debts. A few schools provided meager incomes, but other schools were conducted gratuitously, and the farm could not support the community.

Little is known about the summer of 1869, other than that Agnes was again elected superior. Filled with misgivings, she left Barton that fall to return to her teaching assignment in Marytown, but it became impossible for her to continue the status quo. By the end of November 1869, Agnes had grown convinced that it was her duty to leave and reside at the motherhouse in Barton. Prepared for the inevitable conflict, the twenty-two-year-old sister left Marytown on November 25. Sister Agnes was concerned about fundamentals. The sisters were not getting proper meals; their religious and intellectual formation was inadequate; their mission appointments were not always suitable; and the congregation did not have an accepted rule. The motherhouse sadly lacked the peace and order that should distinguish a convent. If the community were to survive, she would have to live at the motherhouse, institute a regular religious life, and establish a novitiate. A firm yet loving hand was needed, and Sister Agnes knew she was obliged to fulfill her role as superior according to her own conscience and the advice of the friars in Marytown.

STRAINED RELATIONSHIPS

These convictions of Agnes were not shared by Father Rehrl, who was driven by the needs of the thousands of German immigrants arriving every year in Wisconsin. If the faith were to survive in a hostile environment, the children needed to be educated as Catholics and there was no time to waste. Sisters were to be sent out as soon as possible.[38] It also speaks volumes of Father Rehrl's idealism that in the midst of all these difficulties, he attempted to convince his friend, Father Joseph Rainer, to teach the sisters Spanish for his projected missions in Mexico. Inevitably, it was not long before the visions of the two strong-willed leaders would clash.

The information we have of the relationship between Father Rehrl and Sister Agnes is culled from her correspondence to Marytown immediately after she had returned to Barton. Some letters were written to the group of sisters at Marytown, but most were to her friend, Sister Gertrude Laughlin. They present a picture of a young woman determined to make the community a true religious institute, but aware that she could not succeed without challenging the decisions of the society's founder, whom she respected as a priest and a dedicated missionary. Hastily written, blotted, and full of misspellings, the letters chronicle those few months of frustration when both parties moved closer and closer to an irremediable break. On his part, Father Rehrl had Sister Catherine Spenthoff "secretly appointed (elected) prefect."[39]

In her first letter from Barton, her basic disagreement with the director was clear. According to her, Father Rehrl did not believe in the girls knowing much about spiritual life. He cared only if he could send them out to teach. But she promised to "stick to what is right" although she expected "a great deal of trouble."[40] On December 1, 1869, Sister Agnes wrote again to the sisters in Marytown. There was good news from the candidature. Sister Alphonsa Birkenmeier, the directress, was training the candidates well. Agnes had procured brown veils for them to wear to church and chapel, and they wore little collars for everyday use. After that bit of brightness, however, she spelled out woe upon woe. She had promised to send Sister Cecilia to them but was unable to fulfill that commitment. "Rev. Father takes so many missions and has no one to send out but we shall make a stop sometime."[41] She added, "I have a great deal more that I could say but he is old and getting childish. He bought a press to print that will cost about twelve hundred dollars in all ... and we have so many debts to pay ... and need a house ... he runs us into debts."[42] She could not say much about Barton but believed the sisters there were doing their best.

A week later she wrote to her friend Sister Gertrude about her difficulties. Rehrl had wanted to send an unprepared candidate to St. Joseph in Appleton, the English Catholic school, and change other sisters' assignments. Sister Agnes protested. He told her that he had not established the convent for praying "but only to teach the ignorant children."[43] Saying that everything had gone wrong since the Capuchins had preached a retreat for the sisters, he blamed them for his conflict with Sister Agnes. "But sisters," she wrote, "I let him know after that it made me feel very bad."[44] The next day all seemed well. Father Rehrl "was so good and kind to me," Agnes said, and he praised the Capuchin Fathers and spoke as if nothing had happened. He told Agnes that he would trouble himself no more. They could do as they think right before God, but he had to fulfill the commitments he had already made.[45]

Three weeks later Agnes wrote a newsy letter to Gertrude. There were twelve candidates who were learning well and were "kept in good order so far." One candidate, Margaret Lethert from Pennsylvania, was proving to be a most excellent scholar and teacher.[46] She was pious and had good sense. Agnes had never found so "good-hearted a girl" since she had been in the convent. Sister Cecilia was out collecting in Port Washington, but another sister might have to be sent home because she was no use to the convent. Agnes missed Marytown and her friends there. It was only her faith that kept her going. "Last year Father Pacificus was with us yet and this year we are all separated from each other. Next year who knows? .... My pleasure in this world is gone and I don't care for it any more. I can only say my God and myself for he is the only one that will not leave me if I seek him."[47]

Christmas came and went, bringing more difficulties.[48] Candidates were coming and Sister Agnes wanted them trained in the fundamental knowledge and practice of religious life, as Father Pacificus had trained her.[49] Agnes feared that a "very nice girl of twenty-one with property" who had just arrived from Milwaukee, would not stay because Father Rehrl would send her out before she was prepared. "He did not want a novitiate. The first sisters didn't have one and the new ones didn't need one, either. He said he would answer for it all before God; he would do what he thought was right and the sisters that didn't like it ... could go somewhere else.[50] Without the support of the friars at Marytown at this time, Sister Agnes could probably not have remained firm. With their advice and the example of a regular religious life before her, she told the sisters that she would "go the way that Father Pacificus taught her."[51]

The tensions between Father Rehrl and Sister Agnes added further distress to a community already struggling to hold itself together. There were the inevitable problems on the missions. The community was in the process of making a major decision—accepting its first out-of-state mission in Defiance, Ohio. When appointments were made, sisters could not be sure whose views would prevail, the priest's or the sister's. And who could blame the sisters if they took advantage of the situation to press for their own preferences? At the

same time several promising young women were testing their vocations, and Agnes must have spent many hours praying that the community would be worthy of them and that the young women would
have the strength of will to remain in spite of the tremendous difficulties they were facing. She also worried about at least one seriously ill sister. It is little wonder that, in several letters, Agnes mentioned
being ill herself. Sister Agnes had also been facing some difficulties
with the diocese. A letter from Father Kundig in March sheds little
light on the precise cause, but it would not be unlikely to assume that
it was related to the obvious instability in her community. Kundig
wrote, "Our Bishop ordered me today to let you know that he wishes, with the help of God to work well with you and that we will all
remain true to our calling and vows. Up to now he appeared very
reticent in regard to you as if I had taken too much liberty in forming a friendship with you. But today that was changed ...."[52] The letter, double-edged as it may seem to present readers, must have reas-
sured Agnes for it is still extant.

A CRITICAL MEETING

That spring, an invitation to cook for the priests who were giving a
Lenten mission at nearby St. Bridget Parish in Wayne, Wisconsin,
had to have been welcomed by Agnes. The mission was to be given
by two Capuchin friars: Father Solanus, her old friend and mentor,
and Father Francis Haas, one of the founders of the community at
Mount Calvary. Agnes expected to have a chance to talk about the
problems she was facing and to receive the counsel she so sorely
needed from priests who were also members of a religious order.
     Although this was the first time Agnes met Father Francis, she
was aware both of his role in the history of the Capuchin foundation at Mount Calvary and of the awe the friars had of him. When
she met him, she, too, had the same reaction. Standing at 6'1" and
bearded as every Capuchin was obliged to be, his eyes were piercing
and his bearing, self-assured. He had brown hair, blue eyes, a large
nose, a medium mouth, and a long face.[53] Strong-willed, he had
placed his faith in God and had done the improbable. As a secular
priest, he had left Switzerland and, with a fellow priest, had established the centuries-old Capuchin Franciscan Order in the United
States. He was deeply spiritual; he had an ardent devotion to the

Sacred Heart and lived out the implications of that devotion. As an ascetic himself, he had a strong belief in the efficacy of trials and delighted when he saw others given the chance to be strengthened by them. A dry sense of humor and broad understanding of human nature gave his personality the balance that made him an effective spiritual director. His meeting with Sister Agnes that spring would lead to a relationship that would have a profound impact on her life and the survival of her community.

Agnes found in Father Francis an excellent confessor who was perceptive, kind, and supportive beyond her expectations. She met with him at least twice during the mission and left both times heartened and full of hope. She could not have known that his first impression of the society had been far from favorable. Through Father Pacificus, Francis had heard enough of the struggles of the sisters to become convinced that their venture would be fruitless, so he had attempted to discourage Pacificus from helping them. It was his meeting with Sister Agnes and her sisters, however, that finally impressed him with their sincerity, good will, and dedication to their work. It was also clear to him that Agnes, although young, possessed much of his own energetic zeal.[54] Before the mission was over, he had encouraged her to move to Fond du Lac.

A CRITICAL DECISION

As someone experienced in laying the foundation for a community and well aware of the practicalities that needed to be addressed, Father Francis saw opportunities for the society in Fond du Lac. He told Agnes to buy some land near the town, which had schools in which the sisters could teach. Although Fond du Lac was a railroad hub, its land was still cheap. Much larger than Barton, with fewer than fifteen persons in its entire township, Fond du Lac was the state's second-largest city. Father Francis added that Barton was a miserable place for a motherhouse, an opinion he did not withhold from Father Rehrl.[55]

Agnes saw in the counsel to build a motherhouse only twelve miles from the Capuchin monastery an implicit promise that they would support the community with spiritual direction and advice.[56] It was this support that she and her sisters desperately needed. She therefore lost little time in going to Fond du Lac, where she talked to Father Nicholas Pickel, pastor of the town's German church, St. Mary's.[57] They got along famously. She played the organ for him and they talked together for four hours. He, too, advised her to move to Fond du Lac, where she would be welcomed by the other two priests to teach the town's six hundred Catholic children in need of an education. There was suitable property she could buy, a large brown frame house together with six lots for five or six thousand dollars. Father Pickel would find a good man to act as intermediary because he suspected the "Yankee" who owned the land would not sell it to be used as a convent. He urged Agnes to make up her mind quickly because the Notre Dame Sisters in Milwaukee had been "spying for Fond du Lac" for a long time. On her part, Agnes thought that Catholic school tuitions, sewing lessons for the Protestant girls, and craft fairs would bring in over two thousand dollars each year. The property would be paid for in six or seven years.[58]

Agnes needed little encouragement. After talking the matter over with Father Rehrl in Barton, she returned to Fond du Lac with Sister Catherine Spenthoff, the superior of the motherhouse, to investigate further. They were both very pleased with the results of their trip. Sister Agnes and her assistant, Sister Barbara Lishka, then went to Milwaukee to discuss the projected purchase with the vicar general of the diocese, Father Martin Kundig. Evidently agreeing with the decision that Fond du Lac would provide more opportunities for the sisters, Father Kundig commanded Sister Agnes in obedience to transfer the motherhouse there.[59]

The E. Phillips property that Agnes bought on June 8, 1870, reveals her as an astute businesswoman. Instead of taking for five or six thousand dollars the house and five or six lots that had been suggested by Father Pickel, she purchased for six thousand three hundred dollars twelve city lots that extended from East Division Street to the center of Sheboygan Street. The final agreement included a two-story frame house, a new barn, and a new stable. The community was able to make an initial payment of $1,500 because of substantial dowries brought from Europe the previous year by two new members, Rosalia and Crescentia Immler.[60]

A Hopeful Spring

In April of 1870, while all these negotiations were going on, the community experienced a most promising event in the arrival of eight high-spirited Irish candidates from St. Mary Parish in Appleton, Wisconsin. Over time the story of their journey to Barton became part of community lore. Sister Magdalene McKenney, the girls' best-loved teacher, accompanied them.[61] The young women boarded a train in Appleton at 8:00 a.m. and traveled as far as Burnett Junction. They stayed at a hotel there and enjoyed visiting with an Irish family. The next day they got the train to Hartford, where they ran around, bought candy, and altogether had a final fling. Then they procured transportation on a lumber wagon with a spring seat. Sister Magdalene sat with the driver and two trunks while the eight girls sat on the six trunks in the back. When Margaret and Catherine Murphy got out to walk for awhile, the driver hurried up the horses and the two girls fell headlong while trying to catch up. Toward sundown they arrived at Barton and were greeted by sisters wearing faded brown veils. For supper they consumed dried apple sauce, bread, butter, fried pork, and a little tea. The girls thought the sisters must have been housecleaning and expected that things would be better the next day. However, the sisters' apparel did not improve, and as the meals became more and more frugal, they realized they had been welcomed royally, according to the sisters' standards. Later, after two of them broke the teapot doing dishes, tea was no longer served.[62]

The new candidates were fortunate in that some of them had completed considerable high school work and had been able to study under the direction of the superintendent of the Washington County schools. After their arrival, education in the convent was placed on a more regular basis. Rehrl taught Scripture when he was home, and the seminarian, J. E. Halbenkann, was hired to teach music and philosophy.

News from the new mission of St. John in Defiance, Ohio was glowing. About one hundred pupils were expected to enroll in the school, and the parishioners were in the process of finishing a house for the sisters, who were to be consulted about household goods.

Meanwhile, Kundig and Rehrl discussed the future of the community. It is not clear what was said in the discussion, but Sister

Agnes received a surprising letter from the vice-chancellor, in which he laid down the following directives:

> Inasmuch as the Reverend C. Rehrl has given the rectorate of your Institute into my hands, himself continuing as Chaplain and Confessor, I hereby submit to you the following rules which are to be observed in strict obedience: 1. You will build nothing nor undertake the erection of any new building without my approval and consent. 2. By election, choose six sisters to form your council without whose sanction no money shall be expended. 3. With the authorization of the Sisters you will provide sanitary housing and wholesome nourishment for the inmates of your institution. 4. The Sisters shall not devote themselves to agriculture unless to the extent of cultivation of vegetable or flower gardens, as they may desire. 5. Matters which are of importance to the Sisters alone, you need confide to me only if you judge it necessary.[63]

What Sister Agnes thought on receiving this letter is not recorded. She could hardly have helped feeling relieved. Father Rehrl would remain as their chaplain and confessor, but his plan to spend $1,200 for a printing press would be frustrated; the sisters in Barton would not be forced to do the heavy work on the farm; and, most importantly, they would have adequate housing and nourishing meals.

A DISAPPOINTMENT FOR FATHER REHRL

Where was Father Rehrl in all of this? The impact of events on Agnes' life was clear. At the beginning of Lent in 1870, the energy that had moved her back to Barton at Thanksgiving had been slowly dissipating as she dealt with financial problems, concern for the new entrants, grief that good women were leaving, complaining letters from Marytown, more frequent encounters with Father Rehrl, and personal loneliness and frustration. For his part, the priest returned to Barton exhausted from his mission trips, but knowing that he would have to deal with Agnes and her dreams for the society he had founded.

Then Father Francis entered the picture, and Agnes overflowed again with life. The revered Capuchin understood her and believed in her and her plans for the society. He gave her advice. The community would do better in Fond du Lac. When she went there, she was warmly received. She talked to Father Kundig. While it is doubtful that he was enthusiastic, he put no obstacles in her way. We know only that Father Rehrl was kept informed and that he, too, made no objections to the plan—but eventually he resigned the directorship of the community in favor of Father Kundig.[64]

The community that he had prayed for, that Saint Agnes had promised to him in Rome, that the Holy Father had encouraged him to found, that he had besought his fellow priests to support, that he had instructed personally—this community had, in effect, rejected him.

A Retreat and Its Aftermath

At the time of Father Kundig's letter, the sisters were planning another joyful event. In July 1870, they would participate in a summer retreat, which would end with the profession of three novices and the investing of eleven candidates. When Sister Agnes learned that Father Rehrl had asked Father Francis to give the retreat, she felt it was an answer to prayer. She had been worried for some time that the community had no approved constitutions. Although Father Rehrl's rule contained inspirational passages and good counsel, much more was needed if the stability and order required for a regular religious life were to be attained. On the first day of the retreat, she asked the Capuchin to write a rule for the community that could be submitted to Rome. He agreed, but asked that the retreat be extended so that he would have eight days in which to complete the task.[65]

On the last day of the retreat a sense of joy filled the community, even though four of the thirty-two members could not be present because of the distance they would have had to travel, while two others had refused to participate.[66] Father Rehrl was expected and Father Kundig, in answer to an invitation from Father Rehrl, had written that he would be in Barton on Saturday, July 23. When Father Kundig arrived as promised, Agnes was struck by his somber demeanor. After the minimum formalities, he informed her that he had decided to disband the Sisters of St. Agnes.[67] He gave two reasons for the decision: the community, twelve years old, still had not received canonical approval, and it as yet had no constitutions.[68]

It was also apparent that the prospects of the society were bleak. Father Rehrl had neither the time nor the experience to form women religious. It would not have been just to receive young women into a society that had no discernible future. There were other more stable congregations in the diocese, which readily admitted candidates and adequately prepared them for teaching. In any case, Kundig's decision retained elements of ambiguity.[69] Although it is not clear if the absent Bishop Henni, who had always shown great regard for Father Rehrl, knew of the vicar's decision, later developments seemed to indicate that he did not.

The shock and dismay that Sister Agnes felt when the vicar told her that he had come to disband the sisters can scarcely be underestimated. The community had purchased property in Fond du Lac with the permission of Bishop Henni, but she could not appeal to him because he was attending the First Vatican Council in Rome. Father Francis was Agnes' one ray of hope.

It was her only chance to save the society. Agnes told Fr. Kundig that Father Francis was writing the constitutions for the community and requested that he discuss the situation with him, but if he still decided to disband the group, the sisters would submit to his will. Father Francis, upon hearing of the matter, asked the Vicar to discuss it with him privately. As the draft of the constitutions proved satisfactory to both Father Kundig and Father Rehrl, it only remained for the sisters to meet and accept the document.

A SUDDEN REVERSAL

The next morning Father Kundig informed the sisters that he had found the constitutions acceptable. He then read the document to the assembly and solemnly addressed the sisters, "Those who under the inspiration of the Holy Ghost, Whom we have just invoked, feel that they wish to ratify these Rules and Constitutions and of their own accord are determined to live under these precepts may rise and say 'I accept.'" Without hesitation, the sisters all arose and gave their consent. The Society of St. Agnes was then empowered to "exist under these Rules and Constitutions and to function as a duly-authorized organ of the Church for the honor and glory of God and the salvation of souls."[70]

To the end of their lives, the sisters present recalled the Solemn High Mass and the emotion-filled sermon that followed. Father Francis spoke of the renunciation, sacrifices, and devotion their lives would demand, and he choked with tears as he recalled the pain he had felt as he had left his country, family, and friends. It was a sorrow that everyone present had known and would continue to experience.

The investing and profession ceremonies, according to the new constitutions, were presided over by Father Kundig. The eleven candidates who were invested were joined by the three novices who were professed that day. In accordance with the constitutions, the novitiate program Sister Agnes had struggled so hard for was now a reality.[71]

After dinner the professed sisters gathered together to fulfill one final obligation, the canonical election of the superior. Sister Agnes was elected unanimously. Father Kundig announced that she was to be known as Mother Agnes, "Mother" being the title given to the superior geneal in the constitutions. She appointed Sister Barbara Lishka and Sister Gertrude Laughlin her assistants. Father Rehrl's name is not mentioned in the account of the festivities.[72]

A RIFT

The next few days were jubilant ones for the sisters. Father Kundig had set August 1, 1870 as the day for the move to Fond du Lac. Among the many remaining tasks were supervising the remodeling of the house and barn in Fond du Lac and packing up the mission in Barton. In the midst of all this activity, Father Rehrl approached Mother Agnes to tell her that he would not accompany the sisters to Fond du Lac but asked to tell the sisters himself. Agnes was stunned, but, even in the midst of her emotional turmoil, she must have realized that more collisions would have been inevitable between the two of them. Strained as the previous two years had been for her personally, Mother Agnes must have spent the night searching her soul. Still, when the next day came, she again approached Father Rehrl and begged him to come with the community. It was no use. Father Rehrl was adamant.

At a meeting of the professed sisters the next day Father Rehrl gave one reason for his decision not to move with them. When Father Kundig had taken over the directorate of the sisters, Kundig had not stated nor had he implied that he wished Rehrl to remain with the sisters. Therefore he would remain where he was and take care of his mission churches. He promised continuing interest and care for the community; he then blessed the sisters and wished them Godspeed.[73] The sisters were shaken, for it was inconceivable to most of them that their founder would leave them. When the day came that twenty-six sisters left for Fond du Lac, six remained behind with Father Rehrl: Sisters Genevieve and Euphrosine Popp, Elizabeth Schmitz, Theresa Kraus, Susanna Gersbach, and Philomene Wild. Father Kundig had reluctantly given them permission to stay.[74]

By this time Father Rehrl had come to blame Agnes for the difficulties the society had been facing. Even before the final break, he had written to the Bishop of Green Bay, the Most Reverend Joseph Melcher, who, in turn, had written her "a pretty hard letter"[75] about the sisters. For her part, Agnes complained that Father Rehrl was doing all he could against them, including "writing one letter after another"[76] to the bishop. Not unnaturally, Father Rehrl was trying to dissuade other women from joining the Fond du Lac group. One sister, who had promised to teach for Agnes, told her that Father Rehrl had written to tell her "never to join us never and never."[77]

Although statistics given in the Catholic Almanac are very confusing for the next few years, the two groups were considered two separate institutes.[78] The women associated with Father Rehrl were known variously as the Society of St. Agnes (1864) or Ladies of the Community of St. Agnes (1865-1880) or simply as the Agnes Sisters. In 1874 the publication places the Barton and Fond du Lac groups together under the notation, "Academies of the Sisters of St. Agnes at Fond du Lac and at Barton, Washington County, Wisconsin," adding that "these Sisters have charge of over thirteen parochial schools."[79] In 1877, under the heading "Female Academies and Schools" both the Congregation of Sisters of St. Agnes at Barton and the Community of St. Agnes at Fond du Lac were listed. The sisters in Barton claimed seventeen sisters, four novices, five parish schools; the Fond du Lac group numbered seventy-five sisters, ten novices, and ten postulants. The next year Barton claimed twenty-one sisters, while Fond du Lac had eighty-two. The numbers in Barton did not change in 1879 and 1880.[80]

In Barton, Father Rehrl and the six sisters who remained with him were doing the best they could. For a time they were even able to get new recruits. But the community's problems were insurmountable. Father Rehrl the missionary, could not be at the same time director, mentor, and spiritual guide of young women. Equally ominously, Sister Gertrude Laughlin, the superior, had begun to spend a great deal of time at her mission, St. Patrick in Janesville. Rehrl wrote to her complaining about the neglect of the farm and the animals and asking that she return to Barton. Apparently, Sister Genevieve Popp, who had been in charge of the farm for years, was no longer there. The sisters wrote to the superior and begged her to return to them in Barton, where conditions were no better, if not worse, than they had been eight or nine years previously. It was no use. When the superior attempted to move the motherhouse to Janesville and began receiving candidates and professing novices there, it was clear that the community remaining behind at Barton had slipped away from its founder, too.

Even so, it took a long time for Father Rehrl to realize that directing a group of religious, even though he was its founder, was not his vocation. He clung to what remained of the society. Finally, when matters were becoming worse instead of better, he went to St. Francis Seminary to talk matters over with his friend, Dr. Salzmann. The advice he got was not what he wished because the priest told him to give it up. "Can't you see for yourself that it would no longer work?" It was advice that he could not accept. He left the room and visited Father Rainer, who later remarked Rehrl had said, "I'll never go to Dr. Salzmann again for any counsel. He told me to give it up."[81]

Meanwhile Father Rehrl continued his rounds of the missions, directed the society as best he could, and worked on his farm. He built a barn, complete with his initials on it, that is still standing today. Like the house he built, it is well-proportioned and built to last. He was respected by his neighbors for his charity to the poor, whatever their religion. One of his neighbors who occasionally worked for him spoke of the missionary's practice of collecting money for widows and putting it in the old red handkerchief he always carried.[82] A typical anecdote about Father Rehrl describes an occasion when he, wearing new shoes that must have been the gift of a benefactor, came across a poor man wearing a worn-out pair. He immediately took off his shoes and offered them to the man. The man hesitated, and then said, "I'm not a Catholic." The priest put on the old man's shoes and said, "I didn't ask you." The man was left with a new pair of shoes and a sense of bemusement at both Father Rehrl's charity and his taciturnity. Judge Patrick O'Meara had the final word on his character, saying, "He had all the qualities of sainthood. He was regardless of his own comfort in the service of religion more than any man I ever knew."[83]

There is also evidence that Father Rehrl possessed a sense of humor, dry to be sure, but evidence that he could enjoy life's little surprises. On April 24, 1875, he wrote back to his home diocese: "It may well be that many of my acquaintances in my Mother Diocese have already traveled to their eternal homeland, but I, I who have been listed as dead three times, and once even the newspaper carried a written report about my death—I am still living!"[84]

DAY OF RECONCILIATION

The denouement of the story of Father Rehrl and Mother Agnes came unexpectedly. Almost nine years had passed since Mother Agnes and her sisters had left Barton. There had been many tears shed during those years, many trials overcome, and many prayers and sacrifices offered. By 1879 the congregation numbered eighty-eight professed sisters, five novices, and fifteen postulants. It sponsored twenty mission houses located in five states: Wisconsin, Michigan, Indiana, Illinois, and Pennsylvania. Scarcely eighteen months previously a new four-story motherhouse had been dedicated in Fond du Lac.

By March of that year, the sisters at the motherhouse were preparing to celebrate the feast of St. Joseph with a sense of gratitude for all of their blessings. As the often-told story recounts, on the morning of March 18, Mother Agnes and Sister Regina were standing at a second-floor window admiring the early spring day when they saw a bobsleigh enter the convent property. Then followed scenes worthy of a nineteenth-century melodrama. The prosperous-looking driver was accompanied by an obviously poor man, but only the driver approached the convent door. Mother Agnes remained at the window but directed Sister Regina to find out what the men wanted. Sister Regina returned with the information that it was an old friend, a certain Mr. Annen from Barton, who had come to extend greetings to some of the sisters. Mother Agnes, of course, told Sister Regina to offer Mr. Annen hospitality and dinner and added that she should offer the poor man who was waiting in the yard a meal, because he was probably ashamed to ask for something to eat. Again, Sister Regina went off on her errand, and this time, Mother Agnes saw her speaking to Mr. Annen, who emphatically shook his head. Then Agnes set out to meet Regina, who was returning very quickly with astonishing news. It was Father Rehrl with Mr. Annen and the two had refused the invitation to remain for dinner.[85]

At that moment, Mother Agnes looked out the window and recognized Father Rehrl. The reunion was touching and the reconciliation complete. Father Rehrl accepted an invitation to remain the night to celebrate St. Joseph's feast the next day with the sisters. Even in the midst of all the emotion, Mother Agnes' sense of the practical did not desert her. She delegated several sisters to make him a new cassock, biretta, and shirts to be ready for Mass the next day. They stayed up all night sewing in the dim light of the oil lamps. The next morning his outfit was completed by the addition of a coat, hat, and shoes.

Father Rehrl sang the High Mass for the feast day and Father Francis celebrated the reunion in his homily by expressing the hope that "the occasion would be an enduring tie between the two branches of the Sisters of St. Agnes."[86]

According to Sister Julia Dullea, a few months later Father Rehrl met some of the clergy in the vicinity of St. Lawrence, Washington County. They noted his new clothes with surprise and pleasure. Rehrl, with tears welling in his eyes, replied, "I have been visiting my spiritual children." Not long after, the sisters learned that Father Rehrl had given his new coat to a shabbily-dressed man he felt sorry for.[87]

As Father Rehrl compared the thriving, peaceful convent in Fond du Lac with the uncertainties and irregularities of the little group in Barton, he came to the painful conclusion that he had to lay the whole matter before Archbishop Henni.[88] On September 1, 1879, he announced that the archbishop had decided to dissolve the Sisters of St. Agnes at Barton. The sisters were told they were free at the end of the expiration of their yearly vows to join either an approved religious community or to secularize. Seven sisters from Barton were admitted to the novitiate in Fond du Lac in September of that same year.[89] The next week in writing to a fellow priest who was looking for sisters, Rehrl sent the address of the sisters in Fond du Lac. His final remark was, "Not I left the sisters but they left me."[90]

For some time the parishioners of the churches the missionary had served had arranged a relay system to help him on his mission visits. Young men met him at assigned places and escorted him to his next stop. The process continued throughout his trip until his safe arrival home.[91] This was also the year when Father Rehrl, realizing that he could no longer keep up his extensive mission rounds, limited himself to serving at St. Matthias Church, Auburn. When the sisters left Barton, Mother Agnes—concerned about his increasing frailty—sent him a teacher for the parish school and three sisters to assist him.

Sister Clara Rehberg, the first young woman to become a Sister of St. Agnes, was one of his initial caregivers. She described Father's daily regimen to the sisters. He got up each morning at three; then he did the morning chores, milking the cows and driving them to pasture. Returning home, he slipped off the wooden shoes he had worn to do the farm work and put on his slippers. By then it was five o'clock and time for Mass. He prayed and meditated until his breakfast of milk soup, cheese, and potatoes at seven. If he did not have a sick call or visitors in need of help, on weekdays he was ready to work on his writing or in the print shop. No longer printing his little booklets for elementary children, he worked on his meditation book, printed a catechism, and a child's booklet of prayers and hymns arranged for each day of the week. His last work, *A Book for Thinking Christians*, was not completed to his satisfaction when he was forced to discontinue working on it.[92]

FATHER REHRL'S LAST DAYS

For the next two years, the missionary, then in his seventies, continued as best he could. One of his last projects was making arrangements for the school of St. Matthias, which he believed would be an important school for non-Catholic children. He had appointed the directress of the parish's Ladies Society to meet and take care of the sisters. He planned to build a small house near the church there "as I do not want to live any longer with families." He asked Mother Agnes to come with the sisters to Barton so he could visit with her and "talk over many things."[93]

The visit did not take place. On August 28, 1881, he said his Sunday Mass at St. Matthias while obviously very ill. Tuesday he conducted a funeral, but he could barely finish the prayers at the cemetery. A chair had to be provided for him at the grave. On Wednesday morning he came down to the convent in the pouring rain and said to the sisters, "I am so sick." The doctor from West Bend was called in. He administered a sedative and told the sisters that there was little he could do because Father had a serious heart condition. On Thursday, the doctor suggested that the sister call a priest for the Last Rites. On Saturday, September 3, he was visited by two priests. One was a Capuchin who had been one of Father Rehrl's first communicants, Hyacinth Schommer. They stayed all morning and Father Rehrl gave them directions regarding his Masses and other pending obligations. They left him sitting in an armchair while they went over to the convent for lunch. They had been gone only a few minutes when they were called back by Sister Genevieve. The missionary was slumped on the floor. The priests placed him gently on the bed and then as they blessed him, they heard him say, "Oh Jesus, be thou with me at this my hour of death. Oh dear St. Agnes!" As the Angelus was ringing, he died.[94]

He had a "fine funeral," which was attended by the priests and people of the surrounding territory.[95] Non-Catholics as well as Catholics would miss the familiar figure in his cylinder hats and worn pants and coat, along with the red handkerchief he always carried to hold the money he collected for widows.[96] Mother Agnes was in Indiana and not able to attend, but other Sisters of St. Agnes were present. Father Francis preached in German to the hundreds of people who attended, and Father Dominic Thill preached in

English. Father Francis spoke of the missionary's tireless efforts to preserve the Faith among the new settlers, finding no effort too strenuous, no deprivation too great. A true apostle, Father Rehrl's life was devoted to the salvation of souls. Protestants and Catholics alike paid him honor as a man of great charity, love for the poor, and zeal to spread the word of God.

His will proved to be simple: "The East half of the South East quarter Section no. Ten (10) ... together with all the buildings, I give and bequeath to the Rt. Reverend John Martin Henni and his successors in office for the use of the Sisters of St. Agnes in the village of Barton .... And that the said house be kept up for the purpose of educating children in the Catholic Religion, and for the people in general ...."[97]

The archbishop, however, did not agree with this disposition of the estate. According to directions from the archdiocese, the two mortgages on the property were foreclosed. A sheriff's sale was held and the property was sold for $784.90.[98] Father Rehrl's personal effects were sold at auction. Among the many books auctioned off was a Bible printed in 1574.[99]

Subscriptions for five dollars were offered to raise the funds to print the prayer book that he had been preparing, *A Book for Thinking Christians*. His friend, Carl A. Bruderle, who financed and distributed the book, wrote in the introduction that it was "the result of strenuous work, continual care, and material sacrifice."[100] Unfortunately, Father Rehrl was not given the time to complete the book as he would have wished. Its contents, a mixture of treatises on prayer and the sacraments, passages from Scripture, thirty visits to the Blessed Sacrament, and church history, needed stringent editing; the printing was irregular, and the book lacked an imprimatur. It was treasured only by his friends.

Father Rehrl was buried in St. Mary's Parish cemetery in Young America, a small village one mile north of Barton. Mother Agnes placed a simple marble headstone with the initials "CR" on it. Later he was removed to the new cemetery, then a plot for the priests. The original simple headstone was replaced by a monument bearing on its front the name of Rehrl. The sculpture on it represents a chalice, a lamb, a cross, a sword—and the words Agnus Dei. A cross was repeated on all four sides of the stone, and inscribed on the west side in German was a quotation from St. John:

"I am the resurrection and the life ...."(11:25-26).
Father Rehrl's name was on the south side.

In 1968, on the 87th anniversary of his death, the community acknowledged and honored their founder by removing his remains to St. Joseph Springs Cemetery in Fond du Lac. He lies there near the graves of Mother Agnes and the pioneer sisters of the congregation. Today, no one would question the role of Father Caspar Rehrl in founding the Sisters of St. Agnes. But, as the Golden Jubilee of the congregation was celebrated in 1920, it does not seem that the Sisters of St. Agnes officially considered him their founder.[101]

FATHER REHRL'S LEGACY

Father Rehrl loved God and God's creation; he loved the church and desired nothing more than to serve God through preserving and intensifying the faith of God's people.[102] Scholarly by nature and education, he realized the necessity of adapting the church to the needs of the time.[103] He lived a life of physical exertion and hardship, believing that, "No step is lost, no drop of sweat is in vain, if one lives in grace and acts through love of God."[104] He loved the poor; he was charitable, persevering, and stubborn. He was not political and he was not tactful.[105] He never sought his own glory. "Only his true and disinterested and ardent love induced him to continue his work among strangers, living in a scattered lot, so rich in sorrow and poor in spiritual grace,—and to do real Samaritan work amongst them."[106] The spirituality that undergirded his life was the spirituality of the immigrant church with its emphasis on Christ crucified and the church's role as moral teacher. This love of God was expressed primarily in ways that gave form and substance to his life—in the whole-hearted performance of his priestly duties and in love of neighbor expressed in his commitment to education.[107]

A list of churches he served is imposing: St. John Baptist, Johnsburg; St. Nicholas, Mount Calvary; St. Mary's, Marytown; St. Anthony, Allenton; St. Martin, Ashford; St. Matthias, Auburn; St. Matthew, Campbellsport; Mater Dolorosa, Fredonia; St. John of God, Farmington; St. Andrew, Leroy, Wisconsin; St. Mary, Mayville; St. Matthias, Nabob; Sts. Peter and Paul, Nenno; St.

Matthew (St. Bartholomew), Neosho; Holy Trinity, Newburg; St. John, Rubicon; St. Kilian, St. Kilian; St. Lawrence, St. Lawrence; St. Michael, St. Michael; Immaculate Conception, Saukville; St. Peter, Schlesingerville; St. Theresa, Theresa; St. Augustine, Jackson; St. Bridget, Wayne; Holy Angels, West Bend; Immaculate Conception, Barton; St. Mary, Woodland; St. John, Kohler; St. Mary, Port Washington; Holy Cross, Holy Cross; and St. Finbar, Saukville.[108]

He gave the Sisters of St. Agnes a spirit of daring, a sense of dedication, a willingness to undertake hard and unpopular jobs, and an indifference to worldly success. He inspired in the sisters a respect for the church and the clergy, a commitment to education and a love of liturgical music that would mark their formation for the next century. The qualities of a rough-hewn, honest, hard-working pioneer were his, coupled with a willingness to give all without counting the cost. Sisters who were his contemporaries or who lived close to the founding period always spoke of him as "holy Father Rehrl."[109]

What did it mean to work as a missionary priest in the United States along the Midwestern frontier in the mid-nineteenth century? It was to live where little immigrant dwellings were buffeted by icy winds, where summers were humid and thick with insect life, where hard-working German and Irish farmers struggled to create new lives in a not always welcoming environment. It was to grieve when countrymen lost their faith and their children went uneducated. It was to do all in his power to bring to others what he most valued himself—the knowledge of Jesus Christ and the blessings of an education.

What did it mean to found a religious community of women? It was to suffer as aspirants came and went, unable to endure the privations he accepted so stoically. It was to have the joys of teaching the candidates when he returned from his mission trips. It was to see a little community grow, only to feel deserted as the community turned elsewhere for leadership. It was, finally, to overcome the pain of shattered relationships and to seek reconciliation with the sisters who had rejected his leadership. It was to find—to his joy—that they still revered and loved him.

What is it like to be a missionary and a founder of a religious community? In the long run, it is to be an imperfect human being, prone to the mistakes and faults that are the burden of the human race. It is also to be filled with a strong faith and a conviction that the work that lies before one is God's work.

Chapter III

=== ❦ ===

Mother Agnes in Charge

On the first day of August, 1870, Mother Agnes Hazotte descended from a lumber wagon and took formal possession of a farm on the outskirts of the city of Fond du Lac, Wisconsin—the new home of the twenty sisters, fourteen novices and the seven candidates who comprised the Sisters of St. Agnes.

Twelve years had passed since the first three members had been gathered together by the missionary, Caspar Rehrl, to help him in his work of spreading the faith. Father Rehrl was no longer with them; the few women who had lived through those twelve years had undergone numerous hardships; the society was still pitifully small in numbers. The community had survived, but it had yet to establish the strong spiritual foundation which could give its members the support and strength needed to sustain them in their very difficult lives. But a new day was beginning. The women were idealistic and self-sacrificing and the charismatic Capuchin friar, Francis Haas, offered them the guidance they so desperately needed; but it was Mother Agnes, aged twenty-three, who was responsible for the formation, welfare, and ministries of the sisters as well as the spiritual health and financial stability of the congregation. It was her hope that the move to Fond du Lac would afford a home for the community and sustain its spiritual and economic growth.

FOND DU LAC AND THE WORLD BEYOND

Fond du Lac was only thirty some miles north of the village of Barton in a location that seemed ideal for the motherhouse. It bore little resemblance to the place where, twenty-five years previously, Rehrl had spent the night at the French trader's hut. In 1870 it had a population nearing thirteen thousand; but like the sisters themselves, the town and surrounding areas were still undergoing transitions. Lumber was outstripping wheat as the basis of prosperity in the region; and dairy farms, thanks to the superior care the German immigrants gave their cattle, were increasing. Grist mills, foundries, a farm implements factory, a blast furnace, and over a dozen carriage and wagon factories also contributed to the economy. The car shops of the Chicago Northwestern Railroad employed around four hundred men. The nature of the population was changing also as the original "Yankees" were selling their overworked lands and moving further west, but new immigrants had more than doubled its 1860 population to 12,640 in 1870. The newcomers were just as hard-working and family-oriented as the older inhabitants had been. Religion played an important role in the lives of the citizenry; nine churches represented the major Protestant denominations and four churches, the Catholic.[1]

Ethnicity determined much of the social interplay in the Catholic population. Almost all of Fond du Lac's immigrants were German and Irish, although the first Catholic church was named St. Louis after the saintly king of France to pay tribute to the national origin of the area's first Catholics. That church had been established in 1847 or 1848 when thirty settlers met with Father Rehrl to build it. By 1854, when the number of Catholics had grown to two thousand and a new church was necessary, a number of temperance Irish withdrew from St. Louis and established St. Patrick's Parish.[2] The Germans, true to their belief that "the school will build the church," established St. Mary's School for their children in 1857 and then chartered their church in 1865.[3] While Fond du Lac had an established public school system with its fifty instructors teaching in forty-two public primary schools, four grammar schools, and a high school, the only Catholic school was unabashedly German. Because there was no other religious community in Fond du Lac at that time, the struggling Sisters of St. Agnes believed the town would provide opportunities for them.

In 1870, Queen Victoria reigned in England; Ulysses S. Grant was President of the United States; and Reconstruction was transforming the American South. It was only five years since the United States had been torn by Civil War and little more than a year since the transcontinental railroad had united the continent. Less than two weeks before the sisters' move to Fond du Lac, the Franco-Prussian War had begun with the French invasion of Germany. On the very day of their arrival, two events occurred, both heralding major trends in American history: John D. Rockefeller founded the Standard Oil Company, and women in Utah, given full franchise, voted for the first time.

The first church council in almost three hundred years was still in session. On July 18, 1870 the bishops had solemnly defined the primacy and infallibility of the Roman pontiff.[4] While those other worlds of national politics and international relations seemed far from the Wisconsin prairie, those events inevitably were woven into the fabric of the sisters' lives.

ADJUSTING TO NEW CIRCUMSTANCES

While Mother Agnes had counted and been grateful for the blessings showered on the community, she could not have shared fully in the high spirits of the younger sisters. Securing a future for the congregation had come at no small cost. Father Rehrl had been deeply wounded by the sisters' decision to leave Barton, and Agnes could not have been impervious to his pain. The older sisters were torn by the rupture; six chose to remain with their founder and no doubt many were left wondering if they themselves had made the right decision.[5] It was not that Agnes regretted the move, but she realized that now the community had to adjust to a new rule of life and prove that it belonged in the same company with the time-honored congregations of the church. Moreover, if the sisters were to survive, she had to gain the respect and credit of the Fond du Lac business community.

It was a daunting task that Mother Agnes faced. The euphoria that the sisters had felt after their rescue by Father Francis Haas would not last if the community could not provide basic physical and emotional necessities for its members. At the same time, Agnes herself had a great need for support. In January, there was another flare-up with Rehrl, who also needed sisters to take care of his schools. When Sister Librada wished to join the sisters in Fond du Lac, he wrote an acrimonious letter to Mother Agnes, "who wrote him a good answer back."[6] At the same time Agnes, who could bear to see no one suffer, asked the sisters to "Keep a nine days devotion for Father Rehrl for his intentions, but tell no one .... Pray for poor Father, he has trouble enough with his congregations here. Let the school children pray every day three Aves for him, but don't tell them why and for whom."[7] That Agnes made the effort to convince him to remain with the community after that final ordeal says much about her character, determined and unswerving, but willing to forget hurts and disappointments and try again.

Surprisingly, Agnes now had a supporter in Father Kundig. When she told the vicar that Rehrl was "cutting up," he invited her and her sister companion to dinner and told her not to trouble herself, for Father Rehrl could not "do anything."[8] While that may have been the case, Agnes neither was of a nature to live comfortably with unresolved situations nor was she without feelings. Moreover, she never lost the respect she had for Father Rehrl as a priest and as the founder of the society.

WELCOME SUPPORT FROM THE CLERGY

At this juncture, Father Kundig was administrator for the Fond du Lac sisters pending the return of Bishop Henni from Rome. Father Nicholas Pickel, pastor of St. Mary's Church, was their ordinary confessor until January 21, 1871. Because it was not possible to secure a priest to say Mass daily in the convent chapel, the sisters attended Mass at the local parishes, St. Joseph's, St. Mary's, or St. Patrick's, where they had also begun to function as organists. At the direction of Father Kundig, both Father George Willard of St. Joseph's Church[9] and Father Pickel interested themselves in the community's welfare. Father Pickel helped Mother Agnes secure the proper titles to the property and conduct other necessary civil transactions with prudence and care. Father Willard assisted in the hearing of confessions, said Mass at the convent as often as possible, and gave a conference every Sunday at 5:00 p.m. for the sisters.[10]

While the priests of the city were assisting the community, Mother Agnes was also relying on the counsel of Father Francis. When Bishop Henni returned from Rome, he found two groups of women claiming St. Agnes as their patron. Initially, the bishop, who valued Father Rehrl as a man and as a missionary, was cool toward the convent in Fond du Lac. By March, however, he realized that the sisters had more stability and direction in their lives as religious as well as more opportunities for greater service to the church.[11] On December 20, 1870, he informed Agnes that he had authorized Father Francis as rector and protector of the institute to act in the bishop's name in everything concerning the welfare of the congregation. On March 31, 1871 he gave Francis official notice of his appointment.[12] By July of that year, Father Francis, pleased with the progress the sisters were making, was able to write to Bishop Henni, "I cherish a firm confidence in the vitality of this Congregation of St. Agnes. Its spirit is unassuming, but sound ...."[13]

MAKING ENDS MEET

According to the community's mission lists, in 1870 the sisters served at St. Mary, Appleton; St. Joseph, East Bristol (Columbus); St. Peter, Ashton; St. John of God, Farmington; Trinity, Brothertown; St. Joseph, Appleton; and in Town Ten. They had one out-of-state mission, St. John in Defiance, Ohio. The move to Fond du Lac had cost the society sixteen missions.[14]

The income from the missions that the sisters still had in their care was scarcely enough to provide for daily necessities, let alone payments on the mortgage. The establishment of the novitiate meant the immediate additional expense of providing for fourteen novices (more than one-third of the community) for the year, as well as the loss of income they could have earned during this period. Even before the sisters moved to Fond du Lac, the community was in such dire need of money that Agnes had written to Rev. Martin Kundig, the administrator of the diocese, asking for permission to send sisters on collecting missions[15] as well as to beg for alms in Milwaukee.[16]

In his reply Kundig expressed perplexity that the sisters did not appeal to the citizens in Fond du Lac for help. Moreover, sisters from as far away as Buffalo had just been collecting in the diocese at a time when the diocese itself needed money for church repairs. He concluded by telling them to collect around the countryside because "every farmer will give you a bit of lamb, wheat, oats, chickens, or other help."[17]

Begging was not new for the sisters; in fact they could not have survived in those early days without the generosity of the settlers. While they were at Barton, the sisters often went begging, bringing back such things as a live pig in a sack, if they were lucky, and bags of barley or wheat. In 1873, although initially they were not paid a salary, the sisters accepted St. Peter School in Malone, Wisconsin. Instead, each fall a parishioner would take a lumber wagon and go to each family to collect produce or other articles for the sister. A sister would ride on the wagon, and at times, suggest a needed article.[18] Until the community was better situated, both Sister Domitilla Briesgen and Sister Catherine Spenthoff gave themselves selflessly to collecting alms around the countryside. At the motherhouse, the sisters raised money by using every available minute making quilts, lace, wreaths, and embellishments for First Communion veils. They would make whatever they thought would sell at their fairs and bazaars.

As early as 1869 Sisters Agnes and Gertrude had gone to New York to raise money and recruit candidates. There is no record of the outcome of their fundraising, but they did return with three candidates, two of whom, Mrs. Catherine Pingeon (Sister Vincent) and Margaret Brady (Sister Augustine), remained with the community.

Sisters of St. Agnes went east to beg for alms in New York; north to beg in Michigan and Canada; and south to Ohio, Indiana, Georgia, and even Cuba.

The sisters could often count on the support of many of the sisters' own families. Family help showed itself in a variety of ways and often in very difficult circumstances. In spite of the emotional distance their daughters were enjoined to keep from their parents, the mother of Sister Stanislaus, Mrs. Carroll, paid for her daughter's music lessons and "cared for our sisters who had to wait for hours for train connections at Appleton .... If any sisters arrived, she would go out to Appleton Junction to meet and welcome them to

her home where board, lodging, and motherly hospitality was gladly extended to the travelers."[19]

THE CONTEXT OF THEIR LIVES

The farmhouse with its outbuildings remained the motherhouse for
the next nine years. In retrospect we see Agnes at its center with the
flame of her zeal setting on fire the hearts of others who, as she was
doing, offered their lives as oblations. She had chosen, or been set
on, a difficult path. Both she and her sisters had to arrive at deeper
understandings of each other; their life together, and their obligations as vowed women. Above all, they had to learn to trust each
other. It took time. As late as March 1871, she complained, "I can't
do anything with our sisters."[20]

There was one thing that could be done for the sisters, however,
and Mother Agnes did it. Shortly after their arrival in Fond du Lac,
Mother asked the newly invested Sister Antonia Schmitz to design a
new habit. The uniformity of the habit would give the sisters a sense
of pride and identity as well as identify their community to the outside world. Sister Antonia's design was worn until the 1960s.
According to tradition, the habit consisted of a pleated black dress
with a cape and a black veil. Mother Agnes loved the large white
collar of the Notre Dame Sisters, but the cost of linen dictated a
much smaller collar for the Agnesians. The candidates wore a bonnet similar in style to the colored bonnets worn by the Amish
women.[21]

The responsibilities that Mother Agnes was bearing could have
been overwhelming. Supplying food, shelter, and education to a
fluctuating community with inadequate financial resources was no
small task. Agnes also had to earn the confidence of the pastors,
shaken in many cases by the community's estrangement from Father
Rehrl. And, until the community reached some measure of stability, the continued departure of well-loved companions was a persistent reminder of the fragility of the bonds that united the sisters.
Above all, whatever the difficulties, Agnes had to struggle to maintain the morale of the community. Only five months after the move
to Fond du Lac, the death of a novice, Sister Laurentia McCormick,
on January 29 in Defiance, Ohio, was a particularly hard blow.[22] It
was the first occasion at which the sisters experienced the same

sense of loss for themselves and the same joy that would forever continue to mark the entrance of one of their own into eternal life.

MINISTRIES AND DIFFICULTIES

Immediately after the sisters had arrived in Fond du Lac, Mother Agnes rented a house a few doors west of the convent and in September opened St. Agnes School, a boarding and day school. Students attended classes in the barn; boarders lived in the rented house. Many communities at that time established such a "select school" for paying students to help support schools for the poorer children. That same year a select school for children from any parish was opened by the pastors of the non-German churches on First Street off Main.[23] In 1872 Sisters Cecilia Ferstl and Antonia Schmitz "opened"[24] St. Mary's School. Two years later, Mother Agnes made improvements in St. Agnes School by building a two-story brick veneered house at a cost of $338.79. The first floor was used for the school; the second floor became the chaplain's residence.[25]

Although Mother Agnes was making an effort to establish the sisters in town, the Sisters of St. Agnes had their roots in the rural schools. Father Rehrl's intention to provide teachers and catechists for the rural areas when he had founded the society had always been of special interest to Bishop Henni.[26] The schools were also important to the many sisters who had themselves grown up in the one-room schools that dotted the countryside. Mother Agnes had to find new schools quickly for the community as the Barton sisters naturally retained Rehrl's mission schools. Almost always the list of mission houses and schools shows that the community provided two teachers and, as church work and organist is ordinarily listed among their contracted duties, at least one of the sisters had to have some musical training. Given the heavy schedules demanded of the teaching sisters, both of prayer and work, house sisters were an absolute necessity.[27]

Bishop Henni, meanwhile, was discovering that the sisters on the missions were still facing serious difficulties stemming from their past lack of preparedness. On March 21, 1871, Agnes received a disheartening letter from him informing her that more women were requesting to be released from their vows. His note was brief: "I received the notice from Reverend priests Wilson and Herbert that Sisters Agatha and Theodore in Port Washington[28] and Sister Celestine in Columbus and her companions plan to leave and will ask for a dispensation from their vows. We must have the reasons or we cannot give in to this."[29]

ONE SISTER'S STORY

The bishop must have received their reasons, and these reasons were good. The story of Mary Helena Bath is a poignant reminder of the hardships that young sisters endured in the early years of pioneer congregations. Mary Helena was born third in a family of eleven children in 1849. Her father was Catholic, but not her mother. In October 1864, her mother entered the church, and a month later Mary Helena left her home in Addison, Washington County, to join the little community in Barton. It was her fifteenth birthday, November 12, 1864. After a little ritual beside the kitchen stove, she received the dress of the sisters and the name Agatha. She was immediately sent to help teach in the little select school of which Sister Mary Agnes was head teacher.[30]

Those days were happy ones. Agatha praised Agnes, "who took it upon herself to teach me all she could and I felt pleased with my lot, as I had a very hard time to obtain the permission to leave home .... There was nothing too hard nor too much for me although extreme poverty was our lot all the way."[31]

That fall, with an even younger postulant as a companion, Agatha was sent to teach at St. Bridget. Their teaching was not a success. December found her at St. Anthony to teach in the public school there while an older sister taught in the parish and school. That experience was successful and she returned to Barton in the summer to continue her studies under Sister Agnes. In October, she and two other sisters were sent to Port Washington to teach classes in English in a parish school while a German sister taught in German. It was another dismal experience, for Agatha wrote, "All in all we did not prove to give satisfaction and the parish priest made use of the summer to politely let us understand that we need not return."[32] Her next assignment was at St. Xavier where she was to teach in the public school. All seemed to go well until the spring of 1868 when the pastor, unhappy with his parishioners, ceased attending to the parish. The sisters were withdrawn and Agatha was sent to the neighboring St. Augustine Parish.

There she remained until October 1869, when she was sent to St. Joseph's in Bristol, where she taught in the public school until May 1871. That month she left the Sisters of St. Agnes on the advice of her confessor, the Reverend Anthony Foeckler, who, seeing the insecurity of the community, advised her to join the Benedictine Sisters in St. Joseph, Minnesota. Sister Agatha had taught in seven schools in her six and one-half years as a Sister of St. Agnes.[33]

MOVING FORWARD

Although the instability in the community was a source of great anxiety to Agnes, when Bishop Henni wrote to Agnes about a problem in Defiance, Ohio, he added words that he must have intended to be encouraging, "You should compare this problem with that of the Benedictines in Minnesota."[34] The days were not all gray. In July, the community had the happiness of witnessing the first profession of at least twelve sisters.[35] Now real, although tiny, mission houses could be established, and better prepared sisters could go out on mission as teachers and house sisters.

In Fond du Lac, the sisters were working hard to make the St. Agnes Academy a success. Sixty years later Mother Evangelist (Lydia) Holcomb,[36] a Sister of Mercy, wrote an account of her school days at the convent academy:

> The school was frequented by children from the best families in Fond du Lac, Catholic and non-Catholics. We Catholics wanted to help the non-Catholics acquire a knowledge of our faith, so during the lunch period at noon we would say, "Let's learn languages," and then proceed to say the Our Father in English, German and Latin. The motto which the sisters exemplified was the time-honored "Ora et labora."[37] It was inspiring to see Sister Stanislaus walking up and down the aisle as she taught or supervised the study of the pupils. Sister Cecilia had a lovely voice and she led us all in the songs and hymns we loved to

sing. The May gatherings and the annual picnic at
Lake De Neveu were sources of joy to both sisters
and pupils. We were delighted to help in paying the
debt on the convent by planning and working for the
bazaars that were held and by contributing our mite
toward them. What chattering and laughing there
was as we gathered in the classrooms to make quilts
or aprons to be sold! How proud we were to act as
hostesses on the occasion of the sales![38]

WOUNDED WOMEN

In the fall of 1871 the sisters' relative peace was shattered. Mother
Agnes received word from Bishop Henni that he was obliged to
intervene in congregational affairs one more time. This time the
matter was much more serious both in its content and in its effects.
The facts, as we know them, can be found in a letter from the archbishop to Father Francis and in a set of directives from Father
Francis to the sisters, as well as in statements that appear in the
Annals of the Congregation. Much later, Mother Agnes wrote: "During
the first year when all seemed prosperous, through the ambition of
two of the members, a party spirit was aroused within the community which disturbed the peace and harmony."[39]
        Certain unidentified members of the community had made
eleven charges of a serious nature against Mother Agnes. Nowhere
is there evidence of the nature of these charges. But, given human
nature, it is not difficult to find some possible explanations. While
the *Annals* attribute the whole affair to ambition, there were possibly
other factors also at play. Father Rehrl had been the founder of the
community, and more sisters than those who had remained in
Barton felt a strong sense of loyalty to him. Furthermore, the lack of
constitutions and Rehrl's absences had allowed them to become
accustomed to much more self-determination than was now possible, so some sisters must have felt that the rule was imposing new
and sometimes onerous obligations upon them. Sisters formerly
close to *Sister* Agnes were now distanced from *Mother* Agnes as she
turned to Father Francis for advice and support. Undoubtedly, some
were bewildered and hurt. Among them were Sisters Ursula Hofen,
Gertrude Laughlin, and Aloysia Lethert.

We have met these sisters before. Sister Ursula was the blind sister who, in 1861, had been the sole sister remaining with Father Rehrl. Sister Gertrude (Catherine Laughlin) had been the best friend and confidante of Sister Agnes. Sister Aloysia had been "Margaret," whom Agnes had praised so highly when she was a candidate at Barton. These were women, who for one reason or another, were significant members in the community. Why they experienced such profound disaffection for Agnes has been a question that later sisters have never been able to answer satisfactorily.

Gertrude Laughlin remains the greatest enigma. The Irish Gertrude and the French Agnes often must have supported each other as outsiders in this very German society. Together they had been professed, then sent to Marytown, where they spent several formative years. They were close friends, and when Agnes left Marytown to return to Barton, it was to Gertrude that she poured out her anguish over the problems of the community and her difficulties with Father Rehrl. It was only after Agnes left Marytown in November of 1869 that there began to be rifts between Gertrude and Agnes. By St. Agnes Day, only two months later, when the sisters from Marytown went to Barton to celebrate the community feast day, Gertrude chose to stay home.

The following day, when Agnes wrote to thank Gertrude for the money she had sent from the mission, she expressed her distress over the difficulties between Lidwina and Gertrude. Agnes did not take her sister's part but asked Gertrude to be patient with her. After unburdening herself of her own problems, she assured Gertrude of her friendship. Agnes wrote hastily and from her heart: "Come down soon. You know we have been so long together and [we are]now parted. It does seem lonely to me anyhow, but I must keep it to myself. Many a tear I have shed since we parted, since we knew how to get along together. If we had faults ... we did not keep our anger in our heart. We talked it over. In a minute it was gone .... Pray for one another. God has laid a hard burden on me. I must think of His holy will or else I could not stand it here."[40]

From the next letter it appears that matters must have improved between Gertrude and Lidwina, because Agnes, after inviting Gertrude to come for a visit, simply asked about Lidwina.[41] But in a letter written only one week later to an unnamed sister, Agnes enthusiastically described her trip to Fond du Lac, her interview with Father Pickel, and her visit to the proposed site for a mother-house when she cautioned, "Now don't you mention anything to Gertrude or to any one. You may tell Lidwina but keep it very secret."[42]

A week later, Agnes wrote a long letter to Gertrude. There were difficulties with a candidate and a Capuchin brother over school affairs, but most of all over her sister, Lidwina. "My heart aches," she wrote, "and I feel sick from nothing but troubles." In spite of her own suffering, she tried to counsel Gertrude. "I know that you had troubles enough up there since I left …. Look at your Lord especial-ly in this holy time how he suffered for us poor sinners. In the sweat of Jesus you will find consolation—not from people. You may believe if it wasn't for Jesus here in the Blessed Sacrament I could not live …. I get consolation and if He doesn't console me I think he is near by me and wants me to feel that I must suffer if I want to enter in the kingdom of heaven …. "[43]

Yet whatever happened, it appears that Gertrude no longer shared the confidence of Agnes although Gertrude was elected her first assistant in July. By August it was too late to mend matters. By this time it was Mother Agnes and Father Francis who were recre-ating the society. Perhaps from Gertrude's point of view, she had been badly used. First, she missed Agnes. At the same time, her friendship with Agnes had been put under a great strain by Sister Lidwina. She believed she had done her best to deal with that situ-ation until Agnes found in Father Francis a mentor, hero, and con-fidant. Gertrude was deprived both of her closest friend, almost the only human comfort she had at that time, and of some small share of influence in the community.

As for Sister Ursula, it is possible that, while she joined the sis-ters who left Barton for Fond du Lac, she had never been thorough-ly convinced that it was right to leave Father Rehrl. An underlying uneasiness could have made an alliance with the discontented sisters a means to get out of an uncomfortable situation.

Why the recently professed Sister Aloysia became so disaffected is also unclear. When she first came, she had been a candidate with great promise, both intellectually and spiritually. Well-versed in German and Latin, she had been given the responsibility of trans-lating Father Rehrl's rule.[44] She had taught grammar and music and did both well. Agnes had held high hopes for her, finding her a "most excellent scholar." Agnes wrote exuberantly to Sister Gertrude that she had never found such a good-hearted and pious girl nor one with such good sense "since she had been in the Convent."[45] Whether the intelligent and perceptive Sister Aloysia had simply developed a loyalty to Sister Gertrude and empathized with her pain, or believed that the society's difficulties were so great that the bishop should be called in, is now only a matter for speculation.

RESOLUTION AND AFTERMATH

Whatever the reasons, in the fall of 1871 Sister Gertrude and several other sisters wrote to Bishop Henni making serious (and still unknown) accusations against Mother Agnes. The Bishop enclosed the letter to Father Francis and appointed him and Rev. John Huber, the convent chaplain, to investigate the charges. He also wished Father Francis to inform Father Huber of the charges against Agnes so that Huber could "admonish her on several points in which she could have exposed herself, but this should be done in secret and in kindness."[46]

After questioning all the older sisters individually in the presence of Father Huber, Francis determined that the accusation was slanderous, "the corrections of the Superior unfounded." The archbishop immediately wrote to Father Francis, giving him full power to make any changes necessary. In addition, the archbishop added that Sister Cecilia Ferstl was to replace Sister Gertrude as assistant immediately and Father Francis was either to bring Gertrude to repentance or dismiss her. On January 29, 1872, three sisters were released from their vows and dismissed from the congregation. Sisters Aloysia, Gertrude, and Ursula returned to Father Rehrl at Barton; a fourth, unnamed, must have expressed repentance. The community was forbidden to have anything to do with the three who were dismissed. Father Francis further commanded each house superior to read a letter to the sisters and then "reply without delay expressing in a written assurance her personal loyalty to me; also the written expressed loyalty of each subject with her own signature. All those, who within a month's time, will not have done this will be excluded from the Congregation."[47]

Early in 1874, Gertrude devised an advertisement for a boarding school she was planning to open in Barton. In it she explained
to the Catholic population the difference between the sisters in
Barton and those in Fond du Lac. It was to be placed in the *Catholic
Weekly*, the *Catholic Popular Paper*, and the Milwaukee Catholic paper:

> The Motherhouse of the Sisters of St. Agnes is at
> Barton, Washington Con., Wis. While the most
> Reverend Bishop of Milwaukee was at the *Concilium*
> in Rome, most of the sisters by instigation of their
> superior here accepted different rules and have
> moved their Motherhouse to Fond du Lac without
> the knowledge of their Bishop who was still in Rome.
> He heard about the change after his return. The
> bishop permitted that the remaining sisters at Barton
> continue the novitiate under the Old Rule ....[48]

Mother Agnes must have been both hurt and humiliated by the
affair. There was scarcely an emotion she had not experienced during the previous two years, but of all feelings the sense of betrayal
is, perhaps, the most wounding and penetrates the deepest into the
human psyche. Although she must have received some consolation
from the loyalty of the majority of sisters and the support of Father
Francis, her suffering must have been intense.

Agnes noted these events very briefly in *The Annals of the
Congregation*, but she gave no clue as to her feelings. The shock had
come just as she was able to have some justifiable satisfaction in the
community's recent progress. The community had been saved;
Father Francis had provided the counsel that only an experienced
religious could; the priests in Fond du Lac had been happy to assist
them in any way they could; their newly-established boarding school
had looked promising; they had been successful in establishing a
mission in Ohio; Bishop Henni had been proving himself a kindly
pastor. To discover that there were depths of dissatisfaction in the
congregation so profound as to lead Sister Gertrude, who undoubtedly had a following, to make serious charges against her to the bishop must have turned her world upside down. Where had she gone
wrong?

It is probable that Agnes had been so immersed in circumstances that were life or death for the congregation that she had forgotten that community spirit was upheld by all the sisters together. The declining morale of some had either passed unnoticed or been dismissed by her; perhaps, like Father Rehrl and Father Francis, she believed that individuals should be able to sublimate their emotions through prayer and sacrifice.

FATHER PICKEL'S PLAN

Early in 1872, Mother Agnes was stunned to discover that the rightful ownership of the Fond du Lac property was now being questioned by at least one of the priests in Fond du Lac. In a letter written on February 14, 1872, Father Nicholas Pickel wrote to Father Rehrl as the founder of the Sisters of Saint Agnes, expressing the concern of the clergy for the welfare of the sisters and strongly encouraging him to come to Fond du Lac, contending that the St. Agnes Community in Barton was the rightful owner of the Fond du Lac property. He advised Rehrl to claim ownership of the property, and added that "with the acknowledgement of the house, all the missions will also be yours."[49]

Father Pickel was mistaken if he thought that money for the down payment on the property had been wrongfully taken from Barton. It is not clear what his motivation was, although later events strongly suggest that his resentment of the position and influence that Father Francis Haas had as rector of the Sisters of St. Agnes had much to do with this move. Father Pickel had also written to the bishop. The bishop's reply, "Do you want this property?" was ambiguous.[50] In any case, there is no record that Father Rehrl acted on the matter.

The incident does show, however, that the warm relationship between the congregation and some of the priests in Fond du Lac was breaking down and it is not difficult to see one source of tension. Francis had provided the counsel and the structure the sisters so badly needed for survival, but his position as their director upset the relationships that the sisters had established with the parish priests in the area.

The priests of Fond du Lac had welcomed a community founded by a fellow priest to provide teachers for the parish schools. The diocesan priests, actively ministering their parishes must have desired sisters who would take direction from them and respond to their needs. They must have been disappointed when the sisters were placed under the direction of a friar. Furthermore, the practices and daily schedule suitable for the monastic life did not serve the apostolate well. While it was unfortunate that Agnes, in effect, had to choose between the friar and the parish priests, it is undeniable that Francis had much to offer the community that was impossible for the parish priests to provide.

FATHER FRANCIS AS DIRECTOR

From the day he was appointed as director, Father Francis did everything in his power to guide the young women placed under his care. He gave them retreats, counsel, and practical advice on hundreds of matters. He celebrated their feast days with them; he was present at their investing and profession ceremonies; he wrote their rule. Eventually, the sisters came to know him simply as "Pa." Mother Agnes, faced with a problem on one of the missions, wrote to one of her councilors, "I do wish Pa would come to give the sisters a good retreat."[51] Sister Magdalene, lonesome in far away Yankton, South Dakota, wrote in 1887, "I feel homesick when I think of Papa, Mama, and you all together .... "[52]

The letters Father Francis wrote to Mother Agnes through the years give us an insight into his character. Matter-of-fact and often concerned with matters of health, his letters to her allow us to catch a glimpse of his common sense, his insights into human nature and its many foibles, his occasional flashes of dry humor, and his dedication to the welfare of the Sisters of St. Agnes. Early in his relationship with the community, he made a commitment that never wavered: "I consider you and each individual member of your community as my children, and I shall always be ready to assist you to the best of my ability .... From now on, then, you will have a paternity in me that transcends everything temporal, a paternity blessed by God, a spiritual Fatherhood that loves, and also saddens when offended.[53]

One of Father Francis' first counsels was to "take care of quickly and in all seriousness" the providing of a thorough education for the novices and candidates.[54] Because the necessity of providing for the education of the young women was one of the points of Agnes' disagreement with Father Rehrl, it was a piece of advice that hardly needed saying. Yet it was comforting to be sustained in such an expensive venture at a time when every sister teaching was providing much needed support for the community.

There must have been times when Father Francis' counsel on the value of the redemptive power of suffering was difficult to appreciate. Although often he certainly sympathized with her, his advice must have seemed overly bracing at times. He wrote, "I love to see that you are always being tested in some way."[55]

He warned Agnes that age was no protection against foolishness; he told her of a remedy used in dealing with malcontent friars in Bavaria, where it was rumored all the grumblers were put together in one house and the worst one made guardian.[56] He received some amusement from Sister Antonia's "cycle of accelerated raptures,"[57] and offered an explanation for Sister T's recent bout of kleptomania: "Perhaps it is a maternal yen. It is good that you understand this."[58] His understanding of the frailties of human nature never led him into trying to repress the emotions of those whom he counseled. Francis never tired of reminding Agnes that "each person's traits are God-given, and in order to understand oneself and be understood by others there must be communication. Where communication fails to improve situations, I would prefer to let Divine Providence take over, in love and gentleness."[59]

Father Francis was convinced that "the person who does not love or feels no need to be loved must be very unhappy, I believe he cannot love God either."[60] He wished to help others direct the capacity to love ardently to loving God with all the fervor of their being; he did not believe in crushing or deforming natural human capacities.

Always central in the thinking of Francis was the solemn duty that Mother Agnes had in fulfilling her role as superior. On February 2, 1872, he wrote:

> Let me have the assurance that you act with firmness and determination in all things and that you put aside every bit of human consideration as soon as duty or order demands. That will give me confidence, and then everything will proceed well. You

> must act, not feel. Always pray in important mat-
> ters—then proceed bravely! Human faint-hearted-
> ness would spoil everything. I know that you are
> being sorely tried and that you suffer; but I cannot
> consider that now—you are the Superior![61]

And again: "We superiors must be ready to endure much but not yield anything when it comes to our rights and duties. We must openly defend the authority of superiors. However, one must differentiate this from getting the better of [the other party]."[62]

Throughout the years, Francis offered his comments, always perceptive and sometimes amusing. Yet if he detected a tendency of Mother Agnes to rely on him for advice, he was quick to admonish her. "What frightens me is that you have to depend on me. No plan is good if I have to criticize it; hold your own."[63] It must be said, however, that even Father Francis showed concern if he felt Agnes was overburdened. He advised Sister Seraphine to "take good care of the Mother Superior. Do not let her be unhappy. She often takes small things too seriously."[64]

No one can doubt that for the rest of her life, Agnes took the advice of Father Francis seriously. *Courageous, brave,* and, for a later generation, *risk-taking* have become words associated with her. She had those qualities when she got on the train to Fond du Lac and when she clashed with Father Rehrl, but it was Father Francis and his constant demand that she "put aside every bit of human consideration"[65] that gave her that last bit of steel she needed to see her through to the end.

EXPANDING MINISTRIES

In spite of its uncertain beginning, the sisters made some progress in 1872. They had not lost any more schools; a sister was teaching the German-speaking children at St. Mary's in Fond du Lac; Sister Stanislaus Carroll was taking lessons from Father George Willard, as well as teaching in the school the pastors of Fond du Lac had opened for non-German speaking children; and still another, in St. Catherine's School in Granville County. A second out-of-state school was accepted in New Haven, Indiana. On week-ends, Sisters in Fond du Lac frequently went to near-by parishes to teach catechism or play the organ for Sunday liturgies.[66]

That same year Mother Agnes brought six-year-old Anna Carey, whose stonemason father and mother had both died, to live with the sisters. Anna was but one of the orphaned children Mother brought into the convent during those years.[67] However, her preference was to find a suitable home for a child. Consequently, when a gentleman in Fond du Lac applied for an orphan girl to adopt, Agnes found ten-year-old Margaret Hickey, who was being cared for by the Grey Nuns at St. Anthony's Orphanage in Toledo, Ohio. She brought the child to Fond du Lac and placed her in a family.[68] When she learned that the child was not receiving a proper Christian education, she removed her immediately from the family and brought her to the convent. With new tenants such as these and the increasing membership of the community, an addition had to be built on the house, which, of course, further stretched their already overextended budget.

A most surprising and heartening letter came from Bishop Henni in September 1872. After an assurance that he was interested in the progress of the community, he commented that he heard little from Fond du Lac. Observing that "there is no doubt that life in the convent will blossom forth if the right nourishment and care is given it, in other words, where there is the fundamental humility and penance as ground material."[69] The bishop warmly affirmed the work of the sisters and continued: "You have in Fond du Lac as good an opportunity as the Notre Dames have in Milwaukee. In four weeks you had the mayor, who is of the Lutheran religion, ready to listen to the Sisters. With many hundreds, he was astounded by the exhibition at the end of the school year and could not help remark that Milwaukee residents would be lucky to have such progress in their city!"[70]

When Christmas came that year, all problems were forgotten for a few days. Father Willard, one of the strongest supporters of the sisters, had painted the convent altar white and Sister Lidwina had decorated it with the words *Gloria in Excelsis Deo*. The sisters had barely absorbed the beauty of the chapel when the choir from St. Joseph's Church arrived to sing the midnight Mass. It was a Christmas to be remembered forever.

Within a week the sisters were shaken to hear of the death of Sister Julia Bell.[71] The first professed sister of the community to die, she was twenty-four years old. Sister Julia had been sent to Defiance to open the mission there; she had been there two years when, on December 23, she suffered a stroke and died six days later.

STEADY GROWTH

The congregation showed steady, if unremarkable, progress in 1873. Four new missions were accepted that year: three in Wisconsin (St. Mary, Pine Bluff; St. Peter, Malone; and St. Thomas, Beloit) and one in Pennsylvania (St. Michael, Hollidaysburg). In November, Mother Agnes' relative, John Hazotte, came for a visit. Because the convent needed someone to take care of the horses, Mother Agnes begged him to stay, and "Convent John" was much appreciated by the sisters for his kindness and sociability. For forty-three years John's horse and wagon was a common sight at the town's railroad station.[72]

Another good year for Mother Agnes and the sisters was 1874. Mother Agnes' tasks had been lightened by the previous year's appointment of the community's first secretary, Sister Seraphine Morrissey.[73] The opening of St. Agnes Convent School for the candidates and novices marked the fulfillment of one of the community's most important goals. The school offered upper elementary subjects and teaching methods. A professor from the archdiocese's normal school, Professor John Morrissey, came from Milwaukee on a weekly or bi-weekly basis to teach physics, classics, the Constitution, and pedagogy to the novices and geometry to the sisters.[74]

Music had always been one of the most important areas of study in convents.[75] It was needed for the daily liturgies in the motherhouse; sisters were frequently expected to be organists in the parishes; and, because no nineteenth-century social gathering was complete without music, music teachers brought a small, but needed, income into the community. Agnes secured the services of Professor John Baptist Singenberger, one of the most important figures in the Caecilian movement.[76] Bishop Henni had brought the Swiss professor to Milwaukee to reform church music by teaching chant in the Holy Family Normal School and Pio Nono Institute. On Friday evenings Professor Singenberger arrived in Fond du Lac to give lessons in organ and piano to advanced students, to teach harmony and vocal music, and to work with the choir. Thorough and exacting, he trained organists, choir directors and composers. His contribution to the musical education of the Sisters of St. Agnes cannot be measured.

SPIRITUAL PROGRESS

Of great significance to the sisters was the consecration of the community to the Sacred Heart of Jesus on February 21, 1874. The devotion had originated in France in 1673 when St. Margaret Mary Alacoque reported visions in which Christ had asked her to venerate an image of his heart of flesh to make reparation for the world's indifference to his love and mercy. Fridays became special days of prayer and penance for the conversion of sinners and the reparation of sins. It was Father Francis who had aroused in the sisters zeal for this devotion, according to his biographer, Father Celestine Bittle: "The Sacred Heart was the source of all his personal piety, the inspiration and motive of all his labors, the beginning and end of all his endeavors."[77] The Sisters of St. Agnes accepted this devotion wholeheartedly: the Litany of the Sacred Heart was recited every Friday, the practice of receiving the Eucharist on nine consecutive First Fridays was meaningful, and images of the Sacred Heart were common in convents. For the sisters, increased devotion to the humanity of Jesus put a further emphasis on the necessity of sacrifice and increased prayer. Some of the community's best loved hymns became those dedicated to the Sacred Heart of Jesus.

During that same year of 1874, Francis finished the arduous task of writing the constitutions. He often wrote in the little room in the priests' house, and the sisters knew that he never began to write before kneeling in prayer. He was said to have written the chapter treating of religious profession and professed sisters, on his knees. Bishop Henni approved the draft and then sent it to Rome for approval. On February 26, 1875, the Sacred Congregation of the Propagation of the Faith decreed the sisterhood to be "praiseworthy" and Pope Pius IX approved this decision on March 28, 1875.[78]

AN ACCEPTABLE RULE

The rule follows the way of life of the Capuchin friars. Many of Fr.
Francis' regulations came directly from the Capuchin *Constitution of
1643*.[79] The sisters promise, as is the duty of every Christian, to imi-
tate the life of Christ. With the approbation of the Church, they
were to promise holy poverty, chastity, and obedience under entire
submission to the pope and the bishop in whose diocese the motherhouse was located.[80]

One section was devoted to each vow. The vow of poverty was
first. The sisters were to live the kind of life that the poorer middle
class lived in the world. The fare would be the same for all; however, on festivals an additional dish could be granted by the superior.
Like the Franciscans, the sisters' garb should be of undressed
woolen cloth. Once the dress was prescribed, it could be altered by
no one. The sisters should avoid grandeur in their buildings. Their
finances should be conducted according to the spirit of holy poverty. If ever there should be an excess of goods, the sisters should
establish educational institutions for poor girls. Father Francis
exhorted the sisters to combine modest demeanor and sincere charity to rich and poor "whom those natural graces, inseparable from
piety and Christian love of the neighbor will adorn far more richly
than any worldly finery can do."[81]

His discussion of chastity emphasized the importance of the
cloister. On leaving the grounds, the sister should procure a blessing.
The parlor was open only for real urgencies of business or propriety. No seculars could be lodged in sisters' quarters.[82]

The sisters should follow Christ in their practice of obedience
and obey in all things not contrary to conscience and the rule.[83]

The obligatory prayers were similar to those of the Capuchins
except that the teaching sisters were to say daily the "approved and
recommended" *Little Office of the Blessed Virgin Mary*[84] in Latin, and
the house sisters were to recite fifteen decades of the rosary. They
should make two meditations each day: the first in the morning followed by the *Angelus* and the Litany of the Holy Name; the second,
at night, followed by the Litany of Loreto. An examination of conscience and spiritual reading had to be done in the afternoon. In
order to enable them to observe their Holy Rule the sisters should
have as their spiritual patrons Mary, under the title of the

Immaculate Conception; St. Joseph, her glorious spouse; St. Agnes of Rome, Virgin and Martyr; St. Francis; St. Clare of Assisi; the Holy Innocents; St. Cecilia; and the holy Guardian Angels.[85]

Part II contains the Constitutions of the Congregation. It dealt with matters such as the qualifications and elections of superior and administration, the motherhouse, its aim and arrangement, the instruction of girls entrusted to the sisters, the training of postulants, novices and candidates, professed sisters, and the missions. The document concluded with a blessing :"And whosoever shall follow this rule, peace upon them and mercy, upon the Israel of God. And whoever shall persevere to the end shall be saved."[86]

In brief, this was the rule written by Father Francis Haas for the Sisters of St. Agnes. On the 26th of February 1875 it received a Decree of Praise from Rome and final papal approbation on July 11, 1880.

TWO EVENTFUL YEARS

By 1875 the fire that was burning in the heart of the little society was attracting other young women eager to share in lives so clearly dedicated to serving God and nurturing the faith through service to God's people. That year, when thirteen sisters made their first profession, the community numbered fifty-eight professed sisters in all. The additional members allowed Mother Agnes to accept four new missions: St. Cloud, St. Joseph, and Lebanon in Wisconsin, and East Liberty in Pennsylvania. They were all poor parishes. As, initially, the sisters did not insist on adequate housing, the community was attractive to pastors of poor parishes.

At the motherhouse, more classrooms and a house for priests were needed. In May of that year, Mother Agnes thriftily met both needs by building a two-story, brick-veneered house with some rooms to serve as a rectory and others as classrooms for the projected school for the candidates.

In 1876 the congregation numbered eighty sisters and nine novices. In March all of the professed sisters who resided at the motherhouse were received into the Third Order of St. Francis.[87] Now they could feel even closer to their patrons St. Francis and St. Clare and the Franciscan spirit Father Francis had encouraged them to love.

In July of that same year the congregation held its second canonical election. Because there were not yet sisters in perpetual vows, all the sisters in septennial vows[88] and the local superiors were invited as delegates. Sister Agnes was again elected superior general and Sister Josephine Maurer, her assistant. The other members of the council were appointed by the superior general, a procedure that was changed before the succeeding chapter. Sister Lidwina Hazotte was appointed novice director. Sisters Regina Deiler and Seraphine Morrissey were appointed to serve as councilors and to teach at the motherhouse; Sister Cecilia Ferstl was appointed to the council and to teach at the academy.

While the spiritual life of the community was vigorous, financial problems were a constant worry. Despite ongoing expenditures and mortgage payments, assuming the cost of erecting a motherhouse became a priority as more women entered the community. That meant the acquisition of more land. Despite the fact that Mother Agnes could barely make payments on the land that had already been acquired, she purchased an adjoining two and one-half acres (the Amory Block) for fifteen hundred dollars. When five hundred dollars were remitted as a gift, plans for a new convent began in earnest.

Mother Agnes then began to immerse herself in building projects. She borrowed hundreds of dollars in five-dollar sums from benefactors. When she began drawing plans for rooms in the new buildings, she soon found that Father Francis did not consider designing buildings suitable work for a woman or a superior. He wrote a stiff note to her: "Allow me to tell you to throw away the thought of your own plans. The builder prefers to take my advice for an ordinary simple building. With regard to the measurements of the rooms, superiors should be the first to forget building plans. If in your confession you cannot overcome your own ideas, then try to forget it all."[89]

That was impossible. Mother Agnes could not forego building projects. A new motherhouse was an absolute necessity as the number of women and children for whom she was responsible was rapidly approaching one hundred.

Whether Mother Agnes or Father Francis was victor in this particular confrontation is unknown. What is clear is that the responsibility of paying for buildings belonged to Mother Agnes and the community. As is not uncommon in building projects, the task became more difficult as time passed. The plans for building had been made during a relatively prosperous interlude, but 1876 brought a panic that created economic havoc throughout the country. Fortunes vanished; farms were lost; unemployment soared; interest rates were exorbitant. Many parishes were simply unable to pay the sisters in currency. Mother Agnes, however, had already engaged a rising young architect, Wilhelm Schickel, who had trained at the Beaux Artes in Paris and was beginning an illustrious career in church architecture.[90]

The congregation was fortunate because Schickel designed for the future. The plans for the four-story building were E-shaped, although only the right wing which contained the most necessary living and office facilities could be erected at this time. The temporary chapel was housed on the fourth floor of the building.[91]

THE HIGH COST OF FUND-RAISING

With the elections over and the government of the congregation in place for the next six years, it was time to deal with finances again. Father Francis, much as he disliked the idea, gave Mother Agnes permission to send the popular Sister Patrick Walsh out on still another collecting tour. Sister Patrick, with her good humor and gifts for storytelling, was the community's most gifted fund-raiser. Born in Ireland in 1849, she had entered the community in 1872. Sister Patrick collected from Canada to Cuba, traveling on every possible vehicle, including a trip north on a railroad hand car. No place seemed too far or too unlikely for her visits, and every benefactor received an *Agnus Dei* [badge] and a few good stories.[92]

On her return from trips she delighted in relating her experiences to the sisters assembled for recreation. When the sisters were gathered, she would tell them, "Now, let ye all make *Agnus Deis*, Mother said so and I will tell ye a story." And off she went, describing with verve her hair-raising adventures with trains, buggies, bishops, priests, and the usual runs of bad luck that accompanied traveling in the hinterlands.

In 1876 Sister Patrick was found to have cancer of the tongue. She vowed, if cured, to spend the rest of her life collecting money for the orphans Mother Agnes was bringing into the motherhouse.

She was cured and attributed it to the fact that Father Francis had prayed over her.[93] In September of that same year, she left with Sister Martha Manning, professed the previous year, as her companion on a trip to the South.[94] On the train, the twenty one-year-old Sister Martha contracted yellow fever and died in a hospital in Savannah, Georgia. In spite of her grief, Sister Patrick could not be dissuaded from continuing her money-raising expeditions.

FURTHER JOURNEYING

Another highlight of 1876 was the addition of four new missions: Epiphany Parish, Menominee, Wisconsin; St. John's, Menominee, Michigan; St. Charles Borromeo, Grant County, Wisconsin and a parish in Bloomfield, Pennsylvania.

Accepting the mission in Bloomfield ended up playing a role in the congregation's unfortunate relationship with the Right Rev. John Tuigg, bishop of Pittsburgh. In 1875, Sisters Alberta Wolsiffer and Barbara Lishka, with their housekeeper, Sister Ludovica Richli, had opened a school in East Liberty, Pennsylvania, at the request of the pastor. The following year, informed that their services were no longer required, the sisters moved to a neighboring school in Bloomfield, Pennsylvania. It was only then that they discovered they had offended Bishop Tuigg by opening a school in Pennsylvania without consulting him. Furthermore, they learned that he had wanted only diocesan communities for his schools. Sister Alberta wrote to Mother Agnes in consternation, "They do not want us here; to what direction shall we now turn?"[95] Before returning to Wisconsin, the sisters received an offer from Father Joseph A. Schell, pastor of St. Mary's, a German parish in Altoona, Pennsylvania. Father Schell had received permission from his bishop to invite the three sisters.

The good pastor's prudence was rewarded. The sisters arrived to face an unusual schedule. In order to keep alive the German language, all subjects of the six grades were taught to the boys in the morning in German, and in English in the afternoon; the schedule was reversed for the girls. Sister Alberta usually taught in English; Sister Barbara, in German.[96]

Another request for sisters arrived in 1876 from a mission as far to the west of Fond du Lac as Altoona was to the east. The

Capuchins from the Pittsburgh province, who had become acquainted with the Agnesians during their stay in East Liberty, asked for sisters to teach in Herzog (later named Victoria), Kansas. Teachers were needed for the children of twenty-three Volga German families who had recently arrived from Russia. Because the Pittsburgh friars had enlisted Father Francis to plead their case, Mother Agnes agreed to send sisters there as soon as possible. She was able to fulfill the request three years later, in 1879.

While the sisters in Fond du Lac were journeying east, another religious community was invited into Fond du Lac by Father Willard, who gave them St. Joseph's rectory as their convent. They were Sisters of Mercy, five professed sisters and four novices. They opened a school in the basement of St. Joseph's Church and, at the request of Father Willard, established a highly-regarded orphanage in Fond du Lac.[97] Their Sister Alphonsa Monaghan proved to be an excellent teacher of English for the St. Agnes Convent School; in return the Agnesians gave her German lessons.

BUILDING A MOTHERHOUSE

By 1877, the construction of a new convent could be delayed no longer. Excavation for the foundation began on May 1, 1877. In the presence of the mayor, Edwin Galloway, Father Francis laid the cornerstone on May 27.

Meeting the bills remained a burden. Mother Agnes could not ask the sisters to do with less, for they were already living as frugally as possible. She could and did, however, devise small ways to save money. Her natural kindness combined with her common sense led her to the conclusion that supplying hot coffee and fresh bread to the workmen would make for more contented and productive workers. She also came up with another plan. Evenings at recreation, after the workmen left, she and the other sisters went out to the huge pile of bricks at the building site and formed assembly lines. When the masons came the following morning, the bricks were in readily accessible piles.[98]

The cost of the first wing of the building was $41,373.33. With much satisfaction Mother Agnes noted in her diary that the "Archbishop [is] much pleased with [the] new convent and progress of the Sisters since coming to Fond du Lac."[99]

The History of Fond du Lac County, written shortly after the building was erected, described the brick and stone motherhouse as "one
of the largest and finest buildings in Fond du Lac."[100] The article
reported that 120 sisters belonged to the convent and twenty-two
orphan children lived there. Neither were the finer things of life
neglected there. The reporter admired the needlework in particular,
writing that: "The needle and fancy decorative work turned out is
remarkable in design, beauty, and quality. Everything in the convent
betokens system, culture, genius and comfort. Pictures and plants
are in all the rooms in which also dwell courteousness, cleanliness
and cheerfulness."[101] Some years later Sister Claude Feldner offered
an occupant's view:

> The building was imposing on the outside but simple
> in construction. The kitchen, refectories, vegetable
> cellar, and trunk rooms were in the basement. The
> first floor contained administration, chapel, and the
> assembly hall. The second floor had a balcony look-
> ing over the chapel for the infirm and sisters' rooms
> and dormitories. On the third floor there was a huge
> wooden water tank which sometimes overflowed.
> The candidates slept in a dormitory on four-and-a-
> half, an attic with wooden rafters, primitive wash-
> room facilities (pitchers and basins) and ever-present
> bats. The sisters still had corn husk mattresses; when
> they made their beds, they poked their hands
> through the slit in the center to dig around and fluff
> up the husks.[102]

DAY TO DAY STRUGGLES

From October 9 to October 12, 1877, a three-day fair was held to
raise money and celebrate the opening of the convent.[103] On
November 3, Father John Huber blessed the new structure but
Mother Agnes was unable to celebrate wholeheartedly. The strain of
the building program and the debts had been taking a toll on her
health, and she would never be entirely well again. Much as she disliked disappointing the sisters, she was forced to delay for a few
months her projected tour of the missions. Even so, she arranged to

accept Sacred Heart School in Sterling, Illinois and St. John's in Hilbert, Wisconsin.

The sisters, who loved her visits, were disappointed. Agnes agreed with the Capuchins in emphasizing the importance of community recreations and brought to them a sense of excitement and fun. If the sisters were out of sorts, she would say, "This house needs a good cleaning; let's all get together and clean." They all pitched in and the house cleaning turned into a big party. Then she would tell the cook sister, "You have money. Go out and buy some treats for the sisters." The next day she might go to the kitchen and bake a strudel for a treat or even the full meal. Agnes loved sweets and was famous for her strudels, sometimes baking them for thirty or forty sisters.

More than that, Mother Agnes was known to take over classrooms for sick sisters, sometimes for as long as two or three weeks. Her own experiences in the little country schools had given her an understanding of the hardships that the sisters on mission underwent. Knowing her concern for them, the sisters found it easier to face the difficulties of daily living. In the following letter, Mother Agnes showed a compassionate concern for one of her sisters ... as well as a remarkable (if perhaps erroneous) assessment of her own spiritual poverty: "Keep up your courage and teach your school well.... No matter what comes along we must suffer in this world or there is no heaven. Trust in God and keep up well, when lonely go to our Lord. He will give you more consolation than I can give you. Pray for me. I am so bad I need it."[104]

MILESTONES

In 1878, the Sisters of St. Agnes passed a major milestone. For the first time, they were permitted to vow *for life* poverty, chastity, and obedience in the Congregation of St. Agnes. It had been possible to fulfill the canonical requirement of seven years in temporary vows only with the establishment of the novitiate. At last the sisters could feel that they were members of a permanently established congregation with an assured future.[105] One new mission, St. Patrick School in Milwaukee, was accepted that year. All in all, 1878 was a much-needed quiet year.

1879—A YEAR OF CONTRASTS

On St. Agnes Day in 1879 a novice, Laurentia McCormack, died in Defiance, Ohio. That sad event was soon followed by the deaths of four sisters. From January to November, the community had barely adjusted to one loss before there was the sad news that another sister had gone to God. The reconciliation of Father Rehrl with the community, described in chapter two, could scarcely have occurred at a better time than on the eve of the feast of St. Joseph that year. No one can doubt that Mother Agnes and the older sisters had said many a fervent prayer for the return of his friendship. When it finally came, the community experienced the enveloping peace that follows a heartfelt reconciliation.

May brought the congregation the delightful news that Father Francis Haas was appointed pastor of St. Mary's Parish in town.

Although Mother Agnes must have known that the acceptance of Herzog, Kansas, at least initially, would prove costly, the community was able to honor its commitment to the Pittsburgh Capuchins in August. Even with clergy rates on the trains, the congregation's travel was expensive and the potential to acquire additional income through the mission in Herzog was dubious. Even so, on the 27th of August, Sisters Agatha and Aurea arrived in Herzog, Kansas. With their coming, the congregation reached approximately eight hundred miles to the west and seven hundred miles east to St. Mary's in Altoona, Pennsylvania.

TEXAS

The congregation did not neglect the Southwest in this decade of expansion. Before 1879 was over, Mother Agnes made a decision to send sisters almost a thousand miles to Texarkana, Texas. The decision was the direct result of one of Sister Patrick Walsh's collecting expeditions. While in Texas, Sister Patrick and her companion, Sister Ottilia Hess, met Father A. Barbin and, through him, Bishop Claude Marie Dubuis. The bishop, anxious to have a Catholic school, offered the community property in the town of Texarkana for as long as the sisters would teach there.[106] Texarkana had been formed in 1874 from two towns, one in Texas and one in Arkansas.

That same year a Catholic church was built there. The town was poor and undeveloped, but it could be reached by rail from St. Louis, and the bishop's enthusiasm over the prospect of having sisters was most contagious. Sending sisters there, however, was a decision that would prove to be unfortunate in ways that no one could have predicted.

Because neither Arkansas nor Texas had made provisions for public education, it could not be said that the town had an educational system. Although there were private schools in town, the parish, Sacred Heart, established a parochial school in 1874. The school met first in a boarding house and then in the dining room of one of the parishioners. By the time the sisters arrived, the children met in the lower floor of the newly-built church. Sisters Clementine Venner, Thomasine Carney, and Delphine Keenan arrived in time to teach at St. Agnes Academy for the school opening in January 1880. They were soon joined by Sisters Eugenia Hickey and Ignatia Spaith, a music teacher. The orphaned Anna Carey, now fourteen years old, was sent along with them to run errands and attend school. The first months were difficult. They found the school to be much poorer than they had been led to believe it would be. For a long time, bread and molasses were the mainstays of the sisters' diet. Even so, the school was successful and became even more so under the leadership of Sister Thomasine, who became principal in 1882.

After a chaotic start probably having to do with finances, Sister Thomasine was running a "good school, and she knew that she did."[107] In the spring of 1883 Mother Agnes, who had not been well, went to Texarkana in the hope that her health would improve in the warmer climate. She found the people so indifferent to religion that she felt as if she were living among infidels. Even though she wrote home that the sisters had nothing but bread and meat to eat and asked that one or two trunks full of vegetables be sent, she nevertheless was so pleased with Texas that in 1884 she sent Sisters Borgia Kelly, Seraphica Carey, and Helen McGlone to Immaculate Conception School in the town of Jefferson. There the sisters taught twenty-two children in the parish school. Even though they received salaries from the Texas Public School Fund,[108] their financial situation was so precarious that they felt obliged to take boarders into their convent.

A CRISIS IN FOND DU LAC

Back in Fond du Lac, St. Mary's Parish was well-known for the difficulties the hard-headed parishioners had with their pastors. Some of the difficulties experienced by pastors at that time can be traced to the legal structure of the parishes. Like many American parishes, St. Mary's had been organized and governed by lay boards of trustees. It was a structure common to Protestant churches and it conformed to the American democratic spirit. In the face of the nineteenth century's increasing authoritarianism and clericalism, lay members of ethnic parishes fought hard to maintain control of their parishes; they saw this as part of their struggle to maintain their own culture in an increasingly diverse American society.[109] Canon law, on the other hand, placed control of the parish in the hands of the pastor and bishop.

In 1879, the latest pastor to lock horns with the trustees of St. Mary's Church was Nicholas Pickel. Whether the original difficulties stemmed from personalities, unfortunate situations, or power conflicts, they ended with the transfer of the pastor to Marytown and the appointment of Father Francis Haas in his stead.[110] The Fond du Lac *Journal*, commented that the appointment was "much to the satisfaction of the congregation, with whom that estimable clergyman is deservedly popular."[111] However, instead of bringing peace to the parish that appointment exacerbated difficulties. Father Francis had been the subject of "persistent public defamation"[112] over a ten-year period in that parish.[113] Under the circumstances, it would seem that both Father Francis and the archbishop should have considered the offer of the pastorate of St. Mary's Parish more carefully. However, the recommendation of the friar as pastor by some prominent parishioners may have been a deciding factor in the archbishop's decision. For his part, Father Francis might have been encouraged to undertake the risk by his recent success in bringing peace to another difficult parish, St. Joseph's in Appleton.

The story of the moves and counter-moves of the principals has no place in this narrative, but highlighting some events may give us insight into the difficulties engulfing Father Francis over several years of continual pain and embarrassment. Evidently, the parishioners' initial contentment with his appointment lasted only a few days. On the first Sunday of his arrival, Father Francis asked that the collection monies be turned over to him in accordance with the law of the archdiocese, but the trustees refused. The battle was on and would not end for the friars until 1882.

Father Francis immediately laid the matter before the archbishop. The archbishop replied that the monies should be turned over to the pastor. The trustees saw the letter, but refused to comply. On September 2, 1879, the archbishop transferred St. Mary's Church, along with some property in Milwaukee, to the Capuchins. The trustees cancelled the transfer, withheld the pastor's salary, and advised him to resign for the good of the church. Francis then deposed the trustees and appointed new ones. The original trustees complained to the archbishop. The archbishop decided that the original trustees could stay. On October 7 the trustees went to the civil court and incorporated the parish as a civil organization.[114]

By November the controversy had become so heated that police were present at divine services. Two men who were members of a group that had held secret meetings on parish property were charged by the police for trespassing. The newspapers covered the altercation with enjoyment. On December 5, the vicar general of the archdiocese, Monsignor Leonard Batz, came to Fond du Lac to confer with Father Francis. Their very private meeting was held at the convent and, while no local priests were asked to attend, Mother Agnes was not only invited but also requested to record the meeting.[115] The vicar general relayed a message from the archbishop, who proposed that if the friars would relinquish St. Mary's, they might purchase another site in Fond du Lac on which to build a church and found their own parish. Then Father Francis might accept anyone who wished to come to him as a parishioner. If the divine services were obstructed again at St. Mary's, the church would be closed. Monsignor Batz also revealed that the archbishop had been receiving angry and threatening letters from secular priests and members of the parish.[116]

Events moved quickly the last few days of December. On December 28, Father Francis announced that, if the trustees did not surrender parish records, that service would be the last in the church. Members of the trustees' party then broke open the church, nailed up the pews, and notified their pastor he was to leave the rectory. Francis refused; on December 30, the church was placed under interdict. When Father Francis asked other pastors if he could use their church for the Feast of the Circumcision, a holy day of obligation, they refused.[117] It was then that Mother Agnes offered the use of the convent chapel.[118] About ninety families, two-thirds of the parish, attended Mass in the convent that New Year's Day. At the Mass, Father Francis announced that with the aid of the loyal members of the parish he would build a new church. The Capuchins, promised by the archbishop that the new parish would supplant St. Mary's, had purchased a site with two "patched up shanties" at Main and Merrill and, at the end of February, dedicated the makeshift structure as Sacred Heart Church.[119]

On May 30, 1880 a notice from Archbishop Henni was read in the Catholic churches stating that it was his wish that no new parishes be formed in the city.[120] His reversal can only be attributed, charitably, to the fact that the archbishop was ill and confused.

AN UNSATISFACTORY CONCLUSION

In a letter dated June 23, 1880, Mother Agnes left no doubt about her support of the friars and her skepticism regarding the local priests: "Although the Capuchin Fathers are persecuted, still I am thankful to God that we are under their guidance; they are truly good and pious; I presume this is the reason they are persecuted. The priests here it seems have so much to do the last few days to keep their own positions, that the poor Fathers are left in peace."[121]

It is possible that Mother Agnes received some measure of consolation from a group of women parishioners who were such ardent supporters of the friar that they boarded a train to Milwaukee to meet with the archbishop. Instead, they met with the coadjutor of the archdiocese, Bishop Michael Heiss. Some years later, Archbishop Heiss gave his version of their visit. It is of interest, if only because it clearly shows the dismissive attitude toward women that usually marked the hierarchy's relationship with them: "Some time ago this congregation [St. Mary's] was quite demoralized by factions. The women were the worst; they did not want to give up the priest who had been partly the cause of the trouble. A deputation of seven or eight women came to me in Milwaukee and I found it quite hard to get rid of them. Soon after, when coming back to Fond du Lac I spoke to the congregation without any mention of the women. 'Now see,' said they, 'he has not said a word about us. If he had only scolded us but he despises us.'"[122]

Because Archbishop Henni was too ill to act, and Bishop Heiss was unwilling to meddle in the affair, the Capuchins appealed the entire case to Rome. In April 1881, Heiss received a letter from Cardinal Giovanni Simeoni, prefect of the Propagation of the Faith, to the effect that some pastors in Fond du Lac had sent a writ of complaint against the Capuchins charging them with fomenting discord among the Catholics. Heiss in turn proposed that Rome take the matter in hand. Although both parties agreed that it would not be proper for the Capuchins to remain in Fond du Lac against the wishes of the clergy, the Capuchins maintained that they must be indemnified in regard to their financial loss and their honor.

In September, 1881 Heiss succeeded Henni as archbishop and, in 1882, he created a commission of four priests to answer three questions in regard to the settlement of the matter: Is there need of further investigation of the situation in Fond du Lac? May the Capuchins remain there longer? Should the Archdiocese indemnify them for expenditures made? The commission gave a negative answer to all three questions in reporting to Archbishop Heiss. They agreed that the Capuchins would be compensated mainly by promoting their interests and safeguarding their honor in leaving Fond du Lac by means of an appropriate official declaration.

ARCHBISHOP MICHAEL HEISS

Michael Heiss had come to Wisconsin from Bavaria in 1844. He was chosen as the first rector of St. Francis Seminary and then named the first bishop in the diocese of La Crosse in 1868. In 1880 he was sent to Milwaukee as coadjutor in preparation for his next assignment as archbishop. His interest in education led him to form the first archdiocesan school board. Although he did not wish the children to lose the language of their parents, he demanded that every parochial school under his jurisdiction teach English and teach it well. While he encouraged American-born women to enter religious communities as teaching sisters, he would not allow sisters to teach in public schools because it would favor schools originated in infidelity."[123]

It appears that although the relationship between Archbishop Heiss and the Sisters of St. Agnes was correct, it was never warm. Whether the difficulties stemmed from the unfortunate disturbances at St. Mary's in Fond du Lac or a matter internal to the congregation is a matter of conjecture, but only a few months before the death of Archbishop Heiss in 1889, Francis expressed his concern over the archbishop's assessment of the community.[124]

When caught up in the affair at St. Mary's, the sisters clearly sided with Father Francis, and in that position they, too, must have suffered some inevitable pain and embarrassment. It seems that Mother Agnes had become an unwilling catalyst in the mutual dislike of the pastor and the friar. Opening up the convent for Mass for the parishioners loyal to Father Francis, who, it must be remembered, had been appointed by the archbishop, would seem reasonable. But from a purely political standpoint she may not have realized, or perhaps cared, that the other pastors in Fond du Lac would almost inevitably stand together. In any case, the wisdom of detachment from parish affairs had been made evident to the congregation and became a guiding principle for the future.

Some years later, however, Mother Agnes must have been pleased to read these words from Father Francis: "The printed news of the progress in Fond du Lac pleases me. Your congregation is partly responsible for the peace there because you didn't leave the city when it was hopelessly disordered."[125]

Chapter IV

Coming
of Age

Whether Mother Agnes and her sisters were aware or not, the United States had moved from a rural economy to an industrial one. The worker was experiencing low wages, long hours, and poor and hazardous working conditions, while the small farmer was fast becoming the victim of high interest rates, the railroads, and corporate influence on the government. It was an aggressive period in American foreign policy as the country, fueled by commercial interests, began extending its reach around the globe.

Immigrants from Catholic countries were still pouring into the United States, making the Catholic church the largest single denomination in the nation. At the same time that the church had to deal with aggressive anti-Catholicism from the outside, within its own ranks a controversy was raging over the question of its identity in American society. The issue was clear. Should the church assimilate into American institutions or continue down a separatist path? Among the precipitating issues were the church's stance on unions, social reform, ethnic assimilation, and the parochial school system. Conservatives and liberals attacked each other with a vitriol that would not be seen again until the theological disputes that followed the Second Vatican Council.[1] As for the Agnesians, situated in predominantly German and rural parishes, their attitudes were simply those of their families or the everyday Catholics among whom they lived and served.

THE AGNESIANS

Ten years after the Congregation moved to Fond du Lac, there were ninety-three professed sisters, sixteen novices, and fourteen postulants. Three more missions were accepted that year: St. Alphonsus in Greenfield, Michigan; St. Paul of the Cross in Colombia City, Indiana; and Holy Trinity in Kewaskum, Wisconsin. There was also a fourth in Fond du Lac, the projected school for the very short-lived Sacred Heart Parish.

On August 16, 1880, the congregation's revised rule was approved by Pope Leo XIII. The congregation was no longer simply dependent on the will of the bishop of the diocese; it now had access to Rome and could expect its own cardinal protector. It was an honor received with joy and pride.

Another reconciliation touched the hearts of the community the next year. On February 21, 1881, after an absence of ten years, Sister Gertrude Laughlin rejoined the Sisters of St. Agnes. After her dismissal from the congregation, she had rejoined Father Rehrl in Barton. Soon the talented Gertrude was elected superior and for a short period things went well. Sister Hildegard Popp was running the farm while Gertrude attempted to open a boarding school at Barton. An educator with vision, Gertrude developed an elaborate curriculum for young ladies. Gertrude had a special interest in helping handicapped youngsters. She developed a special curriculum to give deaf, blind, and crippled children unusual opportunities for the time.[2] The boarding school, however, did not materialize. It is probable that the increase in the number of one-room schools in Wisconsin at the time made boarding schools a less desirable option.

When Father James M. Doyle invited the sisters to staff St. Patrick's School in Janesville, Wisconsin, recently vacated by the Sisters of Mercy, Gertrude happily accepted the offer.[3] There, in a larger town, she found much better prospects for the future of the society. The school, however, was over one hundred miles from Barton, and without Gertrude's leadership the convent there had little stability. When she began to receive candidates and to profess

novices, in effect moving the motherhouse to Janesville, Father
Rehrl announced in the summer of 1879 that, with the permission
of the archbishop, the society was to be dissolved.[4] Gertrude had to
decide whether to leave religious life, ask to return to Fond du Lac,
or join another community. At what point in this process her relationship with Mother Agnes was renewed is not clear. It may have
been when she, as superior, contacted Mother Agnes regarding the
decision of six Barton sisters to ask for admission into the Fond du
Lac community.[5]

Again there is little information. The first letter we have is the
reply of Mother Agnes to Gertrude's request that one of the sisters,
who was considering transferring to Fond du Lac, be allowed to
make a retreat with the community. In response to Gertrude's indecision regarding her own future, Agnes wrote, "I suppose you have
decided what you intend to do by this time and will soon be at rest.
We are keeping a devotion to the Sacred Heart and I remember
you."[6]

Just two days later, Mother Agnes learned that Gertrude
Laughlin had decided to enter the Dominican convent in Racine,
Wisconsin. This time the response of Mother Agnes was much
warmer, "Let us pray for one another and do all we can for God
while we are in this world, so that our meeting in Heaven will be a
joyful one. Wherever you are remember your old friend, who so
often thinks of you and of the many happy days we spent while once
together. Write to me occasionally, if you are allowed ... Your ever
loving friend.[7]

Gertrude remained with the Dominicans for seventeen months,
and "not finding the peace and contentment she longed for, humbly
begged to be admitted to the novitiate."[8] She returned to the
Agnesians on February 21, 1881, receiving the name of Bernardine.
Father Francis spoke at the occasion of her temporary vows and
likened her profession to the return of the dove to the ark bearing
an olive branch.[9]

Seven years later, when Mother Agnes celebrated her silver
jubilee,[10] she remembered that she and Sister Bernardine had made
their first profession together: "I shall never forget the evening when
we knelt at the little altar, poor as it was, and offered our first vows
to God .... The path we trod was often darkened with trials but He

kept his eye on us and brought us to light .... Let us be thankful and strive to labor more and more for Heaven."[11]

Those notes speak volumes about both women. Given what we know about her character, there is little doubt that Gertrude had believed that her grievances had been real; yet, ten years later, she was able to beg to return as a novice, and accept, in effect, a new identity. She must have wondered if she would ever again receive the trust of the community or of her dearly loved friend. That the naturally sensitive Agnes was able to disregard the past and open her heart again to an old friend is perhaps, of all her legacies, the one that touches the hearts of the sisters most deeply.

THE END OF AN ERA

Three deaths marked the end of an era for the congregation. On September 3, 1881, Father Rehrl died in Barton, and four days later Archbishop Henni died in Milwaukee. Both had played significant roles in the early days of the community, and their deaths brought a profound sense of loss to the community. The third death was that of Sister Patrick Walsh.

On Sister Patrick's final trip she and her companion were attempting to beg for money in Cuba, which was still a possession of Spain. On their way the two sisters collected wherever they could. Their last stop before Cuba was the Convent of Mary Immaculate in Key West, Florida, with the Sisters of the Holy Names of Jesus and Mary. Soon after the sisters arrived in Cuba, however, Sister Patrick contracted a fatal case of black smallpox. In a letter of condolence to Mother Agnes, Sister Felicite, SNJM, of the Key West convent wrote:

> I received the tidings of dear Sister Patrick's death, both she and Sister Cornelia had endeared themselves to our little Community, during the few weeks they spent with us, by their piety, charity, and devoted zeal for their Sisterhood, and we all sympathize deeply with those by whom Sister Patrick's loss must be keenly felt. She had, I think, some presentiment of what was to be, for she often said how repugnant the trip to Havana was to her, and only her strong desire

to aid her community could have prevailed over her feelings.[12]

Mother Felicite had enclosed $130— the amount Sister Patrick had collected and left in their convent for safekeeping. Sister Patrick was thirty-two years old.

THE COST OF PROGRESS

In 1882, Mother Agnes Hazotte was reelected as superior, Sister Josephine Maurer as vicar and Sisters Cecilia Ferstl, Seraphine Morrissey, and Regina Deiler as councilors.

Between 1881 and 1882, Father Rehrl's last parish school, St. Matthias at Barton, was accepted as were St. Joseph in Decatur, Indiana; St. Joseph in Hays, Kansas; and St. John in Waunakee, Wisconsin. In 1882, three more schools were accepted, all in Wisconsin: St. Mary, Pine Bluff; St. Anthony, Allenton; and St. Lawrence, St. Lawrence.

Six schools were added to the mission list in 1883. Two were in Indiana: St. Aloysius School, Sheldon, and St. Mary, Crown Point. Four were in Wisconsin: St. Charles, Charlesburg; St. John Baptist, Jefferson; Holy Angels, Darboy; and St. Mary, Lomira. Mother Agnes also extended the motherhouse property by buying additional land extending to Gillett Street, except for thirty feet to be used as Sheboygan Street.[13]

Everyone could recognize that the congregation had achieved a degree of stability. But it was not without cost. Both Mother Agnes and Sister Josephine had been plagued with health problems which they tried to deal with as best they could. For Sister Josephine's difficulties, Agnes asked that she be given toast at every meal and lean meat, fried or roasted but not boiled, as often as she could take it, except during Ember Weeks and the last week of Lent. Josephine should eat nothing sweet but she could eat celery, carrots, and sauerkraut, and take red wine after dinner. Agnes was happy to say that she had not had an attack of colic recently, but a priest had given her a good remedy for it, which she planned on trying soon. He advised fifteen drops of laudanum in half a glass of water. Agnes commented that it should be a remarkable remedy. In the meantime she was using Lourdes water.[14]

Fortunately, laudanum, remarkable as it was, never became the remedy of choice. The more usual remedies were teas: wormwood for stomach and intestinal ailments; chamomile and peppermint for colds; elderberry blossoms for bronchitis, coughs, and respiratory infections.

A PILGRIMAGE

A dream came true in 1884 for Mother Agnes when the council decided that a personal expression of gratitude to His Holiness Pope Leo XIII was a sacred obligation in recognition of the outstanding favors granted by him to the Congregation of St. Agnes.

Mother Agnes chose her secretary, Sister Seraphine Morrissey, as her companion. Because anticlerical laws were in force in France at the time, the Sisters of St. Agnes had to justify their existence before being allowed into the country.[15] Agnes was incensed. She wrote back to the motherhouse: "Our sisters go out as mission sisters and we teach the poor and have orphans. We take such places where many other communities would not take. We do all we can to labor in charitable works. I think our sacrifices are just as much as the Franciscan sisters in Milwaukee, the Fond du Lac Sisters of Mercy in Chicago, and many others."[16]

Mother Agnes must have been able to make her case. The two sisters left in a flurry on April 4, 1884, for Altoona, Pennsylvania where they would stop before proceeding to New York. They had scarcely left Fond du Lac, however, when Agnes discovered she had left behind her father's hare foot in one of her large desk drawers, with the bishop's letters. It was not easy getting the talisman to New York before the vessel sailed, but it arrived in time for the sisters to board the French steamer, *Normandie* peacefully.[17]

Upon boarding the ship, the sisters found the second-class accommodations so unsuitable that they had to secure a first-class stateroom. Although they were plagued with seasickness the first two days on board, they were well taken care of. On board they visited with several Capuchin friars and a Sister of Providence who was returning to France from Texas. In the evenings the three nuns sat together in the tiny stateroom, two on the sea trunk and one on a canvas chair. They chatted as they ate fruit and drank lemonade and found that the Sister of Providence had taught relatives of Mother

Agnes, the Hazotte and Klein children, for five years in Altroff. Sister Seraphine wrote, "It seems to me we know them all and the customs of the people before having seen them."[18] Overall, the sisters had a pleasant voyage, although one of the friars found Mother Agnes crying with homesickness one day. On April 25 they arrived at Havre and left for Paris, the first stop on their six-month pilgrimage.

On May 15 the sisters, by then in Rome, had the privilege of an audience with the Holy Father, which Sister Seraphine described with pleasure:

> A Man clothed in spotless white, attended by Monsignor Macchi and another person in purple, enters the throne room. It is Pope Leo XIII. All fall on their knees, but a signal from Monsignor Macchi bids them rise. After speaking a few words to several who are nearer the door than we, he comes to us. The Reverend Schulte introduces us, tells him the object of our visit, begs his blessing for each member of our congregation as well as for our relatives and friends. He answers, "Everything you ask is granted!"[19] He graciously accepts the piliolum[20] Mother Agnes offers him, removes the one he is wearing and gives it to Mother, replacing it with the one she has given him. Noting that we are Americans, he says, "America, America," and places his hand in benediction on our heads. He makes several inquiries about our congregation, during which time Mother Agnes holds his venerable hand in hers. After we had kissed his hand again, he proceeded to the next in line …. After the benediction, one of the officials who accompanied His Holiness, seeing, I presume our wistful looks, beckoned us to come again. So we had the pleasure of pressing the Holy Father's hand once more to our lips before the white-clad figure vanished from our sight to gladden those in the next room with his gracious smile. We left the Vatican filled with indescribable feelings of joy.[21]

Father Francis had encouraged the visit, which he saw as contributing to both Agnes' physical and spiritual health. He wrote to
her soon after her arrival to assure her that all was going well at the
motherhouse. He enlivened the letter with a few observations on the
Europeans, whom he saw as neglecting their old spirituality, but
nevertheless encouraged her to visit the art and architecture in the
"living rooms" of old Europe. He concluded by giving her a list of
his friends to greet should she visit in their area.

With the good news of the community putting their minds at
rest, the sisters embarked on pilgrimages to centers of Catholic
devotion, Assisi, Padua, and the Marian shrine of Loreto, where
Mother Agnes prayed that Father Francis would give the community permission to erect a hospital. In France they visited the shrine at
Lourdes and the Chapel of the Visitation in Paray-le-Monial, where
the seventeenth-century apparitions of the Sacred Heart to
Margaret Mary Alacoque had taken place. From there, they visited
the Benedictine abbey, Maria Einsiedeln, in Switzerland and then
went to a villa on Lake Constance, where they visited with Doctor
Otto Zardetti, a former professor at St. Francis de Sales Seminary
in Milwaukee. They went to Vienna next, then reached their final
destination, Ireland. After a week or so in the homeland of Sister
Seraphine's parents, they embarked from Queenstown on August
27.

Even with Mother Agnes abroad, missions were accepted:
Sacred Heart in Yankton, Dakota Territory;[22] Immaculate
Conception in Jefferson, Texas; and Sts. Peter and Paul and St.
Bridget in Washington County, Wisconsin. The community accept-
ed only one mission in 1885; it was the little town of Munjor,
Kansas, where the Agnesians again joined Capuchins in their work
with the Volga Germans.

RESPONDING TO GROWTH

During the following year, 1886, Mother Agnes not only agreed to
send sisters to Holy Family School, Mitchell in Dakota Territory at
the request of Father George Willard,[23] but she bought land there as
well. She also accepted an offer from the Capuchin friars to staff
Our Lady Queen of Angels, a new parish school in Harlem, New
York City, then a largely German neighborhood. It had not been

easy for Father Bonaventure Frey to convince Archbishop Michael Corrigan, who preferred the already established communities "for whom no house had to be built," to accept the Agnesians into the archdiocese.[24]

Father Bonaventure pleaded his case by arguing that: 1) the sisters were especially well trained in the order; 2) they were obedient and would ask for no extra pay to look after the welfare of the school and do church work; 3) they would train the children in "Caecilian" music; and 4) they would be diligent and maintain an ideal school. "The Archbishop gave in but not without stipulating that the sisters 'not spend their time visiting but give a good example,' and 'that they follow a printed rule.'"[25] Sisters Leo Ankenbruck and Julia Dullea, accompanied by the housekeeper, were allowed entry into the archdiocese, where they opened the school in September 1886. The next year, Mother Agnes bought a house and lot for ten thousand dollars on East 112th Street as a convent in the parish. When a more convenient two-story brick house was found on East 113th Street, she was able to make an even exchange.[26]

Back home in Fond du Lac, the increasing numbers of sisters in Fond du Lac prompted the building of the chapel wing, which had been designed as part of the convent's original plan. It was built on five and one-half acres of land Mother Agnes had purchased in 1886. The wing was completed the following year. The much admired chapel had a three-story-high vaulted ceiling with Gothic arches.[27] An eleven-foot oil painting of St. Agnes had been done by Tertulliano Giangiacomo in Rome, but it proved too small for the chapel. Three years later, the German-American artist, Wilhelm Lamprecht, painted a fresco of the martyrdom of St. Agnes in the sanctuary.[28] Lamprecht had already achieved a measure of fame in the area with his fresco, "The Triumph of Christianity" in the Capuchin church of St. Francis Assisi in Milwaukee.[29]

Before the chapel was dedicated, Archbishop Heiss had paid the convent a visit. Writing on December 9 to a fellow cleric, he spoke warmly of his visit to the sisters: "In the evening I went to the convent of the Sisters of St. Agnes in the outskirts of the town, where I was again received "sicut angelus Dei" [like an angel of God] (Gal.4:14) so that I felt ashamed of myself. The community is of recent foundation and has the approbation of Rome. Last summer they enlarged their convent and built a new, beautiful, and spacious chapel ...."[30]

LOSSES AND GAINS

The year 1887 brought unwelcome news to Mother Agnes. Father Francis had received word that, on the recommendation of the general definitory of the Capuchins, the Holy Father had named him as definitor general, seating him on the board of consultors of the entire Capuchin Order. She knew she must rejoice in his honor, but because the position demanded he must reside in Rome, her feelings were decidedly mixed. It was not that she still needed mentoring; she had learned much over the years, just as the young women who had so naively and hopefully joined her over the years had grown in dedication and loyalty. But there was no denying that they all would find life different without their spiritual director.

Meanwhile, although Father Francis was in Rome, he did not forget Mother Agnes and the community in Fond du Lac. He continued to give her advice, encourage her, and showed a constant concern for the progress of the community. When Agnes worried because her friend Bishop Zardetti had told her that Fond du Lac was not the place for the Sisters of St. Agnes "if you want them to be a first class community," Francis replied with his own hopes and expectations of the sisters: "I thought that an honorable profession as teachers and living the religious life with fervor gave the sisters a good name. It is for these they would be sought out, not for the highest salary and the largest motherhouse."[31]

There is evidence that the Sisters of St. Agnes were establishing credibility in the field of education from the letter that Sister Magdalene wrote to Sister Seraphine from Yankton on January 17, 1887:

> His Lordship[32] seemed greatly pleased with our progress. He wanted the sisters to write a course of study based on the Fargo public schools for the Vicariate. He wanted: "Our schools to be a model in Dakota." I am with Rev. Redmond's help arranging the course according to our method of teaching and which I am glad he thinks exactly like that which he

wants. I showed him the report we must fill every two
months and told of the examination of teachers,
every year after retreat. He told all this to Father and
the trustees at New Year; and praised our community as a teaching body.[33]

Best of all, the sisters had a sense of humor and could tease each
other, if this anecdote from Sister Magdalene Callaghan can be
offered as evidence: "I must tell you that we teach 'the use of alcohol and its abuse' in connection with Physiology in obedience to his
Lordship. Sister Philomene's nose is so red that we feared she would
make no impression on the pupils so it fell to my lot."[34]

Three new missions were accepted that year in as many different states: St. Lawrence in Muncie, Indiana; McKeesport in
Pennsylvania; and St. Ignatius in Houghton, Michigan, the first free
school in the diocese.[35]

It was 1888 and time for another community election. Mother
Agnes, by then forty-two years old, was elected unanimously. It is
inconceivable that she would not have been re-elected. With no limitations on terms at that time, the founders in the early Wisconsin
communities retained their positions for most, if not all, of their
lives. To what degree this was due to the mystique of religious life
and authority is not clear. In any case Sisters Josephine Maurer,
Seraphine Morrissey, and Regina Deiler remained on the council,
while Sister Antonia Schmitz replaced Sister Cecilia Ferstl.[36]

TROUBLE IN TEXARKANA

The year 1888 proved difficult for the congregation. It was not all
bad, for the congregation had been happy to accept St. Martin
school in Ashford, Wisconsin and St. Peter Claver in Sheboygan,
Wisconsin. But the closure of St. Agnes Academy, the community's
first foundation in Fond du Lac, must have saddened the sisters.
Even worse, Mother Agnes' attempts to recall the sisters from
Texarkana to Fond du Lac became the cause of the biggest rift in
the congregation since its removal from Barton in 1870.

The troubles began when the coadjutor bishop of Galveston,
Nicholas Gallagher, visited Texarkana, Texas, to administer the
sacrament of confirmation. At this time there were seven sisters in

Texarkana and three in Jefferson, Texas. At the confirmation, the pastors and sisters took the occasion to inform the bishop that the sisters were so disaffected with their congregation that they wished to be affiliated with his diocese, independent of their motherhouse. Within a few days Bishop Gallagher made the 1,400-mile trip from Galveston to Fond du Lac to confer with Mother Agnes. *The Annals* note that in May 1888, "Bishop Gallagher of Galveston called at Fond du Lac to see if we were in favor of the formation of an English-speaking province." Mother Agnes told him that the plan was impossible, claiming that "the Constitution of the Order would not permit it."[37] He returned to Texas and told the sisters "positively that their plain duty as Religious was simply to submit to the orders of their superior, and that they must not hope for any encouragement from me to do otherwise."[38]

Sister Thomasine Carney with Sisters De Sales Carney, Alexia Carney, Borgia Kelly, Helen McGlone, and Petronilla Malloy refused to return to Fond du Lac but did not inform the motherhouse.[39] Meanwhile, as the sisters loyal to Fond du Lac had no money, they were unable to return to Fond du Lac. Finally, Sister Appollinaris Daub slipped out a letter, via one of the boarders, to Mother Agnes. She, in turn, sent Sister Paula Bohn to Texarkana to bring back the loyal members of the community.

Sister Thomasine did not welcome Sister Paula and told her that there was no money to pay for train fare to Fond du Lac. However, as she would not permit the sisters to take their own trunks, she finally gave Sister Paula fifty dollars to buy trunks. In the meantime, the sisters, who wanted to go with her had washed early that morning. They were forced to gather their few belongings out of the washtubs and wrap them in old pieces of oilcloth. Because the returning sisters had received only enough money for train tickets, they had nothing to eat until they arrived in Fond du Lac.[40]

The pastor in Texarkana was content because the sisters, who were excellent teachers, remained with him. The pastor in Jefferson refused to find other sisters for his parish and asked to be released from the bishop's jurisdiction. The people, angry at the withdrawal of the sisters, protested to Bishop Gallagher and then to Cardinal Giovanni Simeoni, the Prefect of the Propaganda in Rome. [41] With the permission of the bishop, Sisters Thomasine, Helen, and De Sales eventually formed a diocesan community, the Sisters of St.

Rose of Lima.[42] They had a mission for a while in Oklahoma, then left Texarkana for Hope, Arkansas in 1908, and later disbanded.[43] The name of the school in Texarkana later was changed from St. Agnes Academy to Sacred Heart Academy to conform to the name of the church.[44]

Three sisters eventually returned to Fond du Lac. Sister Borgia Kelly returned in 1888; Sister Helen McGlone, in 1892; and Sister Petronilla Malloy, in 1893.[45]

THE 'MYSTERY' OF TEXARKANA

Although the Sisters of St. Agnes were in Texarkana only nine years, three sisters died there: Sisters Ignatia Spaight and Eugenia Hickey of typhoid and Sister Justine Schodron of consumption. They also left behind a "mystery." Why did a group of the sisters missioned there leave the community?

In fact, it was not uncommon in that period for any given group of sisters, for a myriad of reasons, to leave their community and form another. Distance from the motherhouse had much to do with some decisions, along with the reality that the further the administration was from an immediate situation, the less able it was to understand local situations and problems. Ethnic tensions, widespread among the immigrant groups, were common in many convents and monasteries, particularly in the Midwest, and in this case the Agnesians, although American in their foundation, seem, as a group, to have become more strongly German over the years. The Irish frequently differed from the Germans majority in temperament, attitudes toward authority, and even their sense of the ridiculous.[46] With the exception of the liturgical prayers in Latin, Agnesian communal prayers were in German. German was spoken by choice in many of the convents, and many of the schools classes were taught in German as well as English. Most of the sisters stationed in Texarkana were Irish and must have felt more comfortable as the majority in their small local community. Sixty years later, when the Sisters of St. Agnes taught in an ethnically diverse school such as St. Joseph's in Fond du Lac—if the Irish-German combination could be called diverse by that time—the Irish pastor encouraged Irish girls to enter a congregation he deemed more ethnically compatible.

Ethnic prejudices also had much to do with the congregation's withdrawal from Mitchell in Dakota Territory. Although the community did not withdraw from the school until 1896, Mother Agnes had written in 1888 to the superior to tell her of the difficulties the pastor, a Father Sheehan, was creating for her. Not only did he give her to understand that the people did not want German sisters there, he also demanded teachers, for whom he could not pay, for a high school he planned to open. Although Mother Agnes did her best, promising him a teacher the following school year, it was clear that the community would never be able to meet his expectations.[47]

THE LEO HOUSE

In 1889, the Sisters of St. Agnes were given permission to undertake an apostolate far removed from education. It was the first time, but not the last, that the sisters responded to a plea for help and courageously undertook a new ministry. Following the Civil War, more than two million immigrants had poured into the United States. Many were Germans, and many disembarked into their new country overwhelmed, homeless, and considered by some of their countrymen ripe for exploitation. Their plight became a concern of the Central Verein, a union of many German Catholic societies.[48] The organization's goals were ambitious: to unite their energies in defending the attacks on the church in the United States, to promote Catholic religious activities, and to mutually aid and benefit each other.

Around 1868, the Central Verein undertook the care of German arrivals in New York and Baltimore by employing trusted men to meet the newcomers at the ports. When a socially active and prominent wealthy Mainz businessman, Peter Paul Cahensly, came to the United States, he realized that much more was needed to meet both the physical and religious needs of his countrymen. On his return to Germany, he interested a group of fellow businessmen in forming a society dedicated to helping the German Catholic immigrant "in every possible way before he sailed, during his voyage, and at the ports of debarkation."[49] The men named the society the St. Raphaelsverein after the archangel, Raphael, patron saint of travelers. A branch was established in the United States in 1883. One of its principal goals was to establish a hostel where the new

Father Caspar Rehrl
December 31, 1809 -
September 3, 1881
Crayon sketch by Sister
Julienne Rompf, CSA.

Mother M. Agnes Hazotte, CSA
May 7, 1847 - March 6, 1905
Hazotte Family Portrait, Left to Right: Anne Marie
Hazotte, Marie Potier Hazotte, Victor Hazotte

Father Francis Haas, O.M.
November 24, 1826 -
June 21, 1895
Oil portrait by
Tertulliano Giangiacomo
Roma, Italy, 1888.

St. Agnes Convent, Barton, Wisconsin, 1858 - 1870
In 2007 the building still stands on the original site. The property is own
by the Washington County Historical Society.

other M. Agnes Hazotte, CSA
Superior General
1864 - 1905

St. Agnes Hospital, East Division Street, Fond du Lac,
Wisconsin, was dedicated June 23, 1896, and opened to
patients July 1, 1896.

St. Mary's Springs Sanatarium, including the Annex (left) built for hydrother 1902 - 1909. In 1909 these buildings were converted into St. Mary's Springs Academy and named St. Agnes Hall (left) and Boyle Hall (right).

Sister Bernardine (Gertrua Laughlin, Superior at St. Mary's Springs Sanatar

Mother Antonia Schmitz, CSA
Superior General
1905 - 1916

*St. Joseph Orphans House for Boys and Girls, Assinins, Michigan,
was accepted by Mother Antonia Schmitz in April 1906. The first sisters
arrived there June 25, 1906. Msgr. M. Faust, pictured above with some of
the children, served as director for many years.*

St. Anthony Hospital, Hays, Kansas, first opened August 25, 1909, in the converted Beach House. A new hospital was built in 1916 and this addition to it was dedicated on January 21, 1931.

School children at St. Francis School, Munjor, Kansas, pictured around 1915 or 1916. Candidates as seen in this photo (upper left) were sometimes sent for a year or two to join the faculty at a school where a professed sister was unavailable.

St. Agnes Convent
390 E. Division Street
Fond du Lac, Wisconsin
1877 - 1975

Photo shows, from left to right,
the 1877 building, the 1887
chapel addition, and the 1909
addition.

"The Martyrdom of St. Agnes of
ome" rose above the main altar
St. Agnes Convent Chapel,
0 East Division Street.
other Agnes Hazotte
ommissioned New York artist
ilhelm Lamprecht to create
e mural in 1890.

*Mother M. Marcella Kettner, CSA
Superior General
1916 - 1926*

*Left to right: Novice, Professed
Sister, Postulant pictured
wearing traditional garb.
The traditional habit designed
in 1870 by Sister Antonia
Schmitz was essentially
unmodifed until 1960.*

arrivals could be taken for a day or two and then helped to reach their new destination. With the help of Bishop Winand M. Wigger of Newark, New Jersey, the society bought a site at 6 State Street in Castle Garden Park, near where the immigrants were processed.

The year 1887 marked the fiftieth anniversary of Pope Leo XIII's ordination to the priesthood, and American Catholics, particularly those from the Midwest, had been most generous in collecting a large gift of money for him. The pontiff, in turn, donated the gift to the St. Raphaelsverein for the establishment of a shelter for immigrants. The society responded by naming the hostel they were building after the pope.

In October 1889, shortly before the Leo House was to open, the directors found they had no staff. A group of Swiss religious had promised to staff it, but New York's Archbishop Michael Corrigan was opposed to allowing more religious communities into his archdiocese. Appeals to New York congregations of religious were in vain. At that point, Wilhelm Schickel, the vice-president of the Leo House board and the architect who had designed their motherhouse, thought of the German-speaking Sisters of St. Agnes. Because the sisters were already established in Harlem, there could be no objection from the archbishop.

Time was running out. The building would be dedicated on December 7, and it was already October 25. Schickel quickly contacted Mother Agnes. The St. Raphaelsverein asked for three sisters: a superior "who would have to be a practical person, with plenty of common sense, capable of handling all kinds of people,"[50] a sister to take care of the kitchen, and another, the house. The sisters could hire a female servant as well as a porter. The sisters would have a chapel and a chaplain, who would have nothing to do with the management of the house, but would receive and dispatch the immigrants to Castle Garden. The sisters would not be burdened with financial matters, and the building would be debt-free in two years. They were also assured that they would come in contact with good German Catholic families and would be in a position to assist the many German girls who were coming to the city.[51]

There was not much time, but Mother Agnes, eager to accept a challenge and always in need of money, discussed the matter with her council and wrote to Father Francis, who was in Rome. Although Francis, fearing that sisters would be taken away from the schools, would have preferred that the offer to manage the Leo House had not been made, it "would have been clumsy to refuse it."[52]

The matter was not yet over. Because accepting the Leo House would mean that the congregation would have to alter its original mission, the matter would have to be referred to its cardinal protector. Action was taken quickly. Mother Agnes received permission to accept the work and immediately wired Schickel. It was November 15. Schickel asked her to attend the annual meeting of the board with Archbishop Corrigan on November 20. At the meeting, she accepted the Leo House on conditions, the most important being that the sisters never lack the opportunity to carry out their religious exercises.

Mother Agnes remained until after Christmas, helping to clean and prepare the house for the newcomers. Writing to the sisters, Mother Agnes gave a brief explanation of the history of the Leo House to the sisters and described its mission: "The house was instituted for the protection of German immigrants, so that they may not be led astray. Sad experience teaches that many have lost their faith for want of such an institution. Here they receive the sacraments and are directed to places where there are Catholic churches and schools."[53]

The superior, Sister Paula Bohn, had much to do: formulate policies and procedures; give work assignments, put rooms in order, organize the kitchen, and follow directives from Bishop Wigger. The relationship of the sisters to the chaplain was of great concern to the bishop. They were to treat the chaplain with the deference that was due to him. They were warned not to get involved with the spiritual business of the chaplain, and there were directions on any conversation the superior might have with a person waiting to see the chaplain. While recommending that there be little variety in the food served, the bishop also said that it should be of the quality and kind that the immigrant would accept. He noted, without additional comment, that people just off the ships usually had good appetites.[54]

In the end, the bishop concluded that Sister Paula was the right person for the job and that the sisters were hard-working. The Board of Regents was well satisfied. In its first year, 1889-1890, the Leo House served 3,970 immigrants and 241 other guests; it offered

2,493 free meals and 845 nights of free shelter. Furthermore, eighty weddings had been performed in the chapel.[55]

That Christmas Father Francis sent from Rome paintings of St. Agnes, the Sacred Heart of Jesus, and the Immaculate Heart of Mary. He also sent a smaller painting of himself carefully giving the sisters instructions to put it where no one but they could see it. He particularly did not want it in the priests' dining room.[56]

THE NOT-SO-GAY '90S

For some Americans, the 1890s conjure up images of wealth expressed in high fashion, elaborate balls, and fancy horse-drawn rigs. Others think of discoveries and inventions, such as the wireless telegraph, moving pictures, and Ford's first automobile. On a more modest level, town dwellers were enjoying electric lights, paved streets, and electric trolleys. But the decade that opened with such promise very shortly produced a depression that turned into a panic.

A major railroad failure precipitated a financial crisis on Wall Street. Six hundred banks failed, and one-third of the country's railroads went broke. Unemployment rose to 18 percent and Coxey's Army[57] was but one manifestation of the labor unrest that struck the nation. In the West an ongoing agricultural depression deepened, spreading misery throughout the farmlands. As the depression expanded, the dollar lost its value and interest rates on loans reached as high as 20 percent. One of the worst hit areas in the country was Kansas, where many a farmer lost everything and was forced to look for a job in the city. There the situation was so desperate that, in order to keep up the parishes as well as support the sisters, the Capuchins were forced to send begging letters to charitable societies in Europe.[58]

Within the community, Mother Agnes had always made an effort to insure that the sisters were as self-sufficient as possible. They continued to make their own necessities such as soap and candles, and members were also apprenticed to learn other useful trades. Mary Leuchinger (Sister Alcantara), who had come from Germany, was apprenticed to Mr. Peter Feldner in St. Cloud to learn the cobbler's trade.[59]

For the Sisters of St. Agnes, the beginning of the decade brought another general chapter. Although a change in the administration was unlikely, Mother Agnes must have breathed a sigh of relief when the chapter of 1890 left the general administration of the congregation in the same hands. The sisters were congenial, and Sisters Josephine and Seraphine were close friends of Mother Agnes. In five consecutive elections beginning in 1876, Mother Agnes, Sister Josephine, and Sister Seraphine remained in office. Sister Paula Bohn was a member of the council in 1876 and Sister Cecelia Ferstl in 1882. Both Sister Antonia and Sister Regina were chosen in four of the five elections. With the same leadership in place, elections caused scarcely a ripple in the community. Throughout the period, Sister Josephine was in charge of the convent, Sister Seraphine took care of the finances, and Sister Joseph Wolford was responsible for the education of candidates and novices.

For Mother Agnes, the stability in the council must have been a comfort because she was besieged with problems related to her own health and that of the sisters. On March 15, 1890, the community was shocked to learn that two sisters, Sister Alacoque Kraemer in Altoona and Sister Stilla Walz in Defiance, died that day of tuberculosis. Mother Agnes also worried about the health of Father Francis, who was not doing well in Rome. By that time used to the direct and unsophisticated ways of Americans, he felt unsympathetic to Italian mores and found the climate enervating. His health, uncertain for years, was beginning to worsen. He had scarcely settled down in Rome when he was overcome by malaria. His constitution was undermined by the damp, unheated rooms of the *Generaltiate*.[60] As with Agnes and so many others of the time, tuberculosis had ravaged his family, and he, too, in all likelihood, was its victim.

THE FRIENDSHIP OF ARCHBISHOP FREDERICK XAVIER KATZER

While Father Francis was gradually withdrawing from an active life, new people and new ventures began to crowd the days of Mother Agnes. The consecration of the Most Reverend Frederick Xavier Katzer as archbishop of Milwaukee in 1890 marked the beginning of a warm relationship between the two.[61] The new archbishop proved a strong supporter of Catholic schools and ethnic parishes.

He was also a friend to women's religious communities and the Agnesians were no exception. Nevertheless, in 1894 the Archbishop felt obliged to forbid the making of perpetual vows for an indefinite time because several sisters in perpetual vows had left the congregation.[62] Katzer was interested in its success, and the advice he gave Agnes was based upon a sound view of human nature and economic realities. No doubt the Sisters of St. Agnes found both him and his agenda compatible with their mission. He enjoyed coming to Fond du Lac, and when he celebrated St. Agnes Day with the community, he sometimes extended his visit for a few extra days for relaxation and reflection.

Their friendship, however, did not mean that Mother Agnes and the archbishop always saw eye-to-eye. When Mother Agnes indicated that she did not wish to accept a school at Boscobel, Wisconsin, the archbishop responded, "If I have to bow to you in this matter, I will permit other sisters to come to Fond du Lac. Who knows? This would be for English and other [language] speaking sisters who have the same mission as the Agnesians."[63] However, a few months later a compassionate archbishop wrote to Mother about a poor German girl in trouble with her community. The girl had tried to commit suicide. The archbishop wanted Mother Agnes to "look her over" and take the girl under her wing.[64]

THE RETURN OF BISHOP OTTO ZARDETTI

During the same decade Bishop Otto Zardetti[65] reappeared in the life of Mother Agnes. She had met him when he was Dr. Zardetti of the faculty of St. Francis de Sales Seminary in Milwaukee and, during her trip to Europe with Sister Seraphine, had stopped at Lake Constance to visit with him and his brother Eugene. In 1891, he presided over the St. Agnes Day liturgy at the motherhouse and delighted the sisters with an eloquent sermon. He then went to Chicago for a few days and returned to celebrate his forty-fourth birthday with the sisters. "Every Bishop has his own favorite Sisterhood," he wrote, "the Sisters of St. Agnes are mine."[66]

The bishop was charming, complex, and controversial. John Joseph Frederick Otto Zardetti had been born on January 24, 1847, just a few months before Mother Agnes, into a family of successful merchants in the German-speaking canton of St. Gall in

Switzerland. While he was studying for his doctorate in theology at the University of Innsbruck, he was invited to accompany his bishop to the Vatican Council. There he met Bishop John Henni. Ordained in 1870, he was appointed a professor in the diocesan seminary and soon established a reputation as an eloquent orator. Well on his way to a distinguished career, he was influenced by the example of his boyhood friend, Sebastian Messmer, who was then in the American missions. In 1881, after a visit to the United States, he accepted an invitation by Bishop Henni to teach dogmatic theology at St. Francis Seminary in Milwaukee. There he was a colleague of Professor Johann Baptist Singenberger, who, in all probability, introduced him to Mother Agnes.

In 1887, the Bishop of the Dakota Territory, Martin Marty, invited the professor to be his vicar general. Zardetti's rise to eminence was swift. In September 1889, he was appointed the first bishop of St. Cloud, Minnesota, but Zardetti did not find the position to his liking. After only five years in St. Cloud, he was transferred to Bucharest Romania, even though it was highly unusual for bishops who had served in America to be sent back to Europe. Unfortunately, he did not like Bucharest, either, and came to regret having left St. Cloud.[67] Although Zardetti resigned as Archbishop of Bucharest within a year, he was never reappointed to a See in the United States. Instead, he was named the titular archbishop of Mocissus, an extinct see in Asia Minor. Shortly before his untimely death in 1902, he was being considered for the position of first apostolic delegate to Canada.[68]

It was probably in 1894, on his transfer to Bucharest, that he involved Mother Agnes in a complicated financial relationship that she eventually had good reason to regret.[69] The financial disasters of 1893 had wreaked havoc in the financial world and the value of Zardetti's investments, particularly in land, were adversely affected. The bishop had three brothers, and it appears that he had made investments for all of them.

While Mother Agnes was not his primary agent in America, he had made her responsible for forwarding money every six months to Europe. She was to bank it for him, see that his wealth grew, and even take care of a magazine subscription for him. He wanted her to make inquiries about (and possibly purchase) property he had looked at in Yankton. Land values had plummeted and the land was to be sold for taxes. He wanted her to borrow any of his surplus funds at 4.5 percent interest. Until a few months before his death, Mother Agnes received letters that grew more and more peremptory as he became more distraught over the dwindling value of his investments.[70] How, as time went on, Agnes must have dreaded seeing mail from Switzerland.

DECISIONS

The motherhouse continued to buzz with activity, and Mother Agnes at its hub was continuously busy. Sisters came home to recuperate from illnesses and traveling religious and priests were always welcome. The school was active, and there seemed to be always someone practicing the piano or organ. When burdened, she let the sisters know that she relied on their prayers. She seemed to take particular consolation in the prayers of Sister Pacifica Eckhart, who would spend hours praying before the Blessed Sacrament. "I feel assured that all will be well, when I remember that good Sister Pacifica is praying in the Chapel."[71]

Four schools were accepted in 1891: St. Luke in Two Rivers, Wisconsin;[72] St. Joseph in Wyandotte, Michigan; St. Joseph in Mansfield, Pennsylvania; and St. Andrew in Potosi, Wisconsin. In 1892 St. Joseph in Sinsinawa, Wisconsin, was accepted as was Sacred Heart in Yonkers, a Capuchin parish school. In 1894, St. Nicholas in Evanston, Illinois, was accepted, a mission the sisters maintained until 1996.

The Catalogue of the Congregation of St. Agnes, printed in 1893, listed 173 professed sisters, twelve novices and thirty-eight candidates. The congregation conducted forty parochial schools in which 5,718 children were taught and one "immigrant house."[73] In the period from 1871 to 1890, the congregation withdrew from St. Peter, Malone; St. Thomas, Beloit; St. Charles Borromeo, Cassville; St. Louis, Fond du Lac; St. Patrick, Lebanon; St. Patrick, Milwaukee; St. Mary, Pine Bluff; St. Lawrence, St. Lawrence; St. Charles, Charlesburg; St. John Baptist, Jefferson; Holy Angels, Darboy, and Sts. Peter and Paul, Nenno, Wisconsin. The congregation also withdrew from St. Agnes in Texarkana, Texas; Sacred Heart in Yankton, Dakota Territory; and schools in McKeesport, East Liberty, and Bloomfield, Pennsylvania.[74]

Reasons for withdrawing from a mission were various: parishes being unable or unwilling to support a school; inadequate housing for the sisters; disagreements with the pastor over personnel;[75] excessive demands made by the pastor or simply his preference to work with a community with which he was familiar; a shortage of sister personnel; or even the desire of the bishop for his own diocesan community. In at least one case, the school burned down; in another, the superior, who was both principal and organist, died and could not be replaced.

Mother Agnes believed in progress, even though she knew that any steps toward modernization would draw criticism from conservatives, religious and lay alike. In 1892, the sisters at the motherhouse were elated when electricity was introduced and the old kerosene lamps were discarded, except, of course, for the many emergency lamps scattered around the house and chapel. That same year the congregation was incorporated by the state of Wisconsin with the general purpose of providing for the "advancement of education, learning, Christianity, and educating and instructing young girls and all such other business as is properly, legally, and necessarily incident thereto or connected therewith.[76]

Perhaps because the Panic of 1893 depressed land values, Mother Agnes purchased additional land that year. She acquired ten acres of land extending from East Division Street to Gillett Street for $1,350 and the next year bought a house and two lots across from St. Mary's Church on Merrill Street for $1,000.[77]

A MORE PENITENTIAL LIFE STYLE

In 1895, the congregation printed a list of regulations.[78] That there had been gradual changes in the daily life of the sisters during the last few years was obvious. Many elements of freedom and spontaneity seemed lost. The tiniest details of their lives were prescribed. Sanctity could be found in small deeds and small acts of obedience. Religious life implied sacrifices, and each sister made them hour by hour and day by day.

Each sister and each local mission group was isolated. No communication was allowed with other missions. Strict silence was to be maintained on the way to church and school. Within convent walls silence was observed throughout the day. Only a short period of recreation after supper and celebrations on feast days gave the sisters an occasion to talk about events of the day. Each sister was to attend to her own affairs and not ask for help or information from others. They were not allowed to discuss congregational affairs. They were advised to spend more time in pious reading. Only educational newspapers were allowed. Sisters were not to write letters, even of congratulations, to other sisters. Sisters of the same family could visit only once or twice a year. There were to be no visitors or private lessons after 7:00 p.m. The music played in church was to be strictly controlled. Nothing could be played except that approved by the church; there could be no marches or other worldly music. To discourage communications with the choir members, the sisters were not permitted to take part in any treats given to the group. The tightening of regulations seems to have been general and it appears that ecclesiastical authorities had much to do with it.[79]

THE LAST DAYS OF FATHER FRANCIS

Meanwhile, in January 1892, an epidemic of influenza swept Rome. Francis, already suffering from tuberculosis and Bright's disease, was stricken and soon contracted pneumonia. Close to death, he was anointed at the beginning of February and recuperated to some extent, but could not leave his bed until March. Unable to continue his work, he asked to return to Wisconsin to recuperate. On his return, after he had visited some Capuchin houses, he moved into the chaplain's house at St. Agnes Convent. He intended to return to Rome to finish his term as definitor general, but others quickly saw the plan's impossibility. In July, Mother Agnes wrote of his condition to Father Bonaventure, "I find him very weak. He could hardly give Holy Communion to the Sisters. If he could only remain in America! I believe his days are numbered."[80] In October, he resigned his office but continued to live at the chaplain's house. His resignation was not accepted.

The last public presence of Father Francis with the sisters was at their chapter in the summer of 1894 when again the entire generalate was re-elected. He lived in pain. As his weakness increased, he could no longer say Mass. Finally, the guardian at Mount Calvary came to be with him during his last days. As Father Bittle tells the story, one great joy was accorded Francis shortly before his death. A priest came to see him, but refused to give his name. His nurse, Sister Romana, therefore got his permission to usher in the name-less guest. Bittle continues:

> [Sister Romana] remained at the door, watching the two. Father Francis stood in the room, his expectant eyes focused on the man who entered. The latter stepped inside, looked a moment at the bent figure before him, walked over with brisk steps, and exclaimed: "Father Francis!" A smile lit up the face of the sick man, and then both extended their arms and embraced each other. The visitor was Father [Pickel], the bitterest opponent of Father Francis in his Fond du Lac days. The meeting was a source of great consolation to both, and they parted the best of friends.[81]

As Francis grew weaker, his only wish was to die on the feast of the Sacred Heart of Jesus.[82] Visitors were unwelcome interruptions to his solitude. On one occasion, he requested Mother Agnes to leave the room because he did not care to see anyone. She left, but felt it very keenly and was heard to say, "After this I'll love no one but Jesus."[83] Father Francis died on the feast of the Sacred Heart, June 21, 1895.

The letter Mother Agnes wrote to the community after his death gives little hint of the pain she felt:

> Our dear Father Francis' wish is fulfilled. He died a peaceful, happy death at five this afternoon, the feast of the Sacred Heart. At his bedside were the Very Reverend Fathers Bonaventure, Anthony, and Lawrence. "I should wish to die on the Feast of the Sacred Heart, but I am not worthy of so great a grace," he often said. God judged otherwise, and he has gone to celebrate a never-ending Sacred Heart Feast in Heaven. He looks so peaceful and happy that one feels he needs not our prayers, still I wish you all to offer the same suffrages for him that our Holy Rules prescribe for members of our

Congregation. Our gratitude and love for our dear, venerated Father will prompt us to pray more than this for him, he deserves it all.[84]

THE FOUNDING OF ST. AGNES HOSPITAL

For more than ten years, Mother Agnes, the superior of a congregation of teaching sisters, had been begged by Fond du Lac businessmen to establish a hospital in Fond du Lac. The plea was clearly a testimony to the reputation that the Catholic sisters had established as nurses since the Civil War. On her pilgrimage to the shrine of Our Lady of Loreto in 1884, Mother Agnes had prayed that Father Francis might look favorably on the erection of a hospital. It turned out that, whether or not Father Francis approved of the project, the congregation lacked both the funds and the sisters for such a major undertaking. In 1887, St. Paul's Hospital was established under Episcopalian auspices, but within the year financial difficulties had forced its closure.

Meanwhile, Dr. Frank Wiley[85] had made several attempts to reopen the hospital. In 1894, Dr. Wiley visited Mother Agnes again, accompanied by John and Henry Boyle, two prominent Catholic businessmen, and Father J. J. Keenan, pastor of St. Patrick Church. This time she was able to promise that the congregation would give the project serious consideration provided that appropriate support would be assured. In January of 1895, the Fond du Lac Business Men's Association voted to appropriate $55,000 for the erection of St. Agnes Hospital. The money would be raised through loans from "reliable sources."[86] The minutes of the board of directresses of January 25, 1895 state that because the doctors and citizens of Fond du Lac petitioned the sisters to build a hospital, "it appears ... that the erection of a Hospital and its management by the Sisters would be a work of charity and humanity ... for the care of the sick regardless of religious denominations."[87]

In March, after discussing the matter with the general council and Father Francis, and after Archbishop Katzer had approved the necessary expenditures, Mother Agnes began the preparations for its establishment. Not only had money to be raised and buildings to be built, but because Catholic hospitals in those days were staffed almost entirely by sisters, the commitment to prepare and staff a hospital was a major undertaking for any religious institute.

Mother Agnes selected Sisters Evarista Ulrich, Amanda Hildebrand, and Charitas Schnitzler to study at St. Joseph's Hospital in Chicago. There they would spend eight months acquiring the fundamental principles of nursing and surgical techniques under the direction of Dr. Nicholas Senn. Dr. Wiley would take postgraduate courses in Europe to prepare himself as chief of staff. The friars at the motherhouse would act as chaplains.

It was not long before the opponents of the plan became aware that Agnes intended to keep the pledge—and there were opponents.[88] Sister Vera Naber told one such story of a day when Mother Agnes was visited by three men who attacked the plan with every verbal argument possible, including the fact that St. Agnes was a teaching order. Finally, Mother Agnes rose:

> "Gentlemen," she said, "when Christ was on earth He not only preached, He also healed the sick on many occasions and in great numbers. Would you say that He did a good work in that?"
>
> "Well, yes," they answered in unison. "But you're not Christ," snapped one of her antagonists.
>
> "No, indeed, nor do we pretend to be," she said, "but Christ has called us to continue His work on earth, and as long as God permits illness, He will also expect His creatures to care for the sick. We have considered the matter and have decided to undertake the building of the hospital. We shall not reverse our decision. Good day, gentlemen. Thank you for your interest."[89]

On March 4, the day after the visit, *The Daily Reporter* noted that the plans for a hospital in charge of the Sisters of St. Agnes had not been dropped. On March 13, Mother Agnes placed a brief notice in the paper: "General Hospital. Patients admitted regardless of denominations. Physicians are welcome to join the staff. Patients permitted to choose their physicians. Signed: M. Agnes."[90]

Fortunately, those gentlemen were in the minority. Mother Agnes was able to write on June 1, 1896, "Fond du Lac people are all anxious for the opening of the Hospital. Both Protestants and

Catholics are well disposed.">[91] The first donation was from Mr. John Boyle. His brother Henry also gave a generous loan to help pay the construction costs.[92] Wilhelm Schickel, who had been the architect for the motherhouse, proceeded as quickly as possible with plans for the building. The cornerstone of St. Agnes Sanatarium, as the hospital was called until 1900, was laid in August of 1895; the building was completed and blessed by Archbishop Katzer on June 23, 1896. The building itself cost $32,000; the actual cost of the hospital with equipment and furnishings was $47,965.[93] The hospital, a colonial-style building, was situated on ten acres of lawn. A small area was designated a "croquet lawn." A number of oak and elm trees scattered about the lawn presented a pleasant vista. The first floor contained a reception hall, parlors, a doctor's office and a pharmacy, as well as a dining room and rooms for male patients, both private rooms and a ward of eight beds. The second floor contained a chapel and rooms for female patients; the third floor was the surgical department. Private rooms, board and nursing, were provided at $8, $10, $12, and $15 a week. A bed in a ward was $5. In case of an operation an additional charge of $5 was made for dressings, etc. The rules for admission were clear:

> Emergency cases would be received any hour; other patients desiring admission should make application to the Sanatarium, through their attending physician or some reputable person, between nine o'clock a.m. and six o'clock p.m. No cases received who, from the nature of their disease, would occasion discomfort to other patients. Sufferers from contagious diseases, or those afflicted with insanity, are not admissible. Physicians are cordially invited to send patients to the St. Agnes' Sanatarium, where they can, if they so desire, direct their entire medical treatment.[94]

There was no electricity in the building; small oil lamps were lighted in each room while the nurses used lanterns to go through the halls. Cooking was done on small kerosene stoves, and the elevator was operated by hand pulleys. In spite of everyone's efforts, not all the needed items were furnished. When Sister Evarista found it difficult to serve the patients without tray tables, she got logs from

the carpenter shop and made them herself. There was one telephone in the building, while speaking tubes connected the various
rooms. The fear of fire was allayed by the wide iron balconies,
which while "inviting opportunities for pleasant promenades, greatly facilitate the escape of the inmates in case of a conflagration."[95]
    The hospital was officially opened July 1, 1896, but on the day
before, typhoid fever brought seven-year-old Otto Schmidt from
Mount Calvary as its first patient. At first, patients were reluctant to
come because of the association of hospitals with dying. Only two
babies were born at St. Agnes the first year, and with only eighty-
two patients, lanterns were often placed in unused rooms to indicate
business. Frequently, as well, someone would drive a team of horses
on the gallop up Division Street to give an impression of activity in
the almost empty hospital. Even with so few patients, there were
times when the three trained nurses were overworked. Nurses stayed
with post surgical patients for three days and often were relieved for
only four hours in a twenty-four-hour period. It also became apparent that laundry facilities were inadequate; the problem was solved
the next year by building a laundry and bakery for the joint use of
the hospital and convent. It had taken time but, by the next year
there were 257 patients and from then on the growth was steady.[96]
Increasing numbers of sisters brought mounting responsibilities. *The
Catholic Directory* for 1895-1896 lists the Sisters of St. Agnes as numbering 220 professed sisters, seventeen novices, and twenty-four postulants. The congregation was responsible for one teacher training
school, one music academy, one hospital, and forty-two schools.
Candidates and novices still came and went; weeping or excited
young women continued to be sent out on their first missions; and
pastors still had to be informed that they could not have a school
with all experienced teachers. Mother Agnes and the council prayed
that they were making the right decisions in their placements. They
must have asked themselves many questions as they deliberated.
How would a young woman from New York City survive in St.
Cloud, Wisconsin? Who could be prudent enough to be responsible
for a school and a convent, deal with a pastor and parents, and
simultaneously keep everyone content? Which group of women
could provide [both] the [nourishing] climate and [the] challenges
in which this young woman would flourish?

Establishing the hospital did not divert the congregation from broadening its educational mission. During 1895 and 1896, three schools were accepted: St. Mary in Oshkosh, Wisconsin; Holy Trinity in Jericho, Wisconsin; and St. Ann in Monterey, Indiana. Holy Ghost School in Chicago, Illinois, was added in 1897. In 1898 St. Catherine in Catherine, Kansas and St. Ann in Castle Shannon, Pennsylvania, were added. Immaculate Conception (St. Mary's) Grade School in Elmhurst, Illinois, opened in 1900.[97]

St. Joseph's Springs Farm

As hospital occupancy increased and food became more expensive, so did the need to supply more provisions for the patients at less expense. A large farm was the answer. In March of 1898, Mother Agnes bought Cold Springs Farm for $31,000. She had sold forty acres of land outside the city limits for $5,250.[98] Then, when Owen A. Wells offered to sell 293.5 acres of land on the outskirts of town with house, barns, sheds, and farm animals for $24,000, the council decided that, in the long run, the farm would pay for itself by supplying milk, eggs, and vegetables for both convent and hospital. The name of the property was changed from Cold Springs to St. Joseph's Springs. In September 1899, the congregation purchased an additional 117 acres of land from Mr. Wells.[99]

The farm was on land that Father Rehrl had come upon on his journey to Fond du Lac nearly a half century before. Full of excitement, he had written:

> On the ledge east of Fond du Lac there are seven springs. I saw one of them and then looked for others. It is a beautiful piece of land. One comes upon it suddenly when coming down from Calvary. There is a high hill three miles east of Fond du Lac. I strolled through the woods admiring the natural beauty of the land. Suddenly I discovered a rushing spring of cold water. I was thirsty and lost no time drinking my fill of God's gift. I found spring after spring, seven of them! I blessed them and prayed that God might keep these springs flowing to quench the thirst of travelers. Oh how I wish that the Agnes

Sisters might some day live on this beautiful land
watered by the springs.[100]

The hill Rehrl climbed proved to be part of the Niagara
Escarpment.[101] Its height gave travelers a magnificent view of the
land below while the woods of red ash, American elm, oak, and
hickory trees added to its natural beauty.

The wooded land with its adjacent stream also proved to be the
ideal place for the sisters' cemetery. Until this time, the sisters had
been buried wherever their deaths occurred.[102] Now the sisters had
their own cemetery, dedicated to St. Joseph, patron of the dying. For
many years, travelers on County Road K could see the rows of simple white crosses marking the lives of the many sisters who had chosen to cast their lots with each other in God's service.

THE TURN OF THE CENTURY

Causing scarcely a ripple in the life of the sisters, the 1900 chapter
again returned the entire previous administration to office. During
that year one of the first actions of the council was the purchase of
the sisters' old convent and four adjacent lots in Herzog, Kansas,
from the parish because the Capuchins, who were responsible for
the parish, could barely make payments on their own properties.
The sisters staffing the school moved into a new convent; the old
convent was used for sisters suffering from tuberculosis.[103] Around
the same time, sisters were also sent to St. Louis School in Jefferson
(Besancon), Indiana.

In Altoona, Pennsylvania, St. Mary's School had become so
overcrowded that the pastor built St. Joseph's School, a branch
school in a remote part of the city. The sisters lived in a nearby
house during the week and spent their weekends at St. Mary's. In
1901, Mother Agnes was able to build a convent for the ten sisters
teaching at St. Mary's parochial school in Fond du Lac. The two lots
on which the convent was built had been purchased for that purpose
in 1894.[104] The three-story brick building also housed St. Cecilia's
Academy of Music, with the building itself being known by that
name.[105] It was a period when young ladies were interested in learning the guitar, the mandolin, and other stringed instruments.[106]

The year 1901 was also the year that the Vatican issued the Normae (Regulations) for approving religious institutes and their constitutions. While the observance of the cloister was mitigated, the Vatican frowned on nuns teaching boys, nursing maternity cases, or working in seminaries. As the works were necessary, these regulations had little effect on the ministries of American sisters.

ST. MARY'S SPRINGS SANATARIUM AND BOYLE HOME FOR THE AGED

Neither poor health nor financial burdens prevented Mother Agnes from embarking on still another risky venture the next year. Mr. John Boyle, one of the gentlemen who had supported the St. Agnes Hospital project, had come to the conclusion that the St. Joseph's Springs property would provide an ideal place for a memorial to his mother. He told the sisters that he would like to provide a sanatarium or rest home for people recuperating from tuberculosis and other sicknesses. If he could use stone and sand from the quarries on the property, he would erect and equip the building and then turn it over to the congregation to staff and maintain.

After receiving permission from the council to accept the gift, Mother Agnes was required by canon law to get permission from the archbishop for the project. Archbishop Katzer's thoughtful reply shows a practical concern for the issues that could be involved in running the type of building he believed Boyle had in mind. While the archbishop rejoiced with the sisters over the generous gift, he was opposed to the plan, which he saw as compromising the "true spirit of the sisters."[107] In his eyes, the farm should be a place of rest and relaxation for the sisters. He did not want them to work hard during the school year only to spend their summer in a job demanding their "greatest physical strength." He was worried about the kind of person who might be attracted to the place and was afraid that it might become a kind of summer resort. And, of course, there was also the question of its financial feasibility.

Mother Agnes and Mr. Boyle must have explained the sanatarium in a way that took care of the archbishop's objections because the project quickly got underway. By March 12 news of the projected $25,000 sanatarium was in *The Daily Reporter* and the cornerstone was laid by Archbishop Katzer on June 12, 1901. The twenty-eight room sanatarium, built entirely of stone, was completed on June 14, 1902. Mother Agnes named her old friend, Sister Bernardine Laughlin, as superior. Meanwhile, it became clear that St. Agnes Hospital was ill-equipped to carry on the process of hydrotherapy because more space was needed; the problem was solved when the council decided to add a two-story annex to the sanatarium utilizing the ledge's natural spring water. St. Agnes Hall, built entirely of rock-faced stone quarried out of the ledge, was built next to Boyle Hall to provide a department of hydrotherapy. Boyle contributed an additional $5,000 to the projected $14,500.[108]

The sanatarium was located on the eastern edge of the city of Fond du Lac on the same Niagara Escarpment as St. Joseph's Springs. The two stone buildings, one with twin towers overlooking the town, were impressive; the woods and streams were peaceful. The buildings were a sufficient distance from the convent farm to allay the archbishop's fears. Both Boyle and the community had every expectation that the project would be a fitting memorial to his mother and a contribution to the health of the people of the area.

Another contribution to the welfare of the people of Fond du Lac was placed under the care of the congregation in 1903 when John Boyle's brother, Henry, decided to join his brother in acts of philanthropy. Concerned about the growing number of elderly in the area, Boyle gave money to the congregation to erect the Henry Boyle Catholic Home for the Aged with the stipulation that it could be used only for the aged. In addition to the house and property, he gave bonds worth $34,500 and $5,000 in cash for current expenses.[109] For almost one hundred years, the Boyle Home fulfilled its purpose of serving the elderly.[110]

DEEPENING SHADOWS

In 1902, Mother Agnes was fifty-five years old and had been struggling for years with colitis, tuberculosis, diabetes, and a heart ailment. Thoughts of death were more frequently part of her meditations as the first eleven months of that year saw the death of a novice and three sisters. Just two days before Christmas, Mother Agnes lost one of her closest friends, and the congregation, one of the women without whose self-sacrificing labor the Sisters of St. Agnes could not have survived. At the age of twenty, Sister

Josephine Maurer had entered the community at Barton. Only a few months older than Agnes, she had taught at schools in Hartford and Schlesingerville before the congregation's move to Fond du Lac. There she had taught household arts to the candidates and novices. At the chapter of 1876, she became vicar assistant to the mother general, a position she held the rest of her life. She was characterized as having a kindly disposition. She was genial and friendly to everyone. Mother Agnes, although ill herself, accompanied Sister Josephine to a sanatarium in Indiana only to find that nothing could be done. Sister did not live to complete the return journey and died after two weeks in a Chicago hospital. Mother Agnes, who had relied absolutely on her sturdy, even support, never fully recovered from her death.

Mother Agnes, perhaps because of her own ill health, recognized signs of illness in others. Archbishop Katzer was present at the February 10, 1903 dedication of the Boyle Home. Although he was not yet sixty, the archbishop was obviously in poor health. Mother Agnes learned that his doctor had advised him to take time for peace and relaxation. Mother quickly invited him to recuperate at a suite of rooms in the convent. He came in April. Sadly, he was more ill than anyone had realized. After four painful months, he died July 20, 1903, on the same day as Pope Leo XIII. The sisters placed a memorial tablet in the convent chapel to honor their friend and spiritual leader. Freely translated the tablet reads:

> In holy memory of Frederic X. Katzer, pastor of the church, of highest merit, ornamented with apostolic virtue, illuminating clergy and people, teaching by example what he preached by word. Mortal illness overtook him as he was patiently seeking health here among Sisters of St. Agnes, his devoted daughters. Soon after, he left to be in the sight of the Lord. His spirit entered the celestial mansions on the twentieth day of July, 1903.[111]

Mother Agnes already knew the new archbishop, Sebastian Gebhard Messmer,[112] as bishop of the Green Bay Diocese where the sisters had missions. He was the last foreign-born archbishop of Milwaukee. In spite of her very poor health, Mother Agnes continued the tradition of inviting the archbishop to celebrate St. Agnes Day with the community in 1904. The sisters arranged songs and skits, and the talented Sister Julia Dullea read a poem composed for the occasion. In August of that year, the archbishop was again honored at the community's investing ceremonies. Two young women from the archbishop's former diocese henceforth were to be known as Sisters Sebastian and Gebhard.

The months dragged by for Mother Agnes. In September 1904, Sister Seraphine wrote to Sister Agatha Beschta, "It is hard for an active, energetic person like Mother to be confined to bed for more than five weary months. Hard for the community to be deprived of her ministrations, still we are in the hands of God."[113] When the leaves began to fall in October, Mother Agnes wrote to Archbishop Messmer requesting an extended absence from the community. She had fallen in love with Texas during the days the congregation was in Texarkana and was convinced of the beneficial effects of the warm climate. After receiving permission from the archbishop, she left the motherhouse in the company of Sister Seraphine, her vicar since the death of Sister Josephine; Sister Antonia Schmitz, a councilor; Sister Victoria Wolsiffer; Sister Hortulana Leiker;[114] and Sister Bernardine Laughlin.[115] By the time the group reached Hays, Kansas, Mother Agnes was too ill to continue the journey. As a place to recuperate, she bought a house from the Beach family, which she intended for eventual use as a rest home for tubercular sisters, and received permission to have a chapel there.

TOO SOON

For a short time the thin pure air of Kansas proved beneficial, but by February it was clear that Agnes had not long to live. Confined to her bed, she refused to take anything that would alleviate her pain despite intense physical suffering. Although her last hours were peaceful, death did not come easily to someone who saw so much work yet to be accomplished. Her last words were: "So soon?" On March 6, 1905, she died simply, as have so many Sisters of St. Agnes, after receiving the Last Sacraments and while hearing the prayers of her sisters kneeling by her bedside. Several days later in Fond du Lac, the vicar general of the archdiocese of Milwaukee officiated at the funeral Mass. The reading he chose, "Who Shall Find a Valiant Woman?" (Proverbs 31:10), embodied her spirit and the spirit of the women with whom she lived, worked, prayed, and established the Sisters of St. Agnes.

The short biography of Mother Agnes is the 62nd in the community's *Annals*. Sister Louisa Wolsiffer, who had been appointed councilor after the death of Sister Josephine, wrote:

> Mother Agnes possessed a strength and nobility of character which commanded the love and esteem of the sisters. In the government of the congregation she manifested great wisdom and prudence, and met difficulties fearlessly and with courage. She accomplished much by means of prayer; her devotion to the Holy Eucharist, our Blessed Mother Mary and to good St. Joseph was remarkable ... Mother Agnes was charitable not only to members of her household, but also extended her charity beyond the precincts of the convent. She cared for orphans, assisted poor students for the priesthood, and cared for the destitute parents of the sisters.[116]

Although Agnes had received many significant blessings, not the least of which was a childhood spent in a loving and pious family, at no time was her life free of the pain of misunderstandings and criticism. She had been forced to challenge a priest whom she revered, uproot an already struggling community, and attain credibility in a new environment. She had felt betrayed by friends whom she had never thought to mistrust. She had suffered an investigation into her character and actions by the order of the bishop. It was not possible to have remained unaffected; her health suffered. For the last twenty or more years of her life she endured sporadic, and sometimes incapacitating, bouts of pain.

She can only have been sustained by an intense spirituality. As a very young woman, in the midst of a critical juncture in her life, she had written to a dear friend:

> Look at your Lord, especially in this holy time at how he suffered for us poor sinners. In the sweat of Jesus

you will find consolation, not from people. If it
weren't for Jesus here in the blessed sacrament I
could not live. I get consolation from Him and if He
doesn't console me I think he is near by me and
wants me to realize that I must suffer if I want to
enter in the kingdom of heaven. You must do so also.
May the will of God be done and have patience,
dear Sister....[117]

Years after her death, Melanie Dulso, the Sister Thecla who had
invited Mary Hazotte to come to Barton, said simply that Agnes
"developed into such a grand sister." Elaborating on that statement
Melanie added that Agnes possessed a fine character, had a real
vocation, and was "devout and earnest in keeping rules."[117] The
words are simple but not easy to live.

Today Mother Agnes is seen as one of the founders of the
Sisters of St. Agnes although that had not been her wish. She was
insistent that always and at all times Father Rehrl be regarded as
founder.[118] The community today, however, does not agree with
Mother Agnes. She is admired for her courage, for her loyalty, her
refusal to dwell on past injuries, and her humility, which must have
warred with a certain imperiousness in her character. Sisters of St.
Agnes knew her as a "woman in full" and a saint in the making—
and as their sister.

Chapter V

Women of Courage,
Faith, and Vision

Rose McKenney was four years old the summer the Society of St. Agnes began its uncertain existence. Her father was Richard McKenney, one of many hundreds of thousands who had fled Ireland during the black days of the potato famine. Her mother was Ann Hoffman. Rose was born in Milwaukee in 1854; her father probably farmed north of the city while she attended the boarding school in Barton. There she met and grew to love her teachers. A school such as St. Agnes Academy, stumbling along without enough benches, desks, or books for every student, could rely only on the love and devotion of the teachers. But that was all Rose needed. When she was twelve years old and well aware of the hardships the sisters cheerfully faced every day, she decided to cast her lot in with theirs.

Her biography in *Life Sketches of the Sisters of St. Agnes*, brief as it is, is a touching example of the heroic life of a very young sister. In 1868, when she was fourteen, Rose became Sister Magdalene, a professed religious. A few weeks later, she went to teach in Little Chute, Wisconsin. The next year, fifteen-year-old Rose and another

young sister, Thomasine Goggin, were sent to open St. Mary's
School in Appleton. The biographer tells her story simply:

> The two young sisters there gave much edification
> and attracted many young girls to the Religious life.
> In April of the same year, Sister had the happiness to
> accompany eight young girls, aspirants for the
> Convent, to Barton, Wisconsin. One of these died as
> a novice; four made their profession in the commu-
> nity, becoming some of its most zealous and useful
> members. Returning to the motherhouse at the close
> of the school term in 1870, Sister Magdalene was
> taken sick with spine trouble. A large growth formed
> on the center of the spine, which caused intense suf-
> fering; in the course of time the growth had to be
> lanced, and remained, as a running sore for five
> years. All this time Magdalene bore her sufferings
> with heroic patience and resignation. During the first
> year she was able to walk about, but gradually, losing
> control of her limbs, she was obliged to be carried
> about in a chair. She would insist on being carried to
> the chapel every morning in order to assist at Mass.
> A missionary priest, visiting the Convent, was con-
> ducted to the little infirmary; after speaking a few
> words to the patient sufferer, he turned toward
> Mother Agnes and said, "Mother, I perceive now
> that God's blessing rests on this little Community;
> and you will prosper. It is the suffering members who
> draw down God's blessing." These words brought
> great consolation to the Mother and the young
> Community just struggling for existence. Sister
> Magdalene preserved her spirit of cheerfulness to
> the end; grateful for every service rendered, she gave
> edification to all.[1]

Rose McKenney died in Fond du Lac November 9, 1875. She
was twenty-one years old.

STRIVING FOR SANCTITY

The story of Rose and the hundreds like her are a reminder that a congregation is much more than the story of its founders, its administrators, or its institutions. It is the story of pioneer women, girls even, who were willing to sacrifice everything they possessed to respond to a call to follow the gospel. Today, it is the responsibility of living community members to reclaim the worth of these early sisters' lives. Since the 1960s, the feminist movement has made people acutely aware that women's concerns and achievements have been excluded from much of recorded history. As a result of concerted efforts, the level of public awareness of women's place in history has been raised. At the same time all religious, men as well as women, have been charged by Vatican II to study their founding charism. It is hoped that, by reconsidering the women whose lives provided the underlying structure of the congregation in its early years, their successors today will fulfill an obligation to the past and carry into the present and future their bold and generous spirit.

Like most religious communities of women founded in the nineteenth century, the Sisters of St. Agnes were founded in response to the societal needs of the time. The initial intent of preserving the faith through the establishment of schools was an attempt to respond to the religious aspirations of the immigrants and to give their children the tools to live well in their new environment. Father Caspar Rehrl, educated as a priest and a teacher, pursued these goals with his whole heart. When young women eventually joined him, they were inspired by his zeal, even when they chose a different path to attaining his vision. Robert Shuster asked the fundamental question: What so fired the group that others were inspired to join in their endeavors? Shuster believes that the question cannot really be answered satisfactorily. He observed that the central mystery at the heart of the spiritual events that inspire us place us in a realm that is by its nature, transcendent, spontaneous, and ahistorical.[2] Records tell us only that of which our experience is made and not what it actually is.

It is given, then, that we can never recapture the central mystery of the congregation's charism, yet we can get occasional flashes of insight in rediscovering the meager evidence of their lives. Women who entered religious life were lost to society. Given new names, they were no longer identified as members of a particular family. They lived in a closed world with regulations that prevented them from forming ties with non-community members; even maintaining close ties with members of their own family was difficult. Sisters of St. Agnes had stringent restrictions on correspondence, and sisters were encouraged to destroy the letters they received. They kept no diaries, journals, or other scraps of evidence of their inner lives. Parishioners referred to them as "Sister," often unable to call them by name or even the name of the community that served their parish. When they died, there was little left but an account book in which the community secretary had written a brief sketch of a sister's life. And yet a spark had been ignited that has remained for nearly 150 years.

WHO THESE WOMEN WERE

Like other women in pioneer Wisconsin, the sisters at Barton lived in a hostile environment. Not only the severe winters and sultry summers of frontier Wisconsin but also, frequently, the insufficient food and inadequate shelter made the women vulnerable to every kind of illness. Malnutrition, disease, and overwork were a routine part of their lives. Yet if pioneers' lives are made too comfortable, if they are robbed of the opportunity to, acquire positive qualities, they sink into a commonplace mediocrity or worse. These women had the opportunity to develop the virtues of pioneers. There was much to overcome, but their goal was set; they were flexible, willing to cope with difficult circumstances, and showed a courage in oppressive conditions that would have led the less Spirit-driven to despair.[3]

In a materialistic age it is more difficult to understand the sisters' passion for God and those moments of clarity and union that gave meaning to their arduous lives. Their brief biographies try to recapture the spirituality of their subjects—sometimes a characteristic virtue is praised, a favorite devotion is mentioned, or attention is given to their dying days and hours—but there is something missing.

The known facts of the lives of these women can be quickly summarized. Of the 132 professed Sisters of St. Agnes who died before 1910 or entered before 1891, 73 were born in the United

States, and almost all were first-generation Americans. Thirty-five were born in Wisconsin; nine, in Indiana; six, in Pennsylvania; six, in Ohio; five, in Michigan; four, in New York; three, in Illinois; two, in Kentucky; and one, in Massachusetts. Fifty-nine were foreign-born. Bavaria and Prussia claimed eleven each; Ireland, nine; Bohemia, eleven; Baden, four[4]; Canada, three; Austria and Hanover, two each; and Puerto Rico and Switzerland, one each. Two sisters did not know where they were born.

Census reports from 1860, 1870, and 1880 listed occupations of their fathers and mothers. The majority of the fathers were farmers. Other occupations named were blacksmith, bricklayer, mason, gardener, stone mason, machinist, shoemaker, carpenter, railroad worker, saloon keeper, and grocer. The mothers were housewives. The families were large according to today's standards, although it is impossible to tell the total number of the children born into each family because infant mortality was high and other children may have left home by the time the census was taken.[5]

Early members did not necessarily meet canonical requirements for entrance. More than a few were older; there were women with physical challenges, the blind Sister Ursula and the crippled Sister Justine Schodron; at least one sister was born out of wedlock. At least two widows entered, one of whom was rumored to have a living husband.[6] There were no dowry requirements. One who was French-speaking spoke little English or German.

In the congregation's early years, 83.3 percent of the members received only an eighth grade education.[7] The best-educated members came from Europe as adults. In sketches of their lives, we learn that Sister Regina Deiler received her early education at the Academy of the Ladies of the Sacred Heart, Altoetting, Bavaria and "was accomplished in advanced college studies, as well as in domestic arts,"[8] while Sister Marcella Kettner also had attended an academy for young ladies. The education of very few sisters is mentioned, but Sister Stanislaus Carroll is one exception. She had been a student at Appleton High School when she entered in 1870 and continued her studies under Father George Willard in Fond du Lac. By far the greater number of entrants completed their elementary education at the convent school.

Early members of the congregation could not have expected a long life. The median age of death of the first fifteen members who died in community was twenty-two years. Over half (52.2 percent) died before the age of forty-six. In the group who died before 1931, 7.3 per cent lived to celebrate their seventy-fifth birthdays. Chronic illnesses were part of the sisters' lives. Fifty-one died of tuberculosis; thirty-seven of cancer, heart disease, and stroke; nine, of pneumonia; six, of influenza; four, of typhoid fever; and one each, of yellow fever and meningitis. Six, who had been constantly plagued with poor health, were listed as dying of general debility and old age.[9] While these statistics are not heartening, they can only be viewed realistically in terms of the demographics of the day.[10] In Massachusetts, for example, the average life expectancy of a woman born in 1850 was 40.5 years[11]

Of all health problems, tuberculosis was the greatest scourge of religious congregations at that time. The story of Sister Florence English is illustrative of the problem. Mary English was from New Haven, Indiana. In her early girlhood she contracted a severe cold from which she never entirely recovered. Admitted into the novitiate in 1896, no one, including the physician who examined her, realized that she had developed tuberculosis. She taught school nearly two years in Muncie, Indiana, before her health failed. Her case was pronounced most contagious and she was ordered to be isolated. Within a short time after profession, six of her associate novices were discovered to be infected. They were Sisters Laura Wax, Albina Kuhn, Imelda Schmitz, Leona Thalhammer, Chrysostoma Stangl, and Seraphia Fellenz. All, with the exception of Sister Seraphia, died early of tuberculosis.

WHY THEY CAME

Why some people feel called to a religious vocation has always been a mystery. However, although we do not know why a person feels called to religious life, sociological factors inevitably play a role. While some writers attribute religious vocations to motives such as "escape from poverty or brutality, distaste for marriage and child-bearing, dread of spinsterhood, an unhappy home situation, rootless widowhood, desire for respect and status, opportunity for education and professional training, an outlet for talents, sheer loneliness or boredom, sense of adventure, need for security," there also have to be factors beyond the initial impetus that compel women to remain.[12]

While the specific sociological factors for a given sister are, for the most part, unknown, we do know of some circumstances that placed a woman in community with the Sisters of St. Agnes. Clara Rehberg, whose lack of a dowry had prevented her from entering a convent in Baden, came to the United States in order to join a religious community. Because the priests in the area were aware of Father Rehrl's plan to form a religious society, her pastor directed her to his doorstep. She wrote home and invited two friends to join her; they became Sisters Paula Bohn and Ameliana Hochaus. Later, Sister Paula's two nieces came from Germany to join her. Another sister who came to the United States with the intention to enter religious life was Sister Aurea Sellner, who had made her way from Bohemia to Schlesingerville, Wisconsin, then to Barton where she joined the society in 1866. Sister Justine Schodron, born in Prussia, entered that same year. Sisters Caroline and Michael, the two Immler sisters from Niedersouthofen, Bavaria, whose dowries did so much to make the move to Fond du Lac possible, were directed to Father Rehrl by their cousin, Father Francis Uhlmeyer.[13] Priests who admired the sisters, like Sister Evangeline Donovan's Capuchin brother, recommended the society to their relatives.[14]

We know a little more of Mother Agnes. She had come from a devout family and attended a sisters' school. Orphaned young, she seized upon Melania Dulso's invitation to join her in Barton. Whether it was because Melania, very probably a friend of Agnes' deceased older sisters Theresa and Appoline, reminded Agnes of earlier happy days before death had wreaked havoc with the family, we do not know, although her unhappy circumstances must have played a part in her decision to go to Barton.

Sister Gertrude Laughlin, who had attended the boarding school at Barton, was but one example of the hundreds of girls inspired by their teachers. Sister Magdalene McKenney, so close in age to the young Irish girls she taught in Appleton, inspired them to seek religious life. Three of the four orphaned Kreuder girls whom Father Rehrl had brought back to Barton with him decided to become sisters, as did Anna Carey and Margaret Hickey, orphans given a home by Mother Agnes. As long as sisters taught in the schools, their influence was the most important measurable reason why women came to the convent.

It was also common for members of the same family to enter religious life, although they did not always enter the same community. To name only a few blood sisters who entered the Agnesians, Sister Alberta Wolsiffer was joined by three of her sisters, and Mother Agnes' sister Lidwina followed Agnes into the society. Two Moreth sisters and their four nieces entered. Genofeva (Sister Genevieve) and Euphrosina (Theresa) Popp were unusual; forty-five-year-old Genofeva and her twelve-year-old daughter entered together.[15]

Mary Schumacher (Sister Rufina) attended her sister's profession ceremony in 1889. After the ceremony, she told her mother she would like to stay and she did, leaving her mother to return home alone. She was trained as a domestic, but in 1892 the community was so desperate for teachers that she was put in the classroom. She left the schoolroom forty-three years later, having proved to be a "marvelous teacher."[16]

Women already in the working world would sometimes go to pastors or retreat masters for help in discerning their vocation. When Father Francis was in New York in 1875, he directed Magdalene Buggli, a young woman from Baden, to apply to Mother Agnes. Several years later Magdalene entered the convent, where she received the name of Francis upon profession. In a short time she was appointed mistress of the postulancy where "she devoted herself with great earnestness to the education of the young aspirants entrusted to her care, exercising them in humility and mortification on all occasions."[17]

Honora Dwyer (Sister Elizabeth) was recommended for admission into the congregation by a Jesuit pastor who praised her as "the saint of his parish" in Milwaukee.[18] Reverend Chrysostomus Stangl, pastor at Straubing in Bavaria, recommended two groups of aspirants to come to America in 1894 and 1895. Among those Father Pacificus Berleman recommended were Anna Eckart (Sister Pacifica) and Mary Deiler (Sister Regina).

Margaret Brady (Sister Augustine), on the other hand, had a very different experience. As a very young girl she had been chosen to teach catechism at St Michael's Church in New York. Her biography notes that "Margaret had long cherished the desire of consecrating herself to the service of God ... but her Pastor, unwilling to lose his catechist, or, perhaps, to test her vocation, detained her at home for six years."[19] By 1869, Margaret had grown very impatient with the delaying tactics when she met the Capuchins, Bonaventure and Pacificus. They advised her to meet Sister Agnes, who was in New York at that time with Sister Gertrude to raise funds and look for vocations. Sister Agnes whisked her away to Barton along with Mrs. Catherine Pingeon, with whom the sisters had been boarding. Mrs. Pingeon (Sister Vincent), was described as a "widow of advanced age."[20]

It was not only pastors who placed obstacles in the path of young women who wished to join the Sisters of St. Agnes. The first bishop of the Toledo Diocese, the Rt. Rev. Joseph Schrembs, D.D., demanded that every young woman who was planning to enter religious life come to him for an interview. He would then try to persuade them to enter the Sisters of Mercy, a diocesan community, where they would work only in his diocese.[21]

The Spanish-American War was the indirect cause of the vocation of Henrietta Rios. An Army Chaplain, the Rev. E. J. Vattman, brought some Puerto Rican young women to the United States to have them educated for their own country. Henrietta, instead, felt a call to the religious life and was professed as Sister Edwarda. Still a novice, Sister Edwarda contracted consumption, and, although ill, was permitted to make temporary vows with her group. She died four months later.

There were times, though fortunately not often, when a girl came to the convent to fulfill the wishes of a parent. Just as frequently, parents placed obstacles in the way of their daughters' plans, maybe to test their vocation or perhaps to prevent them from doing something that was simply not part of the parents' plans for their daughter's future. Why fifteen-year-old Margaret Paas (Sister Julia) decided to enter a convent is unknown, but we know that she "suffered much resistance on the part of her father, who, being very much attached to his daughter, strongly opposed her leaving home. She, however, courageously overcame all obstacles. Even after she had entered the postulate her father tried to induce her to enter the married state, but she remained steadfast in her resolution of becoming a spouse of Christ."[22]

When a woman entered religious life, she was neither perfect then nor would she be perfect when she died. She did not join a group of women whose lives were exempt from the common struggles of humanity. If she joined the Sisters of St. Agnes she participated in the human story, one filled with misunderstandings and even conflict. It was also a story filled with forgiveness, reconciliations, and the accomplishment of great good. It is a story of women of purpose.

A woman who undertook to enter a religious congregation believed she would live among others who had taken seriously the answer to the question posed by the *Baltimore Catechism*: "Why did God make you?" She wanted her life to count and she wanted to be valued as a person. While the aspirant expected to make the sacrifices demanded by the vows, she also expected to make friends in community and to accomplish good in her ministry for God and the church. Simply stated, she expected to find an inner peace and happiness in becoming closer to Christ and fulfilling God's will for her.

BECOMING A SPOUSE OF CHRIST

Once a young woman had made her decision and was accepted as an aspirant in the community, she soon found that rules would govern every aspect of her life. In the earliest days, she immediately shared in the life and hardships of the sisters. Candidates and novices shivered with cold during the long Wisconsin winters and sweltered in the humid summers while they studied and learned the rudiments of religious life. They were not well nourished—in part due to the times, in part due to religious discipline, and to some extent the never-ending community indebtedness.

An entering candidate was placed under the care of "a Sister, mingling gravity with mildness of character, inspiring, therefore, to her inferiors both love and fear."[23] Although a girl may have entered at thirteen or fourteen, she was not allowed to be invested as a novice until she was sixteen years old. After 1870 and the establishment of the convent school, the candidate usually spent the greater part of the day in classroom studies. They lived a modified version of the rule, which included Mass, the rosary, the stations of the cross, noon visits, spiritual reading, night prayer, and meditation. They were not obliged to pray the office. Ideally, the candidate spent her time entirely in the motherhouse. In reality, the needs of the missions were so great that she was frequently sent out to help and, whether as a homemaker or a teacher, to do the same work the professed sisters did.

At the end of the period of candidature, usually lasting about a year, the candidate could enter the novitiate if that was her desire and if she had been accepted by the community. As part of the entrance ceremony, the novice was given the name of a saint or a title of the Blessed Mother[24] and her religious habit. The novice was given the one year and one day required by canon law as the formal period of initiation into religious life. It was a period of probation when both the novice, and the community decided if she had a vocation to the congregation. "There they were to become practically acquainted with the means of acquiring humility, self-denial, interior and exterior mortification and the love of God and their neighbor."[25]

During that time, she was first of all to develop her relationship with Jesus Christ. It was also the time when she was incorporated into the charism and lifestyle of the community. She studied theology, the vows, and the constitution. She became used to silence, which, except for a brief period of recreation at noon or after supper, was maintained throughout the day. A half hour was devoted to listening to "spiritual reading" during which time a sister usually performed some quiet task such as mending. Recreations were always group activities. Friendships with particular individuals were discouraged as inimical to community living and a danger to the vow of celibacy. The novice did not speak of her family and seldom shared her thoughts and opinions. In the words of Sister Joan Chittester they: "lived alone together."[26]

The novice in the Sisters of St. Agnes was left remarkably free to be herself in comparison to some communities of European origin. There was little attempt to impose uniformity in handwriting, carriage, or patterns of speech; instead, she was kept busy with much physical work—undemanding intellectually, but it allowed her to focus her mind on the presence of God while she and the community decided if she was called to commit herself to Christ as a Sister of St. Agnes.

One of the first lessons an aspirant to the religious life was to learn was the practice of detachment. All her energies were to be focused on following the crucified Christ. Affections that divided the heart were to be rooted out. By the 1890s the asceticism of the monastery had begun to prevail in the congregation, as can be seen from the heroic efforts of two young sisters to practice this virtue. Adeline Schurman (Sister Pius) was twenty years old when she entered the convent in 1883:

> [She] was a fervent novice who made her vows with the determination of becoming a good religious, cost what it may. The sequel proved that she was in earnest. Obedience, humility, and charity were her most cherished virtues and in piety she was exemplary. She recited many vocal prayers, and herein gathered strength to overcome many obstacles in her strife [sic] for perfection. Our dear Sister was subject to one fault which proved a hindrance to her progress; she entertained an undue natural attachment to her mother, sisters and brother. When her eyes were opened to the danger of this fault, she struggled against it heroically, and thereby acquired a perfect detachment from her relatives. Herein she has left us a beautiful example.[27]

Twenty-six-year-old Sister Raymond Heiser was dying of tuberculosis. "Her good parents went to Waunakee to pay her a visit during her illness. After their first visit, she requested them not to come any more, saying that she had made the sacrifice of her life to God and did not want to retract it."[28] Distressing as this story is, it is even sadder to learn that the Heisers had another daughter in the convent.

There were many opportunities to practice obedience, a virtue particularly prized by the religious communities. When a young sister died, comments like these were common: "Obedience and humility were her favorite virtues" and "Obedience, humility, charity were her most cherished virtues."

Some may think that perhaps Sister Crispine Bonlaender carried the virtue of obedience beyond permissible limits. The sisters at Defiance, Ohio, were to make their retreat in Decatur, Indiana.

Sister was ill at the time of their departure, but "made no complaints, as she desired to make the retreat and reap the merit of obedience. In spite of the fact that her condition was growing worse from day to day, she attended all the exercises of the retreat with great fervor ...." At the end of the retreat, "she was obliged to be taken to bed, from which she never arose. The doctor was summoned, who pronounced her illness to be a malignant case of smallpox."[29]

Cheerfulness and devotion to duty were other valued virtues, while melancholy and withdrawal from community gatherings were sources of worry to superiors. Sister Alvera Soether, who had "a cheerful, happy and congenial disposition and a keen sense of humor... [who] knew how to bring sunshine in the family," was the ideal member of a community; she was also a homemaker. For homemakers the words "humble, dutiful, and self-sacrificing" were often used as the highest praise; nurses were praised for selflessness in the care of the patients as well as for their tactful manner and sympathetic understanding. Teachers were praised for impartiality in their treatment of students.

Those novices who passed the "scrutiny"[30] were allowed to make temporary vows. At the end of a three-year period, vows were renewed for seven years. What happened if a sister became involved in some kind of difficulty? Ordinarily she was sent to another mission and given a chance to redeem herself, or perhaps she or the community decided it was an indication that she was not suited to religious life. She was free to leave after the expiration of her vows. It was only after ten years of living the life of a Sister of St. Agnes that the sister was allowed to make a lifetime commitment to God and the community through vows of poverty, chastity, and obedience. It was on the missions that the greater number of sisters lived out their lives. It was there that their good intentions and their ability to live community life were challenged.

MISSION DESTINATIONS

Setting forth on a new mission required courage, whether the sister's destination was a few miles down the road or as far as Kansas or New York. A young woman raised on the Indiana prairie could find herself looking every morning at the soot-covered houses precariously balanced on the hills of Altoona in Western Pennsylvania, the quiet of her Indiana farm home giving way to the railroad town's "chugging of locomotives, ... screeching of whistles, ... clanging of bells and ... jarring crash of coupling cars."[31] Or she could find herself among the Germans in Harlem where, since the 1880s, in the time-honored way of immigrants, a large number of German Catholics had moved to escape the alien ways of the latest newcomers to New York City. Or, more than likely, she would find herself in any of the villages and small towns where the Sisters of St. Agnes tended to be located, such as the Wisconsin farming communities of Malone, St. Cloud, and Waunakee. In these places the newly-professed sister from the big city could find herself as much at a loss as the farm woman overwhelmed by the density and clamor of a city.

Whether rural or urban, the missions had one thing in common: they were poor and the population they served was poor. But the people, most of them immigrants, were hard-working and devout; church and school were among their first priorities. An example can be found in the story of the seventy-five German Catholic families in Mansfield (Carnegie), Pennsylvania. When the price of coke escalated from ninety-five cents to three dollars a ton in January 1880, the newly prosperous parishioners asked the bishop for permission to establish their own parish church and school. St. Joseph's Parish then became the center for the Catholic Germans in Carnegie.[32]

The pastors, frequently overworked, were struggling to find a way to support their schools and churches. Often they had high expectations of the sisters, who were required to do church work, play the organ, sing at Mass, direct a choir and, of course, run a good school.[33] The accommodations provided for the sisters were not always adequate, although usually the women in the parishes did all they could to make the sisters feel at home. Most pastors provided the needed support for the sisters although a few did not.

Because so many sisters were afflicted with "delicate health" and "consumption" and labored under the burden of chronic ill health and less-than-nutritious meals, they must have found that it took their utmost strength to perform their daily duties with the cheerfulness and good will demanded of the good religious. Pastors who lost a teacher during the year because of illness were often dismayed when an inexperienced young postulant showed up to finish out the school year.

We are able to catch a glimpse of one young girl's first mission.[34] While it was by no means the norm, Mary Leikem's first mission experience was memorable enough to be recorded. In 1870, Mary was thirteen years old and Anna Schmitz was sixteen when they were told to leave immediately for Sts. Peter and Paul Parish in the village of Nenno. Anna was to teach; Mary, too young to be certified, was to cook. Nenno was only thirteen miles south of Barton, but to get there, the candidates had to take the train twenty miles to Hartford, then a coach or carriage five miles to Slinger, where Sister Agnes assured them they would be met by the pastor who would take them north again. The two set out. They took a train to Hartford, then a coach or carriage to Slinger. It was almost 5:00 p.m. when they arrived. It was a dark autumn day with a storm rising, and no one was there to meet them. They found Rosenheimer's Hotel, where they looked for a ride. No one could take them to Nenno, but they were pointed in the right direction, and they started the ten-mile walk to the church. A good while later, a farmer came along and offered them a ride. They had to sit down flat on the box wagon while their rescuer drove furiously over the rough road. About two miles from the church, he left them off to walk the rest of the way. When Mary and Anna arrived cold, hungry, and tired, they were met by an irritated pastor who chided them for being late and then sent them to the housekeeper for supper and bed.

The next morning the pastor sent them down to the sisters' house. There was not a piece of furniture in it. With their trunk still back in Hartford, Mary and Anna had nothing. The people of the parish were decent and tried to provide for them, but the sisters remained in Nenno for only one school term.

When their time was mercifully over, they left for Hartford, where they got word that Anna was ordered home. Because Mary, now fourteen, had taken and passed the teachers' examination, she was sent to Town Ten to teach in the public school there. The two sisters who had been teaching in St. Xavier Catholic School in Town Ten were in bed with typhoid fever. In the morning Mary made breakfast for the sick sisters, then walked three quarters of a mile to school, where her first task was to ring the big school bell. It did not pay to ring it late. She taught all day, and then, back home, took care of the sick sisters. Undaunted by her experiences, Mary was invested as a novice when school was out and given the name Sister Aloysia.

The three sisters who opened the mission in Defiance, Ohio, had a very different welcome. Sister Benedicta Victor was in high spirits when she wrote back to the motherhouse:

> We had a very happy journey. The weather is very fine here, everything is green. We have a very good Pastor who care-fully [sic] attends to everything. The house is not quite finished, so we have to stay with some good people here for a few days. They did not buy anything for the house as yet because they want us to have everything according to our own needs. They are so good! We shall have over a hundred pupils in school. Nearly all the studies will be in the English language. The organ is rather large, having two registers. I suppose we shall have the nicest mission of all ....[35]

The mission experiences of the congregation, in relation to the number of members, have always been varied. Because the first missions were rural schools, there was never a large aggregate of sisters in one place; for years many missions had three sisters: two teachers and one homemaker.[36] This would mean, of course, that only fifty sisters were responsible for sixteen different missions. Because the congregation was not diocesan, the Sisters of St. Agnes were not limited to accepting missions only in the Milwaukee archdiocese. That freedom was counterbalanced by the fact that the community was never under the special patronage of any prelate.

At the same time, through the opportune intervention of Father Francis in the community's history, there developed a friendly connection between the Agnesian sisters and the Capuchin friars. The Agnesian rule was written by him, and many spiritual exercises and devotions followed closely that of the friars.[37] Both communities were predominantly German-speaking, hard-working, and devoted to service wherever needed. As soon as they were able, they would not hesitate to spread out into other areas. Because the assistance of sisters was a necessity in many of the developing parishes, it seemed natural that the Sisters of St. Agnes would sometimes be asked to teach in parishes staffed by Capuchins.

KANSAS AND THE VOLGA GERMANS

From the Capuchins came the call to Kansas. One hot July day in 1876, Father Hyacinth Epp of the Capuchin province in Pittsburgh, Pennsylvania, wrote to his fellow Capuchin, Father Francis Haas, asking him for Sisters of St. Agnes to staff a mission in Herzog (Victoria), Kansas. In 1873, the Capuchins in Pittsburg were among the thousands of religious who had left Germany because of the *Kulturkampf*.[38] They were answering the request of Kansas City's Bishop Louis Mary Fink, who had invited the Order to take charge of a group of recent immigrants in Ellis and Rush Counties.

The newcomers had an unusual history. Called "Russians" by their Yankee neighbors, they were from Russia and yet were German-speaking and had a German heritage. Their history went back to the time of Frederick the Great, ruler of Prussia from 1740 to 1786. Revered in history as the greatest of the "Enlightened Despots" of the eighteenth century, Frederick's military conquests nevertheless placed intolerable burdens on the peasantry. Meanwhile, Russia's German-born Czarina, Catherine the Great, appalled at the economically backward condition of her adopted country, decided to encourage immigration from Germany to Russia. Hoping to import the more advanced Western European skills, she lured new settlers, promising freedom from military service, exemption from most taxation, religious freedom, self-administration, and loans to aid their original settlement. Dissatisfied Germans began the migration into the steppes of Southern Russia in 1763. In a little more than a hundred years, the original population of an estimated eight thousand German families grew into hundreds of thousands. Living in an isolated region, the "Volga Germans," both Catholic and Protestant, were able to retain their own language, customs and religion until the growth of nationalism in nineteenth-century Russia prompted campaigns to force the "foreign" colonists into the mainstream. An edict particularly galling to the German population made their men subject to the draft.

Looking for a place to settle, four representatives of the Catholic

Volga Germans came to the United States in the summer of 1874. Their report was favorable enough to encourage a number of their people to take a chance on a new country, and Western Kansas became the choice of this group of Catholics. They were used to a monotonous landscape and treeless plains. With its short grass, cattle could be raised, and the soil had the potential of growing some of the best wheat in the world.

The first group to settle in Ellis County left the Volga in October, 1875. After wintering in Topeka, Kansas, they arrived in Ellis County in March 1876. By April members of the group had selected land and established a community they named Catherine after their former home in Russia, Katharinenstadt. On April 8, 1876, another contingent of Volga Germans made a settlement that they named Herzog after their Russian hometown.[39] The Russian Germans, moving in large groups and founding their own social and religious communities, proved to be one of the most unusual and distinctive groups of immigrants to the United States.

Ellis County had been true frontier territory. Hays, the county seat, had been founded in 1867 after Fort Hays had been established to protect Union Pacific railroad workers from Indian attacks. At Hays was one of the most rambunctious cowboy towns in the West, infamous for its staggering number of homicides. However, by the time the Volga Germans arrived, respectable farmers were moving in.

Until the settlers could acquire the money to buy wheat farms or cattle, many of the men worked for the railroad or for the "English" ranchers. Meanwhile, the women built the sod houses and kept them whitewashed inside and outside. The homes usually contained but two rooms. One served as a combination entry, storage, and fireplace, while the other functioned as a kitchen, living room, dining room, and bedroom. They had almost nothing in the way of furniture or even kitchen utensils. They dressed as if they were in Russia; the men wore their hair long topped with little visored caps, and the women wore headscarves instead of hats. In the winter the men wore the heavy fur-lined coats they had brought from Russia.[40] Although their thrift and hard-working culture gradually earned them respect, their religion, language, and ethnicity combined to keep them isolated from other, earlier settlers. The need for education was obvious. When the Capuchins arrived they saw procuring "a capable Catholic Sisterhood inured to privations and of solid stock"[41] as a way to solve that difficulty.

Father Hyacinth Epp had become acquainted with the Agnesians in East Liberty, Pennsylvania, and, in the short year they were there, had grown to like them. His letter to Mother Agnes attempted to be realistic:

> For the beginning, conditions are not inviting, but it is not all bad. The school which the Sisters are to direct is a public school whose students are Catholic children. The yearly salary for the teacher is $300, free living quarters at first in a rented house; the next year, in a house built by the church and presently occupied by the priests. The present church is to be converted into a school with room left for a chapel for the Sisters. I truly believe that in time the Sisters will have more schools in Ellis County, for the need is great and will not lessen. Presently the people are poor but every beginning is hard. I do not doubt that the Sisters coming would not be in vain.[42]

It was three years before Mother Agnes could fulfill her promise to send sisters to Kansas. When Sisters Agatha Beschta and Aurea Sellner[43] stepped off the Kansas Pacific train on the night of August 27, 1879, they were disappointed to find that they could see nothing in the blackness surrounding them. There were no houses with welcoming lights; there seemed to be no town at all. The Kansas Pacific land agent, A. Rotelheimer, put them up that night,[44] and the next day, the pastor arrived "on foot," as Sister Agatha remembered years later. There was little to see in Herzog: a few frame houses, some sod houses, and the small stone church that the Hon. W.C. Maxwell had built for the Russian Catholics. When the sisters came to town, the large family of Alois and Catherine Dreiling moved into a sod house, so that the sisters could have their frame house.[45]

The first year the sisters were in Kansas, there was no rain for nine months. The only salary that the sisters received consisted of victuals that the generous parishioners offered them. Often the most necessary things were wanting, such as wood and coal. The sisters then were obliged to gather prairie chips and twigs to make fires for cooking their scanty meals.[46] This situation continued for some years in the Kansas parishes. Father Raphael Engel told this story:

> It happened in the early eighties when the Sisters'
> salary was so pitifully low that an unidentified bene-
> factor loaned them a cow for their own use. Now in
> those days a milk cow on the premises was a valuable
> asset to any household furnishing fresh milk, cream,
> butter, cheese, etc. Nearby there were many vacant
> lots lush with grass and weeds on which the cow was
> tethered and taken care of by the Sisters. Some of
> the Sisters grew up on Wisconsin farms so the milk-
> ing chores presented no problem. In the fall the
> Sister Superior wrote the following note to the
> owner: "Dear Friend: As you know we have neither
> a shed nor fodder for the cow during the winter
> months. We kindly ask you to come and take her
> home. May God bless you for your generosity and be
> assured of our prayers for you, Sincerely yours, the
> Sisters of St. Agnes.[47]

Times did become better. Sister Stella Schmidt, who grew up in Catherine, wrote that she was the errand girl for the sisters when she was a child. Whenever they wanted something, the sisters would hang a red rag from their bedroom, then her storekeeper-butcher father would send her to inquire what was needed. Whenever the family butchered, the sisters in Catherine and in Hays always got big dishes of sausages, liverwurst, and bratwurst.[48]

As there was no schoolhouse, the church, St. Fidelis, also served as the school. Even when the number of sisters rose to three, they continued to teach in the body of the church. The children spoke no English and, according to the pastor, poor German.[49] He requested that the lessons should be in German whenever possible and that the children must be taught to write in German script.[50] The classes, however, were bilingual; instruction was in German in the morning and English in the afternoon. Because there was no ceiling under the big roof, the church was bitterly cold during the winter. A child would stand near the stove and stuff in corn stalks to provide some heat. The classes would alternate going to the stove to keep warm. At first there were no desks; the children sat on benches with their slates in their laps. The benches that were used as pews in the church on Sundays were used for the school during the week.[51] Tuition, fifty cents a month for each child, was a burden for many to pay.[52]

At the end of May 1880, the Capuchin pastor of St. Joseph's Church in Hays, Father Anastasius Mueller, remarked, "*Es ist kein Leben für die Kirche wo kein Schwestern sind, keine Katholische Schule.*"[53] He therefore requested that the sisters in Herzog, nine miles away, come for the summer to teach catechism and prepare the children for their First Holy Communion. Immediately after the festivities of August 15, however, Sister Aurea became very sick. It was believed that she had yellow fever. A week later, Sister Agatha also became ill. When Sister Aurea died nine days after the onset of the disease, the people, who had loved the jolly Sister Aurea, provided a coffin and took care of her funeral. Girls dressed in white accompanied the body to the cemetery.

Meanwhile, Michael Haffameier's Irish wife, Kate, had taken in Sister Agatha; then both Mrs. Haffameier and her niece became ill. Father Joseph and Father Anastasius did all they could, leaving money at the store to provide for Agatha and requesting to be informed each time it was used up. Back in Fond du Lac, Mother Agnes wrote to Sister Agatha that she was greatly perplexed. Much as she wished to send another sister to Kansas, she did not wish to expose other sisters to contagion. Fortunately, the situation soon resolved itself. Agnes received a wire from Kansas with the news that the disease was not yellow fever, but malaria.[54] When the question arose as to the advisability of abandoning the missions in Kansas, Sister Constantia volunteered to go there and continue the good work.[55] She was accompanied by Sister Martina Engel.

The sisters lived in Herzog, but traveled back and forth over the dusty roads to Hays to teach in the church there. In December 1881, three more sisters (Pudentia Baier, Adriana Heinz and Seraphica Kraemer) arrived. With this addition, three of the sisters could move to Hays. Sister Martina, meanwhile, was suffering from lung trouble and, although described as having a delicate constitution, "cheerfully submitted to trials and hardships incident to the missionary work in Kansas." She contracted typhoid fever and after a lingering illness, "which she bore in a spirit of penance and resig-

nation," died in Hays on July 27, 1882. A month later Sister
Seraphica Kraemer fell ill. She had helped establish the mission in
Hays, and, although she had a strong will, the strain was too much
for her delicate constitution. She was recalled to the motherhouse,
where she died five months later on January 23, 1883.[56] In the three
years the Sisters of St. Agnes had been in Kansas, they had lost
three sisters. Hard beginnings, however, presented no obstacles to
vocations in Kansas. Five years after the first sisters arrived,
Catherine Dreiling left Herzog for the candidature in Fond du Lac.
The following year Amalia Kuhn and Margaret Quint joined her.[57]

By the summer of 1884 the parochial school system had been in
operation for four years. The religious program was an undoubted
success; the children knew their catechism and were fascinated by
Bible stories. The secular subjects were another matter. Father
Hyacinth wrote: "Both the school and the convent rivaled each
other in inconvenience and poverty. If the school building was
unsatisfactory, so too was the achievement of the sisters in charge.
In view of the efficiency of the public school one would expect the
Catholic School to be a strong rival. This however was not the case
in this instance. In time however this situation was reversed."[58]

Father Raphael Engel charitably gave a reason: "We need not
be surprised at the results. The facilities were poor if there were any
at all. No desks, no blackboards, no maps, not even a dictionary.
One teacher taught at one end of the room and another at the other
end without even a partition between them."[59]

The Volga German parish of St. Francis in Munjor was the next
mission in Kansas to be accepted by Mother Agnes. The founders
had arrived in July 1876 and settled along the west bank of Big
Creek, naming their village "Munjor" after their old town in Russia,
Obermunjor. It was the pastor, Father Franz Carl Strobl, who decided
that the children needed some form of organized instruction.
Reversing the usual process among the Volga Germans, Strobl first
convinced the parishioners to build a convent for the sisters he
hoped to attract there.

Mother Agnes sent three sisters to Munjor in the fall of 1885.
They taught religion on Sundays and holydays in the old church.
When the new church was dedicated in 1890, the old church
became the first parish school. Parish historians wrote that establishing the school was very difficult because few of the settlers had an

interest in any school and even less in the prospects of their parish schools. Convincing the people of the value of education and the worth of a parish school "was a long and difficult task." Because the pupils spoke only German at home, the sisters also found the extra work involved in bilingual education a problem. Parents saw no benefit in educating children whose labor was immediately useful and whose lives, they thought, were to be lived on the farm. In the beginning the school year was only five months long, and even then the classes were poorly attended. When the school year later was expanded, attendance in the fall and spring was very poor because the children were kept home to work in the fields. It was not until 1915 that the complete school year was well attended.[60]

Settlers had come to Catherine, Kansas, with their schoolmaster, Jakob Schmidt, an important personage in their community. He began teaching the children in his own home. When a school was built and the sisters came in 1899, he was free to pursue his own goals, but he still taught the children religion for three weeks every summer. An account of early school days under the sisters is provided in the history the parishioners compiled to celebrate the parish centennial:

> The school day of the early 1900s began with Mass every morning. When arriving at school, the drinking water was pumped and each child received one cup for the day. In the winter, the boys started a fire using dried sunflower stalks. The children then proceeded to their desks, boys on one side and the girls on the other side. They were taught reading, writing, and arithmetic. The German language was used in the morning. The afternoon lessons were taught using the English language. There were three 15-minute recesses in which baseball, jump-up, rabbit and other games were played. If the weather was too cold or nasty, the rosary was said during the recesses. The nuns maintained discipline with the help of a ruler or by requiring the child to kneel in the center of the room holding his arms straight out to the sides.[61]

The sisters were also sent to St. Anne's School in Walker, Kansas. The town, four miles east of Victoria, was established by a small group of Catholic colonists who had emigrated from the German state of Hanover to Ohio during the *Kulturkampf*. With the exception of their religion, they had little in common with the Volga Germans, although they were members of St. Fidelis Parish and sent their children to the parish school until they could provide their own. They opened their own school in 1902 with two Sisters of St. Agnes. However, Mother Antonia was forced to withdraw the sisters in 1907 because of a personnel shortage.

The Agnesians did not arrive at St. Mary's School in Ellis, Kansas, until six months after the death of Mother Agnes. In 1870, Ellis had been established as the Kansas-Pacific Railway's central division point between Kansas City and Denver. (Division points were established where locomotives could be serviced.) From 1876 to 1878, large numbers of Volga Germans settled there. In 1886, a resident pastor arrived, and in 1889, St. Mary's Church was dedicated. The first school was established in 1901 with lay teachers; four years later the Sisters of St. Agnes arrived to teach 52 boys and 56 girls.[62]

OTHER MISSIONS

St. John the Baptist Parish in Waunakee, Wisconsin, blessed with zealous parishioners, was typical of a small-town Catholic parish in Wisconsin. It was founded in 1874 when nineteen Catholic families who had been worshipping at two other towns were given permission by Bishop John Martin Henni to found their own parish. Money was scarce, but the parishioners were able to erect a one-room building that served both as church and schoolhouse. Only one year later a separate school was built and staffed by lay teachers. Mass was celebrated twice a month until 1881, when the parish, a mission of a nearby larger parish, finally was able to have Mass weekly. It was then that three Sisters of St. Agnes were missioned there in a comfortable new convent provided by the parishioners. By 1889 approximately one hundred students were attending the school. When enrollment increased in 1896 a second school was built.

Wherever the missions were located, the convents were usually very safe places, but this did not prove to be true in the case of the convent in St. Alphonsus Parish in Greenfield, Michigan. It was in the middle 1880s when Sister Ludgarde Hoefler awoke to find a man standing beside her bed with a club in hand, threatening to kill her "if she refused to consent to his evil designs." Written a few years after her death, her story continued:

> With the help of God she came forth victorious. She resisted her enemy courageously, but seeing that she could not otherwise escape, she opened the window and leaped from the second story down. Margaret Quint, a candidate who slept in the adjoining room, becoming frightened, also jumped to the ground. Both were badly injured and Sister was obliged to creep on hands and knees to a neighboring house. The good people cared for the Sisters until they recovered from the injuries sustained. Indignant at the affront offered the good Sisters, the people of Greenfield wanted to lynch the villain, but he escaped their hands. Later, however, he was detected, prosecuted and sentenced to imprisonment for a number of years.[63]

Perhaps the parish school in New London, Wisconsin, was one of the more typical Agnesian missions. In 1879, sisters first came to teach in Most Precious Blood School. They had been there for only two years when a new red brick school was built, proudly described as having "comfortable and commodious proportions."[64] Years later, Terence O'Donnell, who had been a schoolboy there in the 1890s, affectionately described his parish. It was poor, he said, and included a motley collection of nationalities:

> Culturally the town, while Western, was of New England, having been settled by droppers-off from some Oregon trek. Later came the Germans, Irish and Poles, and as it was in Wisconsin, there was a sprinkling of French-Canadians. The religious division was sharp; the New Englanders attended the

Congregational Church; the Germans were part
Lutheran, part Catholic; and the Irish, Poles and
French-Canadians were of course Catholic. The
New Englanders represented whatever "society"
there was in the community; the others were the
under-strata. And it was the children of those various nationalities that attended the parish school.

Now remember that ours was a pioneer town,
and all the pioneer conditions obtained. In the spring
the logs came down the river in great jams, and with
them came the lumberjacks. In the wake of the log
jam came the cook-shack on its raft, and the red
underwear and gaily colored mackinaws hanging
drying on its line made it seem to childish eyes like
some veritable galleon out of the days of romance.
Before the logs came down the river, when the ice
had scarcely gone, the men of the town would go out
at night with torches and spear sturgeon. For weeks
thereafter you would smell sturgeon smoking in the
smoke-houses. Everyone had fried sturgeon roe for
breakfast, and by rolling string endlessly about the
rubbery snouts from the sturgeon heads we boys
could make fair baseballs .... On Sundays the town
was very busy, people riding twelve to twenty miles
from their farms for Mass at the parish church.[65]

Each town the sisters served in had its own unique character, but
as a rule, sisters were prevented by rule and customs from intermin-
gling with the people and experienced it mainly through the children in the classroom.

THE SISTER NURSE

Neither the sixty-bed St. Agnes Hospital in Fond du Lac nor the
short-lived sanatarium proved to be an easier mission assignment
than one in any of the parish schools. While the absolute necessities
were there, there was no thought of providing for the comfort of the
staff.

The sisters worked long hours; it was customary to stay with post-surgical patients for three days, the nurses often being relieved only four hours in a twenty-four-hour period. It proved even more difficult for the sister nurses to abide by the quasi-monastic schedule of the motherhouse, and it was years before the congregation made adjustments to accommodate a different lifestyle.

Sister Blandine Brogan's life illustrates the self-sacrificing lives of so many of her companions. Mary Brogan was born in 1873 in Olyphant, Pennsylvania. She came to the convent when she was twenty-five years old. Described as an "obedient and docile child ... she seemed to grow in virtue and gave hopes of future sanctity."[66] After profession, she was sent to St. Agnes Hospital. In spite of her delicate constitution, she willingly deprived herself of her much needed night's rest in order to serve the sick. After three-and-a-half years of nursing, it was discovered that she was suffering from both tuberculosis and heart disease. At the request of her parents, she was permitted to return to the East, where she spent six months. On her return she resumed her work in the hospital, where, after one year, her health failed again. Sister Blandine died on July 19, 1905, five years after her first religious profession.

AT HOME IN FOND DU LAC

By 1905, the results of the congregation's twenty-five years in Fond du Lac were apparent. The St. Cecilia Academy for Music Students was located near Main Street. The convent was an imposing brick building on Division Street. Adjacent to it was St. Agnes Hospital. St. Joseph's Springs Farm was two miles to the east and, looking over it from the ledge was St. Agnes Sanatarium. The Henry Boyle Catholic Home for the Aged was situated on Park Avenue a few blocks east and north toward Lake Winnebago.

When Mother Agnes died in 1905, there were 276 sisters in the community. Sixty-one professed sisters had preceded her in death. From 1858 to 1905, the sisters had served in numerous parish schools as well as four institutions dedicated to either health care or social work: St. Agnes Hospital, St. Agnes Sanatarium, the Leo House, and Holy Family Orphanage. They had engaged in a variety of tasks: teaching, caring for orphans, nursing, operating an artificial flower industry, printing, running a farm, and administering the institutions they worked in. The sisters had been prepared to make the congregation as self-sufficient as possible. They cooked and laundered in small houses and institutions, nursed, kept house, trained altar boys, played the organ, directed parish choirs, taught a complete curriculum during the school year, then taught religion classes in the summer. They mentored the novice teachers assigned to their mission.

Measured by the standards of the world, these women wasted their lives. However, if happiness is a criterion, it was their evident joy that led other young women to join them. The sources of their happiness were many. They experienced the peace that comes from responding to what they believed to be their vocation in life. They had friendships with other sisters which gave them support and strengthened their commitment to their chosen life. They were valued by the parishioners whose children they taught, the priests they worked with, the students who remembered them fondly, and the patients who never forgot their kindness as nurses. They saw themselves as having a special role in the life of the church, and this gave them an identity and an emotional security that was a source of strength and pride. Above all, they maintained their commitment to follow the gospel of Jesus Christ through their personal vows of poverty, chastity, and obedience.

Chapter VI

Ordinary
Time

In the church's liturgy, ordinary time is that period in the church year in which there are no major holy days. It is a time to live God's word and experience God's grace in everyday life, in "ordinary things." With the death of Mother Agnes, the high drama of the founding years of the congregation was over. For the next few years, the congregation would experience years of simplicity, order, and quiet growth.

MOTHER ANTONIA SCHMITZ

If any sister should have had an understanding of the congregation, it was Anna Schmitz. Anna was one of seven children born to Peter and Susanna Schmitz of Marytown, Wisconsin. When Anna was ten years old, Sister Agnes arrived to teach at the parish school in her village. Four years later on her fourteenth birthday, November 25, 1869, Anna left her family and, with her friend Margaret Ester (Sister Angela) and another aspirant, set out with her teacher, Sister Agnes, for the sisters' motherhouse at Barton. It was an exciting birthday for Anna. They started at 3:00 a.m. Margaret's brother loaded his passengers on to the bobsleigh, then his team of horses took off on the snowy road. They stopped in Dotyville for breakfast and pressed on to New Cassel (Campbellsport) for lunch. Fourteen hours and thirty-eight miles after they had left Marytown, the party arrived in Barton.[1]

At that time Anna was unaware that this day would prove critical to the life of the society she was joining; Sister Agnes was returning to Barton where she intended to become superior in fact as well as name. During the following months in Barton, Anna must have witnessed, without completely understanding, the human drama behind the society's move to Fond du Lac.

Two years later Anna, by that time Sister Antonia, was assigned to Sts. Peter and Paul in nearby Nenno. In 1876 she was elected to the council and two years later sent to teach at Epiphany Parish in Menomonee, Michigan. In 1879 she was recalled to the motherhouse where she would spend the rest of her life. She had received some education in music and would for many years be an organist at the motherhouse and at St. Mary's Church in town. An expert housekeeper and a skilled needlewoman, she was in charge of the artificial flower industry that Mother Agnes hoped would produce an income. It was apparent that here was a quietly competent and resolute woman who could and would do anything required of her.

Although her life at the motherhouse would not permit her the experiences of most sisters, young Sister Antonia reveled in change, excitement, and learning new skills. In 1882, she went with Mother Agnes to New York to learn new patterns and methods of making artificial flowers. Agnes wrote back to the motherhouse of the delight Antonia took in sightseeing and "riding on subways and elevators."[2]

As a member of the council, Sister Antonia went to Kansas in 1905 with Sister Seraphine Morrissey to be with Mother Agnes in her last days. When the two returned to Fond du Lac, the first task of the council was to choose an acting superior general until a general chapter could be convened. Sister Seraphine, who had been on the council since 1876 and vicar assistant since the death of Sister Josephine Maurer, was chosen. She, together with Sister Antonia, Sister Regina Deiler, and Sister Joseph Wolford were responsible for the congregation until the chapter delegates met on July 15, 1905.

All of the sisters in perpetual vows attended the chapter. The general chapter lasted one day; the elections were held in the morning and the financial report was read in the afternoon. Archbishop Sebastian G. Messmer presided over the election. Sister Antonia Schmitz was elected superior general; Sister Seraphine Morrissey, vicar assistant; Sister Joseph Wolford, first councilor; Sister Louisa Wolsiffer, second councilor; Sister Marcella Kettner, third councilor. There were more new members elected to the council than had been elected since 1876, but every sister chosen had been closely connected with the motherhouse for years.

A New Century

The new century had scarcely begun when Mother Antonia took office, but how different the world looked from that day in 1863 when the first superior general, Agnes Hazotte, was appointed to lead the Agnes Sisters. From a country immersed in the bloodiest war it had ever experienced, the Union had been saved and it was now larger by fourteen states and territories, the Philippine Islands, the Hawaiian Islands, Puerto Rico, and Alaska. In 1893, Frederick Jackson Turner claimed that the frontier was closed and a new era in American history had begun. With the mechanization of agriculture, fewer farmers were now required to feed the nation. While villages had grown into towns and towns into cities, the increasingly industrialized country was swallowing up labor for the factories, mines, and railroads.

Automobiles were beginning to be familiar sights on the dusty roads, and, if you were fortunate, an airplane. The first millionaires had emerged and the names of tycoons who ran the businesses were often more familiar than the names of the men who had been elected to run the country.

The population of the United States in 1905 numbered 83,822,000 and immigrants were still pouring into the country. Italians and Poles, no longer Irish and Germans, were now the majority of new Catholic immigrants. With thirteen percent of the population Catholic, the Catholic Church was gaining power and prestige and developing into the "strongest single denomination in the land."[3]

There was a dark side. The South, devastated by the Civil War, was still struggling to rebuild its economy and used segregation as an excuse to drive its most difficult social problem out of sight. Native Americans had been banished to reservations. The average American worker made only $12.98 for fifty-nine hours of work per week. The workers' low wages and abysmal working conditions precipitated over two thousand strikes in 1905. Large cities were experiencing the problems brought about by poverty: slum housing, crime, abused and deserted women and children, prostitution, and drunkenness. Women, allowed to vote in only four states, were beginning their fight for suffrage although with very little support from the Catholic community.[4]

The Sisters of St. Agnes were no longer attempting to live a religious life with no approved rule, no role models, and little direction but, with the approval of their constitution, they had the assurance that the life they chose to lead was approved by the church itself. During Mother Antonia's life the society had grown to three hundred professed sisters; it had spread to other states and was serving in other ministries besides teaching.

As for the sisters, their ethnic background was predominately German, although very few were German-born. The average age of eleven sisters professed in 1905 was a little less than twenty-four. The oldest woman in that profession group was thirty-two.[5] They were from large farming and working families and had received the average education of their period. They were religious, although not all of them were pious. They chose Mother Antonia to lead them, but they were looking forward with some apprehension to the first transition of power in their young congregation.

GOOD ORDER: THE FOUNDATION OF ALL GOOD THINGS

On July 15, 1905, Sister Antonia took the place of the woman who had done so much to determine the direction of Antonia's own life. The spiritual and temporal welfare of the 276 professed sisters in the community was the object of her greatest concern. That their talents were used for the glory of God and the welfare of the church was now her responsibility, but her greatest concern was that the sisters grew together in holiness. She exhorted the sisters to love each other and the community: "Pray for one another;

where there is union of hearts there is strength ...." "*As long as the flame of home-love* and *home-interest* burn brightly, *we never need fear for our congregation*" were words frequently on her lips.[6]

All the sisters, but Mother Antonia in particular, must have been distressed as they noticed the neglect of the convent home during the long illness of Mother Agnes. The pigs and cows wandered all over the property, and the piles of stone and lumber gave the convent grounds a ramshackle appearance. Mother Antonia soon banished the animals to the farm, and within the next few years lawns and flower beds eventually provided a more seemly environment for the sisters. But the most urgent need of the congregation was the reestablishment of credit with the business community. On September 6, 1905, she sent a letter to each mission house asking that the house procure one hundred dollars to enable the congregation to pay off a debt of $7,500.[7]

The following day, she consulted with the Capuchin provincial, Father Laurentius Vorwerk, about the observance of some points in the rule which, she believed, had not been kept for some time. Not surprisingly, he advised her to require the strict observance of even the most minute points.[8]

The visitation of the missions was Mother Antonia's next priority. Stationed at the motherhouse since she had been a young sister, she knew the sisters well and considered each a friend, but she had little direct experience with life on the missions. As quickly and efficiently as she did everything else, Mother Antonia set out to remedy the situation. She was fortunate that there was a group of dedicated and talented women who were familiar with and well able to take care of the daily affairs of the motherhouse. Two months after her election, she was ready to begin her tour of the missions. She waited until classes were underway and then began her visitation at her former mission in Menomonee, Michigan.

From September 23 until December 18, the greater part of Mother Antonia's time was taken up with official visitations. She traveled to missions in Michigan, Wisconsin, Kansas, Indiana, New York, Pennsylvania, and Illinois. At each mission, she took notice of how the rules were kept, particularly the rules for times of prayer and those of companionship when outside the convent. She also observed how friendly and charitable the sisters were to each other. She then made inquiries into each sister's work, health, happiness, and daily challenges. Finally, she gave individual permissions relating to specific circumstances. At the close of visitation, she met with the sisters and shared with them what she liked or did not like about the mission, what she would like to see changed, and what general permissions were to be granted. She also encouraged the sisters to be faithful to the rules of the congregation and to regular observances.[9]

In the meantime, every house in the community had sent the requested money. Those dollars were only a small start, for the struggle to survive was constant. The past debts and the new debts the congregation was forced to incur in its efforts to fulfill its mission of service were to haunt Mother Antonia every day until the end of her life.[10] It is easier to understand the financial problems facing religious communities when it is realized that sisters in the early twentieth century received only 43 percent of the salaries paid other working women and only 32 percent of the salary paid public elementary school teachers.[11] A public school teacher, usually a female, received $325. Teaching brothers received nearly twice as much as teaching sisters.[12] Pastors did not always pay the full salary. Sometimes the sisters were able to make it only through the efforts of the music teacher who could earn twice as much money as the classroom teacher, as well as through annual performances given by the children.[13] It must be noted, however, that the sisters were able to rely on the generosity of the many parishioners who provided vegetables and fruits in season, cuts of meat, and even financial help in the upkeep of the convent.

CHANGING EDUCATIONAL NEEDS

Integrating the children of immigrants into American society was the most pressing problem schools had to face, but other educational needs were being created by an increasingly complex society. While industry needed more highly educated workers, compulsory education and child labor laws kept more children in the classrooms. Better education was required of elementary teachers as the graded-class organization was established. As late as 1918, a report noted that one-sixth of public elementary teachers did not even have a tenth-grade education.[14] After 1890 middle-level education increased as the high school evolved from the academy, and new subjects, business courses, household arts, and manual training sciences, were introduced to prepare students for all areas of living. Teaching became more professional as normal schools were established and teachers organized into associations that together, in 1870, became the National Education Association (NEA).[15]

Integrating Catholic immigrants into American society through parochial schools became one of the most important societal roles of the church. Catholics had made a commitment to a separate school system in the nineteenth century, but the ideal of each parish having its own school as directed by the Third Council of Baltimore could never be fully implemented. Because a school added between thirty and fifty per cent to the cost of operating a parish there was never enough money.[16] Parochial schools were able to exist only because sisters subsidized them through their low salaries.[17]

Less than one-half of Catholic children were in parochial schools; nevertheless, when Archbishop John Ireland of St. Paul proposed working out a compromise with the public system, a bitter controversy ensued.[18] In any case, at the beginning of the twentieth century, parishes were establishing schools; children were to be taught and sisters were to be there to teach them. For many, if not all teaching orders, there was a continuous crisis in vocations. There were never enough sisters to staff the country's schools. In their attempt to provide teachers, religious communities seemed to operate on two assumptions: the first was that, with the exception of house sisters, every young woman who presented herself at the door of a convent had a vocation to teach. Second, if the sister was told to teach in obedience, she would receive the necessary grace to carry out her assignment.

By the 1880s, Catholic schools lagged behind public schools for a number of reasons.[19] One reason was philosophical. Although there was great intellectual ferment among the educational theorists around the turn of the century, Catholic education fell behind through its blanket refusal to attend to any new ideas.[20] As Catholic men's universities did not accept women, sending sisters to state campuses for their education was the only option available to sisters.[21] In 1884 the Third Council of Baltimore urged the establishment of normal schools for teacher training, but each motherhouse wanted to educate its own sisters, which, of course, limited the offerings that any community could afford. In 1904 the Catholic

Education Association was founded in St. Louis to bring Catholic educators together to resolve common problems and plan future progress.[22] It later changed its name to the National Catholic Education Association. It urged dioceses to create departments of education headed by school superintendents "who would oversee teacher training, educational standards, the development of a standardized curriculum for parish schools and the interfacing of the Catholic schools with developments in public education."[23]

The education of the sisters was a critical issue to be addressed during this period. A report issued in the *NEA Journal* in 1899 states that 75 percent of the teachers in the United States had been entering upon their work without any special training whatsoever and that the training of much of the remainder had been far less extensive and less satisfactory than that required for any other profession.[24] While it can be argued that because of the opportunity for in-service training, religious communities provided better preparation and support for their teachers than the majority of public school teachers received, it was clear that societal changes were forcing higher standards of admission upon the teaching profession.[25] If religious were to remain effective educators, they needed to receive more education.

In Fond du Lac, the sisters were doing what they could to advance the education of their new members. The *Annals* of September 12, 1907 note that Professor Morrissey of the Catholic Normal School in St. Francis had begun a course in physics, classics, the Constitution, and pedagogy for novices and candidates and a class in geometry for sisters.

AN UNEXPECTED CHANGE

The beginning of 1906 brought an unwelcome change to the community. Toward the end of the previous year, Archbishop Messmer had informed the congregation that the Capuchins would no longer be the chaplains of the motherhouse. The news was a blow to the sisters. Mother Antonia was disturbed because Messmer did not give her a reason for the change.[26] Although not yet professed, she had been in the society when the intervention of the Capuchin friar, Father Francis Haas, had insured the future of the Sisters of St. Agnes. His spiritual guidance and that of his successors had helped the community through its formative years. Their rule, written by Father Francis, was closely related to that of the Capuchins.[27] Many sisters had ministered in Capuchin parishes in New York and Kansas. Some had come to the community because of the counsel of a Capuchin spiritual director. The relationship between the two communities had always been important to the sisters. Why then the change?

One reason given was that the Capuchins were too overworked and understaffed to continue with the sisters, although the Agnesians never seemed able to find that reason satisfactory.[28] It was also the wish of Archbishop Messmer. In September 1905, when the Discalced Carmelites from Regensburg, Bavaria came to the United States to search for a suitable place for a foundation, the Archbishop offered them Holy Hill in Hubertus as a site. For years, beginning with Archbishop Henni, Milwaukee archbishops had been trying to interest religious orders in accepting the site.[29] It was a place of pilgrimage where a version of the grotto at Lourdes had been built. The archbishop also offered the Carmelites responsibility for the spiritual guidance of the Sisters of St. Agnes. They quickly accepted the charge and the Reverend Eliseus McKenna, OCD assumed the responsibility of the chaplaincy on January 3, 1906.

St. Joseph Orphanage

In June of that year, at the request of Bishop Frederick Eis of the diocese of Marquette, Michigan—and in spite of some reservations—Mother Antonia sent ten sisters to staff the diocesan St. Joseph Orphanage in Assinins, Michigan.[30] They replaced the Sisters of St. Joseph who had been missioned there since its opening in 1881. That the bishop intended the orphanage to be self-supporting says much about the poverty of the diocese.[31]

The buildings, one for the boys and one for girls, were of fieldstones, but both were dilapidated and inadequately furnished. The children were accepted from infancy to age sixteen. The sisters cared for an average of fifty children a year from ages two to sixteen and provided them with elementary education, as well as supervision in their arrangements for their secondary education.

Through the long Michigan winters the sisters shoveled snow, carried water, and got up twice in the night to tend the furnaces.

The janitor and the superintendent would go out with the older boys to help with the milking and work in the gardens. The girls helped around the house and did fancywork. When Mother Antonia learned of the circumstances, she was very concerned about their situation. When she inquired, she was relieved to discover that, in spite of their circumstances, the sisters there were happy. The community remained.

The summers offered a whole new world to both sisters and children. There were woods that the children loved and Keweenaw Bay where they could swim. The sisters with the children would take long hikes in the woods. "Then the children would disappear, about twenty of them. Where they were, we didn't know. We would sit down and read a book but when it was time to come back we'd blow the whistle and we'd count the noses. And they'd—everyone—they'd come from all different directions and were all there."[32]

Because almost all of the available personnel had been sent to Assinins, the only other new mission accepted in 1906 was St. Mary's School in New Richmond, Wisconsin.

NEW ERA OF REFORM

After her visitation to the missions, Mother Antonia followed the advice of Father Eliseus. On November 13, 1906, she wrote to the sisters containing a list of regulations designed to ensure that the wall of separation between sisters and laity would grow higher and stronger.[33] The sisters were not allowed to correspond with priests, families, or pupils of their former places. Boat riding or riding in cars with women friends was not allowed. If such permissions had been granted, they were revoked. They were not to play cards or games with seculars. Their visits with seculars were limited to those prescribed in the rule. They were not allowed to help out in the priests' houses. There was to be no visiting from one mission to another without special permission. The sisters were not to do fancywork, but use the time for study and self-advancement.[34] When they left a mission, a trunk and satchel should be sufficient for all of their belongings. They were reminded that chapter, the discipline, [35] and all other penitential exercises prescribed by the rule should be observed. Superiors were reminded that they would be answerable to God if they neglected to enforce those rules.

Classroom teachers were reminded that they were "not to impose prayers on children as punishment, lest a dislike for this necessary means of salvation be thereby engendered in the hearts of the little ones" and "not to use corporal punishments, but to study some other means of correcting their pupils."[36]

Christmas was special in 1906. The charitable John Boyle gave Mother Antonia a gift of $600. This unheard-of prosperity allowed Mother Antonia to provide the sisters, besides their usual Christmas present of candy, a half-dozen linen handkerchiefs at fifteen cents apiece, a toothbrush, and six holy pictures.[37]

Even as she enforced some regulations, Mother Antonia sought, without success, to loosen strictures on home visits. The month of September in 1907 brought a measure of excitement as the community began to prepare for a four-day visit from the Right Reverend Archbishop Heiss. During this visit, Mother Antonia, in response to the sisters' requests, asked for permissions that had been refused previously and would be refused again. The sisters asked for more contacts with their families; they wished to visit their homes on occasion and attend family religious celebrations such as baptisms, weddings, and nephews' ordinations. Most bishops around the country were not in favor of letting the sisters leave their convents. In this instance Heiss followed the general line by allowing sisters to visit their homes only in case of the serious illness of their parents. He permitted the sisters to take charge of boys in spite of a general prohibition against letting sisters teach boys. The congregation could receive Indian girls into the community "if their parents were of good character," and he promised to provide a cardinal protector for the sisters. However, when Mother Antonia asked the archbishop to keep a canonical visitation at the motherhouse, she received only a vague statement that he might do so "sometime."[38]

CONTINUING IMPROVEMENTS

In spite of the debt under which the congregation was laboring, improvements of existing facilities continued. In 1907 and 1908, the old barn west of the convent was demolished, and a new barn of red brick was built on Sheboygan Street. A pipe organ and vestment case were installed in the chapel. Reevaluation of suitability of the missions for the congregation prompted the withdrawal from schools in Walker, Kansas; Menominee, Michigan; and Besancon, Indiana; but a new school was accepted in a Slavic Franciscan parish in Rockland Lake, New York.

In 1909 the increasing number of sisters required the congregation to add two wings to the motherhouse at the cost of $85,165.87. The long-needed elevator was installed, as well as a music department with practice rooms.[39] More land was needed, so the council bought property adjoining the convent, then moved the original frame convent and remodeled it for use by hired help in the convent and hospital. The upstairs rooms were used by sisters' guests who stayed overnight in Fond du Lac. These improvements, small but not unimportant, reflected the value Mother Antonia assigned to creating a home for the sisters, their guests, and the laymen and women who worked with them.

Snowstorms sometimes brought unexpected guests to the motherhouse. The annalist writing on February 2, 1915, seems to have found some humor in the predicament of two friars "who were obliged to remain overnight as the trains did not leave for Calvary. They left this am [sic] the 2nd but returned to us at four o'clock. They started again this evening and must have reached their destination, for like the dove at Noah's time, they did not return, but must have found a dry place to rest their feet."[40]

ST. MARY'S SPRINGS ACADEMY

A new item on the administration's agenda became the establishment of St. Mary's Springs Academy. The school had its origin in the financial failure of St. Mary's Springs Sanatarium.[41] The benefactor who had made the two buildings of the sanatarium possible, John T. Boyle, was an excellent businessman. When it became clear to him almost five years later that the sanatarium was unsuccessful in attracting patients, principally because of its distance from town, he proposed a new project. If the Sisters of St. Agnes would staff and administer a boarding school for girls and young ladies, he would fund the cost of restructuring the buildings. Mother Antonia and the council agreed to the proposition. Because there was no boarding school in the area, it was time for the congregation to enter the field of secondary education.[42]

On October 7, 1909, Archbishop Messmer dedicated the boarding school. The school's curriculum was a staggering one, but not atypical. It provided for grades one through eight, a two-year commercial course, and a four-year classical curriculum. Music, painting, sewing, and cooking were also offered.

The choice of the council for principal was Sister Angeline Kamp, who had already proved to have the necessary academic and administrative abilities, as well as the drive and energy, to head such an important new venture. A thirty-four-year-old native of New Haven, Indiana, she had previously been missioned at Our Lady Queen of Angels in New York, where she had served as teacher and principal. In 1907 she was appointed principal of the new school at Rockland Lake, New York, but circumstances necessitated the sisters' leaving the school after only two years.

Sister Angeline was assisted by Sister Marcella Kettner, the sister with the most sophisticated educational background in the congregation. Her childhood experience in a European convent boarding school, her successful teaching career, and, most importantly, her dedication to education provided the necessary scholarship and experience for this new venture. In addition, the two sisters visited academies in Green Bay and Chicago, where the administrators and teachers generously shared their expertise with the Agnesians.

Before the school could be opened, Sister Angeline not only had to become familiar with the organization of a boarding school and an academy curriculum, but also had to prepare the faculty of thirteen sisters and a chaplain. Two sisters were sent to the Gregg School in Chicago to learn methods of teaching commercial subjects.

Sister Angeline also had to recruit pupils. With a companion, she spent days visiting the pastors in the town and countryside to request their support. By opening day, September 9, 1909, seventeen pupils had enrolled. Room, board, and tuition for the year amounted to $75. A month later, three more students joined the others; by the end of the year the enrollment almost doubled. The academy was going to be a success and Sister Angeline's leadership had much to do with it.

By 1914, sixty students from Wisconsin, Illinois, and New York attended the academy. The turreted, four-story stone building overlooking Fond du Lac was most impressive. The academy's motto,

Virtute et Scientia, ignored neither virtue nor knowledge, but printed descriptions of the hoped-for outcomes of an academy education gave more weight to virtue:

> The plan of education followed at the academy is designed to develop mind and character. The training given to the disposition and character is designed to qualify the young women to do credit to themselves and others, in the position determined for them by God ....
>
> The discipline of the academy is mild but firm. It gives a reasonable latitude and yet is conducted with such vigilance and energy as to secure order and regularity, without which little can be accomplished. Pupils are expected to conform to the regulations, cheerfully and promptly knowing that their own success and welfare depend upon the regularity of the institution.[43]

Recreation was highly important, as the school brochure stated: "During recreation hours, study is absolutely forbidden. This is a decree from which there is no appeal. Exercise in the open air during all seasons is indulged in three or four times a day."[44]

With such a philosophy to uphold, it should be no surprise that Sister Angeline proved to be a demanding principal. Rules and order were extremely important to her and she applied them equally to faculty and pupils. The little country boarding school was run like one of the strictest convent schools in the country. The pupils, wearing white lace veils, attended Mass at 6:00 a.m. and were expected to behave with the utmost decorum. There was a certain elegance, and perhaps even elitism, about the place; the sisters who taught there were known for years as "the Academy ladies." [45]

ST. ANTHONY HOSPITAL IN HAYS, KANSAS

Establishing St. Anthony Hospital in Hays, Kansas, was the second major decision of 1909. It will be remembered that when, in 1904, Mother Agnes was unable to continue her trip to Texas, she had remained in Hays. One of her last acts was the promise to do all she could to establish a hospital in Hays, Kansas. The nearest hospitals to the people in Ellis County were two or three hundred miles distant in Denver, Topeka, and Kansas City. The Capuchin pastor of St. Joseph's Church and the local doctors, aware that the congregation had established St. Agnes Hospital in Fond du Lac, soon importuned her to establish a hospital in Hays.

Mother Agnes died before she could fulfill her pledge, but there had been some discussion regarding converting the Beach house, where she had been residing, into a hospital. Meanwhile, Mother Antonia offered the parish free use of the house, provided that the Fathers said Mass there twice a week.[46] In 1908, Sister Cyrilla Lauer wrote to Mother Antonia and asked the community to consider the hospital project. When Mother Antonia replied that the congregation was not in a financial position to undertake such expansion, Sister Cyrilla was able to assure her that the expense of the conversion of the house into a hospital would be assumed locally. It was then that Mother Antonia agreed to provide the nursing staff for the new hospital.

The doctors moved quickly; they organized the medical staff and elected the dedicated Dr. Joseph U. Catudal as chief of staff. The congregation provided eight sisters: one to administer the hospital; two to nurse the sick; two to cook; and three to do laundry, general work, and baking. When the hospital opened on August 25, 1909, the operating room was on the second floor and there was no elevator. When a patient was unable to climb the stairs, Dr. Catudal carried him on his back. The sacrifices made by doctors like Dr. Catudal, together with the efforts of the sisters who collected food for the patients around the countryside, played a large role in clearing the debt of the hospital in two years.[47]

In the 1920s, one patient's recovery and gratitude for St. Anthony Hospital was dramatic enough to merit a local newspaper article:

> Nine years ago a stranger was picked up on the highway many miles east of here, his body broken and mangled, and brought to St. Anthony Hospital. Although physicians despaired of his recovery, he was slowly nursed back to health. A few days ago an operating light, one of the most expensive pieces of

surgical equipment on the market, arrived at St.
Anthony Hospital direct from France. The hospital
authorities were delighted, as the lamp was a piece of
equipment long needed, but they were completely
mystified .... Then early this week, a letter, couched
in terms of gratitude that had not diminished in nine
long years, arrived at the hospital. The letter and the
lamp were from W. Wallace Kellett, American representative from the Henry Maurice and Farman
Airoplace Company of France, the patient of nine
years ago ... hospital authorities recall with some
amusement that, when Mr. Kellett regained consciousness and found that he was in a Catholic hospital, he said quite frankly he would rather have died
than to be brought to a Catholic hospital. Before he
left the hospital, however, his prejudice had fled, and
in its place, had come a deep gratitude.[48]

With the addition of St. Anthony Hospital, the congregation
was now faced with the challenge of providing sufficient nursing
staff for two hospitals. Sister Seraphia Fellenz, assistant superintendent and director of the school of nursing, penned a laconic statement in her notebook: "Saint Agnes Hospital School of Nursing
was inaugurated on October 3, 1910, with Doctor F. S. Wiley as
principal speaker.[49] Mother Antonia and twenty Sisters were present, eighteen being members of the nursing staff."[50] The first faculty consisted of three doctors as lecturers and two sisters as instructors. The community room at the convent was the first classroom.
Frequently, faculty and students were needed so badly to help with
patients when the hospital was crowded that classes were discontinued until the rush was over. Dedication and hard work were rewarded when two years after it opened, the school was accredited by the
Wisconsin State Board of Nurses. From 1910 to 1918, thirty-one sisters completed the required courses and became registered nurses.
In January 1917, Sister Frances Clare Kohne was the first Sister of
St. Agnes to write the Wisconsin State Board examination for nurses.
     The accomplishments came at a price. It is little wonder that
both Mother Antonia and Sister Seraphine became ill in 1910.

Sister Seraphine, described as having a "delicate constitution," was threatened with tuberculosis. She spent most of the year in a fruitless search for better health. She lived in San Antonio from February to May, in Fond du Lac in the summer, and in Houghton, Michigan, during September. That fall, Mother Antonia, who had been quietly enduring her own health problems, underwent surgery.

THE EDUCATION OF A SISTER

The young women who entered the community in the early part of the twentieth century differed from those who had entered a quarter of a century earlier. The harsh ideal of almost complete psychological, as well as physical, separation of the sisters from their families seemed to be disappating. Sisters Pius Schurman, Raymond Heiser, Crispine Bonlaender—each of whom had entered between 1878 and 1883—saw ties of family and friendship as destructive of their goal, total union with God. In 1909, when Myra Bodah entered, the congregation clearly had committed itself to its mission and spirituality. For many sisters the discipline of professional preparation and continuing dedication to their ministries, along with their prayer life in community, would achieve the same end of total union with God. They were willing to undergo privations, but did not see the complete severing of family ties as desirable.[51]

The letters Elmira (Myra) Bodoh wrote to her family between September 1909 and December 19, 1919, depict a picture of one of the first young women in the congregation to receive a thorough scientific education. Born on a farm near New London, Wisconsin, Myra loved the countryside all her life. When she was twenty-two and sent East to teach, she could not keep from crying when she saw the little children playing in the dirty New York streets. Her family was devoutly Catholic and the pastor of the parish church was a close family friend.[52] The fourth of thirteen children, Myra was happy at home and happy at the parochial school where she grew to admire the sisters, particularly the principal, Sister Marcella Kettner.

In 1909 Myra entered the convent. Over a ten-year period, she wrote home faithfully from the motherhouse in Fond du Lac; the schools in Two Rivers, Wisconsin, and Yonkers, New York, where she taught; and from Marquette University and the University of

Wisconsin, where she studied for advanced degrees. It is from her letters home that we can get some sense of the development of a sixteen-year-old into a sister in an active religious community.[53] It is disappointing that Myra made no attempt to depict convent life, but she told relatives the happenings of her convent would not be of interest, so she would not write about them.[54] Occasionally, however, a conviction, an attitude, or a belief surfaced in her writing, and we catch a glimpse of a determined young woman, serious about her religious life, her professional development, and the obligation she felt for the welfare of her younger brothers and sisters.

LETTERS HOME

Myra's first letter home was written on September 2, 1909, shortly after she entered the convent in Fond du Lac. She loved writing and she had a strong sense of the comic. Both characteristics were evident in her first letter which included a description of her trip to Fond du Lac. The sixty mile journey involved taking a train from New London to Oshkosh, then taking a streetcar for a twenty-mile ride to Fond du Lac. Myra decided that she did not like the streetcar as well as the train, nor was she favorably impressed with the women she saw. "I can tell you I saw the Biggest [sic] crowd of foolish, homely and gaudy looking women at Oshkosh than I ever did before."[55]

Myra was disappointed to find Sister Marcella away, but she was fascinated by the candidates' dormitory and the five flights of stairs she had to climb to get there. Even in the new surroundings, her thoughts, as they always would, went back to the farm and she wondered how her little sisters would like "to go to bed here." She found the twenty candidates "the jolliest crowd of girls I ever met." They studied "algebra, chemistry, physics, physical geography, rhetoric, orthepy [sic],[56] Latin, German, and Catechism." The candidates studied or were in class seven hours a day and had an additional class in drawing on Saturdays. She said her lessons were quite hard, "but Sister Marcella said we weren't used to study yet, and would get our lessons better in a few months."[57]

Much as one could wish for Myra's uncensored observations on the convent and her new life, her monthly letters home were read by the candidates' mistress and revealed therefore very little of her feelings except those of close attachment to her family. She loved to hear about the younger children, their grades, the prizes they won at the fair, how the work at the farm was going on, and the health of the farm animals, although she was able to take the death of one of the family's horses very philosophically. She said, "It's too bad Kate died, but it's a good thing it wasn't one of the best horses. If I can't see her when I go home, I can see her hide."[58]

When her parents began to worry about her, she wrote, "You asked if the letters made me homesick? On the contrary it makes me glad to know you all are getting along so nicely .... But though I am sometimes lonesome for you all, I know this is my vocation. I do my best, and am happy."[59]

THE CANDIDATE AND NOVICE

Attachment to her family did not prevent Myra from participating wholeheartedly in the life of the candidature. She studied hard; she enjoyed feast days; and she got excited over Christmas. (In 1909 each candidate received a book, nuts, candy, popcorn, bananas, an orange, and fifteen holy pictures.) She delighted in jokes. On one occasion, Myra became the victim of her own joke. She wrote to her family that she had gotten another candidate to write a letter to her grandmother in German, "I can't write that good yet, so when I got Grandma's letter in German, Sister Justin said, 'Good for you, now crack your brain over that German.' I had to get somebody to read it for me, but don't tell her I didn't write it (and couldn't read hers!)."[60]

Her sense of humor must have seen her through many hard times. When one of the sisters in New London provided her family with news of her, Myra wrote, "Sister Ambrose is right. I am growing fatter every day, but you don't need to make the doors bigger for when I come home."[61]

Myra was in the candidature two years. With the exception of her classes—geometry, physics, algebra, Latin, German, rhetoric, agriculture, and the theory of teaching—the following year of the candidature was much like the first. Her letters become more formal. Instead of writing to the "Folks at Home," she began her letters with "My Dear Parents."

Myra never became as sentimentally pious as some novices were apt to be, but after a year and a half in the convent she uncharacteristically wrote:

> Again I will beg of the little child Jesus from His humble crib to raise His tiny hands to bless you all. No one can tell you of the joyful feast we will spend here in our dear convent home, but do not think that I do not wish to be with you, for time nor distance cannot change the love I bear for you all. When you kneel before the crib in church do not forget to ask the little Infant to make me a good sister and I in turn will ask many blessings and gifts for you all.[62]

THE SISTER AND TEACHER

Almost two years after she entered, she was invested and given the name Sister Jeannette. During the novitiate, letter writing was curtailed, but before her profession Sister Jeannette sent a formal letter to her parents:

> Now I am preparing to make my vows. Less than two months and the great day to which I have long looked forward will be here, and the greatest desire of my life will be accomplished. Since, my dear parents, I am about to take this final step, and believe it to be God's will in my regard, I beg your pardon for all the pain and sorrow I have caused you, and thank you for all you have done to aid me in my vocation. I know if it were not for your parental love and solicitude for our spiritual welfare, I would not have the happiness of responding to the call of the celestial Bridegroom. Do not think that I am indifferent to the many sacrifices you have made for me.[63]

Because Sister Jeannette's family was present at her profession, there were no further letters until after she arrived at her first assignment at nearby St. Luke School in Two Rivers. The ten teachers there were responsible for five hundred children. Sister Jeannette was amused by her fifty pupils: "They are lively, and keep me busy as a bee."[64] She found everything to admire, the school was well-equipped, and there were "grand priests who took an interest in the school."[65] The children brought her so many apples that she was worried about her weight. It was while she was in Two Rivers that on Ascension Thursday Sister Jeannette had her first ride in an automobile. Observant as always, she noted that the trip to visit the Franciscan Sisters in Shiocton took twenty minutes, or two and a half minutes a mile.[66]

After only one year at St. Luke, Jeannette was told that she would teach at Sacred Heart School in Yonkers, New York. The next morning she and eleven other sisters were up at 3:00 a.m. to take the 4:40 a.m. train to Chicago. Because the sisters were always expected to keep their trunks packed and their possessions limited, this mode of operation was not unusual. It also guaranteed that sisters would arrive at a new mission with few preconceived ideas about the place or the people. Sister Jeannette, who always analyzed new experiences, was glad that she had not been born in Chicago, which she found dirty and crowded, but liked Detroit, which she found very clean. She was excited by her first ferry ride, crossed the border into Canada, and greatly enjoyed sleeping in an upper berth. She heard but did not see Niagara Falls, but she did see salt beds in Syracuse, the streets of New York City, and then eighteen miles of highway north of the city to Yonkers.[67]

It took time to become adjusted. Writing home after a trip to the city to attend a Catholic school meeting, she observed, "I can tell you the style seen on Broadway is certainly the limit. In observing the crowds, one sees downright wickedness stamped on the faces of more than half I meet."[68] By May, Sister Jeannette was discovering that not all was wickedness in New York. Sacred Heart Parish was known for its beautiful processions and liturgies. During the procession for Forty Hours' Devotion,[69] schoolchildren, priests, and members of parish societies participated. The little boys wore white suits with big red silk sashes; the little girls wore wreaths of flowers; the larger girls wore veils; and all carried flowers. Each morning the boys in her class brought more fresh bouquets of lilacs and bunches of violets than she knew what to do with.[70]

PLANS FOR A CAREER CHANGE

Meanwhile, because the projected pathology laboratory at St. Agnes Hospital was in need of a director, Sister Jeannette Bodoh was to be prepared to take charge. In the summer of 1915 she returned to Wisconsin to begin her education by taking a six-week course in technical laboratory work at Marquette University in Milwaukee. Student that she was, Sister Jeannette loved the courses and the three doctors who taught it, although she was the loser in a little interchange with a professor. This professor always called on her as "Miss Bodoh." Sister Jeannette made an appointment and asked him to please call her "Sister." The professor replied that he had but one sister whom he loved dearly. He regretted it, but he could not think of calling another woman "Sister."[71]

Towards the end of the semester, Sister Jeannette wrote:

> It hardly seems possible that school is over. It was too short. But that is always the way; everything pleasant to us seems short, and I enjoyed my work so much and found it so interesting. However, I am glad my studies do not stop. Reverend Mother has engaged an excellent Catholic Doctor to be pathologist in the hospital for the next two or three years, and at the same time to be my guide and teacher in laboratory work ... by that time retreat will be over and I shall have my Seven Year Vows made. How time does fly! It does not seem as if I have been in the convent six years. It is like yesterday that I left home for the first time. I certainly, never for one moment, had occasion to regret that first step which has brought to me such happiness.[72]

STUDIES IN MADISON, WISCONSIN

Sister Jeannette was then enrolled in the University of Wisconsin in Madison, where she took classes in pathology, bacteriology, physiological chemistry, and water analysis with the medical students. In spite of her heavy assignments, she liked her work and found it "not so hard on the nervous system as teaching."[73] She planned on becoming a registered nurse as well as a pathologist and bacteriologist. She lived at St. Mary Hospital with the sisters, who treated her as one of their own. She needed to study a great deal and spoke of being often discouraged, but the sisters there encouraged her and told her that if she could not make a success of her work, nobody could.

Sister Jeannette loved her classes at the university, but adjusting to being the only sister in the class was somewhat difficult. She did, however, find that the professors and pupils were very respectful and kind and they tried to make her position in class pleasant. "Being the only Sister attending school here is a little embarrassing in the beginning, but when the boys get used to me, it will be easier. Many of them never came in contact with a sister before, and have to find out that I am like other folks, before they stop looking at me."[74]

In her Christmas letter of 1916, Sister Jeannette reflected on the war then waging in Europe:[75] "If the people of Europe stop, on this bright feast, to compare it with former Christmases, must they not shudder at the terrible reality of the present day."[76] She was going to Fond du Lac, but was not expecting a restful vacation:

> Dr. Clark gave each of us the job of making a general bacteriological survey of our town ... I guess he thought we might rust. Besides that, I must buck for two final exams which will take place the second session in the new year. After that must type 100 pages in Pathology and tear apart and wash my two habits. How do you think Christmas vacation sounds to me with all this staring me in the face?[77]

In February an aunt died, and again Sister Jeannette wrote to her family on death:

> 'Tis another of life's lessons for us. Soon it will be our turn. "Today we are, and tomorrow we are not," and this world, for which we have slaved goes on as jolly as ever, and forgets that we ever lived. We do not need much wisdom to realize that a person who serves the world at the expense of his eternal welfare is a fool. And how many of them there are in this

world! I have seen so many sad deaths, I mean deaths of worldly, sin-loving people, that I thank God over and over again that my home was not in the city, for if I had been brought up the same as some of these poor persons, I would turn out even worse. A person cannot fear death when he knows the true picture of life.[78]

A golden afternoon for Sister Jeannette was the day that she received an important visitor:

Mother Marcella from Fond du Lac passed through the city and stopped off to see me. She was here from Friday evening until just now, I have just returned from taking her to the depot .... She was very, very much pleased with my studies here. I am so glad she picked me out for this work, I like it so much that I could work in the laboratory night and day without ever thinking of feeling tired or hungry. I only hope that my eyes will hold out. They do not trouble me as much as they used to, still Mother says I must consult the best oculist in the city at once. She is going to have the Sisters pray for my eyes. I trust in prayer, and I feel I shall be OK.[79]

AN "AWFUL" RESPONSIBILITY

Sister Jeannette was to spend six weeks studying in Rochester, Minnesota, then return home:

After that I shall try to shoulder courageously and trustworthily the responsibility of the hospital. I shall take complete charge, and shall begin to instruct a sister or two as my assistants.
The responsibility of that post is something awful. Life or death may depend on my diagnosis, for I am the one to decide whether or not a disease is malignant, and, in many cases, what kind of an operation will be necessary ... Still, in spite of all that, I am not

nervous or afraid about it. I have been trying hard
here, and the professors and doctors say that I am
trustworthy for the place. I have been doing the diag-
nosing for the doctors here just for practice—they let
me do it to help me along. I made only one mistake
during the whole year, and the man was already
dead when I made the laboratory diagnosis.[80]

On July 10, 1919, Sister Jeannette vowed for life poverty, chastity, and obedience.[81] She was prepared to do her share in furthering
the mission of the Sisters of St. Agnes to care for the sick. Her story
is but one and not, perhaps, typical. It does, however, provide some
insights into the experiences of an intelligent young woman who
loved her life as a Sister of St. Agnes.

The letters Sister Jeannette Bodoh wrote to her family between
1909 and 1919 reveal a picture of the maturing and education of a
sister in circumstances far different from the life she would have led
if she had entered fifty years previously. The unchanging horarium,
habit, and quaint customs presented a picture of convent life that
made it appear more static than it actually was. The sisters, regardless of rules and regulations, could not be enclosed. They had ministries; most of these ministries demanded professional preparation
and continual study. Removed as they were from the world in some
respects, their life and aspirations were affected by the needs of the
times they lived in.

MOTHER ANTONIA'S SECOND TERM

The year 1911 had provided the community a breathing space. In
the six years after the death of Mother Agnes, the congregation had
progressed both spiritually and materially. Its lifestyle, customs, and
government would not change appreciably for the next sixty years.
Both Mother Antonia and Sister Seraphine seemed to be in better
health. Only one mission was accepted; the Sisters of St. Agnes
returned to Marytown. At the general chapter that summer, there
was no substantive change in administration, but this time Sister
Marcella Kettner was named vicar and Sister Seraphine Morrissey,
second councilor.[82]

After the chapter, the congregation could no longer delay attending to the needs of St. Agnes Hospital. The success of the hospital in Fond du Lac and the surrounding area had created a critical need for more space and more services. With little hesitation, the council voted to build a new wing. Mother Antonia signed a contract for $109,774[83] and borrowed $75,000 from Henry Boyle for the building,[84] which eventually cost $134,138.55.[85] The new east wing, completed in 1913, allowed the sixty-bed hospital to accommodate more than twice as many patients as it had in the past.[86] Services were also increased: an x-ray laboratory was added that same year; a pharmacy, in 1914; and a bacteriology and pathology laboratory in 1915. This placed a considerable burden on the congregation because a sister had to be prepared to staff each department.[87] In 1920, when the first classification of hospitals in the United States by the Joint Commission on Accreditation of Health Care Organizations was undertaken, St. Agnes was awarded a place in Class A of the accredited hospitals in the country.

St. Agnes Hospital was fortunate in that Sister Seraphia Fellenz was an outstanding and far-seeing administrator. Sisters of St. Agnes attended the organizational meeting of the Catholic Hospital Association (CHA) in 1915, and St. Agnes Hospital was among its first institutional members.[88] It is noteworthy, although typical of the Sisters of St. Agnes, that once the decision to operate a hospital was undertaken, there seems to have been little or no discussion on the propriety of religious participating in such meetings.[89]

MORE SCHOOLS AND MORE SCHOOLING

In the meantime, Mother Antonia did not allow the attention she had been placing on the hospitals to distract her from her concern for the schools. When she was on a visitation to the Leo House in 1912, its chaplain, Father Urban Nageleisen, was being transferred to the German parish of the Holy Family in the Bronx. When she realized that Holy Family had no parochial school, she urged him, should he establish a school, to ask her for sisters to staff it. A month later he purchased a large house on Blackrock Avenue to serve as a convent. In 1913 the school was opened with six sisters. Four classes were held in the basement of the church; two others, in the convent. That same year, Mother Antonia agreed to staff two more schools in Wisconsin, the last of her administration: St. Bernard in Watertown and St. Florian in the tiny industrial suburb of West Milwaukee. The sisters by then were teaching in forty-three schools located in eight states: Illinois, Indiana, Kansas, Michigan, New York, Ohio, Pennsylvania, and Wisconsin.

At the same time, changes in the public school sector were having an impact on parish schools. Some pastors were beginning to think of adding high schools[90] or at least commercial courses beyond the eighth grade. In addition, St. Mary's Springs needed more sisters with an advanced education. In the past, few sisters had had educational opportunities beyond those offered at the motherhouse, although Sisters Louisa Wolsiffer and Mercedes Kennedy had studied music and art in other convents. No one had yet been sent for a bachelor's degree. The issue worried the council. Not only was education expensive, but there was a fear that it would prove divisive in the community itself. But the decision was inevitable; some sisters, at least, had to have a university education.

There were also pastors who were anxious to advance the educational standards of their parish schools. It was through the creativity of an exceptionally education-minded pastor that the sisters arrived in Watertown. St. Bernard Parish was Irish in a town noted for being a center of German culture; its well-established school dated back to 1857. When the Sisters of Mercy withdrew, the pastor, Thomas Hennessey, CSC, immediately began searching for another community. When he learned that the motherhouse of the Sisters of St. Agnes was only fifty miles away, he took his junior choir of grade school and high school girls for a visit to the convent in August. The girls liked the sisters; the sisters liked the girls. When school opened in September, four teachers and one house sister greeted their new scholars.[91]

St. Florian had been established by the Capuchins, but because the Order had other needs and duties, they suggested that the Carmelites take over. Accepting St. Florian's School was a costly venture for the sisters because both the Carmelite Fathers, who had accepted the parish, and the parish itself were struggling, but Mother Antonia provided seven sisters, including an organist and a sister who had charge of the choir, as well as $5,750 for a house and lots for the sisters' residence.[92] The residence, however, was also to be used as a house of studies for the sisters who were beginning to attend Marquette University in significant numbers.

Reflecting the changes in teacher preparation in the country, the education of the sisters began to change about this time, also. The Agnesians attempted to formalize their own teacher training classes by initiating a normal school. Both Mother Antonia and Sister Marcella[93] were anxious to take advantage of the opportunity to prepare sisters for their bachelor's degrees. Finances would allow only one sister to attend at that time; but, after much thought, Sister Clare M. Goodwin[94] was sent to Catholic University for her bachelor's degree.[95] She later received an M.A. degree from Loyola University and a doctorate from Fordham.

While the community was growing steadily, with an average of sixteen women invested each year from 1905 until 1916, the number did not seem nearly enough to meet the expanding responsibilities of the sisters. By 1913, Mother Antonia was ready to consider the suggestions of Sister Marcella to recruit vocations in Europe. Because other women's religious communities in Wisconsin were receiving entrants from Europe, there seemed no reason why the Sisters of St. Agnes should not be equally successful. It was through her urging that Mother Antonia sent Sister Marcella and Sister Bernadette Wax to Germany to recruit for vocations. The two Sisters left the motherhouse with a grand fanfare one day in June and five months later returned with eight potential vocations. The congregation never repeated the experiment. Unlike most other communities in Wisconsin, the Agnesians had neither a European motherhouse nor close ties with Europe. Candidates had no opportunity to become acquainted with the sisters nor the sisters with them. Too, the World War started the following year, followed by the restrictive immigration laws of the 1920s.

IMPROVEMENTS AND INVESTMENTS AND TRIVIA

It seemed that it was always time for improvements. Increasing numbers of sisters made enlarging the convent chapel imperative by moving the communion railing several feet forward. At the same time, Mother Antonia had new lighting fixtures installed.[96] To beautify the chapel she purchased etched glass doors and twelve statues.

She also had a summerhouse built where the sisters could do their spiritual reading, sewing, or simply relax.

When Bishop Frederick Eis of the Sault Sainte Marie-Marquette diocese approached Mother Antonia for sisters to staff the new Holy Family Orphans' Home in Marquette, Michigan, she was glad to consent. He had inquired about securing sisters previously, and she sympathized with the struggles he had endured for over a decade to build a new orphans' home. He had begun the project with $24,000 subscribed from priests who had attended a diocesan retreat in July 1903, but it was ten years before the project actually got underway. The four-story brick home finally opened in 1915 with a staff of thirteen to care for the forty children who had been transferred from St. Joseph Home in Assinins.[97] The Native American children remained at St. Joseph's. The sisters—whether teachers, nurses, domestics, or house mothers—took care of the physical, educational, and spiritual needs of the children. It did not take many years for the number of children to rise to two hundred.

Not all of the children were orphaned. Some children were there during a temporary family crisis. Others were from broken homes. Still others were neglected or abused, and placed there by court order. The diocese provided several big parties for the children during the year. Charitable neighbors would sometimes have children stay with them a few days for a visit.

Accepting the care of any institution was a tremendous undertaking for a community. Like the hospitals, an orphanage or a boarding school like St. Mary's Springs demanded a greater number of personnel for staffing. Unlike the parochial schools, these institutions required a personal commitment of seven days a week and twelve months a year for the sister working in them, with the sole exception of the five to eight days allowed for her annual retreat. That much was true, at least, of the institutions that only the sisters staffed. Being financially responsible for the hospitals and St. Mary's Springs also meant tremendous financial investments that the community did not have.

It was not only big decisions that made up the life of the Superior General. A glance at Mother Antonia's "diary" shows these entries written in 1912. Her comments are straightforward, perceptive and not without an ironic twist:

Feb. 6—This was a day of trouble and trials.
Feb. 10—I bought Cora Ensweiler a new coat.
March 1—Sister Vicaria went to Oshkosh to straighten matters between the rev and sister. The latter is not submissive, she talks too much.
April 28—The Archbishop [Messmer] gave permission to let the sisters go home for Golden Jubilee, First Masses, and if parents are very old, and are expected to die any minute. I need not ask him again.[98]

As Mother Antonia looked at the congregation's commitment of personnel around the country, the need for more vocations was always on her mind. She continually prayed for more vocations and asked others to do the same. In 1913 she asked the candidates, novices, and sisters at the motherhouse to pray to St. Joseph for more candidates—one for each day of St. Joseph's month, March. More than that number came that year. It was that group which, on St. Agnes Day in 1914, discarded the old-fashioned bonnets in favor of short black veils. At this point, too, Mother Antonia was concerned with a much more serious problem—that of certification for the teachers. The congregation's schools in Kansas were almost closed because of the lack of certification of the teachers.[99]

MOTHER ANTONIA'S LAST DAYS

August 28, 1915 was an ordinary visiting day for the candidates, a day when families were allowed to come to the convent and visit with their daughters who were candidates. When Mother Antonia stopped to visit with Stella Maeder and her family, her arm snapped when she picked up Stella's ten-month-old nephew. Years later Stella, by then Sister Agnes Therese, wrote a touching account of events and of Mother's kindness to her: "My relatives were grieved at the report and I was inconsolable. Mother sent for me the next morning and tried to make me see that it was God's will that it should happen that way. The doctor said she could have broken the bone by turning a door knob, as it was thin as a needle."[100]

Mother Antonia was taken to Chicago for tests. X-rays showed that she had carcinoma of the bone at an advanced stage. The doc-

tor told her that she had only four or five months to live. Agnes
Therese continues:

> After Mother returned, she took her meals in her
> office. She looked very pale, and I recall that she car-
> ried her left arm in a black sling. Often she called me
> to do some little thing for her. Though her face was
> lined with pain, she would smile and speak cheerful-
> ly, sometimes presenting me with a sweetmeat or a
> piece of fruit.
>
> I have beautiful memories of her. She allowed
> me to enter the convent at twelve years of age after I
> had written twice. Her answer to my first plea stated
> that I should see more of the world and come to the
> convent at fifteen. I replied saying that I knew the
> world as I was a Chicago girl. I am sure she must
> have laughed heartily over that letter, for I didn't
> even know the score at that age.[101]

By Christmas, Mother Antonia was bedridden and suffering
from intense pain, extreme nervousness, and desolation of spirit.[102]
In January she called a council meeting. When the sisters met in her
sick room, she asked the reluctant Sister Marcella and council to
assume her duties and make the arrangements for a general chapter. On St. Agnes Day, Archbishop Messmer came to visit Mother
Antonia. Sister Seraphine wrote on that day:

> He said to her that God favored her in sending a
> long and painful sickness. If he had one wish for
> himself it was that of a prolonged sickness, before his
> death that he might have time to prepare for the end.
> Our dear mother is suffering a martyrdom. She can-
> not use her left arm and neither of her legs. She is as
> if nailed to the cross. Her patience and resignation
> are marvelous.[103]

Even in the midst of her pain, Mother Antonia remembered the
needs and suffering of the sisters. Sister Jeannette Bodoh wrote to
her mother:

> Our dear Reverend Mother Antonia died today at 4
> p.m. .... Please pray for her and have the children
> pray for her. She was so kind and suffered so very
> much. When she heard that Mama was to have the
> operation, she had all the sisters in the Convent offer
> communion for Mama, and told me she would say
> her prayers and offer communion for her too. [This
> was only two weeks before her own death.] When
> Henry [Sister Jeannette's brother] died she came
> over to the Hospital and told me how sorry she was,
> and that she had offered communion for him ....
> When I left on April 18 from my visit, she gave me
> her dying blessing and said she would remember me,
> though she would never see me again.[104]

Mother Antonia died on May 2, 1916. Archbishop Messmer
gave the eulogy, which perhaps says as much about the archbishop
as it does about Mother Antonia. He said, "I have always admired
in Mother Antonia her reverence and deep intellectual submission
to the authority of the Church. She did not aspire to an undue
expansion of the Congregation, but rather desired the growth and
preservation of a good religious spirit among the sisters."[105]

Her sisters said that she was a model religious, that she governed
the congregation with prudence and foresight and that she was zealous for the preservation of a good religious spirit and for mutual
harmony among the sisters. She herself said, "I never knew any sister who was not my friend."[106]

Two of Mother's notes to the sisters show her deep understanding of religious life. At the end of 1909, she asked the sisters to unite
in prayer for special graces for personal renewal and for the right
community spirit. And then she asked of each sister, "What have we
done for God's interest during the past year? To us as Religious, it
must be the perception of our inner self; more understanding of
sacrifice; a keen sense of the depth and breadth of purity and deepest love."[107] Toward the end of her life Mother Antonia wrote:

> How fast time flies, and as we look on the vanished
> years, we sometimes feel how empty they have been.
> Perhaps they are not so empty as we suppose; for it is

not only the labors that make an outward show that give value to our lives, but much more are those many *acts of the heart of which God alone takes note*, and reckons as good works. Let us set about heaping up a great store of *these riches*. They do not need great talents, for they are gained, *not by the head, but by the heart*.[108]

Chapter VII

Increasing
Expectations

After its chaotic beginning, the Congregation of Sisters of St. Agnes by 1905 had emerged as a respected congregation. Its members were women whose characters had been formed in hard-working immigrant households and in daily efforts to live the vows of poverty, chastity, and obedience. They had struggled for physical and economic survival. They had worked together to form a community which prided itself on doing whatever church or society asked of it. They had a spirituality which owed a great deal to the missionary spirit of their founder, Father Caspar Rehrl, the Franciscan influence of Father Francis Haas, and the energetic commitment of Mother Agnes Hazotte in meeting the spiritual and corporal needs that came to hand.

During the twenty years after the death of Mother Agnes, the congregation was led by only two women. Both had a significant influence on the life of the congregation. Mother Antonia Schmitz had shown her sisters the value of a hidden life devoted to quietly loving God and promoting harmony among those whose lives she touched. Mother Marcella Kettner, devoted to her vocation as religious and educator, was untiring in her efforts to lead the congregation to higher levels of professional competence.

IMPACT OF WORLD EVENTS

During the eleven years of Mother Antonia's administration, with the possible exception of the depression of 1907, national events had little direct effect on the lives of the sisters. The San Francisco earthquake, Henry Ford's Model T, the first transcontinental airplane flight, the landing of United States Marines in Nicaragua, and even the election of Woodrow Wilson were scarcely noted.

International events, however, were of more importance. When Mother Antonia died, the United States was on the verge of entering World War I. The war, which had begun in August 1914, was the result of nationalism, imperialism, economic rivalries, and an arms race that had led to an unstable system of entangling alliances. When the heir to the throne of Austria-Hungary was assassinated by a Serb, alliances eventually drew almost all the countries of Europe into the fray. England, France, and Russia were the principal players against Germany and Austria-Hungary, although eventually the non-European world was drawn in. Opinion in the United States was already divided because of conflicting economic and policy interests, but the traditional animosities that millions of immigrants brought over from Europe intensified the debate. Wisconsin, with its large immigrant population, was deeply divided. Senator Robert La Follett, Congressman Victor Berger, Mayor Daniel Webster Hoan of Milwaukee, and Archbishop Sebastian Messmer were among the many prominent Wisconsinites opposed to the entry of the United States into Europe's struggle. Although the congregation supported the war effort after war was declared, there is little reason to believe that the sisters, as a whole, would have differed from the archbishop in his initial pacifism.

MOTHER MARCELLA KETTNER

During this period the first and only foreign-born superior general of the congregation was elected—on July 15, 1916—by all sisters in perpetual vows. With 239 electors, the sisters anticipated that arriving at an immediate decision would be difficult, but Sister Marcella

Kettner was elected on the first ballot. The only new member elected to the council was Sister Meinrad Heiser who, on the death of Mother Antonia, had been appointed to fill the vacancy on the council.

In retrospect, it seems providential that Mother Antonia's vicar, Sister Marcella Kettner, became the next superior general. Her background, talents, character, and unwavering dedication to the rule made her the obvious choice to succeed Mother Antonia. Sister Marcella was also uniquely qualified to implement the necessary improvements in the quality of teacher preparation in the community.[1]

Anna Francisca Wilhelmina Kettner was born the daughter of Franz Friedrich Kettner and Anna Haettenbacher in Donaueschingen, Villingen, Baden on April 3, 1857. Her maternal grandfather had been Spanish; her paternal grandparents, German. When Anna was five, her mother died and she was placed in an academy under the direction of the English Ladies.[2] The product of a strict European and religious upbringing, Anna would always place a high value on order and obedience; but the early loss of her mother had left her with a compassionate heart not readily apparent in a young woman of such dignity and reserve.

Anna came to the United States when she was twelve years old. Why the family chose to leave the attractive Donaueschingen is somewhat of a mystery. If the testimony of a later visitor to the town was correct, the Kettner stables were larger than many a French chateau he had seen.[3] At some earlier point in her life, Anna had entered and left a religious community "in one of the Dakotas." Whatever the reason, her confessor told her that "maybe God doesn't want you in that community."[4]

Anna next joined the staff of St. Nicholas School in Evanston, Illinois, and then, at the age of twenty-eight, the Sisters of St. Agnes. While teaching as a novice in the convent school, the newly invested Sister Marcella began the task that would last the rest of her life—broadening the educational horizons of her sisters. After profession, she taught in Menominee, Michigan, then in New London, Wisconsin. It was while she was in New London that she would teach a youngster who, years later, would provide a grateful and loving insight into the Sister Marcella the children had met in the classroom.

Years later, the student, Terence O'Donnell, described the teacher who had influenced his life in so many ways.

> Her complexion was fair and her face had that shrewish air which can easily mislead one, for it is actually not shrewish but shrewd. It is a capable, kind sort of shrewdness that is straightforward. I have found it a peculiar attribute of a certain type of fair complexioned people, who by nature and desire can only be termed instinctively chaste; this of course is a comparison I draw in later years, with more knowledge of human nature. Besides being the Sister Superior, she taught our classroom, gave music lessons to such as desired them, played the organ in church and was the choir director. Her hands were beautiful. I used to see her fingers spanning a full octave on the organ. Between the fingers the skin often was cracked, especially in winter. This is not surprising since the Sisters made their own soap from the wood ashes in the school stoves, and it was strong soap, with a lot of lye, naturally injurious to the skin. Then, too, our winters were severe; whole weeks went by at twenty below zero.[5]

Like Sister Marcella, Terence had also lost his mother at an early age. Soon after the O'Donnell family had emigrated from Ireland, his mother had died and the father remarried. The situation was a most unhappy one for the neglected children. Terence would go to school with the front of his shirt brown from scraping the potatoes, his morning task. For special occasions, Sister Marcella would see that the house sister would wash, starch, and iron the little boy's shirt so he would not be embarrassed. Terence told how she would "punish" the O'Donnell children with work after school and on weekends and holy days to keep them from their unhappy home. She would have them work for her in the school or convent:

> When she found I liked to draw I was asked to the Sisters' house before Easter to help them paint rabbits on the Easter eggs. Looking back now I realize

the Easter eggs that the nun painted were artistic masterpieces ... I myself liked the *Agnus Deis* the nuns tinted superbly in water color with images of the Blessed Virgin and with the Sacred Heart. My nun made the large ones we received for good conduct or superior class-standing. These were edged with handmade lace. It was not until years later in Brussels I realized how exquisite that lace edging was. All this contact with art was vital for students in a poor frontier parish."[6]

Terence benefited not only from Sister's concern, but also from her remarkable breadth of knowledge and unusual ability as a teacher. Because the pastor wanted to keep the children in the parochial school, Terence wrote,

[Sister Marcella] concocted a sort of synthetic "9th grade," the subjects and the periods of time and history covered being not like anything else encountered anywhere by anyone on land or sea. Where Sister Marcella got it all I don't know, but I was bumping into a lot of the material even in the first 2 years of a liberal arts course at Indiana U. I left about that time because it was World War I, but I "made" ensign at Pelham Bay in the company of full-time college graduates, taking the equivalent of the 4-year Annapolis course in 8 months ... something entirely owing to some of the material Sr. Marcella had taught (including a sumptuously illustrated scrap book of an armored destroyer and what made it "tick").[7]

Following the death of Mother Agnes, Sister Marcella returned to the motherhouse as third councilor. Her paramount responsibility was the convent school, although she also replaced Mother Antonia as convent organist. As a councilor, she encouraged Mother Antonia's efforts to increase the educational level of the sisters. Primary teachers were to complete eighth-grade work, while eighth-grade teachers were to complete high school and college work. She believed firmly in the discipline of public, oral examinations. Sisters were obliged to take quarterly examinations at the motherhouse until they had taught at least twenty years.[8] She also did her best to promote an interest in literature and drama. She engaged the services of a Shakespearean actor who occasionally came to the convent to present different plays in monologues. Seventy years later those monologues were still remembered with pleasure.

In spite of Sister Marcella's demanding standards, one sister remembered, "We younger religious felt no generation gap in her communication with us. She had a special warm spot for the young."[9] When St. Mary's Springs Academy was founded, Sister Marcella's own life as a child in an excellent convent boarding school provided her with a background that proved invaluable in its opening years.

Mother Marcella began her duties as superior general on July 15, 1916. She was fifty-eight years old, and it was clear that she had experience, vision, and determination. On the one hand, her efforts to maintain the sisters at a distance from the world around them spoke of the ideal of a cloistered nun. On the other, her determination that the sisters be as well-educated as the community could afford spoke of her conviction that they must be professional women. To her the two ideals were complementary and attainable. To later generations they frequently would seem impossible.

Characterized as "sternly uncompromising,"[10] she was not slow to give penances for some minor infraction of the rule. More than one sister was sent early to bed for two weeks. At the same time she took her own title as "Mother" seriously and insisted that the house sisters treat the sisters in the house in a "motherly fashion."[11]

Although Mother Marcella neither underwent the trials of founding the community, as had Mother Agnes, nor the financial struggles of stabilizing it, as had Mother Antonia, her years in office could not have been easy. The year after she was elected, the United States and her native land were at war with each other. It is not difficult to imagine the pain of those who saw their adopted country at war with their homeland or their sorrow at news of battles fought where they had played as children. Mother Marcella worried about friends and relatives and grieved over the lost lives, the broken families, and the material destruction of war. She did all she could to procure stipends for needy priests and help the nuns and children in orphanages who were suffering from want. The congregation bought what war stamps and liberty bonds it could afford but beyond that, Mother Marcella and the sisters could do little but pray for a speedy peace and concentrate on the work at hand.

Just over a month into Mother Marcella's term, the Carmelite Fathers left. They had accepted the chaplaincy of the motherhouse intending to build a monastery in Fond du Lac. In the end the town proved unsuitable, and because it was against the Carmelite rule to have two or three monks living permanently outside a monastery, their general chapter voted to withdraw the priests stationed in Fond du Lac. The motherhouse had been notified in April, but in the interim between the death of Mother Antonia and the election of another superior general, it had not been possible to contact another Order for a chaplain. At the August retreat, Mother Marcella was so impressed with the ability of the Precious Blood priest who had preached it that she spoke to Archbishop Messmer about securing the services of the society. The archbishop contacted the provincial at Carthagena, Ohio, and the matter was speedily arranged. The Carmelites left on August 30, 1916, and Precious Blood Fathers Ulrich Mueller and Hugo Lear arrived on September 4.[12]

LEADERSHIP

Mother Marcella's annual Christmas letters were the principal means of informing the sisters of the general spiritual and financial state of the community, with, of course, pleas of prayers for special intentions. Her first Christmas letter, in 1916, reported a great deal of illness among the sisters and requested prayers for them, for peace, and for vocations. The letters give some insight into her spirituality as well. In asking the sisters to pray for vocations, she added, "The reward is ... a home here on earth under the same roof as the Prisoner of the Tabernacle, a home beyond the grave in the everlasting home of His Father."[13] In 1918, she wrote, "To insure this happiness, nothing is more conducive than the faithful observance of the holy vows and the rules; therefore, I earnestly wish to remind each one of these all important duties."[14]

Like Mother Antonia, her predecessor, Mother Marcella, was convinced, after only a year in office, that a certain laxity had crept into the congregation. In September 1917, she sent to the community a list of customs and usages which were to be observed by all the sisters.[15] Perhaps she was inspired by the memories of the English Ladies she had so admired in childhood as many of the regulations seemed less suited to the American temperament. Shopping was limited to four times a year; sisters were forbidden to stop at stores on the way to a doctor or dentist; they were permitted to visit other convents in the same city but once a year. They were allowed two automobile rides a year, but could not stop off for a visit at any place enroute. Merchandise was to be purchased at wholesale. Petty purchases could be made only by telephone or by messenger. Only in urgent cases could sisters go to the butcher, baker, or grocer.

One prohibition that many sisters found difficult was Mother Marcella's ban on card playing.[16] In most of the convents, it was one of the preferred ways to spend the half-hour or so allowed for evening recreation. During the long Midwestern winters card playing was a way to relax, and the sisters from the rural areas in particular had grown up playing cards at family recreations. Mother Antonia herself had enjoyed a game of pinochle at recreation.

Two years later, Mother Marcella rescinded any permissions she had given in that circular because she said "their *abuse* led to laxity and disorder." The sisters' lives were even more restricted. Only the superior or her substitute was allowed to go shopping. Correspondence was limited strictly to business. Mother Marcella emphasized that all sisters had to contribute their share to the observance of the holy vows and rules, the means by which they would keep aloof from the spirit of the world.[17]

While rules and regulations were important to Mother Marcella, she did not believe in indiscriminately maintaining old European customs. She stopped the practice of kissing the superior general's ring. While rank among the sisters was still maintained, she did everything in her power to treat house sisters in the same manner as school sisters.[18] Mother Marcella also considered the health of the sisters and mitigated customs accordingly. An unheard-of privilege was granted when she allowed the sisters a rest either in the morning or the evening once or twice a week. They were encouraged to take a fifteen or twenty-minute walk three times a week. She took the advice of Dr. Frank Wiley and asked for permission from Archbishop Messmer[19] for the nurses to discard their white woolen habit and adopt the Catholic Hospital Association habit.[20] It was with profound gratitude that the sisters donned a habit that could be washed daily.

EDUCATIONAL PROGRESS

From the time she returned to the motherhouse, Mother Marcella had worked ceaselessly to advance the education of the sisters. When in 1917 she heard rumors that teachers in all schools would soon be obliged to take state examinations, she must certainly have agreed with the Department of Education and made use of the occasion to raise the educational level of the sisters. She wrote: "I, therefore, urge upon each and every teacher the necessity of making use of every spare moment to advance in her studies; this applies equally to those engaged in hospital work. Any help the Motherhouse can give is at your disposal. Let us first of all be religious, humble, self-sacrificing, and teachers striving daily for greater efficiency so as to be better able to advance the interest of Christ."[21]

More informally Mother would say to the sisters, "See that you are a good teacher—not only a good teacher, but an intelligent teacher."[22] By 1918 sisters were attending summer school at colleges in Kansas, Michigan, and New York. She engaged professors from the Oshkosh Normal School to supplement the faculty at the motherhouse. On Saturdays sisters living nearby were required to take classes there. In her efforts to make the sisters more professionally-minded, she ran counter to the prevailing convent ethos when she told them to hang up their certificates saying, "We must blow our own horn! Nobody else will do it for you."[23]

Predictably, Mother Marcella became a strong supporter of the high school movement. The Agnesians agreed to staff three high schools during her administration. The first was a girls' high school in Hays, Kansas. In 1917, concerned that Catholic education for girls stopped with the eighth grade, Father Dominic Schuster, OFM, pastor of St. Joseph's Church, assembled a committee to remedy the situation. After securing the Sisters of St. Agnes to staff the new school, the committee was successful in raising enough funds to open the first two years of girls' Catholic High School in September 1918. There were two sisters on the faculty and twelve girls, eight freshmen and four sophomores, in attendance. The second year,

three business courses were added to the curriculum and the enrollment increased to nineteen. By 1922, the student body numbered
forty-two, enough to justify building a four-room school building.
The faculty was increased by one more sister and the school became
fully accredited by the Kansas State Board of Education.[24]

Since 1881, Agnesians had been teaching at St. Joseph's School,
the parish school of St. Mary's of the Assumption Parish in Decatur,
Indiana. In 1915, a commercial course was added to the elementary
school curriculum, and five years later Decatur Catholic High
School was organized by the parish. In Yonkers, New York, where
the sisters had been teaching at Sacred Heart School since 1893, the
sisters established a two-year commercial course that, in 1923,
became the nucleus of Sacred Heart High School.

Meanwhile, with the success of Catholic University's program
for sisters, the Jesuits had begun to look for ways to admit sisters to
their colleges. In August 1917, sisters who were teaching at St.
Nicholas in Evanston attended a lecture in the school auditorium on
the state of the Catholic Church in Mexico. "Since in those days no
sister would think of mingling in the audience with lay people, they
sat in the dressing room listening to the speaker .... The door ...
opened quietly and a strange priest tiptoed into the room." Asking
to speak to the sisters, he inquired, "How would you like to go to
school?" It was the president of Loyola University in Chicago. He
had come with a plan. Loyola University planned to open an extension center in a convent in Wilmette, Illinois, to accommodate the
sisters. Courses would be held on Saturdays and credits would be
granted by the university. From that time on, every Saturday saw
numbers of sisters attending the convent campus of Loyola
University.[25]

The sisters could be sure that Mother Marcella monitored their
progress carefully. At the beginning of 1919, she wrote: "Enclosed,
find school work for the year. Again I wish to impress strongly upon
all that each Sister is expected to do her utmost toward her own
advancement, for the honor of God and for the reputation of the
Community."[26]

As states began to demand higher and sometimes unique
requirements for teacher certification, it was becoming more difficult to prepare sisters who might be required to teach in any of eight
different states. Mother Marcella found a solution. Because

Michigan's stringent requirements for certification allowed teachers licensed by that state to be accepted in other states, she sent a number of sisters to Northern State Teachers College in Marquette, Michigan. In the summer of 1921, ninety sisters were attending summer schools at Duquesne, Fordham, and Marquette universities and at state normal schools in Indiana, Kansas, Michigan, and Wisconsin.

NEW STUDENTS AT THE SCHOOL OF NURSING

In an effort to help alleviate the shortage of nurses caused by war, St. Agnes Hospital inaugurated a six-month training program for fifteen young women in 1917. The success of this program—but more importantly the increased number of patients who were straining the resources of St. Agnes Hospital—led to a decision to admit lay women to the School of Nursing. A full-time lay nurse and graduate of St. Mary's School of Nursing in Milwaukee was engaged as the first director of the program. Three lay applicants entered on May 1, 1918. By the end of September, they were joined by fifteen more young women, and the three-year curriculum began.

Before the classes had started, but not before the curriculum had been designed, the lay director resigned in order to join the Red Cross Nursing Service in the Army Nurse Corps. She was succeeded by Sister Frances Clare Kohne. The faculty included the hospital chaplains, the sister faculty, and ten physicians. In addition, there were nursing supervisors in all of the hospital's units: medical and surgical; obstetrics; pediatrics; the pharmacy and laboratory; and public health nursing.

An ad that appeared in the *Fond du Lac Daily Commonwealth* in June of 1919 set forth requirements for admission to the school: "Applicants must have completed two years of high school, be of good character, and between nineteen and thirty-five years of age."[27] These students would be given tuition, room, board, laundry, and an allowance for incidental school expenses.

Housing the students would be a problem throughout the early years. Half of the first group was housed on Sheboygan Street where John Hazotte had lived for many years; the others, in sun parlors in the hospital. Then the congregation purchased a large three-story residence and remodeled it for thirty students.

For the first three months, the probationers were required to bring four washable dresses of any color; at the end of the period they were given the regulation gray-and-white striped uniform with a stiff white collar and cuffs, a white bibbed apron, and a plain white cap. Only when they graduated could they wear a white uniform.

POSTWAR CHALLENGES

Immediately after the war, a great influenza epidemic raged throughout the world. During 1918-1919 more than 675,000 people died in the United States and more than 25,000,000 people died around the world. At both St. Agnes and St. Anthony Hospitals, sisters, doctors, and staff worked long, hard hours. At St. Agnes, patients were isolated as much as possible in special corridors with a selected corps of sisters and students to care for them. No members of the medical or nursing staff lost their lives, but the majority of boarders and some sisters at the academy were stricken, as were twenty of the twenty-seven novices. Three sisters and one candidate died before the epidemic ended.

Early in 1919, another tragedy struck the congregation. During the night of February 27, a fire broke out in the Henry Boyle Catholic Home, burning the entire second and third floors of the building. Three of the residents died of smoke inhalation, and six others were injured by jumping or falling in an attempt to escape the flames. Sister Patrice Lahey was injured in her attempts to rescue an elderly patient; the superior of the home, Sister Delphine Keenan, died of shock and exposure a week later.[28]

In July of that year, Mother Marcella visited Archbishop Messmer of Milwaukee to obtain permission for the sisters to attend first Masses of nephews or cousins. For years the sisters had requested the privilege; for years it had been denied. Mother Marcella must have had some hope that this time the archbishop would relent. Instead, he restricted the reasons for a sister's visit home to the illness or very feeble health of a parent and the first Mass of a brother *only*. He forbade them to go home to attend family reunions. Mother Marcella reported that "His Grace also said, 'Sisters always want more liberties ... no further petitions will be considered, since this ruling is final."[29]

There was some good news that year. The appointment of Andrew Cardinal Frühwirth as protector of the congregation was a matter of satisfaction, as was the sisters' record-breaking fiscal year, which showed only $39,000 remaining to be paid on the convent mortgage.

REVISION OF CANON LAW

In 1917 the church's canon law, codified for the first time in six hundred years, was promulgated by Pope Benedict XV. Congregations of religious were told to revise their constitutions accordingly for submission to Rome. Mother Marcella secured the assistance of a canon lawyer, Charles Augustine, OSB, to bring the CSA constitutions in line with the new code of canon law.[30] In addition, she conferred with Archbishop Messmer regarding changes in the constitutions. Among the requests two would have made the constitutions more liberal. She asked for the equalization of rank and rights for all sisters and that sisters be allowed a home visit once every five years. The archbishop approved most of the requests but he thought a "periodical home visit would bring laxity into the community."[31]

The more that women's religious communities came under hierarchical control and management, the more limited their autonomy became. Regulations became even more stringent and detailed as the application of its prescriptions to the minute details of daily life became a science engaging a whole corps of priest experts.[32] Set times for prayers and daily Eucharist were imposed and "reaffirmed the view from Rome that religious life takes place in the convent, as opposed to streets, hospitals and homes of the poor."[33] The regulations, applying to all congregations, had another unfortunate result—that of destroying distinctions between religious congregations.[34]

Once the community's revised constitutions were in place, superiors were obliged to submit responses to a detailed Vatican questionnaire that measured how well the community was following the new canon law.[35] The Sisters of St. Agnes certainly felt the impact of the changes, and decades later sisters would comment on how much stricter the life they were living had become as compared to the time when they had entered.

THE TWENTIES

The Allies had won the War, but while Germany and Austria had been defeated, the harsh terms of the Treaty of Versailles ensured a future war. The Republican landslide of 1920 expressed the xenophobic and isolationist spirit that was sweeping the country. It was the period of the Jazz Age, silent movies, "the lost generation," bootleg gin, flivvers, flappers, the Charleston, and prohibition. At the same time the country was suffering from disillusionment and paranoia, evidenced by the Red Scare, the revival of the Ku Klux Klan, and severe restrictions on immigration.

By 1920, Catholics knew that their patriotism could no longer be questioned when statistics showed that Catholics served in the armed services in greater proportions than their fellow Americans. As American Catholics were becoming more prosperous, upwardly mobile, and more self-assured, they began entering the mainstream. They established more parishes, built more schools, and supported Catholic organizations; and religious vocations, while not plentiful, were prospering.

The congregation celebrated its golden jubilee in 1920.[36] The sisters found many reasons for gratitude. For the first time, the property and buildings of the congregation were free of debt. The celebration lasted three full days. The chapel was festooned with garlands of gold roses."[37] There was a special Mass honoring the twelve living pioneer sisters and celebrating the lives of the departed. Two dining rooms were filled with business people and benefactors, who were served a grand feast day dinner.

"There were three galvanized wash tubs full of potatoes, one hundred pies, and in New London old Sister Anna Von Feld from Kansas, the superior, baked fruit cakes in dish pans which the pastor brought in his truck. The candidates and novices who served and did dishes ate standing around the kitchen."[38] There would not have been a celebration without a celebratory poem and the singing of the novices and candidates. And it is impossible not to wonder if Sisters Clara Rehberg, Lidwina Hazotte, and Bernardine (Gertrude)

Laughlin did not quietly meet and recall Father Caspar Rehrl and his dream for the Agnes Sisters.

SISTER JEANNETTE ON STAGE

On August 30-31, 1921, the second annual meeting of the Wisconsin Conference of the Catholic Hospital Association of the United States and Canada met at St. Mary's Springs Academy.[39] Hosting this event was to the intense pleasure of the Sisters of St. Agnes and, indeed—if the local newspapers were correct—to the whole city of Fond du Lac. One of the speakers was Sister Jeannette Bodoh, who was in charge of the pathology laboratory at St. Agnes Hospital. In the reporter's assessment, her speech "not only proved a big feature of the convention but ... created much interest among persons interested in the hospital."[40]

Sister Jeannette's lengthy paper ranged far beyond the limited topic assigned and proved beyond doubt that she remained the straightforward young woman who had embarked on her life as a sister only twelve years previously. After a discussion of laboratories and the work of the technician, she criticized a sister-technician for remarking that too much was being demanded of them. She was appalled: "I cannot perceive that too much is being demanded of us. I think we should be grateful for the work, and we should thank Almighty God for bestowing upon our scientific workers talents to solve problems and to work out new methods .... Should we not be glad that we have brains, and hands, and eyes, and health with which to serve God and aid suffering humanity?"[41]

A little later in her talk, however, she assailed hospital administrators for the amount of work they were expecting of some sisters:

> One of the greatest impediments of progress in our hospitals lies in the fact that one Sister is sometimes given charge of too many departments .... I know a case in which one Sister, in a moderately large hospital, is in charge of the pathological laboratory, the X-ray laboratory, the pharmacy and the record department; her only aid being such as one partly trained assistant is able to render .... To promote reasonable enjoyment the work will have to be lightened so as to

give sufficient time ... for the practice of the prescribed religious exercises, for meals and sleep, for
quiet study, reading ... experimental work, outside
diversions and recreation.[42]

While Sister Jeannette's comments addressed the problems of
technicians, her remarks could have been, and undoubtedly were,
applied to the work of sister nurses as well.[43]

PROGRESS IN EDUCATION

In 1921, Wisconsin organized its Bureau of Nursing Education. Its
director, Miss Ada Eldridge, initiated sweeping changes in the state's
schools of nursing. She initiated the requirement that all nursing
school applicants complete a four-year high school course. She
demanded an organized health service for student nurses, a shorter
working day, two weeks of vacation annually, employment of more
graduate nurses for general duty, a more adequately prepared teaching staff, and a closer correlation of theory and practice through the
ward-teaching program. The program was enthusiastically accepted by the St. Agnes School of Nursing. The congregation met its
responsibilities by adding more faculty, improving facilities, and
preparing more sisters as nurses. The appointment of Sister Digna
Desch as director of the school to meet the new standards of the
National League of Nursing curriculum proved to be critical in the
life of the institution. During her twenty-six years of service, Sister
Digna earned the reputation of holding the School of Nursing and
the students to the highest professional standards.

In 1921 Mother Marcella reported great progress in strengthening the sisters' education.[44] As the sisters attended outside colleges
and universities, the community's economic burdens increased, nevertheless six thousand dollars had been expended on the sisters' education that year. It was her belief that the money would be well-
spent if the results meant better service and greater efficiency in the
works to which their lives were consecrated.[45] It was time, though,
for the congregation to have its own accredited teacher training
institution. Mother Marcella, determined that Agnesians meet and
preferably surpass educational standards, began the process of

obtaining normal school accreditation from the University of Wisconsin.

The most serious problem was the shortage of vocations. Mother Marcella, convinced that prayer was the answer, begged the sisters to pray that more young women would find their vocation in the congregation. She had been disappointed that only thirty candidates had entered because she had set her heart on fifty. By 1922, she was only three short of her goal of fifty when forty-seven young women entered, comprising the largest group ever to have joined the postulancy in one year. There remained the challenges of welcoming the candidates, discerning their fitness for religious life, forming them as community members, preparing them for their life's work (as teachers, health care professionals, or home-makers), and giving them appropriate mission assignments.

Mother Marcella was also looking forward to contributions the community could make to the field of education in the future. On September 29, 1921, the *Articles of Corporation(sic) of the Congregation of St. Agnes, Fond du Lac Wisconsin* were amended to give the congregation the "power to confer all such literary and scientific honors and degrees as are usually granted and conferred by similar institutions of learning, schools, academies, normal schools, colleges and schools for nurses."

Mother Marcella's first term ended in the summer of 1922. On June 26 of that year, St. Agnes High School was accredited by the state of Wisconsin. Before that date students of the high school had written certifying examinations for the Catholic University of America.[46] During this period the community added to its care St. Joseph High School (later called Decatur Catholic High School) in Decatur, Indiana and Girls' Catholic High School (later called Marian High School) in Hays, Kansas. The sisters also began staffing two parochial grade schools: St. Boniface in Richfield, Wisconsin, and St. Joseph in Fort Wayne, Indiana.

MOTHER MARCELLA'S SECOND ADMINISTRATION

It was time again for a general chapter. The new code of canon law[47] mandated that the general chapters of the congregations be composed of elected representatives instead of, simply, all perpetually professed religious. Preparing for such a radical change involved a great many decisions because the method of choosing delegates and their number was left to the individual institutes. The council decided that superiors of the larger houses were ex officio delegates and that smaller missions should be divided into groups and vote for one representative from each group. This was clearly a conservative decision because it made, in effect, members of the current administration the majority of chapter members. At the chapter, the twenty-seven delegates re-elected Mother Marcella and her council.

The chapter met on June 26-27, 1922.[48] The perennial issue of home visits was discussed.

There were other issues of greater and lesser moment. The use of the discipline was again raised. Although five sisters voted against it and twenty one to abolish it, the medieval practice remained. Several sisters objected to receiving persons of illegitimate birth into the community although the practice was sanctioned by canon law. It was agreed to pass over the matter in silence. The novice mistress favored a longer postulancy than was prescribed by canon law, but she was not successful in making the change. She also reiterated the need for simplicity in the motherhouse, especially in the cells. After a spirited discussion, it was finally agreed that black under-sleeves and gloves would be allowed and could be worn at any season.

The chapter voted against requiring uniforms in the parochial schools in which they taught because of the expense to the parents. A discussion ensued on the arts and, it was decided that preference would be given to those that were most useful.[49]

In 1922, forty-seven sisters received their state certificates as registered nurses. The assurance of sufficient personnel gave Mother Marcella the courage to continue with necessary building programs, as did her conviction that healing the sick was an important part of the gospel message.

1923—AN EVENTFUL YEAR

Journeying with Mother Marcella for a few months in 1923 and 1924 presents a picture of convent life that was far from that of the otherworldly, detached nun so beloved of nineteenth-century fiction. She spent the first few weeks of April on visitation at St. Agnes Hospital. While there she discussed plans for a $650,000 addition to St. Agnes Hospital with the architect.[50] That same month, twenty-four men raised a barn at St. Joseph's Springs, to the joy of the sisters who relived their own early days on family farms by cooking and serving a big dinner for them.[51]

With Mother Marcella in charge, summer time had become a time of study as well as a time for annual retreats.[52] A retreat in English was attended by 155 sisters, nineteen novices, and eighteen postulants. On June 28, the postulants were invested in their religious habits. Summer school followed with classes in English, Latin, algebra, geometry, language, pedagogy, and civics taught by the sisters while a professor from Marquette University taught physics.

Only one new school was accepted in 1923—and that one, rather unenthusiastically. Not only had other congregations refused St. Mary's School in Nanty-Glo, Pennsylvania, but Agnesians also were dubious about accepting work in a mining town. The pastor, Father John O'Connor, prevailed, and soon Mother Marcella was inquiring why the food bills were so low there. The sisters, delighted to be in Nanty-Glo, reported that the people there were most generous and "wonderful, even grinding flour for them."[53]

In August the general council met from August 18 to August 25 to arrange the personnel on the missions for the following year. An invitation to re-assume charge of St. Joseph School in Fort Wayne, Indiana was accepted, but distance prevented the council from sending four sisters to a parish in Spokane, Washington. Those decisions were important, but ordinary. But an additional decision had far greater repercussions than could have been predicted. On August 27, the council decided that since fifty or sixty postulants, novices, and sisters did not speak German, morning and evening prayers and sermons on Sundays and holy days would be in English. While in retrospect it seems extraordinary that the congregation did not come to this decision during the war, when so many churches stopped providing sermons in German, this seemingly innocuous decision threw the community into a turmoil that created repercussions for years to come.[54]

On August 31, Mother Marcella made that announcement to the sisters at the motherhouse. Although the council had expected some "*slight* opposition" because of the few sisters from Germany who had been in the United States between twenty and sixty years, the intensity of the reaction among some of the sisters was astonishing. The reasons for this opposition are obscure, although it was noted that some sisters were under the impression that German was the language spoken in heaven. The original three or four sisters in opposition were joined by a Bavarian, a Hungarian, and a German-American, all of whom spoke English. The council mistakenly thought that the furor would soon be over, but the faction soon grew to twelve, and included more American-born sisters. They would speak only German at recreation, "when they attended it." Furthermore, the *Annals* state that "according to their own testimony they annoyed the confessors in season and out of it."[55]

As the days went by, the level of civility of the insurgents further declined and their behavior became even more appalling. There were confrontations, even threats of physical violence.[56] Finally, one of the sisters behaved in such a shocking manner that, when Mother Marcella reacted calmly and kindly, "She was seized with remorse and falling on her knees craved pardon for her outrageous conduct …. Mother told her that she might retract publicly in the refectory after supper and make the Way of the Cross once in reparation for the public scandal she gave."[57] A few days later, Mother Marcella reminded the sisters that if they wished to send some of their belongings to the sisters in Europe, they had her permission. One of them again attacked her: "You want to contribute toward sisters in Europe, but you want to drive your own old German sisters out of the house..."[58]

The arrival of the extraordinary confessors for the Ember Days confessions gave the insurgents another opportunity to create trouble. They went from confessor to confessor to learn how much each knew, greatly scandalizing the fathers in the process. The council came to the conclusion that open rebellion seemed imminent. When the convent chaplain advised Mother Marcella to choose the lesser of two evils by quietly beginning the next week's prayers in German, she thought it best to accept the suggestion of resuming prayers in German "at the sacrifice of *principle* for the sake of peace." The secretary added the further comment that "during those weeks of intense suffering, neither Mother Marcella, nor any member of the council nor any of the English speaking sisters even showed resentment in any way nor said an unkind word to those sisters who so deeply offended against justice."[59] On October 6, the community resumed prayers in German.[60]

ILLNESS AND OTHER MISFORTUNES

On January 20, 1924, Mother Marcella was taken ill after Mass with severe pain, vomiting, and a fever of 103 degrees. She recovered in a few weeks to face another series of problems. The plans for the hospital addition were going forward, but financing such a major project was difficult. While still under the doctor's care, she had to deal with negotiating the loan. The definitor general of the Capuchins, Father Antonine Willmer, gave her directions for asking the Holy Father for permission to seek a loan of $600,000.[61] The congregation was to state the amount of the debt to be contracted, the purpose of the loan, the amount of the present indebtedness of the congregation, the time in which the loan was to be paid and about what percent of it each year, and whether all the congregation's property was sufficient to cover the debts. The archbishop's consent also had to be included with the congregation's letter.[62]

On February 15, a tragic accident happened at St. Joseph Spring Farm. A young man of eighteen was killed while working in one of the sand pits. The frozen sand caved in on him and struck him on the abdomen, causing a hemorrhage. The last rites were administered and it was noted that "he resigned his soul to its maker, without regret."[63]

Summer came and with it the heaviest precipitation on record in Fond du Lac. The *Annals* reported that a cloudburst of eight inches of rain deluged the city on the night of August 3. Both branches of the Fond du Lac River overran their banks and torrents of water from two to three feet deep flooded the east and the west sides of the city filling basements with sewage, causing heavy damage. De Neveu Creek overflowed and poured fifteen inches of water into the basement of St. Agnes Hospital flooding the storerooms and kitchen, putting all gas and electric stoves out of order, then entering the X-Ray department, spoiling delicate equipment and destroying photographic plates filed in the cabinets. The pathology laboratory suffered equal damage. The tunnels, new and old, leading to the motherhouse, were filled with water and these flooded the whole convent basement to a depth of eight or more inches. Both motherhouse and hospital suffered considerable damage. Trains were ditched between Fond du Lac and Milwaukee and miles of track were washed away. Property loss in the city was estimated to exceed a million dollars.[64] The devastation was quietly accepted as an act of God. The flood was never again mentioned in the *Annals* but a retaining wall was constructed between the creek and the hospital.[65]

In September a happier occasion was the formal opening in the motherhouse of a long-desired accredited normal school. Under the charge of Sister Clare M., six students studied algebra, arithmetic, English, grammar, composition, spelling, psychology, physiology, educational methods, and American History. Another forty-six students were in high school. Sister Angeline Kamp was principal and also taught English III and IV and Latin I, II, and III. Sister Regina Wallesch taught algebra I, mathematics II, physics, German I, and penmanship. Sister Borgia Kelly taught English I and II, American and Medieval History and arithmetic. Sister Mary Luke Shouse, a novice, taught grammar and geography to the seventh and eighth grades.

RENOVATIONS AT ST. AGNES HOSPITAL

In the meantime, the company that the congregation had employed to install the electric lights in the powerhouse had become insolvent, and other plans had to be made to complete the project. The great expense of the renovations made it impossible to follow all the suggestions made by the medical staff for renovating St. Agnes Hospital. However, discussions continued; the floor plans were rearranged; and the chapel was enlarged and its location changed. Eventually, everyone was reasonably satisfied with an addition that would bring the capacity of the hospital to 250 beds.

There was, fortunately, support from the Fond du Lac community. An article in the *Daily Commonwealth* pointed out that the hospital had handled 38,273 cases and 1,725 births between its opening in 1896 and the end of 1923. According to a tabulation of the 3,402 patients treated there during the year 1923, more than 2,000 were non-residents of Fond du Lac. Sixteen states and forty-six of Wisconsin's seventy-one counties were represented on the hospital's roll of patients.[66] In a speech of support, Episcopalian Bishop Reginald H. Weller said:

To my mind the whole responsibility for the hospital
rests upon the Sisters of St. Agnes. It is their broad
vision and their timeless work and support that has
made this institution possible. The Sisters have not
asked the community for the $700,000 which has
been necessary to invest in the building of the addition. It is going to cost a very large sum, however, to
equip this addition for it must be equipped with
apparatus and furniture that will make it possible to
render service of the highest order .... The drive, to
secure this fund, $100,000, is soon to start. Support
it in a generous manner. God's blessing will rest on
those who give to relieve human pain and to prolong
human life.[67]

That these improvements could have been made only at the cost
of the personal sacrifices of the sisters out on the missions is clear
from the letters Mother Marcella wrote to them. On October 7,
1924, Mother Marcella wrote to account for the financial status of
the congregation. She began by informing the sisters of the debt the
congregation had assumed to modernize St. Agnes Hospital:

The amount of the contracts is $550,000. They went
beyond our expectations, but this is usually the case,
so there was nothing left but to shoulder the burden
bravely and trust in God. Since May 1920 when the
debt which rested on the congregation at the beginning of this administration was wiped out the
Congregation has paid the following: For farm buildings and improvements $31,000; on account new
Power Plant, $142,000; on account contracts for new
wing $98,000. We have in the banks, $130,000. On
October 1, 1924 the Congregation assumed a debt
of $250,000 at 6 percent interest for the erection of
the hospital addition. This leaves about $100,000 to
be made up within the present school year.
    Around the first of each month the architects
issue certificates showing how much of the contract
price each contractor is entitled to for the work done

within the month previous. Shall we be able to meet these obligations? It rests with you and you have never failed us. It will be a great help if you will arrange to send a check for what you can spare each month. Every little bit will help, so don't wait until you can send a large check. In this way we hope it may not be necessary for us to assume a new debt.[68]

Meanwhile, a group of doctors and prominent businessmen launched a hospital community fund drive to raise $100,000 for the furnishing and equipping of the new addition. It was not just those who could offer financial support that were important to the success of the hospital. The congregational *Annals* for October 21, 1924 praised four women who had met weekly at the hospital for five years and "spent entire days there" making hospital garments band-ages, surgical dressings etc. The women were the nucleus of the women's auxiliary that has provided the hospital with a constant and dedicated group of supporters through the years.

The annual Christmas letter further updated the sisters on the hospital project. Noting that the hospital addition was enclosed and heated, she wished that the sisters "could see the noble building made possible by [their] united savings .... We need hardly say how we appreciate your loyal cooperation and the promptness with which your monthly contributions reach us." Mother Marcella went on to ask the missions to help furnish the hospital rooms with each mission making two pairs of pillowcases ornamented with a crochet insertion size 22 1/2 x 36 inches. Other items would be welcomed such as dresser tops, 19x40, washable goods, table tops, 19x32, etc.[69] The following Easter, Mother Marcella reported that the congrega-tion was financially sound but did need money.[70]

HONORS AND DISAPPOINTMENTS

When she reported on the finances, Mother Marcella added an additional piece of news that, although it must have gratified her, was nonetheless delivered almost apologetically. She wrote that because the *Catholic School Journal* had mentioned a prize-winning book written by a Sister of St. Agnes, she felt she should give the sis-ters some background on the volume. The Knights of Columbus had sponsored a writing contest open to teachers in normal schools. The subject was to be the teaching of history coordinated with the teaching of civics and national responsibilities in the elementary schools. Sisters Angeline Kamp and Clare M. Goodwin had collaborated on the prize-winning volume. They not only received $750, a large sum at the time, but one of the judges insisted the work be published. The book, *History Curricula by the Sisters of St. Agnes*, appeared under the Macmillan imprint. The cost was seventy-five cents plus postage. Sisters Angeline and Clare M. were invited to teach the following summer at Catholic University, but community needs prevented them from accepting the invitation.[71]

At this time, it was not customary for Sisters of St. Agnes, nor indeed for any religious, to attract the attention of the public. A student at the time, Sister Claude Feldner, provides another case in point. A public performance was required before she could receive a degree in music from Fort Hays Kansas State College, but it took a great deal of stretching the rules by the college's music department before the congregation allowed Sister Claude, invisible to the audience, to fulfill the requirements for her degree.[72]

An unexpected disappointment came as the sisters worked on the revision of the constitutions when a question arose regarding the validity of their membership in the Third Order of St. Francis. From the time Father Francis Haas had been their director, the sisters had treasured their connection with St. Francis Assisi and their tie to Franciscan spirituality through their affiliation with the Capuchin Third Order. To support their claim to Third Order status, the congregation sent photographs of the pertinent documents to the Capuchin provincial in Detroit and to the definitor general in Rome. However, on January 10, 1926, Mother Marcella received a letter from the definitor general, who seemed to be "of the opinion that our Community has not been aggregated to the Third Order of St. Francis."[73] Then a few days later the community was heartened by a letter from the Capuchin provincial "encouraging us to continue our practice of gaining the precious privileges of the Third Order of St. Francis, as were heretofore accorded us."[74] Another encouraging letter arrived from Detroit, but finally on Sunday, January 23, the convent chaplain made a disappointing announcement based on a strict reading of one particular canon law: "Whosoever has pronounced vows—in any religious institute cannot simultaneously belong to any Third Order, even though he was once enrolled in such a one. The Sisters of Saint Agnes, who at one time, were enrolled in the Third Order of St. Francis, are severed from this enrollment by the above mentioned Canon."[75]

MOTHER MARCELLA'S LEGACY

Mother Marcella had enjoyed remarkably good health until December 1920. She was visiting the houses in New York when she was stricken with double pneumonia. Her life was preserved at this point, possibly because of the sacrifice of another. Her brief biography noted:

> Our good Mother grew worse, and when the physician pronounced her case hopeless, Sister Geraldine (Mary Connelly) betook herself to prayer, and kneeling before the statue of Our Lady besought God, through the intercession of His Blessed Mother, to be pleased to accept the sacrifice of her own life, and to spare Mother Marcella for the good of our Congregation. Apparently our dear Lord was pleased with her prayer. Mother recovered from her illness, but before the lapse of one year our Sister was no more.[76]

Although Mother Marcella remained active after her illness, her health did not return. In December 1924, she was discovered to be suffering from pernicious anemia. That same year St. Joseph's School in Fort Wayne was opened and nuns joined the staff of Sacred Heart High School in Yonkers, New York and St. Mary High School in Oshkosh, Wisconsin.

In January 1925 Sister Seraphine Morrissey died. One of the last of the pioneer sisters, her death was a severe blow to Mother Marcella. As the year wore on, Mother's health worsened, but she attended the dedication of the addition to St. Agnes Hospital on July 21, 1925. Within a week she became seriously ill. From that time there were crises the sisters believed she could not possibly survive, then periods when she rallied and attempted to continue her work. She lived for eighteen more months continuing in her office as best she could. "Her death was peaceful as was the life that preceded it. She rendered her soul into the hands of her Creator at 9:30 a.m. on June 9, 1926."[77]

As a spiritual leader, Mother Marcella had done all that she could to emphasize the importance of the rule. She believed that there was nothing more conducive to the happiness of the community than the faithful observance of the holy vows and rules, and she did all in her power to uphold them. She believed in the ideal of nuns serving the world, but not being of it. As an educator, she did all she could to raise the educational standards of the congregation and to prepare her sisters for the future. Responsible for the well-being of the sisters and their ministries, she was a faithful guardian of the goods of the congregation. As a human being, she had disciplined herself in the practice of the virtues she revered, particularly charity, which she maintained even when tried most sorely.

In the short sketch of her life, Mother Marcella's biographer wrote that she "possessed a truly noble character, was broadminded and liberal and by her amiable and gentle manners endeared herself to her Sisters and to all who had the good fortune of her acquaintance, both in and out of the Convent. She was zealous for regular observance of the Constitutions and for the practice of charity among the Sisters."[78]

Sister Vera Naber, who knew her well, wrote, "Without doubt she was a great soul, and no matter what tribute was paid to her it could not equal, much less exaggerate, the beauty of her life. Her deeds live after her and speak for her."[79]

There was much that was similar in the characters of Mother Antonia and Mother Marcella. Although one was the daughter of a German immigrant farmer and the other was the daughter of a prosperous German gentleman, the two were alike in their prudence, their steadfastness, and their trustworthiness. While they were strict, they were kind, and they did not ask more from others than they were willing to give themselves. They were loved because each in her own way was the prudent woman of scripture. They did their duty quietly and loved their community. Mother Antonia's task had been to follow the path laid down by Mother Agnes and to stabilize the congregation. Both Fond du Lac, Wisconsin, and Hays, Kansas benefited from Mother Antonia's willingness to meet the health care needs of those communities. Mother Marcella, far more aware of the world, tried to maintain the spirit of religious life while doing all she could to develop the sisters professionally as well as spiritually. Both did much for the congregation they loved, but it was their "acts of the heart" that were their real gifts to the Sisters of St. Agnes.

Chapter VIII

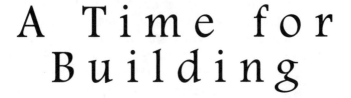

A Time for Building

Although the women chosen by the Agnesians to lead them during the years before Vatican II were alike in their fundamental values, their desire to conform their lives to God's will, their dedication to their sisters, and their willingness to support congregational ministries, their individuality guaranteed that the legacies they left were uniquely their own. The first and most revered of those sisters was Sister Joseph Wolford.

The America that existed the day that Sister Joseph Wolford became superior general bore little relation to the America of 1861, the year she had been born. By the time she assumed office, the United States had emerged from a civil war, had become an empire, fought in World War I and had almost completed the Second Industrial Revolution. The modern city had taken shape. Mass production was leading to the creation of an America in which individualism was sacrificed to conformity and workers were controlled by rules rather than by individual relationships. The immigrant church was becoming an American church as Catholics who had rooted themselves in American soil developed a distinctly American style of living their faith. Society had benefited from the labor of Catholics as well as through their churches, hospitals, orphanages, and schools. Despite a significant degree of anti-Catholic hostility remaining in the country, Catholics were proud of their church and their country and optimistic about the future.

MOTHER JOSEPH WOLFORD

The daughter of John and Catherine Rufin Wolford, Philomene Wolford, was born September 4, 1861, in Louisville, Ohio. While she was still a child, her parents moved to Plymouth, Indiana. There she had the opportunity to attend nearby St. Mary's Academy at Notre Dame, Indiana. By the time she was nineteen, she had become a schoolteacher. While she was teaching in northern Indiana, she met the Sisters of St. Agnes, who had been at St. Mary's Parish in Crown Point since 1882. When she sought counseling regarding her vocation from the pastor, Philip Guethoff, OM Cap., he suggested that she might fit in with the Agnesians who were young, struggling, and in need of help.[1] Although Philomene was certainly acquainted with better-established communities, she chose on February 15, 1886,to cast her lot with the poor and relatively unknown Agnesians.

After her religious profession in 1888, Sister Joseph was sent to Our Lady Queen of Angels in New York City, where she taught until 1892, when she was assigned to teach at the motherhouse. During the day she taught the novices and candidates; on Monday nights, the sisters living nearby came to the motherhouse for her classes in education.

Sister Joseph was an excellent teacher, but from the stories her students told she may not always have found it easy to restrain her naturally quick tongue. She never preached but taught by virtue of her own example. When she spoke to the candidates and novices about writing letters, she said, "Write those things which you would say if you had an opportunity for a ten-minute conversation; do not be frivolous nor use slang expressions; on the other hand, don't preach a sermon either; but never close a letter unless you have said something which directs the mind of the reader to God."[2]

With the death of Mother Agnes in March 1905, Sister Joseph was unanimously chosen as third councilor to fill the vacancy in the generalate. In 1909, following the death of Sister Regina Deiler, she became first councilor and left her teaching duties to serve as administrator of St. Agnes Hospital for one year. She was re-elected councilor in 1911; in 1916 and 1922 she was elected to serve as vicaria under Mother Marcella.

Upon the death of Mother Marcella, it was Sister Joseph's responsibility as vicaria to assume the duties of the mother general until her successor could be elected. The congregation's next step was somewhat unclear because the new canon law had changed rules regarding chapters of election, and the revised constitutions, although sent to Rome, had not yet been approved. To clarify matters, the congregation applied to Archbishop Messmer for guidance. Asked to set the date and preside over the election, the archbishop chose December 30, 1926. He extended the present term of office to six years and six months, both to allow the next general chapter to take place within the summer vacation and also because the new constitutions had yet to arrive from Rome. [3]

According to the new constitutions, only sisters in vows for ten years, counting from their first profession, were entitled to be delegates. The delegates would all be superiors of houses in which there were twenty-four perpetually professed sisters, besides one delegate to be elected by and from among the members of this house. Such houses constituted separate units. All other houses which were not separate units were to be divided into districts. [4]

The *Annals* do not reveal the number of delegates, but Sister Joseph Wolford was elected superior general; Sister Aloysia Leikem, vicar assistant; Sisters Germaine Cassin and Louisa Wolsiffer, councilors; Sister Angeline Kamp, councilor and secretary general; and Sister Meinrad Heiser, treasurer general.

When Sister Joseph's election was announced to the community on December 30, 1926 and the *Te Deum* of jubilation was sung, the sisters must have felt quietly relieved. They knew Mother Joseph; they had seen her quietly carry out the wishes of Mother Marcella. They were not expecting changes of any import, and they were accurate in that assumption. The constitutions had been revised and accepted. It was her duty to follow them herself and encourage others along the way. She sought no glory for any sister or for the congregation as a whole, and the words she wrote to the sisters she applied equally to herself: "May you always be humble handmaids of Jesus, working and sacrificing for Him, in your simple Convent

Home, wherever it may be, like Joseph and Mary in their home at Nazareth."[5]

Sister Joseph was remembered by the sisters as a tiny round woman with red cheeks and sparkling eyes, busy, at times abrupt, but always kind. In her history Sister Vera Naber, who knew Mother Joseph as well as she would allow herself to be known, wrote that "she conformed her every action to the prescriptions of the Rule even to the minutest detail.[6] She was exact with herself without being exacting with others."[7] It was said that when she changed bedrooms, she carried all of her possessions in her apron. "Obedience seemed to be her forte, and she rendered it exactly and unquestionably to the spoken word and the printed precept alike....Although she had a keen intellect, she chose as companions during recreation the older Sisters, some of whom because of deafness or senility had some difficulty in following conversations. If a sister asked for advice, she could be sure of receiving just what she needed, but Sister Joseph rarely imposed it upon anyone unsolicited, even after she became mother superior."[8]

Mother Joseph "rarely spoke of herself, her opinions, her interests, and the principles which motivated her actions,"[9] wrote Sister Vera; but the retreat notes, resolutions, and quotations that Mother Joseph had collected and treasured throughout the years reveal the path she chose to attain union with God. All spoke of the emptying of self, which she saw as indispensable if she were to achieve her goal of union with Christ in his passion and death. A paper entitled *Resolution: I Will Practice Union with God by Complete Surrender to the Will of God* listed eight areas that could provide occasions of surrendering one's own will to God's: humiliations, poverty and privations, obedience, prayer, suffering, recreation, employment, and daily routine. Another list, was called *Catalog of Trivial but Regular Mortifications Which May Be Performed in an Unassuming Way*. The seventh practice on this list reads: "In general, I shall seek to have conditions a little short of comfortable. I have found out, from experience, that I am almost most well when not quite well. Therefore, during spiritual reading, I shall never sit. When sitting, I shall never use the back of the chair. I shall never sit with knees crossed. I shall never use the banister. I shall never take more than one step at a time." Number thirteen reads, "If I happen to wake up during the night, I shall (just once in one night) make a prostration at my bedside, towards the nearest Blessed Sacrament. (Kneel with hands on floor, and touch the latter with forehead.) The whole act of penance is to last about twenty seconds, in atonement for sins committed by priests and religious especially."[10]

Years later Sister Muriel Tarr wrote of receiving a few minutes of spiritual guidance from Mother Joseph. She was leaving chapel when Sister Joseph called to her:

> "Dear Sister," she said, "Do you know how to spend every hour of your day in union with the Passion of our dear Lord?"
> "No," said I, "except by a general intention."
> "You come to me tomorrow; I'll have a scheme written for you."
> The next day she gave me a tiny spiral notebook that had been used for advertising purposes and in it she had written the hours of the day from rising until night prayer, paralleling each hour with some action of the Passion. When I thanked her for taking time to write that out for me, she said, "That's all right, Sister, just remember that the real meeting place of lovers is on Calvary."[11]

While Mother Joseph found her ideals summed up in a statement she had copied from a publication, *The True Religious*, others found there a description of the way she actually had lived her life: "The cornerstone of the character of every religious must be prayer and calm; and her whole life must be dominated by the rule of her sacred vocation, the practice of true charity, her spiritual exercises, meditation and rosary, tranquility and peace in selfless resignation in wrongs and trials, recollection and union with God."[12]

For twenty-one years Mother Joseph had lived in the motherhouse, and it was from that vantage point that she had seen the life of the community. Now she was to acquaint herself with every mission, the needs of the institutions, and the needs of the sisters active in ministry. This she did with a style of her own. Terse, prompt, and decisive, she was considered an excellent administrator and once she had decided upon a course of action, she was inflexible. Archbishop

Stritch[13] said often that he would like to have transferred her to the archdiocesan chancery.[14]

Mother Joseph did all in her power to prepare the sisters for teaching. She taught methods classes and the philosophy of education; she made sure that the sisters made every effort to become certified by the state. Yet she differed from her predecessor in one significant respect. She "had no inclination to further the cause of higher education for the sisters."[15] She believed that affording more opportunities for some sisters than for others would create distinctions among the sisters. However, distinctions in the community already abounded. Domestic sisters were differently ranked from teaching and nursing sisters. A clear distinction existed between *superiors* and *inferiors* (at least the blunt vocabulary was honest), and still another existed between elementary and high school teachers. And, of course, hospitals were intrinsically hierarchical.

SISTERS IN A CHANGING WORLD

With the exception of the demands of their ministries, the sisters had little to do with the rapidly changing world about them. By 1926, the year that Mother Joseph assumed office, two cultural changes pointed out even more clearly the gap between women who had left home for the convent and their sisters who had stayed behind. Hemlines that had risen above the knees, an obvious indication of a broader liberation of women in general, made the sister's unchanging habit a sign of greater symbolic distance between her life and society's. By that same year of 1926, the radio, invented in 1907, had become part of the ordinary American household, widening as well as distorting the nation's view of the world. Needless to say, it would be some years before the radio would be introduced into convents.

It seems probable that Mother Joseph spent little time reflecting on the changing culture of American society. As she saw it, her role was to uphold traditions, customs, and, most important, the rule—which she saw as a powerful means of bringing one closer to God. All the great rules, of which the *Constitutions of the Sisters of St. Agnes* was but one offshoot, contained fundamental prescriptions that had been worked out through the centuries and had given great spiritual blessings to the church and society, as well as to the individuals who had embraced them. The constitutions deserved respect and even reverence. When a sister was buried, the little black book that had prescribed some of the minutest details of her life was placed in her coffin. On her head was placed a crown of thorns, a symbol laden with meaning and clearly indicative of the cost of the faithful following of the way of life she had vowed to embrace.

VISITATIONS

Mother Joseph officially began her duties on December 30, 1926; in actuality she had been the guiding force in the congregation almost all of the previous two years. Only two weeks after her election she began to visit the convents. The five hundred sisters in the community were her first priority. On January 15, Mother Joseph visited the missions in New York: Yonkers, Harlem, Unionport (The Bronx), and the Leo House. In Pennsylvania she visited Altoona, Carnegie, and Nanty-Glo, returning to Fond du Lac on February 26. In March she held visitation for three days at St. Agnes Hospital and in April, at St. Mary's Springs Academy. On April 18, she traveled to Michigan, visiting missions in Menominee, Marquette, Assinins, and Houghton, not returning until May 7. The summer was filled with sisters coming back to Fond du Lac for retreats, summer school, and medical attention. Remaining in Wisconsin, she visited the Boyle Home in September and Kewaskum, Hudson, and Two Rivers in October. On October 28, she left for Kansas, not returning to the motherhouse until December 6.[16]

With all Mother Joseph's traveling, community business often had to be conducted by mail. During one of her absences, the perennial issue of home visits arose again. It had proved difficult to interpret the new canon law. As she later told Archbishop Messmer, "We thought that the term 'grave reasons' seemed to restrict our privileges in regard to Sisters' visits to their parents' home, rather than to give them more latitude as the Sisters desire."[17] The archbishop prudently advised her to refer the matter to the definitor general of the Capuchins at Rome. Father Antonine, in effect, told her that the mothers general had more latitude to grant the sisters permission to visit their parents under the new canon law.[18] It is doubtful that this was the answer she would have preferred.[19]

NEW HORIZONS IN FORMATION AND HIGHER EDUCATION

One of the most marked effects of the 1917 revision of canon law was the extension of the novitiate from one year to two years. The first year, to be known as "the canonical novitiate," was to prepare the novice for her vows. The classes were to be exclusively directed to that end. Ideally, the second-year was to be devoted to professional preparation; in actuality most second-year novices were sent out to teach. Novices frequently were assigned to nearby missions so that they could take evening and Saturday classes at the motherhouse in addition to their summer classes. This necessitated planning a curriculum that would satisfy both the standards for normal schools in the state of Wisconsin and the requirements for the universities where the sisters would ordinarily complete their degrees.

In 1927, the motherhouse ended its elementary program [20]and intensified its efforts to attain accreditation for its teacher education program. In March of that year, a representative from the Department of Education in Madison visited the normal school in the convent to make recommendations.[21] That same month Mother Joseph and Sister Angeline went to Loyola University in Chicago to arrange for the transfer of advanced credits from the convent to Loyola University. The sisters must have been taken aback when the Jesuits suggested college algebra, solid geometry, trigonometry, history, science, and languages for the first two years' work. Philosophy, which had to be reserved for a college student's last two years, had to be taken at a Catholic university. Fortunately, the congregation was able to make arrangements with the extension division of the University of Wisconsin for college work completed at the convent during the months of July and August.

Edward Fox, SJ, president of Marquette University in Milwaukee, was also approached to recommend professors to teach summer school at the convent. Although the university's own needs made loaning any of their professors impossible, he promised to send representatives to Fond du Lac to examine both the convent normal school and the school of nursing with a view to accrediting them to Marquette. This would give the convent the right to employ its own teachers to teach in the school and to accept the three years of training in the nurses' school as an equivalent of freshman and sophomore college work. The president also suggested changing the identity of the institution from normal school junior college.[22] The last suggestion was never acted upon.

MORE CHALLENGES

The year 1927 was not without other unexpected and expensive problems. When almost half the eighty-three cattle on the farm were discovered to be tubercular,[23] purchasing milk and butter for the hospital and motherhouse created additional expenses. More than an ordinary amount of illness spread among the teaching sisters that year. Postulants were sent out to teach to fill their empty places. The assignment was hard on them, the other sisters in the school, and, not infrequently, the pupils. Worse, the addition of the two-year novitiate caused a sister shortage so acute that some pastors were asked to hire secular teachers and, although they were councilors, Sister Angeline was again given responsibility for St. Mary's Springs Academy, while Sister Vera was sent to St. Joseph's in Decatur. Mother Joseph gave up her projected four-month tour of the missions in Indiana and Ohio and returned to Fond du Lac in less than a month.

Exactly one year after her assumption of office, Mother Joseph followed in the footsteps of her predecessors by issuing directives that emphasized the observance of the sisters' enclosure. Letter writing was restricted. Sisters could write relatives once or twice a year and parents more frequently. If a member had a blood sister also in religious life, she could write that person three times a year, but to other sisters only when necessary. She could write to former pupils only when asked for advice or counsel, and to other laypersons, only in regard to business. Meals were ordinarily to be taken in silence. At the noon meal, the table reading should consist of the *Roman Martyrology*,[24] part of the gospel, and a short reading from some spiritual book. At supper, the reading should consist of part of the *Acts of the Apostles* or the epistles, a short sketch from the life of the saint for the day, or a reading from another spiritual book. The community was observing monastic practices as much as was possible for sisters engaged in active ministry.[25]

Although Mother Joseph considered maintaining the separation of the convent from the world a priority, a great deal of the time and energy of her administration was spent in maintaining the quality and standards of congregational institutions. St. Mary's Springs Academy, St. Agnes School of Nursing, and St. Anthony Hospital in Hays, Kansas, all needed additional buildings at the same time. Even the Henry Boyle Catholic Home for the Aged needed a larger chapel.

The two buildings that St. Mary's Springs Academy occupied had originally been a sanatarium. Not only was it time to erect an up-to-date school building, but because the school had been opened to day students in 1927, a small but increasing enrollment made a new building a necessity. Mother Joseph wasted no time. She negotiated with an architect and construction began. Meanwhile, when the pastor of St. Joseph's Parish in Fond du Lac applied for teachers for his new school, in spite of the "great dearth" of sisters, she deemed it advisable to accept St. Joseph's School even at the cost of personal sacrifice.[26]

By the time the new building at the Springs was dedicated, Mother Joseph had it entirely paid for through some combination of financial expertise and wizardry.[27] That proved fortunate, because within a month of its completion, a delegation of eight gentlemen from Hays, Kansas called on her to discuss building an addition to St. Anthony Hospital. Emphasizing the necessity of a bigger facility, each man in turn gave a talk on the growth and prosperity of western Kansas and especially of Hays. Mother Joseph informed them that the congregation could not at present assume such a large financial obligation, but added that the council might consider the proposition if Hays and vicinity would contribute one-half the cost.[28]

That same year, after the hiatus of 1928, a class of novices double the usual size was professed. Sisters who were doing the work of two were given assistance; a few elderly sisters retired; and it was possible to accept two parish schools, Presentation School in North Fond du Lac and St. Ann High School in Walker, Kansas.

THE DEPRESSION

Suddenly, beyond the convent walls, the once booming stock market crashed on Friday, October 25, 1929. Nevertheless, in the face of the precipitous drop in stock values, bank failures, and rising unemployment, the following May found Mother Joseph and Sister

Aloysia looking over the plans for the new unit to St. Anthony Hospital.[29] After the usual trimming of ambitions, they found that the addition would cost approximately $235,000. It would add fifty more beds, a laboratory, a chapel, a maternity department, rest rooms for the doctors and nurses, a new refrigeration plant, a nursery, diet kitchens, enlarged engine rooms, and a laundry. On March 12, ground was broken. In May and again in September, Mother Joseph made the trip to Kansas "to look after the progress" of the new building.[30]

Also at this time Julia Boyle, wishing to erect a memorial to her husband Henry, agreed to add a wing to Boyle Catholic Home to serve as a chapel. On October 1, 1930, a new chapel seating seventy-five people was dedicated. After the Solemn High Mass, Rt. Rev. Monsignor B. G. Traudt conducted a ceremony of investiture in which Mrs. Boyle received the Golden Cross from His Holiness, Pope Pius XI. The medal of distinction "Pro Ecclesia et Pontifice" was bestowed in recognition of the many benefactions that had been made over the years by the Henry Boyle family.[31]

The *Annals* of 1930 and 1931 show Mother Joseph continually making small but regular payments for the construction of the hospital addition. In January 1931 the building was dedicated. The *Annals* recorded the event with justifiable pride in the congregation: "They [Mother Joseph and her companion] report that the new structure is nearly perfect—no criticisms having been made by anyone, including the architect .... The people of Hays are proud of their hospital and contributed fifty thousand dollars towards its erection. They have already furnished twenty-two rooms and the nursery apartments."[32]

The same month that the hospital was dedicated, Mother Joseph received permission from the archbishop to build a nurses' home for St. Agnes School of Nursing. Its projected cost was between $200,000 and $250,000.[33] The five-story brick building was dedicated in December 1931. The first two floors had classrooms, a combination gymnasium and auditorium, lounges, and a library. The three upper floors had private rooms for 137 students, a number that would allow for a reasonable increase in students. It was a tremendous project to undertake almost simultaneously with the academy building, but Mother Joseph wanted to save on costs by purchasing large amounts of supplies at a discount.

By the early 1930s, more sisters were attending universities.[34] The Knights of Columbus of Milwaukee provided eight scholarships for sisters to attend summer school at Marquette University. For several years, Norbertine Fathers conducted summer school at the convent. In 1930, 120 students were enrolled: eighty sisters and forty novices and postulants. Of these, sixty-eight students were doing college work and fifty-two were still in high school. In the next year, the total number of students rose to 150.[35]

Meanwhile, the archbishop was making plans for the education of the sisters of the archdiocese. His goal was to preserve the Catholic philosophy of education by providing a Catholic program of teacher training for the sisters. He wanted to provide extension work in certain convents with the faculty composed of secular teachers, priests, and sisters who would also belong to the Marquette faculty. "The idea," he said, "is to have mass education among the Sisterhoods, not only the individual who goes to Washington to get her Ph.D."[36] He also promoted inter-community cooperation by forming a representative committee of seven sisters to plan for the benefit of all of the sisters in the archdiocese.

For the congregation, 1930 and 1931 were years much like 1929. It was not until another year or two had passed that the full effects of the depression were felt. Around the country the number of jobless continued to rise. Mortgages on houses and farms were foreclosed, and real property values diminished. Grocery stores that had extended credit to their impoverished customers found themselves overextended and had to close. At the Leo House in New York, the congregation consented to forego salaries rather than see its collapse.[37] In Fond du Lac, the hungry began to approach both the hospital and the convent. Mother Joseph asked the sister cooks to serve a substantial meal to anyone who asked for it. In the month of August 1931, over 1,200 meals were given to the hungry at the hospital and about four hundred meals were served at the motherhouse.[38]

The hospitals had fewer patients, although no one was denied an emergency surgery whether the doctors were paid or not. At St. Agnes Hospital one floor had to be closed. The sisters found dismissing faithful workers, particularly the cleaning girls who had no other means of support, extremely difficult and kept on as many as they possibly could.[39]

Throughout the early thirties, the downward economic spiral continued. One-fourth of the work force was unemployed; steel production was down to 12 percent of capacity; the gross national product fell to 67 percent of the 1929 level. Shanty towns sprang up around the country. Working men became hoboes. Families went without meat and fresh vegetables for months while crops rotted in the fields because prices were too low to make harvesting worthwhile.

Parishes were hard hit. Those hardest hit were in Kansas, where the sisters went for months without salaries. The troubles had begun in March 1931 when Ellis County experienced one of its worst blizzards ever. Next came damaging heat with temperatures often hovering around 100 degrees. The year 1933 brought a poor wheat crop. Then came the dust storms.

Decades of plowing up the grasslands to plant wheat had led to the loss of ground cover. When years of drought came, strong winds whipped the remaining topsoil into appalling dust storms that afflicted the southern plains for nearly a decade. Sometimes the thick dust turned the skies black. Housewives would cover the windows with sheets, towels, washcloths—anything to keep the dust out. After a storm passed, dust outlined infants' mouths and noses. Dust got into the lungs of animals and humans. Hundreds died of dust pneumonia. By 1935 almost 9,000,000 acres of farmland had been affected. The sisters in Kansas thought the smell of dust would never leave their schools and convents. Yet the majority of farmers, determined to survive, continued to plow the land and pray for rain.

Parishes and schools suffered. In Ellis County it became evident that the parents could not continue to give their children a parochial high school education. After much deliberation, it was thought necessary to establish a public school district but leave the Sisters of St. Agnes in charge. In 1935, St. Fidelis in Victoria changed to a public school. Both the parish high school and the grade school in Walker became district schools in 1940. Due to a succession of crop failures, St. Joseph's Parish in Hays was forced to appeal to the Kansas state school system for aid in January 1940. In the fall of that year, St. Joseph's joined the public school system under the name of Jefferson School and remained in that status until the spring of 1945, when parishioners again assumed responsibility for it.[40]

It was more usual for parishes to close their schools as did St. Joseph's parish in Green Bay. In Fond du Lac, two teachers were eliminated from the staff at St. Joseph's School. Nine sisters were left responsible for 468 pupils. The pastor of St. Florian's Parish in Milwaukee, Wisconsin, called at the motherhouse to speak with Mother Joseph about reducing the salary of the sisters during these hard times. Instead of doing so, Mother Joseph gave him one teacher gratis. At a meeting, Archbishop Samuel Stritch had told mother superiors that they should try to help priests by giving a sister or two to teach free of charge or by making a donation, but added some shrewd advice: "The Mother Superior should not, however, agree to lower the salary of any sister, because it would be too difficult to get back to the salary again in better times. It would take at least ten years to get back to the present day salary."[41] He added that "the Mother Superior should see that the Sisters in their convents and missions should economize as much as possible, because times are very hard and the people are in dire circumstances. Many of the priests are getting no salary."[42]

THE ARCHBISHOP, THE ACADEMY, AND A NATIONAL CRISIS

Despite the new school building for St. Mary's Springs, the expected influx of day students from Fond du Lac never materialized. When in 1932 Mother Joseph and the principal, Sister Angeline, visited Archbishop Stritch, the Springs became the main topic of their discussion. There were only 123 students: fifty-six boarders and fifty-seven day students. The archbishop was very willing to wrestle with the problem. He immediately dismissed the amount of tuition as a problem, focusing on transportation to the school as the big obstacle. It was his belief that if a bus was provided, a hundred girls from Fond du Lac would attend the academy. For their part, the sisters were told to arrange a dinner and inform the local priests that their presence was requested by the archbishop.[43] Asking the priests of Fond du Lac to support the academy when all parochial schools were suffering because of the depression showed a certain amount of courage on the part of Archbishop Stritch. Furthermore, building a Catholic boys' high school in town was considered by many to be the greater priority.[44]

The dinner was held, the priests came, and the archbishop spoke to them on the value of Catholic education during adolescence and the necessity of the priests supporting the school. Even if the students paid full tuition the school could not pay the expenses.[45] The archbishop's efforts, however, proved futile. It was not until the academy became coeducational in 1939 that enrollment gradually rose.

Even as the archbishop was speaking, the country's banking system was approaching collapse. President Herbert Hoover refused to take bold action to end the crisis. The voters elected the first Democratic President since Woodrow Wilson when they made Franklin Delano Roosevelt the thirty-second President of the United States. On inauguration day, March 4, 1933, banks were closed in thirty-eight states. Roosevelt's quick action saved the nation's banking system, but the economy remained fragile. There would be years ahead with government programs designed to revive agriculture and industry before a world war would assure the country's prosperity again.

Mother Joseph was greatly concerned, but there are only two entries in the *Annals* at this time that directly refer to the situation. An entry on March 27 notes that "Mr. George Hutter called at the Motherhouse to confer with Mother M. Joseph regarding conditions in the Banks of the city of Fond du Lac."[46] The second entry, dated June 9, noted that representatives of one bank in town "called to ask us to invest in Common Stock. Mother M. Joseph told them that we do not favor this step. However, Mother offered to leave our money in the Bank for one year. This proposition was gladly accepted by both gentlemen."[47]

At the end of Mother Joseph's administration, she had received and tried to make the revised constitutions the community's own. She had spent months visiting the missions, talking with sisters and interviewing pastors. She had spent countless hours over the accounts. The *Annals* record sums loaned and borrowed. No amount was too small to borrow to pay the large sums constantly expended. She endured the endless meetings with architects and contractors that such projects involved. At the close of her administration, built and paid for were a new building for St. Mary's Springs Academy,

St. Agnes School of Nursing, and an addition to St. Anthony
Hospital.

By 1932, Mother Joseph felt she had done all she could. At seventy-one years of age she felt she was too old and her health too
fragile to be considered for re-election. She begged permission from
the archbishop to withdraw her name from consideration. The
archbishop consented to having her notify the delegates of her wishes, but he stipulated that with her notification she must enclose his
letter to her, which stated that if she were elected, it was her duty to
accept the office.[48]

MOTHER ALOYSIA LEIKEM

The delegates respected Mother Joseph's wishes but not apparently
because of "her advanced years." They elected seventy-five year-old
Sister Aloysia Leikem, who had refused to be considered for the
position when Mother Marcella died.[49] Sister Joseph was returned to
her former position of vicar assistant, and Sisters Germaine Cassin,
Angeline Kamp, and Vera Naber were elected councilors.

Sister Vera Naber, who was present at the election, paints a
touching picture of Mother Aloysia's reaction:

> When she repeated the formula for acceptance …
> the tears ran down her cheeks, and her utterance was
> choked with sobs as she said, "Most Reverend Father,
> I accept the office entrusted to me by the wish of the
> Sisters, and with the grace of God and the help of
> my assistants, will comply with the duties it imposes."
> Archbishop Stritch tried to comfort her by saying,
> "After all, Mother, it is not you who will govern the
> Congregation. It is God. Leave it in His hands, and
> all will be well."[50]

The new superior general was one of the pioneers of the community. Her parents, Frederick Leikem and Catherine Theisen,
were among the early Prussian immigrants drawn to the fertile lands
of southeastern Wisconsin. Their daughter was born on April 12,
1858, in Sauk City, a village along the Wisconsin River. Mary was
brought up as a typical German Catholic farm girl, hard-working,
uncomplaining, and able to put her hands to any task. Less than a

month after her twelfth birthday, Mary had entered Father Caspar
Rehrl's society of Agnes Sisters. While among them, it was Mary's
good fortune to find herself surrounded by other energetic and
cheerful young women. There was Sister Magdalene, only four
years older than she but already a professed religious and the object
of the admiration of the group of Irish girls who had just arrived
from Appleton. There was Anna Schmitz from Marytown, three
years older and also destined to become superior general one day.
There were the Kreuder girls orphaned and grateful for the care
given them by Father Rehrl. There were older sisters from German
states: Sister Clara, pointed out by the others as being the very first
Sister of St. Agnes, and Sisters Caroline and Michael. Sister Agnes
was very much a presence, but at that time she was so involved in
community business that Mary admired her from afar.

A helpful child, Mary had been placed in charge of the convent
geese and was forever after remembered as the convent "goose girl."
When she was thirteen and sent with Anna Schmidt to St. Peter and
Paul's Parish in Nenno, she as cook and Anna as teacher, she was
able to survive a series of misadventures that would have undone
most beginners. At sixteen she was professed, and the new Sister
Aloysia continued in the rural schools in Wisconsin until 1881, when
she was sent to open St. Joseph School in Decatur, Indiana. There,
for thirty-eight years, she was principal, teacher, and organist.

In 1919, Sister Aloysia was sent to St. Patrick in Hudson,
Wisconsin. The next year she was sent to St. Joseph School in Hays,
Kansas, although she did not yet possess all the requirements for
teacher certification in that state. She fulfilled the requirements,
including a class in plays and games, at Fort Hays College and graduated from that institution in 1922 at sixty-two years of age. In
1926, she returned to the motherhouse and was elected to the council as vicar assistant.

Mother Aloysia had a smile for everyone. She was interested in
the sisters and "when she saw someone going the right way she
trusted her and pushed for her."[52] She loved to see the sisters enjoy
themselves. The ban Mother Marcella had placed on card playing
was rescinded. Mother Aloysia simply said, "You may play cards,
but I forbid you to fight."[53]

The younger aspirants called Mother Aloysia "Grandma."
Sister Alvis Jacobs and thirteen other little girls were given over to

the charge of Sister Isabelle, a dear friend of Mother's. Although Sister Isabelle was an organist, she had a serious foot problem and was unable to play the old pump organ in the room given over to the "little novices," as they called themselves. The girls soon found that if one of them would sit on the floor she could take the place of Sister Isabelle's foot at the organ. They were often joined by Mother Aloysia, and the whole group would have a rousing good time singing all evening.[54]

Mother Aloysia's inherent humility and ability to accept the advice of others was one of her greatest strengths in her new job. As vicar, she had become only too aware of Mother Joseph's struggles to keep the congregation afloat financially. At one of the first meetings, Mother Aloysia asked the council to allow Sister Joseph to continue to guide the financial decisions of the congregation. This would allow the general treasurer, Sister Seraphia Fellenz, to continue in her position as administrator of St. Agnes Hospital. As for Sister Joseph, the sisters had complied with her desire to relinquish the position of superior general, but did not accede to the spirit of her request. Although she was a victim of spinal arthritis, Sister Joseph was again responsible for the financial health of the institute in a situation that was being made even more difficult by the ever-worsening economic crisis of the country. Yet, true to her principles, she accepted another six years of bearing a great part of the burden of keeping the congregation and its institutions both solvent and up-to-date.

Mother Aloysia found herself beset by the same problems that faced every superior general, but unlike her predecessors, she did not mark her first year in office by reminding the sisters of old regulations or imposing new ones. The role of "mother" was much more congenial than that of "superior." Aspirants and candidates never forgot her warm welcome on the day they entered. She loved recreations and the company of the sisters, and, as long as her health remained, she enjoyed visiting the missions. Not a visionary herself, when a project proved to be necessary, she would delegate the work to those involved and support them to the fullest extent.

Providing higher education for the sisters was the next challenge. More young women were entering the candidature ready to begin their college work. Although St. Florian Convent in Milwaukee had been built to serve as a house of studies for sisters attending

Marquette University, as well as a residence for the sisters teaching in the school, the house had soon become overcrowded. After a great deal of discussion, it was determined to send the candidates and novices needing higher education to the State Teacher's College in Oshkosh, which offered a two-year teacher preparation course. Every day the convent chauffeur drove five candidates and four novices to their classes in a Pierce Arrow motor car. They carried a suitcase full of lunches and ate in the classroom the president of the college kindly provided for them. It appeared that Oshkosh was providing a satisfactory solution to the problem of educating the young sisters.

The year 1933 ended on a satisfying note. The congregation was pleased and honored to learn that their new cardinal protector, Pietro Fumasoni-Biondi, had been appointed. The fifth apostolic delegate to the United States, he was a well-known figure in ecclesiastical and political circles.

BUSY YEARS

As a member of the previous administration, Mother Aloysia was weary of construction and its attendant problems, but she was responsible for two building projects that had not yet been completed when she took office. The motherhouse had again become too small. It was time to build the wing that Wilhelm Schickel had projected sixty years previously. It would house the aspirancy, the candidature, and the novitiate. A new residence was also needed for the chaplains. The two projects began with a minimum of fuss, a few meetings with the local contractor, and the hiring of an architect. Soon another large building project was underway.

There was congregational business as well. The first item on the agenda for the new year was the visitation of missions. In January 1934, Mother Aloysia left to visit the six missions in Ohio and Indiana. Three weeks later, on February 16, she was stricken with a serious heart attack. Although she recovered quickly, the *Annals* noted that illnesses of various sorts began afflicting her with increasing frequency.

In her visits to the schools Mother Aloysia witnessed sisters teaching with little in the way of supplies or books and with pupils whose parents were too poor to provide them. Offers like one that came from the pastor of St. Lawrence Parish in Muncie, Indiana, were not uncommon; he informed her that "he would keep the eight teachers in his school, providing that Mother Aloysia would be satisfied to agree to his offer of twenty-five dollars a month for each teacher or two hundred dollars a month for all until times pick up." The *Annals* added, "Upon receipt of the above, Mother M. Aloysia wrote to Rev. E. J. Houlihan and assured him that she accepted his offer."[55]

Even so, the congregation was able to accept St. Alphonsus in New Munster, Wisconsin, in 1934 and, in 1935, St. Jude's School in Wauwatosa, Wisconsin, while Immaculate Conception Parish in Elmhurst, Illinois, added a high school curriculum.[56] But Presentation School in North Fond du Lac, which had opened in 1929, was forced to close in 1933, as did St. Ann High School in Walker, Kansas.

From 1935 until 1947, only one more elementary school was opened, the long-awaited St. Patrick School in Fond du Lac. The parish had been struggling to build a school since the pastorate of Father T. J. Cosgrove in 1911. In the 1920s the parish had looked at building sites, drawn up plans, estimated costs, and even asked for bids when the market crashed. Early in 1930, the Henry Boyle family offered to give a matching grant of fifty thousand dollars. Parishioners, barely making it in the depression, were not immediately able to contribute. Even so, the pastor started another campaign in 1934, and finally enough funds were pledged for construction to begin and the new school to be dedicated on August 28, 1938.[57] The Sisters of St. Agnes had been promised that parish since December 17, 1937. Two sisters had called on Archbishop Stritch in regard to another matter when he informed them that St. Patrick School at Fond du Lac was to open in September, 1938, and the pastor was asking for six sisters. The sisters were immensely pleased to hear him say, "Fond du Lac belongs to the Sisters of St. Agnes."[58]

FOUNDING OF MARIAN COLLEGE

Meanwhile, Sister Vera, in charge of the young sisters' educational program, believed that the problem of completing their education had been solved by the arrangements made with Oshkosh Normal School. Then came a shock. In January 1936, as the time approached for the students who were completing the program to begin their student teaching, she was informed that the sisters could not wear their habits in public school classrooms. When her visit to the president's office proved futile, she reported her failure to Mother Aloysia, who replied, "Well, now what shall we do? Sister Vera, you brought the bad news. It's up to you to find a way out. What would you suggest?" Sister Vera had already thought through the options. She told Mother Aloysia the community could either build a house of studies near a Catholic college or, alternatively, open a college at the motherhouse. Mother Aloysia called in the novice mistress, Sister Frederica Spuhler. Sister Frederica expressed her conviction that the only way to keep the Agnesian spirit alive was by establishing a community college. Mother Aloysia, who had been happy to see the east wing of the motherhouse nearing completion, agreed with Sister Frederica, simply saying that she preferred not to think of building a house.[59]

Given the history of the congregation, it is not difficult to see why establishing another educational institution, even in the midst of the depression, held no terrors for the council. Sisters with a minimum of education had opened grade schools that proved successful. Without one nurse in the community, the sisters had committed themselves to building and staffing a hospital. They had opened a home for the elderly and agreed to staff the Leo House with no prior experience in either field. They had founded an academy and a school of nursing. There is no evidence that there was a single doubt or hesitation about embarking on another new project. On the contrary, they believed that with the help of the Holy Spirit all difficulties could easily be overcome. Because the new wing in the convent provided plenty of space for classrooms, there was not a building problem. The faculty positions could be filled by the few sisters who had earned higher degrees, along with those who had always helped the sisters from Marquette University and St. Norbert's College. Perhaps the college could even employ a lay teacher or two. At the same time, founding their own community college was a decision that many other congregations had made and were making.[60] From 1920 to 1942 the number of Catholic colleges for American women had risen from 54 to 117.[61]

There are only two references to Marian College in the *Annals* before it opened. We know that Sister Vera went to Racine,

Wisconsin, in March to discuss college problems with the dean of the college there.[62] And we know that Mother Aloysia informed the council on June 16 that it was absolutely necessary to open a junior college at the motherhouse.[63]

On September 8, 1936, the entry in the *Annals* reads, "Today, the birthday of our Blessed Mother, is also the birthday of our 'Marian College.' It was opened with an appropriate program consisting of speaking, music, and singing."[64] It had been named Marian College after Mary, the Mother of God. Its seal, referring both to Mary and the mission of the college, carried the words *sicut lilium inter spinas* ("as a lily among thorns") and the symbols of a torch of learning, thorns, and a lily. The student body numbered twenty-one full-time students and twenty-five part-time students.

Sister Vera Naber, a woman of drive and determination, was appointed dean. The faculty consisted of four sisters and two priests, one of whom was the college chaplain, and the other, a biology professor from St. Norbert College. In pursuit of her goal to acquire a competent, if small, faculty, Sister Vera negotiated with the Precious Blood Fathers to send degreed chaplains to the motherhouse. Marian College's principal purposes were to prepare students for state certification in the teaching profession and to offer classes in general education and theology. There was a great deal more flexibility in the courses students could take than in those the Department of Public Instruction allowed sixty years later. The classes offered that first semester were German, history (area unspecified), algebra, apologetics, English, biology, Latin, Advanced Latin and Latin Composition.[65] The curriculum in the second semester included art, psychology, and music.

A MYSTERIOUS ILLNESS

Barely ten days after the opening of the college, on September 17, 1936, two candidates suffered spells of dizziness. They were put to bed at once, and an intern from the hospital was called in. Then more candidates began to complain of pains in the back and neck, muscular weakness, nervousness, sleeplessness, and loss of memory. The doctors were helpless and even considered the possibility of mass hysteria. The sisters at the motherhouse were both extremely embarrassed and extremely worried.

By September 28, fifteen candidates showed symptoms. A doctor was called who placed the infirmary under quarantine and reported the case to the State Health Department. That night a sister and a senior novice also showed symptoms of the disorder. Two doctors came from Madison to investigate conditions at the motherhouse. Teachers were summoned and questioned, even in regard to their mode of presenting various subjects. Mother Aloysia ordered a novena of Masses to be said in the convent chapel for the suppression of the epidemic.

On October 1, the convent high school and Marian College were closed for an indefinite time. More novices were struck down; then a sister who did not live in the novitiate house became another victim. This brought the Fond du Lac health officer to the motherhouse. It took all of Sister Joseph's charm to prevent a quarantine notice from being placed on the convent's front door. As a compromise, sisters were prevented from leaving the motherhouse, and business calls could be transacted in the parlor only.

Two doctors then came from the State Board of Health to investigate the kitchen, refrigerators, and store rooms. The sisters in the kitchen were mortified. As an experiment, half the novices and candidates were given convent food and the other half, hospital food. On the fourth day of the experiment, a junior novice who had eaten food from the hospital instead of the motherhouse was taken down with a light case of the epidemic. The outcome of the experiment removed a great burden of worry from the convent cooks.

On the eighth of October, two specialists were brought in from Milwaukee. They pronounced the case a form of influenza and predicted that the sufferers would be up and around in a few days. On October 14, the Fond du Lac physician called at the motherhouse to inform Sister Joseph of the serious state of affairs regarding the novices and candidates in the infirmary.[66] He suspected encephalitis. On October 17, a representative of the United States Department of Public Health arrived. Two days later, he reported that "he was certain that they had none of the three diseases which they were supposed to have." He said, too, that "their illness was neither contagious nor serious."[67]

Overall, thirty-five young women between the ages of fourteen and twenty-one were involved. The college was quickly re-opened, but the sisters regarded the entire episode as discreditable. It was never mentioned. At the time, Sister Vera undoubtedly spoke for many when she asked, "Was the entire episode an ingenious machination of the evil spirit?"[68]

Years later, Berton Roueche included this outbreak of the disease in a series of articles on cases of medical detection. He found that the Department of Public Health partially solved the mystery when it was discovered that several similar cases had occurred in different parts of the world—the first, in Iceland. The disease (epidemic neuromyasthenia) is extremely rare.[69]

PROGRESS AT MARIAN COLLEGE

The year after the college opened, Mr. John Callahan, the Wisconsin Superintendent of the State Board of Education, requested that any qualified woman be admitted into Marian. After securing the consent of the archbishop, the Board of Trustees acceded to the request.[70] For the next five years the University of Wisconsin provided Marian with supervision and guidance. As a result, the curriculum changed and requirements were modified: for example, the first college bulletin had stated that a Bachelor of Arts from Marian required sixteen hours of Latin and sixteen hours of a modern language. Marian also followed the state teacher's colleges in offering a two-year teacher certification program for rural teachers.

Introducing a college into the motherhouse was not without problems. Everything was done to keep the college from interfering with motherhouse routines. The halls, even in the college section, were to be kept quiet. Novices and candidates were not allowed to socialize with their lay classmates. A room, called the "lounge," was given to the lay students, who played innumerable games of hearts in it. Only a thin partition separated the lounge from the office of the academic dean, who firmly discouraged loud noises and adolescent hilarity. Smoking, a popular activity at the time, was not allowed in the building. The students developed a degree of decorum that remained characteristic of Marian students for many years.[71]

The candidates and novices did not need a lounge; they cleaned and prayed instead. Their brief recreation was after supper, when they could go outside and take short walks. Lunch hours were long to allow time for prayers. Afternoon classes were scheduled to end on time for spiritual reading.

Members of the faculty did not find the situation easy. Because communication between professed sisters and those in formation was strictly limited, instructors had minimum contact with their students. The horarium of the motherhouse took precedence over the teachers' professional lives. A member of the college faculty dreaded being late for prayers or meals because it was considered disruptive to the rest of the community. For years the sister faculty spent the noon hour on Monday folding wash in the convent's large industrial laundry.

The faculty meetings, complete with minutes, were held. (True to form, one of the first meetings concerned grading.) For the sisters teaching in vicinity schools, classes during the academic year were held two evenings a week and on Saturdays; in the summer, sessions for them lasted six weeks. Very quickly the sisters were joined by many rural school teachers who had not yet completed work for their bachelor's degrees.

FOUNDING OF ST. CLARE HOSPITAL, MONROE, WISCONSIN

Although in 1937 the depression was far from over, the congregation was considering establishing another hospital. The sisters were offered opportunities in Chicago; Decatur, Indiana; and Monroe, Wisconsin. It had been forty years since St. Agnes Hospital had been established and over twenty-five years since St. Anthony Hospital had opened. The congregation possessed both experience and a body of personnel anxious to branch out into other locations.

The decision to build a hospital in Monroe was made in a relatively short time. On October 19, 1937, Mother Aloysia received a letter from Dr. C. E. Baumle of Monroe, informing her that the physicians there were in favor of having the Sisters of St. Agnes build a fifty-bed institution. He added that he and another physician would be glad to come to the motherhouse to discuss the possibilities of such a project.[72] The doctors, who had exhausted other sources for aid, had appealed to the pastor of the city's Catholic

church for suggestions. Father Eugene C. McCollow, who previously had been an assistant at St. Joseph's Parish in Fond du Lac, knew
the work of the sisters and recommended them. Acting on his suggestion, the doctors had contacted the congregation.

Monroe, located in the rolling hills of southwestern Green
County, possessed several advantages. Only 120 miles from Fond du
Lac, it was relatively accessible.[73] The Swiss immigrants who gave
the area its distinctive cultural heritage were a hard-working, stable
people; the town, with its scrubbed houses, reflected their sense of
order. Although there was another small hospital in the town, it was
unable to meet the growing needs of the area. The physicians were
eager to make Monroe a medical center for that part of the state
and, in fact, were in the process of establishing a clinic there.

Two letters later, Doctors Baumle and W. G. Bear arrived at the
motherhouse on October 24 to discuss the project. In another two
weeks, Sister Joseph and Sister Angeline visited Monroe to explore
prospects for building a hospital. (Mother Aloysia was on visitation
in Kansas.) Dr. Bear then sent a letter signed by all of the doctors
from Monroe and from some of the surrounding territories; in it,
they promised to cooperate in building the hospital. Furthermore,
Dr. Bear and his son, Dr. Nathan Bear, promised to donate ten town
lots that would, with additions, provide the necessary land for the
building.

On December 7, Mother Aloysia called a meeting of the council to discuss the matter and make the decision. The council decided to accept the offer from Monroe in preference to the other two
offers. The next step was to obtain permission from the archbishop,
who agreed to a meeting on December 17. Mother Aloysia and
Sister Joseph undoubtedly returned pleased with their visit because
the entry in the *Annals* reads, "His Excellency encouraged Mother to
build there as much good may be accomplished spiritually."[74]

Once a decision was made, Mother Aloysia moved on it immediately. On January 5, 1938, the architectural firm was chosen; three
days later the architect was in Fond du Lac to discuss plans. The finished design was for a sixty-bed hospital with eighteen bassinets. In
July, the building contract was awarded and construction began.
Then the problem of furnishing the hospital arose. On September
2, two gentlemen from Monroe, accompanied by Father McCollow,
visited the motherhouse to solicit patronage for the furnishings that

St. Clare Hospital would require. Fortunately, Dr. Bear and Mr. Emery Odell, editor of the *Monroe Evening Times*, had already taken leadership by starting a successful drive to help raise funds for new hospital equipment.

Because this was the first major project the sisters had ever undertaken in a locale where there had been no prior Agnesian missions, Mother Aloysia assigned four sisters to live on the premises while the hospital was being constructed. In the middle of May 1939, these sisters set out for Monroe. They lived on the second floor of a laundry. They had four rooms: two bedrooms, a kitchen, and a small room used as a chapel and living room. With a stove equipped with a single burner, their cooking was primitive. They had been given very little money and much of that was used to pay freight and express on the frequent deliveries of supplies. Breakfast was the bright spot in their day as they were "invited to share a real breakfast, table linens and all," with Father McCollow after morning Mass.[75]

It became difficult even to raise money to pay the workers and strikes threatened. The sisters pleaded with the workers not to go off the job.[76] Fortunately, the necessary monies were raised, the workers continued to work, and the hospital was completed. The building together with the driveway had cost $289,601.48; equipment, $40,596.83; and hospital supplies, $21,547.01. Various other payments amounted to $3,976.59. The entire cost amounted to $355,221.91.[77]

On August 1, 1939, St. Clare Hospital was dedicated. One floor was designated for congregational members who needed care. The staff included eight sisters, thirteen doctors, twenty-three registered nurses, thirty-three nurse's aides, and five male employees and auxiliary personnel. The first baby was born at 1:00 a.m. that morning; three hours later a patient's appendix was removed.

In spite of the positive support from the local newspaper, the sisters were not well received by everyone in the town. Many were unfamiliar with nuns in habits, and the historic Swiss suspicion of Catholicism ran deep.[78] For a long time the sisters had to get used to seeing townspeople cross the streets to avoid them, but eventually the good work done in the hospital overcame local prejudices. Through it all, the sisters could take some comfort from Mother

Aloysia's reminder: "We did not choose Monroe, Monroe chose us."[79]

FOUNDING OF ST. THOMAS HOSPITAL, COLBY, KANSAS

St. Clare Hospital was still in the process of construction when there came a plea for help from a little town in western Kansas. Kansas was still reeling from the drought, dust storms, and depression, and for isolated places like Colby in Thomas County, providing adequate health care was a continuous problem. More than 200 miles from Denver and 110 miles from Hays, Thomas County had been "plagued by adversity throughout its history."[80] From 1895 on, groups of doctors had attempted to establish a private hospital. An act passed by the Kansas legislature in 1923 had made possible the organization of county hospitals through public funds, provided that a petition be signed by not less than 25 percent of the freeholders of the county.[81] At the time internal squabbling among the physicians themselves was causing many problems, but in 1929 the doctors of Thomas County asked the county commissioners to call a special election for the purpose of voting an appropriation. The petition was supported by the local newspaper, whose editor stated that "the public should understand also, that such a hospital would not be run by the doctors and there would be none of those nasty doctors' fights in connection with it."[82]

Although a petition had been signed, enough other funds could not be obtained. In 1931 the last private venture failed even though the number of patients had increased. When the Works Progress Administration (WPA) was established in 1935, funds finally became available to support the construction of public building projects.[83] The combination of these funds and private bequests made the founding of a hospital possible.

But the WPA would not provide funds until reliable management and responsible administration of a new hospital was assured. Because St. Anthony Hospital in Hays was already well-known for its good management, members of the committee tried to persuade its administrator, Sister Frances Clare Kohne, to accept the responsibility. Although Sister Frances Clare was in favor of the project,

Mother Aloysia was not. Sister Vera provided a bit of the exchange between a representative of the committee and Mother Aloysia:

"Finally she [Mother Aloysia] said, 'Yes, Mr. Ferguson,[84] we know you need a hospital in Thomas County; yes, we realize that it is a good cause; yes, we appreciate the fact that you are paying us a compliment when you ask us to take over the administration. The answer, however, to your appeal is 'NO.' Can't you understand 'NO'?"

"No," said Mr. Ferguson ....[85]

The committee was nothing if not persevering. When a delegation from Kansas arrived at the motherhouse, the council capitulated. On September 12, 1938, the council agreed to undertake the management and staffing of the hospital.[86] Although it was to be built by the WPA, the congregation was obliged to assist financially to complete the work. The facility was furnished largely by local contributions and staffed by the sisters. A state representative in the legislature secured the passage of a special bill authorizing for one dollar the granting of a ninety-nine-year lease on the property to the Sisters of St. Agnes,[87] with the understanding that the congregation was to be sole administrator of the hospital. If Thomas County ever should wish to take over the hospital after the lease expired, the county would be obliged to reimburse the congregation.

BOYS AND GIRLS TOGETHER

One of the last decisions of Mother Aloysia's administration led the academy into the future. In May 1939, St. Mary's Springs announced that the school would open its doors to boys. Archbishop Stritch had "yielded to the pressure of Fond du Lac parents"[88] in asking the sisters to make this change. The congregation believed that it was to be a temporary arrangement until such a time as Fond du Lac accumulated enough funds to build a boys' school.[89] Whether the sisters agreed with the decision or not, it put the school on the right track.

By the thirties, the Springs had developed a distinct culture with its own traditions and customs. The girls wore black skirts, white

middies, and white sweaters as needed. For gym classes they wore
black bloomers, black stockings, and white sneakers. The same gym
outfits were worn for swimming in the outdoor academy pool.
Boarders wore as a Sunday uniform a black dress with a white collar and plaid tie. (The early requirement that the students wear a
uniform Sunday dress, however, was soon dropped.)

People in Fond du Lac had become familiar with the yellow
academy bus that picked up the town girls. A sister always accompanied the bus driver on his rounds.[90] But it was the boarders who
experienced the full flavor of the school. For an hour after school,
the students who worked for their tuition did their chores while the
others took leisurely strolls. After supper it was time to walk again
around the roof garden. When it was really cold, the girls wrapped
towels around their heads while trotting after Sister Emma and her
flying veil. Their lives were strictly regulated with many periods of
silence. Tuesday afternoons the boarders went to the ironing room,
where they found their clothes washed and placed in damp little
bundles. They ironed their clothes in silence. On Saturdays the girls
were taught ballroom dancing to the clicking castanets of Mr. Cleo
Smith. Although the academy had a phonograph, it was reserved
for listening to music on Saturday nights. In one dormitory the students were allowed to listen to the top ten musical hits on the radio.

The school sodality was important,[91] and it was always a great
honor to be the student chosen to crown a statue of the Blessed
Virgin Mary in May. Yearly events included a German play, a junior dance in the autumn and the traditional senior prom in the
spring. As in most Catholic high schools, the formals the girls wore
provided many occasions for skirmishes between them and the
nuns. Inevitably some girls were given scarves or veils to drape over
their bare shoulders.[92]

Despite the best efforts of the sisters to retain the academy culture, the entrance of eleven boys in 1939 changed forever the
atmosphere of the school. The boys, three seniors and eight freshmen, had their own study hall.[93] Until the local newspaper got the
story, the boys and girls used separate stairways, but the merriment
resulting among the town's newspaper readers brought a quick end
to that experiment.

A DARK INTERLUDE

In April 1938, Mother Aloysia had reached her eightieth birthday. Her health was becoming precarious, but in September she again began visiting the missions. She went to Sheboygan and then on to St. Luke's and St. Mark's in Two Rivers. Early in October, she left for Pennsylvania and New York, where she planned to spend three days on each mission. From there she intended to proceed directly to Kansas and return to the motherhouse around Thanksgiving. On November 22, the council wrote to her telling her that it was very urgent that she return home as soon as possible as several difficult problems had arisen. Back in the motherhouse, Mother Aloysia suffered a cerebral hemorrhage on December 23. On December 28, the attending physician with two consultants decided that Mother's condition was hopeless. After two difficult weeks and a slight stroke on January 10, 1939, she began to improve, but slowly. On January 26, she suffered a severe heart attack. The doctor advised her to put her affairs in order because she was in imminent danger of death. Again, she recovered, but she was exhausted and depressed.

In 1939 the council was busy preparing for the general election in June while taking care of only the most pressing business. The staff for St. Clare Hospital was chosen. Mother Aloysia's health remained precarious at best. That year it was hard to believe that spring was coming. Pope Pius XI died on February 10; on March 25, Sister Dominic Engler, a senior novice, died of tuberculosis. On April 3, Sister Louisa Wolsiffer, one of the last of the pioneer sisters, died. On April 16, Mother M. Aloysia suffered a series of severe heart attacks and received the Last Rites. Again, she rallied, but the next months were exceedingly painful for her and the community.

The election of the new administration came as a great relief to Mother Aloysia. A week after the election, she left the motherhouse for St. Clare Hospital, where she had decided to make her home. With her new freedom, her health improved and until February, 1941, she was able to contribute to the morale of the hospital and lighten the burden of the sisters. In that month, she asked to be taken to the motherhouse as she wished to die there. She died on April 16, 1941. In delivering her eulogy Monsignor Joseph J. Seimetz from Decatur, ended with these words: "There is not much more to say except that she was an ideal Sister of St. Agnes. She was always a 'Mary' in the house of God, a 'Martha' in her own. Her life had its exacting details, its annoying difficulties, but these never penetrated beyond her calm demeanor or disturbed the deep serenity of her heart."[94]

The life of Mother Aloysia seems to exemplify the virtues that were most commonly attributed to the congregation, whether by themselves or by others—that is, simplicity and humility. She was able to delegate power and to share it; she used her position to empower others to implement the congregational agenda. She responded to the demands made upon her, whether professionally or personally, competently and quietly. Of her life it was written, "Yet her outstanding virtue was a childlike guilelessness which endeared her to the sisters and charmed casual acquaintances."[95] To use a word Agnesians always used as a compliment, she was "common"—one of them.

With the death of Mother Aloysia few ties to the pioneers who had founded the Sisters of St. Agnes remained, but if there was one certainty, it was that its members did not wrestle with the questions of identity and charism that so absorb today's members. Their Constitutions clearly stated, "The special end which they have in view, besides their own sanctification, is with the purest intention, to take charge of the little ones of Jesus Christ, and to instruct those committed to their care in the devout exercises of Christian life."[96] As a congregation of almost 668 women,[97] they were responsible for four hospitals, a school of nursing, a college, an academy, a home for the elderly, the Leo House staffing, two orphanages and parochial schools.

They lived a life of few physical comforts, but they were sustained by the conviction of their vocations, the bonds they had with each other and the belief—common to so many of their generation of Christian women—that fidelity to life's duties was both a sacrifice and a privilege.

Chapter IX

Stability in a Chaotic World

During the summer of 1939 Europe was again poised on the edge of war. Only twenty years previously, World War I had ended, leaving a legacy of nearly 38,000,000 casualties, widespread devastation, and shifts in the international balance of power. As a result, the nationalism and militarism that had plagued Europe during the nineteenth century had intensified, leaving the continent vulnerable to both fascism and communism.

Americans wanted nothing more than to stay out of European affairs and its warring ideologies. They were slowly emerging from the trauma and had made some progress in providing a social safety net through such legislation as the Social Security Act and the minimum wage law.

In the midst of the depression, American Catholics had continued to find support in their church. Increased devotion to Jesus and the Eucharist led to more frequent reception of Commuion. Marian devotions such as the recitation of the Rosary, novenas, and the sodality movement played important roles in parish life. Parish missions and retreats were popular. The liturgical movement arrived in the United States during the 1920s and began to influence church music, art, and architecture.[1]

The papal encyclicals, *Rerum Novarum* (1891) and *Quadragesimo Anno* (1931), which had condemned both socialism and unbridled capitalism, were having an impact on Catholic social philosophy.[2] Catholics were better accepted and more prominent in politics. In 1928 Al Smith had been the Democratic Party's nominee as president; and during the thirties, Father Charles Coughlin's radio advocacy of economic reforms was heard around the country.

According to Sandra Schneiders, the Catholic Church in America from the end of World War I through the forties experienced a period of extraordinary stability: "Faith was laid out in catechism-clear propositions that no one questioned. The liturgy was rich and invariable; authority structures were clear and effective; the status of Religious in the society of the Church and their role in its apostolic work were well-defined and unchallenged."[3]

The stability of religious life was grounded in the three vows interpreted through centuries of the development of canon law. That the interpretation of the vows would necessarily change according to the circumstances of time and place was seldom a consideration. On the contrary, there was a general assumption that convent life was and should be separate from the considerations and turmoil of the world in which it found itself. It was the obligation of the superior general to maintain the environment that safeguarded the living of the vows as well as to support the community's ministerial activities.

MOTHER ANGELINE KAMP

Margaret Kamp was born on February 23, 1875, in the farming community of New Haven, Indiana. In 1890 she entered the convent in Fond du Lac. After profession, Sister Angeline was sent to Our Lady Queen of Angels School in Harlem, first as a teacher, then as principal. In 1908 she became principal at a school in Rockland Lake, New York; the following year she returned to Fond du Lac to open St. Mary's Springs Academy. In 1926 while she was superior at the academy, she was elected to the general council. Not re-elected to the council in 1932, she remained at the academy until 1939, when, at the age of sixty-four, she was elected superior general.

At a conference for community superiors that Mother Angeline held in June of 1944, she quoted this commonly understood definition of the role of the superior. "She is bound by her office to promote the regular observance of the Rule and to aid the Congregation in attaining its end, namely, the sanctification of its members, according to its peculiar spirit, and the preservation of this spirit and traditions."[4] She added, "Consequently, every superior has the right and duty to teach and train her subjects; to direct them according to the Rules; to watch over them and to ward off what is dangerous to them; to secure the rights of each according to distributive justice; to see that they discharge their duties in the right spirit; to provide with tender and maternal care for their bodily and spiritual support; to correct and punish them when necessary—in a word, she is the very head and heart of the religious family."[5]

The ideal sister was docile, obedient, and humble, and demonstrated those virtues by her punctilious adherence to the rule, customs and regulations. This point of view was fully supported by Archbishop Stritch of Milwaukee. On the day Mother Angeline was elected, he praised the Sisters of St. Agnes: "I have great respect for the Congregation of the Sisters of St. Agnes and for those who have governed it. The tradition established by the Mothers Superior up to the present is fine. They have been progressive but prudent. They have not been carried away by a desire to do something spectacular. With the Sisters of St. Agnes I feel that virtue means more than credits. They have not yielded to the ambition to do things beyond their ability." He added that "professionalism has the tendency to crush the desire for perfection. In a religious family it is important to keep as the dominant idea the desire to become perfect while we conduct our exterior works as best we can."[6]

Living the Vows

The vow of obedience was the cornerstone of religious life. It was no accident that Archbishop Stritch emphasized the virtue of obedience in the remarks he addressed to the delegates. "The superiors have been just as fair as is possible for them to be ... There may be mistakes in judgment because of a lack of requisite information ... it is in the acceptance of these judgments that the sisters learn how to bear the cross. There is nothing better than that, the virtue of real, interior obedience even if, or perhaps because it costs a pang to render it."[7] The emphasis on conformity and obedience that marked the universal church of the period was heartily endorsed by Mother Angeline.

Mother Angeline interpreted the vow of poverty "as having those things of life which people of the middle class would enjoy." That meant sufficient food, austere convents, frugal use of goods, no luxuries, and an absolute minimum of personal possessions.[8] There were few books of any kind.[9] The sister was not allowed to call anything hers. All of her possessions should fit in one trunk.[10] Nevertheless, Mother Angeline did not forget the importance of charity, particularly in regard to the families of the sisters. "If parents, brothers or sisters are very poor—in dire need—it is permissible to give them something with the permission of the superior. This is given as alms."[11] This could have been a major commitment in 1939 as the sisters came from large families.

Then as now, vows were lived out in the real world and society's socio-economic systems necessarily affected the day-to-day living of the vows. Because women did not enter the Sisters of St. Agnes with large dowries and only a very few received a sizable inheritance, it was the salaries of the teaching sisters and the surplus remaining from the operation of the hospitals that provided the congregation's principal means of support.[12] Salaries during the 1930s and 1940s were usually a dollar a day—that is one dollar for each of the twenty teaching days in the month. Music teachers could still bring in fees for private tuition; sometimes organists would receive a fee. The domestic sisters did not receive a salary although many laundered the church linens and baked altar breads. Sacristans sometimes received a monetary gift at Christmas.

Many pastors as well as parishioners treated the sisters generously the year round. In some places there was a special day to give food to the Sisters. Thanksgiving was the time of the "can roll." A day or two before the holiday the classroom door would open and the pupils would have a merry time rolling cans of soup and vegetables down the aisles. Often the older boys would arrive with live poultry. The event, important to the economy of the convent, was always a "surprise." There were also doctors and dentists who cared for the sisters gratis. After movies became popular, the owner of a local cinema might treat the sisters to an especially inspirational movie; in some places bus or trolley drivers refused to take fares from the sisters.

Missions were not assessed the amount of money to be sent to the motherhouse. The missions were expected to send in their surplus. Inevitably there would be a superior who was concerned more about the money sent in than the welfare of the sisters.

Only superiors or treasurers carried a purse. Although Sister Joseph insisted that the sisters carry five dollars with them when they went out, "because you never know when you may need it," it was not unheard of for sisters to find that they were caught a few cents short of the cost of some needed article. Food served in the convent refectory was plain. Breakfast consisted of cereal, bread, and coffee or milk. After breakfast the sugar bowl was removed for the remainder of the day. At mid-morning and mid-afternoon bread, jam, coffee, and milk were available for those who needed it. Meals suited Midwestern tastes. Fruit was a rarity.[13] Desserts were served on feast days, although on some missions the cooks might give the sisters a large cookie on Friday nights. Candy was so rarely in evidence that some sisters saved theirs for summer school.

A sister was never to ask relatives or friends for anything. If she received a gift, she was to show it to the superior, who could decide to incorporate it into the common supplies. If the sister wished to use the gift, she was to ask for it. However, if the donor stipulated some special use for the gift, the donor's wishes were honored.

On a sister's name day,[14] she would receive a dessert provided she had asked for a penance the night before. She would also be greeted by a plate of holy cards. These cards were recycled so many times that the more hideous ones became legendary. Even procuring holy cards for the sisters was not always easy for the superior. On one mission, for example, the superior had so little money that she scraped the advertisement off the backs of the cards she gave the sisters. Sisters in perpetual vows were honored with a table bouquet— frequently of artificial flowers.

The vow of poverty was supported by the common life.[15] Every detail of clothing was prescribed. Being singular in any respect was not applauded. Each sister had three habits: an everyday habit, a work habit, and a Sunday habit. Blue and white striped underskirts were for everyday use, black was worn on Sunday. A colored apron was worn for cleaning; a black apron for school. Shoes at this time were still being repaired by Sister Alcantara Leuchinger. Not only did Sister use pieces of old rubber tires but she was known to cut up straw floor mats for the soles. Shoes had to look and be in very poor condition before a sister got new ones. Clothes were in constant need of mending. During spiritual reading shoulders on capes and the tops of veils were patched and re-patched; stockings were darned and habits were put back together.

The vow of chastity was supported by the cloister. Only the parlor was accessible to visitors. If visitors stayed for a meal, they ate alone. Relationships outside of the community were not encouraged and particular or exclusive friendships were strongly discouraged within the convent. A sister's life was bounded by her convent, work, and church. She did not attend night gatherings, even school sports events. If a sister saw a film, it was probably with a class of students or on the rare occasions when it was religious or inspirational. Sisters could visit their parents at home for a week every five years, but at no other time, even if she lived nearby. Families found a way around the problem by inviting a whole local mission to a picnic in their family garage.

RULES, CUSTOMS, AND SPIRITUALITY

From after night prayer until after breakfast, when the superiors greeted the sisters with, "Praised be Jesus Christ, good morning, dear sisters,"[16] the "Great Silence" was observed. During the day, there was silence in the chapel, sacristy, bedrooms, and refectory and at almost every meal. At the weekly chapter of faults, when sisters accused themselves of infractions against the rule, breaking the silence, walking heavily, and slamming doors were among the most frequently mentioned infractions of the rule.[17]

Vanity was strongly discouraged. Mirrors were proscribed. Novices were taught not to peek into windows or glass doors to see if their veils were on straight. However, they soon discovered that shiny toasters made excellent mirrors. When they arrived on mission, they usually found a mirror or two in the house because most superiors preferred their sisters to leave the house with the complicated pieces of their habits tidily arranged.

While sisters did study for higher degrees, there was little opportunity for intellectual development, beyond doing assigned readings.

The diocesan newspaper was often the only paper in the house; fiction was not read. There might have been a professional journal or a religious magazine in the house; often there was not.

The life of the church, especially the liturgical cycle of the Eucharistic celebrations, offered spiritual and aesthetic sustenance to the sisters. Special visiting confessors during Ember Days gave the sisters opportunities for more counseling and guidance.[18] The great feasts of Christmas, Easter, and Pentecost as well as that of St. Agnes were celebrated with great ceremony at the motherhouse. Many other special days and events marked the liturgical year. There was the blessing of the Christmas crib, the blessing of the house on the feast of the Epiphany, the blessing of wine in the chapel on the feast of St. John the Evangelist, the blessing of buns on the feast of St. Agatha, the blessing of candles at Candlemas, the blessing of throats on the feast of St. Blaise, the marking of the forehead with ashes on Ash Wednesday, the processions on the feasts of Corpus Christi, Pentecost, and Forty Hours Devotion, with its forty hours of prayer honoring the Blessed Sacrament. Everything was directed at making beautiful and appropriate worship the center of the sisters' lives.

The day new members are received is a very special and joyous occasion for every religious community. For Agnesians that day was the feast of the Assumption of the Blessed Virgin, August 15. On the eve of the feast, postulants received the religious habit and entered the novitiate for a period of two years. On the feast itself, in the presence of their families, friends, and the community, women vowed poverty, chastity, and obedience as members of the Congregation of St. Agnes.[19]

A retreat was an important part of a sister's year. Ordinarily retreats were scheduled for five days; on some important occasions such as making her first profession or perpetual profession, a sister made an eight-day retreat. The motherhouse scheduled several retreats during the summer and one in winter. Other retreats were scheduled in New York. Sisters usually arrived for their retreats exhausted from their year's ministry. Some slept almost continually the first day or two. If they were making a summer retreat in Fond du Lac, they found themselves and seven other sisters sitting sideways, squeezed into a pew meant for six persons.[20] Retreat masters from various religious orders were brought in from all parts of the country. They ordinarily gave three conferences and a sermon each of the days and were available for confessions. Sincere, hard-working men, they often came bearing the message of some favorite cause, such as devotion to the Sacred Heart of Jesus. Most had developed a series of lectures on the three vows. There was seldom an attempt to develop the scriptural or theological understanding of the sisters.

The Franciscan spirituality of Father Francis was still readily discernible during this period. Rudolf Bierberg, a priest of of the Congregation of the Most Precious Blood,[21] when asked to characterize Agnesian spirituality, had no doubt that it was "Capuchin more than anything ... Father Francis had more to do with forming the spirit of your community than Father Rehrl."[22] However, the influence of chaplains, professors, confessors, and retreat masters from other congregations should not be overlooked.[23]

DIRECTIVES

In September following her election, Mother Angeline sent her first circular letter to the congregation. Her first words summarized her agenda. "This circular is being sent for the purpose of reviving our zeal for religious life. I beg of you to try to lead a life worthy of a religious ... If the observance of the rule in all its details demands a sacrifice, make it cheerfully and God will bless you. I have every confidence in you, dear Sisters, that you will do your best to observe the rule faithfully and so become more Christ-like."[24]

She then laid down twenty-five directives. The sisters were cautioned against carrying tales to the priests, asking the children or people of the parish for "eats," reading novels, attending night school, riding on Sundays, going to a movie unless it is with the school children or a performance for sisters only, and having particular friendships. Many regulations involved visits, gifts, and the use of money. Letters were always to be read by the local superior with the exception of letters to the superior general.[25]

Sisters had asked for permission to recite the office privately, which was refused; and some missions asked to make meditation during the afternoon. She was unable to grant the latter permission because "according to the rule, meditation is to be made in connection with night prayer at 8:00 or 8:30 p.m." Later, at a separate meeting with superiors, she gave the sisters permission to write to the motherhouse if there was anything in the document which admitted of constructive criticism.[26]

In June 1941 Mother Angeline informed the sisters of her interview with Archbishop Moses E. Kiley.[27] The sisters had asked for more opportunities to see family members, especially the sick, and attend religious events, such as ordinations of family members. "I sent you a circular last fall. The councilors and I prayed. We made novenas in order to know what to put in it, and I went to the Archbishop and on my knees begged him for the permissions, but he couldn't give them. He said, 'I will go through your rule and get a Doctor of Canon Law and I will grant you all I can. Don't come and ask other permissions. I can't grant them. I didn't make the rule, but I made a vow to keep the rule and you did too.'"[28]

She gave advice to the local superiors: "Superiors should never correct a sister in the presence of the children, no matter what the occasion may be. Tell the sisters what you want them to know. Don't give directions about classroom procedures by sending a note .... Don't try to dictate so minutely ... that the sisters have no liberty to carry out plans of their own. Call a meeting of the sisters occasionally and discuss matters with them. Let them exchange opinions and talk over classroom situations. Create a feeling that each sister is interested in everything that concerns the school, not only in her own classroom and pupils. No good comes of being dictatorial."[29]

Addressing the sisters on charity after a retreat in 1941, Mother Angeline asked the sisters to: "Pray vespers and compline for me ... that I will be just to every sister. I want to be a mother to each one. Pray for me. I pray for you. I beg of you to pray for me. If you have complaints, make them to me .... If you do not want to tell me, tell the other council members. I will not be angry if you can tell any of the councilors better than you can tell me."[30]

On another occasion, she advised the sisters to ask themselves three questions daily: "How many times did I mortify myself? How many times did I do an act of charity for another? How many times daily did I speak kindly to someone?" She added, "Give a report on that to me sometime."[31] The reader is left with the sense of a woman almost lost in the morass of the details that had come to make up the sisters' daily lives but determined to do her duty and see that the rule—the key of heaven—was kept, whatever the cost.

Two relaxations of regulations meant a great deal to the sisters. Every sister could have a one-day outing annually. However, the permission was not exactly a carte blanche. No one should go out alone or make arrangements with outsiders for a particular outing. A family spirit should prevail. If other outings were desired, they must first get permission from the motherhouse and be home by 8:00 p.m. in the summer and 6:00 p.m. in the winter. After the outing, they must write and tell Mother Angeline where they went. There was also permission to take one long ride and no more than three short ones annually. Unfortunately, on one Kansas mission, trips to the doctor counted as a ride and one of the local doctors was a firm believer in the efficacy of shots of various kinds. One young sister had scarcely arrived on the mission when she discovered that she had been chosen to administer the shots. It seemed that the sisters would rather risk their lives than use their three short rides for trips to the doctor.

Even with the numerous regulations that burdened the sisters, they managed to have a great deal of fun. They celebrated feast days, enjoyed numerous private jokes as well as each others' foibles and took pleasure in their outings to an extent possible only to those who seldom went anywhere but church, school, or hospital. On occasion they found that even Mother Angeline could enjoy a little levity. Four sisters whose names all contained some variation of "Rose" were all stationed one year on a mission in Indiana. Not unnaturally, they began to call themselves the Four Roses after the well known Kentucky bourbon. Not to be outdone, the remaining three sisters, termed themselves the Three Feathers after another popular whiskey. On a day when the sisters were in a particularly giddy mood they had to send a letter to the motherhouse. They dared themselves to sign the letter "The Four Roses plus the Three Feathers equals Schenley's 'Seven and Seven'" after a popular highball of the period. Of course, after the letter was in the mail, the sisters had second, third, and even fourth thoughts, none of them happy. When the reply finally came, they were astounded to read that Mother Angeline was happy to know that there was so much cheerfulness on the mission.[32]

THE WORLD OUTSIDE

On December 7, 1941, the Japanese attacked Pearl Harbor, and the United States was again at war. Like other Americans the sisters prayed constantly for the safety of the men and women in the armed services. They too lost brothers, uncles, nephews, and friends, and were affected by shortages of food and fuel; but in the absence of newspapers, newsreels and radios, they often felt cut off from the day-to-day progress of the war.

Less than a year after the United States entered the war, a Capuchin priest, Rev. Theodosius Foley, called to solicit sisters for missions in Nicaragua.[33] Foley was speaking for the Apostolic Vicariate of Bluefields, a territory of more than 22,000 square miles that comprised the eastern third of Nicaragua. Since 1913, the territory had been the responsibility of Spanish Capuchins, but Capuchins in the United States had been asked in 1938 by the Propaganda Fide[34] in Rome to take responsibility for the territory. They now needed help to provide a school and a clinic for the Miskito Indians living along the Rio Coco.

Father Foley left disappointed, but the following year the new bishop of the Vicariate, Rev. Matthew Niedhammer OFM, Cap., a pupil while Mother Angeline was principal at Our Lady Queen of Angels, Harlem, came to renew the request. He left with the assurance that Mother Angeline would bring the matter before the general chapter in 1945 provided she had the assurance that the sisters themselves would be willing to work in the missions.

MINISTRIES

The great amount of attention Mother Angeline gave to the Rule did not prevent her from being keenly interested in the works of the congregation and its usual business. When she went on visitation, she enjoyed time in the classrooms and exerted her considerable charm on the children. A child at that time still remembered more than fifty years later the excitement her visit aroused in Carnegie, Pennsylvania, and her pleasure when Mother Angeline noticed and praised her individually and asked about her family[35]

In the first few months of her administration she had conferences with pastors regarding the staffing of their parishes. She and

Sister Vera arranged a high school program with William J. Plunkett, the new pastor of Immaculate Conception parish in Elmhurst, Illinois. With only three hundred families in the parish Msgr. Plunkett had immediately set about to raise the funds to establish the first coeducational Catholic High School in Du Page County. Immaculate Conception Grade and High School became one of the congregation's largest missions.

THE SISTER TEACHER AND THE SCHOOLS

There was no doubt that Mother Angeline had had a successful career as teacher and administrator in the schools, but she had little to say to the teachers on the subject of teaching. The reason very well could have been because she saw in the constitutions a philosophy and a plan of action which, when followed, would form teachers of no little merit. The pertinent sections read:

> Since, after their own personal perfection, the instruction of children is the secondary end to which the Sisters of the Congregation are bound by the rule of the Institute, it is imperative that Superiors appoint to this sublime duty only such Sisters as they deem worthy and qualified because of character, conduct, and talent.
>
> It is the daily duty of the Sister to teach the children to memorize the words of the catechism; to exhort them to revere the mysteries of faith; to observe the precepts of Religion in the love and fear of God; and to hate sin. They shall not waste time in idle surveillance of the children nor amuse them with stories. They shall conscientiously teach during school hours, and, thereby, gradually develop the capacity of the children, that they may advance in the sciences. Thus, their schools, with the blessing of God, will merit well-deserved recognition.
>
> The Sisters shall make no distinction, through human respect, among the children committed to their care, but seek rather to win the indocile by gen-

tleness, sweetness, and motherly affection, than to
discourage them by undue severity, much less by corporal punishment.[36]

On some missions there were days when the teachers must have
worked very hard to find the sublimity in their profession. At times
the numbers of pupils reached as many as fifty or sixty in one room.
Agnesian schools were designed principally for two grades in one
room. When a teacher taught several grades in a classroom, combi-
nations could be unusual and difficult: first grade and one-half of a
third grade, the third grade and the overflow from the fifth grade. A
sister might teach single grades, double grades, or four grades in one
classroom; or she might be in a departmentally organized school.
Textbooks were handed down to brothers and sisters and relatives
because of lack of funds. Wall charts were a "must." Sisters often
found that constant repetition and memorization was the key to
learning. Classroom cleaning was usually, but not always, the janitor's job. There were still country places where the sisters cleaned
everything, including the outdoor toilets, on Saturday.

In the 1930s and early 1940s school libraries were not common
and not all classrooms had library shelving. The sisters often made
do with used orange crates. The first Agnesian school that had a
room set aside with shelving for a library was at St. Joseph's in
Carnegie, Pennsylvania. A friend and benefactor of the sisters,
Charles Fleck, provided the industrial shelving which had sat
unused in some warehouse. With the advent of libraries, some sisters began to take special training for library certification.

In the smaller schools, the children attended the parish Mass
before class. In the larger schools, classes attended Mass in groups.
They prayed before classes, made little sacrifices to please the baby
Jesus during Advent, attended the Stations of the Cross during Lent,
put their money in little boxes for the poor or pagan babies, learned
Gregorian chant, and in some places sang the Requiem Mass at
funerals. They did not eat meat on Fridays and went to confession
regularly. They were more familiar with the lives of the saints than
they were with the exploits of Greek gods and goddesses. On the
whole, the schools fulfilled their mission of giving the children a
strong sense of their identity as Catholics.

HOSPITALS AND BUILDING PROGRAMS

It was three years after the Sisters of St. Agnes had agreed to staff the projected Thomas County Hospital in Colby, Kansas, before the WPA completed the building project. On October 8, 1941, the Thomas County Hospital was dedicated and given the name St. Thomas Hospital.[37] It had a capacity of thirty-two beds and thirteen bassinets. Everything possible had been done for the medical staff and the patients, but the eight sisters who were assigned there found that no provision had been made for them. Three sisters lived in a cottage and the other five planned to sleep in a ward, but the hospital often was so fully occupied that the sisters gave up their beds and spent the night in chairs. In the morning they walked six blocks to the parish church. As soon as possible, the hospital obtained a chaplain, and the congregation bought a two-story house that was transferred to the hospital grounds.[38] The hospital had scarcely been opened when the need for a new building became clear. The new building cost $150,000. The Sisters of St. Agnes provided $100,000. Individuals and civic organizations furnished the rooms.

St. Agnes Hospital faced a critical shortage of space. The need to care for the elderly was one reason. Although elderly persons still usually lived with relatives, it was not possible in every case. In Fond du Lac, for example, there was the Fond du Lac County Home but there were few other options for the elderly. If the county home could not care for the medical needs of the patients, they were sent to St. Agnes Hospital, where they sometimes lived for many years. There were also other persons, financially able to provide for themselves but with no place to live, who chose to reside in the hospital. The congregation itself needed more infirmaries to care for aging and sick sisters as well as more bedrooms and a community room in the hospital for the sisters who lived and worked there. It was time to enlarge St. Agnes Hospital.

However, Archbishop Stritch as early as 1939 had informed Mother Angeline that he would give no permission for any other building projects until the hospital had a suitable chapel. Even the advent of World War II would not move Archbishop Kiley, his successor. Although both materials and good labor were in short supply, the addition went up and the chapel was dedicated to the Sacred Heart of Jesus in May 1943. The neo-Gothic chapel was designed to provide an atmosphere of serenity and peace; its marble high altar was a gift of the Saint Agnes School of Nursing Alumnae. Its simple design and light colors were in contrast to the exceptionally striking stained glass windows depicting saints known for their compassion to suffering humanity.

The strain of financing and overseeing yet one more building program had proved too much for Sister Joseph, who was still vicar general as well as responsible for the congregation's financial affairs. On Christmas Day 1943, she succumbed to the flu. She said nothing to Mother Angeline, who was planning a trip to New York. After the travelers were out the door, Sister Joseph sent immediately for Sister Vera, the first councilor, in order to bring her up to date on the business affairs of the congregation. She was still working the next day when the doctor called and advised that she receive the last rites. She died on January 5, 1944.

THE SISTER-NURSE

Whether at St. Agnes, St. Anthony, or St. Clare Hospital, the sisters still assumed the burden of administering and staffing the hospitals alone. Around the country, "The sister supervisor in the nursing units, for example, made rounds with the doctors, addressed all problems, managed the nursing staff, and directed all care of patients in her unit, as well as seeing to the needs of their families."[39]

For the sister at St. Agnes Hospital a typical day began at 4:40 a.m. The sister-nurse, wearing her black serge habit and face veil, hurried to be at morning prayer at 5:10 a.m. She prayed the Litany of the Saints, the first three Hours of the Little Office and then meditated for half an hour. Mass followed at 6:00 a.m.[40] She went immediately to breakfast and usually had time for only toast and coffee. Then she rushed back to her bedroom to change into a white habit. If the sister was on night duty, she put a black mantle on over her white habit to attend Mass. Sister was usually the nurse in charge, whether of the operating room, the nursing unit, or nursery. Care of patients, physically and spiritually, was her priority, but she might also wash sheets and scrub floors. The sister in the nursing unit took care of the equipment, patched rubber gloves, boiled syringes, and sterilized enema tips. She sharpened needles and made her own I.V. tubes. No task was too small or too difficult.

It was the responsibility of each head nurse to manage the nursing unit in its care of patients, carrying out of doctor's orders, serving of meals, administering of medicines—in short, in doing everything that needed to be done to keep the unit going. Because there was no Nursing Service Department until 1950, each head nurse was able to run her unit with little or no interference. There were also very few nurses on a unit. Usually there was one registered nurse assisted by student nurses. By Christmas time, a freshman student nurse was often the only nurse in a unit, although there was a night supervisor to call upon for aid. Private duty nurses were quite common in that era, and are still fondly remembered for their generosity in helping out sisters and students.

Sister-nurses had only a few minutes to eat dinner at noon, worked until it was time for spiritual reading, or, more often, until the work was done. During spiritual reading, the sisters usually mended their clothes. Then it was time for vespers and compline, supper and recreation. For most sisters, recreation was truly a re-creation. They played cards, took walks, celebrated feast days, or just enjoyed each other's company. The three short and one long automobile rides the sisters were allowed yearly were deeply treasured. With the exception of the one week allowed for a retreat, this was their schedule for the year. Before World War II, there was no such thing as an eight-hour day for the sisters, nor did days off exist.[41] The woman who was able to maintain such a rigorous schedule with grace and fidelity "considered her work to alleviate the sufferings of their fellow brothers and sisters to be for the honor and glory of God … without giving a thought that a monetary value was being placed on her work. A pay check never entered her mind."[42]

ST. AGNES SCHOOL OF NURSING

The administration and staffs of the hospitals and St. Agnes School of Nursing were affected more directly by the entrance of the United States into World War II than was any other segment of the congregation. The shortage of nurses increased work loads for the already overworked hospital personnel. During this period Red Cross Grey Ladies and Girl Scout volunteers were trained to aid in a variety of tasks. The School of Nursing participated in government programs subsidizing both the education of students who promised to engage in essential nursing services for the duration of the war (Cadet Nurse Corps) and also schools of nursing willing to accelerate their program of study to provide student nurses with their primary training in two and one-half years.[43] Between 1943 and 1948, St. Agnes graduated 240 cadet nurses.

The three-year diploma program for RN's had never been anything but successful. But as health care became more scientific, there was a demand from within the profession for nurses to obtain bachelors' degrees. Furthermore, the cost of the nursing program to the hospital was becoming prohibitive. The St. Agnes School of Nursing administration was beginning to realize that discontinuing the three-year program was almost unavoidable. Although not everyone was convinced that the degree program would produce nurses of the proven quality of the graduates of the three-year program, the administration began to study the integration of nursing and college programs.[44]

Sisters in health care were being sent to universities for advanced training by the end of the 1930s although it was not until the 1950s that sisters who were registered nurses were formally prepared as administrators.[45] Other administrators before them had been teachers or employees from the business office. One had been a dietitian, and another had been in charge of the operating room. At the age of eighty, Sister Bertha Flanagan, a former teacher, was chosen to administer a hospital. Not all administrators were personally successful, but teamwork on the part of the rest of the staff pulled the hospitals through.

SOCIAL CHANGES

Scarcely noted by the busy sisters, the war years had been bringing about a social revolution. More strains were placed on family life because more than sixteen million men and women served in the armed forces. Six million women entered the workplace. Families were uprooted from familiar and supportive environments. It was not long before society's disruption was shown by increases in divorces, mental illness, family violence, and juvenile delinquency.

Political differences were muted temporarily as the nation threw its resources into defeating the Axis powers. Minorities had more opportunities for decent wages; women were employed in factories and shipyards; Black Americans left the South for good-paying jobs in Northern factories and West Coast shipyards. Higher incomes allowed more Americans to go to the movies, read books, and seize opportunities for cultural experiences.

Atom bombs ended the war in 1945, but the United States and its former ally, the Soviet Union, were soon embroiled in the Cold War. Threats of a third world war followed. The fear of a nuclear holocaust unleashed by communists haunted many an American. Catholics worried about the communist menace and many a parochial school child was frightened by the message of Our Lady of Fatima and the threat of the blood of martyrs on the streets of American cities.[46]

PROGRESS IN EDUCATIONAL MINISTRIES

Following the general custom among sisters' colleges at this time, the superior general frequently served as the president of the congregation's college as well. Although Mother Angeline bore the title of president, Sister Vera Naber, appointed dean, bore the responsibility for the college's development. In 1941 Marian College was accredited by the University of Wisconsin as a four-year elementary teacher training college. That year also marked the college's first commencement with eight graduates receiving the degree of Bachelor of Science in Education. In 1949 the college affiliated with Catholic University, and was admitted to membership in the National Catholic Educational Association as a senior college. In the same year the students became members of the National Federation of Catholic College Students and the Alumnae Association was organized.

In those early years, Marian College was blessed with an excellent, if little known, faculty. Among them were Sister Muriel Tarr, who, as academic dean, brought a breadth of vision in literature and the arts; Sister Clare M. Goodwin, who made history come alive for the students; Sisters Mary Anthony Keller and Gerald Vodde in the science department who gave students a thorough preparation in the basic sciences; Sister Mary Constance Busch who was unrivaled in her ability to clarify mathematical concepts, and Rudolph Bierberg, C.PP.S., an excellent theologian and professor. Originally these professors had no rank, no tenure, and no money.

There were no secretaries, not even for the academic dean. The faculty room contained two or three typewriters for faculty use. Instructors duplicated examinations on little pans of gelatin.[47]

The year 1950 was a banner year, because the faculty acquired a hectograph. The first official faculty meetings complete with minutes were held. Typically, during the early 1950s the faculty discussed philosophy of education, the papal encyclical *Humani Generis*, Aristotelian philosophy, Christian humanism, and the social thought of John A. Ryan[48] and Mortimer Adler.[49] A continuing concern during the early years was the small number of upperclassmen because most lay students completed either the two-year rural program or the three-year elementary program, and the newly professed sisters were sent out on mission. Although the majority of students returned to Marian to complete their degrees, they came back in the summers or on a part-time basis.

In 1950, there were 86 full-time and 145 part-time students. In the summer, as sisters returned to the motherhouse to complete their bachelor degrees, enrollment hovered around two hundred. By 1951 there were three curricula: the four-year teacher training course, the two-year course for the licensing of rural teachers, and a nursing degree completion program.

Twenty years after Marian College opened, Sister Vera wrote an apologia in her history: "At present the Congregation cannot point to a prepossessing building as the culmination of its efforts in the field of teacher education; however, all the Sisters fondly hope and fervently pray that an adequate Marian College plant may materialize ... when the finances of the congregation justify the expenditure."[50] Marian's greatest strength was its clear sense of mission and a dedicated faculty. Founded for the preparation of teachers, it was able to focus on its goal and do it well, but time was needed to build up the library holdings, the laboratories, and financial resources. But in light of the congregation's educational apostolate, the college was necessary, and the community was willing to make a commitment even though it would prove to be a constant drain on its resources.

St. Mary's Springs was gradually adjusting to the increasing number of male students. Father Joseph Herod was assigned there in 1942 as its first athletic director as well as religion teacher. The school joined the Fox River Valley Catholic Conference and intramural sports played an important role in the life and morale of the school. The school had also changed in other ways. By 1955, the boarding school had been slowly phased out. The primary grades were discontinued in 1945; in 1946, the intermediate grades; the seventh and eighth grades in 1947, and eight years later, the last boarder left.[51]

Accepting new missions meant stretching the sisters as far as possible. It was not unusual for a sister to teach seven days a week, five in the parochial school and then catechism classes on Saturday in the parish for the children who didn't attend the parochial school and Sunday in another parish. They trained the altar servers, frequently took care of the church, and organized many parish celebrations such as Forty Hours, Corpus Christi, May Crowning, and the feast of the special patron of the parish. Some pastors wanted the sisters to take on more duties. When a monsignor requested that the sisters also do the church wash, Mother Angeline pointed out that "the sisters were breaking down on all sides because of an excess of work."[52]

The election, on the other hand, was creating a great deal of anxiety in the congregation. Mother Angeline was in her seventy-first year and her health was beginning to show signs of strain. In addition, her arbitrary decisions were causing anxiety. But on June 15, 1945, Mother Angeline was returned to office in spite of the many predictions that she would not serve again.[53]

By far the most far-reaching act of the delegates was to approve the decision to send missionaries to Nicaragua.

MISSION TO NICARAGUA

Ninety-one sisters volunteered to serve in a country they had to look up on a map. Realizing that the congregation was enthusiastic about the missions, Mother Angeline, well before the chapter, had chosen Sister Mary Agnes Dickof, a fifty-one year old dietitian from Marshfield, Wisconsin; Sister Pauletta Scheck, a teacher from Germany, who was also fifty-one; Sister Francis Borgia Dreiling, thirty-nine years old, a teacher and organist from Victoria, Kansas; and Sister Agnes Rita Fisette, a thirty-year-old house sister from Marquette, Michigan. The criteria for service were simple, good health and permission of the sister's parents.

With good hearts, a modicum of knowledge and not a little trepidation, the sisters began to prepare for their great adventure.[54] They began to study Spanish; Sister Mary Agnes received some lessons in midwifery from a local physician, Dr. Joseph Devine. They packed numerous boxes of supplies that they placed under the care of appropriate patrons. The Blessed Trinity and Mother Cabrini were assigned general supplies; Our Blessed Lady was to look after the sewing material, dining room ware, kitchen goods, tablets, pencils, dispensary material, and laundry supplies; St. Benedict was assigned tools, farm implements, and books; while Guardian Angels and the Infant Savior were to look after games and sundries.[55]

The friars had invited the sisters to work with them in a country that was known for its history of instability and oppression. About the same size as Wisconsin, Nicaragua is separated geographically, ethnically, culturally, and religiously between its Pacific and Atlantic coasts.[56] In 1945, more than three quarters of its approximately two million people lived in the Pacific lowlands. The majority of people were of mixed blood but the national culture reflected its predominantly Spanish heritage.

Nicaragua had been independent of Spain since the Latin American revolutions in the 1820s. It was governed by Anastasio Somoza Garcia, who was supported by the United States. The country's lack of economic development and poverty coupled with the wealth of the ruling class was making it a fertile ground for revolutionary activity.[57]

The east coast, where the sisters were missioned, was isolated from the west. Pine forests covered much of the area and little of the land was suitable for agriculture. The Miskito people lived in eighty villages along the 450-mile Río Coco and comprised the largest ethnic group where the sisters would be missioned.[58] Because of their isolation, the Miskitos had been able to retain much of their own language and culture. They had also been cut off from the limited technological and scientific progress of the rest of the country. Education and health care were primitive. The people were Christians—the majority were members of the Moravian church.[59]

The missionaries left for New Orleans on August 16, 1945 attired in black serge habits, veils, face veils, and mantles. They stayed ten days with the Sisters of Charity in New Orleans where their Mother Stanislaus had arranged to have professors from

Tulane and Louisiana State University give them a short course in parasitology. Sister Mary Agnes learned about amebiasis and bacillary dysentery, ascarides and worms, malaria and fevers.[60] She, who was given two bottles of aspirin and one bottle of quinine to start a clinic,[61] had also received some instruction in appropriate medications.

When the sisters arrived at the Colegio de Asunción in Managua, Nicaragua was relatively peaceful. Bishop Niedhammer had arranged that the Sisters of the Assumption provide lessons in Spanish and an introduction to Nicaraguan culture for the missionaries. In exchange their guests taught English to the high school girls.

That night after the missionaries arrived, Sister Mary Agnes wrote a wryly brief comment in her Journal: "The first night away from the U.S.A., in Nicaragua, the land of revolutions."[62] The following morning the sisters had their first glimpse of the class distinctions prevalent in Nicaraguan society. It was a minor incident but it made an impression. The sisters had walked to Mass, and Sister Mary Agnes, as superior of the group, was offered a ride home with the Madres. When Sister indicated that she would rather walk with the other sisters, Madre Carmen insisted that she must ride, "You must keep up your dignity." Sister Mary Agnes noted the incident, remarking that "such customs did not fit into Agnesian life."[63]

On their first walk through Managua, the sisters were shaken by the destitution they encountered. "Walked through the streets—the sight was terrible. Pigs, chickens, brushed against you, mud was a foot deep, vendors half-clothed sat on walks, despicable sight. This was a taste of our work in Nicaragua."[64] Commenting on the absence of electricity for the ordinary person, Sister Mary Agnes wrote, "but up on the side of the mountain is the presidential estate and it practically sparkles all night with hundreds of lights. Reason alone tells the need of a day of reckoning."[65] The next morning after a visit to the city of Leon, she predicted an inevitable "revolutionary movement … it won't be long before Nicaragua is going to be active, as Communism is rampant in every quarter."[66]

Accustomed to North American ideas of time and order, the sisters found it difficult to get used to the laid-back approach of Nicaraguans: "We have now come to realize that no real system prevails in anything," she wrote.[67] Three weeks later the sisters witnessed a political protest. The University students were rioting against the President, an event neither too unusual or too serious. The *Guardia*[68] quickly restored order but it was an omen of the future.

Waspam—The Cradle of Their Apostolate[69]

On December 7, 1945, the missionaries began their three hundred-mile journey with the beds, tables, chairs, desks, and dressers made for them in Managua. The bishop had arranged for them to travel to Puerto Cabezas, the principal city on the east coast, where they spent two weeks getting acquainted with fellow missionaries and other Americans. Located on the Caribbean Coast, Puerto Cabezas is a town in an area of great natural beauty. The population, numbering about ten thousand, was then mainly Black and Hispanic, but the culture had been strongly influenced by the English. Even in a town that size, immediate communication with the outside world was possible only through radio.

On December 20 the sisters flew to Waspam. The village was only forty-nine miles from Puerto Cabezas, but as it was a four-hour ride over very rough roads, flying often proved more practical.[70] At that time there were only a few houses there, but the Standard Fruit Company had its center in Waspam, and a road was being built between Puerto Cabezas and Waspam.[71] When the sisters arrived, they were met by "close to five hundred" excited villagers.[72] Everyone joined in a solemn procession behind the cross, as Bishop Niedhammer led the way to the parish church of San Rafael.[73]

Three Capuchin priests were stationed at Waspam, one in the town itself and one in the villages up the river, the other working in the villages down the river. In all they were caring for thirty missions along the Río Coco.[74] It was fortunate for the sisters that their first missionary experience was with a Capuchin community. Not only had the Agnesian rule been written by a Capuchin, but both came from much the same geographical areas; were familiar with some of the same parishes and people, and came from much the same kind of families. Brother Gaul Neumann, for example, was in charge of the buildings of the Waspam mission; church, school, clinic, convent, and the *casa cural*.[75] He was carpenter, plumber, and electrician and would become their valued friend. Sister Agnes Rita cooked for both sisters and friars. The friars' meals were carried in a *portavian-das*[76] to their house.

It was the river that was important in Waspam. The sisters soon found the truth of the words a visitor would later write, "It [the Río Coco] is the Miskito's river—it is their road, their livelihood, the graveyard of their ancestors. They have tamed it, they have named it; they live on it, they love it."[77]

The people in the village lived in the small rectangular houses of split bamboos or sawed lumber and grass roofs built on pilings about four feet off the ground. The height was a protection against insects, animals, and snakes. Most houses had only one room and little furniture. People sat, ate, and slept on the floor. Some houses had a smaller cook-house attached to the main house. Because the only farming land was along the river, men would leave the village early in the morning on their long, flat-bottomed pit-pans,[78] returning later with bananas, rice, or beans, the staple foods of the Miskito Indians. There were fruits in abundance. Their staples, rice and beans, were harvested twice a year in April and November. Usually the rice and beans were turned over to merchants in payment for credit granted on items purchased during the year.

The sister's convent stood isolated. A hurricane had driven a banana company out of business there in 1937. The company returned to the states leaving behind an office building on stilts which the Capuchins had converted into the sisters' convent.[79] There was not a soul within calling distance. At night they waited in their little community room, trying to study the language. "Not a sound was heard except the call of the night-birds; there was the absence of noise," Sister Mary Agnes wrote, "There was the absence of everything that bespoke civilization. We were alone with Him Who stilled our fears."[80]

Underneath the house was the clinic. From the beginning, it was clear that there was far more to be done than even the most willing hearts could accomplish. More than half of the babies born did not reach adulthood and infectious diseases, mainly enteritis, malaria, and tuberculosis were a constant problem. Worms were endemic among the children and malnutrition was chronic. The nearest hospital was several hours away and, in any case, most people could not afford the care. Drunkenness was a problem together with its related difficulties of fighting and domestic abuse. However, left behind as they were by industrialization, the people still had tribal and family structures along with the traditional economic and social values that had guided them for generations as well as a spirituality that could often put the more sophisticated to shame.

The poverty of the people tore at the sisters' hearts. After the pastor took her to homes to visit the sick who were not able to walk to the clinic, Sister Mary Agnes wrote: "All my experience in hospital work in the States seemed to have left me void. I never saw humanity in such a miserable state as I witnessed it now. It was a revelation of an abject poverty in its worst form. I had no supply of medicine to speak of—a little supply of quinine, a small bottle of atabrine, a little of this and little of that was nothing to handle this crowd of festering humanity until further supplies came in from friends at home." It was not long before the dietitian from St. Clare Hospital in Monroe, Wisconsin was performing the duties of midwife, surgeon, dentist,[81] and general practitioner.

Of her experiences, she wrote: "In one home was a young girl, with pneumonia, cuddled up in a home-made hammock too small for her size. In one corner of the same room, lay a young boy with a burning fever. Next to him on the floor lay another youth, in the last stages of tuberculosis, using a wooden block for a head rest; he died a few weeks later. In the adjoining hut was a corpse wrapped up in two burlap sacks ready for burial. The woman died in the morning and would be buried in the afternoon. With this initiation, I returned to the convent and found refuge in the chapel, the powerhouse of the place. The task ahead was a tremendous one and only the Almighty One could work the miracles needed to change this desperate situation."[82]

Of a particularly poignant incident, Sister wrote that she had directed a woman to come for treatment for worms. "She was there before the sisters rose. With her two children she lay on the ground inside the fence and slept. She broke a stone into bits and gave them to her children to eat."[83]

The sisters followed the life and horarium of the motherhouse as much as possible. Neither Mother Angeline nor Sister Mary Agnes believed in exceptions to the rule. At first the sisters wore the traditional habit of five to seven yards of heavy serge and a mantle. The veil with its starched lining was a perpetual penance, as was the linen collar. Sister Mary Agnes spent much time and energy establishing a fenced-in enclosure that the sisters were not to venture leaving after 4:00 p.m. Their religious obligations added to their professional duties made them very busy women. Visitors were infrequent and opportunities for recreation were extremely limited. At Thanksgiving, Sister Mary Agnes complained that she spent fifteen cents each for candy bars for the sisters. "It was terrible," she wrote, "but a treat for the sisters is necessary."[84] The life the missionaries led was one of prayer and hard work. Yet, years later Sister Francis Borgia commented, "It was a life that had more joy than sorrow—joy because they were so accepted by the people."[85]

Opening of School

Enrollment in the school began on May 19. It took more than two weeks before the one hundred twenty-nine children of Miskito, Chinese, and Spanish-speaking backgrounds had registered. Some little boys, following the Miskito custom, came to school without clothes. The sisters made some clothes in a hurry. The children returned the next day in the same state. They had given the clothing away. Even so, the opening day was a triumphant one, dignified by a talk by the lieutenant *comandante* and the blessing of the Nicaraguan flag. The difficulties of teaching in a school without enough benches, school supplies, and books were endless. Although education was not compulsory, the classes were large. Sister Pauletta had fifty primary pupils, some of whom were sixteen and seventeen years old. Sister Francis Borgia had fifty-two children in her intermediate class while Señorita Lilliam Cruz had fifty-seven advanced children. They studied the same subjects as North American children did.[86]Sister Mary Agnes added principal and teacher of hygiene to her roles as superior and administrator of the clinic. Attendance could be irregular. Many of the children walked several miles to school and arrived hungry and tired, but when they did come, frequently rain-drenched, muddy, and bedraggled, they were friendly and enthusiastic. Worms were so commonplace among them that during one hygiene lesson when the children were asked what was in the human body, one child replied, "A heart, some food, and worms."[87]

Half the children spoke only Miskito and the missionaries had not yet learned the language.[88] The teachers had to use all their creativity to devise ways of communication. Sister Francis Borgia was fortunate to have in her class a very bright tri-lingual girl who translated her instructions to the other children in Spanish and Miskito while she taught Miskito to her teacher. She also devised charts in the hopes that pictures would help her get her points across. Astonishingly, when the inspector of schools visited in July, he was pleased with the school and the performance of the pupils.[89]

Nevertheless, the sisters held on to their determination to make the *colegio* a proper grade school just like the ones in the States. Sister Francis Borgia managed to get friends to send uniforms and band instruments to the little school along the Río Coco. The parish church and liturgy began to show the effects of the sisters' labors. Friends also sent dresses for the first Holy Communion of the little girls, while the altar boys looked resplendent in red cassocks. Snapshots show children dressed for plays and entertainments looking just as they might have in Wisconsin or Kansas. By the time the Fourth of July rolled around the little scholars could sing "The Star Spangled Banner" in English and one young lady read the "Preamble to the Constitution of the United States."[90]

CHANGES

Before the missionaries had been in Nicaragua six months, Mother Angeline wrote to tell them that she would send two more sisters. They could choose either two teachers or a teacher and a nurse. The sisters chose the latter, but when Bishop Niedhammer[91] visited the motherhouse, he asked for the two teachers. The following March Sisters Tarcisia Ullrich and Constantia Esterbrook were welcome arrivals. The curriculum now included sewing and manual arts. Sister Mary Agnes, freed from her duties at the school, continued in the clinic alone.[92]

In 1948, when the first Nicaraguan women applied for admission to the community, Sisters of St. Agnes everywhere felt that their work was being blessed.[93] Sister Teresita Inés Argüello from Bluefields on the Atlantic Coast, and Sister Rosa Inés Silva, from San Marcos near Managua, became the first Sisters of St. Agnes from Central America. While they experienced the hardships that North American women unwittingly imposed upon their Nicaraguan sisters they were fortunate in that they realized their director, Sister Tarcisia, really loved them.[94] In spite of her lack of knowledge of their culture, she gave them a firm grasp of the Agnesian style of religious life[95] while they heroically learned a new language and culture, along with the equally foreign traditions and customs of religious life.[96]

CONGREGATIONAL CONCERNS

On April 23, 1947, the Sisters of St. Agnes received a rescript[97] from the Sacred Congregation of Religious which permitted precedence in a religious house to rank from the day of first profession, or, if two sisters were professed the same day, the date of birth. There would be "no distinction in occupation because all types of work, performed in obedience under the sanction of the religious vows, are equally pleasing to God. Previously house sisters were ranked below the other members of the community. As sisters were assigned their places at meals, chapel, etc., according to rank, the practice, imported from Europe, created an obvious class distinction."[98] It was a document that could be greeted only with relief by American sisters who had always been uncomfortable with the custom.

Religious congregations were bombarded with pleas to open schools and hospitals. The Sisters of St. Agnes were no exception. Scarcely a week went by without Mother Angeline writing a letter to another pastor or hospital board regretting her inability to supply teachers or build a hospital.[99] Four schools were exceptions: Our Lady Help of Christians in West Allis, Wisconsin was accepted in 1949, and, in 1950, Beloit Catholic High School and St. Thomas School in Beloit, Wisconsin, and the Capuchin school, *Colegio Niño Jesús*, in Puerto Cabezas, Nicaragua.

At the end of the 1940s, it was becoming clear that more and better facilities were needed to take care of aging sisters who were either living at the motherhouse or at St. Agnes and St. Clare Hospitals. Mother Angeline attempted to alleviate the problem by buying a large house on the Ledge near the Springs. Unfortunately, the sisters soon found that the hilly grounds were unsuitable for the infirm and that, when winter came, the house became so cold it had to be vacated. The property was sold in July 1950.

Archbishop Kiley, aware of the increasing number of elderly sisters, encouraged the congregation to build a residence for the elderly or mentally ill sisters. After much thought, the council decided to put an addition to St. Clare Hospital for the purpose, especially because more space was also needed for hospital purposes. Monroe was in the Madison Diocese, and the congregation soon found that Bishop William P. O'Connor did not look favorably on their request. Not only did he think that a million-dollar hospital was pretentious in a small town, he had also been hearing from clergy and laity that the hospital was understaffed and that too heavy a burden was placed on the sisters.[100] Despite the bishop's concerns, he accepted the assurances of the sisters that the project was necessary. The permission was given and he graciously dedicated the addition on May 29, 1951.

That same month, the council received a letter from one of the doctors at St. Clare in regard to admitting alcoholics to the hospital. Alcoholics Anonymous was becoming more widely known at this juncture, but it was clear that the congregation was not ready to face the problem. The *Annals* noted that because "we were not permitted to do it, we wrote him saying that the higher authorities would not give permission for a sister to undertake the work on account of the moral and physical risk."[101]

Sister Blandine Eisele did not agree with this position. In 1936, only one year after Alcoholics Anonymous was founded, she attended a convention in Cleveland where she became acquainted with the program.[102] It was not long before she became involved and made it her personal mission to work with alcoholics. She would face years of misunderstanding before the work she did with persons afflicted with the disease was understood and respected.[103]

The establishment of a school of nursing in connection with St. Anthony Hospital in Hays was the last large project of Mother Angeline's administration. For some time the sisters there had been eager to fulfill the request of the bishop to open a Catholic school of nursing for western Kansas. A nurses' training school in the area would help the hospital conquer the problem of the lack of qualified nurses. Sister Digna Desch, who had been director of the St. Agnes School of Nursing for many years, was sent to Hays to organize the St. Anthony School of Nursing. It opened on August 19, 1951 with twelve students.

THE FIFTIES

With the advent of the 1950s, the country entered into an era of consumerism. The economy was booming as people began to make up for the deprivations of the Depression and the war years. The first credit card appeared. As people rushed to the suburbs, tract housing spread across the land. Automobiles became a necessity; gas stations multiplied; the fast food industry took off, and the first shopping malls appeared throughout the country. A visit to any part of the country revealed a depressing sameness which was soon symbolized by "the man in the gray flannel suit."[104] College students, when profiled, were found to be more interested in security and income than in public service or the helping professions.

Everyone seemed to agree that a woman's place was in the home. Sister Muriel Tarr, dean of Marian College, expressed the dominant ideal to the graduating class of 1951: "A woman's social destiny is to save the family; her dignity is to be found in preserving and fostering her distinctly womanly characteristics." Even so, 40 percent of American women were working outside the home, often out of economic necessity.

As the decade advanced, social critics began to point out that the United States, with only 6 percent of the world's population, was consuming almost half of the world's goods; racial problems were escalating; poverty still existed at home. The fear of communism increased with the possibility of nuclear warfare. The country was ripe for another Red Scare when Wisconsin's Senator Joseph McCarthy's charges of a communist conspiracy led to a witch hunt, congressional investigations, and the infamous loyalty oaths. As for Catholics, whose worries about atheistic communism had pre-dated those of most of their fellow Americans, far too many were happy to be in the mainstream of political sentiment, and became ardent McCarthy supporters.

While middle-of-the road American churches were experiencing a kind of revival of Christianity that downplayed sin and evil and preached Americanism and fellowship, members of the Catholic intelligentsia who had achieved a secure place in American society began to look more critically at the church and its institutions.[105] A new theology emerged according to Charles Morris, which "emphasized the individual's relation with Christ, sought the authentic meaning of the Scriptures, tried to recapture the spirit and simplicity of the liturgies of the primitive church, and groped for an inclusiveness that made the Eucharist a shared meal, rather than a distant ritual on cold marble altars."[106] Thomas Merton's[107] story of his conversion, the best-selling *The Seven Storey Mountain*, introduced a welcome and highly personalized form of Catholic spirituality.[108]

MOTHER ALBERTONIA LICHER

On June, 27, 1951, when the delegates to the 15th general chapter of the congregation elected Sister Albertonia Licher as superior general, they were not looking for either theological or liturgical innovations. They were choosing a woman whom they loved and trusted to bring serenity, peace, and affection to the community. She was the youngest woman in the position since Mother Agnes and, without a doubt, the gentlest and most tender of heart. A woman who felt as her own the wounds of others, she demanded much of herself, little of others. With her councilors, Sister Sebastian Schaller, Sister Fidelis Karlin, Sister Anaclete Entringer, and Sister Lucile Herman, she would serve 705 professed sisters, 50 novices, and 50 candidates in sixty-one cities in the United States, and two missions in Nicaragua.

Agnes Licher was born August 19, 1899, the fourth of the eight children born to Albert and Anna Licher in Anderson, Indiana. The children were taught by the Holy Cross Sisters at St. Mary's School there. Like so many other families after the financial panic of 1907, the Lichers struggled to get by. When Agnes was in the sixth grade, the family moved to Muncie, where her father found work in a wire mill. There she attended St. Lawrence School where she became acquainted with the Sisters of St. Agnes. After graduation, she attended a business school in town and then worked for a firm of lawyers.

Although Agnes had become convinced by age eighteen that she had a vocation to the religious life, she was worried over the effect the loss of her income would have on the struggling family. Even as a young girl, she had felt responsible for the other children. The family never forgot that Agnes had put cardboard in her shoes so that another child could have a new pair.[109]

Years later her sister wrote, "Her one worry on entering the Sisters of St Agnes—was she feared taking from dad and mother the weekly salary she was then earning. They needed it so much. As an absolute fact, we can state, 'Dad gave her the last quarter we owned.' And when we say last, we mean that very thing. There was not a cent in the house until dad received his next check. But from that memorable day on, things changed in our family. It is a perfect example of Our Lord's promise, 'I will not be outdone in generosity.'"[110]

The newly professed Sister Albertonia was sent to Our Lady Queen of Angels in Harlem and then to St. Fidelis High School in Victoria, Kansas, where she taught commercial subjects. In 1935 she was given charge of the commercial department at Decatur Catholic High School in Decatur, Indiana. At the same time, she attended Purdue University and became licensed as a school librarian. In 1944, after the death of Sister Joseph, the Secretary General, she was chosen to be third councilor and general secretary of the congregation.

While Sister Albertonia was on the council, she endeared herself to the sisters by participating in their lives. Instead of going immediately to recreation after supper, she went to the kitchen to help the house sisters with the dishes. She could be found snatching a dust cloth from a novice and helping her dust the wainscoting in the basement hall. Working in the yard was her delight until she became superior general, when members of her council advised her that yard work was not fitting for a superior general. When she had to go out, she took an elderly sister with her whenever possible to give her a chance to get away. She visited the elderly often when they were sick, always bringing along a little gift to make them feel better.

Seven years on the council had acquainted Mother Albertonia with the problems that faced the community. There were the usual financial decisions to be made regarding the hospitals. There were also, of course, seven hundred sisters for whose spiritual welfare she was responsible, and, it must be admitted, there was also a problem with morale within the congregation.[111] Twelve years of narrow legalism coupled with a deep-rooted conviction that superiors were always right in relation to their subjects had created an atmosphere that often contained more fear than love. Willing to make any sacrifice to bring harmony and joy to the community, Mother Albertonia was convinced "that a Mother Superior must suffer to bring the utmost of blessings on her community."[112]

A letter written by the convent chaplain, her confessor, spiritual director, and trusted friend, encouraged a style of leadership compatible with her own temperament and spirituality. In fact, Mother Albertonia would have been capable of no other.

> The whole problem of improving religious life, therefore, boils down to the practice of the virtues and the counsels .... The emphasis must be upon the practice of virtue by the individual religious. Practically, this cannot be done by listing abuses as Father Hagspiel[113] does, nor by a get-tough policy on the part of superiors, nor by any external means. ... And unless we individually desire their perfection, we shall never cooperate with the actual graces of God to do so .... Contrary to Father Hagspiel's method, then, I suggest as best means for perfecting life among the Sisters such things as: sympathy, understanding, encouragement, inspiration, example, teaching, etc. In three words, believe, hope, love ... and never be content with the degree to which we have attained. In this way, not only will the abuses be done away with, but prudence and common sense will prevail among superiors and subjects.[114]

In November 1951, Mother Albertonia was admitted as a member of the Association of Victim Souls Who Immolate Themselves in Union With the Sacred Hearts of Jesus and Mary. Members "abandon themselves unreservedly to the Adorable Heart of Jesus, that He may dispose of them according to His will. Desiring only whatever He wishes, they accept beforehand and in a spirit of reparation, all the pains and sufferings of soul, mind and body that He may be pleased to send them, with the intention of helping, by the immolation of themselves, to extend the reign of the Sacred Heart of Jesus, and to obtain the triumph of holy church, abundant graces for priests and the salvation of souls."[115] Mother Albertonia was convinced that when one has love in one's vocation, one's work and love for one's fellowmen nothing else matters. She "was ready to pay the price, but she did not foresee the pain she must endure."[116]

Within a few months after her election, Mother Albertonia suffered her first mental breakdown. Her health never fully recovered, and she suffered frequent recurrences during her tenure as mother superior. Even so, the Christmas letter of 1951 to the congregation portrays a pleasant picture of community activities. There is also evidence of a more open response to the world because each sister is asked to participate in some program for the diocese in which she is missioned.

Because Mother Albertonia's health did not improve sufficiently, members of the council made visitation to the local missions in the spring of 1952. The Easter letter reported that they were "unanimous in praising the spirit of our sisters everywhere. Wherever they went they were impressed with the astounding amount of work expected of the sisters and edified by the spirit of sacrifice with which the sisters meet these expectations."[117]

BROADER HORIZONS

There were other stirrings in the congregation. Sister Fidelis Karlin had been appointed president of Marian College in July 1951, and she had proven to have the necessary vision and drive that was needed to move the college forward. She created the first lay advisory board to the college; she increased the number of faculty members; she named the first Dean of Students. She purchased a large colonial-style house on Division Street from the Fannie Thornton estate as housing for the lay students, a center and curriculum library for the Education Department and a meeting place for Alpha Omega, the college sorority.[118] Her interest in and compassion for people of third world countries led her to educate several sister-students from India.

Sister Fidelis encouraged the development of courses in English, history, and biology as the first liberal arts majors. The education department began to be an important asset to the lay teachers, particularly graduates of the state's two-year normal program, to complete their work for a bachelor's degree. The department networked with country and city schools so that lay students could have student teaching experiences in the public school system. In 1956 students at St. Agnes School of Nursing began taking their basic freshman courses at Marian. It was the beginning of the process that would eventuate in Marian College assuming full responsibility for a collegiate program of nursing.

Whether it was because of the times, the effects of higher education on the community, or the influence of Sister Fidelis on the one hand and, Father Bierberg, on the other, sisters were beginning to take a more active interest in world affairs. However, the insecurity many sisters felt when making a political decision was revealed in the November 1 statement in the *Annals* which reported that the convent chaplain met with sisters to give them instructions so that they could vote more intelligently.

TRANSITIONS IN HEALTH CARE

Inevitably, St. Agnes School of Nursing also had to face the inevitability of change. The three-year diploma program for registered nurses had never been anything but successful, but as health care was becoming more scientific, a demand arose from within the profession for nurses to obtain bachelor's degrees. The faculty of the school of nursing came to the conclusion that one year of college work should precede nursing. In addition, the cost of the nursing program to St. Agnes Hospital was becoming prohibitive. Discontinuing that program was becoming unavoidable. Sister Mary Agreda Touchett was given the charge of studying the integration of nursing with college programs. It would be only a matter of time before the nursing program would be offered by Marian as a degree program.

Health care was undergoing a revolution as fast as, if not faster than, changes in education. The Hill-Burton Act (1946), the nation's major health facility construction program, had originally been designed to provide federal grants to modernize hospitals. In return for partial federal funding, hospitals agreed to provide services free or at reduced charges for persons unable to pay. Hospitals were no longer serving only the acutely ill. By the late 1940s patients with chronic illnesses were coming as well as patients admitted in order to prevent or forestall sickness or illness. The focus of hospitals became one of preventive medicine. New specialists, new equip-

ment and new facilities had to be added along with new technolo-
gies.[119]

When the 1896 wing of St. Agnes Hospital was found to be
unsafe, there was nothing to be done but to remove that section and
rebuild. It was an opportunity to add the necessary operating rooms,
waiting rooms, and pathology, X-ray, and medical technology
departments. The ground was broken for the building on April 20,
1954. Funds were not easily raised, although St. Agnes Hospital did
receive $100,000 from the Hill-Burton Program. Costing
$3,800,000, the eight-story addition to the hospital was the largest
building project to date in the history of Fond du Lac. Mother
Albertonia, agonizing over the debt the congregation had incurred,
was not able to attend the dedication.[120]

All the Agnesian hospitals benefited in 1955, when each
received funds from the Ford Foundation to assist non-profit hospitals extend their services: St. Agnes Hospital, $157,000; St. Anthony
Hospital, $60,300; St. Clare $61,800; and St. Thomas Hospital,
$20,200.[121] The hospitals also benefited occasionally from bequests.
Emery Odell, publisher of the *Monroe Evening Times*, left the bulk of
his estate to St. Clare Hospital. The $87,000 bequest was used for
the construction of an addition which allowed for an ambulance
entrance, a blood bank, equipment for premature and newborn
infants, storage rooms, a new lounge, and a locker room.

With the diversification and specialization of services and the
increasing ratio of lay nurses to sisters, the need to adapt to new
demands became more pressing. Superiors of religious congregations were being forced to wrestle with a question affecting their
very mission. What would become of the sisters' traditional place in
the hospital, assuring that the hospital care for patients' souls as well
as their bodies?

While the congregation's energies and money were engaged in
building projects, money was scarce on the local missions. The sisters were asked to be as frugal as possible. Every small expense was
discouraged. The missions were asked not to buy any religious articles, spiritual books or magazines; the serving of fruit was curtailed;
the occasional dish of candy disappeared.

TWO MORE SCHOOLS

Two schools both dedicated to St. Joseph—one in Berlin, Wisconsin and the other in Rosemount, Minnesota—had been acquired in 1953. Accepting the school in Minnesota was the direct result of the enthusiasm of the pastor, Father James Fury, and Mother Albertonia's devotion to the Sacred Heart of Jesus. Father had announced to his parish that he was leaving the next day and was not going to return until he had sisters to staff his school, even if it took him a month.[122] The first place he visited was Fond du Lac. After talking with Mother Albertonia and promising to consecrate his parish and school to the Sacred Heart if she would give him sisters, he returned the next day with the promise of sisters for his school![123] Other parishes were not as fortunate. The pastor of St. Mary's Parish in Altoona, Pennsylvania, was irate because the community could not provide a commercial teacher for the school. "It seems strange to us that the Parish which holds the distinction of sending more girls to the Sisters of St. Agnes than any other should be shorthanded for sisters in it's [sic] own parish school."[124] At least two other pastors wrote of their shock because their parishes had just built large new convents and there were no sisters to fill them.

In 1954 the juniorate[125] was opened in order to provide more spiritual and professional preparation before the sister began her professional career. In 1955, St. Mary in Hays, Kansas and St. Mary in Eden, Wisconsin, were opened. In 1956, St. Mary's Parish in Fond du Lac started the CCD (Confraternity of Christian Doctrine) program with three lay teachers to provide religious education for children who attended the public school. St. Mary's Springs High School closed its boarding facilities when it became abundantly clear that the congregation could not meet all the educational needs of even their historical commitments.

CSA AND OTHER WOMEN RELIGIOUS

On November 24, 1956, Sisters Fidelis Karlin and Lucile Herman traveled to Chicago to attend a meeting that would later prove of great importance to the women religious of the United States. Throughout his reign Pope Pius XII had frequently expressed his concern that religious, both men and women, remain or become relevant to the life of the church.[126] Following several other meetings, in April 1956 the Vatican's Congregation of Religious asked the women religious of the United States to form a national conference. The United States sisters' committee invited the major and provincial superiors of pontifical institutes to an organizational meeting in Chicago. Sisters Fidelis and Lucile were members of the group that unanimously agreed to establish the Conference of Major Superiors of Women as a means to provide a forum to share common problems such as health and finance and ideas about religious life.[127] Its stated goals were to promote the spiritual welfare of sisters in the United States; to insure increasing efficacy in their apostolate; and to foster closer fraternal cooperation with all religious of the United States, the hierarchy, the clergy and Catholic associations.[128]

The congregation also supported the second important organization for women's religious institutes, the Sister Formation Conference. Originally established as a sub-committee with the National Catholic Educational Association, its intent was to promote the holistic education of women religious to enable the sister to develop intellectually while she was being formed as a woman religious.[129] Many congregations established juniorates for their young sisters, and approximately 150 institutes established degree programs for their sisters during the 1950s. *The Sister Formation Bulletin*—which carried pertinent articles designed to update the sisters on issues related to theology, sociology and psychology— became very much in evidence at Marian College during the latter part of the 1950s and early 1960s.

Sister formation was a goal that Sister Fidelis, as president of Marian College, enthusiastically supported. As a member of the general council she was able to translate her zeal for the project into almost immediate action. At considerable sacrifice to the congregation and after much negotiation with pastors, in 1953 she was able to release from their mission assignments a group of eleven young sisters to the motherhouse to complete their degrees as well as continue their religious formation.

Mother Albertonia's health was still a constant concern. The rising expenses of the congregation overwhelmed her. By February 1, 1954, she had had three illnesses that had necessitated her absence from the motherhouse for months. The hospital building program was a burden that she could not escape. But there were other expenses looming, such as the cost of sending forty sisters away that summer to various colleges and universities.[130] The pressure became so great that in May her physician advised her to stay away from the motherhouse for the summer. Although the councilors met to see if they could find a solution for the problem in canon law, in the long run the situation remained unchanged.

The question must be asked: why in 1951 did Mother Albertonia accept the office of Superior General? Sisters who knew her agreed that it "was a sheer sense of obedience" to the whole congregation.[131] It is possible, and perhaps known only to her spiritual director and herself, may have been her intent to immolate herself as a "victim soul." Either or both reasons would have been sufficient for her to sacrifice her own will and desires.

MOTHER ALBERTONIA'S LAST MONTHS

The last months of Mother Albertonia's term of office were filled with pain. On May 6, 1956, she was on her way to St. Clare Hospital in Monroe for medical attention when she was involved in a serious accident. The two councilors with her were also injured. Later it was discovered that Mother had a fractured clavicle. It was eight weeks before she was able to return to the motherhouse. On July 12, her health worsened, so she was again hospitalized. By July 27, she was able to go to her family home in Muncie for a month.

Meanwhile, the councilors continued as best they could. It could not have been easy for the sisters on mission with the constant messages from the motherhouse asking for prayers. They could not fully understand the situation and a few worried that the councilors were usurping her power. In November Mother Albertonia visited the missions in Indiana and Ohio but became ill shortly after her return to the motherhouse. On November 30 she was diagnosed with endocarditis and an infection in the bloodstream. On December 1, she received the Last Sacraments. She rallied, but was never able to resume her duties.

On January 8, 1957, the council, without Mother Albertonia's leadership, began the very important task of preparing for the general chapter which was to be held at the end of June. At that meeting, for the first time missions were invited to send suggestions regarding issues to be considered at the chapter.

Mother Albertonia's ordeal as superior general ended on June 27, 1957. For six months she found a great deal of joy in working again with high school students as librarian at Immaculate Conception High School in Elmhurst, Illinois. Then, on December 28, 1957, the feast of the Holy Innocents, she suffered a fatal heart attack.

At her funeral on December 31, Father Bierberg offered this final reflection: "Her life is symbolized, as you all know, by a heart. That heart stood for her love of all God's children with whom she came in contact. She loved all her spiritual daughters with a greater love than most mothers have for their physical children. Sister Albertonia made the kind of sacrifices that are called for by Almighty God from few mothers in the world. Her motherhood was very real and, also, very hidden. So today, then, we are at the funeral of a woman who achieved her destiny in time; to be a mother in a real, full, and perfect sense of the word."[132]

Chapter X

Changing World, Changing Church

Founders of religious congregations have never led easy lives; still less have their reformers—but religious leaders caught in a period when a community's most cherished values are challenged, its way of life disparaged, its members divided and its certainties questioned, must endure a special anguish.

MOTHER ROSITA HANDIBODE

It was to be Mother Rosita's fate to lead the Sisters of St. Agnes at the beginning of the most critical years the congregation had experienced in more than a century. Adelaide Marie Handibode was born July 16, 1897, in New York City, the oldest of four children born to Irish immigrants, John and Helen Kenny Handibode. She attended public schools and, for a brief period, St. Gabriel's School on 34th Street where she was taught by the Sisters of Charity. Around the time she was in the fourth grade, the family moved, and a neighbor encouraged her mother to send Adelaide to the parochial school, Our Lady Queen of Angels.[1]

In a brief memoir, Adelaide recalled making her debut as public speaker as valedictorian of her eighth grade class. The pride of her family was apparent. For the next few months she "had to deliver that speech at every family gathering." It was about this time that she began to think about being a sister, but when she asked her mother if she could go to the convent, her mother answered her with a decided, "No, you are too young to know your own mind." The idea was tabled and she became a wage earner instead.

The family was poor, but as Adelaide said, not the "hopeless kind." She wrote: "Our state was one to work out of rather than to get bogged down in. As soon as we finished the elementary school, we went to work if we could find a job. I found one and earned five dollars a week." In the fall of 1912 she enrolled in courses at night school, where she eventually earned her diploma.

One evening at a time when the nineteen-year-old Adelaide was happy, confident of her ability to make friends and succeed in business, she was at a dance when: "I was overpowered by the feeling of emptiness that I experienced. In the midst of the dancers I was unhappy, so I asked my escort to take me home. The spirit said within me, 'It is time to make a decision one way or the other.'" Soon after this, she made her way to the Agnesian convent to talk to Sister Celeste, her eighth grade teacher. Sister Germaine, the superior, immediately went into action to prepare her to leave for Fond du Lac. Again Adelaide asked her mother for permission to go to the convent. This time the answer was a reluctant "Yes," but her father said, "No." For the first time in her life she took a stand against her father. The next six weeks were very painful ones, but she left home on July 2, 1916.[2]

After profession, Adelaide, now Sister Rosita, was sent to New London, Wisconsin, to open a two-year commercial department. Concerned about teaching students older than herself, she talked to her superior who told her: "Worry doesn't come from the Holy Spirit."[3] There she had the opportunity to be with the first sisters who had attended summer school at Oshkosh State Teachers College. During the school year she attended Saturday courses given by Oshkosh professors. Six years later, she was transferred to the commercial department at Defiance, Ohio, a pleasant interlude because she had to take some courses in methods at the Gregg School in Chicago. In 1928 she was transferrred to St. Mary's Springs Academy, in Fond du Lac where she spent the next twenty-three years, first in the commercial department and then in the English department. In 1951, she was sent to Immaculate Conception High School in Elmhurst, Illinois as superior and principal, and in 1955, in the same capacity, to Sacred Heart High School in Yonkers, New York.[4] In June of 1957 she was one of the seventy-seven delegates to the chapter, and on June 27, 1957, she was elected superior general of the congregation.

Twenty-two years later Sister Rosita wrote that she had arrived at the chapter retreat directly from her mother's funeral, "psychologically unprepared for a Chapter."[5] She had never been a chapter delegate before and wrote that "[I] most likely would not have been one except that I was an ex-officio delegate because I was superior of a house that had sisters in perpetual vows."[6] Mother Rosita neglected to mention that she had earned a great deal of respect as superior and principal. She was stunned to find herself elected as the head of eight hundred or more sisters and added that the community was probably as shocked as she herself was.[7] For the first time in the congregation's history the superior general had not been a member of the council nor had she ever been directly connected with the motherhouse.[8]

The new superior general did what she had always done. She prayed and then evaluated her experience and abilities. Focusing on her experiences as superior and administrator in Elmhurst and Yonkers, she commented that "these two assignments gave me administrative experience that was challenging and different from classroom experience where I had been, through God's help, singularly successful.[9] Every assignment I had been given was beyond my capabilities, or so I thought. Hence I developed from earliest years in religion a strong reliance on the Holy Spirit for guidance. This was one characteristic that I brought to the task as I plunged immediately into my duties as superior general. If I made any mistakes it was not the fault of the Holy Spirit, but my own impulsive nature to get the job done."[10]

Sister Rosita was one of those fortunate people who could be all business when it was time for business, recollected when it was time for prayer and able to laugh heartily when she heard a good joke or enjoyed a good game of pinochle or bridge. Her speech and letters show both the precision of a business woman and the love for the English language that her years of study and teaching had given her. Her natural tendency for order was reinforced by the strict regimen imposed upon her by diabetes.

THE CHAPTER OF AFFAIRS—1957

In her first address to the general chapter after her election, Mother Rosita "admonished" the delegates to consider the outcome of the chapter as having been the work of the Holy Spirit.[11] Then she presided over six chapter sessions. Thirty-two proposals had been presented to be considered and voted upon by secret ballot. When the issue of updating the habit arose, a topic that would bedevil subsequent chapters until 1981, the assembly voted down any changes in its external appearance. To the relief of the community, the face veil[12] was eliminated and the wearing of a mantle was discontinued except as need arose for individual sisters. Because wearing the mantle had been governed by the calendar rather than by the weather, this mitigation proved to be a great relief.

The proposal that a chapter on hospitals and institutions be included in the constitutions clearly indicated a growing awareness and concern with the political and economic climate which was beginning to impact those ministries. An equal awareness was evidenced with the statement that sisters assigned to hospitals should be given the advantage of a general education as well as professional preparation.[13] Other changes were directed towards facilitating the spiritual growth of the sisters. The sister formation program was extended to include non-teachers.[14] The daily horarium was adapted; all money received by the sisters was to be incorporated into the goods of the congregation. Every three years, sisters were asked to make a retreat at the motherhouse. Monthly conferences[15] were required, but if that were impossible, the sisters were to have three hours of recollection. Instead of common spiritual reading every day, the sisters could read spiritual books of their own choosing three days a week. Although there was some discussion of a revision of the constitutions, the matter was postponed for further consideration.

ANOTHER BEGINNING

Mother Rosita's first priority was to call the community to a "new beginning". She saw the community as having "been chastened in the previous administration by the illness of our much loved Mother Albertonia."[16] During the previous months a great deal of the usual business of the council had been set aside in order to allow the new superior general to set her own direction. The day after the chapter ended, Mother Rosita held her first council meeting. She soon found that her councilors, representative as they were of different segments of the congregation, would serve her well. Sister Anaclete Entringer, the vicar, had been on the previous council and had also been novice mistress. The other councilors had full time jobs in addition to serving on the council. Sister Fidelis Karlin had been on the previous council and was president of Marian College. Sister Mary Anthony Keller was a professor at Marian College and Sister Mary Josephine Escher was director of nursing service at St. Agnes Hospital. The council met for days to draw up the mission assignments, appoint superiors, consider applications for admission into the community, make educational decisions regarding the newly professed, consider offers of new schools, and handle personal requests from the sisters.[17]

THE CENTENNIAL

Fortunately, what could have been another burden was transformed into a blessing. The year 1958 was the centenary year of the founding of the congregation.[18] A celebration of some magnitude was what the community needed to revive fallen spirits. Every sister was involved in a series of year-long activities. The goal of the celebration was "Unity through fidelity to the Evangelical Counsels." Determined to emphasize spiritual values, Mother Rosita began by asking permission from Archbishop William E. Cousins to allow all-day exposition of the Blessed Sacrament in the motherhouse for adoration on all Fridays and Sundays of the year.

The festivities began in May of 1958 with a trip by Mother Rosita and Sister Seraphica Mulvihill to Rome in order to solicit the blessing of Pope Pius XII on the centennial celebration.[19] They also used the occasion to request that there be perpetual adoration in the motherhouse chapel, that the community use the short breviary in English, and that Nicaraguan sisters be allowed to make their perpetual vows in their own country.[20]

The trip to Rome exceeded Mother Rosita's expectations. The two sisters were granted an audience with Pope Pius XII. Twenty years later, she recorded the event in her Memoirs. Years later her sense of awe remained evident:

> After going through the routine of showing credentials at every few feet, we finally found ourselves in an Audience Hall where on our knees we awaited His Holiness, Pope Pius XII. We were face-to-face with the personification of holiness when the door opened and tongue-tied we awaited our turn to speak. We succeeded in getting our message across when we presented the spiritual bouquet from the Community, and His Holiness, graciously granted our request for his blessing on each member of the Community. He included the Sisters' relatives on his own initiative. We had not been so bold as to ask for this favor.[21]

For a Sister of St. Agnes, no visit to Rome would be complete without a visit to the tomb of St. Agnes where Fr. Rehrl had prayed so earnestly for success in founding a community dedicated in her honor. For Mother Rosita, like so many of her sisters, that visit proved to be a source of a profound insight. She wrote, "With a visit to the tomb of St. Agnes behind me, I could begin to see that every problem hid an opportunity, for the Community was in much more competent Hands than mine .... All developments could be traced to problems .... Recognition of the fact that there were available sources of expertise, lessened the worry connected with costly projects, and shared responsibility prepared us for Vatican II."[22]

Sister Fidelis Karlin was in charge of the activities in Fond du Lac throughout 1958 and 1959. They ranged from an exhibition of the art of the sisters, the compiling of a book of reflections on the constitutions written by the sisters; *To Him Alone*, a book of the sisters' verse edited by Sister Muriel Tarr; and a pageant depicting the life of St. Agnes and the early missionary days of the community.

Decision for Happiness, a short film promoting vocations, was filmed. There was a special institute for homemakers and Sister Vera Naber was commissioned to write the history of the congregation.[23]

Mother Rosita, found the sisters' response to the challenge so gratifying "I eventually had the conviction that there was no problem so big that CSA couldn't solve if we all pulled together. Morale was high. Trust in God and one another grew with each passing year. The pioneer spirit of the Founders was still alive."[24]

The centennial year of the Sisters of St. Agnes marked the zenith of the congregation if the point of reference is the size of its membership and the number of its institutions. There were more than eight hundred professed sisters, a goodly number of aspirants, candidates and novices, a high school, a school of nursing and a college, and two missions in Central America. There were continual requests for the services of the sisters but there was, a faint forewarning. Although there had always been members, who, for varied reasons, decided that religious life was not the life they were called to lead, the numbers of those making that decision began to increase. In 1950, one woman left before her final profession, in 1958, eight women withdrew from the congregation.

THE CHANGING WORLD

The year 1958 proved to be of great significance for the Catholic world, and, indeed, for the world at large. On October 28 of that year, seventy-six year-old Angelo Roncalli was elected Bishop of Rome and took the name John XXIII.[25] Elected to provide a safe transition to the next pope, on January 25, 1959, he exhilarated some Catholics and dismayed others when he announced his intention to call an ecumenical council. The council was to consider measures regarding the renewal of the church and the reforms that had been promoted by the ecumenical and liturgical movements. This call for aggiornamento would set in motion the greatest changes in the Catholic Church since the Reformation.

The election of a Catholic, John F. Kennedy, to the presidency of the United States was an unmistakable indication that the social assimilation of Catholics into the mainstream of American life was not only accelerating but had occurred. The immigrant church with its fortress mentality was breaking up; the parish was rapidly losing its position as the focal point of Catholic social and spiritual life; the pastor was no longer assumed to be the best educated man in the parish, and "Sister says" was not necessarily gospel. Young people who, a generation earlier, might have gone to Sunday vespers, a parish dance or a CYO game, now had spending money, access to the family car, and whole new worlds of adventure.

Although the sisters were not completely unaware of the social changes that society was undergoing, for the most part religious congregations were concerning themselves with meeting the increasing demands for their services and caring for the increased number of vocations that followed World War II. While a number of communities responded by building houses of formation and new motherhouses, the Sisters of St. Agnes were constrained both by their innate economic conservatism and the immediate necessity of providing for retired sisters and educating the young sisters.

Whatever was going on, inside or outside the church, the ministries of the congregation had to be supported. Mother Rosita recognized that the day had passed for considering the administration of institutions a matter of common sense. She sent sisters to universities to prepare for administrative positions whether in the schools and hospitals or in the college. It had also become clear that the advice of experts was needed to negotiate the complex regulations of government programs now providing much-needed funds. In 1958 the congregation secured the services of an auditor who was charged with preparing an annual consolidated report of the entire congregation, an attorney who was well-versed in canon law, and a consultant to the community hospitals.[26]

That same year the congregation accepted St. Louis School in Fond du Lac[27] and St. Henry in Fort Wayne, Indiana; in 1959, St. Margaret Mary, Milwaukee, Wisconsin and Sacred Heart in Fond du Lac. At the Boyle Home a new wing was completed in 1959, which provided a recreation room, dining room facilities, and eight more guest rooms with fireproof stairway accommodations. The additions had been made possible largely through bequests, for the most part that of Mrs. Emma C. Cavanaugh, who had willed $53,000 to the home.[28]

At the decade's opening, the congregation could be described as being in a very satisfactory condition. Although there were never enough members to accomplish all their dreams, sisters were faithful to their constitutions and were devoted to their ministries. Women entered the congregation every year, never in sufficient numbers to cover the apostolates adequately, but enough to evoke gratitude that the community was growing.

FOREIGN MISSIONS

On January 6, 1960, Mother Rosita left for her first visit to Nicaragua. Three weeks later she returned to report that on the whole she was well pleased with the work of the sisters in the mission field. As a result of her report, the council determined to send more sisters to Central America. The North American sisters would be given the opportunity to return to the United States every three years for spiritual renewal, and the sisters' house in Puerto Cabezas would be renovated to accommodate an aspirancy and candidature for native vocations. The decade would see the launching of eleven ventures in Latin America.[29]

That same year the decision to accept the offer of the Christian Brothers to take charge of the Infantile section of their school, Instituto Pedagogico de Varones in Managua was, perhaps, more momentous than it appeared at the time. Managua, the largest city in Nicaragua, was described as "impetuous" and "the prodigal son of the nation, the most unruly, hotheaded, and outspoken of the nation's family."[30] It had become the nation's capital in 1857 and rapidly became a city of political and business opportunists, with a small clique of wealthy families dominating the political and economic life of the nation. However, the masses of the people lived in abject poverty. Although Mother Rosita hesitated to send sisters there, the city's university and school of nursing provided both opportunities for further study and a place for sisters to stay when they were in the city for medical reasons or traveling to the States.

There were few cultural similarities between the life the missionaries were experiencing on the Atlantic Coast and the life they would find in Managua. Along with the ethnic and cultural dissimilarities, the most striking difference was poverty. Poverty marked the lives of the people in Waspam and Puerto Cabezas; but the grinding poverty in Managua existed side by side with the ostentatious wealth of the ruling class. The Christian Brothers' School was designed to accommodate 1,400 boys from kindergarten through secundaria. The greater portion of the families was from the wealthy and powerful segment of Managua, although the poorer class often made great sacrifices in order to send their boys there.[31] The great disparity between the classes of people was a continual source of concern to the sisters. In the schools on the Atlantic Coast, they taught all the children; in Managua, their source of income came from teaching the sons of the affluent.

The three sisters and four lay persons taught 413 small boys in the first three divisions of the school. The sisters were on duty from 7:30 a.m. to 11:15 a.m. and from 1:30 p.m. to 4:15 p.m. They spent an hour and one-half of their noon rest period playing with the children of Acahualinca.[32] During vacations and when time permitted, the sisters visited the barrios where they catechized the children or they visited the eighty or so lepers at the *Leprosaria*.

When Mother Rosita visited Managua in 1963, she found that the sisters had been living three years in a house where the only bathroom was a sink facing the open patio. She went immediately to the brothers and demanded a new residence for the sisters. Two years later Mother Rosita visited again. She was given the best bedroom in a house that faced a printing press. She found that the clanking of the machinery made sleep impossible either at the time for siesta or at night. The sisters were moved to another equally unsatisfactory house. It was at that point the Agnesians purchased a house adequate for their purposes.[33]

CHANGES AT HOME

St. Joseph's farm was the source of one of the most appreciated benefits the motherhouse enjoyed. Everyone there had enjoyed the milk, fresh eggs, and sweet butter that the farm had provided. When it became apparent that there were no longer sisters available to replace those who were unable to continue working at the farm, a cloud of melancholy drifted over the sisters at the motherhouse. On February 20, 1960, a Mass in the chapel at St. Joseph's Farm marked the end of the sisters' services there.

That same afternoon, and generating even more conversation, the novices appeared in a new veil. The event carried more significance than might have appeared to the casual observer. Finally, religious congregations were beginning to listen to the Pope's pleas for modernization of the habit. The change was hastened by revolutions in the American way of life. In cities and towns public transportation was being replaced by the automobile. Cars were becoming a necessity. Everyone had to acknowledge that the large stiff veil was a hazard on the road.[34] The congregation had been asked its opinion on the topic. When the answers were tabulated it was found that an overwhelming 501 sisters voted for a soft veil.[35] Most votes were driven by the stiff veil's sheer discomfort and inconvenience.[36]

Making the change was an arduous process. Since the form and material of the habit were prescribed by the constitutions, permission had to be obtained from the Holy See to change. Then a committee had to accept the design. The decision was not made quickly; the veil chosen was the eighteenth model attempted. Inevitably, there were many and strong opinions about it, but six months later the Sisters of St. Agnes had a new look. Precisely at 6:30 p.m. on August 2, 1960, eight hundred sisters in nine states and Nicaragua appeared wearing the new veil and a soft collar of considerably more modest proportions.[37]

CURRENTS OF CHANGE

In 1960, making such a simple change as the design of a veil was an earth-shaking event. The young women who had entered the community had had no expectations of change. Few had even considered such a possibility, yet each year from 1963 through 1969 sisters experienced changes or modifications in their prayer life, horarium, social life, clothing, community practices, and even their individual opportunities for enrichment and renewal. Sisters were encouraged to participate in renewal institutes, rededication exercises, and Scripture study. They were freed from the regular schedule for one day of the week; they could obtain drivers' licenses[38] and attend night meetings when necessary. They could visit institutions Catholic or not, and they could vacation at a summer cottage if one were offered to them. Sisters were beginning to consider their own individuality. For some the loss of uniformity and anonymity was traumatic as they were forced to make their own decisions; others were beginning to find themselves for the first time. With the disappearance of a quasi-monastic life style, some were beginning to wonder why they had entered a convent. There was going to be a lot to sort out.

The well-publicized Nixon-Kennedy debates in the fall of 1960 were noteworthy for the sisters at the motherhouse because for the first time they were free to watch television after night prayer.[39] The time had come to recognize that television was playing an important role in American life and that it was necessary for sisters to be aware of the world they lived in. Watching the evening news became as much a part of life in the convent as it was in other households. Other programs soon became part of a house's routine. In many convents, watching Lawrence Welk was as predictable as any religious activity, and even was referred to by the irreverent as the "Saturday night holy hour." By 1968 viewing television had become a personal responsibility along with the time for retiring.

During the year, the congregation accepted two new schools in the United States: St. Charles School in Bensenville, Illinois and, since the congregation was already established in Colby, Kansas, the parochial school there. St. Joseph in Hays, that had been part of the public school system, was returned to the parochial system.

On July 6, 1960, the *Annals* proclaimed: "a Red-Letter-day". Marian College was granted accreditation by the North Central Association of Colleges and Schools." It was the culmination of five years of hard work. The first two applications for accreditation were rejected, the first in 1957 for failure to include sufficient evidence for evaluation, and, in 1958, for the lack of a long-range plan. With the help of a representative from North Central, the college administration and faculty prepared an acceptable report. With accreditation achieved, the congregation felt it realistic to erect a college campus separate from the motherhouse. That same month, George Hutter, Jr., a Fond du Lac building contractor, donated 14.7 acres of land for a residence hall for Marian students.

In 1961, the decision of a group of lay men and women in Yonkers to launch a money-raising project for the community marked a new form of collaboration between religious and lay people in the mission of the congregation.[40] The Yonkers story deserves mention not only as a tribute to one particular group, but also as an example of the support that friends and benefactors have given to religious congregations. In the summer of 1961, a group of parents from Sacred Heart Parish in Yonkers, New York, were visiting their daughters in Fond du Lac. Someone suggested doing something for the "good Fathers," the Capuchin Friars of the Province of St. Mary, Garrison, New York. But someone else counter-replied, "Why not do something for the 'good Sisters?'" It did not take long before the parents decided to help the sisters with the new infirmary building. The women were planning a penny social, but the Chronicles note, "that along came Joe Gurdak, full of love and faith. Joe said, 'No Penny Social, we're going to run Bingo games, and make $50,000 a year for the sisters.' This was indeed a bomb-shell. Al Petrosino asked Joe what kind of needles [drugs] he was taking. 'Why, everyone knew the State was investigating Bingo and had found illegal practices (to say the least). There had to be a Bona Fide organization; this group hadn't even had a name yet. Why you almost had to be a Saint to get a Bingo license.'" Members were recruited, the Agnesian Auxiliary was formed and "Joe Gurdak then hounded City Hall, Yonkers, for a Bingo license ...."[41]

Then came the big night. Joe and a few other workers pooled several hundred dollars of their own money to cover expenses. That first night, September 9, 1961, the Agnesian Auxiliary made $987.50. The first check for $9,000 was sent to Mother Rosita for the Infirmary on December 18, 1961.[42] Within seventeen months the Sisters of St. Agnes received their first $50,000.[43]

There were changes, too, in the mission to Latin America. With the election of Pope John XXIII there was a new urgency in the church to evangelize in the less developed countries. In 1961, the new pontiff asked religious congregations to send 10% of their membership to Latin America. It was a suggestion that the Sisters of St. Agnes would take seriously indeed. In a short time, Sisters Raymond Grieble and Bertha Bumann were sent to St. Mary's College in Mankato, Minnesota where, for five weeks, they studied Spanish and the geography and anthropology of Nicaragua.

In 1961, after sixteen years of service to the people along the Río Coco, Sister Mary Agnes returned to the United States to die. Sister had developed the clinic insofar as it was possible in the circumstances, but little had changed over the years.[44] There was never enough medicine and medical supplies, but the most serious problem was not one that could be solved in Waspam. To reach the clinic, many patients had to travel hours on foot; some came more than 150 miles by canoe, travel time taking as long as seventeen days.

Often they had to leave before treatment was completed, either because they had no food or because their family or their crops needed them.

It was not until the following year that Sister Anne Jude Van Lanen arrived.[45] A registered nurse, she had prepared for her ministry by spending three months studying and working with the Sisters of Charity in Dallas, Texas, and she had come eager to teach basic health care practices and preventive medicine. She was convinced that the only way to achieve real progress was for the people themselves to learn to be responsible for their own health care, but found she had time only to train one or two young women to work with her in the clinic. Together with Gregory Smutko, OFM Cap., and other missionaries, she designed a comprehensive program for the development of the people along the Río Coco.[46]

The group decided to emphasize programs fostering women's potential for leadership. The Catechetics-Evangelization program already in place for the men was extended to include women; leadership programs were given to develop health leaders, midwives, agricultural leaders and leaders of cooperatives; a program for deacons and their wives was initiated.[47]

Meanwhile in Puerto Cabezas, the establishment of an aspirancy had become an immense benefit for the town itself. The year after high school classes were established for the aspirants in 1962, Sister Kenneth Struckhoff took advantage of the original permission to establish the school and opened a high school to all qualified girls. The next year the Christian Brothers established a boys' school in the town. On May 22, 1967, the two schools united and there was now one school open to all the youth of the area. The school was the second high school established on the Atlantic Coast. At the same time the sisters added classes in teacher education, making Puerto Cabezas a significant educational center in the region.[48]

Nineteen-sixty-two was the last full year of Mother Rosita's first administration. There was one important financial decision made when the congregation opted to self-insure its members rather than enroll in a commercial health insurance plan,[49] but, on the whole, it was a time to slow down and thank God for the success of many projects. Two were especially meaningful. On June 3, Regina Hall was dedicated by Archbishop Cousins. It was the first completed building on a projected campus for Marian College and on October 19 the St. Agnes Hospital debt was liquidated.

Throughout the previous five years, Mother Rosita had provided spiritual leadership, had made modifications in the life of the community that were both needed and welcomed, and had proved herself to be an astute business woman. If many sisters found her distant, and indeed, she could scarcely be expected to have more than a superficial acquaintance with more than eight hundred women, she could show an understanding and appreciation of their work in her letters to them.[50] The congregation was undoubtedly in good order.

For the remainder of the Catholic world, 1962 would be remembered as the beginning of *aggiornamento*. After four years of preparation, the twenty-first ecumenical council was convened on October 11, 1962. The church was ready to reflect on divine revelation, the sacred liturgy, the laity, missionary activity, Christian education, and the renewal of religious life, in sum, the role of the Church in the modern world.

In the 1960s, the world saw many shifts in allegiances, many discoveries and inventions, and many unexpected deaths. It was a decade of conflict. American society was divided as the establishment was challenged by Blacks and women, and a counterculture grew up among the young based on free love, drugs, and protests against the war in Viet Nam and the military-industrial complex But the year 1963 contained such striking events that the British poet, Philip Larkin, dubbed it *Annus Mirabilis*, or Year of Wonders. The wonder-drug Valium launched the era of blockbuster medicines. In January, France and Germany signed a treaty ending 400 years of conflict. In February the Beatles released their first album; in April, Michael DeBakey was the first to successfully transplant an artificial human heart. In May, the first television pictures were transmitted from space. In June, Pope John XXIII died, to be succeeded by Pope Paul VI.[51] In August, the United States, Great Britain and the Soviet Union signed the Limited Test Ban Treaty. November saw the assassination of two presidents, Ngo Dinh Diem of South Viet Nam and John F. Kennedy, the president of the United States. That same month Lyndon Johnson succeeded to the presidency of the United States and launched the Great Society and soon after, the War on Poverty.[52]

STIRRINGS

Whether the new spirit would lead humankind to advance further along the path of unity and peace or to further chaos and violence was yet to be determined. Meanwhile, a few tentative breezes of change were stirring among the Agnesians. The movement for reform in religious institutions had begun in the 1950s. By the 1960s, the sisters spending summers on large campuses were becoming acquainted with new trends in theology and electrifying new books. One book was R.W. Gleason's *To Live Is Christ* which argued for the proper integration of nature and grace in the light of modern psychological knowledge.[53] His humane and positive approach to spirituality and the religious life, including his startling recommendation that sisters wear contemporary clothing, gave many sisters a fresh outlook and a receptivity to new ideas.

On the university campuses *The Nun in the World* by Joseph Cardinal Suenens[54] was even more vigorously discussed. In the volume, written while he participated in the deliberations of the Vatican Council, he argued that nuns were living in a closed world of "dusty old wax flowers [that] should be replaced by living blooms drawing nourishment direct from the earth."[55]

Suenens saw sisters in the health care and teaching professions in danger of "officialism" or sinking to the level of being mere functionaries. Religious engaged in obscure jobs and menial tasks were diverting their energies from apostolic jobs of far greater importance. Commenting on aging communities, he attributed the decrease of vocations in large part to the absence of religious from the adult world. He saw among the young religious many concerns. They wanted, for example, recognition of the values appropriate to the world they lived in. They wanted outmoded customs dropped. They wanted a spirituality rich in biblical life and communal liturgies as opposed to "spiritual exercises" and non-liturgical prayers.

One of the most important means to effect the changes Cardinal Suenens envisioned was the general chapter. He wrote that chapters were ordinarily ill-prepared and unrepresentative, concerned almost exclusively with maintaining tradition. Instead he believed that if communities understood that the chapter, while it was meeting, was the highest authority in the congregation, it could be a powerful instrument for change. Furthermore, he said that the delegates should understand that as representatives of all the sisters, it was their duty to check their government. He emphasized that superiors should be replaced more frequently and that chapters should meet more often. Equally important to him were professional and community meetings that he believed to be essential for apostolic growth.

Suenens concluded that, in order to fulfill her proper mission, the sister in the world needed to exercise the theological virtues of faith, hope, and charity to a greater extent than at the present. "The heart," he said, "can only expand when the horizon widens and one can breathe deeply of tonic air. A great joy will follow her acceptance, and a great hope will arise in the Church! Let her not be afraid."[56] To those who were feeling the dissonance between their professional life and their religious ideals, his vision seemed both liberating and attainable.[57]

Members of religious congregations also found much to ponder in Pope John XXIII's encyclical, *Pacem in Terris* (April 11, 1963). Regarding issues pertaining to truth, justice, charity, and liberty in matters of governance, the pontiff had emphasized the importance of structures that would ensure consultation and input at every level. It was inevitable that many sisters, restless under out-dated authoritarian structures, would re-examine their own congregational governance.

While these fairly advanced ideas regarding dress, apostolate, or government structures were circulating among some segments of the congregation, Mother Rosita and her council were encouraging the members of the community to grow in union with God. Of their efforts she wrote later: "Retreats for superiors … provided a forum for airing opinions of customs that were not conducive to the renewal being called for by Pope Pius XII even before Vatican II. Superiors were encouraged to present their views, that were gratefully considered by the generalate and sometimes changed to something better suited to the changing circumstances of life in 20th century America. Two summer sessions of Re-Dedication Exercises were conducted by Gerald Walker, OFM Cap., and an assistant, who was either a scripture scholar or a theologian …. The custom of 'once a superior always a superior' was declared obsolete and replaced by the rule of a three-year term with option of renewal on the same mission …. Workshops on Canon Law, Spirituality, or

other relevant matters were attended by members of the Generalate
…. This remote preparation for the 1963 chapter made the chapter
acts more relevant to changing conditions."[58]

THE CHAPTER OF 1963

In her letter convoking the Eighteenth General Chapter of the
Sisters of St. Agnes, Mother Rosita wrote: "In view of the needs of
our times, it would seem that the main objective of the chapter
should be to answer the question: What can the Sisters of St. Agnes
do to increase their effectiveness as instruments for the work of the
Church today?" She then suggested that each delegate read carefully Suenens' *The Nun in the World.*[59] It was a remarkable recommendation for one who had lived and loved the religious life as it had been.

While the preparations for the chapter were going on, 1963 had
seen some important decisions. An indication of changing times was
the closing of Holy Family Orphanage in Marquette, Michigan.[60]
This move released enough sisters to make the acceptance of St.
Zachary School in Des Plaines, Illinois, possible.

Mother Rosita was re-elected as superior general in 1963. She
later wrote that "the vote of confidence gave me the courage to
accept the responsibility for another six-year period, though if I had
been able to look into the future I might have recoiled at the
prospect."[61] A new group of councilors, whom she would term
"providential," were chosen: Sisters John Baptist Shaja, a secondary
school science teacher; Sister Evangeline Kodric, principal of St.
Mary's Springs Academy; Sister Imogene Palen, a science professor
at Marian College, and Sister Bonita Willnecker, a secondary school
teacher. The chapter elected Sister Mary Daniel Egan first full-time
secretary general for the congregation.

One of the first items of business was setting the direction for a
new spirituality in the community. With little fuss the congregation
discarded the remnants of and accepted the liturgical reforms of the
twentieth century. A new resolution proposed: "that the Sisters of
St. Agnes live the life of the Church in the framework of the Mass,
the Breviary, and Mental Prayer; and that all other devotional practices be included in this framework." The chapter made the long-
awaited decision to use the English breviary instead of the *Little*

Office of the Blessed Virgin. At the same time, the chapter approved the administration's decision to seek funds for moving forward on decisions in matters that had been the topics of community concern or interest for some years—plans for building both a retirement home and the campus for Marian College.[62]

Sister nurses were allowed to serve the sick in their homes whenever necessary.[63] Non-serge habits were adopted; both the constitutions and the book of customs were to be revised to accommodate to the changes of the previous few years. Although the financial report showed great indebtedness and high expenditures, a percent of the hospital sisters' salaries was set aside for charity in an effort to be more available to the poor. St. Joseph's Cemetery was to be improved with new roads, stone markers, and landscaping.

The chapter's closing note, however, addressed the critical goal for the congregation, "that we may strengthen the bond of unity in the spirit of peace."[64]

Chapter XI

Gathering Clouds

Mother Rosita's second term began in July 1963 in a period of high hopes. The *Chronicles* of 1964 noted eight hundred professed sisters who served in fifty-six elementary schools, six high schools, a college, four hospitals, a small hotel, and in two foreign countries. There were forty-six novices, fifty postulants, and 113 aspirants in their formation program. There seemed to be only one cloud on the horizon. In the foreword to the 1964 congregational *Chronicles*, the community secretary, Sister Mary Daniel Egan, wrote that "The dearth of personnel now forms our great obstacle to what might have been unusual growth in our works of the apostolate."[1] If more good were to be accomplished, it was clear that more young women should choose to serve God in religious life.

VOCATIONS

When Mother Rosita took office, there were two significant sources of vocations to the congregation. The majority of girls came from the schools of the congregation; a significant number of other entrants had relatives in religious communities.[2] An occasional older woman entered, but the congregation did not accept anyone over the age of thirty-five. A few of these women were registered nurses. Fewer were college graduates. Because parochial schools were the source of so many vocations, attention was given to promoting vocation clubs where girls could get acquainted with the sisters outside the classroom and in which they could ask questions about religious life. Immeasurably more important than a vocation club was the girl's experience with the sisters throughout her education. If a girl thought she might have a vocation, and if her parents were willing, she might choose to enter the aspirancy after graduating from the eighth grade.[3] The question of the advisability of early entrance into religious life was, however, being raised more frequently.

By the 1960s, society's changing values and growing materialism were having an impact on vocations. At the same time, young women were being presented with more vocational opportunities for service. Combined with a growing restlessness among some religious, these factors were beginning to affect adversely the number of young women choosing religious life. It seemed time for the community to take its answers to those questions to the Catholic population as well as to young women considering religious life.

In 1964, Mother Rosita appointed Sister Michaela O'Brien as vocation director. Her principal task was to educate the laity, particularly parents, about the value and relevance of religious life. In the past, the restrictions of the cloister had militated against even the most sincere well-wishers acquiring an understanding of religious life. The ongoing religious renewal had awakened a curiosity in the laity, and, with the relaxation of rules, the sisters were able to attend meetings, give talks to parish organizations and civic groups, and welcome visitors to their convents. Moderators were appointed whose special mission was to reach girls not in schools, and each sister was encouraged to participate to the best of her abilities. There was little congregational interest at this time to interest women beyond high school age or college age in the possibility of a religious vocation.

Not for vocation recruitment, but related to it, was a two-week summer camp for young girls the community sponsored at Camp Vista. The camp on Cedar Lake, only twenty miles southeast of Fond du Lac, had been built over the years by a diocesan priest, Father Joseph Fischer, who believed that young people could achieve a closer union with God as they contemplated the majesty and beauty of nature. Religious communities were given access to the camp for their programs in Christian leadership. Each summer an average of ninety girls attended the Agnesian-sponsored camp where they enjoyed the usual camp activities, swimming, canoeing, ball games, art, and music. The program's emphasis was placed on helping the girls attain self-knowledge, the development of their own spirituality, and leadership skills.

THE ASPIRANCY

While many religious communities discontinued their aspirancies, the Agnesians continued theirs. Although some sisters believed that the usual high school, dating, and job experiences of the American adolescent were a necessary part of maturing in contemporary society, no one could deny that some of the most solidly religious and level-headed women in the community had made, and never regretted, the decision, made in their early teens, to enter the convent.

As late as 1957, St. Agnes Convent had its own high school in the motherhouse. Aspirancies, like minor seminaries, provided a secondary school education as a means of providing a religious environment for girls attracted to religious life. There they were almost completely immersed in the convent culture. They wore black dresses and veils; they grew used to hours of silence and living in a group; their every minute was scheduled from morning Mass to night prayers. In order to graduate in three years, the girls attended classes the year round, but they did return home for summer vacations. At the end of their second year in the aspirancy, they could, if they chose, enter the candidature where they would complete their high school program.

However, as more religious were influenced by the work of theorists like Adrian Van Kaam, CSCp., whose work in human development emphasized the connection between psychology and spirituality, the decision was made to close the convent high school. In June of 1958, St. Agnes High School graduated its last class of ten aspirants.

Mother Rosita's philosophy was clear:

> They [aspirants] are the same all over ... and we
> expect that not all those who come will stay. We can
> make our standards very high because *these girls must
> grow during the years they are with us*."[4] To the sisters she
> wrote: "Its aim [is] to develop young women, who
> are interested in becoming sisters, into mature
> dynamic Christians. Every means will be used to
> promote their spiritual and physical growth. Each is
> to be treated as a unique individual and will be given
> opportunity to develop her God-given talents ... and
> to learn to use them for others. Every effort will be
> made to assist the girls to become emotionally, intel-
> lectually, culturally and socially well-balanced."[5]

In September of 1959, the aspirants enrolled in the coeducational St. Mary's Springs High School "in order to gain the hetero-
sexual relationships that some say are so essential to maturation."[6]
Meanwhile, Sister Michaela attended Marquette University to study
theology and counseling in preparation for the position of aspirants'
director. The aspirants lived in the motherhouse but there was an
attempt to make the aspirancy more home-like and comfortable. At
school, the girls were indistinguishable from the other girls as they
wore the Springs' uniform of black skirts and white blouses.
Although Sister Michaela's efforts to provide a normal teen-age life
for the girls were frequently frustrated by the motherhouse culture,
initially the program was successful in terms of the number of
enrollees.[7] Before 1960, the number of aspirants had hovered
around thirty; in 1960 the number rose to thirty-six; to seventy-five
in 1962.

In 1963, Mother Rosita had attempted to make religious formation more relevant to the times by calling upon members of the
community for suggestions and advice in preparing a formation
handbook.[8] The manual proved useful as a guide to formation personnel who were struggling to maintain the essence of religious life
while they acknowledged the changing values of the young women
born after World War II.

Gratifying as the increasing number of aspirants was, it stretched community resources to care for such a large number of girls. At the same time, because St. Mary's Springs did not have the space to accept all the local applicants, those students were chosen by lottery, creating lasting public relations problems for the school.[9] With so many aspirants at the motherhouse, in 1963 it seemed wise to establish a second aspirancy in Hays, Kansas. Prospects were excellent that vocations would continue because Kansas had always been most generous with its daughters. Two other factors made the plan attractive: the projected closure of St. Anthony School of Nursing in July 1964 had left the students' residence empty; the Agnesian-staffed Marian High School would provide a very satisfactory education.

When 102 aspirants enrolled in the Fond du Lac program that year and twelve girls entered the program in Kansas, the decision seemed more than justified.[10] Sister Mary Neff was placed in charge of the twelve girls who had enrolled in the program. The girls there followed a schedule at least as demanding as that of the aspirancy in Fond du Lac, but it was not long before what had been considered an advantage, the proximity of the girls to their homes, proved to be a disadvantage. Without the support of the motherhouse atmosphere, the girls, living near their relatives and attending school with their old friends, lacked the necessary distance for immersion in their new life to take place. As a small group in the high school, they were overpowered by the interests of the rest of the girls.[11] As time went on, some of the aspirants, instead of developing more independence, became overly dependent on the director. The mounting expenses of the program to the congregation had to be another consideration.

The growing confusion in the church and religious life as well as the number of sisters and priests leaving religious life were intensifying the problems of vocation recruitment. The concept of aspirancies was even more seriously questioned in religious communities as well as the Catholic press. By September 1966, most communities had closed their aspirancies, but the Agnesians remained ambivalent about eliminating their program. There were half as many aspirants in Fond du Lac as there had been three years previously. In Hays, while the number of the previous year's seven aspirants had risen again to the original number of twelve, it was becoming progressively clearer that, at the least, the congregation would have to make serious modifications in the program. In Fond du Lac, although the younger girls were not greatly affected, "seniors," Sister Mary Daniel Egan wrote "have been jolted into a rethinking of vocation and their place in the plan of God."[12]

The congregation had been redoubling its efforts to make the education of the aspirants relevant to contemporary society. In March 1965, the seventeen senior aspirants in Fond du Lac began training for a six-week summer job as nurse aids in geriatrics, pediatrics, maternity, and adult care at St. Agnes Hospital. The program offered two advantages. The aspirants would be able to pay for their entrance into the postulancy and would gain experiences that could not fail to help them mature.

In 1968, a new model, the home aspirancy was tried in Kansas. Aspirants lived at home, but each had a counselor. They met together four times each year at the Aspirancy Center for recollection days and once each year for a three-day retreat. Other obligations included attending the bi-monthly sodality meetings; attending Mass daily if possible, but at least once or twice a week other than Sunday; and having a regular confessor. In addition to praying the rosary daily, they should try to have fifteen or more minutes of daily mental prayer and ten minutes to one half-hour of daily spiritual reading. It was hoped that the girls would bond together as they learned to make their own decisions with regard to their spiritual life, social life, and personal orientation to school and home.[13]

This program proved to be even more difficult to manage than the previous one. Living at home could not give the aspirant sufficient distance from family or peers to eradicate confusion concerning social relationships, especially dating. It became increasingly difficult to arrange individual meetings with the girls, but the greatest difficulty was to inculcate a love for the liturgy and assist the girls in a growth in prayer

The difficulties inherent in the program led the congregation to discontinue the home aspirancy program in 1971.

THE POSTULANCY

Traditionally, the postulancy was the "time for the young woman to learn the spirit of the community and to prove through docility in cooperating with God's precious graces, her earnest desire to fulfill His Holy Will in her regard."[14] The goal remained, but the program began to undergo incremental modifications that were changing its character. Formation personnel were also beginning to read the urging of psychiatrists to consider the psychological adjustments that candidates to the religious life would experience. A candidate needed to cope with the loss of her sense of identity; the emptying of the affections; the struggle for control of the will; and the loss of a philosophy of life.[15] Older candidates especially found the process extremely difficult. In 1959, in response to the new concern on psychological health, the postulants were given the Minnesota Multiphasic Personality Inventory (MMPI) to assist with the diagnosis of major personal and emotional disorders.

After 1958, as the young women must have completed high school before entering, the youngest postulants were now in their late teens instead of fifteen or sixteen as in previous years. Their life experiences and greater maturity could not help but affect their attitudes even though the basics of the program remained much the same—the daily instruction period by the director, the chaplain's monthly instructions, and the emphasis on their college classes and hard work as preparation for their ministries.

Societal changes were also affecting the postulancy. Young women who had entered the postulancy in 1964 were more influenced by events within the church itself, as well as national and international events, than their predecessors had been. A postulant of that year wrote:

> I think our postulancy was influenced by a number of national and world events. We were the first of the baby boomers[16] that resulted in, I believe, the largest group of postulants to start in September; we were 44 at the start. I also think the Vatican Council changes and national unrest, due to the Vietnam War, made us more outspoken in our opinions. We saw things changing or being challenged, and it gave us a mentality that some CSA routines could be questioned, too.
>
> I think it was a time of great idealism and questioning, and our group seemed to epitomize some of

that. The group's size challenged the postulant and novice mistresses to figure out what to do with all of us. The plan was to keep us busy physically with painting, yard work, helping at the farm and Nazareth Heights.[17]

Mother Rosita was a distant, proper woman who was interested in our report cards, but she didn't have a clue about where we were coming from. We ourselves were all over the place in terms of how we viewed religious life and the world around us, but we knew things would change. Our idealism was channeled toward the new church that was evolving, and how we would minister within that new church.[18]

These women reflected other signs of the shifting attitudes toward religious life. Beginning in 1943, for example, the postulants had worn the traditional bridal gown at their investing, symbolic of their intent to become brides of Christ. The later postulants' decision to wear their uniforms and a white mantilla instead of bridal attire was clearly a statement that the spirituality symbolized in the traditional ceremony held little meaning for the contemporary woman.

As the sixties progressed, directors began to prepare the girls for anticipated changes. A more other-directed program was offered to the candidates of 1965. From four to five-thirty in the afternoon they worked as nurses' aides at St. Agnes Hospital in alternating shifts. They could apply their wages toward tuition at Marian College. However, by 1967 the council had become concerned that nursing-students in formation were becoming more college-oriented than service-oriented and decided to limit their courses to those essential to their profession. The lighter program would also allow the students to earn their board by working at the hospital.

THE NOVITIATE

Described in the *Formation Handbook* "as a way of love and recollection," the two-year novitiate was and is "a time set aside in that the novice comes to know and love better the Lord to Whom she will give herself completely on her profession day. It is a time for strengthening ideals and convictions, examining desires and purifying intentions, forming mind and heart in the nature, spirit, and ideals of the religious life of a Sister of St. Agnes." Junior novices received instructions in spiritual formation, theology, ethics, and church history. They spent time working in the hospital laundry and cleaning at the farm and Nazareth Heights as well as the motherhouse. The seniors had the opportunity for both spiritual and professional development. On Saturdays, they taught religion to public school students, but as few novices had finished college, the greater part of their time was devoted to their professional preparation.

Novices felt that the novitiate was "on hold." Instead of the usual study of the constitutions, the novices read Örsy's *Open to the Spirit* and received instructions on sexuality from a senior novice. One novice remembered her group as becoming rebellious because changes were the decision of the general chapter.[19] Their frustrated director observed that: "Novices showed a much greater assertion of independence and were less amenable in accepting direction in their novitiate formation. This is probably one of the results of the fast-moving changes in today's world... but this spirit poses a problem of striking a balance and coping with community life as the congregation struggles through the changes that are already in the making."[20]

At the end of their novitiate, the women made vows for a three-year period. A juniorate had been established at the motherhouse in 1960. The juniorate year was designed to be a continuance in formation—spiritual, professional, and apostolic. It was also a year of adjustments to the community when the young women were given the opportunity to live out lessons learned in the novitiate. They could mingle with the other professed sisters and usually recreated with them. At this point, if one looked at the statistics, they appeared to be a very stable group. They had survived a very challenging training period and were looking forward to their lives on mission. Their futures seemed reasonably predictable. At the end of three years in temporary vows, they would renew their vows annually for another three years and then vow to observe poverty, chastity, and obedience in the congregation for life. During the period of temporary vows, the sisters would usually experience living on several different missions.

FORMATION IN NICARAGUA

The formation of the Nicaraguan women began with the same spirit that had always motivated the missionaries; they would do their utmost and somehow the grace of God and their own good will would see their works through. To an extent that was true, but as time went on, it was obvious that some changes had to be made. Although the young Nicaraguan women had all lived for several years with North American sisters in Nicaragua, the problems they faced when they arrived in Fond du Lac in regard to language, culture and ignorance on the part of the North Americans were enormous. In addition, the rigorous formation program of the period demanded a uniformity and preferably a homogeneity that even the North American candidates found forbidding. In an attempt to remedy the situation, on October 11, 1962, a house of formation was opened in Puerto Cabezas. The program began with the establishment of an aspirancy in 1962; three years later, on April 30, 1965, the first novitiate in the country was opened with five young women, one from Puerto Cabezas and four from the Pacific Coast of Nicaragua.[21]

The formation program got off to a bad start. It is possible that the unrest of the sixties had also begun to affect Nicaragua. Novices and aspirants grew restless and four professed sisters left the community.[22] Some problems can be traced to the lack of preparation of formation personnel. The director of the program was given one day's notice to prepare for her responsibilities. She immediately asked for and was given a native sister as an assistant, but both sisters felt the lack of preparation keenly. The aspirants, twelve native women, aged fifteen to twenty-eight, with levels of education ranging from professional to elementary, were difficult to form into a cohesive group. The development of the high school and normal school programs, positive as they were in themselves, created tensions in some of the women who dreaded the demands of the teacher education program and did not always feel capable of pursuing their studies and coping with examinations. It was not long before the program was discontinued. Of the eight young women in the program, only two novices continued their preparation in Managua. They made their first profession of vows on St. Agnes Day, 1969.

BUILDING PROGRAMS

At the end of the 1963 general chapter, Mother Rosita moved swiftly to implement its decisions. Two decisions involved major building projects. In undertaking them she had to allay a new set of fears—the chapter had voted to build both a retirement home for the sisters and a campus for Marian College. The burden of two large building programs in addition to the congregation's indebtedness incurred by the building program of St. Agnes Hospital was a formidable undertaking and frightening to some of the older sisters.

From the standpoint of the material welfare of the sisters, the most pressing task was building a residence for retired, sick, and infirm sisters presently residing at three sites—the motherhouse and both St. Agnes and St. Clare Hospitals. The new building, soon named Nazareth Heights, was built on the ledge adjacent to St. Mary's Springs High School. The building, designed to fit into the landscape, commanded a view of Lake Winnebago. In the two inner courts, white birch, flowering crabapple, Juneberry, Russian olive, mountain ash, and Cotoneaster multiflora provided a serene setting for meditation and recreation. Honey locust, Austrian pine, bittersweet, creeping sumac, and Pfitzer junipers were planted near the front entrance.

Nazareth Heights, dedicated on September 1, 1965, was designed for one hundred residents. Of the first sixty-eight sisters assigned there, fifty were residents and eighteen sisters were staff members. First and foremost, the goal of the Heights was to provide a setting for prayer. Next came the provision of activities that emphasized helping the sisters to retain their independence and usefulness; to feel needed as members of the community; to improve their strength and lessen the medical needs of old age; and to fulfill their needs for recognition and success. The funding for its operation came from interest on the trust fund of the congregation; estates of deceased sisters; income from mission sisters' vacations spent at Nazareth Heights; and income from mission sisters who recuperated there.[23] As was to be expected, the number of residents continually increased. By the end of the decade the number of residents rose to seventy-eight.

Since Marian College had been founded, it was clear that if it were to continue, its facilities needed to be expanded. The college still occupied the east wing of the motherhouse and consisted of eleven classrooms, two science laboratories, one language laboratory, and five administrative offices in the motherhouse and the use of the gym in the St. Agnes School of Nursing. Through the efforts of Sister Fidelis Karlin, the chapter had approved the construction of a college campus designed to accommodate six to seven hundred students.

On May 1, 1965, ground was broken on the twenty-eight-acre campus for the first phase of the building program—the construction of the administration and humanities building, the science building and the library. The buildings, set among evergreens, lilac bushes, flowering crab and dogwood trees were of Wisconsin stone construction. The college received a grant of $540,876 from the United States government. The sum represented about one-third of the original cost of the academic buildings under construction.

The student center, containing dining facilities for 300 students, and an additional residential hall for 134 students were built during the second phase of the construction at a cost of $1,600,000. In addition, Marian received $1,025,000 in a United States government loan for the second phase of construction of the college.[24] Father Benjamin Blied donated $10,000 towards the chapel fund on the condition that it be named after Dorcas, the seamstress whom the apostle Peter had cured at Jaffa.[25] The total cost of the six-building college campus was four million dollars.[26]

Improvement of existing buildings likewise absorbed the energies of the congregation during the next few years. The buildings at the motherhouse were sand blasted and trim painted. Extensive playground lighting was installed; a complex fire alarm system covering the entire motherhouse was installed on the grounds. A 950-foot well was dug on the ledge east of St. Mary's Springs to insure a pure water supply and fire protection for the ledge property. The well was dug just in time. In November, a heavy fire destroyed a large storage barn that housed two cars, a truck and other equipment. The cause of the fire was never determined.[27]

BREWING STORMS

The *Annus Mirabilis* of 1963 had most decidedly given way to the *Annus Horribilis* of 1965, and the years following. Civil disturbances over race and the Vietnam War were playing increasingly large roles in American society. The congregation's *Chronicles* of 1965 present a bleak picture. "As a result of the changes of Vatican II, authority, both civil and ecclesiastic, has been attacked and undermined .... Even our Blessed Lady herself has not escaped this destructive criticism .... The Prefect of the Sacred Congregation of Religious found it necessary to voice concern over the drastic changes to modern dress designs introduced by a number of sister groups ... when a renewal of religious spirit should be of major concern. Times within religious life reflect the confusion, insecurity, spirit of criticism, striving for independence and loss of true values pervading the atmosphere of the world. The number of defections both among the clergy and the religious was alarmingly on the increase ...."[28]

In a society that emphasized self-fulfillment, religious life with its vows of poverty, chastity, and obedience, could have held little attraction. For some, doubts about the relevance of religious life led to requests for exclaustration or dispensation from vows. More fields of service were open to women. They could enter, at least theoretically, any profession they chose. Even the priesthood seemed a possibility. By 1966 the Sisters of St. Agnes were facing the crisis in religious life that some congregations had faced earlier. In 1964 five dispensations were granted to Agnesian sisters; two in 1965; five in 1966; eleven in 1967; sixteen in 1968 and twenty-one in 1969. And, if the experience of other congregations was taken into account, more women were considering leaving religious life.

While the formation personnel were trying to adjust to the "new"entrants, many sisters were using their new freedoms to become involved in activities that took them away from the convent culture. In 1965, some helped to establish Project Headstart in Fond du Lac. Others worked with children and youth in the government-sponsored "Summer in the City" program in New York. In the following year, sisters volunteered as camp counselors, art teachers, nurses, and assistant cooks at Camp Vista. They began working in Appalachia and the slums of Cincinnati. Sister Juliana Kohne was employed in a government anti-poverty program, the Woman's Job Corps. Sister Benedict Dorey, a registered nurse and midwife, was invited by a Daughter of Charity, to join her in a clinic in the all-black town of Mound Bayou, Mississippi.[29]

Other sisters were using their freedom by ministering in traditional apostolates in non-traditional ways. Sister Judith Schmidt, still filled with much of the exuberance of the sixties, wrote:

> I came to St. Bernard's at age 28 as principal of the school and superior of 7 nuns (sisters). (We were called nuns in those days.) I was enthusiastic, filled with the spirit of adventure, and ready to take on anything. So, I taught 8th grade and was principal of 300 plus students, supervised 8 teachers and auxiliary personnel ....
>
> St. Bernard's Parish *is* and was for me the richest experience of my professional and personal career. Maybe it was because I was young, vulnerable, and mold-able. But it was because of all of you who allowed me to change, grow, make mistakes, start again, laugh, cry, try different things, such as march with Father Groppi[30] in the 60s, visit the 'coffee houses' in my full habit, walk the railroad tracks at 4:00 a.m. with one of the sophomores at the Public School, plan junior high retreats with a variety of youth groups ... play volleyball with a group of women one night a week in the school gym, put on 8th grade class plays using many after school hours (getting to know the 'kids' better), developing the beginnings of parish councils (working sometimes until 4:00 a.m. to 'fight' through the issues), gathering students from grades 1-8 in the gym each Friday—sitting on the floor—singing songs with guitars... and in general doing 60s things.[31]

Mother Rosita and her council found sisters leaving community works for other apostolates difficult to understand. It was not that they did not find the works the sisters were engaging in worthwhile, but decisions to engage in individual apostolates would inevitably have an adverse effect on living community—to many sisters one of the essential elements of religious life. And, of course, congregational, institutional commitments weighed heavily upon the council.

Activism may have been more visible than the sisters' increased interest in updating their own theology and their teaching methods, but at the appeal of two-thirds of the sisters, Mother Rosita requested that Marian College inaugurate a program in Religious Education.[32] Many sisters became avid readers of such publications as the recently founded *National Catholic Reporter* as well as the traditional *Review for Religious* and *Sponsa Regis*.

A CALL FOR PRUDENCE

In 1966, Pope Paul VI issued *Ecclesiae Sanctae* mandating all religious to hold special chapters of renewal within the next three years. This document was followed by the issuance of the norms guiding renewal by the Vatican Council.[33] Concerned over the "eagerness with which apostolic religious were pursuing renewal, this document called for prudence and care in putting the Council's teaching into effect."[34] Religious congregations were cautioned to promote spiritual renewal before adapting their way of life. Chapters of renewal were mandated, not just to make laws, but to foster apostolic and spiritual vitality. Constitutions were to be revised in keeping with "the evangelical and theological principles concerning religious life and its incorporation in the church," and the recognition of the spirit and aims of its founder. The council made a list of specific points regarding renewal and adaptation. Praying the Divine Office was recommended. Religious were to engage in acts of penance and mortification. They were to practice poverty both in spirit and fact. The "greatest importance" was placed on community and living in common. Formation programs were to be adapted. Collaboration among communities and national conferences of major superiors was encouraged.[35]

One more document was promulgated before the Sisters of St. Agnes held their renewal chapter, *Instruction on the Renewal of Religious Life (Renovationis Causam)*.[36] Intended to provide congregations with norms for the formation of new members, it stressed the primacy of consecration over mission and emphasized the statement in *Perfectae Caritatis* that "no adaptation to modern requirements should be put into effect, which is not inspired by spiritual renewal."[37]

In order to make the liturgy more accessible, there were changes in liturgical worship: English hymns could be sung at Benediction and prayers for the distribution of Holy Communion to the sick were to be said in English. The traditional fast before receiving the Holy Eucharist was reduced to one hour instead of a fast beginning at midnight. The congregation educated itself. There were institutes, conferences, and tapes. Mother Rosita enthusiastically supported the Movement for the Better World and for several years the congregation published bulletins to encourage the sisters to participate in the program.[38]

From the perspective of Mother Rosita "dissident voices" were introducing secular patterns of life into religious living. It was her fear that "the difference between meeting the 'secular world' and that of secularizing religious life itself was not being discerned."[39] The council arranged regional meetings and brought in speakers to answer questions and address doubts that were becoming increasingly disturbing.

It was a dilemma that Mother Rosita found exceedingly difficult to deal with because there was no one reason why sisters were leaving religious life. Sisters who had obediently and uncomplainingly risen before 5:00 a.m., lived in cold and drafty convents, taught as many as sixty children in a classroom or worked seven days a week caring for patients, were now, when their lives were becoming more tenable, asking to return to the world. They were discarding vocations that she and hundreds of her sisters had paid "not less than everything" for in their certainty that they were following God's holy will. She had taken their vows in her hands and had been chosen to be their "mother." Had the new directives diluted religious values? Had the community failed these women? If that were true, in what ways? What responsibility did she have for the welfare of their souls?

There were times when her own nature, impetuous, logical, impatient with ambiguity, got the better of her. One young sister approached her to talk over her difficulties, when to her surprise, Mother Rosita opened the bottom drawer of her desk and gave her a form to complete for a dispensation. There were other instances when women who had not made the final decision to leave the congregation suddenly found themselves back in secular life. When communication seemed impossible, women with a genuine love for the community felt called to follow their Christian vocation in other ways.

MODERNIZING CORPORATE STRUCTURES AND THE INSTITUTIONS

The decision to incorporate the hospitals, the college, and the academy as separate entities was a giant step toward modernization and protecting the institutions themselves. Until this time, all institutions were part of the motherhouse corporation. Each institution now had its own board of trustees and its separate financial arrangements. Sisters who were employed at the institutions constituted the membership.

Increasing professionalization in the administration of the community-owned ministries led to other changes. Recognizing that the administration of institutions had become highly professionalized, Mother Rosita had already begun to insure that sisters were being prepared to administer schools, hospitals, and the college. The internal administration of the congregation also needed updating. There were also improvements in maintaining internal records. Since records had frequently been incomplete and haphazard, the first duty of the new secretary general was to put the archives in order.[40] For the first time in congregational history, a personal file was provided for each sister.

In addition to the general chapter decision to incorporate institutions separately, two events had an impact on the college in 1963. The passage of the Higher Education Facilities Act provided construction grants to church-sponsored higher educational institutions, greatly aided in constructing the Marian College campus. The second was the appointment of Sister Mary Sheila Burns, a sociology professor, as its president. Marian College was no longer the responsibility of a member of the congregation's council. For the first time it had a full-time president and a small, but adequate and well-designed campus. The college was almost thirty years old and it was time for it to assert its own identity.

There was another major change, although not everyone regards change, even if an improvement, as progress. This was particularly true of the alumnae and faculty of St. Agnes School of Nursing who found it difficult to so regard the end of the diploma program and the inauguration of the degree program at Marian College. The closing of the School of Nursing in 1966 was the result of a long, and for many graduate nurses, heart-breaking process. Of the institutions under the aegis of the Sisters of St. Agnes, it was the School of Nursing that had formed alumnae with the greatest bonds to their school. The close association the nurses had for their three years as students with role models provided a formation for which they were always grateful.[41] They also grew close to each other. For three stress-filled years the students lived, studied, and worked together in an exceptionally strict and demanding environment. The rules were strict—and expulsion for their violation was not unknown. But students took pride in the excellent reputation of their school and appreciated the fact that their services were in high demand.[42]

A long history led up to the school's closure. Twenty years previously, the academic dean of the School of Nursing Education at Catholic University had encouraged Sister Digna Desch, director of the St. Agnes School of Nursing, to establish a four-year nursing curriculum. In 1949, she, together with Sister Vera Naber, Dean of Marian College, developed a curriculum that combined general education with professional instruction and led to a baccalaureate degree in nursing. The course of studies was published in the bulletins of Marian College and St. Agnes School of Nursing. It attracted no students.

A few years later, a Special Commission to Develop a State-wide Plan for Nursing Education in Wisconsin, recommended that at least two more collegiate programs were needed in the state. Marian College and Saint Agnes Hospital were cited as the most likely center for one such program. In 1956, as a first step, all freshmen at St. Agnes School of Nursing matriculated at Marian College, giving students full college credit for those courses and providing a college background on which to base their professional education. Sister faculty members were prepared in clinical specialties on the Master's level while the freshman program was gradually strengthened and expanded. With the approval in 1960 of Marian by the North Central Association of Colleges and Secondary Schools, it became possible to take the final step of developing the curriculum for the new course of studies.

On April 8, 1964, the Wisconsin State Board of Nursing approved the application of Marian College to begin a collegiate nursing program and granted initial accreditation effective upon admission of the first class. Thirty-one students enrolled in the Marian College Division of Nursing in September 1964.[43] Throughout and after the process was completed, there was a continuing debate between the nurses from the diploma program who valued their "hands-on education" and those who held that nurses should understand the theoretical basis of their profession, even at the expense of less time spent in actual bedside nursing.[44]

The introduction of the first class of nursing students on the campus in 1964 brought a welcome burst of energy. Until this time, candidates, novices, and sisters formed the preponderance of students. With the exception of the student teachers organization, they did not participate in extra-curricular activities. More campus organizations were possible and Marian students began to have a higher profile in the area.

The college received a government grant which provided a salary of two years for the instructor of public health while the serious shortage of nurses at the time prompted the government to approve a program by extending loans up to $1,000 to needy nursing students.

Regina Hall became the residence of the more than forty sister faculty and staff. The former St. Agnes School of Nursing was renamed St. Agnes Hall and became the residence hall for Marian students. A large yellow school bus transported students from campus to residence hall.[45] Male students had been admitted to the evening classes in the 1950s. The first full-time male student, an Episcopal clergyman who was allowed to attend class with the novices and candidates, graduated in 1967, but the official decision to become a coeducational institution was not made until 1969. Academically, much of the faculty's effort was successfully directed toward attaining accreditation for the teacher education program from the National Council for the Accreditation of Teacher Education (NCATE) and for the nursing program from the National League of Nursing (NLN).

CATHOLIC SCHOOLS

By the middle 1960s, the Catholic School system was in the midst of a crisis. Although Catholic schools had grown twice as fast as public schools since the end of World War II, the advent of the baby boomers, the growth of new parishes in suburbia and the growing affluence of the Catholic population had created a demand for Catholic education that could not be satisfied.[46] Dioceses were falling further and further behind in educating Catholic children, although the church was educating one in eight children it was turning away thousands. At the same time, increasing educational standards for teachers, the addition of lay teachers in many schools,[47] and the more sophisticated educational tools demanded by parents were increasing the cost of educating Catholic children.[48]

There were other problems in Catholic education. In 1960, the National Catholic Education Association was faced with questions that needed answers. Were Catholic schools as effective as public schools in the secular education of their children? Were Catholic schools divisive? Did parochial schools preserve religious faith and make their students devout Catholics? One of the most influential critiques of the value of Catholic education was made by Mary Perkins Ryan, whose 1964 book, *Are Parochial Schools the Answer?* charged that parochial schools were impeding the church's witness by absorbing the energy, talent, and funds that should be directed toward liturgy, social justice, and the education of older youth and adults.[49]

While the congregation was pouring resources of personnel and monies into Marian College, the focus of its educational efforts remained in the elementary schools. Although in 1964, the *Chronicles* noted that lack of funds and the building of new schools in neighboring parishes were necessitating the closing of small schools and the discontinuance of lower or upper grade levels in other schools,[50] Agnesian schools in New Haven and Fort Wayne, Indiana; and Hays, Kansas; opened new classrooms. In Wisconsin, SS. Peter and Paul School in Hortonville, opened a new eight-classroom building while both Holy Trinity in Kewaskum, and Brother Dutton School in Beloit, had engaged in building programs.

However, the nation-wide drop in Catholic school enrollment was precipitous the following year. Within the world of CSA schools, the downward trend in enrollments began in 1966. Between the 1962-1963 school year and the 1966-1967 school year, enrollment figures in the elementary schools declined from 25,308 to 23,837 in over sixty schools and from 3,372 to 3,068 in the high

*Mother M. Joseph Wolford, CSA
Superior General
1926 - 1933*

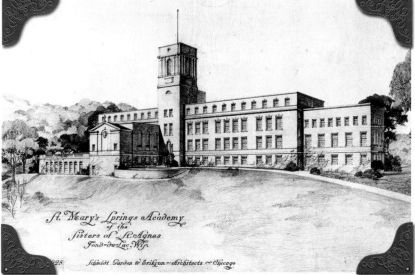

*Architect's drawing of the Main Building of St. Mary's Springs Academy,
Fond du Lac. The building opened in September 1929.*

Mother M. Aloysia Leikem, CSA
Superior General
1933 - 1939

St. Clare Hospital, Monroe, Wisconsin, opened August 1, 1939.

Mother M. Angeline Kamp, CSA
Superior General
1939 - 1951

St. Thomas Hospital, Colby, Kansas, opened October 8, 1941.

L-R: Sisters Mary Agnes Dickof, Francis Borgia Dreiling, Pauletta Scheck, and Agne Rita Fisette opened the CSA mission in Waspam, Nicaragua, in 1945.

The shores of Waspam, Nicaragua, as seen from the Río Coco soon after the pioneer missionaries arrived there.

CSA mission compound in Waspam, Nicaragua, as it was from the inception of the sion. The path led across the bridge up to the church.

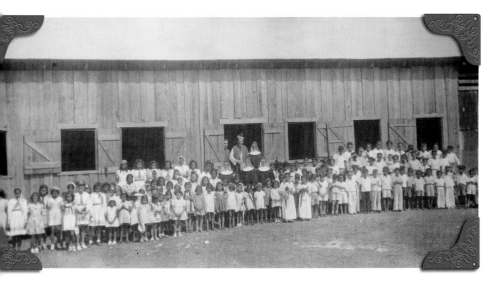

pioneer missionaries visit the school in Puerto Cabezas, Nicaragua. In the doorway Father Roman Ament, OFM Cap., and Bishop Matthew Niedhammer, OFM Cap.

Mother M. Albertonia Licher, CSA
Superior General
1951 - 1957

Having made an annual retreat and attended summer school, Sisters departed from the mother-house after August 15 to return to their previous missions or to begin new assignments.

Mother M. Rosita Handibode, CSA
Superior General
1957 - 1969

ı September 1965 a dream became reality when the first sister residents moved into
ʻazareth Heights Infirmary.

Sister M. John Baptist, CSA
Superior General
1969 - 1973

Marian College of Fond du Lac was relocated to 45 S. National Avenue in September 1966. Shown here, left to right, are the Administration Building, the breezeway, Albert Cardinal Meyer Library and, in the background, the spire of Dorcas Chapel.

Sister Judith Schmidt, CSA
Superior General
1973 - 1985

*This photo
illustrates the
variety in
modified habits
worn by sisters in
the same local
community.*

Sister Maureen Courtney (center) and affiliates Felícita Colomer Kramer and Teresa de Jesús Rosales Dixon (both far left facing front) visited Waspam to greet the people who were preparing to return to their river towns after living in resettlement camps. Photo dated August 17, 1985.

St. Agnes Hospital, Fond du Lac, constructed this addition to the west on Division Stre in 1975 - 1977.

Sister Jean Steffes, CSA
General Superior
1985 - 1993

e Sisters of St. Agnes assumed sponsorship of Waupun Memorial
spital, Waupun, Wisconsin, in 1987.

St. Agnes Convent, 475 Gillett Street, Fond du Lac, Wisconsin. Formerly St. Agnes School of Nursing, this building served as the motherhouse of the congregation during the years 1975 - 1999.

schools. Immaculate Conception at Elmhurst had lost fifty students, but Beloit Catholic gained fifteen students. [51]

In 1967, Sister Mary Daniel seems to have summed up the general feeling at the motherhouse when she quoted from a speech by a New York bishop who prophesied at a national conference: "This may well be the winter of Catholic education." He defended the apostolate of teaching, deploring the talk among religious about phasing out of our elementary schools and getting religious teachers into more "meaningful apostolates" such as "being in picket lines, parading in civil rights marches and peace agitations."[52]

SECONDARY EDUCATION

The secondary schools presented a different picture. With only seventy-five sisters in the field of secondary education, the congregation responded to the bishops' request to release several sisters to teach in diocesan high schools—Bishop Guilfoyle in Altoona, Pennsylvania, and Canevin, in the Pittsburgh area. In schools staffed by the congregation, there were the usual difficulties. In Decatur, Indiana, St. Joseph's was overcrowded and the school's physical plant was inadequate. Not only were there problems with the plant at Beloit Catholic, but also an unwieldy administration and a few board members who delayed just increases in salary for the lay people and needed plant repairs. The sister faculty was constantly complaining because of "priest and male faculty dominance."[53] According to the sister faculty, it was only the exceptional teacher-student rapport in the school of 479 students that made it possible for them to tolerate its negative aspects.

Immaculate Conception High School in Elmhurst had 658 students and a qualified and loyal faculty, but it was overcrowded in spite of its relatively new building. St. Mary's Springs with its 689 students was doing well, but the imbalance between the boys and girls and the weak alumni group were matters of concern. Moreover a movement in Fond du Lac to build a new Catholic high school was leaving the congregation in a highly uncertain state.

Sacred Heart High School in Yonkers, New York, had an unusual history. When the Capuchins took over the parish in 1893, Father Bonaventure Frey secured three Agnesians to open the school. In 1923, four classrooms were added to the building that then served as a preparatory Capuchin seminary. Five years later the sisters added a two-year commercial course. Over the years, the coeducational high school accommodated a little over two hundred students. In 1954 the archdiocese gave permission to increase the space and sixteen rooms, a cafeteria, and a library were added. Father Finian Sullivan[54] then requested money from the Archdiocesan Cardinal Spellman Building Campaign fund, but Sacred Heart was not eligible since it was a diocesan school. But the diocese would consider giving them money if the school would get brothers to teach. Father Finian negotiated with the Christian Brothers—who came. In the process, the Sisters of St. Agnes consented to change the co-educational school to co-institutional. The sisters taught only the girls, while the Christian Brothers, the boys. A new building with a capacity enrollment of sixteen hundred students was expected to be completed in 1967.[55]

Throughout the early sixties, numerous planning meetings were underway with the congregation, local priests, and officials of the archdiocesan offices to build a diocesan high school in Fond du Lac. Although the Springs was painfully overcrowded, the plan to build a new Catholic high school not only failed to materialize, but its prospects were lessening as the years dragged on. A corporation had been formed made up of the twenty-two parishes of Fond du Lac County and the Archbishop. In 1966 a fund-raising campaign, "The St. Mary's Springs High School Crusade" was launched. Its goal of $2,500,000 was to be completed within five years. Eventually, fund raising for three years managed to procure about $1,500,000 in pledges and about $459,000 in cash for the campaign. Eventually an agreement was made to build a new school as an addition to the Springs' original buildings. The Sisters of St. Agnes relinquished their ownership of the Springs by transferring the land and property of the school to the corporation. The consolidation combined more than $2,000,000 assets of the congregation with the $2,000,000 building program contributed to by twenty-two parishes in the county.[56]

A REVOLUTIONARY EDUCATIONAL CONCEPT

There has never been a period in American educational history when there have not been competing philosophies of education nor a time when society has not faced difficulties in educating its children. In the midst of the pervasive problems on the educational scene, several Agnesian educators studying at Marquette University were impressed by the educational theories of Dr. James M. Hanlon. Dr. Hanlon, strongly committed to Catholic education, was concerned about the decline of enrollment in the Catholic schools and equally concerned about a movement in the public sector towards 'value free' education.[57] Hanlon believed that the public schools in embracing value relativity would lose their leadership in education but that Catholic schools with their clearly defined values would provide the spiritual, moral and intellectual leadership needed if civilization itself would survive.

Hanlon believed that education was engaged in a battle between two schools of thought: the first, joined to a theory of learning based on the behaviorism of John B. Watson, held that "the definition of education concerns the processes of socialization and enculturation, or a kind of assimilating of a person into the society, and into the culture,"[58] and the second that "education is the process of self-actualization, or of a human being making himself what he planned to be."[59] The first theory, the principal tenet of which is the stimulus-response theory, holds that humans and other animals functioned purely from physiological and physical bases. The second, or humanistic theory, defines learning as the acquisition of insight and takes into account humanity's highest aspirations. Hanlon held yet a third theory. He believed that the two schools of thought could be united, and while in the long run education is about self-actualization, it is self-actualization in the context of society and culture. Instead of talking about learning, the conversation should be about learning how to learn.

This message so inspired Dr. Hanlon's Agnesian students that they arranged a meeting with the superior general and the president of Marian College. They, too, were impressed and in late August, 1966, Hanlon was asked to explain his program to the educators in town. His ideas generated so much support that the college scheduled his class on administration and theory during the 1968-1969 school year. In 1969 Dr. Hanlon was invited to present his theories to the general chapter.

HEALTH CARE

Hospitals and health care facilities were also adjusting to functioning in a radically different economic environment. Private insurance
grew phenomenally: between 1940 and 1965, coverage rose from 9
percent of the population to 71.4 percent. In 1950 Congress, for the
first time, permitted the federal government to participate in state
programs to provide medical care to needy persons who were
receiving public assistance. The increased demand for health care
led to expenditures in facilities, research, additional personnel, and
increases in physicians' fees. From 1945-1964 personnel grew from
150 to 250 per 100 patients. The resulting rise in hospital costs
excluded millions of people without insurance. Then in 1960 the
Kerr-Mills bill was passed; it provided medical assistance for aged
persons who were not so poor. In 1965 Congress passed Medicare,
that mandated health insurance for Americans over age sixty-five
and a supplemental Medicaid program for the indigent.[60]

Agnesian hospitals were affected in various ways. The declining
pool of religious personnel led to a gradual relinquishing of many
administrative positions to lay persons. Administrators devoted
much time to the anticipated changes in hospital routines and the
expected shift in type of patient, together with increased burdens in
the accounting departments.[61] As Medicare had its deductible and
limitation on days in hospital, the hospitals were forced to emphasize acute care. No longer could long-term patients remain in the
hospital. Hospitals were less able to provide charity for the poor,
leading some religious to the belief that they should relinquish their
hospitals to work in poverty-stricken rural areas, inner cities, or third
world countries.

The *Chronicles* for the remainder of the decade reveal a period of
much hard work, some disappointments, and some achievements in
Agnesian health care institutions. Overall, the 1964 *Chronicles* indicate a degree of pride in the four Agnesian hospitals.[62]

At St. Agnes Hospital, the level of occupancy was satisfactory, a
parking lot had been expanded, and the intensive care unit at St.
Agnes was said to surpass any other unit of its type in the area. St.
Agnes Hospital also became the first Agnesian hospital to enter contracts for Service Master, housekeeping services, and Hospital Food

Management.[63] By the end of the decade electroencephalography was added as a new service to patients.[64]

A high degree of occupancy was noted for St. Clare Hospital and even though a reconversion of the fourth floor provided twenty-three additional beds, the hospital was crowded. Although the hospital was looking to the future by acquiring adjacent property in order to make a long-range plan for expansion possible, two years later the expansion program seemed stalemated. A development program fell far short of the goal and the physicians on the staff were openly in opposition to the planning done by the architect.[65] However, by April, 1968 a plan for expansion was proposed that seemed acceptable to all. As government funds were not available at that time, the motherhouse corporation received ecclesiastical permission to borrow four million dollars and became the guarantor for the six million dollar project.[66]

In Kansas both St. Anthony and St. Thomas hospitals were struggling to survive. St. Anthony in Hays faced rising operating costs and also, in a town with a population hovering around 17,000, the competition of Hadley Hospital.[67] In addition, the hospital's buildings were obsolescent and a new facility was desperately needed. The hospital was making plans to acquire a new campus and build when in the fall of 1966 it was approached by representatives of Hadley proposing a merger with each hospital retaining its own identity. The merging of a Catholic hospital with a hospital affiliated with another religion was, at the time, comparatively rare. The idea was given special consideration by the corporation, but tabled until more information could be procured. Long, drawn-out discussions led St. Anthony's to reject the offer though both hospitals agreed to coordinate and cooperate to prevent unnecessary duplication of facilities.[68]

In Colby, Kansas, the erection of several small hospitals in neighboring towns had reduced the census of St. Thomas Hospital.[69] The hospital was also experiencing great difficulty in procuring the services of a permanent radiologist and physical therapist.[70] By 1969, the conditions were "growing ominously worse" as the resignation of an excellent surgeon had caused potential patients to go elsewhere.[71]

RE-EVALUATIONS

External and internal changes necessitated re-evaluations of several realities. As the number of sisters retiring or nearing retirement increased, the congregation was faced with several issues. Preparing sisters for their retirement years was one; convincing a sister to retire was another; and, perhaps the easiest, was building a retirement home to care for the retired.

In 1965 talk about the future of the Leo House and the role of the Sisters of St. Agnes in it had come to a head. A rumor had been circulated that the sisters were about to withdraw because of the hazardous living quarters they occupied. Moreover, with changes in the immigration laws, the membership of the hostel's sponsor, the St. Raphael Society, had been declining for some time.[72] Mother Rosita met with members of the Board of Directors including Cardinal Spellman's representative. As the Board was anxious to continue the services that the hostel offered in the Archdiocese, it agreed to make needed improvements and Mother Rosita agreed not to withdraw the sisters.[73] Improvements continued throughout the next years. Sisters were moved from a dangerous annex into the main building, while a steady occupancy rate of seventy or eighty travelers a day had paid off the mortgage.[74]

St. John's Rest Home in Victoria, Kansas, like the Leo House, was not a congregational project; however, it provided an opportunity for a new relationship with the people there. The people of Ellis County were badly in need of a home for the elderly. After several unsuccessful attempts to interest the people of Hays, Leo J. Dreiling, Sr. turned to smaller communities in the area and with other concerned citizens formed a non-profit organization to promote and finance construction. Since the congregation was established at St. Anthony's hospital in Hays, the group naturally turned to the Agnesian sisters. A committee met with Mother Rosita and her council in May 1962 and left with the promise of four sisters to staff the home when it was completed.

The Bishop of the Salina Diocese, Most Rev. F.W. Freking, gave his blessing to the project but declined to make it a diocesan project. Eventually the St. John's Rest Home Board was formed with the Sister Administrator of the Home as one of the Directors. When Victoria was chosen as the site, Mr. Dreiling and Mrs. Dreiling purchased land and donated it to the Rest Home Corporation. The first occupants arrived on July 22, 1964.[75]

The expansion of the early sixties benefited the sisters at Sacred Heart parish in Fond du Lac and Immaculate Conception parish in Elmhurst, Illinois. Each parish built a new convent for the sisters.

MISSIONS IN LATIN AMERICA

In 1961, Pope John XXIII had urged religious congregations to pledge 10% of their personnel to Latin America.[76] As the congregation's commitments in Central America had kindled an interest in the continent, there was no question but that the Sisters of St. Agnes would respond to the request as quickly as possible. At a council meeting in August of 1963, Mother Rosita read an invitation by the Salesian Fathers to teach English, religion, music and art in the Cardinal Spellman School in Quito, Ecuador.

Investigation into the project revealed a number of advantages. The people there were enthusiastic about the possibility of having American sisters there; it could be a possible site for the establishment of a native novitiate in the city with a Jesuit University, a Salesian Normal School, a Salesian Sisters High School and a School of Theology. The climate was particularly attractive. Although Quito is very close to the equator, its 9,000-foot altitude provided a cool refreshing breeze, while the mountains protect the city from the heat of the sun's rays the greater part of the day.

After a visit and evaluation by Sister Francis Borgia, the regional superior of Central America, the council signed a three-year contract to provide two teachers and a homemaker to Quito. In October 1963, Sisters Raymond Grieble, Catherine Siena, (Vivian) Schmidtberger and Aquiline (Marcella) Wasinger arrived as the first Sisters of St. Agnes to serve in South America. Thrilled and excited as they were to be there, they were immediately disappointed to find that plans for their residence had not materialized. The congregation had no choice but to buy a house.[77]

The sisters were further disappointed to find that their services were desired as teachers of English only. Each sister taught thirty classes of English weekly. Eager as the little boys seemed to be to learn, the sisters found them difficult to control because of the family background and culture. Cared for by servants, the boys had lit-

tle opportunity to assume responsibility or show respect for authority. On week-ends and during vacations the sisters catechized both
the children of American embassy and military officials and the
poor children in the area.[78]

One of the neediest areas was around the market of Boca de
Los Sapos (Mouth of the Toads), officially Triunfo, near Guyaquil
in Ecuador where the sisters participated in a project sponsored by
the Society of St. James the Apostle, an association of diocesan
priest volunteers sent by their bishops to serve in Bolivia, Ecuador,
and Peru.

It was not long before the sisters in Ecuador had been having
some of the same difficulties faced by the sisters in Managua. As in
Managua, questions arose in regard to the sisters teaching in a
school for the wealthy; furthermore, some of the boys' parents were
disturbed because they were convinced that the sisters were endan-
gering the health of their sons by their contacts with the very poor
of the city and countryside.

Only a month before the sisters' arrival in Quito, the apostolic
nuncio in Lima had invited the congregation to staff a government
hospital there. In February 1964 Sisters Fidelis Karlin and Imogene
Palen visited Peru to evaluate the hospitals that were offered in
terms of the CSA mission. Upon their return in March they reported to the council on evaluations of the ten hospitals they visited and
the communities they served. The congregation leaned toward a
hospital in Puno but no immediate commitment was made.

Home from the missions the following summer, Sister Raymond
reported that some of the Latin American clergy were critical of the
Agnesians because they were teaching in a school for the affluent.
Monsignor Alfred Schneider of the National Catholic Welfare
Conference (NCWC) advised the sisters to break their contract with
the Cardinal Spellman School. Furthermore, he said they should
decline the offer to staff a hospital in Peru, which he saw as over-
stocked with missionaries, and concentrate on the poor of Ecuador.
Other clergy told them that the Agnesians should make contacts
with the rich who would help the poor, but that their work should
be among the poor. Mother Rosita replied that the Agnesian presence at Cardinal Spellman was to form a beachhead and a source
of income for the work to be undertaken among the poor.

Nevertheless, Monsignor Schneider visited the motherhouse on August 1. At that point, the council found his reasons to concentrate the congregation's work in Ecuador compelling. Not only were there twenty-nine religious orders already in Peru, but he pointed out that scattering the community's limited forces and resources would, in the long run, prove ineffective. The congregation's interest in Peru was over.

In January of 1964, Father Raymond Kirk of the Society of St. James the Apostle paid a visit to the motherhouse to show the sisters slides of the work Agnesians were doing among the poor in El Triunfo. In mid-April, he was followed by Father Joseph Lauro also of the Society who came to the motherhouse begging for help. He hoped to open a catechetical center and clinic for the people in his area. Father Lauro and two assistant priests had charge of nine hundred square miles of territory with a population of thirty-five thousand. They were responsible for eighteen missions and held catechism classes in eighteen public schools. On Sundays Father Lauro offered as many as nine Masses. The needs of the priests and people were so obviously compelling and the recommendation of the sisters so affirmative that Mother and the council promised the missionaries the help they needed.[79]

El Triunfo was the poorest mission Agnesians had ever lived in. The humidity, the mud, the smell of the place were appalling. The place seemed to alternate between periods of flooding and periods of aridity. When the sisters stayed overnight underneath the priests' house, sometimes for as long as a week or ten days, their sleep was often disturbed by rats running over their blankets.[80] Nevertheless there was something about the people and the ministry that engaged the affections of the missionaries.

Like other Latin American countries, the land was held by the wealthy and the great majority of people lived in utter poverty. Most of the income for the ordinary person in Boca came from the large market there, patronized by people on their way between the coast and the mountains. As in Waspam, destitution was evident in the illnesses of the people. Wages were poor and drunkenness caused the usual problems. Sanitation was a major problem. Malnutrition was a given, tuberculosis was rampant, and parasites were common. Infant mortality was extremely high.

Although the pastor had done everything in his power to welcome the sisters, life in Boca de Los Sapos proved a challenge for
them. They lived comfortably compared to the rest of the population. The pastor had helped build their house of concrete blocks
filled with mud and had even provided beds by the time they
arrived. Later, unlike the inhabitants, they had chairs and an electric generator. During the rainy season when torrential downpours
converted the streets into rushing streams, the people built little
bridges connecting their bamboo houses and the government provided row boats for the frequently needed rescue missions. The rain
and flooding were hard enough but the long white habits[81] were a
detriment to the sisters' comfort and safety.[82]

The missionaries found El Triunfo difficult but rewarding. At
the clinic in El Triunfo the sisters worked with two self-sacrificing
doctors, one worked full time, and one on week-ends. Medical supplies there were scarce and expensive. The sisters asked for only half
of what they spent for medicine and supplies, but it was often too
much for families who sometimes left a third sick child outside
because they had only four *sucres*, instead of six. But some help came
from benefactors; the sisters were particularly delighted to receive a
small sterilizer from the wife of the American ambassador.

The clinic was open Monday through Friday and a dental service was offered on Saturday evening and Sunday morning. During
the first year the clinic cared for a total of 25,362 patients, made 266
sick calls, more than 250 health education house calls, thirty-nine
emergency hospital runs, and assisted at fifty-three births,[83] and also
cooperated with government-sponsored experimental programs.[84]

Catechizing involved walking around the country from mission
to mission meeting with the people. It was both a source of joy and
physically demanding.[85] As time went on, the sisters were able to put
more emphasis on teaching religion in the schools and efforts to
build a Christian community. They started the day with spontaneous prayers at the beginning of the class; approached the lesson
through the use of modern parables; moved on to the parallel in the
religious topic of the day; and concluded with a summary of various practical conclusions by the children. The children learned simple prayers, religious songs and hymns, and dramatized some gospel
events. When possible, the school was divided into groups: pre-
Communion, Communion, and post-Communion. This was new

because many of the children were accustomed to hearing the same First Communion lesson each year.[86] The missionaries found a real thirst for God on the part of the people and they believed that much had been done to satisfy it through religion classes and participation in the liturgy. The CSA *Chronicles* recorded a comment from one missionary: "Our real success... in walking around the countryside here in Ecuador [is] clearly evidenced by the uplifted morale of the people. As a visiting priest put it in a conference, 'the greatest contribution you can give these people is hope.'"[87]

In their report to the motherhouse, however, the missionaries also indicated areas of frustration. They saw situations that needed, in their opinion, to be changed immediately. Their goals and the goals of the natives were not always congruent. For example, the missionaries were not able to convince the people to take any communal action toward improving their situation. These differences in values between the missionaries and the people, compounded by the North American sisters' elementary understanding of Spanish, added to their problems. Even the presence of two Nicaraguan sisters on the mission for a time did not always guarantee an appropriate level of communication.

When only two North American sisters were left on the mission the isolation and loneliness they experienced proved an insurmountable problem. Early in 1972, after they had applied for a dispensation from their vows, the superior general "with great disappointment and difficulty" had to inform the Provincial of the Society of St. James the Apostle that "we would have to withdraw completely from this work because we had not trained personnel to replace the sisters. In God's providence, however this work on which we had expended so much both in loss of personnel and in financial lay-out was to continue."[88]

Meanwhile a cooperative assistance program had been established between St. Louis University and the Catholic University of Ecuador under the sponsorship of the United States AID to set up a nursing center. Its objective was to train leaders in the nursing profession who would raise the standards of nursing care in the Ecuadorian hospitals. The Sisters of St. Agnes had been invited to participate in the program by Father Edward Justen, SJ, of the Catholic University of Ecuador in Quito.[89] The Daughters of Charity of St. Vincent de Paul would be responsible for designing the curriculum for a hospital nursing division while the Agnesians would participate in a program designed to establish a model hospital associated with the University. The project had immediate appeal. As highly qualified nurses were available, the community could supply the expertise. It was also an advantage that there were already Agnesians in the city with plenty of extra room in their residence.

In the years since the first Agnesians had arrived in Nicaragua there had been significant developments in missiology. Universities had begun to offer programs in missionary formation. Religious to be sent to Central and South America enrolled in programs of missionary formation at the Catholic University in Ponce, Puerto Rico or the recently established Center for Intercultural Formation in Cuernavaca, Mexico. They studied Spanish, anthropology, the nature of culture, Latin American culture in particular, and developed skills in intercultural communication. They learned to respect and appreciate local culture and customs but did not overlook the crushing effects that the "culture of poverty" has on its victims. They became even more convinced that their obligation, above all, was to help each person "come to a realization of his own dignity and potential as a human being and as a Christian."[90]

From February to June, Sisters Laura (Katherine) Knowles, Jean Vianney (Janet) Ahler, and Julie Hoffman enrolled at the Catholic University of Ponce in Puerto Rico; from there they went directly to Quito.

It was a doomed project. The first year little or no progress was made by the planning team. While some of the problems stemmed from critical differences between South American and North American approaches to tasks, the complexities of health care in the city could not be solved by the addition of another hospital. Before that conclusion was accepted, one frustrated nurse returned home in less than a year; the remaining sisters resigned after the director of their team[91] determined that Quito was unable to support another hospital. As neither the university nor the congregation was prepared to give up, Sister Paulette Shaw was sent to be director of nursing at the hospital.[92]

The hospital was finally opened, but was unable to sustain itself for more than a few years.

In the *Chronicles* of 1967 we find an uncharacteristically emotional response to a plea for help. "The coming to the Motherhouse of Juan Diego (John) Parthum, OFM Cap., on February 28 [1966] made a profound impression upon Mother and the councilors since his plea was so sincere and his reason for asking for sisters, a pressing one."[93] Mother Rosita also confided to Sister Dolores Taddy a less public reason: "When I visited Nicaragua I sensed that if we refuse to open this mission in preference to any other, we would offend Bishop Niedhammer and disturb our relations with the very good Capuchin Fathers."[94]

Responding to that call, in May of 1967, Sisters Dolores and María del Rey Cajina were sent to open the Colegio Santa Rosa in the Parroquia of Santa Rosa de Lima in Rosita, a little mining town in the mountains about one hundred and twenty-five miles to the west of Puerto Cabezas. The decision to accept the mission proved to be excellent. Providing Catholic education for the children would prevent their being proselytized by the Protestant school that was being planned for the area and also provide a place for the newly-professed Nicaraguan sisters to begin teaching in their own country. There were additional benefits in Rosita. Although the village was described as "tough" like all mining towns, it had been developed by a Canadian mining company and there was electricity as well as adequate water systems.[95]

When the first students enrolled in the school reached sixth grade, a higher grade was added yearly. Like the school in Puerto Cabezas, it became an important center for education, where students, coming from towns and the large rural area, were prepared for university studies. When Sister Rosa Inés Silva arrived in 1971, she became director of the already established primary school and in 1973 of the secondary school. The schools were financed in a unique manner. Father Juan Diego operated a theatre that provided the only entertainment of its kind for the town. The profits from the operation paid the total salary of the teachers.[96]

Besides teaching in the schools and in the catechetics programs, the missionaries directed programs for children and young people in the town. They went into the rural areas where they worked with the catechists and delegates of the Word and directed the ministry for the sick and aged.[97] They placed a special emphasis on affirming the dignity of the women of Rosita by providing classes in spiritual formation, sewing, cooking, family care, health, and manual arts.[98]

Nuevo Ocotopeque in Honduras provided another example of a project that the Agnesians were unable to sustain. In September, 1968, the great poverty of Honduras prompted the congregation to send two sisters to Nuevo Ocotopeque as assistants to Roderick Brennan, OFM Cap., who was opening a catechetical center there. Father had even provided a convent. The center was opened on September 15, the feast of Our Lady of Sorrows. In January, 1969 the sisters were withdrawn because of more pressing needs elsewhere.[99]

Why was it so difficult to surmount the problems of the sixties? A comparison with the foundation of the Agnesian houses in Nicaragua does point up some critical differences between the two foundations. The sisters there had been sent to an already established mission. Their colleagues were a group of dedicated friars with whom they had a great deal in common. They could celebrate together and sustain each other in crises. With the horarium and the rule nearly identical to that of the motherhouse, the sisters were leading a life similar in many important respects to the life they had led in the United States. While that could be restrictive, it could also be comforting. The few Nicaraguan sisters who entered could more easily be absorbed into the essentially North American culture.

The congregational experience in Ecuador reveals a different pattern. It is possible that the congregation moved too hastily to answer the plea of Pope John XXIII to send more religious to Latin America. Sisters placed in two cities with strikingly divided social classes struggled under a burden of guilt because they were not devoting all of their time to the poor. Sisters were sent to areas where there was little or no companionship to be had. In the case of the hospital in Quito there had not been enough groundwork laid by the sponsors of the project. In any case, the congregation took to heart the lessons learned in the 1960s.

A FINAL ACHIEVEMENT

The centennial celebration of the founding of the congregation had sparked an interest in its early history. In the past the congregation, with the exception of Sister Julia Dullea, might be said to have avoided the topic. Church documents, *Evangelica Testificato* and *Lumen Gentium,* which had asked religious communities to preserve their founding charisms led to an interest in the community's founders. For some time, Mother Rosita and Sister Imogene Palen had regretted that the body of their founder, Father Caspar Rehrl, was not in the community cemetery. Mother Rosita regarded as one of the final achievements of her administration the exhumation and reburial of the remains of the congregation's founder in St. Joseph Springs Cemetery on September 3, 1968. Since that time the congregation has celebrated and honored its founders on September 3.

Chapter XII

An Unknown
Destination

By the time the renewal chapter of the congregation met in 1969, almost seven years had passed since the opening of the Vatican Council. Neither the church nor religious congregations had a map to guide them on the journey they had so courageously begun. Modifications of the habit swiftly turned into the adoption of secular clothing and often became a symbol of the attempts of women religious to participate in the spirit of Vatican II. By the middle sixties, there was scarcely a week in which Agnesians were not inundated by reports of new and dramatic changes in other religious congregations. They saw traditions and customs swept away in many communities; they were shocked when the permanence of vows and the value of their traditional institutional commitments were being questioned. They followed with interest and mixed feelings the struggle that members of the respected Congregation of Sisters, Servants of the Immaculate Heart of Mary (IHM), were having with their conservative bishop over issues the sisters regarded as internal to themselves.[1]

When Agnesians looked back on their own past, they saw a group of women whose sober German heritage of hard work and pragmatism had kept them quietly and obediently serving the church for over a century. If, they argued, observing the rule and customs had produced women of great character, solid achievements, and some of undeniable sanctity, there should be no need to make radical changes.

Mother Rosita Handibode herself felt that the congregation had made every effort to adhere to the spirit of the Council and the call to religious renewal. As she reminded the 1969 chapter: "If there has been any preoccupation in this administration, it has been in the area of the spiritual unfolding of the members, namely, the attempt at renewal of religious life. Taking into account the psychological needs of the sisters, several sets of directives were issued during the administration. Suggestions from the sisters formed the basis for the decisions reached to set aside certain customs which had become obsolete and were no longer achieving the purpose for which they had been originally set up."[2] These measured words could not, nor were they intended to, reflect the anguish that making those modifications caused her.

But many Agnesians believed that if their congregation were by definition an apostolic community, changes would have to be even more radical to make sisters available for ministry in a changing world. And if Pope John XXIII's encyclical *Pacem in Terris* were to be heeded, a major restructuring of the government of the congregation was necessary to respect the individual by incorporating in it the principles of collegiality and subsidiarity.

SETTING OUT

With mixed feelings and in obedience to the direction set by the Second Vatican Council, the community began its preparation for the chapter of renewal. Two studies both provided information and involved the sisters in preparing for their chapter of renewal.

The first was an assessment of community life in the local community sponsored by the Conference of Major Superiors of Women in 1966.[3] The survey, under the direction of sociologist Sister Marie Augusta Neal, SND, was designed to discover the readiness of American sisters for renewal as well as to provide data that communities could use in their efforts to implement Vatican II.[4] Although the survey revealed areas of restlessness, the administration was heartened to discover that data showed the Sisters of St. Agnes were above the norm in satisfaction with their community.

The second study was the congregation's own.[5] In September 1967, Sisters were asked to submit names from which a committee was chosen to structure the pre-chapter preparations. The committee met in December and prepared a congregational self-study that would consolidate the proposals from the sisters. Recommended reading included articles in such periodicals as *Review for Religious* and *Sisters Today* as well as works by Bernard Cooke, Bernard Haring, Elio Gambari, and, most importantly, the Council documents. In September 1968, the sisters were asked for their opinions on the fundamental issues involved in the more than 5,000 proposals submitted during the previous two years. Each section of the questionnaire had been prepared by a committee and each set of questions was accompanied by a brief summary and/or explanation of the ideas and proposals involved. After further group study and discussions, the sisters sent the results of their prayer and study to the committee.

Sisters found that sharing convictions and insights to be much more difficult than anyone could have anticipated. Sisters, who outside their work had lived the greater part of their days in silence, found the bi-weekly discussions almost unbearably difficult. It was the younger sisters, whose recent educational experiences accustomed them to the give and take of dialogue, who quickly found stimulation and enjoyment in sharing ideals and ideas. For many of them, it was a time of expectation and hope.

As Mother Rosita wrote later: "One of the main purposes of the study was to provide a means of opening up to one another in a true sharing of individual insights. Out of this study of the spirit of the congregation, religious vocations, vows, and prayer, were to come proposals from the grass roots. Each sister was to have a voice, for "the Spirit breatheth where He will.""[6]

Sisters in Central America were well-prepared for the teachings of Vatican II, in part because of the pastoral work of Florian Ruskamp, OFM Cap., who initiated renewal there by asking the sisters to join him in studying the Bible.[7] As time went on, the discussion groups also delved into ecclesiology, theology, and the spirit of Vatican II.[8]

In addition, the sisters also studied the renewal and adaptation of religious life in Nicaragua under the direction of Father José de la Jara.[9] The program began with a consideration of the nature and spirit of the congregation and their own religious formation. They developed position papers and made recommendations for consideration by the chapter, but it was the issue of their religious formation that led to their lengthiest and most serious discussions.[10]

As preparations for the chapter proceeded, a few sisters, convinced that the Nicaraguan sisters should be autonomous, requested that sisters live only with members of their own national group. Mother Rosita immediately sent a questionnaire to each sister in the Nicaraguan missions asking if she preferred to live in a house composed only of members of her own national group. Almost unanimously, the women elected "to live as Sisters of St. Agnes not as Nicaraguans or North Americans."[11] In spite of the challenges of intercultural living, the overwhelming majority of sisters considered themselves one and wished to remain so.

In 1968 *Open to the Spirit* by Ladislas Örsy, SJ, was published. This last book of significance widely read in the CSA community before the renewal chapter considered not only the theological implications and applications of the three vows in contemporary apostolic communities, but also the proper role of government in such communities. Ladislas Örsy's recommendations based on a thorough study of the documents and his own experiences as a Jesuit, provided sisters with a practical approach to some of the many problems facing them.

The last major change before the chapter took place on January 1, 1969, when sisters who wished could experiment with a modified, but black or white habit. As no budget was allocated for the project, sisters who chose to do so and who could sew cut up their habits into dresses, skirts, jumpers, and jackets. Many sewed for their friends. The results of their endeavors were uneven and not always aesthetic, and they attracted a great deal of unwanted attention. Houses divided over the issue. Many parishioners were shocked. Some wept as they wondered where their "good" sisters had gone. In Nicaragua, the bishop refused to speak to the sisters who had modernized their dress.[12] The issue caused tension within the congregation for years and almost forty years later remained an issue for some of the Catholic laity.

THE DELEGATES

Of the seventy delegates who had attended the Chapter of 1963, more than half were superiors or ex officio members: the superior general and her predecessors, the members of the council, the general secretary and the general treasurer, superiors and another sister from each of the larger houses, two sisters, a superior and another sister elected from groupings of smaller houses.[13] Sisters professed for ten years or more were eligible to vote or be voted upon. At the request of Mother Rosita, the Holy See granted permission to change the method of electing delegates in June 1968, giving the congregation the privilege of choosing a more equitable process. For the 1969 chapter the sisters chose to reduce the number to forty elected delegates and seven ex officio members. All perpetually professed sisters were now eligible to vote and be voted upon.[14] Sisters eligible to be voted upon were organized according to their "age in religion."[15] The result, of course, was a chapter with a new demographic profile.

Of the forty elected members, fourteen were from the faculty of Marian College; six were teachers in junior or senior high school; eight worked in elementary education; three were formation directors; six were in health care; three were from the foreign missions; and one was a homemaker. While there was some overlap e.g., a nurse might also be a Marian College employee, each was identified by her professional preparation. There was no representation from sisters in temporary vows, nor were there any native Nicaraguan sisters. The constitution gave active and passive voice only to professed sisters, while the Nicaraguan sisters were simply unknown to the community at large.

When the issue was raised, Mother Rosita determined that the delegates could make some adjustments, if they wished. At the same time, she called upon "each mission house in the congregation and *as a house* (not superiors only) to make as clear, honest and realistic an evaluation as possible" of the persons, religious and spiritual life and works of the congregation.[16] As one of the first items of chapter business, sisters in temporary vows and the Nicaraguan sisters were given the opportunity to elect representatives with an active voice in the election and chapter decisions.[17]

In April 1969 the delegates were called together for a two-day workshop. This gave them an opportunity to achieve solidarity as well as to choose the commission on which they wished to work. Each commission would review the applicable proposals and a composite would be used as a basis of a questionnaire to be given to the congregation. Based on the responses received, the appropriate commission would then make its recommendations to the assembly.

Previously general chapters were convened every six years for the election of the officers of the congregation and "also for the consideration of business transactions of greater moment for the entire congregation."[18] Nowhere was there mention of the spirit of the institute or its way of life as topics for general discussions. Now those topics had assumed major importance. In the course of preparing for the chapter as well, delegates had been voicing concerns regarding a number of issues. In addition to the concerns regarding representation, the question was raised as to whether chapter sessions should remain closed as was traditional or whether discussions should be open to observers. When the delegates were given the opportunity to respond to the issues in an opinionnaire, the majority proved to favor open sessions.[19] It was clear to them that the congregation had everything to gain by involving all its members.

OPENING AND DIRECTION SETTING

The chapter opened on June 30 with a retreat given by Kieran Kavanagh, OCD. Msgr. James McDonald, a canonist, was available to give counsel on church law. At the solemn liturgy offered on the first day of proceedings, the delegates, aware that they were representing their sisters, faced the first days with a mixture of feelings. On the one hand, they felt honored to be present and grateful that they were participating in an event of such significance to religious life. On the other, they were awed by the tremendous responsibility for determining the future of their congregation.[20] The assembly had now become the highest governing body in the congregation.

In her first address, Mother Rosita reminded the delegates that:

> The questions before us at this moment in our history are momentous. One of these questions is have we

really achieved the renewal we have been working towards? It is impossible to measure the depth of any person's union with God, but there are certain outward manifestations of this union that are shown in our worship and prayer life. This is a chapter for renewal; therefore it must not lose sight of its obligation to provide the means for true renewal. Without the help of the Holy Spirit we cannot hope to achieve any of the goals we have set for ourselves …. The task before us calls for a mobilization of all our powers. Our intellectual acumen, our practical ingenuity and our spiritual insights must be employed if we are to succeed in carrying out our theme, a summons to sanctity in joyful service.[21]

Until July 31, 1969, the delegates would be in the company of each other as they faced and dealt with what would prove to be a staggering agenda. They had gathered to begin the long process of writing a constitution that would reflect their lives and their hopes. Expectations differed from apprehension to idealized visions of the future. They came wearing traditional habits or short skirts or jumpers and, although they all wore veils, found that the clothes they wore, whether wished for or not, affected the reactions of others to comments or presentations.

Each delegate served on one of four commissions: religious life, apostolate, formation, government. Sessions were scheduled for study and commission meetings in the mornings and the afternoons. In the evenings, commission members met and prepared for the presentation of their recommendations. Unlike most legislatures the chapter was constrained by a rigid time line. Topics must be presented, discussed, and voted upon in a very limited amount of time. The effort demanded painstaking organization and much hard work. It proved to be advantageous to the younger, more reform-minded sisters. Many of them were used to working hard at night, and were energized by the give and take of ideas. The advantage this gave them in preparing and presenting their positions in relation to the usually older and more conservative delegates became much more apparent in retrospect.

Although the chapter opened with a discussion on government, it was soon decided to postpone that discussion until more fundamental matters were decided. Key to the discussion was the identity of the community. The religious life commission then set the direction of the entire chapter dealing as it did with the nature of a religious institute, a descriptive definition of religious life and the identity, nature, purpose, values, and future direction of the congregation.[22] Like other active religious, the Sisters of St. Agnes lived a life combining the elements of ministry to others with a regular, semi-monastic lifestyle. The recent modifications seemed sufficient to the administration and to many, if not most, members. Now the delegates would decide whether to remain satisfied with the accomplishments of the past six years or to move even further away from the monastic tradition.

Three papers had been prepared for presentation by the commission on religious life. It was in an atmosphere of anticipation that Mother Rosita delivered the first paper. Reflecting on the many times she had had to respond to questions about the spirituality of the community, she commented, "I have always felt somewhat *put on the spot* because I was not able to say that we belonged to any of the great schools of spirituality in the Church. I now see this, not as a weakness, but as a strength. Father Rehrl, being a secular priest, knew only the spirituality of the Gospel. This he communicated to the pioneer Sisters ...."[23] She continued, alluding to the revised code of canon law of 1918 and norms: "We became too juridical and lost some of the inspirational quality of our early rule. We are told in the Norms: 'That the task of the chapters is not completed by merely making laws, but especially by promoting spiritual and apostolic vitality.'"[24]

The second paper on prayer life stressed the impossibility of separating the apostolic life and the life of prayer, while the third paper on community life stressed the importance of prayer but also moved toward more flexibility and freedom in choice as well as in the daily living in community.

On July 3, Sister Fidelis Karlin presented a summary paper from the commission, *CSA Fundamental Beliefs: Identity, Nature, Purpose, Beliefs, and Future Direction.* The paper contained ten summary resolutions dubbed "The Decalog."[25] The first statement declared that the congregation was apostolic in nature and mandated changes in life style that would promote true apostolic service. Although the traditional Christian activities of teaching, healing and aiding the needy were reaffirmed, they were to be adapted to changing needs and situations. Room was to be allowed for apostolic service outside institutionally administered works. The governmental structure was to be decentralized to serve the needs of the sisters and to administer apostolic works effectively. Each sister would be given personal consideration in her choice of work, preparation, and continuing education, as well as placement and retirement. In all apostolic works and in every local house there would be wide scope for personal initiative, responsible cooperation, and participation in decision-making.

The congregation recognized "the supreme value of witnessing to Christian community" and urged the sisters "to increase the bond of love which unites all the members through better communication, meaningful assembly, collegial living, and the friendships that arise from these." Above all, prayer and personal communion with God were to be strengthened by fostering the values of authenticity and openness. The concluding statement pointed toward creating a "truly otherward community" and viewing its "mission as one of both giving to and receiving from those to whom we are sent, as well as to and from one another."[26]

The recommendations passed unanimously on July 3.[27] "The Decalog" provided both a foundation for a way of life that was apostolic, more personalistic, and stripped of traditional monastic practices and a lens through which the congregation could examine itself. The delegates now had a framework for dealing with the big issues.

GOVERNMENT STRUCTURES EXAMINED

Because changes in the government structure now seemed inevitable, elections were deferred until that issue could be settled. Whether or not the delegates would accept the concept of decentralization would be a strong indicator of whether the principles of "The Decalog" were actually accepted. However, the hierarchical structure of religious communities had always felt alien to most American religious, and the Sisters of St. Agnes, who prided themselves on their American roots, were no exception. As the congregation had grown, many sisters had felt quite distant from the general administration. Although the original self-study did not have an area specifically related to government, results of the study indicated a level of dissatisfaction particularly high among the sisters in health care.[28] The new emphasis on subsidiarity, providing that decisions take place on the level that was affected, and collegiality, emphasizing cooperative action, would allow for a more complete use of a sister's talents as well as ordinarily assuring better decisions.[29]

Because there had never been a community-wide discussion of models of government, it became the responsibility of the commission to propose a model of government. Members of the commission had accepted the principles of subsidiarity and collegiality as brought forth by Vatican II. It became the goal of the government commission to embody those ideals in a form that would facilitate community ministries and personal responsibility. Decentralizing the government according to different apostolates rather than by geographic regions or by simple numerical division seemed the best way to reach those goals. Although alternate plans were discussed intensely and at length, the commission's proposal was finally accepted.

The philosophy of the new government was expressed in the proposal: "that the Government of the Congregation of St. Agnes be apostolically oriented to unify its members and motivate them to a common vision and goal, namely, the renewal of their religious consecration in Christian community for their service to the Church, vitalized by the inspiration of their Founders and the continuing strength derived from the Scriptures and the Sacraments."[30]

The discussions on the chapter floor revolved around the method of organization rather than the concepts. The commission, mindful of the fact that the congregation had been founded to follow and spread the Gospel through teaching and healing, had organized the government to serve the needs of the apostolate. Two groups challenged the concept. One wished to divide the congregation mathematically; the other to divide the congregation according to geographical regions. The plan to decentralize the government according to the apostolates was accepted. The commission's plan was accepted and is described in the following chapter.

The changes in government had been of such scope that the week-end after the new governmental structure had been accepted, the chapter sent teams to clarify the modifications for sisters who met in regional groups in New York, Chicago, Fort Wayne, Hays, and Fond du Lac. Although it was not possible to describe the new structures adequately, the teams attempted to transmit some of the spirit of the chapter and its decisions to the sisters as well as evince the concern of the delegates in their desire to communicate with the sisters who were not able to be in Fond du Lac.

The delegates returned to elect the new administration. The election of Sister John Baptist as superior general was expected; her councilors were women familiar to and respected by the community: Sister Rachel Doerfler, teacher and directress of candidates; Sister Miriam Therese Putzer, an English teacher who had also done formation work; and Sister Francis Assisi Pielmeier, a professor of education at Marian College.

PRAYER LIFE AND VOWS

Although it was easy to see that there were too many prescribed spiritual exercises, it was prayer that gave meaning to the life of a religious, and it could not be touched on lightly. After long hours of discussion, the delegates agreed that the sisters were to participate in daily Mass and recite together lauds and vespers according to the divine office. They were to remember in their prayers the needs of the church and all the world, in particular the spiritual and temporal benefactors of the congregation, and the deceased and the bereaved. The daily reception of the Eucharist and an increasing emphasis on mental prayer nourished by the reading of the Scriptures were counseled that "we may learn the surpassing worth of knowing Jesus Christ."[31] While the privilege of yearly retreats was retained, there could be experimentation as to place or manner of retreat and local houses were to set aside part of one day a month for recollection. Devotions such as the way of the cross and the rosary were discontinued as community exercises, but each sister was free to "express her love in ways best suited to her."[32]

Modifications were made in the interpretation of the three vows. Enclosure was limited to the sleeping quarters of the sisters and decisions would be made locally on norms allowing for

"Christian courtesy and hospitality" in the convent. No longer was a companion necessary when a sister left the convent although it was suggested that the sisters retain its benefits when suggested by prudence. It seems on first glance that the vow of obedience changed little. The old terminology of "superior" was retained. The sisters were to "show humble obedience to their superiors" who were exhorted to use their authority in a spirit of loving service and with a regard for the human personality that would make it possible for the sisters to obey gladly. Sisters were reminded, however, that they were to be cognizant of the superior's authority "to decide what must be done and to require the doing of it."[33] When considering the vow of poverty, it was resolved that the "Congregation ... possess what is necessary 'for its temporal life and mission,' and that the appearance of luxury and the accumulation of property and possessions be avoided."[34]

Other changes included permission to reassume one's baptismal name and the privilege of an annual vacation. Convents would retain a scheduled recreation but the resident sisters would decide its manner and time. That these changes could be so sweeping and occur so overwhelmingly in such a few days is not always easy to explain. For example, in the *CSA Study Composite* there were a number of proposals regarding silence in the convents: 549 sisters agreed that there should be specified times and places for silence, with only 148 disagreeing; 491 wanted the great silence retained, as opposed to the 129 who wanted it abolished.[35] By the time the chapter was considering the issue the climate of opinion had shifted so significantly the sisters were asked only to be considerate of each other in that regard. The radical changes that actually occurred had never been considered as possible by the majority of sisters.

EDUCATION

One of the critical thrusts the commission on the apostolate proposed was a commitment to renew the spirit of Christ in the community's schools. To that end, one of the first steps taken by the commission was a request to all schools staffed by the congregation for an immediate evaluation of their Christian effectiveness.

A number of resolutions were meant to guarantee that the sisters be well-prepared professionally in the field of their choice and that they pursue graduate work "to assure within the Congregation a wider range of experience and a more diversified knowledge." [36] Teachers were encouraged to prepare for secondary education and administrative leadership while the congregation continued to lend its moral support to Marian College and prepare sisters for its faculty.

Principals and administrators were to be reassessed periodically for leadership qualities while administrative positions in school and convent were no longer to be held by the same sister. Special recommendations were made to assure communication among everyone involved in the school, whether administrators, faculty, staff, students, parents, or parishioners. Furthermore, sisters were to be permitted to visit the homes of students and to participate in the civic and cultural life of the community to the degree necessary to aid the students in Christian growth.

Although many sisters found it wrenching to accept the necessity of retrenchment, a commitment was made to plan for reducing the number of sisters in the parochial schools and schools staffed by the congregation and to participate in efforts of consolidation initiated by the dioceses. The congregation also offered its support and recommended expansion of parish catechetical programs. Sisters who desired to work full-time in the field could receive special training in religious studies. The assembly also established the Agnesian Confraternity of Teachers, later renamed *Project Gift*, a project designed to relieve the shortage of sisters and increase vocations by inviting young women to teach with the sisters for two or three years and receive the same stipend as that of the sisters.

The delegates made several major decisions in regard to Marian College. Men were admitted as full-time students.[37] They suggested considering appointing a layman as president of the college as well as appointing lay persons to the college board of trustees.[38] Also, "to maintain the creativity and morale of the faculty and to share its resources in other areas" the college could consider allowing religious faculty to contract for a specific number of years and be allowed to accept a position elsewhere for their own enrichment, provided the salary earned was used to secure an instructor or to educate another religious.[39] The chapter also directed that the corporate structure of the college be revised.

If there is any one act of the chapter that captures the idealism and optimism of the delegates it was the adoption of a plan designed "to save Christian education within one generation."[40] The chapter voted to implement Dr. James Hanlon's dream to establish a coordinated Catholic educational plan in Fond du Lac as a model for the whole Catholic system. The system would begin in kindergarten and culminate on the graduate level. Fond du Lac, with six elementary schools, a high school, and a college staffed by the congregation, offered an ideal laboratory for this kind of experiment. Dr. Hanlon hoped to consolidate the parochial schools and educate their faculties along with the faculties of St. Mary's Springs and Marian College in weekend and summer seminars. They, in turn, would use his principles in their own classes and construct an ideal curriculum as a model for all Catholic schools. The student emerging from the system, grounded in Catholic teachings and the methodology of the arts and sciences, would be well on the way to achieving self-actualization.

The sisters, most of whom had devoted their lives to Catholic education, were eager to do anything in their power to reinvigorate the Catholic educational system. They knew that there were excellent teachers and administrators among them and they were willing to devote themselves to realizing an ideal. Dr. Hanlon was offered the presidency of the college with the understanding that he would convince the parishes to allow necessary experimentation in their schools. This decision was fated to lead the teachers on every educational level in Fond du Lac into an exceedingly challenging and difficult decade.

ISSUES IN HEALTH CARE

The chapter commission on health care reported on the state and trends of health care institutions in the United States. Its report predicted that the congregation would be facing major decisions in the near future:

> We can establish hospitals or other institutions
> as our primary mode of service with the aim of
> making them model centers of Christian health
> care. Or we can become completely open in our

approach to our apostolate with the missionary
aim of moving into areas of greater need when
we recognize that others can take over, equally
well, what we are now doing. In today's rapidly
changing technological society, it is not sufficient merely to keep abreast with trends, but as
Christian leaders, it seems imperative that we
should become pace setters .... In light of the
fact that hospitals function like 'big business,'
are permeated with technology and professionalism, and other sponsors can own and operate
them efficiently, should the Sisters of St. Agnes
continue to own and operate hospitals? ...We
believe our Congregation with its renewed spirit of mission, its renewed atmosphere of faith
and hope, its renewed traditions of respect and
concern for each individual and his [her] needs,
its renewed profession of love for all, can create
a hospital personality which will be a corporate
witness that Christ lives now. This can be our
unique contribution toward Christ's Becoming
in the world."[41]

The commission asked for a re-consideration of the philosophy
and objectives in the hospitals in the light of Vatican II: a determination on how those considerations should guide policies; how to
help personnel internalize that philosophy; how methods could be
developed to determine the presence of a Christian corporate personality and how that personality might be improved. The need for
pastoral care in nursing homes and hospitals was emphasized. The
congregation should also consider two important trends in health
care: the movement toward more representation from the public on
hospital boards of trustees and the rapid changes in health care
brought about by federal legislation.

The report concluded by asking delegates to vote on three proposals: that, for the present, the sisters continue to operate the hospitals and nursing homes they established; that the institutions study,
and revise if necessary, the board of directors of the corporation;
and finally, that the apostolate to the aged be continued.[42]

FORMATION

As the introduction of new members is one of the most important responsibilities of a community, the formation program was examined carefully. The *Sisters Survey* had indicated a fairly high level of satisfaction with the formation program of the past with an approval rating of 71.7%. However, 9.1% had indicated that they were quite dissatisfied.[43] As was typical of the period, the formation program had been based upon nineteenth century spirituality. According to that philosophy, the aspirant to religious life must strive to empty herself of self-love in order that she might be filled with the love of God. She must be obedient, mortified, and self-sacrificing. As a Sister of St. Agnes, she should strive for the virtues of simplicity and humility. New theological insights, however, suggested a program that was planned to be a positive experience for the entrant "reinforcing a healthy self-concept on which to base a solid spiritual growth."[44] In addition to the traditional objectives, she would be educated to be a true apostolic woman realizing her potential but using it in the service of others. This goal could be realized only by developing a close relationship with Jesus Christ.

Plans were made to modify the aspirancy. Meanwhile aspirants would be allowed to spend week-ends at home. The convent high school would be retained, but after graduation the aspirant would return to her home to work or attend college prior to making a decision regarding her vocation.[45] High school graduates would still be accepted and would receive the type of professional education needed for their chosen apostolate.

It was now clear that formation must not end with profession. In the past when the young sister went out on mission, she was often left to her own resources. Superiors were not accustomed to thinking of themselves as part of the formation team nor were the sisters with whom the young woman lived, even though it was from those sisters that the real community spirit was imbibed. Too often her special needs were overlooked in the midst of the busy, often overly-demanding, life in the local convents. The commission on formation planned to develop a manual designed to acquaint the whole community with the formation process and the personal responsibility of each sister toward the young women considering religious life.

The commission, with the approval of the superior general, was given power to inaugurate experimental programs. Recognizing that the time of readiness differed for individuals, the sister in temporary vows could choose to make her final vows after three years and before nine years of profession were completed.[46] During this period a coordinator on the formation team would map out a program of spiritual, doctrinal, and professional integration "that will help the young woman ... know, love, and live the mystery of her religious call in relation to the whole spiritual life of the Church."[47] Although academic preparation was emphasized, the congregation would provide specialized training for those whose talents lay in other areas.

MISSION ISSUES

The delegates from Latin America had come to the chapter inspired by the Latin American bishops who, at their 1968 conference at Medellin, Colombia, had issued a strong call for social justice. They had come to the chapter determined to make the sisters in North America aware of the fact that third world countries were beginning to experience social upheavals as the injustices inherent in the international economic and political arena were becoming better understood by the millions who were living out their lives in abject poverty. They pointed out to the delegates that in Nicaragua, 92 percent of the population was considered members of the "poor class" but only 2 percent of all the religious in the country worked among the poor, and the majority of that number were Sisters of St. Agnes. They wanted to assure the congregation that it had not only a responsibility to maintain its presence there but also to assist in promoting dialogues among all groups.[48]

They also pointed out that the sisters in the foreign missions were experiencing a period of transition and adjustment. Although North American sisters had been in Nicaragua twenty-four years and native Nicaraguan sisters had been in the community for twenty-two years, neither group had been adequately prepared for intercultural living. They had done much good under the circumstances, but developments in missiology, increased education among the Nicaraguan sisters, and the experiences of all the sisters made this

an opportune time for them to evaluate both their missionary formation and their ministries.

In their report to the chapter, the native Nicaraguan sisters evaluated their religious formation as superficial "because it was
received in another language, another culture, and another religious
mentality." "Nevertheless," they wrote, "the spirit of the motherhouse was intuitively received, accepted and loved."[49] They saw
their years of study in the United States as affording them great distinction in their own country; but as the majority of them had
entered the community before they had completed high school, few
were qualified to enter a program of higher education. "Yet," they
continued, "we have some Sisters in the teaching field who haven't
a sixth grade diploma; but, because they came to the States, are
believed to be qualified teachers."[50]

They attributed some of their current difficulties with interpersonal relationships to the fact that "we evaded our real selves by
finding friendship in the American sisters who were with us. But
once we returned to our country, the difficulties among us arose and
became a real problem in community living."[51] They considered
themselves true missionaries but believed that their formation did
not give them the "restlessness and zeal to return to Nicaragua and
be concerned with the real problems of our underdeveloped country."[52]

Because they concluded that the object of the founders was to
form the "whole person," they believed, that as a group, they should
not be dedicated to the exclusive instruction of children. They asked
that volunteers for the foreign missions be scrutinized carefully, that
foreign missionaries spend part of their time of formation in the
country where they were to work under the direction of a native
religious educated to carry out that formation. This same missionary formation should be extended to the native sisters although
exceptions could be made in the case of belated vocations. They
stated that the church of today "demands that our apostolic work be
directed to the slums," and requested that a community or mission
family be formed and composed of four religious who were of one
mind and soul, who wanted to live an ideal Christian community in
the barrios while living and working in the greatest poverty.[54]

In their preparation for chapter, the North American sisters in
Nicaragua were especially sensitive to the movement of the church

in Latin America. They supported the statement of the Latin American bishops that "the responsibility for a concentrated effort to search for new solutions ... falls on those involved in higher education and the youth."[55] Work with catechists was seen as of prime importance to the church, hence the necessity of doing much more in their preparation. Most compelling of all was the belief that the missionaries themselves must be evangelized before they could evangelize others, returning " to the power of the Word as fountain of the faith."[56] They agreed with Segundo Galilea,[57] who taught that the church must divest itself of much of its property and stated: "We frown upon the possession of property in Latin America, especially as a foreign community ...."[58] They quoted a statement from the Conference of Latin American Women Religious which had suggested that religious should not be bound to the confines of a single private institution but rather become part of the activities of the total Christian community. The ultimate goal "is our duty to strive to place in the hands of the indigenous the responsibility for any given endeavor;" in other words, "to work ourselves out of a job" is a solid concept for missionaries.[59]

LOOKING BACK

Numerous other issues raised in proposals were also brought to the floor and were disposed of expeditiously. Homemakers were to be given more free time and encouraged to meet with each other and attend institutes and workshops. A committee on retirement was established to plan and implement a pre-retirement program. By the time the delegates were ready to pack their bags, they had passed 181 acts into law and had written role descriptions for the local superiors, apostolic councilors, councilors and the superior general, the generalate, the executive board, and the house chapter.

What was the experience like that historic summer? Almost twenty years later one delegate wrote: "For me, this chapter was a milestone event in my own life and in that of CSA. We met as local communities, following a thick manual—sharing, for the first time in my remembering, about things we most valued. I did research on a position paper about the values and spirit of CSA. I was still rather young and it was scary ... I was on fire with the prospect of renewal."[60] Some chapter delegates, while they had experienced much the same enthusiasm and hope for a re-vitalization of the community, recalled, too, the tensions, suspicions, misunderstandings, and fears they had experienced. Yet the community could take a measure of pride in the fact that inexperienced delegates were able to participate with grace and civility in discussions that could, on occasion, be fairly described as incendiary.[61] Issues were discussed with respect, long hours were devoted to framing decisions in language acceptable to all, and, in almost every case, the chapter body had arrived at consensus. The congregation had returned to its apostolic roots as it measured itself against the needs and desires of the modern world.

IMPLEMENTATION

July was over; but the renewal chapter was not. The following summer the chapter would meet again to complete its work. A great deal had been accomplished, but the year ahead would determine the work for the future.

One more significant change took place that summer. On August 15, the sisters could choose to revert to their baptismal names. To some it was a way of reassuming their own identity as themselves or as a member of a specific family; others saw the change as another way in which sisters were losing their identity as religious. For most, the reasons were less philosophical. Some sisters wished to honor their baptismal names; or did it for legal reasons or simply liked their baptismal name better. Although many, generally older sisters, chose to keep their religious names, everyone had to get used to using family names and to distinguish among the numerous Marys, Jeans, Patricias, or Helens, in the community.

While the chapter was in session, Mother Rosita and her council had effaced themselves so successfully during the tense month of the chapter debates, that delegates were frequently unaware of the presence that had been so overwhelming in their lives for twelve years. For them it must have been a painful experience. Years later, Sister Rosita wrote: "We made the mistake of failing to set limits to experimentation in all directions: habit, life style, and government: [Kevin] O'Rourke, OP warned us against this, but momentum once started is difficult to halt. The Decree[62] warned us that 'the best contrived adaptations will be of no avail unless they are animated by a spiritual renewal.' Time has shown that an in-depth study and experimentation take place only when each member of the Community experiences metanonia.[63] Since I was no longer in office, my best contribution to the Community was to cooperate with the officials and give them prayerful support in their efforts to cope with a situation that could become more difficult without specific direction."[64]

Mother Rosita lived eighteen years after she left office. Those years were spent at Nazareth Heights where she assisted in administration until she retired. She continued to study, to pray, to listen to and to counsel those who sought her out. Cancer, diabetes, and the numerous complications of advancing age took their toll. She found letting go difficult but was sustained by her belief that this was the purification that was preparing her for the fullness of life to come.[65] During her last years, she sometimes worried that she may have been too rigid with the sisters. Whatever grain of truth lay in her concern, she did not ask of any sister more than she herself was ready to give. She died on August 21, 1987.

Mother Rosita was praised in her obituary for her "loyal dedication to the principles of religious life and to our own Constitution" and "by her strict adherence to the constitutions in her own religious life."[66] A woman of whom it could be said that there was nothing haphazard in her life,[67] she is to be admired for her struggle to be "open to the working of the Spirit" in the chaotic years when gusts of fresh air blew through the dusty corners of religious life.

Chapter XIII

Continuing
in Faith

The chapter summer, longed for and dreaded, thought about, prayed and talked about, was over, but the old structures, and with them, the old securities were gone forever. Both the charge of Vatican II to renew and adapt religious life and the post-war cultural and societal changes had given religious congregations the opportunity to discard the irrelevant baggage of the past, but it also, and perhaps unintentionally, had begun to transform the ministries of active congregations.

SISTER JOHN BAPTIST SHAJA

Of all the Sisters of St. Agnes, Sister John Baptist Shaja was the one most immediately affected by the decisions of July 1969. Although she herself had no time to absorb the great changes the chapter had accomplished, the sisters were depending on her to be a "sign of unity" to lead them into making a graceful transition to a new understanding of community as it responded to the church's call for renewal. She was rooted in the past, yet in her humanity, common-sense, and openness to people and ideas, she could help sisters feel both secure in the present and hopeful for the future. Born of immigrant parents, she had experienced many of the difficulties common to first-generation Americans. Her parents, Mathias Csaja and Maria Imhof were among the thousands of young Hungarians who had left their country around the turn of the century in search of a better life. They had arrived in St. Louis, Missouri where their only daughter was born on December 16, 1906. One week later the child was christened Kathrina Elizabeth at Sts. Peter and Paul Church.

It was a time when the lumber industry in northern Wisconsin was flourishing and jobs were to be had for hard workers like Mathias. He packed up his family and moved to Jack Lake near Antigo. Along the way, the family name was anglicized and Catherine Shaja entered the local public school. There, Magyar-speaking Katie had to repeat first grade. In October the following year, she contracted diphtheria and could not attend school until May. The next year, she entered the first grade for the third time and again her education was interrupted when the family moved to New London, Wisconsin. Here her teachers at the parochial school were the Sisters of St. Agnes. In September Katie found herself in the first grade for the fourth time. Whatever the problems had been, once the first grade was conquered, her academic progress was more than satisfactory. Katie was allowed to skip the third and seventh grades. Following her graduation in 1922, the sixteen-year-old young lady left New London to begin her life as a Sister of St. Agnes.

Catherine began her teaching career as a candidate at Holy Ghost School on West Adams Street in Chicago. In 1925 she was professed and given John Baptist as her patron saint. Her first mission was at Immaculate Conception School in Elmhurst, Illinois. A year later she was sent to St. Mary's School in Altoona, Pennsylvania, where she taught for twelve years. In 1938 she was missioned at St. Luke, Two Rivers. After six years there, she spent one year each in Defiance, Ohio, and Victoria, Kansas, and then returned to her first mission, Elmhurst, in 1946. She remained at Elmhurst until her election as vicar general of the congregation in 1963. During those years she followed the typical teacher's path of summer schools and night classes, earning a master's degree in physics from De Paul University in Chicago.

Sister John Baptist was a born teacher, but more significantly, as a student from her early teaching days in Altoona recalled, "she allowed us into her heart."[1] She made friends readily and kept them. Through the years she showed a special concern for the young sisters as they adjusted to life on the mission. The warmth and the straightforwardness she brought to her relationships with her sisters and students were quickly observed by the community in her four years as Vicar. There had been no doubt at all that when the time came she would be elected to the office of superior general to lead others "to venture courageously into an unknown born of dreams and visions for a new age without losing continuity with the past."[2]

In 1970 Sister John Baptist wrote in the introduction to the *Interim Constitutions,* "Let us not expect that the coming years will be easy ones. They will be some of the most challenging in our history ...." That these words were spoken in wisdom and truth became more apparent with each passing year. To launch the new government with no working model to follow, based on unfamiliar concepts, with a structure yet to be fully understood, was an overwhelming undertaking. The experimental constitutions could be described as providing motivation but, in Sister John Baptist's words, "broad in general principles, short on detail.[3] As the community together began to learn and to live under a new constitution, she faced torturous questions: "How far do we go? How fast must we move? How to hold that delicate balance between too cautious and too precipitous? What touches the core of renewal and what is mere surface? Where will each move lead us in the future? *What does God ask of us in this whole picture?*" She made two promises to herself. Whatever the years brought, she would maintain her own integrity as a person; she would strive to meet her sisters with understanding and compassion.[4]

One of Sister John Baptist's most difficult and painful responsibilities was counseling sisters who were discerning whether or not they should remain in religious life. Eleven sisters were secularized between August 1 and December 22, 1969, her first four months in office.[5] Worried that young women were making the decision too hastily, at the end of that month, she wrote to all sisters eligible to make their final vows to remind them that the sister is to pronounce her final vows only after having reached "that degree of spiritual maturity wherein she can embrace the life of the counsels as a

means of perfection and love rather than as a heavy burden."
Twenty-five sisters from several temporary profession groups made
their perpetual profession on August 15, 1970.[6]

The decision of the community to emphasize spiritual formation as a life-long process led Sister Rachel Doerfler, formation and
renewal coordinator for the community, to develop a three-tiered
vocation-formation program. The first phase was vocation education and promotion; the second, initiation into religious life from
pre-novitiate through the novitiate; the third, the on-going formation and renewal of the whole community.[7] At a time when the very
idea of life-long commitment was under fire, implementing each
segment of the program was a continuing challenge.

A reality the community was finding difficult to face was the
need of the sisters to prepare for retirement.[8] As a response to a
chapter mandate, a director of retirement was appointed with
broad responsibilities to plan programs and act in an advisory
capacity wherever needed in the community. The philosophy of the
program emphasized the responsibility of the individual to prepare
for retirement "by being a person responsible for her own continued
growth."[9]

THE COUNCILORS: GENERAL AND APOSTOLIC

The role description of the general councilors continued to be
much as it had been. Besides the few obligations determined by
canon law, their responsibilities were delegated. However, as the
concept of "collegiality" had been accepted by the community, sisters now expected that the councilors would exert greater leadership
in the affairs of the congregation and be in touch with the general
well-being of the sisters. One of their first obligations was to assimilate the spirit of the new government quickly and positively according to the mandate of Vatican II and gain a deeper understanding
of Agnesian apostolic spirituality in order to transmit it to others.[10]
Their greatest challenge was to help maintain the unity of the congregation. Besides making themselves available to individual sisters,
they devoted long, painstaking hours to planning and directing
renewal workshops and developing processes and guides for the
education of local communities.

The five apostolic councilors were elected by the sisters in their own ministries. They were concerned with the personal and professional well-being of each sister, counseled sisters in their choice of work and responded to their desires and abilities for higher education, and arranged appointments and summer assignments. As members of the executive board, they were also charged with making recommendations for the expansion or suppression of community works. Commissions elected by sisters in that region provided support for the councilors while membership on commissions gave sisters a chance to contribute their experiences and ideas in planning sessions. The commissions had the authority to make decisions within their respective apostolates.[11] The largest apostolate, elementary education, was bisected into East and West with a councilor heading each section. Health and allied services, secondary education, and the foreign missions each had one councilor.[12]

At the beginning, it was clear that the apostolic councilors occupied a subordinate position in the government structure. They shared an office. They had no car although their work demanded a great deal of travel. Some sisters regarded their visits as an infringement on the role of the superior general, as an extravagance, and a waste of community personnel.[13] A few sisters would not accept a transfer from the apostolic councilor because the vow of obedience, in their estimation, was made to God and to the superior general, not to an intermediary. It took many months before the value of their work became apparent to the superior general and to the community at large.

That the apostolic councilors in elementary education began their tenure in office at the time when withdrawing personnel from schools was necessary made their job extremely difficult. Sisters, pastors, and parishioners all lacked understanding of the changing needs of church ministries and the total personnel picture. They could not accept the reality that replacement of sisters in historical commitments was simply not possible. The apostolic councilors held endless meetings to explain needs, plans and objectives, and to discuss strategies to deal with the problems.

Sisters found it painful to leave the parishes where vocations to the community had been nurtured, where parishioners had supported the sisters for decades, where they had taught and loved the children and their families. Others became hurt or angry when it became necessary for them to leave the classroom. The apostolic councilors had to bear both the burden and brunt of the reality." [14] Time brought greater understanding as well as the development of the philosophy, objectives, and criteria for personnel placement that provided the sisters with the rationale for difficult decisions.[15]

It was not only the departure of sisters from the congregation and the retirement of aging sisters that created difficulties for the apostolic councilors in fulfilling traditional commitments, but the decision of the chapter to broaden the congregation's concept of service by pledging to undertake the spiritual and corporal works of mercy "wherever the church needs us" was leading some sisters to seek individualized apostolates.[16] In 1970, at least ten sisters were employed outside community structures. They included such diverse ministries as coordinating the nursing program in the Colby, Kansas, community college and at the Capuchin preparatory seminary in Victoria, Kansas; organizing religious education for the Archdiocese of Milwaukee; teaching in an inner city school in Milwaukee; and conducting Newman work in Thibodeaux, Louisiana. But only six of the ten sisters earned a salary and contributed to the motherhouse.[17]

Within the apostolate of secondary education, a number of sisters challenged new ideas as 'revolutionary' and suspect because they were coming from restless younger members.[18] In addition, the natural competition for personnel resulted in some strained relationships between secondary and elementary education. It was a difficult beginning, and it was not until the election of the second apostolic councilor that suspicions were gradually allayed and apostolic councilors could be effective for secondary education.

Sisters in the apostolate of health care had been most anxious for decentralization. Historically, leadership roles had been filled by educators. The new government provided them with an opportunity to have a stronger voice in hospital affairs and to make appointments which allowed them to use their professional expertise more effectively. The transition did not happen quickly nor easily. Their apostolic councilor, Sister Lucina Halbur, was challenged to define her role in relation to the role of the superior general. It was months before she was included on the hospital boards.[19]

For Sister Colette Hartman, the apostolic councilor from the foreign missions, the new government provided an opportunity "to give an authentic response to our mission of 'incarnating' ourselves into the life of the poor as directed by Medellin."[20] But both she and her successor, Sister Bertha Bumann, experienced difficulties in being heard and understood by North American leadership. They saw themselves as viewed by the motherhouse simply as contacts in case of crisis and as providing an assurance that all was well on the missions.

Sorting out the relationship between different levels of government was another challenge. Sister Michaela O'Brien, the second apostolic councilor for secondary education, wrote: "Often there was minimal agreement *among* ... and between ... the two groups [the general councilors and the apostolic councilors] regarding expectations and relationships. [They] existed and functioned side-by-side not as an integrated governing body ...."[21] However, when it became clear that, in addition to the usual challenges in the apostolates, withdrawing personnel from the schools involved endless hours of ... planning with pastors and the sisters themselves to ensure a smooth transition for the parish and, in the case of the hospitals, withdrawal from one hospital and endless negotiations regarding merger on the other, the superior general was generous in expressing her gratitude to the apostolic councilors.[22]

NEW EXPERIENCES IN UNITS OF GOVERNANCE

Both at the general and the local levels sisters adjusted to new or changed structures. At the general level, the executive board was a collegial body that included the superior general, the councilors, the apostolic councilors, and a representative of Marian College. The board was "to provide inspiration and enlightenment ... and strive to create a climate in which sisters can develop a deep spirituality and act with responsible freedom."[23] Its members were to discern the spirit of the community. They were to urge renewal of spirit and be constantly aware that the spirit speaks through the members. They were to provide leadership in carrying out the acts of the chapter: assemble and interpret necessary data, allocate funds to meet new or developing needs in the church; support the work of various commissions; and decide on matters of importance that concern the entire congregation, subject only to the veto of the superior general.[24]

The sisters serving at the motherhouse, the retired sisters at Nazareth Heights, and those who were serving outside the institutionally administered works remained the responsibility of the superior general. The sisters at Marian College had a committee of higher education with an elected chairperson who represented them on the executive board of the congregation. Although the executive board was designed to integrate the total government, it was never able to live up to its potential.

On the local level the houses were considered as the primary instrument for making collegiality in the local community a reality.[25] Sisters were asked to hold monthly meetings in which all the sisters were asked to share through consensual acceptance in making decisions that would involve the welfare of their local community. These decisions could involve identifying apostolic needs in the area, evaluating the effectiveness of the apostolate, setting up a house budget, determining the horarium, planning special liturgies, and providing a forum for discussions. The houses were also given power to experiment with methods of choosing the local superior.[26]

CONCLUDING THE CHAPTER OF RENEWAL

On June 1, 1970, the delegates re-assembled to conclude the chapter of renewal. During the year the commissions had had the opportunity to refine their work of the previous summer, and submit proposals for new legislation. Formation, religious life, and the apostolate were each allocated three days for presentations and discussion, while one day was allocated to a discussion of government and the last day was set aside for unfinished business.

Sister John Baptist challenged the delegates with four questions. They concerned 1) the length of time members completely disengaged from the life of the community could still be considered effective members; 2) the extent, in the face of pressing congregational needs, to which the community can proceed in permitting or accepting outside commitments for members; 3) the manner in which members seemingly attached to the freedom they have found in working outside the community can be reclaimed; and 4) the means by which such alienation by any of the members can be reversed.[27]

The greater part of the two weeks was uneventful, as the delegates struggled to rewrite and clarify the work of the previous summer. The role descriptions of the superior general, councilors, and apostolic councilors were all refined and modified.[28] The superior general's role as religious leader of the community was emphasized; the councilors were asked to be "in the forefront of service to the church, thinking, planning ... developing gifts ... to be placed at the disposal of the community and the church."[29] The apostolic councilors, as they conferred with the sisters in their choice of work, were to help them "to live and think with the church."[30] Clarifications were made in regard to local government, and a judicial body[31] was eliminated.

The most difficult discussions involved the habit. Although a considerable portion of the congregation wanted to retain the traditional habit, the delegates compromised. The modified habit could be worn by those who wished, but black and white were the only permitted colors and the veil was part of the habit. Some sisters preferred more choices in color, and there was a growing number who wanted the veil to be optional on some occasions. Neither group attained its goal at this time; but it was the veil, with its heavy burden of symbolism, that became the focus of the deepest emotions of the sisters. To some it was *the* sign of religious consecration. To others it was an unnecessary encumbrance to their apostolic activities and, perhaps, personal comfort. After a prolonged and emotional debate the decision was made to retain the veil.

THE SEVENTIES

The congregation was beginning its experiment with new structures and a new lifestyle in a time of national as well as religious stress. With no national political and economic ideology, the turbulence and political activism of the sixties was not yet over. The country was polarized by the war in Viet Nam. The political corruption that the Watergate break-in exposed and the resignation of both the vice-president and the president had led to a widespread spirit of cynicism. The seizure of hostages from American embassies in Tehran and Pakistan had humiliated the government. On the domestic front, the war on poverty had been abandoned and the battle for civil rights was yet to be won. Family life was in jeopardy as divorces and teen-age pregnancies increased. A landmark decision by the Supreme Court, *Roe vs. Wade,* legalized abortions.

Noting that Americans placed less value on the concept of duty, sacrifice, the work ethic, social morality, and respectability and more value on personal happiness, self-fulfillment, pluralism, leisure, and personal health, the novelist Tom Wolfe called the decade "the me generation"[32] New Age spirituality attracted people who, unwilling to submit to the restraints of organized religion, were reacting to a society in which the accumulation of wealth and status-seeking became overriding values.[33] The first non-Italian pope in 455 years was elected, but soon disappointed many Americans by his opposition to women's ordination. Movements such as *cursillos,* the charismatic movement, the Christian family movement, and marriage encounters were sweeping through the church, but interest in traditional religious life was declining.[34]

Within the community, the story of the Sisters of St. Agnes during the decade reflects much the same confusion that bedeviled American society as a whole. Not everyone understood the reasons for the changes in the church and congregation; certainly not everyone accepted them. Every aspect of religious life was questioned. Women who had consciously put their own desires aside for decades were attracted to the seemingly unlimited possibilities of self-fulfillment in the "world."[35] Departures became common.

Sisters also faced decisions in regard to their ministry. Should they ask to leave a comfortable middle-class school and teach the poor in inner-city Chicago or the Southwest? Should they leave the apostolate for which they were prepared and look for something more stimulating or personally fulfilling? Should they ask to live closer to their families?

There was a growing concern that the community would lose its vision and focus if ministries became too individual. A radical few began to discuss the possibility of divesting the congregation of all its property and giving the proceeds to the poor.

What had begun as the questioning of customs and practices that had lost their meaning or prevented the exercise of personal responsibility or effectiveness in the apostolate was shifting into questions of the meaning of the vows, authority, community, and religious life itself. A common vision was in the process of fading as traditional apostolates were abandoned and new types of apostolates were founded.

At the celebration of her fifty years as a professed religious in 1975, Sister John Baptist captured the feelings of the period when she wrote: "We were really busy. All communities, too, I'm sure have lived the kind of anguish, desperation, and fear experienced in drifting rudderless, anchor cut loose, or with rudders just bobbing around—getting nowhere because the rowers were rowing in different directions. But, with it all, there has been deep, unintermittent prayer, the constant cry, 'Lord, save us. We perish.' And because the Lord's answer hasn't changed since that on the stormy lake: 'Why do you doubt? O you of little faith,' we continue in faith and hope . . . ."[36]

NICARAGUA: PORTENTS OF A REVOLUTION

In addition to the consequences of renewal, the sisters in Nicaragua had to contend with that country's upheavals. Until his assassination in 1956, Anastasio Somoza Garcia, with the help of the National Guard, controlled Nicaragua. In spite of the corruption of the regime, the United States supported his successors as dependable allies in Central America. His elder son, Luis Somoza Debayle, became president, and then, in 1967, was succeeded by his second son, Anastasio Somoza Debayle, former chief of the National Guard. Through manipulation of the government, the Somozas had become the largest landowners in Nicaragua, but the country still lagged far behind its economic potential. Nor were there any major efforts to build up the country's infrastructure or improve the living standard of the people.[37]

For years, both civil society and the church provided ample evidence of a desire of the people for reform. While there had always been opposition to the regime from various sectors of society, the sixties marked the beginning of a new phenomenon—Christian theologians merging with radical revolutionary groups. In 1961 three young men, intent on establishing a new society, founded the *Frente de Liberacion Nacional*, a revolutionary party based on Marxist-Leninist principles.[38] From small beginnings, the events of the following years combined with the party's willingness to use military

means and the courage of its members permitted it to assume leadership in the struggle for political and economic change.

The Catholic Church, which had traditionally supported gov-
ernments as a guarantor of order and protector of religion in society, was experiencing a new awareness of the church in society. The
new emphasis on studying the scriptures and the practice of "theological reflection"[39] encouraged the application of the gospel message to its own reform as well as the correcting of the injustices of
society. In Nicaragua one outcome was the establishment of
Christian base communities with lay leaders educated to organize
groups for the discussion of the gospel and formation of Christian
social consciences. This call to reform and change, particularly "the
option for the poor," inspired the Latin American bishops at their
1968 meeting in Medellin, Colombia, to call upon Christians to be
active in the struggle for human rights and social justice.

The theology and activities of one such people's church, Santa
María de Los Angeles, was confirmed and given impetus by
Medellin. Santa María was organized among the poor in the Barrio
Riguero in Managua by Uriel Molina, a Franciscan theologian.
When their teaching contract for the Christian Brothers ended in
1969, Sisters Bertha Bumann, Colette Hartman and Nancy Chow
moved to the Barrio to assist Father Uriel in working with the poor.
There they became acquainted with a group of students who would
soon become significant in Nicaragua's history. These university students, influenced by Molina's emphasis on liberation theology,[40]
asked to live, pray, work, and discuss political and economic issues
together as a community. The sisters joined them as they worked to
form Christian communities among the six barrios in a parish of fifteen thousand people. The dedication and life style of the young
men and the seriousness of their approach to social issues impressed
the sisters. As Marxian methods of social analysis were used as a
tool to examine societal problems, Sister Colette became convinced
that the imperialistic policies of the United States were the root
cause of Nicaragua's problems.[41] Breaking loose from dominance by
the United States and the establishment of socialism "with a human
face" would be the beginning of a new and more just society. While
Sister Colette was attracted to the dedication and ideals of the
members of the FLN,[42] Sister Bertha found its Marxist orientation
untenable. The very different conclusions on the part of two dedi-

cated women presaged a division in community thinking that would impact the social fabric of the community in Nicaragua for two more decades.

The night of December 23, 1971, Sisters Bertha, Colette, and Nancy, asleep in their apartment, were awakened by the collapse of the ceilings and walls in their rooms. The earthquake[43] endured for two-hours. By the time it was over, Managua was devastated, 20,000 people had died and five square miles of the city had been leveled. The earthquake set in motion events leading to the downfall of the Somoza regime, the triumph of the revolutionary party, and eventual civil war.

Although the sisters had no place to live but a ruined church patio, for the next three months the community organized what goods they could negotiate with other foreign refugees and began the task of helping the people in the area rebuild their lives. In the midst of the desolation the sisters were immediately aware of the import of the events and the promise the cataclysm could offer the future. As Sister Bertha wrote, "We thank God that we are alive and able to help in some small way. What our new role will be depends on how we unite forces and help the people to a liberation never had before. Most of the church buildings are in the area of demolition, but the Church, the people, are with us. With new directions and Christian hope much can be done. The beautiful moon has waned but we know it will wax again. So is our hope for the church here."[44]

While the people in Managua were struggling to survive, help was coming from all over the world. President Somoza seized upon the opportunity to sell off the beans and rice, hoard commodities, sell or rent donated equipment back to the government, and bank money donated to care for the hungry and homeless. The nation and the world were outraged. From that time on, the Somoza regime was doomed.

PREPARING FOR THE CHAPTER OF 1973

By the end of 1972, the congregation had successfully lived more than three years under the experimental constitutions. When the time came to submit proposals for action to the forthcoming chapter, it was heartening to the administration that, of the almost two hundred proposals submitted, the majority were signed by groups of sisters and concerned with continuing, deepening or expanding the present direction of the community rather than returning to the past.[45]

Of necessity, much of the energy of the government had been directed to internal matters. Roles had been established and a modus operandi between its levels had been negotiated. But from the theme of the chapter, "Challenge to Community in Christ," it was clear that sisters had yet to negotiate the tensions of living in community in the midst of enormous changes. One change was apparent in the chapter itself: whereas non-delegates had been gradually admitted during its course, they would now be admitted to all sessions unless an executive session was called.

At a preparatory meeting for the chapter in April 1973, delegates found one of the most useful speakers to be a canonist, Thomas Swift, SJ, who spoke on canon law and the issues of authority and obedience. Swift emphasized the necessity of corporate reflection and his technique of frequently countering questions about legalities with two questions proved most helpful in future deliberations: "What do you as a community want to become?" and "What do you as a community want to do together?"

When the chapter opened in July, the congregation numbered 766 members. During the year, sisters had identified community issues as their chief concern after prayer. In a letter to the community, Sister Francis Assisi noted that "To achieve community we need to share life, vision, and love. This is possible only when we grasp the theological significance of our oneness in Christ and when we eschew all selfish desire in favor of the good of the other."[46]

Sister John Baptist's report to the Chapter of 1973 was a sobering one:

> This administration began when personalism, activism, the demands for independence and freedom were at their peak .... All of us, in the agony of confusion, uncertainty, diversity, have had to lay our lives on the line. We have had to determine what we were willing to give in exchange for our vocation. All of us, in one way or another, used the years—some to reach depths of prayer, community, dedication never reached before; some few to drift more com-

fortably than ever before; a very few, to splash around in the shallow, just happy to be free ....

I don't need to tell you that there is another side—there has been a fair share of anxiety, turmoil, tension, indecision, sometimes downright hopelessness and occasionally, even despair ... I believe that these four years have been an experience toward truth. The difficulty, however, has been that in the throes of renewal and adaptation, CSA's identity has become blurred and clouded. It is now time to once again know who we are. We have come from uniformity to pluralism. It seems to me that out of this pluralism, we have now to build a more powerful force of coordination .... CSA needs to recover an identity .... It is a fact, that to the degree each Sister goes her own way, to that degree will our individual and communal witness value become less and less discernible. There is need for some external, concrete norm, structures if I dare use the word, chosen by us, to truly incarnate CSA's values, to support, defend and maintain the inner reality of CSA's life.[47]

Sister John Baptist continued by noting that she had seen a growth in community interest and involvement in peace and justice issues. She reminded the sisters that: "His kingdom and therefore our kingdom is the world. Its problems—poverty, social justice, the rights of the unborn, the aged and the dying, political manipulation and corruption—all these are our concern. Not one of us is truly free until truth and justice prevail; not one of us is truly religious unless we spend ourselves for the liberty and salvation of every other person we touch, however remotely or indirectly."[48]

FOCUS ON ISSUES

At the chapter discussions, it became clear that the amount of diversity a community could allow was a fundamental question: "We are a community of free people; here unity can allow for diversity for it is freedom of spirit." But, said another, "We don't want uniformity but we want to know what unites us."[49] Some thought that problems would be solved if sisters understood the experimental constitution. "Our main business is to help the sisters know it, love it, and we will have no problems living it."[50] The fear that the community was in danger of becoming a secular institute was allayed by the statement that the "Congregation of St. Agnes [is] a religious institute, apostolically oriented and characterized by consecration through the three vows of poverty, chastity, and obedience." There were further definitions of the three vows including clarification of the vow of obedience quoted from a letter of the Sacred Congregation, which asked for respect for "the obligation and right of a Superior to exercise prudently the role of her authority."[51] Chastity was to be understood "as basic to our way of union with God, and our celibate community as a witness to this union and constant waiting for the Lord Jesus." Poverty should be recognized as a vow that included "poverty in fact as well as in spirit and that we find creative ways to share with the needy, always keeping the needs of the community in mind."

The question of the habit again precipitated many hours of intense, sometime anguished, discussion, but the habit was retained—although there were concessions that could be read as indicating that it would not be for long. Sister John Baptist summarized the situation when she addressed a group interested in religious life. "Our discussions and deliberations proceeded on a surprisingly high level of theological and spiritual considerations; we managed to attain unanimity on most issues without too much conflict and then—well, totally feminine, we balked when it came to dress."[52]

The governmental structure of the congregation was still an issue. A growing number of sisters at Nazareth Heights felt deprived because they had no apostolic councilor. With a view to making adaptations in the structure, an ad hoc committee was formed to study models of government. Interapostolic[53] living was authorized as was intercommunity living when the situation demanded it. Sisters at universities or in individual apostolates could choose to affiliate with a house of their choice. In an effort to maintain some cohesiveness in the houses, common recreations were mandated but their manner and time were to be decided upon by the house chapter. Another directive encouraged the meaningful celebration of holy days and holidays. Sisters indicated a desire for more owner-ship in the congregation by asking for more communication in the form of a quarterly newsletter.

The use of personal expense accounts was evolving into a common practice, while the acceptance of guidelines for diversified life styles was a further indicator of the future. In local convents there could be, with unanimous consent, experimentation with group leadership. The right to vote for chapter delegates was extended to sisters in temporary vows. The executive board had been intended to control and evaluate experimentation, but it was obvious that once a mitigation or change was allowed there was no returning to the stricter rule.

OUTCOMES

As the delegates were leaving, one sister posed the question, "What did we do at chapter?" A typical response was: "We experienced a deepening of our prayer life, grappled with problems of authority and obedience, firmed up our convictions to preserve our corporate commitments and foster extended apostolates.[54] Another added, "When people on the outside ask us what we did at chapter, we can say we hope we will become better religious, we hope to serve the church better. We want to say to each other, 'we really love you; we want you to grow.'"[55]

The first four years of living the new experimental constitution were over. While there is no measuring of the anxieties, the struggles, and even the pain of the sisters who were charged by the community to accept leadership in those troubled times, an article in the chapter bulletin expressed the gratitude of the sisters and some small measure of appreciation for their achievements:

> It is appropriate that we take a moment to ponder on the unique situation which faced our Superior General and her Councilors when they took office in 1969, meeting a challenge that no other Administration had ever faced. With only a new Constitution ... to guide them, they were to be the spiritual and administrative leaders of the Congregation of St. Agnes.

Not very well acquainted with each other, totally
unfamiliar with the new role they were to play, separated by an age span of twenty years, they wanted
desperately to observe the spirit of the decree for
Renewal of Religious Orders, and so joining hands and
hearts, and placing their confidence in God's merci-
ful love, they set out courageously through the
wilderness of those difficult years.[56]

At the election, Sister John Baptist and Sister Rachel were re-
elected as superior general and vicar assistant; Sister Anne Jude Van
Lanen, a nurse and a missionary, and Sister Dianne Bergant, a
scripture scholar and professor, were the newly elected members to
the council. Much had been accomplished during the four-year
term in absorbing the principles of Vatican II, it was now time to
move to a post-Vatican mentality. The council, sensitive to the symbolism of space and place, began the journey by moving away from
the hierarchical ordering of daily life by refusing to sit at a special
table in the refectory or to occupy special places in chapel.

These years of early renewal were a time of workshops, programs, and meetings devoted to religious life, spirituality, Scripture,
and psychology. Workshops were designed to sensitize the community to an awareness of and respect for culture in the role of evangelization. Norbert Brockman, SM, and Lawrence J. Cada, SM,
June 1976, in one of the most discussed presentations, forced the sisters to deal with the historical reality that not all religious congregations have lasted forever. Graphic presentations of the life cycle of
religious communities with their inevitable periods of breakdown
forced the membership to deal realistically with present actualities.[57]
The congregation was realizing that the present was as much of
God's will as an individual would ever discern; that the future was
ultimately in God's hands and that each sister had to make a stringent effort if the Sisters of St. Agnes were to survive spiritually and
materially.

ENDINGS ... AND BEGINNINGS

In 1974 the Precious Blood Fathers terminated their services to the
congregation after fifty-eight years of service. Never again would

chaplains serve the congregation in the same way nor have the influence that they had in the past. Valued and respected as they had been in the past, the history of the past decade and more had placed the destiny of women's congregations in their own hands. With other women, sisters were beginning to find in each other their spiritual directors, retreat masters, scripture scholars, theologians, and canon lawyers.

The decision in 1975 to raze the motherhouse to make room for the expansion of St. Agnes Hospital destroyed both a home and the expression of a distinctive life style.[58] Although it was clear that the motherhouse was too old, too large, too expensive to maintain, and too hazardous to live in, its destruction was, nevertheless, a deeply disturbing event for many of the sisters. That it came at the unfortunate time when other traditions, rituals, and practices were being questioned and abandoned made the decision particularly difficult. The motherhouse was a sacred space made alive with memories of many of the women who had lived and prayed there. Every sister had learned to regard it as the "heart and home" of the community. It was the loss of the chapel, scene of long hours of prayer, magnificent liturgies, and the ceremonies that marked their commitment to Christ that grieved them most deeply. It was there that each sister had experienced both pain and joy; there that they had made decisions that determined the course of their lives. Sisters felt a further sense of loss when they saw their old furnishings, everything from pitchers and wash basins to beds, bureaus, desks, chapel pews, prie-dieus, pictures, statues, and trunks sold or given to charity.

The motherhouse community, administration, and sister residents, moved a block away to St. Agnes Hall, the former St. Agnes School of Nursing. Fortunately, a minimal amount of remodeling was required; a science laboratory became the chapel and the gymnasium the dining room.

On the feast of St. Agnes, January 21, 1975, the congregation initiated a new relationship. Melva Olson, a friend of many sisters, discovering that congregations were beginning to establish an associate relationship with like-minded friends in ministry and faith-sharing, suggested that the congregation also invite people into such a relationship. The administration took time to consider the idea, but after a period of persistence on the part of Melva and discern-

ment on the part of the community, Melva made her first commitment, and within the year three more women also assumed an associate relationship to live the charism and mission of the congregation in their personal lives and gather to deepen their spiritual life,
support one another, and respond to the needs of the church.

One of the most important decisions affecting the financial
health of the congregation was to enroll its members in the Social
Security program. The congregation entered the program
November 1, 1973, with payments retroactive to October 1, 1968.[59]
The health insurance provided for persons sixty-five and older
(Medicare) has proved invaluable to the congregation.[60]

TURMOIL ON A MISSION

The breakdown in religious communities had serious consequences
for Catholic education. Between 1969 and 1977 the number of full-
time teachers and principals in elementary education in the congregation plummeted from 299 to 171, although the total number in
the apostolate decreased by only forty-two. The congregation withdrew from more than a dozen schools.[61] In other schools as the
younger sisters left, aging sisters were serving part time or working
in other areas of service within the schools and parishes. An increasing number of sisters were moving into religious education while
others were changing to new ministries within the congregation.

Societal breakdowns in some areas also affected the schools and
teachers. In the sixties the public schools of New York City had been
torn by the efforts of minorities to gain control of the public school
system. A situation had arisen in the parish school of Our Lady
Queen of Angels in Harlem that a local newspaper would call reminiscent of struggles for community control in the city's public
schools. The school had 670 students of whom more than 90%
were members of minorities. Thirteen sisters were stationed there at
that time. A number of sisters in the house had become involved
with some of the activist members of the black community. From
the perspective of the congregation, their involvement had led to
the neglect of both their classroom and religious obligations. The
combination of divergent philosophies in regard to relations with
the larger parish community and internal tensions within the rectory, convent, and faculty of the school created an environment of

such stress that every religious serving in the parish was transferred.

When the news got out to the neighborhood, the decision generated a great deal of anger among some of the sisters and parents who saw the move as removing good teachers and replacing them with "middle-class whites, who know nothing about us."[62] A committee of concerned parents demonstrated in front of the parish church and parents began a letter-writing campaign to get the support of city officials and political figures, as well as of Cardinal Terence Cooke, in their dispute with the school administration. Even the congregational administration received threats, night letters, telegrams, and phone calls. Black dissidents wrote to Sister John Baptist and threatened to bring her before the civil and ecclesiastical authorities.[63] A small group of sisters refused to accept the congregation's decision. In the long run the incident had little if any long-term effect on the school; its negative impact on several of the concerned sisters was severe.

A PLAN FOR EDUCATION

From 1969 through 1977, every Catholic school in Fond du Lac was involved in the attempt to implement *The Plan to Establish K-16 Model School System Educational Research & Development Center in Fond du Lac*—otherwise known as the Hanlon Plan. As it is beyond the scope of this volume to do full justice to the theory and the history of its attempted implementation in Fond du Lac, the following is only a very brief survey.

Dr. James Hanlon looked upon the subject areas of the school curriculum as tools for the acquisition of each of the seven following processes: 1) the learning mastery system, 2) the world view construction mastery system, 3) the ideal pattern construction mastery system, 4) the decision-making mastery system, 4) the climate creation mastery system, 6) the environment creation mastery system, 7) the cybernetic mastery system. Ideally, the student would graduate from the program as a self-actualizing Christian.[64]

To accomplish the plan he formed the Marian College Consortium with a board composed of forty-two members representing the parishes, Marian College and the congregation, responsible for policy.[65] Dr. Hanlon was director of the consortium schools, president of the corporation, and K-12 superintendent of schools functioning as regional superintendent. A Research and Development Center was to be an integral element of the system. The center would research the body of theoretical knowledge on which the plan was based and evaluate the curricula, syllabi, and guidelines. The greater number of faculty and administrators were expected to come from the congregation, while Dr. Hanlon committed himself to recruit personnel with special skills and to raise funds from organizations, such as the De Rance Foundation, interested in Catholic education.

Meanwhile, before Dr. Hanlon had officially committed himself to Fond du Lac, he was instrumental in having Marian College appoint, beginning the summer of 1969, Dr. J. Lance Kramer as its academic dean.[66] Dr. Kramer was charged to construct a plan for the establishment of the Marian Plan while another committee wrote a plan for obtaining grants to fund the project.

In the fall of 1970, the first steps were taken toward consolidating the six parish schools in the Fond du Lac area to prepare the way for the introduction of the Marian Plan. Dr. Hanlon would soon become, in effect, superintendent of six elementary schools, as well as president of Marian College. Three principals were in charge of two schools each in an effort to move toward a common educational philosophy, curriculum, and textbooks. A unified school board was established with priest and lay representatives from each parish. There were joint faculty meetings with the schools and in every elementary school, teacher committees were formed at various levels as teachers acquainted themselves with the vocabulary and concepts of Hanlon's theory.

In July 1971 Dr. Hanlon became president of the college. To explain and illustrate his theories, he assigned Marian College faculty members to write and produce a series of TV programs, *Thursday's Child*, to explain both the theoretical base and its application. The series began the summer of 1972 on the local TV channel. Before the series was completed, the channel suspended operations.[67]

There were other steps to take before the plan could be fully implemented. Dr. Hanlon had to gain approval from the consortium, from the parishes, the Marian College Board, the Archdiocesan School Board, and the congregational chapter. That accomplished by July 19, 1973, the incorporation process could begin and he could apply for grants. In the fall he began in-service workshops for the teachers.[68] In June of 1974, he gained full authorization from the Archdiocesan School Board to begin operations of the Marian College consortium system for a four-year period.

Numerous meetings were held explaining the plan to the parishioners in Fond du Lac. In February 1974, when a group of lay teachers filed a petition for the election of a collective bargaining agent in an attempt to unionize the schools, Dr. Hanlon worried that his plan might be jeopardized. The union soon found that unionizing was unworkable as each parish, the Springs, and the college paid its own teachers.[69]

Meanwhile, meetings continued. At quarterly meetings the principals presented summaries of the work in progress in their schools to implement the theory. The *Chronicles* reported that there was a lack of understanding of what was to be accomplished and "for all practical purposes the consortium is not functioning as Dr. Hanlon reported it would when it began operation. It is a serious situation for the congregation to face, as it was at the sisters' request that Dr. Hanlon came to Fond du Lac, and at present results are not satisfactory with the majority of people in Fond du Lac."[70]

CATHOLIC SECONDARY EDUCATION IN FOND DU LAC

The enrollment of St. Mary's Springs, now sponsored jointly by the congregation and by the Archdiocese of Milwaukee, fluctuated between 593 and 695 students from 1969 through 1977. At the beginning of the period, although the congregation had relinquished ownership, many sisters still had a strong commitment to the school. A major activity during the next years had to be raising funds to reduce the $1,500,000 mortgage on the building. Faculty and students resorted to telethons, pizza sales, and magazine subscriptions.

Like the other congregational institutions, Marian College underwent profound changes during the seventies. In 1969, it was a small women's college; its board of trustees, president, and faculty were overwhelmingly sisters. The majority of its student body was Catholic, of traditional college age, and Caucasian. Almost every student was planning on teaching or nursing as a career. The financial situation was always precarious as the college relied almost wholly on tuition and the contributed services of the congregation for support.

In the seventies, the president was a layman; men joined the faculty in ever increasing numbers; lay persons were members of the board of trustees; and the college had become co-educational.[71] Many of the college regulations, such as hours and a dress code, had been drastically modified or disappeared. Its student body had become less homogeneous and more apt to challenge the status quo.

Hanlon's plan, based on his own theory of education,[72] was designed to eliminate the traditional college curriculum. The appointment of Dr. Kramer as academic dean brought the first person trained in academic administration to the post. Upon his arrival, the faculty undertook a curriculum study that resulted in a common studies program which ensured all students a basic liberal arts component in conjunction with their professional program.[73]

The enrollment in the fall of 1971 brought sixty-two male students to campus. A little more than half were seminarians from St. Lawrence College Seminary, which had closed at the end of the 1970-1971 school year. The introduction of those men brought a new excitement to the intellectual, extra-curricular, and religious life of the campus. The next year counted ten ex-service men, "serious and determined to make their way in life."[74] In 1972, a sports program was initiated when Marian joined the Wisconsin Independent Colleges Athletic Conference with men's and women's basketball teams. As the budget for sports was nearly non-existent, it was only the dedication of faculty members that kept the program in operation.

New programs were added, increasing the number of majors. Faculty and administration also changed noticeably. Sisters retired and the number of lay persons employed in the college increased.[75] One hundred fifty freshmen enrolled in 1972, creating a demand for student, particularly male, housing. The problem was solved when the college negotiated with George Hutter to build the Greenbrier apartments on National Avenue—a fourteen-apartment complex designed to accommodate fifty-six students.

Meanwhile, Dr. Hanlon's commitment to the high school and elementary schools was proving to be a liability to the college. Although many faculty members[76] found a positive benefit in the dialogues on the nature, philosophy, and goals of education, the majority did not find the system applicable in their own teaching. The academic dean, Dr. Kramer, later wrote: "What seemed like an interesting notion on the K-12 level simply didn't have a reasonable college level extension."[77] Dean Kramer resigned in July of 1975.

The college's problems escalated as America's only peacetime inflation combined with declining student enrollments to create hardships for the faculty, in terms of both salaries and divisional budgets.[78] When, in April of 1976, Dr. Hanlon terminated a philosophy professor's contract because she had distributed a critique of his theory to the students, the faculty became further frustrated. Ten days later, the board of trustees renewed Dr. Hanlon's contract for three rather than five years.

Although the professor appealed on the grounds that academic freedom was violated, the ad hoc faculty senate committee gave serious study to the matter but failed to support the professor—primarily because she had taken the matter to the students rather than to the faculty.

The case was then brought to the American Association of University Professors. The AAUP upheld the college's contention that the professor was attacking its mission. It did, however, recommend that the college clarify its mission statement.

The college also grappled with re-accreditation issues. Although in 1974, the North Central Association had granted Marian continued accreditation for a ten-year period, in 1976 the Department of Nursing was granted only limited re-accreditation. The size of Fond du Lac contributed to the department's most serious problems, the shortage of qualified instructors with a Master's degree in the Fond du Lac area and the limited opportunities for clinical experience. As half of Marian's 490 students at this time were enrolled in the nursing program, the problem was a serious one. By 1977, Marian had barely survived its crises, both economic and philosophical, but was well on its way to even more serious problems.

HEALTH CARE

By 1960 the health care system in the United States had been transformed. In part, this change was caused by the growth of private hospital insurance plans[79] and increased costs of technology. The dramatic increase in hospitals' operating margins led to the growth of for-profit hospital chains that began to compete with the not-for-profit sector. Like similar not-for-profit hospitals, the Agnesian hospitals could no longer rely on congregational funds[80] and monies raised by the local community, but were forced to generate capital-improvement funds, borrow large sums of money, and issue bonds. The administration of hospitals began to resemble that of corporations, with CEOs and "bottom line" rhetoric.

As national legislation and national standardization of hospitals increased and the number of religious serving in the hospitals decreased, preserving the Catholic identity of hospitals was becoming an ever greater challenge.[81] Increasingly, Catholic hospitals were becoming community hospitals, often with heavy non-Catholic staff and clienteles. They were financed through public funds or by appeal to the whole community, and were often enough, the only health facility reasonably available to a community. It was becoming more difficult to deal with controversial issues such as tubal ligations and artificial insemination in a pluralistic setting.

Hospital administrations were forced to consider their moral responsibility in relation to procedures deemed immoral by Catholic teaching as specified by the *Code of Medical Ethics for Catholic Hospitals and the Ethical and Religious Directives for Catholic Hospital Facilities.* Preserving the Catholic identity of hospitals in a pluralistic society had become, and would continue to be, a constant concern throughout the next decades.

THE HOSPITALS AND THE CONGREGATION

By 1970, St. Anthony's expansion program had a serious financial problem. The congregation had opted for a new building and committed itself to 1.5 million dollars for the construction costs as well as to becoming a guarantor of two million dollars from the Knights of Columbus national headquarters. Expected Hill-Burton funds were not forthcoming; meanwhile, the two million dollar loan the congregation had negotiated would not be released until the building was completed, and the current interest rate available for interim borrowing was high. When the congregation was ready to discuss plans for building the chapel and the convent, its financial and legal consultants were "chary in giving any words of recommendation for … assuming any greater indebtedness."[82] By mid 1971, the congregation was considering a proposal from Hadley Memorial Hospital stating that the hospital would be willing to 1) merge, 2) purchase St. Anthony Hospital, or 3) be purchased by St. Anthony.[83]

In spite of endless hours spent in meetings, interviews and conferences to consider how a merger or outright sale could be arranged for the benefit of both parties, no agreement was acceptable to both parties. Meanwhile, St. Anthony was working vigorously to remain viable. Although efforts to build a spirit of cooperation were hindered because of pressures brought to bear by a group of "self-appointed mediators,"[84] the hospital developed active public relation programs and collaborated with Hadley in an effort to reduce costs to patients.[85] In 1973, St. Anthony's advances were apparent. Nearly all the obstetric care in the area was given at St. Anthony Hospital. A neonatology service was also established, unique to Agnesian hospitals. A helicopter service transported almost all of the neonates born in the area to the hospital's state-of-the-art neonatal unit. The recently launched detoxification program was proving successful.[86]

Reports for the next few years were satisfactory. By 1975 hard work had put the hospital on a firmer basis. The new hospital had been dedicated and its census was good. Payment on loans and the principal had been possible; compatible working relations between and among the administration, sisters, lay personnel, and public established; occupancy was higher than budgeted; doctors were added; and innovative educational services provided. There was planning for internal renovations; a cobalt suite was being designed, and a linear accelerator was being considered. St. Anthony remained a hospital actively serving the local area.[87]

St. Thomas Hospital in Colby, Kansas had been beset by problems for years. The hospital was losing approximately $45,000 in operations annually. Over a thirty-year period, the congregation had invested $400,000 in improving the facilities; Thomas County had spent $50,000.[88] In addition, the facilities did not meet standards and the medical staff was inadequate. The sisters working there found the level of health care in the area unacceptable and the morale was low. The hospital had been pinning its chances for survival on the hope that a surgeon and at least one general practitioner could be recruited to join its staff, but the situation at St. Thomas had deteriorated to the point where the question became not "do we wish to remain at Colby?" but "are we abandoning the apostolate if we leave?"

In spite of the sisters' efforts, the problems persisted. Two years later an independent study commissioned by the congregation made the limitations of the health services in the area clear, and efforts to provide adequate medical care by recruiting physicians were unsuccessful. Placement of sisters had become nearly an impossibility.[89] In 1972, circumstances allowed the congregation to discontinue the operation of the hospital. The congregation had compelling reasons: the current administrator had the experience, the expertise, and the public confidence to effect a smooth operational transition; the laymen on the board were giving every evidence of competence and the local community appeared ready to assume governance of their own health care.[90] In addition, Sister Mary Catherine Grief, had set up a practical nurse education program at the Colby Junior College that provided competent practical nurses for the area.[91]

On May 21, 1973, the announcement of the withdrawal appeared in the *Colby Free Press-Tribune* together with the assurance that the hospital's financial position was excellent. The local community requested the congregation to reconsider, but the withdrawal occurred as planned on September 1, 1973.

At the beginning of the decade the hospitals in Wisconsin were in a better situation. At St. Clare Hospital, the congregation had committed itself to a million-dollar loan and was the guarantor for a long-term four-million dollar loan for renovations, but "things moved with cheerful alacrity."[92] Although the town's population was fewer than 10,000 and the county was fewer than 26,000, the hospital employed 317 lay people and the clinic had grown to a staff of forty-seven doctors. It was a matter of pride for the staff that over half of the patients came from a distance, some from as far as one-hundred miles.[93] At the cost of $11,500,000, the hospital remodeled the old section and built a new wing.[94] It was dedicated on January 9, 1974.

Contrary to expectations, St. Clare experienced a drop in occupancy the following year. Malpractice issues were affecting hospital admissions throughout the country. The situation was made even more difficult as St. Clare Hospital was one of the five hospitals in the state that was dropped by its insurance company. The company agreed to negotiate on a month-to-month basis but the administrators at the hospital felt that more coverage was needed, and consequently, took out other coverage at a considerably higher rate.[95] Eventually, the St. Clare benefited when the state issued policies at a considerably lower cost.[96] Difficulties continued throughout the next year: low census, dissension between administrators and physicians, administrators and heads of some departments, combined with unforeseen repair expenses all contributed to an uneasiness abut the future.[97] With all these difficulties, the hospital still found it possible to initiate a continuing education program for personnel and to meet its debt obligations on schedule. The year ended with the good news that the addition of several new doctors in the area was expected to strengthen the services of the hospital.[98]

On July 1, 1971, St. Agnes Hospital celebrated seventy-five years of service to the community. There were only positive entries in the *Chronicles* during the first few years of the decade. Nine physicians joined the staff, and the hospital sponsored a survey of its facilities and services and of the health needs of the local community. The survey included the study of such issues as the replacement of obsolete beds, the provision of outpatient facilities, the expansion of emergency services, and the consideration of the construction of a physician office building.[99]

With the results of the survey in hand, plans were revised to study the possibility of undertaking a building project that would include the construction of a new wing to provide for the replacement of two hundred beds and new, expanded emergency and outpatient services, the renovation of existing areas to meet code regulations, and the eventual demolition of the south wing. The administration began making plans with a consultant, architect, and construction manager but was unable to issue contracts until the hospital board of directors decided it could proceed with a program in excess of ten million dollars without imposing unreasonable costs on the patients. In addition, it was necessary to obtain the approval of the State Health Policy and Planning Council.[100]

The ground was broken for the $13,000,000 project on April 28, 1974. A fund-raising company was contracted with a goal of $1,000,000. Plans were made for a five-story patient tower, an outpatient area, expanded emergency facilities, and provisions for one-day surgeries. As the construction of the building would increase the work load for the administration, the heads of ancillary services, patient services, and personnel services became vice-presidents of their respective departments and the office of executive vice-president was established.[101]

The following four years proved to be exceptionally trying for the administration of St. Agnes Hospital. The medical staff had been resistant to the reorganization into departments/specialties.[102] Although within the next year the campaign netted $38,000 over the goal, and the construction project was moving smoothly, internal problems were also creating a considerable amount of tension among the personnel and between personnel and administration.

At the same time the hospital administration made efforts toward broader visibility in the Fond du Lac community. The administrator, Sister Joan Wirz, served on the county board and city council where efforts were made in regard to mental health and drug and alcohol rehabilitation. She served on the Association of Commerce Board, while another administrator became a member of the local Rotary club to enable the hospital to network with representatives of local business, professional, and vocational interests.

UNREST AMONG THE NURSES

Around the country there was considerable tension within the nursing profession: the nurses' lack of autonomy, low pay, long hours, and overwork led to shortages in some hospitals and strikes and slowdowns in many cities around the country. Unrest among the nurses led the Wisconsin Nurses Association to initiate a movement to organize a Professional Nurses Council at the hospital. At a meeting on January 28, 1976, a group of nurses acquired enough signatures to call for an election. In February, registered nurses voted to be represented by Wisconsin Nurses Association. St. Agnes became one of the few hospitals in the state with a unionized nursing staff. This move led the Local #1199 National Union of Hospital and Health Care Employees, AFL-CIO, to follow suit by attempting to organize other employees.[103] Personnel in maintenance and dietary, as well as technicians, began to negotiate a call for an election. In March, the board approved a decision to hire consultants to inform the members of details of union activities.[104]

The hospital divided into factions. Morale was abysmal. The spirit of cooperation among the employees disappeared as people refused to do more than the minimum demanded by their job descriptions. Meanwhile, steps were taken to remedy the deficiencies that had been identified by the consultants in their study, and the morale of the nurses was improving.

On June 3, 1977, a vote taken at a union election at the hospital resulted in a decisive victory for the hospital as only forty-six nurses voted to join the Professional Nurses Council, with 142 nurses opposing the move. Nevertheless, on March 3, the National Labor Relations Board (NLRB) issued a complaint citing unfair labor practices by the hospital in its negotiations with the Wisconsin Nurses Association. The complaint cited the hospital for refusing to promote an admittedly qualified nurse because of his participation on the negotiating committee of the Nurses Association, for bargaining in bad faith at the negotiating table and for instituting unilateral changes in terms and conditions of employment of the nurses during negotiations.

On June 27, 1978, the hospital board made the decision to stand firm and negotiate only for a compromise on wages, but not on any of the philosophy related to union shop and fair share in those elements that would impinge on the rights of management.[105] On July 28, a settlement was reached, but union activity continued another year. The board continued its concerns for protecting the rights of management. On September 12, it accepted the Patients' Bill of Rights "with regret," noting that there was little choice not to have such a document for the patients.

On February 8, 1980, the regional office of the NLRB at Milwaukee ruled that hospital officials had violated provisions governing union elections. The ruling was appealed but the appeal was denied. A new election was scheduled for March 12 on the grounds that the employer had "interfered with the exercise of free and reasonable choice." At that election, the nurses voted to reject the union by a vote of 104-81 with six contested votes and eight abstentions.[106]

CHANGING AND NEW MINISTRIES

One of the most striking changes in twentieth century society were in demographic profiles. In 1900, the percentage of persons sixty-five and older was only slightly over 3 percent of the population; in 1970, the percentage had risen to slightly over 20 percent. The Henry Boyle Catholic Home for the Aged was becoming unable to meet the demands for rooms. Moreover, although it had been remodeled and updated since its 1903 construction, it was becoming a constant struggle to keep in compliance with state regulations. In 1968, the congregation had established a building fund for a new home; by 1973, the need to improve its facilities had become critical. The room problem was solved temporarily by buying a house next door to the Home for the staff, freeing their rooms for more residents. As a long range program was needed, the congregation formed a Lay Advisory Board to aid in engendering community interest and support.[107]

Meanwhile, the number of persons on the waiting list had risen from thirty-six to sixty. At the same time operating costs had outstripped the increase in revenues, and government agencies were making demands for improvement of the building.[108] By 1975 it was clear to the sisters that they needed additional expertise. For the first time, laymen, Thomas Hierl and Peter Stone, were asked to join the Board of Directors.[109] By the end of 1976, the board had negotiated with St. Agnes Hospital for two and one-half acres of the old motherhouse property. The approval of the Health-Wide Planning Commission and the board was obtained, and loans of $10,750,000 were secured. Ground was broken for the newly-named St. Francis Home on March 17, 1977. The Boyle Home, re-named the Boyle Apostolic Center, retained its mission of ministering to the elderly by becoming a pre-retirement home for the sisters.[110] Sisters there worked in health care, child care, teaching, physical therapy, library work, tutoring, cooking, handicrafts, and ministering to shut-ins by telephone.

Agnesians began a new ministry in 1973 in Mobile, Alabama, a city with a traditionally high percentage of people living below the poverty line, when Sister Lucy Ann Wasinger became coordinator of religious education in the Mobile deanery. Other sisters were soon involved in the summer program for young people that had been established in the area in the hope of strengthening racial and ecumenical relationships. That same year, Bishop John May invited the congregation to continue the work[111] of the departing Italian Missionary Sisters of Verona in the Catholic Welfare Office.[112] The clientele were usually either not eligible for any public assistance program or were experiencing a temporary crisis. In 1976, as little more than 15 percent of the people serviced were not Catholic, Bishop May established an interdenominational advisory committee. In three years the operating budget of the committee rose from $22,400 to $71,000.[113]

The southwest also began to attract sisters. The first sisters to arrive began working on a reservation in Sells, Arizona, in 1969, the first of a migration to the southwest that is still continuing. Committed to working with the poor, they began their ministries on the Navajo reservation and among the poverty-stricken in the city of Gallup, New Mexico.

THE CONGREGATION'S TWENTIETH CHAPTER

As the congregation looked toward its twentieth chapter, it found little reason to be optimistic about the future. On June 14, 1976, for the first time in the history of the community, there were no novices at the motherhouse. Four novices were professed sisters but there were no junior novices to take their place. It says much for the leadership of the previous eight years that the sisters maintained a surprising equilibrium and optimism. The remembrance of those desperate weeks in 1860 when the congregation was reduced to one blind member became a source of hope and inspiration to the community. In March 1977, the community was shocked to open a letter from Sister John Baptist and read: "My Lent has taken an unusual turn and living out the Paschal mystery with our Lord will probably be more real than at any other time in my life. I walk in peace—in His Will is my peace."[114] Sister had been diagnosed with a malignant tumor. These realities colored the context in which Chapter 1977 would meet.

The major purpose of the congregation's twentieth chapter was "to move toward a shared understanding of the meaning of who we are."[115] As Sister John Baptist was not eligible for re-election, there would be a new superior general. The election could be construed as an acceptance or rejection of the changes of the previous eight years.

Sister John Baptist's *Report on the State of the Congregation* provided the community with a balanced assessment of their present circumstances. "There has been growth. This is evident in the thrust of the sisters away from what might have been unreal and superficial in their lives and in the life of the church. This growth has also been in-depth—directed retreats, house of prayer experiences, scripture study, interest in peace and social justice. Vatican II renewal was the core of all this action."

"The constitutions should help the community in three ways: in conscious, personal living of the Gospels; in giving members freedom made through deliberate choices; in providing the minimum structures that aided in the consistency of choices. ...The past years have been given to us to discover, uncover and recover our values, to come to some personal convictions and then bring our lives into conformity with them. Once we have truly chosen, will the price in self-giving, corporate concern, and accountability be more than we can pay?"[116]

Within two weeks, the chapter passed forty-one acts to be implemented by the next administration. Among them was the decision to honor Father Caspar Rehrl by celebrating the centenary of his death. The spiritual life of the community proved to be enhanced by the inauguration of weekly scripture sharing. The congregation's ambivalence in regard to the Hanlon Plan was made clear when the mission/ministry committee of the chapter requested that the consortium be given no special consideration in teacher assignments and that an executive board of the congregation oversee the plan. The same committee accepted a proposal that the congregation respond broadly to peace and justice concerns. This decision concretized Sister John Baptist's reminder in the 1973 chapter that: "His kingdom and therefore our kingdom is the world. Its problems—poverty, social justice, the rights of the unborn, the aged and the dying, political manipulation and corruption—all these are our concern" and would become increasingly significant in ministry priorities in succeeding years.

The community life committee had been charged with many of the most sensitive issues in the congregation. The swift and radical changes effected in 1969 left a wake of pressures, stress and misunderstandings. In an effort to clarify issues that had been sources of difficulty, the committee distinguished between areas of primary values that are basic to community life; secondary values that externalize or symbolize primary values, and the values that admit of variety. Primary or non-negotiable values were prayer, community charism, faith, hope, love, basic commitment to the vows, commitment to the mission of the church, commitment to the apostolate, and an orientation to Scriptural life.[117]

The areas that admitted variety were, for that reason, also sources of tension.[118] The assembly concluded that individuals were to exercise personal accountability but the house meeting should be a source of unity and community.[119]

Two further statements of the chapter, one stating that "within the context of our apostolic religious life those decisions that touch on diverse manifestations be made by the individual sister and be accepted by the community with love, respect and support" and the other, "that the individual sister be free within the context of an apostolic religious institute to re-create herself according to her need for relaxation and personal enrichment" underlined its intentions. Perhaps in an effort to maintain some principle of unity or semblance of authority, a statement was made that the local community should not hesitate to delegate decision-making to the local superior, nor should the local superior hesitate to delegate authority.

The community reflected society's growing interest in the relationship between spiritual and physical wholeness and an increased interest in health issues. The delegates asked the executive board to look into the feasibility of purchasing or renting a house to be used for relaxation and renewal. Home visits were no longer considered the sister's vacation.

It was now the third chapter at which the question of the habit was raised and discussions were becoming more impassioned. While few insisted that clothing was of the greatest importance, it had far more importance than most sisters were willing to admit. It embodied centuries of tradition. Sisters had been revered because they wore it; they had also been embarrassed by attention, usually, but not always, well-meant. It frightened some people and put most people on their guard. Quite simply, it seemed to create a barrier between religious and the rest of the world. When the chapter finally agreed that the veil could be removed in the convent and that the habit is *ordinarily* worn, but that individual sisters could decide if circumstances warranted a reasonable adjustment, the wearing of a distinctive habit was doomed.

On July 25, 1977, the congregation chose another group of women who would have the responsibility of guarding its heritage, and, with its members, envisioning its future.

A little more than a year after the chapter on September 23, 1978, the congregation lost the woman who had steadied it during some of the most turbulent years of its history. Of the source of her strength in living out her office, Sister John Baptist had written: "Over and over again, I've meditated on Jesus' prayer at the Last Supper: 'Father, I have kept those whom you have given me.' Keeping has many manifestations, not bruising the smoldering flax; at other times, uncompromising, demanding, asking everything. To know when, where, how best to 'keep' is the crucial and most difficult part of love. To love as Jesus loves takes courage, selflessness, risk. It takes prayer, yours and mine."[120]

Chapter XIV

Hope in Our Hearts

The election of Sister Judith Schmidt and her council was met with approval by the younger and more progressive members of the congregation, but the delight was not universal. Indeed, in a time of transition that could not have been possible. Sisters were struggling painfully to find their place in the church at a time when the papacy seemed ambivalent regarding the changes brought about by the second Vatican Council. The community was only slowly emerging from the shock of the previous decade of radical changes in its life styles, prayer life, and ministries, and the departure of so many loved members. Sister John Baptist and her council had provided a sense of security as the new government was launched, but there was little possibility that the congregation could soon recover the sense of destiny that had sustained it for over a century.

For the first time in its history the community was presented with an entirely new council. Sister Judith was the youngest superior general since Mother Agnes. The council was also noteworthy for its youth. Its members ranged in age from forty-two to forty-six years of age. Sister Judith and Sister Lucina Halbur had each earned the respect of the congregation, both professionally and as apostolic councilors. Sister Miriam Therese Putzer had previously served as councilor to Sister John Baptist, and Sister Jean Perry had been principal in one of the larger schools of the congregation. But some sisters felt that the council was too young and almost certainly too liberal. At least one generation of sisters considered themselves "passed by." Together with a degree of mistrust in the government, this uneasiness prompted a demand from the disaffected that the delegates meet two years later in a so-called and unprecedented "accountability session."

Sister Judith made it clear in her words of acceptance that she was aware of the difficulties that lay ahead, but, characteristically, was full of hope: "Knowing that we are a pilgrim people, we are always in some stage of growth. We ... accept this in each other and we welcome change and growth and the beauty of who we are and hope to become. We urge one another to fidelity, to risk, to imagination in the design of our passage from stage to stage. Let us be for others a sign as we pass, a sign that the Lord loves and leads us forever .... We must go forth with hope in our hearts ...."[1]

CORPORATE RENEWAL

Now, eight years after the 1969 renewal chapter, an increasing polarization was threatening to tear the community apart as sisters dealt with changes with varying degrees of success. If hope were to be maintained by the new leadership, it would be hard won. The open disappointment with the chapter's choice of leadership by many conservative members was forcing the council to establish a level of trust as one of its first priorities. At the same time the congregation was obliged to formalize its new way of life in a constitution.[2] But before it was possible to write such a document, the community had to reach consensus on its spirituality, the manner in which the vows would be lived out, its expectations in regard to community life, and the structure of its government. It was an obligation that the congregation could meet only if members trusted their leadership and trusted each other.

Rather than attempt to deal with these issues directly, the council chose to focus on an "adherence to the spirit of Vatican II" while continuing the community's search for a fuller understanding of apostolic spirituality in the belief that common understandings would, in time, provide a basis for unity.[3] Borrowing a concept from the efforts of business to renew entire organizations, the council planned a four-year program designed to engage each member in the total venture of renewal through workshops, regional, and formation meetings rather than the traditional format of visitations to local communities.[4]

In November 1977, the corporate renewal program opened with meetings designed to encourage each sister to recognize and accept her feelings about the changes in the community.[5] As the process progressed, the council members were heartened by the positive comments which showed an appreciation of the community's efforts to respond to Vatican II. They found evidence of a deepening spirituality in the community, and a growing sense of openness, acceptance and sharing, together with a heightened sense of self in the sisters.[6] The opportunity for new ministries removed a heavy burden from those who were experiencing burn-out in their present occupations and energized sisters who were anxious for different opportunities for service. But they found others who feared that changes were made without sufficient consideration of consequences, that there was less asceticism in relation to the practice of the vows, that the congregation was ambivalent about genuine change, and that too many individuals had a limited vision about church needs. Above all, the scarcity of religious vocations troubled everyone.

When asked to describe their vision of a revitalized congregation, the largest number of members saw a community evincing a deeper spiritual life, one responsive to church needs and open to new ministries, a growing integration of life among its members, and a sense of zeal and dedication for the kingdom. Responses to the question in what ways the future congregation would be different, fell mainly into the categories of adaptability to the needs of the times, a deepened faith life, varied ministries, diversity within unity, and a broader vision.

In the following meetings each sister reflected on her understanding of apostolic spirituality and of community. The responses generally expressed appreciation for the opportunity for deeper exploration of what it meant to be a member of an apostolic community. Many sisters saw themselves as growing closer to Christ in

His ministry although others experienced struggles in integrating prayer, ministry, and community.[8]

In the fall of 1978 the series of corporate renewal workshops was continued. The goal became an attempt to move the congregation from a primarily cerebral approach to problems to processes such as role playing that engaged the imagination and emotions as well as reflective thinking. One process, for example, gave participants an experience in the process of corporate decision-making through presenting a complex situation in which a decision had to be made whether the sisters wished to continue in a traditional commitment. The discussion led to considerations of mission and ministry and its relationship to local planning and the individual needs of the sisters.

During the spring of 1979 the community explored the meaning of the term, "signs of the times," using the definition of the theologian, José Comblin: signs of times are external manifestations of a message of the Spirit to the world. The problems or needs of an era are not signs of the times in themselves—merely events or trends—but events that impel persons to a positive response. In that response, such as in the movement for social justice, Christ's activity in the world can be seen. These realities must be reflected from a theological perspective. Within those parameters, sisters identified realities that they found to be true signs of the times: efforts at "simplicity of life;" efforts to build a human community (at global, national, regional, church levels); a heightened awareness of issues of dignity of person, human rights and justice; and a heightened appreciation of the gifts of creation.[9] Less-structured prayer, a variety of prayer forms, and varied retreat experiences were seen as both positive and negative as was almost every other aspect of community living. Comments elicited from the sisters by these processes revealed an amazing range of perceptions and opinions. It was plain that the congregation was still struggling through a transition that was not necessarily becoming easier as time went on.

THE "ACCOUNTABILITY SESSION:" CLEARING THE AIR

The accountability session, product of apprehension and fear, was held June 25, 26, and 27, 1979. The first and only one of its kind in congregational history, all of the sisters were invited to hear reports from the various committees on the progress and implementation of each act passed by the chapter of 1977.[10] The session proved to be a turning point for the administration. It had proved itself capable in part because of Sister's Judith's skills as leader to draw on the strengths of other members of the administration. She attributed much of the success of the session to the fact that: "Members could see that we were doing our job, [and] we came together in a non-threatening manner." She added also that "we had a closing reconciliation liturgy that was very meaningful and brought together differing points of view, personalities and opinions. I guess we knew it was OK to differ and still be a community."[11]

No substantive changes were made. The administration's reports on proposals asking for the establishment of a house of prayer, a renewal center and a tertiaryship[12] program led to the conclusion that none of these ideas, worthy in themselves, could be implemented at that time. *Project Gift*, the program which had hoped to involve young women as volunteers working with the sisters in their ministries, proved to be a disappointment. Without a full-time director the program had no hope of success, and as it did not seem feasible to release a sister for the project, it was temporarily allowed to die.

During those summer days, the congregation came to realize that the tenor of the previous two years had been positive, the sisters had agreed to live with their differences, and the pragmatic Agnesian spirit had prevailed. The congregation was doing about as well as could be reasonably expected. No one was completely satisfied. No one expected to be.

NICARAGUA— A TORTURED NATION

One of the most troubling decisions confronting the administration was the position it should adopt during the Nicaraguan insurrection and civil war. Following the December 1972 earthquake in Managua, letters from Nicaragua to the motherhouse depicted the Somoza government growing desperate in its attempts to maintain its power. It was only by using the *Guardia* (National Guard) as an instrument of repression that the government was able to maintain itself. It was not long before almost every segment of society was appalled by the corruption of the regime, but it was the radical

Sandinistas who took the lead in fomenting resistance. Their small forays against the *Guardia* in the countryside led to the dramatic kidnappings of government officials at a Christmas party in 1974.[13] President Somoza responded to the embarrassment by the imposition of martial law on the country, intimidation, and, in some cases torture and murder.

The government's reaction strengthened support for the Sandinistas, who were training and converting *campesinos*[14] in the mountains near the mining towns of Rosita, Bonanza, and Siuna where Agnesians were working. Sisters and friars in Siuna became increasingly concerned as their campesino parishioners, suspected by the *Somocistas* of sympathy to the Sandinista cause, began to disappear. The evidence of abuses and torture, imprisonment and deaths in the rural mountain communities by the Somoza government was so compelling that sympathy for the Sandinista cause grew.[15] When more and more *campesinos* disappeared, the Capuchin friars took action.[16] The list of victims which they sent to the Speaker of the House of Representatives of the United States, Tip O'Neill, shocked the world.

During the next few years the Somoza government continued its violent campaign against a growing number of dissenters. In January 1978, the assassination of a leading critic of the Somoza regime and editor of Managua's independent newspaper, *La Prensa*, triggered a general strike and brought the moderates and Sandinistas together in the effort to oust Somoza. The Nicaraguan Episcopal Conference, led by Managua's Archbishop Obando y Bravo, called for the resignation of Somoza, political freedoms, and the establishment of a new economic order. Government atrocities had become so deplorable that the United States withdrew economic and military aid from the government for its violation of human rights. By February 1979 a national coalition supported by the banking and financial interests, industry and the Nicaraguan Chamber of Commerce with the FLN was established. In May the Sandinistas launched an offensive and attacked the Guardia throughout the country.

Early in the morning of May 28, 1979, the Sandinistas assaulted the *Guardia* barracks in Rosita and Bonanza. In a few minutes they killed seven National Guardsmen, injured two and captured four. Frightened, the people of a nearby barrio fled and took refuge in Santa Rosa School, which Sisters Josefina Galeano, Guadalupe Ortiz, and Marise Meis had opened to provide shelter. It was not long before government planes arrived and fired into the streets. Fearful that when the National Guard arrived, they would be tortured and killed, nearly 200 people, adolescents, teachers, mine workers, farmers, and catechists, set out early the next morning to join the Sandinistas in the bush. .

Escape was impossible. The group was too large; not everyone was physically able to make the journey; provisions were insufficient. Inevitably the National Guard picked up the trail of the group. On June 3 and 4 a number of youth and adults (the *Guardia* reported fifty-two or fifty-four) were tortured and killed at La Madriguera de la Rampla near Siuna. Some had been caught in ambush, others had turned themselves in, hoping to save their lives. The men and boys in the group were shot immediately, the women and girls were kept overnight and then killed. Later, when campesinos saw vultures flying, they found the bodies. The parish priest received permission to go to the site and cover the bodies. "Stories are told that the girls' bodies had the breasts cut off and pieces of broomsticks or small tree limbs were stuck up their vaginas."[17]

From 1973 until 1979, the sisters continued in their ministries, but agonized with the people as stories of massacres, homicides, even genocide increased.[18] Letters to Fond du Lac begged for prayers. Sister Bertha wrote: "Continue to pray for us; our national picture is more tense by the day. The mother of a political prisoner is asking for relief of torture for her son ... and she is on her 18th day of fast and there is no letup for them. Schools are on strike, people are disappearing, bank assaults day after day, munitions robbed.[19]

In Managua, some of the sisters actively helped the forces of liberation. During the last days, Sister Colette lived and worked at the seminary while she helped refugees, transported activists, and delivered messages for the revolutionaries. As support for Somoza evaporated, the guerillas were able to launch their final offensive.[20] It lasted seven weeks. On July 17, Anastasio Somoza Debayle, with the help and encouragement of the United States, left Nicaragua.[21] The Sandinistas marched into Managua and took it over without opposition. Two days later the party claimed victory.

The rejoicing felt throughout the country quickly turned to disenchantment in the province of Zelaya. The indigenous peoples, never involved in the country's politics, had little to do with the course of the revolution. Communication between the coasts had been even more difficult during the last months of the insurrection, but the people had accepted a Sandinista victory. On July 21, two days after victory in Managua, Sandinistas marched into Puerto Cabezas. The populace, Miskitos with a sprinkling of North Americans, gathered to welcome them. An angry *comandante* addressed them in Spanish, a language not all the Miskitos understood, "You have not shed your blood for the Revolution, therefore you will pay."[22] It was a moment as painful as it was shocking and the opening scene of a tragic episode in the history of the Miskito Indians.

It was not long before the sisters were of two minds about the revolution. A few, sympathetic to Sandinista ideology, saw little but good in the new government's program. Others were less hospitable to its Marxist orientation and were concerned about the erosion of liberties and the treatment of the Miskitos. But in November of 1979, Agnesians in Nicaragua gathered together for a week to respond to their own experiences of the revolution. The theme of their meeting was "Contemplation of God's Word through Our Lives as Women Religious." The women reflected upon four questions: What have I experienced personally with the revolution? Did I think God was in all of this? What have my experiences done to me? How have I dealt with what it has done to me inside? At the end of their assembly they constructed a *Credo*, that attempted to express their commonly held values: the special presence of God, especially among those in need of liberation, the need for the personal conversion of the missionary, prayer and contemplation as essential aspects of mission, the love which bonds the Agnesians, and participation in "the rising of a new dawn for the Nicaraguan woman."[23]

As a group, the participants committed themselves to the success of the revolution when they wrote, "It is the moment for giving our support to the historical process that is in the making, and that the christian [sic] principles that are present will triumph in the revolutionary process."[24] Some sisters claimed for themselves a role in the revolution in the statement: "We are co-responsible for the triumph of this liberating process."[25] The sentiments were those of the enthusiasts; the doubtful at the assembly remained silent.[26]

The Sandinistas, now known as the Sandinista National Liberation Front (FSLN), acted immediately. The FSLN established a highly centralized provisional government run by a Junta.[27] It took over the national army. It confiscated all the TV stations and placed them in the hands of the party. It created the Sandinista Defense Committees, "the eyes and ears of the revolution," on most blocks in the cities. In a short time the Sandinista flag was seen everywhere. School children were required to assemble each morning to sing revolutionary anthems and the school curriculum became a vehicle for Sandinista philosophy. The literacy campaign brought into the country hundreds of atheist Cubans who used the opportunity to teach basic reading skills to introduce the people to atheistic Marxism.[28] The Miskitos, a deeply religious people, were enraged and began demonstrating in response.[29]

In 1980 the state expropriated lands of some of the Indian communities. The Sandinistas, busy restricting private ownership on the Pacific Coast, would not accept the common ownership traditional to the Miskitos. The Miskitos demonstrated. The government was ruthless in retaliation, insisting that the Indians were being manipulated by counter-revolutionary forces. Mass arrests were followed by the murder of some Miskito leaders. All news from the Atlantic Coast was cut off and a special permit was required to travel in the region. In effect the area was being isolated from the rest of the country. The Sandinistas, apprehensive that the Reagan government would invade the country, claimed that the CIA was behind Miskito resistance.[30]

Fearful that the revolution would be compromised, the FSLN refused to allow political opposition. But their economic reforms were unsuccessful; there were problems in agriculture; they were in conflict with the churches. Although they had promised an unaligned foreign policy, they relied on the Soviet Union and Cuba for support. All these factors were exacerbated by politically inexperienced leadership. Deep divisions began to appear among the Nicaraguans as some began to long for the past while others remained captivated by the promise of a new and better world.[31]

Within the church there were disagreements between the "progressive" Catholics who saw in the bishops' guidelines a base for providing more humane social and political order, and the "revolutionary Christians" who had stated their position in a 1980 document that declared "preference and solidarity with the poor in Nicaragua today means to work under the guidance of the Sandinista front."[32] Perhaps anticipating such a conflict, in 1979 the Sandinistas had invited religious and government leaders to participate in a seminar that was designed to show "the compatibility of Christianity and Marxism." Sister Eileen Mahony, who attended the meeting, wrote that "two leaders from Cuba were present to inform us how their country is such an example. To say the least I was and am perplexed."[33]

The Sandinista government appointed priests to government office contrary to church policy,[34] favored liberation theologians and harassed the other clergy. It censored sermons and homilies, and continued its policy of oppressing the Miskito peoples. Archbishop Obando became convinced that the long-range goal of the Sandinistas was to destroy Christianity in favor of Marxism and that the party was using religion and the "Popular Church"[35] to support their cause.

The charge was denied by the Sandinistas. Although they were dedicated Marxists, they continued to maintain that they wanted to bring about a collaboration between Christianity and Marxism. As the disagreements became more heated, they accused the archbishop of "siding with the old Nicaraguan ruling class and a conservative hierarchical Pope against the legitimate striving of the peasantry."[36]

The administration in Fond du Lac was greatly concerned. Some issues centered on the role of the church leaders and the ways in which the sisters could support the people to whom they ministered. Others centered on the sisters' own political positions as they continued to live together through the post-war era.[37] In January 1981, Sister Lucina directed a retreat/workshop to help sisters understand the anatomy of revolutions in the abstract as well as to let them share their own experiences. The sisters, realizing that their attitudes regarding the revolution were shaped by their differing personal experiences, made efforts to transcend their own pain and to remain connected in community in spite of ideological differences.

PREPARING FOR THE CHAPTER OF 1981

The corporate renewal program had been a remote preparation for the 1981 chapter. In November 1979, the congregation had begun to prepare for the next general chapter. Sisters were reminded that a chapter was a church event, "a time of personal conversion, a time for new life in the church, a time for our community's change and growth."[38] Council members shifted their visitations away from "problem identification" to broad issues of renewal and, to facilitate the writing of the new constitutions mandated by Rome, encouraged community wide reflection of all areas of life to surface commonly held values, beliefs and norms. Instead of writing proposals, meetings were held in which the sisters joined in "clusters" for discussion. At the conclusion of the discussion, groups prioritized issues by assigning a weight to each item that had surfaced. The top five were then sent to the motherhouse. Synthesized, they formed the basis of a needs assessment which would be used to identify the key issues to serve as a basis for the chapter agenda.[39]

In an effort to achieve a more diverse group of delegates to the coming chapter, a complex voting procedure was used. After voting from a slate composed of the entire community, a group of eighty nominees comprised the next list, from which thirty delegates were chosen. Then a third ballot listed the final fifty names, from which ten were chosen to complete a list of forty names.[40] There was little discernible impact on the results.

When the report of the results of the *Needs Assessment Survey* was issued, the congregation discovered that internal issues caused the greatest concern: the quality of community life, retirement, formation, and aging. A segment of the community wanted more uniformity, particularly in the habit, in community prayer, and in common recreation; there was also a call to clarify the relationship of physical presence to community and to redefine the vows in contemporary terms. Others asked for a variety of liturgical and prayer choices in types of retreats. Even the definition of membership was debated, as the possibility of a totally temporary commitment to the congregation was raised. Some sisters suggested considering open placement to facilitate planning for a second career.[41]

However, some sisters, becoming restive with what they considered seemingly endless discussions of internal issues, were becoming more concerned with the efforts to build a human community (at global, national, regional, church levels). With a heightened awareness of issues of dignity of person, human rights and justice, they were beginning to increase their efforts at "simplicity of life" and a greater appreciation of the gifts of creation.

Social justice issues began to receive more attention—as did women's issues. There were requests that the role of women religious in the church be investigated as a means of furthering the total appropriation of women, lay and religious, in its ministerial and leadership aspects. Convinced that by responding positively to these signs, Christ's activity in the world can be seen, the sisters asked that the movement toward social justice be continued. However, others, disagreeing with the emerging feminist stance in the congregation, suggested that the congregation send letters to affirm the church's position on issues and that the sisters cultivate pride in being obedient to the pope/church even, they said, when there was disagreement.[42]

At the workshop in December 1980 delegates were introduced to the first outside facilitator for a congregational chapter, Raphael Domzall, a specialist in organizational development.[43] Each delegate could express her preference to serve on one of six committees: dynamics of community living, formation and renewal, government, lifelong apostolic commitment, ministry, or mission/charism. They were intrigued to find that one of their first tasks was to take the Myers-Briggs type indicator.[44] Committees were shaped so that members would represent a range of different styles of working in committees as well as different geographical regions and apostolates.

In spite of the numerous issues to be resolved, Sister Judith announced that the writing of the constitutions would begin: "After more than twelve years of renewal efforts, we are now able to distill from the gospels, from research and study into the spirit and aims of our founders, and from our own lived experience a set of statements concerning our identity, mission, charism, spirit, and commonly held values."[45] The *Identity and Mission* statement, when accepted, would serve as the primary unifier in the congregation as well as a guide to the committee responsible for drafting the new constitutions.

CHAPTER 1981 OPENS

When the delegates gathered in July of 1981, they were challenged by Sister Judith to consider how they walked with Jesus and how they expressed His message. She counseled them to take more time to pray, alone and together, to gather around His table, and to share Scripture. "In other words," she continued, "I am speaking ... of a *personal putting on of Christ*....[That] will enable us to read the signs of the times, to meet the challenges these signs offer without timidity, to devote every fiber of our being to His work in our world—and so to be *prophets in our times*."[46] She spoke of the need to take a critical look at life style, to ask if congregational ministries were meeting the real needs of the real world and to allow new forms of ministry to develop, particularly in the development of lay leadership. Asking if the human community was preserved and enriched because of the presence of the Sisters of St. Agnes, she charged sisters to reflect on probing questions: "1) Does our formation program prepare us for a continually renewed response to the God who constantly calls? 2) Can people see, by the way we live, and that our *vowed life in community* is of the essence of apostolic religious life? 3) Do our *local communities* provide challenges, support and encouragement? 4) Do our *community structures* promote and proclaim our mature religious womanhood? Do they foster and support our prophetic presence in the service of the kingdom? 5) Is CSA's response to our *mission in the kingdom* sufficiently meaningful to explain our presence and to challenge other women to join us and make a real contribution to that kingdom?"[47]

As preparation for chapter, a number of studies had been conducted which generated more discussion than had been originally anticipated. As an example, the struggle for unanimity on one paper, *The Spirituality of the Sisters of St. Agnes*, contained a number of refinements and clarifications which led to a concern that the writing of the constitutions might prove more difficult than anticipated. The decision was made that the material to be incorporated into the constitutions be processed through the community at large. The serious attention and corrections given to the papers eventuated in their becoming statements of substance which reflected the thinking of the delegate body instead of merely background papers for further discussion.

The chapter developed a statement of corporate thrust as an initial expression of the mission of the congregation, namely, that the congregation's fundamental commitment in ministry is to evangelization, especially on-going evangelization in the local church through teaching and healing and related ministries. In carrying out the corporate thrust, witness of life is acknowledged as primary in all ministries; justice demands a renewed and deepened commitment to those whose faith life or human dignity is threatened. The community pledged itself to manifest and to promote a reverence for the sacredness of every human being; a concern for a fair distribution of power and resources, and peaceful social action that enables people to participate in decisions affecting their lives. The community recognized its own need to be evangelized and called one another to develop a critical conscience. Finally, it recognized the universal call of every baptized Christian to spread the Good News, and pledged to cooperate with the laity in their emerging role of co-ministering with the congregation.[48]

The community life committee made two major proposals: the first, that a plan be initiated to improve communication at the local level and the second, that a consistent practice of shared Scripture be established at the local level. Both were accepted.

The committee also developed a list of congregational priorities drawn from church documents pertinent to religious, CSA constitutions, and lived experience, making careful distinctions between values of primary importance, those of importance but which may be adapted to local circumstances, and those that may be left to the discretion of the individual sister. Of primary importance was the theology of the vows, spirituality, and the congregation's corporate thrust; of importance but may be adapted, were the celebration of the Eucharist and Reconciliation, daily office and prayer, the local community, and the ministries of the congregation. Left to the discretion of the individual sister, assuming that she operate within the framework of the constitutions, are her attitudes and ideas, personal expressions of the vows, style of personal prayer, choice of recreation, and religious garb.

Hours of discussion led by the identity and mission committee culminated in a key statement: "As members of the congregation of the Sisters of St. Agnes, we profess to be an apostolic religious institute of women, called by God in the power of the Spirit, to share in

Jesus' mission of revealing the Father's love, through a vowed life in community and joyful service to His people. We are a pontifical congregation within the Roman Catholic Church."[49]

Another important directional statement was the declaration that the "fundamental commitment in ministry is to evangelization, especially on-going evangelization in the local church through teaching and healing and related ministries." Witness of life, commitment to justice, and collaboration with the laity were becoming increasingly paramount values. The congregation affirmed its mission as extending beyond any one culture or nationality, leaving sisters "free to serve in diverse geographic areas, as changing needs indicate and our talents and resources allow."[50]

The chapter also directed that a committee be formed to study the meaning and possibility of alternate forms of membership within the congregation; that a sister be appointed to serve on the formation committee in a consultative and educative role in regard to CSA needs on aging; that a consistent practice of shared scripture be established; and that the definition of simple life style include a consciousness of the needs of others and a "willingness to share ourselves and our facilities, time, and prayer."[51]

A group of nine sisters had proposed that the congregation set up a mission house in which radical gospel poverty would be lived for an experimental period of three years. After a study was made, it was discovered that only two members were willing to participate. The others who expressed an interest discovered, on further consideration, that such a radical life style could not be lived without interfering with their present ministries. The project was dropped.

There was the final disposition of the subject of the veil: "that the religious garb is simple, modest, and appropriate for religious women today. The veil is optional."[52]

Along with the subject of attire, the most controversial issue on the agenda was the structure of congregational governance. A number of community members had always been strongly opposed to the new government. A letter sent to the delegates was a typical expression of their feelings: "The Sisters do not object to decentralization but they do object to the form of decentralization of our community …. [They] regret the closing of a number of missions. Sisters, still well-able to teach, were permitted to leave the classroom, and in some instances, take on an apostolate for which they were not sufficiently prepared .... [Furthermore,] there would not be a need for apostolic councilors if the general councilors would work exclusively for the community as they are chosen to do, and not take on another apostolate."[53]

Unquestionably there had been difficulties and they were increasing. From the beginning there were sisters who missed the old and familiar structures. Decentralization had taken from the generalate its relationship to individual sisters. More importantly, in the decade following the acceptance of the government, the community was undergoing the triple trauma of fewer vocations, more sisters leaving, and an aging population, factors leading to the necessity of leaving historical commitments. The apostolic counselors, who were dealing well with the proliferating problems, were not infrequently seen as the cause of the difficulties.

During the 1977 chapter the subject of governance had been raised, but as reports from the commissions that year indicated that there were no problems that could not be worked out, the preponderance of delegates had voted only to modify the government. However, the ad hoc government committee that was appointed took the major step of discarding government's apostolic orientation. During the months before the chapter, members of the committee had presented the alternative model to the congregation.

The proposed model divided the congregation according to geographic regions, defining the coordinator as an intermediate superior with delegated authority. The local community would be the basic unit in the congregation. A perpetually professed sister with direct personal authority would be local coordinator; otherwise, the regional coordinator would serve in that capacity. Her concerns would be the welfare of the sisters in the region and the promotion of the congregation's mission and effectiveness in the church in her region. The regional coordinator would be a member of an interregional board with no decision-making authority.[54] Members of the local community would share in responsibility and decision-making in their local house.[55] Discussions on the chapter floor were tense. As some delegates seemed to find difficulty in separating the structure and roles from personalities, on the morning of July 11 it was proposed that the government be discussed in executive session without the presence of the apostolic councilors. The proposal passed and the discussion took place although a number of the delegates were outraged at the exclusion of members of the chapter.[56]

As the model presented by the government committee was accepted, although not unanimously, the 1981 chapter did restructure the government.[57] The new government structure is described in the 1985 *Constitutions and Directives* as "a source of unity, [which] enables us to carry out the one mission of Christ according to the needs of the church, the charism of the congregation and each one's personal gifts .... The principles of subsidiarity and decentralization and a commitment to shared responsibility support the structures that channel each sister's initiative, her responsible cooperation, and her participation in decisions affecting her own life, the life of the local community, and that of the total congregation."[58]

Two changes were made in terminology. The title "superior general" became "general superior" and the "generalate" became the "general council." The number of ex-officio delegates to chapter was reduced to four, the major superior and her council. It was apparent that the majority of the congregation favored the concept of shared leadership, but it was determined that if any house wished to experiment, two-thirds of the sisters must agree.

The congregation was now divided into geographic regions rather than by apostolates. The apostolic councilor was elected by members of her apostolate; the regional coordinator was appointed by the major superior from nominations of the total community. The executive board was abolished. Emphasis shifted from the apostolate to the welfare of the sisters. Policy development was at the commission level while the interregional board was responsible for policy implementation. Membership on commissions assisting the apostolic councilor was elected; four members could be appointed on the regional committees.[59]

Did anything positive emerge from the experiment with apostolic decentralization? Among the benefits that might be listed include the fact that the congregation, in applying the principles of decentralization and subsidiarity, built upon the reality of the sisters' lives at that time. The congregation took a giant step toward consideration of the individual in professional and personal matters. Sisters felt invested in the decisions that were made in their apostolate. Strong leadership emerged from the ranks of the elementary teachers who, despite their overwhelming numbers, had not emerged previously as congregational leaders. One former apostolic councilor commented that "because of apostolic decentralized government during that time, we were able to direct and sustain a viable elementary education apostolate in true partnership with the laity."[60] Sisters in Nicaragua appreciated the fact that the new government structure had facilitated their growth toward more autonomy.

With the exception of Sister Jean Perry, who had withdrawn her name from consideration, and Sister Vianney Saller who replaced her, the council remained the same. Six regional coordinators, whose first charge was the welfare of the sisters in their geographic region, were appointed.[61] The 1981 election affirmed the congregation's direction and the revision of the government structure removed some areas of concern for the general council. As the way was now cleared for the writing of the constitution, it was possible to pay increased attention to the sponsored ministries, the continuation of long-range planning, and the development of the vocation ministry along with the continued efforts at spiritual renewal.

NICARAGUA IN A TIME OF WAR

The victory of the Sandinistas had not meant the end of troubles for Nicaragua and the missionaries. It had been difficult enough for Americans to be in a country during a revolution. It became more difficult as the relationship of the Sandinista government with the United States began deteriorating. During the first two years of the revolution, President Jimmy Carter had been sympathetic to the aspirations of the new government but had eventually suspended economic aid because of Sandinista involvement with Salvadoran guerillas. Meanwhile the inevitable counter-revolution had begun. By 1981, a small group of the disaffected, including members of the old National Guard, began to launch guerrilla operations from Honduras. That same year the Reagan administration, with money from the sale of arms to Iran, covertly began to supply aid to the Contras[62] despite a ban by Congress on such aid. By the spring of 1982 the Contras were receiving aid from the United States.

When Sister Eileen Mahony returned to Waspam after her leave in August 1981, she found that she had entered an area that was becoming an armed camp. The Atlantic coast was cut off from the rest of the country. The Sandinistas were responding to the Miskito peoples' resistance to both its agricultural policies and its attacks on religion by imprisoning, torturing, and murdering dissidents.[63] When Miskitos began to cross the Río Coco into Honduras either to join the Contras or for refuge, government retaliation escalated.

By December 1981, war had broken out on the upper Río Coco. Nevertheless the sisters remained. Soldiers were everywhere and as the civil war intensified, the sisters endured many of their anti-gringo taunts as well as their frequent lewd comments. Sister Eileen discovered that she was a particular threat to the Sandinistas because she could speak Miskito while the Sandinistas, who were from the Pacific Coast, could not. Everywhere she went there was a soldier watching her; at night guns were kept trained on her bedroom. The constant surveillance was almost unbearable. Although the sisters were doing what they could to convince the Sandinistas they were not involved in politics, they were in a perilous position and they knew it.[64]

Whatever their ministries or their political convictions, the sisters suffered with the people. Although they tried not to take sides, they could not fail to feel pressured. Sister Maureen Courtney wrote, "Sometimes I feel so 'pulled' to one side or the other that I begin wondering if it's possible to remain open to both. I think there's a real tendency in human nature to want to categorize and we'd all be 'happy' if we could get each other into little boxes with labels on them .... I must admit, too, it was very hard for me at times at the motherhouse to see how much polarization has taken place regarding Nicaragua that each of us must be either 100% Sandinista or 100% anti-Sandinista. The reality is so much more complex. And I believe we must be faithful—not to one political group or the other, but to the gospel, and that gospel can lead us to see good and bad in both extremes."[65] In spite of escalating tensions, sisters remained, praying that all would be well for them and the country as well as the people whom they had grown to love.

In such turbulent times the sisters could not remain untouched. Sister Bertha Bumann was amazed to be called before the papal nuncio and accused of being a CIA agent.[66] Sister Juana de la Cruz Guzmán was upset when she was called to the Nicaraguan State Office and questioned about the congregation.[67] It was the sisters in Puerto Cabezas, however, who experienced the most public difficulties. The town was important as a military headquarters and the convent, which overlooked the Caribbean Sea, was one of its finest buildings. When one of the *comandantes* toured the area, he remarked at a public meeting that he would take over the convent for military use. He was immediately challenged by Sister Kenneth Struckhoff who asserted that a take-over was impossible because the convent was open and belonged to the people.[68] The Sandinistas countered: "But some day it will be ours." The interchange was not unnoticed and was commented on in the press. The *comandante* was incensed, but as Sister Kenneth was widely respected in the area there was little he could do.

Even so, the community was not prepared for the events of January 12, 1982. That morning soldiers arrived at the convent in Puerto Cabezas and informed Sisters Kenneth, Dolores Taddy and Rose Kowalski that they were to leave immediately for Managua. They spent most of the day at the Puerto Cabezas airstrip where they found two Capuchin friars also forced to leave and a few Nicaraguan prisoners. Armed Sandinista soldiers guarded them. After a grueling day, during which they were offered no food, rest breaks, or even information, the sisters were taken to the Managua Immigration Office. Eventually they were told that their papers were not in order, that they were in Nicaragua illegally and that they must "abandon" the country within twenty-four hours. When the American consul was informed, she advised the sisters not to challenge the decision. "I've been in several Nicaraguan prisons," she said.[69]

Early the next morning the sisters left for the airport. Because foreigners could not use Nicaraguan money to buy plane tickets, the sisters in Managua had been trying to find enough American money to buy tickets for them to get them out of the country as quickly as possible. Through the kindness of airline personnel, they were able to get seats on a plane to Miami, which was as far as their money would take them. When later that morning government officials arrived at the convent looking for them, they had already left the country. In an interview with the press, the Minister of the Interior, Tomás Borge, charged that the deported religious were "uncooperative and a threat to the revolution."[70]

Why were the sisters and friars expelled? Although the government was never specific about the reasons, it was obvious that the religious were determined to keep the spiritual life of the people alive. Furthermore, it seems probable that the belief of many of the townspeople that the government deported the North Americans so that the convent could be taken over was correct. The plan was thwarted, however, as Nicaraguan nationals, Sister Nancy Chow and a friend of the sisters, Celia Chow, remained there until Bishop Salvador Schlaefer arrived to take up residence there. Because the property belonged to the Catholic vicariate and the building was never unoccupied, the government did not dare attempt to expropriate it.

When the sisters in Rosita heard the news of the expulsion, they went immediately to Puerto Cabezas to see how they could help. The sisters in Waspam, because their radio had been confiscated, did not hear about the deportation until five or six days later. The following day, while they were eating breakfast, the pro-Sandinista acting pastor told them to leave immediately for Puerto Cabezas. They had time to snatch up only a few personal effects before they were evicted. Before they left, Sister Raymond entrusted the keys of the clinic to Brigida Chow de Zuñiga, the clinic receptionist. When the Sandinistas demanded the keys from her, Brigida told them they would have to kill her first. She held firm until she could return the keys to the rightful owner.[71]

When the nervous sisters were allowed to return to Waspam a few days later, they were met by the sight of soldiers jumping out of the convent windows as they fled in panic at the sisters' unexpected arrival. The Sandinistas had expected them to be deported so they could take over the convent. The sisters were left to dispose of the cigarette ashes, empty beer cans, and the soldiers' dirty clothes. Although the incident had its amusing aspects, it took an immense amount of faith and courage to live and work in such a volatile situation.

Meanwhile, Sister Judith flew to Managua where, from February 2-8, 1982, she met with the sisters.[72] There was no thought of withdrawing the sisters from the country. At the same time, it was essential that the missionaries know that, whatever their political views, they were supported by each other and by the congregation. It was also important that no sister feel pressured to remain in such a dangerous situation. During those days of reflection, they rested, prayed, and recreated together. They spent hours listening to each

others' stories and feelings. Each woman was given the opportunity
to make a choice; she could remain or she could leave. Together
they made the personnel assignments for the next few months.
Although many sisters felt their very lives were on the line, almost
every one felt called to remain. When Sister Judith concluded the
gathering by singing "Be Not Afraid," there was such power in the
hymn and the prayers that the meeting remains one of the most frequently mentioned events by the participants in that emotion-filled
decade.

Sister Judith also made attempts to talk to government officials.
Subjected to classic government stonewalling, she found it impossible to obtain permission from the government either to travel to the
Atlantic Coast or to talk to the FSLN leader, Daniel Ortega. After
the bureaucrats spent two days going through her papers and possessions, it became plain that neither request would be granted. But
when she returned to the United States, she left the sisters with a
new sense of dedication and mission.

The letter Sister Judith wrote to the community on her return to
the United States stated the congregation's position: "And so, in conclusion, I would like to reflect *out loud* on what all this says to us now,
in our Church of today. We could be tempted to get a big press out
of our situation in Nicaragua at this time, for we are a strong missionary force among the very poor in that country. However, we
believe that sensationalizing only puts us in a position to be used by
international propaganda machinery, thus feeding the rationale for
more violence and hatred. Our course is rather to stand for the
sacred dignity of every human being. This shows itself:

-in our ministries among the poor in Nicaragua
-in our public proclamations there on the rights related to
    faith and dignity
-in our tenacious efforts to dialogue with Nicaraguan officials
-in our encouragement of U.S. leaders to permit self-
    determination for Central America
-in our urgent plea for a diplomacy that will end violence and
    promote justice and human dignity
-we believe that the Gospel calls us to this, and that this is *our*
    way of evangelizing by the congregation today."[73]

Meanwhile, more Miskitos along the Río Coco had begun flee-
ing to Honduras. Sister Eileen, working in the clinic in Waspam,
found more Miskitos were coming in "to have their blood pressure
taken" and then whispering a message she should deliver to their
families after they had left for Honduras. Those defections, together with the constant defiance and insurrections, made the government determined to put an end to its difficulties with the Miskitos.
Beginning on January 14, 1982, the Sandinistas began a campaign
to forcibly relocate over forty-two villages along the river in five
resettlement camps.[74] These camps, surrounded by the jungle, were
designed to give the government free fire zones and deny the
Contras local support and intelligence.

Day after day the Sandinistas began dropping bombs on the Río
Coco to prevent the people from crossing to Honduras. When they
realized that the Sandinistas intended to force the people to evacu-
ate the villages along the Río Coco, about half of the Río Coco
population fled to Honduras, but the sisters in Waspam, after prayer
and discussion, made plans to stay with the people as long as the
town existed. Their vehicles were confiscated; they had no means of
communication with the outside world; the Sandinista government
believed an invasion by the United States was imminent, and yet the
sisters remained. They did, however, arrange for a truck to be sent
from Puerto Cabezas in order to save as much from the mission as
they could, as they began to strategize on where and how to serve
the people after the town was destroyed.

The day finally came when the military reached Waspam. The
sisters watched as the people saw their homes, churches, crops, and
livestock destroyed and agonized at the sounds of the planes and
gunfire and the wails of mothers and children forcibly separated
from each other. Each sister retained her own ineradicable pictures
of the scene. For Sister Raymond the memory of the baby chicks
and turkeys, little puppies and cats, and the small bundles of clothes
that the refugees from upriver were forced to leave behind in the
classrooms of the school remained especially wrenching.[75] Most
painful to Sister Eileen is the memory of the plight of a mother and
her newborn child. The woman had just given birth when the soldiers refused to allow her to be cared for in the clinic and forced her
into the truck. There was no way to help the new mother. Forced to
see the woman torn from her newborn baby, pushed into one truck,

the child handed over to a woman in military uniform, Sister Eileen could no longer contain her tears. A female soldier turned and attacked her: "How dare you cry like that—making it worse than it is?"[76] Approximately 8,500 Miskito Indians were forced to march from eleven to fifteen days on their own "trail of tears" to the resettlement camps.

The March 1983 visit of Pope John Paul II to Nicaragua publicized the situation to the world. The FSLN intervened in every aspect of the visit. They disrupted the ceremonies at the public Mass by chanting, shouting, and singing the Sandinista party anthem at its conclusion. The probability of unfavorable criticism from the rest of the world was so great that the Sandinistas confiscated the tapes of the ABC crew which had filmed its proceedings.[77] Reactions were mixed among the sisters who attended. A few considered disturbances as an unfortunate, but unavoidable part of the revolutionary process; others were shocked and hurt by the disrespect and insolence of the Sandinistas and their sympathizers.

On March 29, 1983, in spite of the guerrilla activity along the Río Coco, Sisters Raymond, Patricia Hayes, and Jomarie Zielke, accompanied by a priest and deacon, arrived at the village of Santa Clara, to help with Holy Week services. The Sandinistas were lodged at the school several hundred feet behind the house next to the church where the sisters were to sleep. At 4:00 a.m. the Wednesday of Holy Week, they were awakened by the sound of bullets tearing through the wooden house they had been given for the night. The Contras had crossed the Río Coco from Honduras, planning to lead a group of Miskitos across the river to Honduras. They attacked the *cuartel* to distract the Sandinistas from rescue operations. The sisters were directly in the line of fire. For three hours they lay on the floor praying the *Memorare* as the bullets sped over their heads. When the attack was over, they found bullet holes in their clothes and blankets. A mortar had hit the side of their house and at least fourteen Sandinista soldiers lay dead.

Sisters Patricia and Jomarie, both nurses, assisted by Sister Raymond, took care of the seriously wounded survivors. Then they were separated and evacuated to the army headquarters. Until they found each other that night they lived in terror, both for themselves and for each other. Finally, on Holy Saturday they were given permission to leave and were able to find someone with an "old, old truck" to drive them back to Puerto Cabezas.[78] By eight o'clock that night, they reached the parish church to find the people, believing the sisters had been killed, holding a vigil for them. Later, when Sister Patricia found that plans for the attack had been known by the deacon as well as others in the village, she was left with a profound sense of betrayal.[79]

By this time a few North American sisters knew that they could not "adapt to the Sandinista process" and returned to the United States.[80] Those that remained maintained a surprising equilibrium. Their fortitude came from their vocation and the strong sense of identity with the church,[81] their love of community and the great strength they received from the people with whom they worked.[82] Although they were always careful for fear that any indiscretion might endanger the Nicaraguan sisters or their families, they believed that their place was with the people. Sister Marise Meis, for example, served on a Peace Commission for the municipality of Rosita. Other sisters helped where they could to further peace efforts.[83]

None of the sisters felt that she could do enough, prompting Bishop Salvador to write a few words of encouragement: "It is true that you can't do all that you would like to do—but whatever you do, the people feel supported in their faith, in their suffering and in sharing their lives with persons consecrated to God and the Church … It is not right to be precipitate, but neither is it good to abandon bravery well lived. Onward!"[84]

The plight of the Miskitos in the camps was constantly in the minds of the sisters in the area. Initially, they and the other North Americans in the region, including the Bishop, were not allowed entry, although international teams of observers were welcomed. Finally, Sister Maureen Courtney and two friars, tired of waiting for permission, managed to get on the trucks going into the camps in order to see the situation for themselves. They found the interned living in want, in shelters that were mainly thatched lean-tos or shiny blue plastic tents. When they arrived, the people wept with joy to see them.[85]

PLANNING IN UNCERTAIN TIMES

The increasing number of elderly sisters made careful planning for the future crucial. In order to plan for the future, the congregation engaged a professional firm to do an actuarial study which projected the future number of members as well as future income and expenses. Throughout the years, although contributed services have been the major form of the congregation's contribution to the poor, the church, and society in general, the congregation has also taken seriously the obligation to share its resources. Its history of giving showed that its donations had been in four categories: missionaries and organizations that helped the poor; organizations that promoted social justice; organizations that promoted the arts, education, and religious orders in need; and a sizable percentage to "other" such as the Catholic Communications Campaign. In an effort to direct the congregation's contributions to charity in keeping with its documents and to involve more members in identifying persons who had needs, in January 1983 the board of directors established the ACTS (Agnesian Caring Through Sharing) program. ACTS had four components: donations,[86] grants,[87] alternative investments,[88] and support of CSA ministries in disadvantaged areas.[89]

Much thought was also given to assuring the continuing financial stability of the congregation. With fewer sisters in full-time positions each year, there was an added urgency in balancing the books. In 1982 a financial advisory committee was established, and on October 1, that same year, central financing was begun in order to provide a uniform accounting method throughout the community and give a total picture of CSA finances. In 1983 the decision was made to collect Social Security benefits at sixty-two rather than sixty-five. That same year a financial planner prepared a twenty-year projection.

In 1982 a Long Range Planning committee was established to identify issues in the community that could be grappled with on an on-going basis, instead of being guided and governed by a possible change of personnel every four years. The Committee's *Long Range Planning Report of 1984* had been designed to surface the areas and issues that demanded attention for critical study and planning.[90] The issues and concerns researched were community living, finances, formation, information systems, ministry-personnel, pre-retirement and retirement, role of women religious in the church, sponsorship, vocation.[91] The process also identified the many ambiguities that had rapidly become interwoven in the daily life of many, if not most, of the active religious. The greater part of the report focused on the increasingly significant issue of community living.

A questionnaire had been distributed to all members living in North America. It contained ten questions developed to ascertain present attitudes and values about local community living. There were 570 questionnaires distributed, 450 sisters responded. At that time eighty-six sisters lived in groups of over twenty; eighty-eight sisters lived in groups of ten to twenty ; 168 lived in groups of five to ten; eighty-six sisters lived with less than five; and twenty lived alone. Of the 413 sisters who responded to that question, 62 percent preferred to live in groups of five to ten; 26 percent preferred to live in groups of over ten; and 12 percent preferred to live in smaller groups or alone. Age made little difference in the responses.

Sisters who wanted larger groups saw such possibilities for a more stimulating community, a greater opportunity for at least one meaningful relationship, a greater opportunity for and sharing spirituality, less chance of loneliness and depression, and more people to share responsibilities. Those who preferred to live in a smaller group saw opportunities for greater closeness in community.

"Do sisters foresee that because of diversified ministry commitments and shortage of numbers, more sisters would have to live alone?" An increase in the number was expected by 39 percent of the sisters; 26 percent felt that there would be no increase in that number; and 35 percent made no prediction. The second part of the question asked if increasing numbers of sisters alone would have an impact on the value of community living. Almost three-quarters of the sisters felt that it would, both positively and negatively. Among positive outcomes identified: living alone would deepen appreciation for one another when they did get together; that although there would be a change in the concept of community living, it was not necessarily the value of community as such. Those who saw negative outcomes worried about the economic impact; they saw a weakening in communal values such as sharing Scripture, prayer, ideals, ideas, faith, community, and mission responsibilities. Only 11 percent believed that an increasing number of sisters living alone would not have an impact on the value that CSA places on community living.

The ambiguity of the community regarding sisters living alone was apparent in the statements sisters made about community living. Although the majority were aware of the reality that the fast pace of life would continue to result in a lack of energy in building quality community living, it was clear that living in community was expected, although some exceptions would always occur. Most sisters preferred living in larger groups, but realized that local communities would be smaller in size. They predicted more intercommunity living arrangements; there would be more diverse ministries which would cause continued changes in local community life; the highly mobile life sisters were living would cause strain in developing cohesive local communities and more sisters will live alone due to ministry needs. They believed that some local communities would become more open and inclusive of the laity for mutual support and growth. Other statements include the prediction that the community would become more creative in prayer styles because of common Scripture/Faith sharing experiences. Increased awareness of peace and justice issues would continue to be an incentive for more counter-culture witnessing even though the congregation is ambivalent— in part because of the need to care for its elderly members.[92]

From 1969, the community had been experimenting with the formation program. With religious life in a state of transition, or, as it seemed to some, chaos, one of the most critical areas in the congregation was its formation program. The committee on formation accomplished a critical task by developing a coherent overall philosophy in programs beginning with vocation education/promotion through initial formation, affiliate,[93] pre-novitiate,[94] novitiate,[95] temporary vow,[96] on-going, pre-retirement and retirement. A full-time director of vocation promotion was appointed and a formation manual prepared. There was a change in the pre-novitiate program, when candidates were given the experience of living on various missions. In 1984-1985, three candidates lived together with the community and their director at St. Joseph's convent in Fond du Lac. During those years there was an average of three novices each year. Three sisters made final vows during this period. A role description was developed for a consultant on aging and more importance was attached to continuing formation and the needs of the aging.

Elderly sisters were encouraged to see the value of a "ministry of presence" as well as of service. Interim houses for sisters in "pre-retirement" were opened.[97]

With all the progress made, and some issues, such as the habit, governance, and even, to some degree, the acceptance of diversity resolved, others were beginning to challenge any effort at solution. Should sisters choose ministry over community life? Should they live alone, or live with community members and drive to their place of ministry? Some issues would be resolved simply by continuing to provide room for the community to experiment in such matters as group government, experimenting with differing styles of prayer, the making of vows or promises, establishing a house of prayer, or a house devoted to practicing radical poverty.

SPONSORSHIP AND CORPORATE MINISTRIES

The mandate of Vatican Council II for a true collaboration with the laity in Christian ministry asked that the congregation examine its relationship to its sponsored ministries. By 1981 the changes brought about by declining membership and individual choices in ministry had left religious institutes grappling with the administration of their institutions. Some congregations had turned over their institutions to lay boards and quickly lost control; a few congregations had come to the conclusion that the sisters should own nothing and had divested themselves of their properties. The majority spent countless hours creating viable new structures designed to ensure the maintenance of Catholic identity and the congregational mission. It was a task involving canon law, civil law, business acumen, and sensitivity to the mission of the congregation as well as the institutions themselves.

The congregation envisioned its mission as linked with the mission of Jesus Christ by providing a base from which to advocate societal changes which would help bring about a right relationship between God and the people of God. Sponsorship maximizes collaboration with the laity in the teaching and healing ministries. Through sponsorship "the congregation is publicly identified with these incorporated apostolates, providing governance direction to these institutions, and protecting the resources of each institution for the mission of the Church."[98] The general council, in a needs assessment survey, urged that sponsorship be affirmed as a congregational ministry, asking that qualified members be recruited to become actively involved at the corporate and governance levels.[99] The restructuring and clarifying of the congregation's relationships with its institutions would prove to be one of the most important accomplishments of the decade.

In July of 1982, Sister Mary Mollison was appointed the first corporate director of the congregation. Sisters employed in community-sponsored institutions no longer comprised the corporate membership. Corporate membership of the institutions was changed to the major superior, the councilors, and three other members of the community chosen by the general council. That same year a corporate structure known as Hazotte Ministries, Inc. was established as a non-profit corporation to provide health care and educational programs and services in non-institutional settings. Increasing government regulations and escalating competition among health care providers led to an on-going study to consider the possibility of collaborative and joint sponsorship relationships with other Catholic health care institutions.[100]

By 1979 it was clear that the breach between Dr. Hanlon and the majority of the Marian faculty could not be mended. Although he had been successful in re-engaging the faculty in dialogues on the nature, philosophy and goals of education, his educational theories were proving impossible to implement, at least with the resources available at the college. His tenure ended at Marian College that year.

The college, like many other small Catholic colleges, was suffering through difficult years for other reasons as well. In the 1970s, the number of "traditional age" college students declined as did the number of sister faculty members. Although the enrollment in 1978 was fairly stable, the majority of students were nurses and there had been little effort to diversify the student body or to inaugurate new programs. In 1979, circumstances forced the decision to establish the business program which had been advocated for years as well as a psychology major. An ROTC program was also inaugurated—in spite of intense opposition by a few faculty members.[101]

The nursing division began to plan for a baccalaureate completion program for registered nurses who were seeking the Bachelor of Science degrees in nursing. In spite of opposition on the part of faculty members who would have preferred a fine arts center, the board chose to build a gymnasium in the hope of attracting more male students. During this period enrollment rose slightly to 525, stabilized, but declined at the beginning of 1984 and suffered a precipitous drop to 325 in 1985. One dormitory stood empty. The college was in such great need of funds to continue, that the recently-erected Greenbrier Apartments were sold. The CSA Chronicles noted that: "Some reasons given are the smaller number of college-age men and women, as well as reduced federal funding for college students."[102]

In 1985, the board of directors at Marian College began a formal long-range planning process as threatening trends in Catholic higher education indicated both a further decline in enrollment and substantial increases in tuition.[103]

In October 1979, the congregation began the long process, which eventually resulted in the acquisition of the Waupun Memorial Hospital in Waupun, Wisconsin, a little over twenty miles from Fond du Lac. The School Sisters of St. Francis, who owned and operated the one-hundred bed facility, had contacted several religious orders as potential buyers. The Franciscans, who had only one acute care facility, needed money for retirement but also wished the mission of the church to continue in the area.[104] The Agnesians saw in the acquisition of the hospital an opportunity to serve and to strengthen St. Agnes Hospital.

After many hours of consultations and discussions, the corporate board of the congregation made an offer which was rejected by the Franciscans. However, the community promised to keep the Agnesians informed if they began negotiations with another religious congregation. Meanwhile the hospital proceeded with a renovation project which was to cost 3.9 million dollars.[105] Several years later negotiations were reopened. Representatives from the two boards and administration and sponsors met several times and drew up an action plan for collaboration. The representatives agreed to investigate ways the two institutions could collaborate and avoid duplication of services.[106]

On August 5, 1980, the hospice program was introduced into Fond du Lac. The modern hospice movement had begun with the establishment of St. Christopher's Hospice in Sydenham, England in 1967. The movement, designed to provide supportive and loving care to people who were preparing to die in their family settings, spread quickly to the United States. Around 1977 Frank Murphy, consultant for the hospitals sponsored by the congregation, strongly recommended that St. Agnes hospital become involved in this ministry. Three nurses, Sister Anne Jude Van Lanen, Sister Mary Agreda Touchett, and Mrs. Peg Cerny, friends for many years, became interested. With a grant from the Fond du Lac Visiting Nurses Association, the two sisters studied the hospice program in England.

In January of 1978 the hospital hosted a broad-based, area-wide and ecumenical informational meeting. A committee was established to assist in the needs assessment and to gain and provide public support. Lack of money may have been the greatest obstacle but it was not the only one. A few physicians and local citizens saw hospice as a form of euthanasia while still other medical professionals envisioned it as interfering with their medical and professional services. But the congregation and key members of the St. Agnes Hospital Board provided the impetus to continue and the state approved the program on June 10, 1980.[107]

The first year, from August 1980 to August 1981, there were sixty-seven admissions into the program. A team was trained to meet the emotional and physical needs of patients with a limited life expectancy. Comprehensive services were offered to anyone who needed assistance to live at home. More than thirty physicians were involved and seventy volunteers made hundreds of home visits. Donations of money to the program amounted to $22,157.00. The success of the program was assured and similar programs were soon initiated at both St. Anthony Hospital in Hays, Kansas, and St. Clare Hospital in Monroe, Wisconsin.[108]

OTHER MINISTRIES

The number of Catholic schools in the nation continued to decline. With fewer sisters, the replacement of sisters by lay principals and teachers continued throughout the period. It became the policy of the community to withdraw first from stable parishes with strong Catholic leadership. In 1981, the congregation participated in the consolidation of Catholic Girls High School with Thomas More Preparatory School the Catholic boys' high school, in Hays, Kansas.

On January 9, 1985, Sister Judith met with Archbishop Rembert Weakland and signed papers making St. Mary's Springs High School the sole responsibility of the Archdiocese of Milwaukee,[109] although the congregation could exercise the option of regaining the property should it cease to be a Catholic high school.

The plan for a model school system for Fond du Lac did not progress as the educators had hoped. In 1978, the *Chronicles* reported that the "usual problems of communication among the president, the faculties and the board of directors continue." A revision of the bylaws of the consortium was made in order to reduce the number of board members from forty-two to twenty-two. The following year, the board asked for the resignation of Dr. Hanlon. After his resignation the consortium board unanimously adopted a resolution: "The consortium will continue to exist for the purpose of conducting a unified Catholic school system in the City of Fond du Lac and the Village of North Fond du Lac."[110] Marian College voted to withdraw from the consortium.

Throughout the period of experimentation probably the greatest problem was lack of money. There had never been enough money to hire a professional staff. Furthermore, Dr. Hanlon's theoretical approach combined with his liberal use of Greek and Latin terms in explaining his ideas insured that they would remain unintelligible to all but the most dedicated. However, Dr. Hanlon's theories have had a positive impact on many successful teachers throughout their careers.[111]

Within a short time, the shortage of personnel dictated that decisions be made not to replace principals in Brother Dutton School, Beloit, Wisconsin; St. Nicholas, Evanston, Illinois; Immaculate Conception, Elmhurst, Illinois; St. Joseph, Rosemount, Minnesota, and St. Mary, Eden, Wisconsin. The principal of Sacred Heart School in Fond du Lac was named for one year only and all of the teaching sisters were withdrawn from St. Peter Claver, Sheboygan.

Unity House, founded in 1983, was designed to be a haven for women in an inner-city neighborhood in Chicago that had been almost destroyed by poverty and violence. It would also provide a residence/ hospitality center for lay and religious serving the poor in the neighborhood as well as a site for those seeking to experience cross-cultural immersion. The concept grew out of the experiences of Sisters Judith Vander Grinten and Sharon Baudry while studying at the Chicago Theological Union[112] and working with Shalom Ministries. A condemned twenty-one bedroom house was purchased for $13,500. A great deal of work had to be done to make the house habitable, but the sisters and volunteers through hard work made the house welcoming. Members of the house provided ecumenical prayer gatherings, a clothing pantry, tutoring, assistance for pregnant teens, and a safe place where women were always welcome.[113]

REVIEWING THE PAST AND PREPARING FOR THE FUTURE

Statistics compiled in 1984 showed that approximately 25 percent of the sisters were still engaged in education on some level; 7 percent in health care services; 10 percent in parish services; 6 percent in social services, 3 percent in diocesan services, 7 percent in community services, .03 percent in the foreign missions, and 19 percent sick or retired.[114] Sisters were living in nineteen states and Nicaragua: 364 were in Wisconsin; forty-three in Kansas; forty in New York; twenty-five sisters lived in both Illinois and Indiana.[115] There were five or fewer sisters in each of the remaining states.

Because only half the sisters were engaged in full-time ministries, and stipends, rather than salaries, were the rule in compensating sisters, the question of caring for needy members had to be faced. A history of simple living, conservative financial practices, and careful attention to the care of institutions, had left a legacy of financial security, both in terms of present needs and in preparing for the greater demands of the future. The congregation had lately introduced central financing; it was supporting its own health insurance plan; and was beginning to make plans for hiring a fund manager and initiating a new approach to investments. However, the finances of the sponsored institutions, although not connected legally with the congregation, were nevertheless a matter of deep concern and constant vigilance.

In the summer of 1984 the sisters met for a final review of the constitutions before they were submitted to Rome.[116] Community meetings were held to identify areas of concern or tension and in the fall of 1984, the sisters received the *Long Range Planning*

Recommendations. The theme of the 1985 chapter, "Mission into the Future: Empowerment through Ministry," was a clear indicator that the congregation had disposed of as many internal issues as seemed possible at this time, and was determined to focus on ministerial needs.

In her cover letter of September 19, 1984, Sister Judith announced that the chapter would address issues of church, poverty and justice, women, ministry, and community.[117] To focus the chapter days solely on the significant issues, the council scheduled the chapter of elections several months before the chapter of affairs. This would also provide the opportunity for the new administration to think through with the delegates the most important tasks of the next four years.

On January 12, 1985, the chapter delegates, after reviewing the document with their canon lawyer, voted to ratify the new constitutions. Forty sisters voted yes, three no, and one abstained. The struggle to achieve a common vision while honoring individual diversity was not yet over but a hard-won consensus had been achieved. It had taken the work of four general chapters. The congregation could now try to live out the vision. It was a time of relief and celebration.

As the congregation moved toward new leadership, members were left with the knowledge that the administrations since the chapter of renewal had striven to unify the congregation, give clarity to its vision, and listen and respond to a changing and chaotic culture. They had been responsive to the needs of the individual, most notably in providing psychological and spiritual direction for those who needed or desired it. They had maintained a hope for the future while realistically looking at and preparing for more years of the breakdown.[118] The chapter's theme, "By Paths Unknown I Will Guide Them," was the community's statement of faith in a future that was all too unclear.

Chapter XV

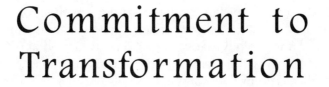

Commitment to Transformation

"Act creatively, courageously, and with hope." With those words Sister Judith Schmidt challenged the delegates at the 21st general chapter of the Sisters of Saint Agnes to take action to help the poor, the marginalized, and the helpless. She urged sisters to enter more fully into the ministry of the church; resist the exploitation of women, and above all, become "contemplatives in action—to discover the Kingdom in our midst while prophetically[1] proclaiming and effecting its fulfillment."[2]

Women religious had been deeply affected by the racism, sexism, poverty, violence, and political and economic oppression that are the burden of so many of the world's people. As the 1970s advanced these concerns were becoming issues in religious congregations and in the sometimes heated debates of the Leadership Conference of Women Religious.[3] Each issue had the potential to disrupt congregations.[4] What did it mean to be a woman of justice and peace? For some it might mean prayer and ascetical practices, for others, civil disobedience and prison. Did responding to the poor mean sharing their lifestyle, or leaving a comfortable position to live on a reservation or in the inner city? Did taking a corporate stance regarding the exploitation of women in society mean challenging oppressive structures in both society and the church even at the cost of alienating friends and benefactors? Did participating more fully in the ministry of the church mean helping in the RCIA program or visiting the sick or did it mean demanding ordination? These were only some of the issues facing women's congregations. Yet the challenge could not be allowed to pass by in silence.

As time passed, it had become clear that private charity and social justice were not the same. Social justice has as its goal giving individuals and groups fair treatment and a just share of the benefits of society. Ronald Rolheiser noted, "Issues such as war, poverty, violation of the ecology, native rights, feminism, and abortion, and racism ... are caused not simply, nor indeed any longer *primarily* by individuals acting in bad conscience, but by huge, impersonal systems that are inherently unfair ...."[5]

The connection between spirituality and justice had become clear to be ignored.[6] According to Michael Crosby the contemporary connection between spirituality and justice can be traced to the exhortation of John XXIII to look at "the signs of the times;" the Vatican Council's mandate to the church to participate in humanity's struggle for peace and justice; and, in 1971, the Catholic bishops' statement, "Justice in the World,"[7] which linked spirituality with justice.[8] Striving for the transformation of the world through doing works of justice was, then, a proper, indeed necessary, activity for religious.

CHAPTER DECISIONS

In April of 1985, the congregation had broken with tradition by electing the new leadership preceding the chapter of affairs. Sister Jean Steffes, the regional coordinator for the sisters in the east and southeast, was elected general superior. An educator, she had also served as director of novices. Sister Mary Mollison, whose professional background included nursing administration and CSA corporate director, was elected vicar; Sister Rhea Emmer, whose resume included clinical nursing and administration, spiritual direction and retreat ministry, as well as research and development for the Catholic Health Association of Wisconsin, was elected second councilor; and Sister Mary Charlotte O'Neill, a college professor and high school administrator, was elected third councilor.

In the sixteen years since the renewal chapter, the congregation's understanding of the theology of leadership had both expanded and deepened. The general superior possessed the highest personal authority in the congregation, but the constitutions also describe her as: "Receptive to the Spirit manifested to her through prayer, the church and daily events ... [she] involves the sisters in discerning with her the ecclesial role that the congregation can fulfill in the world. As the primary voice of the congregation, she inspires, leads and educates the sisters toward increasing unity, holiness and apostolic effectiveness in proclaiming the kingdom."[9] The canonical duties of the general councilors remained unchanged, but they were playing a more active role in community affairs in response to the congregations' desire for a more collegial style of governance. Sister Jean's style of leadership reflected her analytical approach to governance. When she quoted a statement Sister Judith had made at the chapter, "If we ... could address [our] issues more seriously, making ever more concrete and practical the questions we raise and the actions we plan, we would indeed become ministers of change,"[10] she was also describing her own preferred style of administration. As the spiritual leader of the congregation, she, together with her councilors, visited the sisters and the houses of the congregation, she marked important community events in writing letters blending the constitutions, scripture, and current events. She revived the annual reading of constitutions which had fallen into disuse during the experimental period. Underlying all the administration's activities was its consistent effort to connect the congregation's efforts with those of the greater ecclesial world.

The 1985 chapter made a number of important decisions and innovations. Before the Sisters of St. Agnes could "hear the cry of the poor," the congregation had to answer for itself the question, "Who are the poor?" In accordance with Catholic social teaching, the chapter defined "the poor" as those who are unable to provide themselves with the basic necessities of life. With that definition in mind, the chapter embraced Pope John Paul II's "preferential option" for the poor which called upon Christians to look at the world through the eyes of the poor and in solidarity with them. It challenged the community to the radical "conversion of heart" that was needed as well as to find ways to alleviate the problem of poverty through direct service, advocacy, and/or systemic change. The assent was spontaneous, no one could quarrel with the concept—making it concrete would prove more difficult.

The chapter had made other significant decisions: ecumenical/interfaith cooperation was encouraged and sponsorship was designated as a ministry of the congregation. Committees were formed to develop a consciousness-raising process on women's role in society. Processes for determining the nomination of leadership by the whole community and policies to clarify the role of regional coordinators and community living were formulated. After much discussion, the decision was made to experiment with the launching of a group of lay volunteers to work with the sisters in their ministries.[11] The acceptance of its new constitutions had freed the congregation to move into the larger world.

PLANNING: SPIRITUALITY, MISSION AND MINISTRY

At its first meeting, the general council agreed to choose a planning mechanism to provide a blueprint for implementing chapter acts as well as to give directions to the congregation's sponsored institutions.[12] Laying the groundwork for change was characteristic of the administration, which gave a great deal of attention to formulating and modifying policies.[13]

Planning for the spiritual progress of the congregation and its ministries was mandated by the constitutions for the general council, the interregional board of the regional coordinators, and the joint session (composed of general councilors and regional coordinators). In addition, the 1985 chapter, reflecting the concerns of the sisters regarding the proliferation of individual ministries, had established a ministry planning committee charged to develop, implement, and evaluate a twenty-year ministerial plan for CSA.[14]

The Ministry Planning Committee began its work by requesting from each sister her own plan for the future, and only then dealt with the overriding question: "Which on-going ministries do we move out of and which emerging ministries do we move into?"[15] After months of meetings, the committee developed criteria to assist in congregational and individual ministry planning in light of the CSA mission and ministerial priorities. By the time of the 1988 pre-chapter sessions, the committee had drafted five criteria for use in all ministry planning. For the congregation or any of its members, the ministry should promote gospel values and is in keeping with church teachings and the CSA mission; promote collaboration and empowerment; allow for active participation in CSA community life; is located within one of the geographic areas identified by CSA; and is in keeping with the sister's skills and preparation. The committee also developed five priorities for a preferred future in ministry: namely, ministries which influence structures for justice, empower economically and socially marginalized women, facilitate services to those who lack access to adequate health care, provide leadership in economically poor parishes, and educate economically poor adults and children in creative programs in both traditional and nontraditional settings.[16]

Meanwhile, as pastors wanted more control over personnel in the schools and parishes and sisters more choices in where and how they would use their talents,[17] the focus of ministry planning "moved somewhat from what we do to what we are: committed ministers of the gospel."[18] It was becoming apparent that community-wide planning for ministry was rapidly becoming less feasible although the theological basis of mission was becoming clearer. As a result, policies for ministry planning were revised. The whole process of individual ministry and community life planning through which a sister committed herself and the congregation to a particular ministry site took on a new significance. With the help of her regional coordinator, she now discerned with the community "in a manner that gives witness to the values of mutuality, inclusivity and collaboration."[19]

Developing mission statements in congregations is also "the development of the means of 'institutionalizing the reimagination' of religious life," according to Sister Mary Daniel Turner.[20] With that objective in mind, in Advent 1986 the council introduced a new mission statement to the congregation, commenting:"[The] CSA statement of mission reflects our beliefs and hopes, our goals and dreams as a distinctive group of apostolic religious women in the Church dedicated to the promotion of full human life and the building of the kingdom."[21]

The statement affirmed both the congregations's commitment to participate in Christ's mission by responding to those whose faith life or human dignity is threatened and its commitment to minister with simplicity and hospitality in the fields of education, health care, pastoral ministry, and social service. The statement emphasized the commitment to promote justice for the economically poor, to further the role of women in church and in society, and to collaborate with the laity, other religious, the clergy and those of other faith traditions. The statement ended in a promise to support one another that "among us and in our world the Risen Christ be discovered and revealed."[22]

A committee appointed to conduct a congregation-wide study of women in society and the church prepared two videos to help facilitate discussions. *More Than Meets the Eye* launched the project in 1986 by depicting sisters discussing their own experiences relative to the issue; the second, *The Role of Experience in Shaping Spirituality* was distributed in 1987. That year the major theme of the community's summer gathering was feminine spirituality.[23]

THE CONSTITUTIONS APPROVED

With the approval of the constitutions by the membership, it was time to obtain the approval of the Vatican Congregation for Religious and Secular Institutes. By 1983, Rome had retreated from the openness of Vatican II, and in that year, Pope John Paul II directed the American bishops to conduct a study of American religious. He had accompanied the request with a highly conservative document, *Essential Elements*,[24] intended to be a summary of the 'essential elements' of the church's teaching on religious life.[25] Two issues were of particular concern to the Sacred Congregation: that sisters have a local superior and that a religious habit be mandatory. Both the documents of Vatican II and the community's own experience as an American foundation led them to prefer a collegial approach to decision-making and clothing appropriate to the world they lived in.[26] Religious congregations were challenged to obtain approval for their constitutions without changing their own understanding and approach to religious life as it was lived in their own community. The congregation, with the help of a canon lawyer, was able to negotiate language acceptable both to the sisters and to Rome. Eighteen years after the chapter of renewal, the Congregation for Religious and Secular Institutes issued a decree of approbation for the Congregation of the Sisters of St. Agnes on January 21, 1987.

Approval of the constitutions, however, did not mean the end of all differences. The constitutions proclaim that the community is "called by God in the power of the Spirit [to] continue Jesus' mission of revealing his Father's love according to the purpose and spirit of our founders."[27] It is a spirituality that the sisters express through living their commitment to daily participation in ministry, community, and society. In a period of advances in scripture study and developing theologies regarding Christology and ecclesiology, and as sisters were searching for their own spirituality, differences of opinion were becoming more marked. More emphasis was given to seeking spiritual direction and experimenting with different prayer forms but some of the issues seemed to question traditional Catholic theology and practice. There was less emphasis on the sacrament of reconciliation; sisters began to develop alternatives to attendance at daily Eucharist; there were sisters who wished to re-interpret the meaning/requirements of the vows. Not unnaturally, the differences of opinion could and did lead to some tension in the congregation.

EVALUATING COMMUNITY LIVING

The contradictions regarding community living that had surfaced in the Long Range Planning Report of 1984 were becoming ever more apparent. With the collapse of the superior-inferior relationship in communities, governance of local houses had moved to governance by group consensus. Another movement followed shortly, as many sisters saw opportunities for greater personal growth living in small groups. In December 1990, fifty-five sisters were living alone, whether from ministerial necessity or for personal reasons.[28] The break-up of the larger communities had caused some tension, but it soared when a growing number of sisters began to live alone. The possibility had always been permitted for reasons of health, education, or a ministry in the name of the congregation, but it had been unusual. The old ideal of sisters living a common life based on a monastic model was fast disappearing as a growing number of sisters held with Sister Sandra Schneiders that leading a common life was not theologically necessary for a ministerial religious and, that for some, may be unnecessarily physically demanding and psychologically stressful.[29]

The definition of community was also changing. For some members, local community referred to two or more sisters of the same congregation sharing life and faith together in the same house; for others local community referred to two or more sisters of the same congregation living in a geographic area that allows them to gather for meals, faith sharing, community meetings, and recreation on a regular basis. To others it meant being connected to the congregation through phone calls, letter writing, and attending congregational meetings.

Although some sisters would have wished the common life to be the norm in the congregation, because an issue that was so deeply personal could not be resolved by legislation, sisters wishing such permission could request it for either personal and/or ministry reasons from the general superior.

In 1986 and 1987, the members of the general council visited the houses and institutions of the congregation. "The foci of the visitation were the congregation's quality of life in relation to its mission, spirit, charism, traditions, and constitutions: its integration with the church's agenda ... and the progress in implementing the chapter acts of 1985."[30] Despite differing expectations in regard to community living, the councilor's evaluation was generally positive. They found that although change was not rapid, "we do change;" they found dedication to ministry and diversity within it; they found love for the community in participation in community events and a willingness to go beyond what is expected. They were pleased to see simplicity, hospitality, and joy in many local communities. They saw, however, the need for more preparation regarding global and cultural realities and more consciousness of the necessity of maintaining financial stability in the light of aging membership and diverse ministerial commitments.[31]

There were still areas of confusion. Sisters were not always clear about the distinction between the religious and lay state; they did not always understand the implications of "preferential option for the poor;" nor were they always in agreement on what constituted "a simple life style" for the community.[32] The community was united, however, in concern for the small number of vocations to religious life.

THE FORMATION PROGRAM

Sister Jean's years as director of novices had also given her the experience and a philosophy of formation relevant to contemporary life.[33] She was working with women who were determined to breathe new life into the formation program; each had a special interest and enthusiasm and could bring to the program a renewed sense of focus and direction. The council wanted a model that would respect the woman's life experiences and, at the same time, introduce her to a way of life based on mission, community life, and the vows. A woman interested in discerning her vocation would enter into a mutual relationship with a mentor during which time she would examine religious life, her own call, and the way of life of the Sisters of St. Agnes. The process was designed to respect both the integrity of the life style of the congregation and the woman's adult commitment.[34]

That there was no formation program in Nicaragua since 1970 was a major concern of the administration. Nevertheless, the sisters there had felt unable to deny admission as aspirants to several young women. An important part of the committee's work was laying the groundwork for the re-establishment of a formation program in Latin America. The council responded by formally voting to inaugurate a formation program in Latin America. One philosophy would govern the program, but there would be two distinct national adaptations. A joint formation team was created to provide a basis for both unity and diversity. Sisters in Latin America were encouraged to prepare for formation work by updating their missiology, theology, and psychology through programs sponsored by the Latin American Confederation of Religious (CLAR).[35] The first Nicaraguan novices in the new program were received in February 1987.[36]

As in the past, the women emerging from the program would have to be ready to face both challenges and disillusionment of life as well as prepared to find joy in their community and ministry experiences[37] Professed sisters also had much to learn. They would have to become accustomed to women who had grown up in an environment much different from theirs, older than the candidates of the past, and diverse in their faith and theological development.

NEW REALITIES—NEW SOLUTIONS

Within a very few years the traditional ways in which community members had connected in large groups had all but disappeared. Rather than several hundred sisters making the same summer retreat at the motherhouse, sisters were making retreats at their own time and in places of their own choosing. As it no longer took sisters years of summer school to complete their undergraduate work, they were attending colleges and universities around the country. They no longer lived in large convents or hospitals; at times there were only a few sisters in their geographical area. To meet the need for the sisters to connect as a group, annual gatherings were scheduled for the entire community.

The meetings provided "the time, space and even the motivation for claiming and celebrating the larger meanings for which a community stands. An experience of the diversity of ages, ministry locales, perspectives, theologies, ecclesiologies, and philosophies has powerful ability to broaden, deepen and reconfirm the individual and the congregation in the mission, charism and spirit which transcends all differences and energizes each and all … with renewed heart and enhanced zeal."[38] For a few days each summer, sisters took time to pray, to listen, to discuss, to party, and to re-connect with each other. As well as providing an avenue for continuing formation, the gatherings became a time for renewing friendships; for making new friends; and for sharing memories and lives.

The new prominence given to the laity in Vatican II was taken seriously by religious congregations who sought to promote the role of the laity and to collaborate with them whenever possible. Many congregations established associate programs. The associates embrace the congregation's mission, charism and spirit, although they have a lay spirituality that differs from that of the religious. CSA's associate program was relatively new and still in the process of development. A new program for their formation, designed to lead to a deepening and continuing conversion into faith and discipleship, was adopted and broadened by welcoming men and persons of different ecumenical backgrounds.[39] It was also extended to Nicaragua through the efforts of Sister María del Carmen Avendaño. An Associate Coordinating Committee was created, responsible for the growth and development of the group. Although community leadership affirmed the associate program as "one form of witness of life which speaks to the value of religious consecration as well as lay commitment in our own day," total acceptance by the congregation was slow partly because of concerns that the program could bring about a loss of CSA identity.[40]

The success of the Peace Corps and the lay volunteer programs sponsored by religious congregations had created an interest in the congregation to sponsor a similar program for people who would like to combine working with the poor in partnership with Agnesians. There was enough enthusiasm in the community for the 1985 chapter to make a recommendation to the general council to do a pilot program. The committee developed a mission statement for the program and a task force of volunteers developed a survey to determine the community's preference in the design of the program. Instead of the term "lay volunteer" which the task force decided could connote a lack of mutuality, the program was named a co-ministry program. The mixed feelings and opinions regarding the program centered mainly on concern for the commitment of the resources, personnel, and finances necessary to support an ambitious program although there were also reservations about inviting non-members to live with the community. The committee decided to launch a pilot program to test the plan's feasibility for the congregation.[41]

RESPONDING TO THE CRY OF THE POOR

Of all the decisions made in 1985, the decision to embrace Pope John Paul II's "preferential option" for the poor had the most immediate implications. As a first step in its implementation, sisters were asked to strive to understand the meaning of poverty both vicariously in its meaning through meetings, readings, and discussions, as well as immersion in experiences among the poor.[42] From 1986 through 1988, nearly 250 sisters participated in workshops, all of which included the themes of poverty and justice. Sisters were invited to make a personal commitment to the poor by signing a card promising to make efforts of conversion of heart through prayer, suffering, study, and reflection. Some sisters focused on finding ways to commit to the poor through direct service, advocacy, and/or opting for systemic change in society.

The commitment to make a preferential option for the poor accelerated the expansion into new ministries and new ministry settings quickly reflected this commitment.[43] More sisters were attracted to the under-served dioceses of the south and southwest. Sisters were working with the under-served and poor Catholic population in Gallup and Farmington, New Mexico; and in rural Kentucky. In 1986 a three-year commitment was made to a black parish in Chicago, St. Justin Martyr, to provide a pastoral minister, a reading specialist, and a reading tutor.[44]

Two years later the congregation made commitments to two schools serving black populations. The first, St. Joseph's School, was located on Chicago's north side, on the perimeter of the Cabrini-Green Housing Development, one of the four lowest income areas in the United States. Two-thirds of St. Joseph's 180 students resided in that development or in the area immediately surrounding it. The student body was 99 percent black and only 10 percent Catholic. The characteristic student was black, poor, Protestant or unchurched; came from a fractured family; and lacked educational background and support. The second, Holy Child Jesus School, was in the small farming community of Canton, Mississippi a town noted for its inhospitality to civil rights. The Trinitarian fathers staffed the parish and gave some financial support to the school.

By 1988, there were Sisters of St. Agnes living in Mobile and Montgomery, Alabama; Bisbee, Phoenix, St. Michael's, Sells, Springerville, Tucson and Wickenburg, Arizona; San Diego, California; Daytona Beach, St. Petersburg, Florida; Honolulu, Hawaii; Bensenville, Chicago, Evanston, Illinois; Crown Point, Decatur, Fort Wayne, New Haven, Indiana; Colby, Ellis, Hays, New Almelo, Overland Park, Victoria, Kansas; Gladstone, Michigan; Rosemount, Minnesota; Canton, Mound Bayou, Mississippi; St. Louis, Missouri; Farmington, Gallup, Navajo, New Mexico; Barryville, Bronx, Newburgh, New York City, New York; Tarboro, North Carolina: Cincinnati, Northwood, Ohio; Altoona, Nanty Glo, Pennsylvania; Beloit, Berlin, Fond du Lac, Green Bay, Hales Corners, Hortonville, Hudson, Kiel, Lomira, Madison, Menasha, Milwaukee, Monroe, New London, Omro, Oshkosh, Stockbridge, Two Rivers, Watertown, Waunakee, Wisconsin; and Belén, Managua, Puerto Cabezas, Rosita, Waspam, Nicaragua.[45]

DEATH IN NICARAGUA

Of all the people that the Sisters of St. Agnes worked with, the Miskito Indians in Nicaragua were not only the most materially poor but were also suffering from the civil war in their own country. Despite the risk and the traumas suffered by missionaries, the congregation remained. By 1987, the political tide was beginning to turn and Miskito peoples were permitted to return to their villages provided sisters accompanied them. Sisters Maureen Courtney and Teresita Inés Argüello joined the people as quickly as possible. Because the congregation had never officially closed the mission at Waspam, the sisters simply packed up and returned. The town, with its homes, gardens, and livestock, was destroyed. When the sisters searched for the sites of the school and convent, they found only charred remains of buildings—the jungle had reclaimed its own.

As the people began returning to their villages, life along the Río Coco became relatively peaceful, although always the possibility of injury or even death was present. Each person knew it and dealt with it in her own way. Some were able to throw off their fears, but Sister Maureen Courtney wrote, " I believe that I may die one day soon. And I know that neither my life nor my death will have been in vain."[46]

On the first day of January 1990, Sisters Maureen and Teresa de Jesús Rosales Dixon died. Maureen, aged forty-five, had devoted twelve of her twenty-five years as a professed religious in Nicaragua to working with the Miskito people. Teresa de Jesús, one of the first two women of the Miskito people professed in the community, was twenty-four years old and the youngest professed sister in the congregation.

The sisters had attended a meeting on the Pacific coast but were returning to Waspam where the first Assembly of the Vicariate would be held in the Miskito language. They, together with Bishop Paul Schmitz and Sister Francisca María Colomer, were in route to Rosita where they intended to break their trip and end the feast day with Agnesian and Capuchin community members. When dusk was approaching, they asked for and received a reluctant permission from officials in Siuna to continue their journey to Rosita.[47] Around 6:30 p.m. they ran into an ambush at Ojo de Agua. Maureen, the driver, was killed instantly. Francisca María, seated behind, received

serious face and neck injuries and was temporarily blinded by shrap-
nel or glass. Teresa was killed seconds later by bullets from automat-
ic weapons. The bishop, seated next to Maureen, suffered a shattered arm.

The murders received national attention.[48] There were immediate expressions of solidarity and sympathy from around the country.
On April 4, 1990, the Wisconsin Assembly passed Joint Resolution
115 which noted that "her tragic death underscores the nobility of
her life" and resolved that "the members of the legislature of the
state of Wisconsin express their gratitude for Sister Maureen
Courtney's exemplary life and sorrow at her untimely and tragic
death."[49]

Sister Jean, in the name of the congregation, asked for an investigation, although not retribution, by the Department of State.
There were investigations. The Defense Attaché in Managua went
to the area as soon as he was permitted. The FBI was also involved
as they had a capability and an expertise in technology other groups
could not match. However, the Sandinistas would not allow them to
examine their types of weapons and they had no contact with the
Contra group alleged to be responsible for the attack.[50] At least two
independent investigations, one by the Americas Watch human
rights group and the pro-Sandinista Witness for Peace ecumenical
group blamed Contra rebels, based on interviews with two alleged
eye-witnesses. State Department sources said that diplomats were
skeptical of the eye-witness accounts as the witnesses were tightly
controlled by the Sandinistas.[51] Eventually the State Department
announced that the unsolved case was closed.

It was not clear at the time if the missionaries were intended victims or whether it was a case of mistaken identity. Nor had official
responsibility for the act been established. The question of guilt was
far outweighed by the shock and sorrow the congregation has continued to feel over the violent deaths of two dedicated and peace-
loving women.[52]

Throughout the revolution and civil war in Nicaragua, community leaders had visited each ministry and living site and used every
available means to connect with the sisters. They focused on community over and above any political/ideological concerns. They
made appointments to leadership positions independent of political
ideology. They encouraged the sisters to meet and maintain bonds

with each other. They tried to maintain neutrality in congregational communications. As a result the sisters in North America tended to form their opinions based on the experiences of their own friends although the national media, like the pro-Sandinista *National Catholic Reporter* and the commentators on National Public Radio had an influence on some as did the more conservative press on others.

Whatever their political opinions, the sisters pay tribute to congregational leadership. Sisters were free to leave or remain in Nicaragua as they chose. In answer to a questionnaire sent to the missionaries, each woman indicated that she felt totally supported by the congregation. A typical comment was, "I think superiors respected each one and let each one decide who she supported. I don't think there was ever a time when superiors tried to make everyone think completely alike. Even superiors had their views, but they weren't imposed on the others."[53] They praised leadership for remaining optimistic and for reminding each one of her dependence on God and cited community meetings as helpful to all of them in maintaining their faith in their future.

DEVELOPING A PEACE AND JUSTICE AGENDA

During the next few years, the peace and justice activities of the congregation gained momentum. The Justice/Peace/Ecology Committee was established in 1990 to assist in implementing the justice and peace agenda. During the following years, the congregation co-sponsored and supported events through donations and/or participation in a number of justice and peace events such as the Nevada desert retreat and nuclear weapons protests. Peace issues were kept before the community through the *CSA Update* and the *CSA Focus*, a one-page quarterly written by a sister with a special interest in a current and relevant issue.

It was during this period that the congregation took its first corporate stance[54] when it sponsored the posting of nuclear free zone signs on sponsored institutions.[55] Strongly committed to collaboration with like-minded groups, the community held corporate memberships in *NETWORK*, Pax Christi USA, and Bread for the World. Individual sisters were encouraged to write letters to local newspapers and congressmen, sign petitions, and otherwise participate in justice and peace activities in their local areas. Associates were invited to participate in the meetings. *JustPEACE* was initiated as a newsletter for members and associates as a publication which gave members a chance to explore issues in depth.

Convinced that justice for women in society is intimately related to the totality of women's being, including her spirituality, community leadership asked the sisters to engage in theological reflection— to reflect on their own and other women's experiences in the light of the gospel and their own religious heritage. As part of the process they were asked to affirm each other as women and broaden their own concept of God. For many community members the process provided an introduction into feminist theology.[56] For some, the issue became "a compelling one, inspired by the Spirit and imperative to gospel living." But, "a small but vocal segment believe it is destructive and in direct opposition to the patriarchal church."[57]

Aware that sisters' reactions varied, the council chose to begin the use of inclusive language by implementing its use in liturgical prayers and hymns gradually; by appointing an inclusive language task force to develop a morning and evening praise for the congregation; and providing a more inclusive role for women in the liturgy at the community gathering in the summer of 1987. Sisters were chosen to give "reflections" at congregational celebrations and occasionally at other liturgies.[58]

The use of gender inclusive language created the greatest difficulties. Awkward language was substituted for the familiar language of scripture, liturgy, and hymns; translations could raise theological questions. Some sisters were disturbed at the picture of women as victims, others concerned that women might oppress men in their efforts to attain justice for women.[59] It was easier for most sisters to promote educational opportunities for women; recognize the oppression of women, especially in the workplace, or confront prejudice toward marginalized women.

The congregation's commitment to social justice led it to carry its concerns into the area of finance by investing in companies that reflected its ethical values, filing shareholders' resolutions in an effort to influence management decision making, or withdrawing its stock from companies engaging in arms production. The congregation collaborated with Christian Brothers Investment Services, Inc., the Interfaith Center on Corporate Responsibility, and the National Catholic Coalition for Responsible Investing in submitting resolutions at stockholder meetings. The finance office was also charged to develop with the board a financial plan so that ministry choices could be balanced with resources; assess the integration of local budgeting with overall congregational budgeting; and negotiate salaries in keeping with the goal of just salaries for all church employees.

SPONSORED INSTITUTIONS

Throughout the 1980s, the congregation further defined and clarified the functions of sponsorship.[60] It worked with the institutions[61] to integrate the congregational statement of mission into their operations.[62] It institutionalized routine meetings with the chairpersons of boards and the CEOs; established joint task forces to recommend mission-related and care of the poor programs. It established guidelines and programs specifically designed for women and more lay-women were asked to join the boards of directors. It supported ecumenical pastoral care departments in the hospitals; and made inter and intra-institutional cooperation as well as participation in the formation of selected public policy the norm.[63]

By the end of 1988 each hospital had established a mission effectiveness committee. Foremost among their functions was the initiation of employee retreats to enable employees to integrate their spiritual values with their work-life. Some institutions extended their mission. St. Clare hospital in Monroe, for example, sponsored the commodity food distribution program and employees held hospital-wide clothing drives for Unity House.[64]

These changes were taking place in a political climate inhospitable to health care facilities. Beginning in the mid-1980s hospitals around the country experienced losses from the Medicare program because of the drastic reduction of patient-days and the Agnesian hospitals were no exception.[65] Each institution struggled financially but continued to up-date its equipment and services. Nevertheless, the congregation successfully concluded its discussions with the School Sisters of St. Francis and purchased the Waupun Memorial Hospital although its financial picture was bleak and a significant amount of work would have to be done to improve its financial condition.[66] On May 5, 1987, the congregation assumed sponsorship.[67]

As health care costs escalated, many independent hospitals found it necessary to collaborate with similar institutions in order to survive. In 1987, St. Clare Hospital meetings with the Monroe Clinic eventuated in the Monroe Health Service Management Organization.[68] St. Agnes Hospital established partnerships with surrounding clinics, Waupun Memorial Hospital and Consultants Laboratory. St. Francis Home, however, expanded its services by establishing a thirty-unit independent-living facility, St. Clare Terrace.[69]

In Hays, both St. Anthony and Hadley Memorial Hospitals were affected by twin pressures: the need to acquire new technology and the need to keep costs down in the face of Medicare and insurance rules and regulations.[70] St. Anthony Hospital investigated developing a collaborative relationship with another Catholic health system, but found that the project was not feasible. In spite of obstacles, in 1989, the hospital administration was able to retire its debt to the congregation. The hospital was again approached by representatives of Hadley Memorial Hospital. Although St. Anthony Hospital was financially sound, the congregation's belief that it was in the interest of the people of Hays to combine local resources, together with the changing religious climate in the area, made negotiations possible. There were two important commonalities. Both hospitals had religious roots; both were not-for-profit; and both had a mission to the poor.[71] Furthermore, the hospital would operate under the ethical guidelines of the Catholic church.[72] On December 7, 1990 the announcement of the merger was made to the medical staff. Twenty-four years after St. Anthony's Hospital and Hadley Memorial Hospital had begun discussing together the most effective way to provide for the health care of the Hays community, the Hays Medical Center—a new legal entity—was created.[73]

On the educational front in 1986, in the year of the 50th anniversary of its founding, the freshmen enrollment at Marian College stood at fifty students. The precipitous plunge was caused by a number of factors: among them was the college's failure to develop new programs, use new marketing techniques, and respond to the changing demographic picture. Four years later the college had inaugurated a non-traditional, adult degree program in business administration; registered nurses were offered an opportunity to attain a Bachelor of Science in Nursing; the social work program was accredited and the first graduate program—a Master of Arts in Education—was established. Fifteen town houses had been built to care for 105 students. The impressive turn-around began with the determination of Sister Jean Steffes and the general council to save the college, and the congregation's willingness to invest in its future.[74]

One of Sister Jean's first steps was to hire a firm which specialized in helping colleges with such problems as marketing research and communications, student recruitment, and professional development. With the help of a consultant, Dr. Edward Henry,[75] the college launched a presidential search committee. The committee, after reviewing the credentials of eighty applicants, asked Dr. Henry to serve as interim president of the college. The *Chronicles* of the congregation noted his success: "[Dr. Henry] during the short time in which he had been in office [had] a dramatic effect upon the morale of faculty and staff …. a new verve and spirit of excitement over the direction the college was moving" spread over the campus.[76] The hard work of a dedicated administration, faculty, and staff completed the process. Enrollment quickly increased with the influx of non-traditional students. The 1987-1988 enrollment was 39 percent higher than that of the previous year.[77] The new graduate classes in education were a factor in the 600 percent increase in summer enrollment figures [78] By 1990 an aggressive fund–raising campaign helped put Marian College in the black for the first time in four years.

Like other Catholic colleges, Marian was also faced with the challenge of maintaining its values and mission in a changing religious environment as both faculty and students presented a religiously diversified population. Its goal was to present an environment welcoming to other religious traditions while striving to remain faithful to its Catholic intellectual tradition.

THE CHAPTER OF 1989

The hope for transformation within individuals, the congregation and the world was the theme for the chapter of 1989. It is a hope, Sister Jean Steffes told the community, that has its source in faith. "The face of God is, indeed, found in our midst," she said, "in the faces of all those who surround us, but especially in the faces of the poor and the oppressed. Together we humans make up the body of the Christ who transforms us; together we image the God who made us and planted within us the desire for transformation."[79]

Sisters Jean Steffes and Mary Mollison continued in their roles as general superior and vicar; Sisters Mary Christine Fellerhoff, who was serving at Unity House in Chicago, and formerly professor and academic dean at Marian College, and Sister Jovita Winkel who had been the pastoral associate at St. Mary's Church in Stockbridge, Wisconsin after years in various leadership roles in elementary education and parish ministry, were elected third and fourth councilors.

Two resolutions were particularly noteworthy: one authorized a four-year period of experimentation which would give the sisters in Latin America a greater voice in decisions in the area and the other resulted in a corporate statement which committed the congregation to further the role of women in church and society.[80] Of importance too were the four directional statements. The chapter's work also resulted in four statements giving direction to the congregation. The first statement committed the congregation to move toward effecting systemic changes individually and corporately for the quality of life. The second and third statements committed the congregation to work actively toward transformation within itself and to be a catalyst of transformation in the church and the world. The fourth statement committed the members to move toward greater personal wholeness, healthy interpersonal relationships, and a lived understanding of apostolic community as expressed in our Constitutions.[81]

Both the chapter's discussions and the congregation's deepening understanding of the connection between spirituality and justice led to the formulation of a new mission statement. The 1986 mission statement was retained in essence but the congregation's increasing commitment to furthering justice, particularly for women and children, through systemic change was unmistakable:

> We are committed to transformation of the world,
> the Church and ourselves through promoting
> . . .   systemic change for the quality of life
> . . .   justice for the economically poor
> . . .   furtherance of the role of women in church
>   and society
> . . .   mutuality, inclusivity and collaboration.[82]

The mission statement concluded with a statement of the paramount objective of the congregation: "Love binds us together, and by sharing our lives and our faith in community, we support one another to live with singleness of purpose: that among us and in our world the Risen Christ be discovered and revealed."[83]

Since the early 1960s, Sisters of Saint Agnes had responded to the call of Pope John XXIII to open the windows to let fresh air into the church. They had discarded rules and customs appropriate to a world that no longer existed. They had accepted responsibility for the decisions that governed their daily lives. Their spiritual horizons had widened as they struggled to respond to the needs of the poor and the oppressed both as individuals and as sponsors of institutions committed to change unjust societal structures.

The reason for their existence did not change. They continue to believe that they are called by God to participate in the mission of Jesus Christ. They hold fast to their belief in the value of religious life in the midst of the cultural chaos of post-modern societies. They and the courageous women who continue to join them do not know what lies ahead, but they identify themselves with the pilgrim church and are content like Sarah and Abraham to go where God leads them.

The Congregation of Sisters of St. Agnes is only one of the hundreds of religious communities who, when the need was there, undertook responsibility for the parochial school system in the United States in addition to founding hundreds of hospitals, schools, and colleges. Their assets were only their own lives. They did not consider themselves extraordinary. Nor do the Sisters of St. Agnes of today, whose history is told here as *Ordinary Sisters: The Story of the Sisters of St. Agnes.*

484

Front Section [A] of Photographs
A~1
Father Caspar Rehrl, December 31, 1809 – September 3, 1881. Crayon sketch by Sister Julienne Rompf, CSA.

Mother M. Agnes Hazotte, CSA, May 7, 1847 – March 6, 1905. Hazotte Family Portrait, L-R: Anne Marie Hazotte, Marie Potier Hazotte, Victor Hazotte.

A~2
Father Francis Haas, O.M. Cap., November 24, 1826 – June 21, 1895. Oil portrait by Tertulliano Giangiacomo, Rome, Italy, 1888.

St. Agnes Convent, Barton, Wisconsin,1858-1870. In 2007 the building still stands on the original site. The property is owned by the Washington County Historical Society.

A~3
Mother M. Agnes Hazotte, CSA, Superior General, 1864 - 1905.

St. Agnes Hospital, East Division Street, Fond du Lac, Wisconsin, was dedicated June 23, 1896, and opened to patients July 1, 1896.

A~4
St. Mary's Springs Sanatarium, including the Annex (left) built for hydrotherapy, 1902-1909. In 1909 these buildings were converted into St. Mary's Springs Academy and named St. Agnes Hall (left) and Boyle Hall (right).

Sister Bernardine (Gertrude) Laughlin, Superior at St. Mary's Springs Sanatarium.

A~5
Mother M. Antonia Schmitz, CSA, Superior General, 1905-1916.

St. Joseph Orphans House for Boys and Girls, Assinins, Michigan, was accepted by Mother Antonia Schmitz in April 1906. The first sisters arrived there June 25, 1906. Msgr. M. Faust, pictured above with some of the children, served as director for many years.

A~6
St. Anthony Hospital, Hays, Kansas, first opened August 25, 1909, in the converted Beach House. A new hospital was built in 1916 and this addition to it was dedicated on January 21, 1931.

School children at St. Francis School, Munjor, Kansas, pictured around 1915 or 1916. Candidates as seen in this photo (upper left) were sometimes sent for a year or two to join the faculty at a school where a professed sister was unavailable.

A~7
St. Agnes Convent, 390 E. Division Street, Fond du Lac, Wisconsin, 1877-1975. Photo shows, from left to right, the 1877 building, the 1887 chapel addition and the 1909 addition.

"The Martyrdom of St. Agnes of Rome" rose above the main altar in St. Agnes Convent Chapel, 390 East Division Street. Mother Agnes Hazotte commissioned New York artist Wilhelm Lamprecht to create the mural in 1890.

A~8
Mother M. Marcella Kettner, CSA, Superior General, 1916 – 1926.

Left to right, Novice, Professed Sister, Postulant pictured wearing traditional garb. The traditional habit designed in 1870 by Sister Antonia Schmitz was essentially unmodified until 1960.

Back Section [B] of Photographs
B~1
Mother M. Joseph Wolford, CSA, Superior General, 1926-1933.

Architect's drawing of the Main Building of St. Mary's Springs Academy, Fond du Lac. The building opened in September 1929.

B~2
Mother M. Aloysia Leikem, CSA, Superior General, 1933-1939.

St. Clare Hospital, Monroe, Wisconsin, opened August 1, 1939.

B~3
Mother M. Angeline Kamp, CSA, Superior General, 1939-1951.

St. Thomas Hospital, Colby, Kansas, opened October 8, 1941.

B~4
L to R: Sisters Mary Agnes Dickof, Francis Borgia Dreiling, Pauletta Scheck, and Agnes Rita Fisette opened the CSA mission in Waspam, Nicaragua, in 1945.

The shores of Waspam, Nicaragua, as seen from the Río Coco soon after pioneer missionaries arrived there.

B~5
The CSA mission compound in Waspam, Nicaragua, as it was from the inception of the mission. The path led across the bridge up to the church.

The pioneer missionaries visit the school in Puerto Cabezas, Nicaragua. In the doorway are Father Roman Ament, OFM Cap., and Bishop Matthew Niedhammer, OFM Cap.

B~6
Mother M. Albertonia Licher, CSA, Superior General, 1951-1957.

Having made an annual retreat and attended summer school, Sisters departed from the motherhouse after August 15 to return to their previous missions or to begin new assignments.

B~7
Mother M. Rosita Handibode, CSA, Superior General, 1957-1969.

In September 1965 a dream became reality when the first sister residents moved into Nazareth Heights Infirmary.

B~8
Sister M. John Baptist Shaja, CSA, Superior General, 1969-1973.

Marian College of Fond du Lac was relocated to 45 S. National Avenue in September 1966. Shown here, left to right, are the Administration Building, the breezeway, Albert Cardinal Meyer Library and, in the background, the spire of Dorcas Chapel.

B~9
Sister Judith Schmidt, CSA, General Superior, 1973-1985.

This photo illustrates the variety in modified habits worn by sisters in the same local community.

B~10
Sister Maureen Courtney (center) and affiliates Felícita Colomer Kramer and Teresa de Jesús Rosales Dixon (far left facing front) visited Waspam to greet the people who were preparing to return to their river towns after living in resettlement camps. Photo dated August 17, 1985.

St. Agnes Hospital, Fond du Lac, constructed this addition to the west on Division Street in 1975-1977.

B~11, B~12
Sister Jean Steffes, CSA, General Superior, 1985-1993.

The Sisters of St. Agnes assumed sponsorship of Waupun Memorial Hospital, Waupun, Wisconsin, in 1987.

St. Agnes Convent, 475 Gillett Street, Fond du Lac, Wisconsin. Formerly St. Agnes School of Nursing, this building served as the motherhouse of the congregation during the years 1975-1999.

Notes on Sources

The records, documents, letters, etc., of the congregation are found in the archives of the Sisters of St. Agnes. The congregation's founder, Father Caspar Rehrl, kept a few notes on information he found useful or interesting but they contain no references to either his personal life or the congregation. Although Mother Agnes Hazotte was elected superior of the society in 1864 and remained as superior general until her death in 1905, fewer than eighty letters remain as her legacy. *The Record of the First Beginning in Barton until the First General Chapter in Fond du Lac, Wisconsin,* was a handwritten four-teen page summary written by Mother Agnes covering significant events from 1858 to 1878. The most valuable of these are the letters written from 1865 to 1870 to either Sister Gertrude Laughlin or the sisters as a group. The *Record* marked the beginning of the congregational *Annals,* which usually noted financial transactions, events at the motherhouse, visitations of the superior general to the missions, illnesses and deaths. The letters written by Father Francis Haas, OM Cap., to Mother Agnes give a picture of the society from the standpoint of its spiritual director. There are also a few letters from bishops and priests.

Sisters of St. Agnes did not write diaries, journals nor ordinarily keep their correspondence. A valuable and almost the only source of information of the early sisters was the *Life Sketches* of the women who died as professed Sisters of St. Agnes until 1932. Following the incorporation of the congregation in 1892, minutes of the board of trustees were kept. The *Chronicles,* begun with the appointment of the first full-time congregational secretary in 1963, provided an excellent yearly summary of the congregation, its ministries, and sponsored institutions within an historical context. Records were kept of each of the general chapters. Beginning with the general chapter of 1969, extensive records were kept of preparation for chapters and the strategies used to implement chapter decisions.

Histories of other religious congregations, articles in such periodicals as the *U.S. Catholic Historian* and *Review for Religious,* and the resources available through the world wide web provided the author with a much-needed background.

Chapter I~The Missionary

1. Mother Agnes Hazotte, *Circular Letter*, 19 April 1881. Circular letters were written to the entire congregation. They were official letters of the superiors general meant to provide words of encouragement to the Sisters and to preserve their fervor and good religious spirit. All were informative of both the spiritual and material progress of the community.

2. Vincent N. Schneider, *The Rev. Caspar Rehrl, Wisconsin Missionary, 1845-1881*, unpublished M.A. thesis, St. Francis Seminary, Milwaukee, 1937.

3. Rehrl's piety and kindheartedness and the family's rich spirit are cited as "characteristics of the precious heritage of his mother." Corbinian Vieracker, OM Cap., *History of Mount Calvary (Fond du Lac County, Wisconsin), A Commemoration on the Occasion of the Golden Jubilee of the Establishment of the First Capuchin Priory in North America, 25th of June 1907*, trans. Ronald Jansch, OFM Cap., unpublished manuscript, 5. Benjamin Blied wrote that "Pious influences must have been at work in Rehrl because he had Fr. Weninger as a confessor and he also made a visit to the stigmatist of Kaltern, Maria Moerl, who was highly respected in Alpine Austria." *Austrian Aid to American Catholics* (Milwaukee, Wisconsin: by the author, 1944), 136.

4. Rt. Rev. Msgr. J. Rainer, "Reminiscences of the Late Archbishop Michael Heiss," *The Salesianum* 5 (October 1909): 9.

5. Peter Leo Johnson, *Crosier on the Frontier; A Life of John Martin Henni, Archbishop of Milwaukee*, (Madison: State Historical Society of Wisconsin, 1959), 85.

6. J. E. Halbenkann, "Memoirs of the Rev. J. E. Halbenkann on Three of the Early Missionary Priests of the Archdiocese of Milwaukee, Rev. C. Rehrl, his brother Rev. G. Rehrl and P. F. Bermadinger, OMC," *The Salesianum* 4 (April 1909): 18.

7. The Leopoldine Stiftung was founded in Vienna to aid Catholic missions in North America. It was named to perpetuate the memory of the Empress of Brazil, the favorite daughter of Francis I of Austria and wife of Pedro I.

8. Anton Ensmann, *Testimonial of the Prefect of the Salzburg Vicariate*, quoted in Rev. Corbinian Vieracker OM Cap., "The Rev. Caspar Rehrl, the Apostle of Calumet," *Pastoral-Blatt* 53 (November 1919): 161-ff. Typewritten copy, Salzmann Library, 2. Vieracker's paper is especially valuable because he used as one of his sources a long-standing friend of Rehrl, Rt. Rev. Msgr. Joseph Rainer, president of St. Francis Seminary in Milwaukee.

9. Rehrl was the first missionary from Austria to come to Wisconsin. Steven M. Avella, *In the Richness of the Earth: A History of the Archdiocese of Milwaukee, 1843-1958* (Marquette University Press, 2002), 64.

10. Rehrl's passage cost about 600 florins, the fare Rev. Michael Heiss paid scarcely two years previously for the same voyage. That would have amounted to about $2.70 per day in American money at that time. Mileta

Ludwig, FSPA, *Right-Hand Glove Uplifted: a Biography of Archbishop Michael Heiss* (New York: Pageant Press, 1967), f. n. 20, 115.

11. Caspar Rehrl, "Letter from Calumet Village," 5 November 1845 *Katholische Blaetter*, 30 March 1846. Quoted in Sister Julia Dullea, CSA, *History of the Sisters of St. Agnes*, unpublished manuscript, n.d., ch. IV, 8. Without the work of Sister Julia, there would scarcely be an early history of the congregation. A notebook of mainly typewritten scraps of interviews, anecdotes, comments, forms the principal source of its early days. Her history was never completed. It appears to be an ambitious undertaking, but has little value in comparison with her notes. Elizabeth (Sister Julia) Dullea was born on 8 April 1866 in Boltonville, Wisconsin, to Edward and Bridget Collins. At the age of thirteen she became an aspirant in the congregation. She taught in various community schools, was the first sister in the congregation to earn a doctorate, and spent the last years of her life teaching at the motherhouse. She died on March 31, 1951.

12. One of the most severe of all ecclesiastical penalties, the interdict forbade the administration and reception of the sacraments in the place where the penalty was imposed.

13. Dullea, *History*, ch. IV, 18.

14. Rev. Martin Kundig would later play a pivotal role in Fr. Rehrl's life. One of the great missionaries of the Midwest, he was born in Switzerland in 1805, came to the United States in 1828, and later was ordained a priest who served in Ohio and Michigan. In Detroit he forced "upon his community … the duty of charity and help to victims of misfortune and affliction." He organized women to found a society to help the many orphans; began a campaign to clean up the poorhouse; attempted to solve the unemployment problem; and became a public official, the Superintendent of the Poor. George Paré, *The Catholic Church in Detroit 1701-1888* (Detroit, Michigan: Gabriel Richard Press, 1951), 657-665.

15. Peter Leo Johnson noted that Henni's coming to Wisconsin "opened flood gates of bigotry and intolerance." Ibid.

16. Michael Heiss, letter to the Regent, 8 July 1844, in "Letters of the Late Archbishop Michael Heiss," trans. Rt. Rev. Msgr. Joseph Rainer," The *Salesianum* 9 (July 1914), 19.

17. Rev. Leo Rummel, O. Praem., *History of the Catholic Church in Wisconsin* (Madison, Wisconsin: Knights of Columbus, 1976), 256.

18. Rehrl, *Letter from Calumet Village*.

19. Vieracker describes the territory as "170 miles of forests and bogs," *Rehrl*, 4.

20. Bishop Henni to Most Rev. V. E. Milder, Archbishop of Vienna, 8 December 1845. Quoted in Dullea, *History*, ch. IV, 8.

21. Rev. Joseph Salzmann, a friend of Rehrl's who arrived from Austria in 1847, did not find the area attractive. "Salzmann for a long time did not take to the region, and he frequently spoke of its dreariness. The rough and almost impassable roads in particular disgusted him, being used to the beautiful and well-kept roads that intersect Austria in all directions …. thousands of Germans would go back to Europe if the ocean would freeze over." Joseph Rainer, *A Noble Priest: Joseph Salzmann D.D., Founder of the Salesianum*, trans. Joseph William Berg, (Milwaukee: Olinger and Schwartz, 1903), 45.

22. Vieracker, *Rehrl*, 5.

23. Mother Rosita Handibode, *Homily Given for Founders' Day Celebration, September 2, 1979.*

24. Only three years earlier a traveler had described Fond du Lac as the first town of much importance along the road to Green Bay. He saw small prairies, signs of Indians, abandoned wigwams, and sugar houses. In Fond du Lac, which he termed "famous," he found two houses, one a blacksmith's. Increase Allen Lapham, "A Winter's Journey from Milwaukee to Green Bay," *Wisconsin Magazine of History* 9 (September 1925): 93.

25. Middlings, the coarser part of ground wheat separated in the sifting process, was at that time regarded as valuable only for feed.

26. J.E. Halbenkann, *"Missionary Priests,"*19 *The Salesianum* (October 1909): 19.

27. Rehrl wrote of men who in two or three years were able to work for the Americans and save enough to buy their own land. He identified one man in particular who rose from poverty so absolute that he once was obliged to borrow two shillings. Yet, within three years' time, he owned forty acres of land, two oxen, a cow, two pigs, and fifty dollars in cash. Ibid.

28. Vieracker, *Rehrl*, 6.

29. Halbenkann, 20.

30. At a much later period, Rehrl stayed at the cathedral in Milwaukee, where he was given a horse to ride to Germantown. The priests there later found that he had walked to Germantown leading the horse. Dullea, *Notes*, 3.

31. Vieracker, *Rehrl*, 7.

32. Halbenkann, 18.

33. Fr. Stephen Rehrl also wanted to come to Wisconsin, but remained in Austria in deference to his mother's wishes. Rev. Benjamin Blied, "Wisconsin's Founding Priest: Caspar Rehrl—Circuit Rider," *Catholic Herald Citizen*, 25 March 1950, 22.

34. Dullea, *Notes*, 3.

35. "An Apostle of Our Wilds: Father Caspar Rehrl, a Missionary of Washington County and Vicinity," continuation of the <u>Washington Countiana</u> Series. *West Bend News*: 6 October 1920. Quoted in Dullea, *History*, ch. IV, 11.

36. Rt. Rev. Msgr. Matthew Gerend, "Diamond Jubilee of St. Francis Seminary," *The Salesianum* 26 (July 1931): 7-8.

37. Celestine Bittle, OM Cap., *A Romance of Our Lady Poverty: The History of the Province of St. Joseph of the Capuchin Order of the United States* (Milwaukee: Bruce, 1933), 28.

38. Halbenkann, 18.

39. Vieracker, *Rehrl*, 7.

40. Ibid., 6-7.

41. Harry Heming, ed., *The Catholic Church in Wisconsin* (Milwaukee: Wisconsin Catholic Historical Publishing Co., 1895-1898), 699.

42. Maximilian Gaertner, O.Praem., *An Account of the First Synod of the Diocese of Milwaukee, 1847, from the Diary of Maximilian Gaertner, O. Praem., Who Was Present.* trans. by Sister Consuelo Fissler, O., and Julia Careau. Archives of the Archdiocese of Milwaukee, Wisconsin.

43. "Report of the State Superintendent, 1849," in Joseph Schafer, *The Winnebago Horicon Basin: A Type Study in Western History* (Historical Society of Wisconsin, 1937), 195-196.

44. Elmer C. Kiessling, *Watertown Remembered* (Watertown Historical Society of Wisconsin, 1976), 93.

45. Lloyd P. Jorgenson, *The Founding of Public Education in Wisconsin* (Madison: State Historical Society of Wisconsin, 1956), 128-137.

46. Rehrl letter addressed to the people of Tirol, 9 March 1864. *Katholische Blaetter*, (31 [sic] April 1864), 267, 268. Archives of the Archdiocese of Milwaukee, Wisconsin.

47. Harold A. Buetow, *A History of United States Catholic Schooling* (SNCEA Keynote Series No. 2, National Catholic Education Association, 1985), 18.

48. Anthony Urbanek, "Report of the Missionary Priest, the Reverend A. Urbanek, of the Diocese of Milwaukee; in the State of Wisconsin, of the North American Union, Presented to the Archbishop of Vienna, the Most Rev. Vincent Edward Milde, Regarding the Make-Up and Conditions of the Episcopal City, Milwaukee, and also of the Diocesan Population," Report 25, 1853, *Wisconsin Magazine of History* 10 (September 1926): 87.

49. Jorgenson, 122.

50. Johnson, *Crosier*, 118.

51. Caspar Rehrl, *Reflections for Catholic Christians*, bks. 35, 36, trans. by S. Felicitas Dreiling, CSA, 1978-1980. A series of notebooks Fr. Rehrl kept of facts, readings, etc.

52. Halbenkann, 20.

53. Otto Jeron, OM Cap., *The Rise and Progress of the Province of St. Joseph of the Capuchin Order in the United States 1857-1907* (New York: Benziger Brothers, 1907), 41.

54. Vieracker, *Rehrl*, 9.

55. Vieracker, *History*, 15.

56. Jeron, 49-50.

57. Vieracker, *History*, 9-10.

58. Ibid., 11. These young ladies are almost certainly the Moes sisters. The younger, Maria Catherine, became Mother Alfred, OSF. Her career was most unusual. She had entered a convent in Europe; after ten months she came with her older sister to the United States apparently because of her admiration of Bishop Henni. After they left Johnsburg, they entered the Notre Dame convent in Milwaukee. The two sisters later were dismissed for "a lack of religious spirit," then, in 1856, joined the Marianites of the Holy Cross in Indiana. Following a rocky sojourn with that community, they went to Joliet, where Mother Alfred established the Joliet Franciscans in 1865. Eleven years later, because the bishop of the diocese declared her ineligible for reelection, she left that community and eventually established a new community of Franciscans in Rochester, Minnesota. Their story is told in Carmen Kraman, OSF, *Odyssey in Faith: the Story of Mother Alfred Moes, Founder of Two Franciscan Congregations and Saint Mary's Hospital*, Rochester, Minnesota (Rochester, Minnesota: Assisi Heights, 1990), 34.

59. The School Sisters of Notre Dame had come from Baltimore to Milwaukee in 1850.

60. S. Dympna [School Sister of Notre Dame], *Mother Caroline and the School Sisters of Notre Dame in North America*, vol. 1 (Saint Louis: Woodward and Tiernan Co., 1928), 66.

61. Vieracker, *Rehrl*, 12.

62. Dullea, *History*, ch. VI, 3, 4.

63. Dullea, *Ibid.*, 4.

64. Ibid., 5.

65. "In fact among the oddities of the Church 150 years ago was that many people did not see the education of youth as a work that was particularly suitable for sisters. The Pope issued a document somewhere around 1875, casually pointing this out .... " Benjamin Blied, *Father Blied's Address*, 9 September 1968.

66. Vieracker, *Rehrl*, 12.

67. Ibid., 13.

68. St. Ambrose, *On Virgins*, 2. 8.

69. Dullea, *Notes*, 8.

70. Dullea, *Notes*, 67.

71. Caspar Rehrl to "Most Worthy Consistorium," 24 April 1875. Quoted in S. Imogene Palen, *Fieldstones '76* (Oshkosh Printers, Inc. 1976), 115.

72. The population of Barton in 1855 was 1,095, of whom 445 were of foreign birth. It was connected with the railroad before 1857 by daily mail and stage route. An American and a German hotel, three large stores, and

numerous workshops were all in Barton at this time. *History of Washington and Ozaukee Counties* (Chicago: Western Historical Co., 1881), 440.

73. Dullea, *Notes*, 2.
74. Richard H. Driessel, *A History of the Village of Barton, Washington County, Wisconsin: A Nineteenth Century Settlement in Southeastern Wisconsin* (Fern Park, Florida 1992), 119.
75. Caspar Rehrl, *Account Book*, n.d.
76. Archives of the Archdiocese of Milwaukee, Wisconsin..
77. Dullea, *History*, ch. VIII, 6.
78. S. Emily Schug, CSA, *The Story of Clara Rehberg: The First Sister of St. Agnes*, typescript, n.d., 3.
79. Dullea, *History*, ch. VIII, 9.
80. It is possible to find portraits of almost all of the pioneer priests who served in the Milwaukee diocese, but there are no pictures of either of the Fathers Rehrl.
81. S. Leo Ankenbruck, quoted by Dullea, *Notes*, 34.
82. Sisters interviewed by S. Julia gave Mother Agnes as the source of the information. Dullea, *Notes*, 2.
83. Dullea, *Notes*, 72.
84. Mother Agnes Hazotte, *Record of the First Beginning in Barton Until the First General Chapter in Fond du Lac, Wisconsin*, typescript, c. 1876. 1.
85. Dullea, *History*, ch. VIII, 11. Until 1870, the names Mary and Agnes were given in addition to the name of a sister's own patron saint. Later, only the name *Mary* was given, but ordinarily just the initial *M.* was used; e.g., Sister Mary Catherine was called *Sister Catherine*, but her name was written Sister M. Catherine, unless both the names Mary and Catherine were meant to be used. Since 1969, the initial *M.* has no longer been used. The middle letter *M.* is not used in this manuscript.
86. Ibid.
87. The village of Barton is now the north side of West Bend. The property that once belonged to Fr. Rehrl is presently in the possession of the Washington County Historical Society. Dr. Richard Driessel and his wife Margaret, together with the Otto family, had purchased the convent in 1996 for its historic value, with the intent of turning it over to some historic organization. The property contains three buildings: the largest structure, built around 1856, which housed a convent, school, and chapel; a two-story house built in 1858; and a stone barn built in 1878. "Monument Acknowledges Driessel Family's Gift," *West Bend Daily News*, 13 June 2003, A 9.
88. Dullea, *Notes*, 51.
89. It is noteworthy that while the sisters were living in such dire circumstances, Fr. Rehrl could visualize the future and write that sisters should never for-

get the virtue of frugality. There was to be no eating between meals or consumption of "food imported from remote regions." Liqueurs were not permitted, but a little beer or wine was allowed—if the sisters made it or if it was a gift. And "on vacation days they should spend part of the day in studies and cultivating their own faculties, the rest they shall spend in laboring." *Original Constitutions Prepared by Father Rehrl—Literal English Translation.*1858, 1.

90.   Sister M. Vera Naber, *With All Devotedness: Chronicles of the Sisters of St.Agnes, Fond du Lac, Wisconsin* (New York: P. J. Kenedy & Sons, 1959), 35.

91.   Melanie Dulso as quoted in Dullea, *Notes*, 10. Fr. Rehrl was not always consistent in his attitude toward women religious. On the one hand, the women and the society needed the support of the church and therefore had to conform to canon law; on the other, he simply wanted effective Catholic teachers.

92.   Dullea, *History*, ch. IX, 5.93

93.   Rehrl, *Original Constitutions*, 1.

94.   Mary Agnes Hazotte to Sisters, 1869.

95.   Each religious institute has a rule or constitution that sets forth its way of life. It regulates its discipline, practice, and observances. The terms are frequently used interchangeably.

96.   *Original Constitutions*, 3.

97.   The divine office is the official prayer of the church. Its basic structure combines psalms, prayers, canticles, and readings to be said at assigned hours during the day. The traditional names of the various hours are matins, lauds, prime, tierce, sext, none, vespers, and compline.

98.   *Original Constitutions*, 3.

99.   Peter Leo Johnson, *Halcyon Days: Story of St. Francis Seminary, Milwaukee, 1856-1956* (Milwaukee: Bruce Publishing, 1956), 88.

100. Heming, 275.

101. In an interview in his later years, Fr. George Moder spoke of Rehrl's grief. "He pathetically referred to a large blue handkerchief which Father C. Rehrl used and which was wet with his tears for the good son of their devoted parents, for the devoted brother of his heart, for the saintly priest of God so sadly needed in the missionary fields of America." Dullea, *History*, ch. IX, 9.

102. *Record*, 1.

103. Sister Ursula, whose baptismal name was Catherine, can be identified through the 1860 census of Barton as eighteen years old, a servant, and blind. Her family name, however, is indecipherable.

104. Dullea, *Notes*, 72.

105. Dullea, *Notes*, 15.

Chapter II ~ Conflicting Visions

1. Naber, 27.
2. *Directress* as a term does not have the weight of superior. Fr. Rehrl did not use the canonical term superior immediately.
3. Dullea, *History*, ch. IX, 5.
4. On April 10, 1861, Brigadier General Beauregard, commander of provisional confederate troops, demanded the surrender of the union garrison at Fort Sumter. Shots were fired. The union forces surrendered three days later. The Civil War had begun.
5. *Notes*, 10.
6. The first mention of the Sisters of St. Agnes as "Ladies of the Society of Saint Agnes" is listed under "Seminaries, Academies and Schools" in *Sadlier's Catholic Almanac and Ordo* in 1864. The Civil War prevented publication of the volume in 1862 and 1863. That year the number of pupils in the school was listed as sixty. Dullea, *History*, ch. XI, 5.
7. Dullea quoted Melanie Dulso in *History*, ch. X, 1.
8. *Translation of Fr. Rehrl's Rules for the Sisters of St. Agnes, (Drawn up by Father Rehrl in 1862 for Sisters in Barton and never submitted to Rome.)*
9. Liturgical vestments would require costly fabrics and considerable skill in fine needlework. It seems probable that the prohibition regarding the making of vestments was connected to Fr. Rehrl's love of simplicity.
10. Peter Leo Johnson, "School Beginnings," *Centennial Essays for the Milwaukee Archdiocese, 1843-1943* (Milwaukee: Archdiocese of Milwaukee, 1943), 127-142.
11. Dullea, *Notes*, 11.
12. *U.S. Department of Commerce, Bureau of the Census.* The Detroit census in 1860 lists seven members in the Hazotte household: John, twenty-six; Joseph J., twenty-one; Charles, eighteen; Victor, fifteen; Mary, sixteen; and Mary, thirteen. John's occupation was that of clerk in a tobacco store; Joseph J. (a cousin also named John), Charles, and Victor worked in a tobacco factory. The sixteen-year-old Mary was probably baptized Mary Clementine but called Clementine.
13. *The History of Fond du Lac County, Wisconsin ... containing war records ... biographical sketches ... history of Wisconsin*, etc. (Chicago: Western Historical Company, 1880), 618.
14. Ibid., Christmas 1918.
15. Ibid., September 1917.
16. Naber, 41.
17. This is the same Fr. Halbenkann who many years later wrote *Memoirs of the Rev. J. E. Halbenkann on Three of the Early Missionary Priests of the Archdiocese of Milwaukee, Rev. C. Rehrl, his brother Rev. G. Rehrl and P. F. Bermadinger, OM Cap.*
18. Dullea, *Notes*, 11.

19. Much as she must have dreaded Sister Thecla's departure, and although she possessed only two dresses, Agnes offered the better one to Thecla for her journey.

20. Rehrl, "Tirol," *Katholische Blaetter*, 30 April 1860. Rehrl added a practical suggestion: "Sister Thecla can furnish you with a pattern of a Sister's garb for your trip. Homemade personal clothing is exempt from duty or taxes. The same cash for one outfit bought in America, can easily clothe six sisters in European prices."

21. Ibid.

22. "After S. Thecla left, Father Rehrl didn't know whom he would choose as superior. Sister Thecla thought he'd take Genevieve but instead he took Agnes." Dullea, *Notes*, 11.

23. Dullea, *History*, ch. X, 13.

24. Rehrl, *Tirol*, Fr. Rehrl had proudly stated in his letter to Tyrol that the Bishop had already honored the sisters with four visits. *Katholische Blaetter*, April 30, 1864.

25. Bishop Henni must have been puzzled by the fact that, in four years, Fr. Rehrl had placed four different sisters in charge of the community: S. Clara Rehberg in 1859, S. Thecla Dulso in 1860, S. Genevieve Popp in 1861, and S. Emerentia Ryan in 1862.

26. S. Thecla stayed there for seven years, then took charge of the Catholic and public schools at Rubicon for a year. She then went to Detroit to visit her aunt, who convinced her to serve temporarily as housekeeper for a priest in need of assistance. She stayed until his death twenty-nine years later, then returned to Fond du Lac to live in the Henry Boyle Home for the Aged, conducted by the Sisters of St. Agnes. Melanie Dulso lived far into her nineties, dying on April 28/29, 1926.

27. In 1854, the state legislature demanded that specified subjects be taught in English, a requirement that undoubtedly caused difficulties for some of the young women.

28. Haas also had a brother who became a priest and a sister who had emigrated to America and joined the Notre Dame Sisters in Milwaukee. Campion R. Baer, OFM Cap. *Lady Poverty Revisited: A History of the Province of St. Joseph of the Capuchin Order* (Sterling Heights, Michigan: Lesnau Printing, 2005), 7.

29. By way of distinction from other Franciscans, the Capuchins in most countries at this time appended "OM, Cap." after their names, signifying *Ordinis Minorum, Cappucinorum*. When, in 1939, the Latin word for *friars* was added, they appended "OFM, Cap." to their names.

30. Carl Quickert, "Centennial Section," *Catholic Herald Citizen*, 18 June 1985.

31. Sister Imogene Palen, CSA, *Fieldstones: The Story of Caspar Rehrl* (Fond du Lac Wisconsin: Badger-Freund Printers, 1969), 20.

32. Dullea, *History*, ch. X, 6.

33. Naber, 34.
34. "All went fine until L. came." Dullea, *Notes*, 13.
35. Bittle, 203.
36. Dullea, *Notes*, 34.
37. S. Agnes Hazotte to Fr. Caspar Rehrl, 9 May 1869.
38. "Fr. Rehrl didn't let them in the front door before he had them out the back door." S. Francesca Bercher, interview by author, 15 May 1996.
39. Mother Agnes Hazotte, CSA,. *Report from the First Beginning in Barton, up to the First General Chapter in Fond du Lac.* English hand-written translation, 4.
It appears that Fr. Rehrl gave S. Catherine charge of the motherhouse without the knowledge of Mother Agnes.
40. S. Agnes to the sisters at Marytown, 1869. When reading the early, and not well-written, letters of S. Agnes, it is well to remember that French was her first language. At fifteen, she lived with predominantly German-speaking people.
41. Ibid., 1 December 1869.
42. Ibid.
43. S. Agnes Hazotte to S. Gertrude Laughlin, 9 December 1869.
44. Ibid.
45. Ibid.
46. Sisters Agnes and Gertrude had been in New York to raise money during the summer of 1869. They returned with Margaret Lethert (S. Aloysia), Mrs. Catherine Pingeon (S. Vincent), and Margaret Brady (S. Augustine).
47. Ibid., 21 December 1869.
48. S. Agnes Hazotte to the sisters at Marytown, 12 January 1870.
49. Bittle, 203.
50. S. Agnes Hazotte to the sisters at Marytown, 12 January 1870.
51. Ibid.
52. Rev. Martin Kundig to S. Agnes Hazotte, 7 March 1870.
53. Bittle, 18.
54. "With his keen insight into matters spiritual, Francis recognized the high moral stature of Mother Agnes." Ibid., 204.
55. S. Agnes Hazotte to the sisters at Marytown, 18 March 1870.
56. Ibid.
57. John J. Schmitz wrote that Fr. Pickel's greatest service to the church in Fond du Lac was the invitation he extended to the Sisters of St. Agnes to move there. *More Than Brick and Stone: A History of St. Mary's Parish* (Fond du Lac Wisconsin: St. Mary's Catholic Church, 1966), 12.
58. S. Agnes Hazotte to sisters at Marytown, 31 March 1870.
59. Dullea, *History*, ch. XIII, 14.
60. S. Imogene Palen, *Fieldstones in Fond du Lac: The Story of Mother Agnes Hazotte*

(Fond du Lac, Wisconsin: Badger-Freund Printers, 1970), 25.

61. Agnesians had served in that parish since 1864.

62. Five of the young women persevered: Ellen Morrissey (S. Seraphine), Margaret Murphy (S. Petra), Catherine Murphy (S. Bernard), Mary Carroll (S. Stanislaus), and Anna McCormack (S. Laurentia).

63. Rev. Martin Kundig, to S. Agnes Hazotte, 28 June 1870.

64. Naber, 60-61.

65. Naber, 62.

66. The sisters who were so far away were in Defiance, Ohio. Hazotte, *Record*, 10. 118.

67. Bishop Henni was in Rome for the Vatican Council. Whether he had directed Fr. Kundig to disband the group in his absence is not certain. It is certain that he would not have wished to cause pain to such a faithful missionary as Fr. Rehrl. Peter Leo Johnson stated in his biography of Fr. Kundig that Kundig had decided to disband the community because Rehrl had found fault with his (Kundig's) arrangements. Johnson, *Stuffed Saddlebags*, 266.

68. Mother Agnes added that it was because "Reverend Caspar Rehrl did not agree" with Kundig's arrangements. Mother Agnes Hazotte, *Record*, 2.

69. According to Fr. Benjamin Blied, "Kundig was machinating to dissolve the sisterhood." *Wisconsin's Founding Priest*, 22.

70. Naber, 66-67.

71. "A regular novitiate was now established which had not heretofore been the case, so that the Congregation of the Sisters of St. Agnes very properly dates its permanent foundation from the time of its establishment in Fond du Lac on August 1, 1870." Heming, 950.

72. Naber, 69.

73. Naber, 69.

74. *The Minutes of the General Council, 1860-1903,* read, "According to the instruction of the Very Reverend M. Kundig, Administrator and Rector of our Institution, we took possession of our property in Fond du Lac on August 1, 1870. Reverend Caspar Rehrl who up until now had agreed on everything did not wish to leave Barton. Also several Sisters, although they had accepted the rule and had made their profession. This caused a separation." That same day, the United States census was taken for the town of Barton. Twenty women listed as "sister" resided in the convent on that day. They ranged in age from fifteen to sixty-eight. Four children, ages six to twelve, listed as scholars, were also residents. The nine residents from six to fifteen were born in Wisconsin; nine sisters were born in Bavaria, one in Canada, and six in Prussia. 1870 WI Series M593 Roll 1742, 385-6.

75. Unsigned to "Dear Sister," 3 August 1870.

76. Ibid.

77. Ibid.
78. Historical references do not always distinguish between these two groups and the location of the missions they served.
79. Dullea, *Notes*, 127.
80. Ibid., 124-128.
81. Vieracker, *Rehrl*, 15.
82. Dullea, *Notes*, 65.
83. Ibid.
84. Rehrl "To the Consistorium," 24 April 1875.
85. It appears that with the death of Kundig on March 6, 1879, Rehrl felt free to visit the sisters.
86. Naber, 99.
87. Dullea, *History*, ch. XVI, 4.
88. Henni was appointed Archbishop of Milwaukee on 12 February 1875.
89. The initial sketches were written by Sister Louisa Wolsiffer. Sister Louisa was the congregation's secretary and a member of the general council for thirty-one years. *Life Sketches of the Deceased Sisters of the Congregation of St. Agnes, Book I – 1872-1931*, No. 108.
90. Fr. Caspar Rehrl to "Reverend," 9 September 1879.
91. S. Roseann Simon remembered her family in St. Kilian's parish speaking about helping Fr. Rehrl. Interview by author, 2 June 2006.
92. Palen, *Fieldstones in Fond du Lac*, 59.
93. Fr. Caspar Rehrl to Mother Agnes Hazotte, 16 August 1881.
94. Palen, *Fieldstones*, 60.
95. Dullea, *Notes*, 31.
96. Ibid., 65.
97. Quickert.
98. Ibid.
99. A puzzling item in the *General Council Minutes* reads: "June 16, 1882, Council resolved to buy the old convent at Barton from Fr. Rehrl." Whether the item should be dated 1881 is a matter for conjecture. The matter was not alluded to again.
100. Vieracker, *Rehrl*, 17.
101. While the opening of the canonical novitiate in 1870 was considered the founding date, Peter Leo Johnson, in 1943, termed Fr. Rehrl the founder of the Sisters of St. Agnes. *Centennial Essays for the Milwaukee Archdiocese 1843-1943* (Milwaukee, Wisconsin: Centennial Committee), 130.
102. According to Melanie Dulso, "Fr. Rehrl had nothing in mind but the glory of God and the salvation of souls." Dullea, *Notes*, 10.
103. Rev. Benjamin Blied, typewritten homily, 9 September 1968.
104. *The Congregation of the Sisters of St. Agnes, Constitutions and Directives, 1987*, 24.
105. According to Peter Leo Johnson, "Rehrl was informal, accounted by many

as odd, by some as a fool. However, those who worked with him loved him."
Crosier, 86

106. *Golden Jubilee, June 15 and 16th, 1920: St. John's Congregation, Rubicon, Wis.,*
1920.

107. For a discussion on the spirituality of the immigrant church, see Joseph
Chinnici, OFM, *Living Stones: the History and Structure of Catholic Spiritual Life
in the United States* (New York: U.S. Catholic Conference, 1989), 120.

108. Dullea, *Notes*, 120-128.

109. S. Francesca Bercher, interview by author, 9 May 1996. Because S.
Francesca had entered the congregation only fifteen years after the death of
Mother Agnes, she had known well many of the contemporaries of Mother
Agnes and proved to be an excellent source of information.

Chapter III ~ Mother Agnes in Charge

1. On August 3, 1875, *The Fond du Lac Journal* made this claim to the city's
virtue: "Fond du Lac is said to be the best church-going city in the West. A
large percentage of the population attend. The fact that we have numerous
and roomy churches, good preachers, and a moral, sensible, and orderly
population will account for this pious tendency."

2. Fr. Theobald Matthew, a Capuchin known as "the temperance priest," had
inspired millions of Irish to take the pledge in the 1830s and 1840s. He had
come to the United States in 1849 to launch a crusade against alcohol
among the immigrants.

3. Charles R. Morris, holds that most Catholic immigrant groups brought
their church with them; the bishops became involved only after the parish
was powerful. St. Mary's seems to be one such an example. Charles R.
Morris, *American Catholic: The Saints and Sinners Who Built America's Most
Powerful Church.* (Times Books; Random House, 1997), 131.

4. The American delegates, distrustful of Roman authoritarianism and suffering from Protestant suspicions of the Catholic Church, had been fearful of
the damage such statements could do in non-Catholic countries and were
strongly opposed to those proclamations. One American voted in the negative—twenty-two went home before the vote. Morris, 72.

5. S. Julia Dullea wrote: "Rosa Recker, in doubt about having left Barton, is
said to have written asking Bishop Henni's advice as to when she should
return to Barton. He advised her to remain in Fond du Lac." *History*, ch.
XVI, 3.

6. Mother Agnes Hazotte to S. Gertrude Laughlin, 10 January 1871.

7. Ibid.

8. [Mother Agnes Hazotte] to "Dear Sister," 3 August 1870. Agnes did not

specify what "do anything" meant. Presumably, Kundig meant that the society now had another director who was responsible for its spiritual welfare.

9. In the estimation of Sister Julia Dullea, Fr. Willard deserves to be forever remembered by the Sisters of St. Agnes for his help to the young community. *History*, ch. XIV, 8.

10. Ibid.

11. "Our Bishop ordered me today to let you know that he wishes … to work well with you …. Up to now he appeared very reticent in regard to you as if I had taken too much liberty in forming a friendship with you. But today that was changed." Martin Kundig to Sister Mary Agnes, 7 March 1871.

12. Quoted in Bittle, 212.

13. Ibid.

14. St. Agnes Boarding School, Barton; St. Xavier, Cross Plains; Sts. Peter and Paul, Allenton; St. Anthony, Aneo; St. Bridget, Wayne; St. Kilian, Hartford; Visitation, Marytown; St. John Nepomucene, Little Chute; St. Mary, Port Washington; St. Peter, Slinger; St. Lawrence, St. Lawrence; St. Peter, Ashton; St. Kilian, Ashford; St. Peter, Farmington; St. Augustine, Jackson; and Sacred Heart, St. Francis.

15. After the Second Plenary Council of Baltimore of 1866 the bishops were forbidden to allow women religious to travel around the country collecting alms, but the need for money was so great that the bishops were often obliged to make concessions. Fr. Francis was of the opinion that in most dioceses priests have the right to allow collecting without asking their bishop. He was concerned, however, about ethnic issues. He was careful to ask Agnes to warn S. Patrick Walsh that if she should come to New York to collect, her companion should not be German, nor should she mention his name or that of any known Germans there. The Irish Archbishop of New York was not inclined to let money leave his Archdiocese to support German communities. Fr. Francis Haas to Mother Agnes Hazotte, 16 November 1877.

16. S. Agnes Hazotte to Rev. Martin Kundig, 3 July 1870.

17. Fr. Kundig to Sister Agnes, 5 August 1870.

18. S. Irma Reichling, letter to author, 23 September 1994.

19. S. M. Stanislaus Carroll, *Life Sketches*, No. 246.

20. Mother Agnes Hazotte to S. Gertrude Laughlin, 30 March 1871.

21. Sister Antonia Schmitz would save greenhouse flower boxes to make candidates' veils. The bonnets were shaped by inserting into the double front a cut-to-size green cardboard about 5 1/2 to 6" deep and about 18" long. The back of the bonnet was gathered and kept in place by a shoestring. S.

Felicitas Dreiling, *Vignettes of Superior Generals: Mother Antonia- 1905-1916*, 20 December 1979.

22.   Sister Laurentia was one of the eight Irish girls who had entered from Appleton, Wisconsin, in 1870.

23.   *Select* indicated that tuition was charged.

24.   The school had been founded previously, but the term *opened* may have been used as an indication of assumed responsibility. *Life Sketches* No. 31.

25.   *Inventory of Real Estate Owned by The Congregation of St. Agnes Made Mar. 13, 1926.*

26.   Johnson, *Crosier*, 118.

27.   House sisters did the cooking, cleaning, and laundry in the convents. They said the Lord's Prayer and the Hail Mary instead of the Latin *Little Office of the Blessed Virgin Mary*.

28.   The Agnesians were at St. Mary's in Port Washington for only one year. Their housing was unsatisfactory. They could reach their second floor rooms only with the use of a ladder.

29.   Bishop Henni to Mother Agnes Hazotte, 21 March 1871.

30.   S. Aloysia Bath, OSB. *Notebook,* Archives, St. Benedict's Monastery, St. Joseph, Minnesota.

31.   Ibid.

32.   Ibid.

33.   Mary Helena Bath became S. Aloysia, OSB. Six years later the bishop appointed her prioress of her community. At that time she was probably the best educated sister in the community and was considered quite American. In 1889, as a result of the first free election in the history of the community, S. Aloysia again became prioress. At great personal cost, she was successful both as spiritual leader and as an educator in her community. Imogene Blatz, OSB, and Alard Zimmer OSB, *Threads from Our Tapestry; Benedictine Women in Central Minnesota* (St. Cloud, Minnesota: North Star Press of St. Cloud, Inc., 1994), 36. The Sisters of St. Agnes and particularly her mentor, Mother Agnes, can assume a modest amount of credit for the hard-won education of Mother Aloysia. Her story is important for the light it sheds on the trials the young sisters faced in their early years as educators. One can only reflect in amazement that these barely educated girls, in such a short time, became competent teachers, sought-for, and valued.

34.   Bishop Henni to Mother Agnes Hazotte, 15 June 1871.

35.   Records were kept only of the sisters who remained in the community. Twelve members of that profession group remained in the community.

36.   Lydia Holcomb entered the Sisters of Mercy in 1876.

37.   "Pray and Work."

38.   Dullea, *History* , ch. XIV, 11.

39.   "Intrigues of a serious nature arising (instigated) in unsuspected quarters

against the Rev. P. Commissarius [Rev. P. Francis Haas, OM Cap.] and Sister M. Agnes Hazotte, Sup. Gen., which began showing their destructive results the beginning of winter, caused the Rt. Rev. Bishop to renew the jurisdiction which he had previously given to the V. Rev. Father Haas, OM Cap.," Mother Agnes Hazotte, *Record,* 6.

40. [S. Agnes Hazotte] to "Dear Sister [Gertrude Laughlin]," 22 January 1870.
41. S. Agnes Hazotte to S. Gertrude Laughlin, 23 March 1870.
42. S. Agnes Hazotte to [recipient unknown], 31 March 1870.
43. S. Agnes Hazotte to S. Gertrude Laughlin, 7 April 1870.
44. Ibid., 21 December 1869.
45. Ibid., 21 December 1869.
46. Positing that the charges involved an inappropriate relationship between Mother Agnes and Fr. Francis is inescapable, but the fact that the friar was appointed a judge in the dispute seems to rule out that hypothesis.
47. There is no signature on this document, but in the initial information before the directive, Fr. Francis states his power is authorized by the archbishop.
48. *From Barton,* a handwritten document with no signature and no date, CSA Archives. A printed newspaper advertisement has not been found. The sisters were attempting to observe the constitutions rejected by Bishop Henni in 1858. It was signed by Sisters Gertrude Laughlin, Aloysia Lethert, and Mechtildis Brilliotte.
49. Rev. Nicholas Pickel to Fr. Caspar Rehrl, 14 February 1872. On November 11, 1892, Mother Agnes conveyed the property to the congregation.
50. Ibid.
51. M. Agnes to [unnamed recipient], 1 March 1883.
52. S. Magdalene Callaghan to S. Seraphine Morrissey, 1887.
53. Fr. Francis Haas to Mother Agnes, 18 January 1873. The letters were written between 14 October 1872 and 14 April 1895 and translated by Sisters Rosaline Stephanie and Lucida Vorndran.
54. Fr. Francis Haas to Mother Agnes Hazotte, quoted in Bittle, 214.
55. Ibid.
56. Fr. Francis Haas to Mother Agnes Hazotte, 26 October, 1890.
57. Ibid., September 1882.
58. Ibid., 30 October 1886.
59. Ibid., 19 May 1886.
60. Fr. Francis Haas to the community, January 1889.
61. Quoted in Bittle, 214.
62. Fr. Francis Haas to Mother Agnes Hazotte, 10 May 1886.
63. Ibid., 5 August 1874.
64. Fr. Francis to Sister Seraphine Morrissey, 20 October 1888.
65. Quoted in Bittle, 214.

66.   S. Claude Feldner recalled that her mother, born in 1867, spoke of the sisters staying overnight at her home in St. Cloud, Wisconsin. S. Mary Frances Schug, *Music*, typescript, n.d.

67.   In the nineteenth century, orphanages became common in America. Previously, children were taken in by relatives or neighbors; older children were sometimes indentured to a trade. Epidemics and later the Civil War created a demand for orphanages. Tuberculosis, cholera, malaria, small pox, industrial accidents, and the death of women in childbirth continued to fill nineteenth- and early twentieth-century orphanages. The children of Irish immigrants were especially vulnerable because their parents frequently came to this country sadly malnourished. Anna Carey later entered the congregation, making her first profession in 1885.

68.   Margaret asked to enter the community in 1877. She received the name Eugenia and taught for six years. She died of typhoid fever in 1886.

69.   Bishop John Henni to Mother Agnes Hazotte, 3 September 1872.

70.   Ibid.

71.   *Life Sketches*, No. 1. Sisters and novices who died before 1872 are not included. Little is known of their lives.

72.   John could also be abrupt. Sister Dominica Gonsch related the story of her introduction to Fond du Lac: "At the ... Depot a man approached me and said, 'I want you.' I looked at him a little suspiciously and did not answer. Fortunately some kind persons noticed my predicament and said to me, 'Lady, he is the man from the Convent.'" Sister Dominica Gonsch, *My Entrance into the Convent*, typescript, n.d.

73.   Dullea, *Notes*, 36.

74.   The normal school was founded to prepare young men to teach in schools where the German language was dominant. No such opportunities were provided for the growing number of women religious in the archdiocese. Every order had to provide education for its own members, obliging professors like Singenberger to travel to various motherhouses to teach the sisters. The subjects listed here are those Professor Morrissey taught in September 1907. *Annals*, 12 September 1907.

75.   The importance of music in the congregation is witnessed by the fact that the first sister to be sent away for studies, S. Louisa Wolsiffer, studied music for two years under the tutelage of the Dominican Sisters in Racine, Wisconsin.

76.   The Caecilian movement was formed in Germany to reform church music in Europe and in the Americas. Its primary aim was to promote the use of sixteenth-century polyphony and the reform of the chant. Professor Singenberger was later made a Knight of St. Gregory, the highest papal honor for a layman, for his work in church music.

77.   Bittle, 253.

78.   *Rules and Constitutions of the Congregation of St. Agnes V& M* as approved by V.
      Rev. Martin Kundig, Admin. & V.G. of the Diocese of Milwaukee, Wis. On
      the 23rd day of July A.D., 1870, Barton, Wis.
79.   Ronald Jansch, OFM Cap., letter to author, March 2002.
80.   *Rules*, ch. I, 1.
81.   *Ibid.*, ch. II, 1-2.
82.   *Ibid.*, ch. III, 2-3.
83.   *Ibid.*, ch. IV, 3.
84.   This centuries-old office was approved by Rome for sisters. It was usually
      selected by active communities because it did not require rising at night.
85.   *Ibid.*, ch. V and VI, 3.
86.   *Ibid.*, ch. VI, 3.
87.   *General Council Minutes, 1876.* Members of Third Orders are usually lay per-
      sons who strive to capture the spirit of the Order and participate in its spir-
      itual benefits, *Annals,* 23 January 1926.
88.   Septennial vows were taken for a period of seven years.
89.   Fr. Francis Haas to Mother Agnes Hazotte, February 1875.
90.   Later Schickel would design the Stuyvesant Polyclinic Hospital in New York
      City, St. Ignatius Loyola Church in Manhattan, St. Joseph's Seminary in
      Dunwoodie Heights, New York. Several examples of Schickel's work are
      protected by the New York City Landmark Commission. Designer of three
      hundred churches, he has been called a father of church architecture. *New
      York Architecture Images—Stuyvesant Polyclinic Hospital,* <www.nyc-architecture.
      com/LES/LES020.htm.> Internet; accessed 6 June 2006.
91.   In the days before elevators, this decision would cause no small amount of
      hardship to the sisters, as prayer would ordinarily take them to the chapel
      a minimum of four times each day.
92.   A sacramental, an *Agnus Dei* was a disc of wax, impressed with a figure of
      a lamb, usually blessed by the pope at stated seasons. In the prayers of
      blessing, special mention was made of protection from the perils of storms
      and pestilence, from fire and flood, and from the dangers to which women
      were subject at childbirth.
93.   *Life Sketches*, No. 10.
94.   From our perspective, knowing that Georgia was still suffering from the
      calamitous effects of the Civil War and Reconstruction, it seems an effort
      doomed from the start. However, Savannah had a thriving Irish population,
      which may have been the attraction.
95.   S. Alberta Wolsiffer to Mother Agnes Hazotte, *Life Sketches,* No. 18.
96.   Rev. J. D. Wagner, *St. Mary's Parish, Altoona, PA. Chronicle, 1855-1948.*
      (Altoona Mirror Printing Co: *St. Mary's Parish, Altoona,* n.d.), 26.
97.   The Sisters of Mercy who came to Fond du Lac from Janesville, Wisconsin,
      could trace their beginnings to a small community in Sterling, Illinois,

established by the Davenport community in 1868. The community had relocated to Janesville in 1870 in response to a request to staff St. Patrick's School there. Because of financial difficulties, the parish and school were closed. In January 1876, upon the invitation of Fr. George Willard, the sisters left for Fond du Lac to establish their motherhouse there. In 1880, a new pastor in Janesville redeemed the property and the sisters were given a title to the convent. The Fond du Lac property was retained as their motherhouse, but because neither the pastors nor St. Joseph's Church nor St. Patrick's wished to build a school, the community transferred to Milwaukee in 1894. During the years the sisters resided in Fond du Lac, a number of girls of Irish descent entered their order. Sister Mary Josephine Donnellen, RSM, *Chronicle: Early Times to 1925*, Archives Sisters of Mercy, Chicago.

98.   S. Francesca Bercher, interview with author, 9 May 1996.

99.   *Entries in Diary of Mother Agnes.*

100. *History of Fond du Lac County*, 606.

101. Ibid.

102. S. Claude Feldner, interview by author, 12 April 1997.

103. A chart compiled of the society's income and expenses between 1875 and 1884 shows that the sisters received 8 percent of their total income through collecting tours. School salaries brought in 36 percent, 26 percent was borrowed, 10 percent came from the sisters' dowries, 3 percent from their artificial flower industry, 2 percent from music and the organ, and less than 1 percent each from needlework, their annual fair and donations. The chart showed only 90 percent of the income. The society spent 21 percent of its income on building; 15 percent on the community, paid 10 percent on notes, 7 percent on interest, 4 percent on a mortgage, 3 percent on travel, medical expenses and serge; 2 percent on books and stationery; 1 percent on flower material, insurance and music. Dry goods and food related items amounted to about 25 percent of expenditures. *Mother House Accounts 1870-1891.*

104. That Mother Agnes could treat the sisters as equals goes far in explaining the genuine love she evoked from the community. Mother Agnes Hazotte to S. Agatha Beschta, 30 November 1875.

105. Years later, Fr. Francis wrote, "An order or congregation without solemn or perpetual vows, I think, is like a fruit without seed, like a heap of sand thrown together without solid foundation. I can not be enthusiastic about that situation. Most congregations wish and have perpetual vows. The members in perpetual vows are the core of the association. Once you are so far that you can appoint perpetually professed as superiors everything will function better .... " Fr. Francis to Mother Agnes, 23 June 1891.

106. Dullea, *Notes*, 59.

107. "I think S. Thomasine is doing as well as she can since I wrote to her last summer. They have all their debts mostly paid. After that they will be more careful. The order and everything else is much better than any of our English missions. S. Thomasine will do well the older she gets. Sisters respect her and have reason to .... " Mother Agnes Hazotte to Sisters Josephine Maurer and Seraphine Morrissey, 23 February 1883.

108. The sisters were required to pass an examination before the public school board in order to be certified.

109. There are a number of examples of Polish, Lithuanian, and Slovak churches going into schism rather than conforming to the authoritarian mode. A milder example of ethnic tensions was evidenced in the story of Bryan O'Laughlin and Martin Gruenheck, farmers in Fond du Lac county who gave land to build a church in the village of St. Peter. When the German Capuchins were given charge of the church, Mr. O'Laughlin and his family withdrew and joined St. Joseph's in Fond du Lac. 7 December, 2007. Lillian M. Fox interviewed by author.

110. The interested historian is unusually fortunate in that details of the controversy are given from the Capuchin perspective in *A Romance of Our Lady Poverty* by Celestine Bittle, OM Cap. Also, John Schmitz gives the perspective of a diocesan priest in *More Than Bricks and Stones: a History of St. Mary's Parish*, (Fond du Lac, Wisconsin: St. Mary's Parish 1966). Another insight may be gained from a letter in which Agnes reported a remark unflattering to Pickel's school: "R. P. Guardian [Rev. Father] came here but I had no chance to tell him anything. F. Pickel was here. P. G. said here in the presence of F. Pickel that P. Cajetan said the children in St. Mary's did not learn anything for they had to carry water and chop wood the most part of the day they would go and [be] in school a few minutes." Mother Agnes to "Dear Sister," 3 August 1870.

111. *The Fond du Lac Journal*, 5 June 1879, quoted in Bittle, 253, 254.

112. Fr. Aegidius á Cortona to Fr. Daniel, Vicar of Mount Calvary, 28 October 1875. Quoted in Bittle, 252.

113. Although the Sisters of St. Agnes were not directly involved, it is probable that Mother Agnes was an unwilling catalyst in disagreements that had, over time, grown between Fr. Pickel and Fr. Francis. She was certainly aware of the conflict, as a letter Fr. Francis wrote to her on March 16, 1875, attests. He was returning from New York and had "in mind to stop over in Fond du Lac; but— however—will they not stone me there?" Letter of Fr. Francis to Mother Agnes, 16 March 1875.

114. The trustee system began to disappear in the United States toward the end of the nineteenth century when the Irish model of an authoritarian clergy and a deferential laity became the normative model in the United States— except in German parishes. Jay P. Dolan, *The American Catholic Experience: a*

History from the Colonial Times to the Present (Garden City, New York: Doubleday & Company, Inc., 1985), 172-173.

115. In his account of the meeting, Schmitz makes it clear that he found this meeting and the presence of Mother Agnes very odd indeed, 20.

116. These notes were taken from a letter dated December 5, 1879, written by Mother Agnes to Fr. Bonaventure Frey, OM Cap.

117. Because Fr. Francis was in accordance with canon law, it appears that tension between the regular and religious clergy was playing a part in the controversy.

118. Msgr. Batz wrote to Fr. Francis on December 31, 1879, "You acted correctly in this final sacrilegious catastrophe at St. Mary's Church. That you sought and found shelter with the good Sisters, fills me with great pleasure. I thank the kindhearted Sisters; the history of the Church of the Archdiocese will certainly record this noble deed and honor it in the proper fashion." Bittle, 263-264.

119. The words of Fr. Bonaventure Frey, Schmitz, 20. Fr. Francis paid fifty-four hundred dollars for the property.

120. Bittle, 268.

121. Mother Agnes Hazotte to Sister [recipient unknown], 23 June 1880.

122. Letter of 11 December 1887. Quoted in Schmitz, 26.

123. Florence Jean Deacon, *Handmaidens or Autonomous Women: Charitable Activities, Institution Building, and Communal Relationships of Catholic Sisters in Nineteenth-Century Wisconsin* (Madison: University of Wisconsin, 1989), 156.

124. "That dear old man may last a long time yet. His lack of appreciation for your congregation could become very sensitive." Fr. Francis Haas to Mother Agnes Hazotte, 21 April 1889. However, the archbishop did remark to Mother Agnes in a letter dated 23 July 1895: "Your Sisters have an interest in everything even if it is difficult." It is not clear from the context of the letter if he meant it as a compliment. It is certain that Agnesians would take it as one.

125. Fr. Francis Haas to Mother Agnes Hazotte, 5 November 1889.

Chapter IV ~ Coming of Age

1. Morris, 83-85.
2. S. Gertrude Laughlin, *From Barton*, handwritten copy of an advertisement Gertrude had intended to place in Catholic newspapers. n.d.
3. Unknown to the sisters at Barton, the Sisters of Mercy had lost their convent because of serious financial problems in the parish and had moved to Fond du Lac.
4. Naber, 99.

5. Sisters Borgia Kelly, Viridiana Weber, and Sebastian Zehnpfennig were among them. The entry in the sketch of S. Sebastian's life reads, "She belonged to a little community of Sisters, at Janesville, Wisconsin, which was disbanded by Archbishop Henni in 1879." Why was it not identified as Fr. Rehrl's society? *Life Sketches*, No. 43.

6. Mother Agnes Hazotte to S. Gertrude Laughlin, 21 June 1880.

7. Ibid., 23 June 1880.

8. *Life Sketches*, No. 106.

9. The name of Gertrude had been re-assigned to Margaret Loidl who was professed in 1879.

10. The silver jubilee marked twenty-five years in vows. The first Sister of St. Agnes to reach the fifty-year mark and celebrate her golden jubilee was S. Clara Rehberg in 1908. *Life Sketches*, 103.

11. Mother Agnes Hazotte to S. Bernardine Laughlin, 29 June 1888.

12. Mother Felicite, Superior, to Mother Agnes Hazotte, 14 May 1881.

13. *Acquisitions*, 7.

14. Mother Agnes Hazotte to "Dear Sister," 7 February 1883. Laudanum was an opium-based painkiller, popular during the Victorian period for everything from headaches to tuberculosis.

15. France allowed only religious engaged in activities helpful to the state (e.g., nursing) to remain in the country. Mother Agnes had to justify the existence of CSA in those terms.

16. Mother Agnes Hazotte to [S. Josephine Maurer], 10 February 1884.

17. This is not the more famous luxury liner, *Normandie*. However, it had a measure of fame when, in 1840, it was one of the vessels used to transport Napoleon Bonaparte's exhumed body from Cherbourg to Havre.

18. S. Seraphine Morrissey to S. Josephine Maurer, April 1884.

19. "The indulgences I petitioned for were granted. So we now enjoy all of the privileges of the 3rd Order of St. Francis." Dullea, *Notes*, 90.

20. The white skull cap is today preserved in Founders Hall at the motherhouse.

21. S. Seraphine Morrissey, *Circular Letter*, quoted in Naber, 110-111.

22. The council also agreed to buy forty acres of land in Yankton, then in the Vicariate of Dakota, for the erection of an institute. *Council Minutes*, 12 April 1885. The property was sold in 1888 to Bishop Martin Marty.

23. Dullea, 15.

24. Fr. Bonaventure Frey to Mother Agnes Hazotte, 5 August 1886.

25. Ibid.

26. The sisters remained at that address until 1993.

27. The cost of the chapel was $30,509.78. *Financial History*, A four-page typewritten list of acquisitions and selected expenditures from 1888 to 1928, n.d.

28.   The marble high altar was not added until 1903. It was purchased from Hackner and Sons, La Crosse, Wisconsin, for $2,340. Mr. Louis Fromveller donated $2,000 to pay part of the altar with the agreement that a rate of 5 percent interest be paid him annually until the end of his life. Ibid.

29.   Wilhelm Lamprecht is still an admired artist and the fresco restored in 1985 may still be seen. "The theme [the triumph of Christianity] very rare in the history of religious art ... was handled with astounding creativity by Lamprecht." Annemarie Springer, *German American Church Artists*, Bloomington, Indiana, June 2001. <www.ulib.iupui.edu/kade/ springer/Ch6/ ch6p2.html> Internet; accessed 11 April 2006.

30.   Quoted in Naber, 114.

31.   Fr. Francis Haas to Mother Agnes Hazotte, 13 February 1891.

32.   The Rt. Rev. Martin Marty. The original Vicariate Apostolic of Dakota was established in Yankton but upon the division of the territory and the admission of South Dakota as a state in 1889 the diocese of Sioux Falls was established to embrace the entire state.

33.   S. Magdalene Callaghan to S. Seraphine Morrissey, 17 January 1887. The ambitious plans for Yankton did not materialize. S. Magdalene died in June 1888. She was thirty years of age.

34.   Ibid.

35.   St. Ignatius Parochial School is a tribute to the dedication to education of the early priests. As early as 1858, because the public school charged tuition, the pastor taught both Protestant and Catholic children in the sacristy of the church. In 1887 a school was built and entrusted to seven Sisters of St. Agnes. All children were welcomed and "the indiscriminate admission had the sad consequence that the attendance became subsequently as scant as it was in the beginning overflowing." When the system of tuition was abolished in 1896, the situation righted itself, but St. Ignatius had the honor of being the first free school in the diocese. Rev. Antoine Ivan Rezek, *History of the Diocese of Sault Ste. Marie and Marquette*, vol. 2 (Houghton, Michigan, 1907) ch. XX, 5-6 <http://home.earthlink.net/~sdrichman/ ssst-ignatius.html> Internet; accessed 7 July 2004.

36.   At this time, the constitution required that the councilors be elected from among the older sisters who had made perpetual vows and that they reside in the motherhouse. *Rules and Constitutions of the Sisters of the Congregation of Saint Agnes*. In two parts. Fond du Lac, Wis.: Mother House, 1886, Part II, 2, par.1.

37.   S. Amadea Wirtz, CSA. *The Mystery of Texarkana* (Fond du Lac, Wisconsin: St. Agnes Convent Print Shop, 1986), 19-23.

38.   N. A. Gallagher, Bishop of Galveston to His Eminence, J. Cardinal Simeoni, 2 January 1889. Quoted in Wirtz, 19.

39.   S. Alexia Carney left the congregation to care for her aged mother.

40. Wirtz, *Mystery*, 10.
41. Ibid., 22-23.
42. Ibid., 6. In her assessment of the situation, S. Amadea Wirtz saw Sister Thomasine Carney and her staff as heroines of this mystery. S. Thomasine had earned a great deal of respect in Texarkana. In 1975, the congregation received a letter from a gentleman, Max Reynolds, who wrote that he had named his son Kearney after S. Thomasine (Elinor Therese Kearney) because of her kindness to his father during his illness and death. Her community, the Sisters of St. Rose of Lima, was greatly respected, although it failed to prosper.
43. Two of the sisters returned to the world, and the others joined the Little Rock Sisters of Mercy. Ibid, 7.
44. S. Rose Carmel Schorsch, interview by author, 30 January 2000.
45. Wirtz, *Mystery*, 12-14. The sisters who returned, because of their disobedience, were deprived of their rank in the congregation, e.g., they took the last places at table or any other place. S. Francis Assisi Pielmeier remembers that, as a very young sister, she remarked on the old sister who always took the last place. She was told that the sister had refused for a period of time to return to Fond du Lac from Texarkana. S. Francis Assisi Pielmeier, interview by author, 5 February 2005.
46. See Colman J. Barry, *The Catholic Church and German Americans* (Milwaukee: Bruce Publishing Company, 1953) for a treatment of German-Irish tensions in the church.
47. Mother Agnes also mentioned that she felt like getting out of Dakota if Dr. Zardetti did not return. Mother Agnes Hazotte to [S. Josephine Maurer] 12 December 1888.
48. The society was organized in 1855.
49. Dolan, 298.
50. Wm. Schickel to Mother Agnes Hazotte, 25 October 1889. Quoted in S. Amadea Wirtz, CSA, *Haven for the Homeless: The Leo House, 1889-1989* (Fond du Lac, Wisconsin: Badger-Freund Printers, 1985), 24.
51. Ibid., 24-26.
52. Fr. Francis Haas to Mother Agnes Hazotte, 15 November 1889.
53. Wirtz, *Haven*, 11.
54. Rev. Thomas G. Lynch, *History of the Leo House*, unpublished paper, 1996. 38.
55. Barry, 109.
56. Fr. Francis Haas to Mother Agnes Hazotte, 15 December 1889.
57. In order to publicize the plight of labor, in the winter of 1893-1894 Jacob Coxey organized an "army" of unemployed to send to Congress as a living petition. Five hundred men arrived in Washington. Although the leaders were arrested, other larger armies of unemployed were formed throughout the nation.

58. Raphael Engel, OFM Cap., Blaine Burkey, OFM Cap., eds. *"Do You Know?*
     Vignettes on the History of St. Joseph's Parish (First Catholic) Parish in Western
     Kansas (Provincial Archives, Capuchin Province of Mid-America, Hays,
     Kansas, 1989), 84. Fr. Raphael contributed 162 vignettes on the history of
     St. Joseph's Parish, Hays, to the weekly parish bulletin during the years
     1971-1975 and from late 1977 until mid-1978 in the monthly parish mag-
     azine, *The Carpenter.*

59. S. Claude Feldner remembered her mother telling her that Mary Leuching
     wept so copiously from homesickness that she had almost enough water to
     soak the leather for a sole in a pair of shoes. S. Claude Feldner, *Anecdotal*
     Jottings, n.d.

60. Bittle, 342.

61. As a young man Katzer came to the United States, studied at St. Francis
     Seminary in Milwaukee, and was ordained in 1866. He soon joined the fac-
     ulty there and taught mathematics, philosophy, and dogmatic theology
     while earning praise as a man of profound learning. In 1866 he transferred
     to the diocese of Green Bay and eleven years later was appointed bishop of
     the diocese. His eventual nomination to the Milwaukee archdiocese was
     opposed by some who were against German domination of archdiocesan
     affairs. He was strict in his adherence to canon law and his "administration
     was marked by a uniform regard for justice." *Catholic Encyclopedia*, online
     edition, 1911, s. v. "Milwaukee," by J. Rainer. <www.newadvent.org/cathe
     en/10319a.htm> Internet; accessed 18 March 2005.

62. Fr. Francis Haas placed the matter before the Propaganda in Rome. It was
     decided that perpetual vows could be made only after the expiration of ten
     years. In 1893, membership was listed as 173 professed, 12 novices, and 38
     candidates. In 1895 the number of professed was only 171. *Council Minutes,*
     1894.

63. Archbishop Katzer to Mother Agnes Hazotte, 23 July 1895.

64. Ibid, 31 December 1895.

65. See Vincent A. Yzermans, *Frontier Bishop of St. Cloud*, (Waite Park,
     Minnesota: Park Press, 1988), for his biography.

66. Mother Agnes to "Dear Sisters," 2 February 1891. When the Sisters of St.
     Agnes were in Yankton, Zardetti was also attentive to S. Bernardine
     Laughlin. Three letters written to her exist. They are dated 9 January 1888,
     23 July 1888, and 31 July 1888. On July 23, he wrote, "I would prefer to
     spend the day in your house having for my privacy your parlor."

67. "I have not forgiven Leo XIII for taking me from America." Archbishop
     Otto Zardetti to Mother Agnes Hazotte, 8 November 1894.

68. Yzermans, 176-177.

69. Zardetti's letters to Mother Agnes dealing with financial matters are dated
     14 July 1894, 6 November 1894, 11 January 1896, 16 July 1896, 8 [month

illegible] 1897, 12 July 1898, 16 August 1898, 18 June 1899, 8 October 1899, 3 May 1901, and an undated, but similar, letter.

70. The *Annals* of September 20, 1905, recorded that a note of $5,692 was paid to Mr. Eugene Zardetti in Switzerland.

71. *Life Sketches*, No. 7.

72. St. Luke's parish provides a good example of the ethnic mix that made up the parishes in those days. In 1898 there were 349 families in the congregation; 234 were classed as German; ninety as French; twenty as Bohemian, and five as English. In 1889 the Polish families had withdrawn from St. Luke's and established Sacred Heart Parish. Rev. John P. Schmitt, ed. *St. Luke's Congregation, Two Rivers, Wisconsin: a Century of Service to God, 1851-1951* (Two Rivers, Wisconsin: Malley Kanzelberger Printing Co., 1951.)

73. Naber, 122.

74. *Mission List*, draft, 1-5. As records were incomplete in the early years of the congregation, this list is not completely reliable.

75. Problems arose when changes were forced upon Mother Agnes because of sickness of the sisters. One pastor threatened to close the school if the community kept changing teachers. Mother Agnes Hazotte to an unnamed sister, 12 December 1888.

76. Congregation of the Sisters of St. Agnes, *Articles of Incorporation*, 1892.

77. *Acquisitions*, 9,10.

78. *Regulations*, 1895.

79. "In the early years of the period, to take but one example, travel among convents and to the homes of relatives was not uncommon in some communities. But by 1890, an ecclesiastical authority was on record as disapproving of sisters' leaving the convent for visiting or shopping. A decade later, social visiting and visits to the sick were curtailed. By the end of the period, social visits of any kind by sisters were enjoined by the cardinal unless specific permissions were obtained for each visit. Mary J. Oates, "Catholic Sisters in Massachusetts" in *Women in American Religion*, ed. Janet Wilson James (University of Pennsylvania Press, 1980), 167.

80. Bittle, 346.

81. Bittle, 351.

82. It is a day of reparation for sins celebrated on the Friday after the Octave of Corpus Christi.

83. Handwritten note, [S. Romana] n.d.

84. Mother Agnes Hazotte, quoted in Naber, 126.

85. Dr. Wiley maintained a supportive and close connection with St. Agnes Hospital throughout its foundation years. It is unlikely that the hospital would have survived without his support and leadership.

86. *Financial History.* 1.

87. *Minute Book of the Meetings of the Board of Directresses of the Corporation The Congregation of Saint Agnes of Fond du Lac, Wisconsin,* January 25, 1895. The

date of incorporation of the congregation by the State of Wisconsin was November 1, 1892; the date of the first meeting of the corporation was November 3, 1892. St. Agnes was founded as a Catholic hospital in accord with "the master principle of every Catholic hospital," which was "to give the highest expert service not only to the patient's bodily ills but to his mental distress, his conscience's comfort, and his soul's eternal welfare." Rev. Charles B. Moulinier, S J, in Robert Shanahan, SJ, *The Catholic Hospital Association: Its First Twenty-Five Years* (University Microfilms, 1987), 3.

88. This was not the first time that Agnes had been criticized for her decisions. When she received the report of one flurry of interest, the exasperated Agnes wrote, "People are very much interested in our affairs. I wish they would send me money instead." Mother Agnes Hazotte to [S. Seraphine Morrissey], 10 February 1884.

89. Naber, 128.

90. Naber, 129.

91. Mother Agnes, *Circular Letter*, 1 June 1896.

92. The Boyle brothers, sons of Irish immigrants, were born in the state of New York. In 1873, they came to Fond du Lac where they began to manufacture yeast. Eventually the company prospered and both brothers became noted for their philanthropy.

93. *Financial History*, 1.

94. *St. Agnes Sanatarium: East Division Street, Fond du Lac, Wisconsin; in Charge of the Sisters of St. Agnes* (Fond du Lac: the Reporter Presses, 1896), 12.

95. Ibid.

96. Naber, 131-133.

97. The parish was named Immaculate Conception but familiarly was called St. Mary's until 1916, when the United States was dedicated to the Immaculate Conception. The pastor used the occasion to return to the original name. *History of Immaculate Conception Parish*<www.icelmhurst.org/main_xmas.html.>Internet; accessed 4 January 2003.

98. *Acquisitions*, 11.

99. The purchase of the property brought some protests from the public, possibly because of a concern that the sisters would be forced into bankruptcy. Mother Agnes, however, saw the farm as "a means in God's Providence to help us pay our indebtedness." Naber, 134.

100. S. Imogene Palen, CSA, *Fieldstones in Fond du Lac*, 76-77.

101. The escarpment, a steep slope or ridge, runs from Niagara Falls to the upper Great Lakes.

102. Those who died in Fond du Lac were buried in the nearby village of St. Peter, where today the visitor will find nineteen well-kept graves belonging to pioneer sisters and novices.

103. S. Amadea Wirtz, CSA, *The Call to the Western Plains: The History of the Sisters of St. Agnes in Kansas* (Hays, Kansas: Printcraft Printers, 1980), 13.

104. *Minutes Board of Directresses*, 4 October 1894.

105. Ibid., 4 January 1901.

106. S. Emily Schug, *Interviews with Sister Claude Feldner*, typewritten paper. 2003. Mandolins had been introduced into American popular culture by the Italian immigrants. By the turn of the century mandolin orchestras were forming in schools and colleges. *A Brief History of the Mandolin*, <www.mandolincafe.com/archives/briefhistory.html.> Internet accessed 9 March 2006.

107. Archbishop F. X. Katzer to Mother Agnes Hazotte, 20 February 1901.

108. Naber, 142.

109. Ibid.

110. When the sisters vacated the home in the year 2000, the property reverted to Boyle heirs.

111. The tablet is now in the congregation's cemetery.

112. Sebastian Gebhard Messmer was born in Switzerland in 1847. After ordination he came to the United States as a professor, obtained a doctorate in canon law, and in 1891, succeeded Bishop Katzer in the Green Bay diocese. In 1903, he was appointed Archbishop of Milwaukee. In order to centralize authority in the church, he wrote the first *Handbook for Catholic Parishioners* in 1907. Messmer effectively stopped the use of foreign language instruction in many schools and in the transaction of diocesan business. Eventually he became opposed to bilingual programs and eliminated German-English catechisms. Known for his support of charitable organizations, he also played a significant role in education and approved the first ministry to African Americans with the organization of St. Benedict the Moor Church and School. He opposed women suffrage but supported Catholic women's organizations. He founded the *Catholic Herald* and supported numerous Catholic lay organizations. During his episcopacy twenty-nine orders of religious men and women were established in the Archdiocese. "Most Reverend Sebastian Gebhard Messmer, D.D., D.C.I, 1903-1930," http://www.archmil.org/bishops/bishopmessmer.asp.

113. S. Seraphine Morrissey to Sister Agatha Beschta," n.d.

114. The choice of S. Hortulana as companion and homemaker may provide another insight into the character of Agnes. S. Hortulana's obituary notes, "From the time of her profession our Sister was subjected to much suffering. Pain in the feet caused difficulty in walking; her face was disfigured by painful eczema; hands and feet were crippled by rheumatism." *Life Sketches*, 117.

115. S. Regina Deiler, the third councilor, was the only member of the council remaining at the motherhouse.

116. Ibid., 61.

117. Mary Agnes, "Dear Sister Gertrude," 7 April 1870.
118. Dullea, 12-13. Years later, a sister who had entered the congregation in 1906 from Catherine, Kansas, characterized Mother Agnes as "noble." When asked "how that came across," she said that Agnes "was good-hearted and if it had not been for the good-heartedness in running the Community, the Sisters might not have been so obedient and respectful to her or have had as much confidence in her." Clementia Schueler, *OHP*, 001-003.
119. S. Francesca Bercher, interview by author, 9 May 1996. Because S. Francesca had entered the community only fifteen years after the death of Mother Agnes, she had known many of the contemporaries of Agnes.

Chapter V ~ Women of Courage, Faith, and Vision

1. *Life Sketches*, No. 2.
2. Robert Shuster, "Documenting the Spirit," *American Archivist* 45 (Spring 1982): 139
3. It does not do to discount the *Life Sketches* on the grounds that "one does not speak ill of the dead." Pioneers were made of sterner stuff. On several occasions the less edifying was included with the edifying. Consider the life of S. D. who "gave satisfaction in the classroom. ... However, by her proud and overbearing disposition she became a source of grief to her superiors and disedification to her companions." Fortunately, Sister, who had tuberculosis, "lingered for nearly one year, during which time she learned how to suffer with patient resignation. With the help of God she overcame her natural impetuosity and became humble and docile." *Life Sketches*, No. 68.
4. Germany was unified only in 1870. Prussia, Bavaria, Hanover, and Baden were German states.
5. S. Marie Wagner, *Analysis of Census Reports of Barton, Wisconsin, 1860 and Fond du Lac, Wisconsin, 1870 and 1880*, 1981.
6. When the constitutions were approved by Rome, S. Vincent Pingeon, a widow, was not allowed to make final vows; the illegitimate sister, after years of pleading, was finally given permission to make perpetual vows. Unfortunately, ready to board the train to take her to Fond du Lac, she dropped dead. *Life Sketches*, 34.
7. S. Mary Sheila Burns, CSA, *A Comparative Study of Social Factors in Religious Vocations to Three Types of Religious Communities*, (Doctoral Dissertation, Catholic University, 1956), 111.
8. *Life Sketches*, No. 83.
9. S. Marie Wagner, Ibid.
10. Michael Lesy provides a fascinating look at the perils of living in nine-

teenth-century Wisconsin in *Wisconsin Death Trip* (New York: Pantheon Books, 1973).

11. "Expectation of Life at Specified Age, by Sex: 1850-1956," Mass. Series B. 76-91. U.S. Bureau of the Census," *Historical Statistics of the United States: Colonial Times to 1957* (Washington D.C. 1960), 64.

12. George C. Stewart, Jr. *Marvels of Charity: History of American Sisters and Nuns.* Foreword by Dolores Liptak (Huntington, Indiana: *Our Sunday Visitor*, 1994), 176. Stewart lists these factors but comments that, without a call, those vocations could hardly have stood the test of time.

13. S. Michael Immler, *Life Sketches*, No. 58.

14. *Life Sketches*, No. 154.

15. S. Genevieve was a widow who had lost two sons as well as her husband. She sold her property in St. Lawrence, Wisconsin, and entered the society with her daughter. She was devoted to Father Rehrl and remained with him in Barton until the end of her life. Dullea, ch. X, 13.

16. *Life Sketches*, No. 200.

17. Ibid., No. 29.

18. S. Elizabeth received this tribute after her death, "She lived for God and for her sisters." Ibid., 56.

19. Ibid., No. 139.

20. The congregation does not have a record of S. Vincent's birth date.

21. According to S. Jane Zurbuch, the bishop was thwarted by a confessor at the Mercy motherhouse. "He told the bishop that the bishop got the girls in but he'd [the confessor] get them out because the girls were not happy where they were not called." *OHP*, 005-003.

22. *Life Sketches*, No. 4.

23. Fr. Francis Haas, OM Cap., *Rules and Constitutions*, ch. IV, 7.

24. The custom dates back as early as the sixth century. The practice was based on God's changing Abram's name to Abraham to signify the covenant between them (Genesis 17:3-9), Stewart, 29.

25. Haas, *Rules and Constitutions*, ch. IV, 7.

26. Joan D. Chittister, "No Time for Tying Cats," *Midwives of the Future: American Sisters Tell their Story*," ed. Ann Patrick Ware (Kansas City, Missouri: Leaven Press, 1985), 8.

27. *Life Sketches*, No. 32.

28. Ibid., No. 21.

29. Ibid. No. 55. Amazingly, no other sisters are listed as having died of small pox at that time.

30. A scrutiny was a discernment by the general council to determine if the applicant had a vocation to the congregation.

31. Writers' Program of the Works Projects Administration in the

Commonwealth of Pennsylvania, *Pennsylvania: a Guide to the Keystone State* (New York: Oxford University Press, 1940), 525.

32.   *The Diamond Jubilee of S. Joseph Church* (Pittsburg, Pa.: St. Joseph Protectory Print), 1955.

33.   Not every religious community undertook the same tasks. Not every congregation, for example, would undertake church work.

34.   Dullea, *Notes*, 66-67.

35.   Naber, 60.

36.   It would be ungrateful to forget the help of the many women of the parish who helped the sisters in so many ways. In many parishes, the women annually housecleaned the local convent, inventoried the linens and replaced them when necessary after the sisters left for retreat. S. Marie Wagner, interview by author, 30 May 2003.

37.   According to Ronald Jansch, OFM Cap., Father Francis Haas used the Franciscan First- and Second-Order Rules to formulate the Agnesian rule and constitutions. As spiritual director of the sisters, he undoubtedly introduced Franciscan spirituality to the community. The flexibility of the Franciscan rule was an important reason for its popularity.

38.   The *Kulturkampf* (1872-1887) was the struggle in Prussia and other German states against the Catholic Church, which took the form of laws designed to bring marriage, education, etc., under the control of the state. Religious orders were severely restricted.

39.   Herzog was established less than a mile from the English settlement of Victoria. The two gradually connected and, in 1913, they became the single entity, Victoria.

40.   Norbert R. Dreiling, *Official Centennial History of the Volga-German Settlements in Ellis and Rush Counties in Kansas 1876-1976* (Volga-German Centennial Association, Hays, Kansas, 1976), 46-47.

41.   Engel, Ibid.

42.   Ibid.

43.   S. Aurea had entered in 1866. Since her first mission in Marytown, she had served in Defiance, Ohio, and in the Wisconsin towns of Granville, Town Ten, St. Cloud, Pine Bluff, and East Bristol.

44.   Blaine Burkey, OFM Cap., *Schoolmaster Schmidt and His Family Album* (Thomas More Prep-Marian High School: Hays, Kansas, 1986), 64.

45.   It was customary for Volga German families to build one house in town and one on the farm. They spent weekends in town to facilitate attending Mass and other church services; other days they lived on the farm. In this case, the Dreiling family lent the sisters their finished town home and lived in a sod house they had built in the village upon first arriving there in 1876.

46.   *Life Sketches*, No. 13.

47. Engel, 64.
48. S. Stella Schmidt, *OHP*, 005-002.
49. The children spoke a Volga German dialect found in and around Ellis County. It represents a German language-speech enclave established along the southern Volga River during the time of Catherine the Great. Although the Germans had lived in enclosed communities in Russia, their language was influenced by their neighbors. *The German Dialects of Kansas*, http://www2.ku.edu/~germanic/lasgdhomepage/about.htm Internet; accessed, 7 June 2006.
50. S. Amadea Wirtz, *Call*, 13.
51. Dullea, 57.
52. *St. Fidelis Church, 75 Years of Faith and Pride: Diamond Jubilee of the Dedication of St. Fidelis Church, "Cathedral of the Plains," Victoria, Kansas. 25 May 1986.*
53. Dullea, 60. "There is no life for the church where there are no sisters, where there are no Catholic schools."
54. Although both diseases were life-threatening, yellow fever was much more serious than malaria.
55. *Life Sketches*, No. 9.
56. Ibid., No. 14.
57. These women were professed as Sisters Felicitas, Basilia, and Cosma.
58. Engel, 61.
59. Wirtz, *Call*, 13.
60. Earl Meyer, OFM Cap., and Raphael Engel OFM Cap., and Blaine Burkey, OFM Cap., *Saint Francis Parish, Munjor, Kansas, 1876-1976* (Hays Kansas: Print Press, n.d.), 44-45.
61. Edmund Schuetz, as quoted in Debra Schmeidler, et. al. *St. Catherine Church: 100 Years, 1892-1992* (Hays, Kansas: Northwestern Printers 1992), 59-61.
62. *St. Mary's Church: 1986 Centennial Celebration*, Ellis, Kansas, 26.
63. S. Ludgarde was then sent to Harlem. While nursing S. Paula, who was sick at the Leo House, she injured herself lifting the patient. She died one week later. *Life Sketches, No. 27.*
64. Heming, 700.
65. Terence O'Donnell to S. Vera Naber, 5 December 1958.
66. *Life Sketches*, No. 66.

Chapter VI ~ Ordinary Time

1. Naber, 51-52.
2. M. Agnes to "Dear Sister," 1882.
3. Dolan, 167.
4. In 1900 the National American Woman Suffrage Association was able to

list only six Catholic clergymen who supported women's suffrage: Reverends J.W. Dalton, Thomas Scully, Edward McGlynn and Bishops John Ireland, Bernard McQuaid, and John Spalding. None were German. Archbishop Messmer of Milwaukee was outspokenly opposed to women's suffrage. James Kenneally, "Eve, Mary, and the Historians: American Catholicism and Women," in *Women in American Religion*, ed. Janet Wilson James (University of Pennsylvania Press, 1980), 194.

5.   Archbishop Katzer to Mother Agnes, Milwaukee, Wisconsin, 21 February 1889. Archbishop Heiss had expressly forbidden the acceptance of candidates over twenty-nine years old, but it appears that the archbishop had allowed an exception to the rule.

6.   S. Felicitas Dreiling, *Vignettes of Superiors General*, 4. S. Felicitas Dreiling was related to the first S. Felicitas Dreiling, who, in 1884, was the first Kansas woman to enter the congregation.

7.   *Annals*, 6 September 1905. At this time the average worker made two to four hundred dollars a year, and the average wage was twenty-two cents an hour.

8.   *Annals*, 7 September 1905.

9.   Regular and formal scheduling of visitations to the mission houses was not customary until the administrations of Sisters Angeline Kamp and Rosita Handibode. Previously, the Superiors general had usually visited at critical times only. S. Clementia Schueler, *OHP*, 001-003, 1981.

10.   In 1907, Mother Antonia wrote to the sisters that, besides the regular expenses, she had paid $11,600 on old debts and had built a new barn for $3,838.85, an addition to the farmhouse for $2,127.84, a henhouse for $543.30. Also, she had made improvements on the convent for $826.98, bought an additional boiler for the powerhouse for $667.25, and paid $3,313. 92 for street improvements—for a total of $22,918.14. Mother Antonia, *Circular Letter*, Christmas 1907.

11.   Mary J. Oates, "Organized Voluntarism: the Catholic Sisters in Massachusetts." *American Quarterly* 30 (Winter, 1978), 668.

12.   Ibid., 665.

13.   Dolan, 289.

14.   Ibid., 398.

15.   Harold A. Buetow, *Of Singular Benefit: The Story of Catholic Education in the United States* (New York: Macmillan, 1970), 110-111.

16.   Dolan, 289.

17.   Ibid.

18.   In July 1890, Archbishop John Ireland addressed a meeting of the National Education Association at St. Paul. Praising the public schools, he wanted state support for schools with permission for religious instruction in all schools. The archbishop feared that parish schools, especially in German

and Polish parishes, were divisive. Morris, 99.

19. Although not infrequently the Catholic schools suffered from bigotry, an unusual form of discrimination prevailed in the Carnegie, Pennsylvania, school system. Children graduating from the public schools were accepted automatically into the public high school. Children who had attended the parochial school had to take entrance examinations. One year none of the parochial school children passed the entrance examination. At least that was what the high school principal said. That was too much for the superior of the local Agnesian convent. The principal of the high school soon found out what all Sisters of St. Agnes knew, that one crossed S. Dionysia at one's peril. She went to the courthouse and demanded to see the tests the children were said to have failed. Needless to say, the children were admitted to the high school. S. Florita Fleck, interview with author, 10 May 1997.

20. Thorndike was not accepted because of his empiricism; Pestalozzi, because of his naturalism; Herbart, because of his determinism; Froebel because of his pantheism; progressive education, because of what was considered undue permissiveness for the child and forgetfulness of original sin. Buetow, 34.

21. As a result the majority of sisters did not receive a thorough grounding in Catholic philosophy and theology. An exception was Marquette University, which, in 1906, admitted women to undergraduate programs. DePaul University in Chicago, opened in 1914, was the first Catholic coeducational college.

22. Buetow, 180.

23. Avella, *In the Richness of the Earth* (Marquette University Press, 2002), 451.

24. Buetow, 246.

25. S. Emily Power, general superior of the Sinsinawa Dominicans, wrote to her sisters in 1903 to inform them that examinations, certificates, and diplomas would be required by diocesan boards of examiners throughout the country and that it would be necessary to prepare well for them. Eileen Mary Brewer, *Nuns and the Education of American Catholic Women, 1860-1920*, (Chicago: Loyola University Press, 1987), 40.

26. The early Capuchins were known as "good preachers, tender confessors, and down-to-earth pastors." Because it seems more than probable that this was the experience of the Sisters of St. Agnes, their distress at the removal of the Order is understandable. Avella, 86.

27. However, the Sisters of St. Agnes are an apostolic congregation, while the charism of the Franciscans is termed evangelical—which calls for living the gospel life "in solidarity and love." M. Clare Adams, OSC, "Religious Life," in *The New Dictionary of Catholic Spirituality*, ed. Michael Downey (Collegeville, Minnesota: Liturgical Press, 1993), 821-822.

28. Ibid., 491.

29.   Ibid., 86.
30.   Although orphans had been taken into the motherhouse in the community's early days in Fond du Lac, the sisters had had no previous experience with either orphanages as institutions or with Native American children, who formed a significant part of the school population.
31.   S. Jane Zurbuch, *OHP*, 005-003, 1981.
32.   S. Serena Humbel, *Memoir: Congregation of Saint Agnes and Orphanages*, unpublished essay, 1981.
33.   It was typical of Mother Antonia's business-like approach that she conscientiously kept the sisters informed of major events in the congregation.
34.   It was not a regulation that was maintained. For years missions made fancywork as Christmas presents for doctors, dentists, and other benefactors.
35.   The discipline was an instrument for self-inflicted mortification or chastisement.
36.   Mother M. Antonia, *Circular Letter*, 13 November 1906.
37.   *Annals*, 25 December 1906.
38.   A canonical visitation is made by a bishop with a view of maintaining faith and discipline and correcting abuses. Apparently, the Archbishop's four-day visit was more informal.
39.   The transfer of the music school from East Merrill Street to the newly-built wing on Division Street proved not to suit the students. The enrollment declined and the school was discontinued. S. Claude Feldner, interview by S. Mary Frances Schug, February 2003.
40.   *Annals*, 2 February 1915.
41.   In a letter to the sisters, Mother Antonia wrote," Owing to the lack of patronage or rather having not sought such, our former Sanitarium will be known hereafter as St. Mary's Academy ...." Mother Antonia, *Circular Letter*, 13 May 1909.
42.   Naber, 164-165.
43.   Sisters of St. Agnes, *St. Mary's Springs Academy 1927-1928* (Fond du Lac, Wisconsin: P. B. Haber Printing Company), 8.
44.   Ibid., 7.
45.   While the sisters stationed at the academy became known to the rest of the community as "the Academy ladies," the sisters did not live like "ladies." They were totally responsible for their own classes, including such tasks as covering the books of their pupils, taking care of the children after school hours, monitoring dorms, cleaning their own classrooms, cleaning other areas of the buildings, and helping in the laundry. In the summer they helped pick, peel, and can fruits and vegetables, as well as clean and make ready the school for the new year.
46.   Engel, 118.

47. Wirtz, *Call*, 55-57.
48. Ibid., 59-60.
49. Saint Agnes Hospital School of Nursing was one of 203 training schools for nursing opened between 1893 and 1913.
50. S. Digna [Desch], et. al. *A Half Century of Nursing Education and Nursing Service, 1910-1960* (Fond du Lac, Wisconsin: St. Agnes School of Nursing, 1960), 11.
51. It seems that each archbishop of Milwaukee was petitioned by the congregation for some mitigation of rules prohibiting sisters from attending family religious events.
52. The pastor was so close to the family that when her brother went to the seminary, Myra worried that he might have made the decision to please the pastor.
53. Lois Bodeau, ed., *Letters Home*, (Eagan: Michigan: by the Author) 1997. The Bodoh family deserves gratitude for preserving the letters, as does the family genealogist, Lois Bodeau, who arranged and published the letters.
54. Myra Bodoh to her family, 6 February 1915.
55. Ibid., 2 September 1909.
56. Myra meant orthography—a method of representing the sounds of a language by symbols.
57. Myra Bodoh to her family, 10 October 1901.
58. Ibid., 2 January 1910.
59. Ibid., 7 February 1910.
60. Ibid., 1 November 1909.
61. Ibid., 14 November 1909.
62. Ibid., 18 December 1910.
63. Ibid., 1 July 1912.
64. Ibid., 27 October 1912.
65. Ibid.
66. Ibid.
67. Ibid., 29 August 1913.
68. Ibid., 9 April 1914.
69. This was a period of forty hours of continuous prayer made before the Eucharist in solemn exposition. The number forty is reminiscent of the forty hours Jesus remained in the tomb before the resurrection.
70. Ibid., 21 May 1914.
71. Ibid., 15 July 1915.
72. Ibid.
73. Ibid., 12 November 1915.
74. Ibid., 24 September 1916.
75. World War I lasted from 1914 to 1918.
76. Ibid., 22 December 1916.

77.   Ibid.
78.   Ibid., 24 February 1917.
79.   Ibid., 13 May 1917.
80.   Ibid., 9 June 1917.
81.   That profession was unique in the history of the congregation. Septennial vows were discontinued that year. About seventy women made final vows.
82.   According to S. Dominica Gonsch, who had entered the congregation in November 1904, there was some opposition to Mother's reelection—but she made it "after an awful struggle." Mother Antonia was strict and seemed reserved. S. Dominica added that she always had enough to eat, although some sisters said they didn't. *OHP*, 001-004, 1981.
83.   *Annals*, 3 June 1912.
84.   *Annals*, 28 August 1912.
85.   *Inventory of Real Estate Owned by the Congregation of St. Agnes Made Mar. 13, 1926*, 17.
86.   The new wing opened with a reception that provided "one of the largest social functions … held in Fond du Lac in a decade or more." Termed a "magnificent" event, the guest list included all of the social and civic leaders of the city. As the article noted, "It was a splendid testimonial of the good will, encouraging support and spirit of kindliness that the people of Fond du Lac hold toward the Sisters of St. Agnes." There could have scarcely been a greater contrast to that June day in 1896 when the hospital first opened. "Hundreds Assist in Notable Event at Hospital Extension," *Daily Commonwealth*, 11 November 1913, 4.
87.   Nevertheless, the hospital established and donated to the city four free beds to serve the needy, *Daily Commonwealth*, 3 February 1916, 4. The total average daily census of free patients was 7.36 percent of the 76.18 patients served that same year; by 1919 the average daily census of free patients was 10.05 percent with the total average number of patients per day, 99.9 *Daily Commonwealth*, 28 January 1920.
88.   Charles B. Moulinier, S J, and the Sisters of St. Joseph of Carondelet spearheaded the movement designed to aid Catholic hospitals meet the standards established by accrediting agencies such as the American Medical Association. CHA provided a forum for women religious representing the communities engaged in health care. One of the first actions of CHA was to provide summer courses at Marquette University which would enable sisters to keep Catholic hospitals in the front rank of charitable institutions. Unlike those who argued against the propriety of letting women religious attend courses taught by non-Catholics and attended by the laity, Archbishop Messmer supported the sisters' attendance at summer schools and meetings. Moulinier answered objections of those who were afraid of "irregularities or interruptions in the routine of their holy rule" by noting

that when it is a question "of promoting God's greater glory by a more effective and fruitful service of Christian charity in the care of the Lord's sick and suffering brethren [sic] why should these angels of charity not come out for a little while from their sacred solitude?" Christopher J. Kauffman, *Ministry and Meaning: A Religious History of Catholic Health Care in the United States* (New York: Crossroad, 1995), 171-173.

89. However, on the operational level, sister hospital personnel frequently experienced difficulties in convincing superiors that attending to the needs of the sick could prevent them from prompt appearance at community exercises.

90. After the Civil War an increasingly complex industrial society created greater educational needs. High schools became more popular, but remained principally college preparatory in nature until 1917. In 1904, the Catholic Education Association drew the attention of Catholic educators to the movement, and by 1911, the movement for Catholic secondary schools grew. The typical popular high school in 1911 assumed four grades and two commercial grades with a minimum faculty of seven teachers. Buetow, 182-183.

91. Charles J. Wallman, *Built on Irish Faith: 150 Years at St. Bernard's* (Madison: Impressions: by the Author, 1994), 274.

92. *Acquisitions*, 17.

93. S. Marcella had attended Marquette University, where she received an A.B. degree.

94. Sister, whose name was officially Clare Montefalco, was always referred to as Sister Clare M.

95. *Nuns and the Education of American Catholic Women*, 41.ß

96. Kerosene lamps were still in readiness in case the electricity failed.

97. Sheri Livingstone, *The Holy Family Orphan's Home (1915-1963): A Beneficial Institution*, unpublished essay, December 8, 1984, 3-4.

98. The document entitled *Mother Antonia's Diary* is a list of events which occurred between 10 August 1905 and 15 July 1916 compiled from the *Annals of the Congregation*.

99. [CSA], *History of the Sisters of St. Agnes 1910-1940*, unpublished paper, n. d.

100. Naber, 176.

101. Naber, 176-177.

102. *Annals*, 9 April 1916.

103. *Annals*, 21 January 1916.

104. S. Jeannette Bodoh to "Dear Mother" 2 May 1916.

105. *Life Sketches*, 102.

106. Naber, 158.

107. Dreiling, *Vignettes*, "Mother Antonia, 1905-1916."

108. Mother Antonia, *Circular Letter*, 20 December 1912.

Chapter VII ~ Increasing Expectations

1. The movement requiring state certification of all teachers was gaining in strength at this time.

2. The Institute of Mary is the official title of the second congregation of women founded by Mary Ward in the seventeenth century. Determined to found a religious institute modeled on the Jesuits and dedicated to teaching, the first institute she founded was suppressed. It was the second one, sometimes known as the *Englische Frauleins*, that was eventually approved. *Catholic Encyclopedia*, on-line edition, 1911, "Institute of Mary," <www.newadvent.org./cathen/08054a.htm>Internet; accessed 15 April 2006.

3. Terence O'Donnell, "The Nun: Reminiscences," *The Commonweal*, 23 (29 November 1935),123. Although O'Donnell indicates that he himself was the visitor, he wrote later that the experience was that of a fellow resident of New London. His claim was merely for its artistic effect. Terence O'Donnell to S. Vera Naber, 5 December 1958.

4. S. Francesca Bercher, interview by author, 7 May 1995.

5. Ibid.

6. Ibid., 124.

7. O'Donnell to S. Vera Naber.

8. Mother Marcella, *Circular Letter*, 1 September 1917.

9. Dreiling, "Mother Marcella," *Vignettes of Superiors General*, 4.

10. S. Clementia Schueller, *OHP*, 001-003.

11. S. Francesca Bercher, interview by author, 8 August 1996.

12. The Congregation of the Most Precious Blood is an association of secular priests living in community, whose principal aim is to give missions and retreats. The congregation was founded at the desire of Pope Pius VII. Distressed at the spiritual condition of Rome, the pope selected Gaspar Del Bufalo and a few priests to give missions in the city. The society prospered and was introduced into America by the bishop of Cincinnati in 1844. "Congregation of the Most Precious Blood," *Catholic Encyclopedia*, <http://www.newadvent.org/cathen/12373c.htm.> Internet; accessed 30 May 2005.

13. Mother Marcella, *Circular Letter*, Christmas 1916.

14. Ibid., *Christmas* 1918.

15. Mother Marcella, *Circular Letter*, September 1917.

16. Mother Marcella had heard that some sisters "scrapped too much" during tense games. S. Francesca Bercher, interview by author, 8 August 1996.

17. Mother Marcella, *Circular Letter*, 1919.

18. S. Francesca Bercher, interview by author, 8 August 1996. Nevertheless some house sisters had a hard time. S. Carlotta Breister who had been

assigned to St. Peter Claver School, Sheboygan, Wisconsin, told this story: "From August, 1922, to June, 1924, we had a cook sister who every Monday for dinner, gave us soup, meat, potatoes with peelings on and vegetables from a can. No dessert or salad in those days. Every Monday noon, she sat at the table and cried, because she wasn't finished with the washing. She did the washing for ten and it was impossible to be finished by noon ... then, every Wednesday evening, she cried at supper because the ironing wasn't finished." *OHP*, 005-005.

19.   It was originally held that diocesan communities could allow a change in the habit with the permission of their bishop, but pontifical congregations such as St. Agnes would have to appeal to the Vatican for permission. It was finally determined that the requirements of asepsis could justify the change. *The Daily Commonwealth* noted "that as far as can be learned St. Agnes Hospital is the first in the Catholic Hospital Association, where the sisters are habitually robed in black, to adopt the new habit." 8 September 1919. By 1920, because the Vatican no longer considered the United States a mission territory, the congregation came more directly under papal control.

20.   In 1918, the Catholic Hospital Association was attacked for advocating this change as well as others, e.g., encouraging sisters to travel to hospital meetings and conventions. There was fear that the modernization of the hospital sister would mean a deterioration in her religious spirit. Rev. Robert John Shanahan, S.J., *The Catholic Hospital Association: Its First Twenty-Five Years (1915-1940)*. University Microfilms, 1987, 29.

21.   Mother Marcella, *Circular Letter*, Christmas 1917.

22.   S. Dominica Gonsch, *OHP*, 001-004.

23.   S. Francesca Bercher, interview by author, 8 August 1996.

24.   Wirtz, *Call to the Western Plains*, 90-91.

25.   Naber, 173-174.

26.   Mother Marcella, *Circular Letter*, n.d.

27.   Great care was taken to insure that the nursing students met high standards of conduct and appearance. In an old scrapbook, an item snipped from the *Milwaukee Journal* in November 1921 reads, "There are no records of women with shorn locks in Biblical history and there will be none now as far as the Sisters of St. Agnes are concerned. Several days ago six student nurses appeared with shorn locks. This is against the rules of the convent. They promptly were informed that they must either wear wigs or be expelled. The next morning six girls appeared wearing someone else's hair."

28.   Damage to the home was estimated in excess of $30,000. The building was repaired and remodeled soon after the fire. Naber, 193-194.

29.   Mother Marcella, *Circular Letter*, 1 September 1919.

30.   CSA, *History of the Sisters of St. Agnes*, a brief typewritten document, n.d.

31. *Annals*, 22 February 1920. Equality of rank and rights for *all* of the sisters was not attained until the 1960s. One has to admire Mother Marcella for again requesting the privilege of home visits for the sisters so soon after the last refusal.

32. Furthermore, Americans leaned toward interpreting the general rules more stringently than was intended by Roman lawmakers. Mary Ewens noted, "The most obvious change ... when one studies the lives of twentieth-century nuns is in the emphasis on the dangers of 'particular friendships,' and the absence of the warm, supportive relationships with men which were so much a part of the lives of earlier nuns and contributed so much to the success of their work." "Removing the Veil: the Liberated American Nun," in *Women of Spirit: Female Leadership in the Jewish and Christian Traditions.* Rosemary Reuther and Eleanor McLaughlin, eds. (New York: Simon and Schuster 1979), 273.

33. Patricia Byrne and Sioban Nelson, *Say Little, Do Much* (Philadelphia: University of Pennsylvania Press, 2001), 157.

34. As Father Rudolf Bierberg, C.PP.S, observed years later, "What you turned out was a typical American canonical nun .... They were all the same; they were all cut from the same cloth .... That's my judgment." He also commented on the scrupulosity he saw in the Agnesian community. He attributed it in part to the rewriting of rules to make them conform to canon law and the great insistence on keeping the way of life that was spelled out. When keeping the rule perfectly was impossible, as it always was, psychological problems showed up as scrupulosity in some individuals. Father Bierberg had become familiar with several women's congregations during his years of active ministry. Interview by S. Josephine Goebel and S. René Backe, *Notes,* July 1977.

35. *Annals*, 22 February 1920.

36. The celebration marked the date of the congregation's establishment of its canonical novitiate in 1870 rather than the entrance of its first candidates in 1858.

37. The *Annals* note that "reverence was given to the Reverend Founder Caspar Rehrl and Mother Agnes and Father Francis, the assistant founder." The process that the community went through later to claim all three as founders is not clear. 1 August 1920.

38. S. Francesca Bercher, interview by author, 9 May 1996.

39. Sisters of St Agnes attended the organizational meeting of the Catholic Hospital Association in 1915 and St. Agnes Hospital was among its first institutional members. It is noteworthy, although typical of the Sisters of St. Agnes, that once the decision to operate a hospital was undertaken, there seems to have been little or no discussion on the propriety of religious participating in such meetings.

40. *Daily Reporter*, 31 August 1921, 10.
41. Ibid.
42. Ibid.
43. After S. Charles Cummins had completed her nursing training, she and S. Austin Koerperich were sent to Hays, Kansas, and assigned to night duty. "Sister Austin and I were on night duty for years and years. When Sister Austin died, I was alone … I was always on night duty and I was always by myself …. I spent my whole life on night duty." S. Charles Cummins, *OHP*, 004-002.
44. In 1920, S. Marcella had been disappointed when Sisters Clare M. and Angeline reported on the results of an interview with the Fond du Lac county superintendent. They had inquired about the acceptance of one of the sister's credits to teach in a district school. He replied that he wouldn't grant it even if she passed her examinations. He was opposed to parochial schools and claimed that attendance at parochial schools was not recognized by the state. He added that he regarded Catholic school students as not having attended any school at all and that parochial schools were inimical to social harmony. *Annals*, 21 September 1920.
45. At times sisters had to contend with stingy pastors. One can but hope that the experience that S. Francesca Bercher had on her first mission was not a common one. "The pastor was so tight-fisted that he had not yet put electric lights in the church. He set candles on the communion rail to get light to read the gospel. Four sisters had been sent to the mission; the three teachers earned fifteen dollars a month—$45 a month all told. The house sister got nothing, nothing. If the country folks didn't bring in produce they wouldn't have had enough to eat. The organist got twenty-five cents to play a High Mass, fifty cents for a funeral Mass. That parish was so rich that the pastor lent out money to other parishes. He lived until ninety-four or ninety-five—took in two orphans to do his housework, etc. When he died all the money went to his family in Germany. He willed the housekeeper (who had worked for him since she was a child)—the dog. The woman was about forty at the time. The bishop arranged matters so the housekeeper received some of the money." S. Francesca Bercher, interview by author, 8 August 1996.
46. S. Almeda Kuhn, *OHP*, 006-005.
47. Canon Law is the internal law of the Church. Over the centuries the body of legislation had grown to 10,000 canons. Pope Pius X (1835-1914) ordered the creation of the first Code of Canon law, a single volume of clearly stated laws. The codification was completed in 1916 and became effective in 1917.<http://en.wikipedia.org/wiki/Canon_Law> Internet; accessed 6 July 2006.
48. *Minutes of th e General Chapter*, 1922.

49.   Father Francis had strong opinions on the topic. "If the Sisters of St. Agnes should teach the daughters entrusted to them the refined manners of the world, and works and arts calculated to be expensive, rather than useful… what reward would they reap from Him who will severely judge everything?" *Rules and Constitutions*, ch. II, 5.

50.   *Annals*, 10 April 1923.

51.   Ibid., 21 April 1923.

52.   S. Rosemary Hoeffel remarked that "until Mother Marcella, the sisters spent summer having a vacation." *OHP*, 005-005.

53.   S. Francesca Bercher, interview by author, 9 May 1996.

54.   Mother Marcella also experienced some animosity on the part of a few of the foreign-born sisters because she had insisted that they become citizens. S. Francesca Bercher, interview by author, 23 July 1995.

55.   *Annals*, 26 June 1922.

56.   S. Francesca Bercher, interview by author, 9 May 1996.

57.   Nonetheless, the sister was unable to withstand the anger of the dissenters and returned to the clique. *Annals*, 6 September 1923.

58.   *Annals*, 10 September 1923.

59.   *Annals*, 1 October 1923.

60.   Altercations over language were not peculiar to Fond du Lac. Churches in Ellis County, Kansas, also experienced them. Some years ago, S. De Lourdes Foy, an Irish woman from New York, told the author that she had undergone great difficulties teaching in Kansas at that time. She remembered parishioners banging kneelers against the pew when the English language was used. The matter was finally settled when the Vatican asked religious to speak the language of the country in which they served. Wirtz, *Call to the Western Plains*, 53.

61.   In June of that year, the congregation discovered that an abbey in North Dakota, to which they had lent at least $30,000, was hopelessly insolvent. *Annals*, 10 June 1924.

62.   Father Antonine helpfully included the form for the letter: "Humbly prostrate at the feet of Your Holiness the Superior General of the Congregation of the Sisters of St. Agnes, Fond du Lac, Wisconsin, U.S.A., in the archdiocese of Milwaukee, with the consent of her Council, begs permission to contract a debt of $600,000 for the purpose of …."*Annals*, 12 February 1924.

63.   *Annals*, 15 February 1924.

64.   *Annals*, 3-4 August 1924.

65.   *Annals*, April-May 1924.

66.   *Annals*, 18 October 1924.

67.   *Annals*, 21 October 1924.

68.   Mother Marcella. *Circular Letter*, 7 October 1924.

69. Mother Marcella, *Circular Letter*, Christmas 1924.

70. The total cost of the south wing of the hospital was $566,350.94. Furnishings and equipment cost $72,000. *Acquisitions*, 21.

71. Mother Marcella, *Circular Letter*, Easter 1925.

72. S. Claude Feldner was sent out to teach at fourteen. She was then sent to Ohio, where she failed as a classroom disciplinarian but excelled as a children's choir director. When the bishop with three of his priests came to visit the school, Sister was prepared. She had previously attended a workshop where she learned the bishop's favorite hymns. After hearing the children sing, the bishop (himself a musician) called the Superior General and asked to have the young sister trained in music. S. Claude Feldner, interview by author, 10 February 1995.

73. *Annals*, 10 January 1926.

74. *Annals*, 16 January 1926.

75. *Annals*, 23 January 1926.

76. S. Geraldine died on 24 November 1921. *Life Sketches*, No. 128.

77. *Life Sketches*, No. 148.

78. Ibid.

79. Naber, 206.

Chapter VIII ~ A Time for Building

1. Fr. Philip had more than a passing acquaintance with the Sisters of St. Agnes. In 1882 and 1883, he substituted for Fr. Francis at the motherhouse. Fr. Francis Haas to Mother Agnes Hazotte, 24 July 1883. An alternative story is that a "young priest" drove her on weekends to her home in Monterey and told her it was a "young community, she would fit fine." S. Francesca Bercher, interview by author, 23 July 1995.

2. Sister Felicitas Dreiling, *Sisters' Memories of S. Joseph*, 20 December 1979.

3. Naber, 211-212.

4. *Annals*, 20 September 1926.

5. *Sisters' Memories of S. Joseph*.

6. "The rule required 7 1/2 minutes of meditation after the noon visit prayers. When the time was up, Mother Joseph pulled out her watch. There was never a deviation by as much as a second." S. Claude Feldner, interview with author, 10 February 1995.

7. Naber, 213.

8. Ibid.

9. Naber, 212.

10. S. Joseph Wolford, personal papers.

11. S. Muriel Tarr, *Memories of Sister Joseph*, manuscript, n.d.

12.   S. Joseph's "Notebook," quoted in Sisters of St. Agnes, *Summons to Sanctity in Joyful Service: Interim Constitutions, Special Chapter Acts* (Fond du Lac, Wisconsin, 1969-1970), 23.

13.   "His Eminence Samuel Alphonsus Stritch D.D. 19301940" *Former Archbishop Samuel Alphonsus Stritch,* <http://www.archmil.org/bishops/bishopstritch.asp.>Internet; accessed 13 March 2006.

14.   Naber, 215-216.

15.   S. Francesca Bercher, interview by author, 23 July 1995.

16.   Mother Joseph's visits were recorded in the *Annals* as they occurred.

17.   *Annals*, 24 June 1933.

18.   *Annals*, 24 February 1927. Eventually the sisters were allowed a home visit once every five years.

19.   S. Carmel Meyer wrote: "In my own dealings with S. Joseph, I found out she had a proclivity for saying "No." I asked permission for a few things, but invariably the permission was denied ... it did force me into devious avenues a few times which resulted in minor worries—such as, "May the eleventh commandment have full effect—just this time." Mother Joseph Wolford, n.d. [1944]

20.   The lone aspirant in 1927 who had not yet completed grade school attended St. Mary's School in Fond du Lac. She wore a "little habit" and ate her lunch by herself in the convent. S. Rose Carmel Schorsch, interview by author, 30 January 2000.

21.   Normal schools were established exclusively to train teachers for the elementary schools. The first normal school was established in Massachusetts in 1839. Teacher colleges began replacing them after World War I.

22.   *Annals*, 23 March 1927.

23.   *Annals*, 10 November 1926.

24.   Originally, this book was a catalogue of saints who had shed their blood for Christ during the early days of pagan persecutions.

25.   Mother M. Joseph, *Circular Letter*, December 1927.

26.   *Annals*, 17 May 1928.

27.   S. Joseph kept track of every item used in the convent. It was said that each sister was given one bar of soap at the beginning of summer, which was to last for six weeks of summer school and one week of retreat. S. Marie Wagner, interview with author, 23 May 2003.

28.   *Annals*, 27 April 1929.

29.   The architect was R.E. Schmidt, who had also designed the new building at St. Mary's Springs Academy.

30.   *Annals*, 23 May 1930.

31.   *Annals*, 1 October 1930.

32.   *Annals*, 27 January 1931.

33.   *Annals*, 10 January 1931.

34. Whether or not Mother Joseph approved of sisters obtaining higher degrees, both the needs of the high schools the community had accepted and the progress being made in teacher education demanded, at the least, the acquisition of bachelor degrees by some sisters.
35. *Annals*, 1 July 1931.
36. *Annals*, 17 August 1931.
37. Although the congregation did not own The Leo House, many sisters felt very connected to it. At the outset of World War I a suggestion had been made to close The Leo House because immigration had stopped. The congregation was credited with shifting the focus and keeping The Leo House open for women employees of the neighborhood, the Customs House, and Wall Street. *Chronicles*, 1989-1990, 33.
38. *Annals*, 31 August 1931. This is the only reference in the *Annals* to the charity offered during the depression, yet religious houses throughout the country were favorite stops for men looking for meals, and St. Agnes Convent would have been no exception. Hungry men were still visiting the convent as late as the 1960s. S. Charitas Schnitzler, who, according to the sisters, could prepare a tray with a good meal on it, attracted some regular diners.
39. S. Mary Veronica remembered with pain the plight of the working women. "It was very hard to dismiss some of our workers who had been faithful— the cleaning girls. And they had no other means of support. And they couldn't go home to their people. They felt they couldn't anyway because there were younger children at home. And so we tried keeping them on … and many of them agreed to work for as little as we could pay." S. Mary Veronica Heimann, *OHP*, 005-001.
40. Wirtz, *Call*, 14.
41. *Annals*, 17 August 1931.
42. Ibid.
43. *Annals*, 15 April 1932.
44. Fond du Lac was no exception to the rest of the nation. As early as 1897, Catholic schools for girls outnumbered those for boys by approximately three to one. See Kathleen A. Mahoney, "American Colleges for Women; Historical Origins" in Tracy Schier and Cynthia Russet, *Catholic Women's Colleges in America* (Baltimore: Johns Hopkins University Press, 2002), 2.
45. *Annals*, 27 May 1932.
46. *Annals*, 27 March 1933.
47. *Annals*, 9 June 1933.
48. Naber, 224.
49. When S. Marita Becher was asked why the sisters voted for Mother Aloysia when she so obviously did not want the position, she said with amazement at the question, "Why, they loved her." S. Marita Becher, interview by author, 4 November 2003.

50. Naber, 229.
51. *Life Sketches*, No. 240.
52. S. Claude Feldner, interview by author 10 June 1999.
53. S. Francesca Bercher, interview by author, 23 July 1995.
54. S. Alvis Jacobs, 12 October 2004.
55. *Annals*, 20 July 1933.
56. The parish had been founded in 1928. The burden of debt was so heavy
     that the pastor stopped paying the salaries of the Sisters of the Visitation
     from Dubuque. When they withdrew from the school, the pastor procured
     the Sisters of St. Agnes. Finances there were not in order until 1950, Avella,
     532.
57. Mary Ann Wettstein, *150 Years of Catholic Faith: Retracing the Steps* (Fond du
     Lac, Wisconsin: Action Printing, 1998), 53-56.
58. *Annals*, 17 December 1937.
59. Naber, 234-35.
60. In the debate over which method for training Catholic teachers would be
     most efficient—through Catholic colleges, diocesan teacher training pro-
     grams, or religious communities running their own programs—the latter
     became the norm. It had the advantage of costing the dioceses next to
     nothing while the communities could control the education of their own
     novices. Timothy Walch, *Catholicism in America: A Social History* (Robert E.
     Krieger Publishing Company, 1989), 143.
61. Earlier, in 1900, Trinity College in Washington D.C. had been founded as
     a college. Also, several girls' academies begun in the 1890s had evolved into
     Catholic women's colleges. In the Milwaukee archdiocese, Franciscans
     opened St. Clare's College (later Cardinal Stritch) in 1932; the Racine
     Dominicans opened St. Albertus (Dominican College) in 1935; and the
     School Sisters of St. Francis opened St. Joseph's Teachers College (Alverno)
     in 1936.
62. *Annals*, 14 March 1936.
63. S. Francis Assisi Pielmeier had entered St. Agnes Convent in August of
     1934. She wrote, "It was never discussed with us in our day, but apparent-
     ly there had been a normal school earlier and a charter from the state exist-
     ed that empowered the institution to offer college courses. By August 1936,
     the Novitiate wing was completed. Its first floor provided classrooms,
     library, music rooms and an office for the college president. The first floor
     of the original convent provided four additional classrooms, a faculty room,
     dean's office and a girls' lounge. The latter was for the use of several lay
     women who had enrolled. At the west end of the building two basement
     rooms which originally served as high school science labs were converted
     for college use. A large room on the first floor served as an assembly hall."
     S. Francis Assisi Pielmeier to S. Deborah Golias, 14 March 2004.

64. *Annals*, 8 September 1936.

65. *Marian College Class Schedule, September 1937*, Marian College Archives.

66. A physician dealing with a different case was quoted as saying, "You can see why the possibility of a psychoneurotic explanation came readily to mind. Every symptom that poor woman had was conceivably psychogenic, and the same was true of the symptoms of all the other cases. Depression. Terrifying dreams. Crying without provocation. Nausea and headache and diarrhea. Back and neck pains. Imaginary fever. Problems of memory and mentation. Vertigo. Hyperventilation. Menstrual irregularities. Difficulty in swallowing. Fatigue. Fast heart. Imaginary swellings. Paresthesia. And paresis...almost a fear of movement. It was like a hysterical paralysis. But there are no waves or epidemics of hysterical paralysis. They simply don't happen." "In the Bughouse," *The Orange Man: and Other Cases of Medical Detection* (Boston: Little Brown and Company, 1971), 95-111.

67. *Annals*, 17 September 1936.

68. Naber, 236.

69. An internet search in 2003 revealed that the condition is now categorized under many different headings, including "the Disease of a Thousand Names."

70. *Minutes of the Meeting of the Board of Trustees*, 7 July 1937. "After a discussion, it was decided to admit those who seem worthy in as far as moral character and high scholarship are concerned." It was also decided that a tuition fee of $85 per semester plus a matriculation fee of $10 be charged.

71. As late as the 1980s visitors from various accrediting agencies commented on that fact.

72. *Annals*, 19 October 1937.

73. A Sister who endured many a trip to Monroe wrote, "Relatively indeed! I always thought the trip interminable. As S. Wilfreda [the hospital administrator] said, 'Every time you go over a hill there's another in front of you.'" S. Susan Stucki, letter to author, 1 August 2004.

74. *Annals*, 17 December 1937.

75. S. Blandine Eisele, "Thanks for the Asparagus Patch," *St. Clare Hospital Highlights, Fortieth Anniversary Issue*, September 1979, 8.

76. Ibid.

77. *Annals*, 1939, 28 November 1939.

78. Although the majority of the non-Catholic townspeople were not acquainted with sisters, St. Victor's School in Monroe had been opened in 1916 by the Dominican sisters from Racine.

79. "St. Clare Story—Service to Mankind and Monroe," *Monroe Evening Times*, 13 October 1973, 10.

80. Wayne Wingo, *A History of Thomas County, Kansas, 1885-1964* (Colby, Kansas: Thomas County Historical Society, 1988), 122.

81.   *Colby Free Press-Tribune,* 27 February 1930, 1.

82.   *Colby Free Press Tribune,* 25 July 1929, 1.

83.   A relief measure established by executive order in 1935, the WPA offered work to the unemployed on a wide variety of programs, including highways and building construction.

84.   David Ferguson was connected with the Thomas County National Bank. He eventually became a good friend of the sisters. In 1943 or 1944, S. Seraphia Fellenz, the administrator, received a Christmas card she liked very much. In addition to the usual Nativity figures were numerous sheep pictured on it. Sister loved watching the sheep that were herded past the hospital every day. Ferguson took the card and sent it to Chicago to have a statue cast from the Madonna on the picture. The statue became known as Our Lady of Colby. S. Mary Josephine Escher, CSA, Copy of note to Mary Mowry, 26 June 1981. Later, when the statue was to be moved to a cemetery in Colby, the congregation negotiated its transfer to Fond du Lac. There is also an identical statue at the community's retirement home, St. Francis Home, in Fond du Lac.

85.   Naber, 240.

86.   Wirtz, *Call,* 98.

87.   Curtiss Chilcote Cline, *Thomas County, Kansas: The First One Hundred Years* (Colby, Kansas: Prairie Printer, 1973), 79.

88.   Letter to Monsignor Edmund Goebel, 31 January 1959.

89.   Ibid.

90.   For many years that sister was S. Rosita Handibode, who later became the eighth superior general of the congregation.

91.   A society founded in Rome in 1563, the sodality was dedicated to the education and spiritual growth of its members, and it practiced devotion to Mary and community service. Before Vatican II, Catholic high schools and colleges typically sponsored sodalities.

92.   At the junior prom, Marie Wagner had to submit to having ferns pinned on her formal for the sake of modesty. S. Marie Wagner, interview by author, 23 May 2003.

93.   One senior, Jack Burger, died in World War II.

94.   Naber, 244.

95.   *Obituary,* 16 April 1941.

96.   *Constitutions of the Congregation of the Sisters of Saint Agnes, Fond du Lac, Wisconsin* (Techny, Illinois printed by the Mission Press, 1928), 3.

97.   The congregation numbered 668 professed sisters, 33 novices, and 41 candidates. *The Official Catholic Directory* (New York: P. J. Kenedy & Sons, 1939), 113.

Chapter IX ~ Stability In A Chaotic World

1. Jay P. Dolan, *The American Catholic Experience; A History from Colonial Times to the Present* (Garden City, New York; Doubleday & Company, Inc.) 384-389.

2. Barbara Ward, "Catholic thought aims above all at balance, the balance achieved by combining planned economy with individual freedom, State control with private ownership, economic independence with political needs and social justice." Quoted in Morris, 151.

3. Sandra M. Schneiders, IHM, *Finding the Treasure: Locating Catholic Religious Life in a New Cultural and Ecclesial Context* (New Jersey: Paulist Press, 2000), 165.

4. Mother Angeline Kamp, *Conference with Superiors*, 16 June 1944, 2.

5. Ibid.

6. *Summary of Remarks of Archbishop Stritch at the Chapter of Elections*, 30 June 1939.

7. Archbishop Samuel Stritch, quoted in Mother M. Angeline, *Circular Letter*, 30 June 1939.

8. *Regional Meeting of Superiors and Assistants*, New York City, 23 November 1939.

9. One Irish mother was appalled to learn of those restrictions when she heard that her daughter in the novitiate "couldn't read." It was her conviction that the Irish "had to have books." S. Marie Wagner, interview by author, 18 January 2000.

10. Sisters kept their copy of the constitutions and could keep one or two books of devotion. They could not take with them school materials, such as charts that they may have developed for their classes.

11. *Regional Meeting*, 23 November 1939.

12. "The hospital sisters supported the congregation during the depression." S. Mary Agreda Touchett, interview by author, 22 October 2003.

13. Although stewed raisins and cottage cheese was a not uncommon Friday night supper.

14. The feast of her patron saint, e.g., S. Patrick would celebrate her name day on March 17. Birthdays were ignored.

15. The difficulty of the perfect practice of the vow of poverty is illustrated by the following remarks found in the *Annals*. Writing about a conference given by the chaplain, the recorder wrote: "He certainly left nothing undone in trying to bring to our minds the many ways in which we can practice the virtue of poverty and the many ways in which we can violate it." 18 March 1952.

16. "Dear Sister" was the proper form of address from one sister to another.

17. One frustrated sister remembered that as a junior novice, she announced, "I accuse myself of everything." S. Mary Louise Scheuerell, interview by author, 11 December 2004.

18. The intent of special confessors was good, but the outcome of advice depended upon the confessor. Felix M. Kirsch, OM Cap., in his *The Spiritual Direction of Sisters: a Manual for Priests and Superiors* (New York, 1931) warned priests and superiors that "their charges were emotional beings rather than rational ones, distinguishing the essential from the accidental only with difficulty. It was further asserted that they lacked prudence, were shortsighted, and were apt to develop idiosyncrasies." Quoted by James J. Kenneally, *The History of American Catholic Women* (New York: Crossroad, 1990), 43.

19. At her first profession, the sister made vows as a member of the community for three years; when those vows elapsed, she could make annual vows for another period of three years. At the end of six years in temporary vows the sister was permitted to make the vows of poverty, chastity, and obedience for life.

20. A sister might emerge from the chapel on a hot August day with her starched veil or collar bearing dents from her ordeal.

21. Rudolf Bierberg, C.PP.S, was chaplain at the motherhouse in 1942-1944 and 1950-1958. Father Bierberg was a scholar of biblical history, a liturgist, and a theology professor at Marian College and St. Joseph's College in Rensselaer, Indiana. During the 1950s, he had a great deal of influence on the community, particularly on the younger sisters, novices and candidates he taught. In one year, he introduced his students to the great encyclicals of the 1940s, the church, the scriptures and the liturgy—the three mysteries which he termed "the source of our life, the explosion of our life, the manifestation of our life." In the second year the students studied portions of the *Compendium of Thomas Aquinas.*

22. Fr. Bierberg taught "not one particular school [of spirituality] but ....highly flavored always with mysticism. The greatest spiritual teachers in my life were St. Teresa of Avila and St. John of the Cross." Fr. Rudolf Bierberg, interview by Sisters René Backe and Josephine Goebel, Summer 1977.

23. Many sisters kept the notes they took at the conferences, retreats, and days of recollection they attended.

24. Mother Angeline, *Circular Letter*, September 1939. This letter differs from those of the former mothers general in regard to timing. The previous incumbents waited a year before they sent similar letters.

25. Even that degree of privacy was compromised because a sister was obliged to ask her superior for a stamp.

26. Regional Meeting, *Notes*, 23 November 1939.

27. Moses Elias Kiley was born in Nova Scotia on November 13, 1876. He studied in Rome, and then went to Chicago where he worked with homeless men. He had been spiritual director of the North American College in Rome and, for six years, Bishop of Trenton, New Jersey. He was consecrat-

ed as Bishop of Milwaukee on March 28, 1940. He restored the Cathedral, which had been gutted by fire; he rebuilt St. Aemelian's Orphanage and renovated St. Francis Seminary. He died April 15, 1953. He is described by historian Steven Avella, as "a dour old Roman insider...he administered diocesan affairs with an almost Manichean grimness." Avella, 70.

28. On the other hand, the archbishop was very concerned that the sisters take their responsibility as citizens seriously. In 1950 he wrote to Mother Angeline stressing the obligation to exercise the right of suffrage. "Voting is the best means we have of bettering our temporal welfare, we should guard the right most jealously, exercise it at every opportunity, use it discreetly. Since no Church as a juridical being can influence the state directly, the duty then, falls upon individual members of a Church to use every honest political device to ensure the general welfare of all citizens." Archbishop Moses Elias Kiley to Mother Angeline Kamp, 12 October 1948.

29. Mother Angeline, *Conference with Superiors,* June 1941.

30. Ibid., *Address to Sisters,* Retreat, June 22-28, 1941, 7.

31. Ibid., *Address to Sisters during the College Summer Session, June 29-August 1, 1942.* On this same occasion, Mother Angeline attempted to instill a sense of realism in the sisters. "Sometimes," she said, "a priest preaches a sermon and you immediately remark, 'He meant that for me.' Do not be so foolish as to think that you are so important that any priest will preach a sermon for you."

32. Lucile Kaslauskas, interview by author, 27 October 2005.

33. *Annals,* 21 August 1942. In 1940 the United States had only sixty-eight missionaries in Central America. Angelyn Dries, OSF, *The Missionary Movement in American Catholic History,* American Society of Missiology Series, no. 46 (Maryknoll, New York, 1998), 100.

34. The pontifical congregation responsible for organizing the mission activity of the Catholic church.

35. Elizabeth States, interview by author, 4 March 2005.

36. *Constitutions of the Congregation of the Sisters of Saint Agnes,* Fond du Lac, Wisconsin. (Techny, Illinois: Mission Press, 1928), par. 315-317.

37. St. Clare Hospital was opened on September 8, 1941. Two days later the hospital reported having ten patients. *Annals,* 8-10 September 1941.

38. Naber, 241-242.

39. Mary Carol Conroy, SCL, "The Transition Years" in *Pioneer Healers: the History of Women Religious in American Health Care,* eds. Ursula Stepsis, CSA, and Dolores Liptak, RSM (New York: Crossroad, 1989), 153.

40. The hospital sisters followed the motherhouse schedule as closely as possible for praying the office: terce and none at 11:15 a.m., vespers and compline at 1:00 p.m., and matins and lauds at 5:00 a.m.

41. A shift was an eight-hour period of duty: the day shift was from 7:00 a.m. until 3:00 p.m., the evening shift from 3:00 p.m. to 11:00 p.m. and the night shift from 11:00 p. m. to 7:00 a.m. The sisters "pretty much" worked 7:00 a.m. to 7:00 p.m. with a hiatus for spiritual reading and recreation. It was not until early in 1959 that the seven-day service week for sisters was eliminated. S. Christine Schultz, interview by author 20 September 2000.

42. S. Christine Schultz., letter to author, February 2004.

43. The usual fee was $365 for three years training.

44. *Annals*, 22 November 1955.

45. S. Christine Schultz, who attended Marquette University in 1939, said that it was considered a major advance when she learned to take the patient's blood pressure. Until that time, it was a procedure reserved to the doctors. Interview by author, 20 September 2000.

46. Numbers of people believed that the Virgin Mary appeared in 1917 at Fatima in Portugal and predicted the immense damage Russia would do to humanity by abandoning Christianity and embracing communism.

47. To make copies, the purple carbon was placed on the pan of gelatin and pressed down, impressing the ink on the gelatin. The paper was then pressed on the gelatin and frequently copies could be made as long as the ink lasted. When the printed layer was washed off, the pan was ready to run off the next set of papers.

48. John A. Ryan (1869-1945) has been called the "social justice priest." He was an advisor to Franklin Delano Roosevelt and the first Catholic to deliver the benediction at a presidential inauguration.

49. Mortimer Adler (1902-2001) American philosopher and educator, co-founder of the Center for the Study of Great Ideas, was a proponent at the University of Chicago for integrating classics of Western thought into the college curriculum.

50. Naber, 287.

51. *History of St. Mary's Springs High School*, n.d. typescript, 3. Archives St. Mary's Springs High School.

52. *Annals*, 3 June 1947.

53. There is an explanation, possibly, but not probably, apocryphal, which provides an answer. According to this account, Mother Angeline had told various sisters that she would not accept the office for another term. One sister, anxious to have Mother leave on a happy note, convinced the delegates to vote for her on the first ballot. Mother would refuse the honor, and the chapter could then proceed about its business. All went as planned, until the election. The sisters voted for her on the first ballot, re-electing her. The story ends with Mother Angeline graciously thanking the delegates and giving each of them a candy bar.

54. In retrospect it seems scarcely believable that in the mid-twentieth century Americans could be so unaware of the implications of ignorance of a people's language and culture, including the culture of poverty, and the limitations of an assumption of the superiority of one's own culture.
55. *Annals*, 10 April 1944.
56. Although the eastern coast of Nicaragua is frequently spoken of as the Atlantic coast, the greater part of the land is bound by the Caribbean Sea.
57. The United States had been involved in the country's politics since 1855. At that time, and again in 1925, United States Marines had been sent into the country to protect American economic interests. Eventually Nicaragua allowed the United States to remain in order to supervise the creation of the National Guard, a body that functioned both as a police force and an army. It was commanded by Anastasio Somoza Garcia, who was supported by the United States. He was challenged by a nationalist, Augusto Sandino, who was later assassinated. Somoza, in control of the National Guard, was able to secure the presidency in 1936 and eventually established a dictatorship. In spite of the fact that Somoza did little to develop his country, his ability to maintain internal peace and support the interests of the United States ensured him American support.
58. Early in the seventeenth century, British pirates found safety in the coves along the eastern coast. Other Englishmen followed and became involved in local tribal warfare. The muskets the British sold one tribe gave it its name, Mosquito or Miskito. With the help of the British, the Miskitos conquered their enemies. The kingdom of Mosquito was erected under the protection of Britain. The arrival of other Europeans and escaped slaves, created further ethnic diversity but English, rather than Spanish, became the language of politics and trade. In 1860 Britain ceded the territory to Managua with the premise it would be a self-governing region.
59. In 1787, the British House of Lords refused Spanish missionaries permission to work among the Miskito Indians. During the mid-nineteenth century, missionaries from the Moravian church arrived. By 1900 the majority of Miskito communities had become Moravian.
60. S. Mary Agnes Dickof, CSA, *Chronological Data of the Mission in Waspam*, 15,16,17 September 1945.
61. S. Francis Borgia Dreiling, CSA, letter to author, April 1998.
62. Dickof, 22 September 1945.
63. Ibid.
64. Ibid.
65. Dickof, 11 October 1945.
66. *Accounts*, 9 November 1945.
67. Dickof, 1 October 1945.
68. The armed forces of Nicaragua.

69. Salvador Schlaefer Berg, bishop, and Paul Schmitz, auxiliary bishop, "To the Agnesian Sisters," 6 June 1985.
70. In the fall of 2003, the roads had deteriorated to the point that it took twelve hours to travel the same roads.
71. Philip Casper, Capuchin, *From Big Sky to Jungle*, unpublished paper, n.d.
72. S. Pauletta Scheck, *Mission Work in Northeast Nicaragua*, typescript (1954) 3.
73. S. Agnes Rita Fisette, interview by S. Emily Schug, 8 September 1995.
74. During the three months vacation from school, the sisters joined the priests in catechizing the river people.
75. Parish house.
76. A *portaviandas* is a dinner pail.
77. Ruth Baus in collaboration with Emily Harvin, *Who's Running This Expedition!* (New York: Coward McCann, 1959), 256.
78. An average mahogany pit-pan is about thirty-five feet long.
79. Scheck, 5.
80. Dickof, *Mission Work in Nicaragua*, unpublished paper, 1960, 4.
81. In 1973, S. John Baptist met Dr. José Canton in Fond du Lac. He had come to Wisconsin after the earthquake of 1972 to thank the people for the help they were giving to Nicaragua. He told the sisters that when he was a young medic, it was S. Mary Agnes who taught him how to pull teeth and many of the practical things for practicing medicine in his own country. S. John Baptist to "Dear Sisters," 9 February 1973.
82. Dickof, *Mission Work*, 7-8.
83. Dickof, 1 May 1946.
84. S. Mary Agnes Dickof to Mother Angeline Kamp, 27 November 1946.
85. S. Francis Borgia Dreiling, interview by author, 11 November 1997.
86. Scheck, 10.
87. S. Mary Patrick Ferguson could never forget seeing a man choke to death on worms. Interview by author, 7 June 1997.
88. However, the government forbade teaching the Miskito dialect. The bishop requested that the children be taught Spanish and a little English. Scheck, 10.
89. Dickof, 18 July 1947.
90. Ibid., 10 July 1946.
91. Bishop Niedhammer was in charge of the school. S. Francis Borgia recalled this incident. "Because we belonged to the Bluefields Vicariate, the ecclesiastical representatives from Rome held visitation in Waspam, Nicaragua....[he] ordered classes separating the boys and girls. [The bishop] had the Maryknoll Sisters and us discuss our dilemma at a meeting. He told us to go on teaching boys and girls in our classes just as before." The bishop's reasoning: "When God gives a married couple children, he does

not give just boys; but also girls. The same holds good in the classroom."
Sister added, *"The Vicar of Bluefields had spoken*; not, *Rome had spoken.*" S.
Francis Borgia Dreiling, *Options*, 18 January 1999.

92. Dickof, 25 March 1947.

93. However, according to S. Pauletta Scheck, "When the Bishop
[Niedhammer] feels he is ready for it, he intends to have the native sisters
form an entirely new organization with different rules and a different
habit." Scheck, 12.

94. The rigors of interpretation of the rule at this time can be noted by a story
told of S. Tarcisia. One of the sister nurses, called out to deliver a baby, was
told to return by 4:00 p.m. Time went by and the baby did not arrive. A
note was sent over requesting Sister to return to the convent. Sister could
not leave. After the baby arrived, sister returned to the convent to be greeted with the announcement that she could retire without any supper.
S. Paulette Shaw, interview by author, 17 November 1997.

95. In 1954, S. Pauletta wrote that the Nicaraguan sisters are "doing work
there which no American sister would be able to accomplish." Scheck, 12.

96. S. Juana de la Cruz, wrote a brief *Memoir* fifty years later. "S. María del
Carmen and I entered at Waspam in June of 1950 … What I liked about
S. Francis Borgia was her composure, how she walked. And the exactitude
of S. Mary Agnes, the superior. We had to hurry; the hour was the hour,
that is exact. We were in class until 11:00 and at 11:00 the whistle blew at
the factory and we had to be at the table for lunch. The same for the hour
of Mass, we had to hurry. There was a custom that the older sisters left first
and then the younger sisters. We had to hurry to get to church on time. …
One thing we had to do was to go to our room early every night. We had
been used to eating dinner at 8:00 and then staying up for a while before
retiring. But here it was different. At 7:00 we had to be closed up in our
rooms, S. María del Carmen and I. We would play some simple games but
without making noise for fear of being scolded. On Sundays we had time
to play outside, but with whom? With Father. We would play ball or something else. Every time there was a vacation we were sent to the missions on
the river." *Written by S. Juan [sic] de la Cruz in 1995, the 50th Anniversary of CSA
in Central America*, n.d.

97. The document from Rome had been preceded by a request of Mother
Angeline to Archbishop Kiley to make the change in the Constitution. She
had written, "Sisters engaged in domestic labor have reasons to feel that
their work does not count for as much as teaching or nursing." Mother M.
Angeline to Archbishop Kiley, 16 February 1947.

98. *Annals*, 23 April 1947.

99. At times pastors became plaintive. One priest wrote, "Will you please try to
do away with all bad impressions and objections you may have had against

our parish ... I am beginning to like the place and of course a parish is all a priest really has and we desire [to make] favorable impressions especially on the Ven. Mother of the sisters who conduct our school." Rev. Joseph J. Michels to Mother Angeline Kamp, 9 June 1942.

100. *Annals*, 3 May 1948.

101. *Annals*, 3 May 1951.

102. *Annals*, 17 October 1972.

103. The work S. Blandine did in Fond du Lac was publicly recognized when a residence for persons suffering from alcohol/drug abuse was named in her honor. The residence was licensed on 1 February 1980.

104. A fifties bestseller, Sloan Wilson's *The Man in the Gray Flannel Suit* became the catchword for corporate conformism and anonymity.

105. Morris, 279.

106. Ibid.

107. Thomas Merton (1915-1968) became a major influence on twentieth century Catholic thought on peace, social justice, and ecumenism.

108. Morris, 279.

109. Mother Albertonia remained the same. In the 1950s when she was superior general, a sister remembered noticing that she was wearing buttoned high-top shoes, of a type not generally worn since the turn of the century. The sister came to the conclusion that she was wearing out another sister's shoes.

110. S. Anna Marie Licher to the members of the congregation, 9 January 1958.

111. While there is no direct evidence that the rigidity of Mother Angeline's administration affected vocations to the congregation, it is indisputable that of all the major religious women's congregations in the Milwaukee archdiocese, the Sisters of St. Agnes had the least growth between 1940 and 1950. The congregation closest in size to CSA increased its membership by 19 percent—the Agnesians grew by .0161 percent. During the next decade, CSA grew by 103 members or 14.7 percent. Statistics cited in Avella, 643.

112. Naber, 275.

113. Bruno Hagspiel, SVD, at that time a popular author and retreat master.

114. Fr. Rudolf Bierberg to Mother Albertonia Licher, n.d.

115. *Association of Victim Souls Who Immolate Themselves in Union With the Sacred Hearts of Jesus and Mary.* Approved by Pope Pius X in 1909.

116. Naber, 275.

117. Mother Albertonia, *Circular Letter*, Easter 1953.

118. The residence, named Hazotte Hall in memory of Mother Agnes Hazotte, was used as a residence from 1953 to 1962. From 1962 to 1966 it was used as the elementary education center.

119. Stepsis, 152.

120. For Mother Albertonia, who grew up at a time when a few cents made a difference to her family, the strain of incurring such debts was often unbearable. And yet, worried as she was about hospital finances, a bill collector told one of the chaplains that whenever he found a case where it was absolutely impossible for the person to pay the bill, he'd bring it to the treasurer and she would mark it cancelled. Bierberg, interview by Backe and Goebel, Ibid.

121. Mother Albertonia, *Circular Letter*, Christmas 1955.

122. Father Fury was optimistic. That same year a pastor from a town in California wrote that he had written to more than 150 orders of nuns to obtain sisters to teach 222 children in a school the parish had just built. *Annals*, 23 August 1953.

123. S. Jean Perry, interview by author, 1 July 2005.

124. Rev. Donald Wagner, 8 April 1953.

125. In CSA, the juniorate referred to the year immediately after the novice made temporary vows. She ordinarily continued her spiritual and professional preparation for her ministry at the motherhouse.

126. Pope Pius XII (1939-1958) frequently pointed out "the disparity between the charisms and structures of religious communities, between their lifestyles and the conditions of the times, and between formation given to candidates and the needs of their ministry in the mission of the Church" and asked religious communities to adapt according to their distinctive charisms. M. Clare Adams, OSC, "Religious Life," *New Dictionary Of Catholic Spirituality* (Collegeville; Minnesota, 1993), 820.

127. The Conference of Major Superiors of Women was canonically established in 1959. It later became the Leadership Conference of Women Religious. Ann Carey, *Sisters in Crisis: The Tragic Unraveling of Women's Religious Communities* (Huntington, Indiana: Our Sunday Visitor, 1997), 78.

128. Leadership Conference of Women Religious, "Religious History," http://www.lcwr.org/history.htm.> Internet; accessed 11 December 2003.

129. S. Mary Emil Penet, IHM, began the movement in the 1950s. The Sister Formation Conference became a conference under the Conference of Major Women's Superiors of Religious Institutes but, in 1971, became autonomous. In 1976 it became the Religious Formation Conference when it broadened to include male religious and religious from non-canonical groups.<http://www.relforcon.org/2A_rfc_faqs.htm> Internet; accessed 6 August 2006.

130. The sisters attended colleges and universities throughout the country, although the larger number attended Marquette, Fordham, Notre Dame, Loyola, and De Paul Universities.

131. S. Rosaline Stephanie, letter to author, February 2004.

132. Rev. R.P. Bierberg, C.PP.S, *Sermon: Funeral of Sister M. Albertonia, CSA*, 31 December 1957.

Chapter X ~ Changing World, Changing Church

1. *Mother M. Rosita, Autobiographical Sketch, June 1967, 1.* Mother Rosita wrote both the autobiographical sketch and later, the *Memoirs of Sister M. Rosita Handibode, CSA, Superior General, 1957-1969, with Deep Gratitude to God and My Fellow Sisters, Who Placèd Confidence in Me*, November 1979. There is also a draft of the latter document, originally entitled *Memories of Sister Rosita* and also dated November 1979. The word "Memories" is crossed out and the word "Memoirs" is substituted.

2. Mother Rosita, *Sketch*, 1.

3. Ibid.

4. While S. Rosita was teaching in Yonkers, she was often able to help her mother in the Bronx. The mother, who lived across the street from the convent, would call out to the sisters, "It's Friday. Miss Efficiency will be here. I let any of my 'rathers' go down the drain. I have to do what she wants me to do." S. Madonna Dionis, interview with author, 4 August 2002.

5. Mother Rosita, *Memoirs* draft, 1.

6. Mother Rosita, *Sketch*, 2.

7. Mother Rosita noted that rumors had reached her that she was being considered as a candidate for superior general, "but politics had never had any attraction for me." Ibid., 2. In the months before the Chapter, sisters who had been associated with her during her twenty-three years at St. Mary's Springs and her four years in Elmhurst had been advancing her name in conversations about the coming elections. A difficult distinction had to be made between "campaigning"—absolutely forbidden—or having discussions regarding possible choices for office. These discussions were absolutely necessary, the more so as the community grew in numbers, because the elections were conducted in absolute silence. The sister who received an absolute majority of votes was elected. If an absolute majority was not obtained in either of the first two ballots, a third balloting would take place. If no absolute majority was obtained, a fourth and last ballot was cast, in which only those two sisters who received the greater number of votes in the third ballot would be considered. If there was a tie in the fourth balloting, the sister who made her profession first in the Institute was considered elected, and, if both were professed on the same day, the senior.

8. A story that made the rounds of the community shortly after her election tells of her visit to St. Agnes Hospital. One of the very young sisters met the unfamiliar visitor in the elevator and kindly asked, "And who is *this* little sister?"

9.   One of S. Rosita's students, Maureen Daly, had written the still popular *Seventeenth Summer,* sometimes said to have begun the modern period of the young adult novel.

10. Mother M. Rosita, *Memoirs,* Nov., 1979, 1.

11. *Annals,* 29 June 1957.

12. Face veils were drawn over the sisters' faces whenever they attended public church services or went out of their convents. The veils had come into popularity in various communities as sisters began to wear their habits on the street. The significance that the sisters assigned to the habit can be inferred from the statement in the constitution of 1875. "The existing costume dare not be changed either by a Sister for herself, nor by the Mother Superior for the Congregation." *Rules and Constitutions of the Sisters of the Congregation of Saint Agnes.* In two parts. Fond du Lac, Wis.: Mother House, 1886, Part I, par. 5, 3.

13. St. Agnes Convent, *Resolutions Adopted by the General Chapter June 29, 1957.*

14. House sisters, later termed homemakers, were not included at first because the program had been established to continue the religious formation of the young sister as she continued her college or university education.

15. The conferences at the motherhouse were usually given by the chaplain and attended by sisters in nearby missions. Sisters in larger cities had opportunities to hear different speakers; sisters in smaller places often listened to tapes.

16. Mother Rosita, *Memoirs,* 1.

17. *Minutes of the General Council Meeting ,* 6 July 1957.

18. As the congregation had celebrated its golden jubilee in 1920, it seems that in the interim a revisionist version of the congregation's history had been adopted.

19. "One of Sister Fidelis' dreams was to secure the blessing of Pius XII for our Centennial celebration," *Memoirs,* draft, 4.

20. The petition to have perpetual adoration was refused; the two other petitions were answered in the affirmative.

21. *Memoirs,* draft, 4.

22. Ibid., 5.

23. Sister Vera Naber, *With All Devotedness: Chronicles of the Sisters of St. Agnes, Fond du Lac, Wisconsin* (New York: P.J. Kenedy and Sons, 1959.)

24. Years later Mother Rosita wrote that the delegation of authority prepared the congregation for what later became known as decentralization of authority." *Memoirs,* 3.

25. Pope John XXIII (Angelo Roncalli) was fourth of fourteen children of an Italian sharecropper. He was elected pope in 1958. He expanded and internationalized the college of cardinals, called the first diocesan synod of

Rome in history, revised the code of canon law and called the Second Vatican Council to promote mercy, faith and the pastoral role of the church. The council revitalized the church and marked the beginning of a new spirit of openness. Pope John XXIII died June 3, 1963. *John XXIII Biography.* <www.vatican.va/holy_father/john_xxiii/biography/> Internet; accessed 21 March 2005.

26.   Robert E. Englehart, Robert McCormack and Frank Murphy.

27.   This was the third time that St. Louis parish in Fond du Lac attempted to maintain a parish school. The first attempt lasted only one year, 1880; the second time the school survived from 1895 to 1904. The final attempt lasted from 1958 to 1973.

28.   *Chronicles*, 1964, 26.

29.   *General Council Minutes*, 2 February 1961.

30.   Joshua Berman and Randy Wood, "Unbeatable Managua: 150 Years of History," *Nicaragua's Best Guide*, June, July, August. <http//www.guide-ofnicaragua.com/0602/ManaguaEN.html.> Internet; accessed 3 March 2004.

31.   *Chronicles*, 1963, 19.

32.   "Acahualinca is part of Managua on the shore of the lake where the garbage is dumped. What an odor! I remember that at times the sisters were nauseous, but when the children came the sisters dedicated themselves to playing with them." S. Colette (Mary) Hartman, quoted in S. Emily Schug, *Notes from a CSA Meeting of January 1995.*

33.   S. Francis Borgia Dreiling, *Residences in Managua: Casa Marragoot*, typewritten paper, 54, n.d.

34.   It was not only because the driver had been deprived of lateral vision, as a "driver's veil" had been concocted to handle that difficulty. It was also a feat to drive with the rear window blocked by three large veils.

35.   One hundred fifteen sisters were opposed to the change; ninety-three had no opinion. *Annals*, 15 September 1959.

36.   Few sisters escaped without at some time drawing blood from large pins driven into their scalp.

37.   The rest of the habit remained the same. At this time the total cost of a habit was about thirty dollars. Theoretically a sister received a new one every three years. Actually they were worn much, much longer.

38.   The use of parish cars became a common benefit for the sisters around 1965.

39.   This permission did not extend to the novices, who remained in ignorance of current affairs.

40.   There had certainly been many fund raising ventures in support of congregational institutions, but this venture was to aid the sisters directly.

41. At this time a New York State Investigation Commission had just completed a probe of bingo scandals in New York City and Yonkers. S. Germaine Lichtle, *Agnesian Auxiliary, 1961-1979,* typescript, n.d.

42. Joseph Gurdak deserves special mention. Every week for the first six months he was called to the City Hall and questioned by the bingo inspectors—the same questions every week. Ibid.

43. The total amount contributed to the Infirmary Chapel by the Agnesian Auxiliary was $51,810.40. By 1963, pressure was put on the Auxiliary to divide the profits with the Capuchin Friars. As of December 1978, the *total* contribution to the Sisters of St. Agnes was $237,810.40; the total contributions to the Capuchins reached $236,000. Ibid.

44 S. Colette Hartman speaks for those who have a negative view of the accomplishments of the early missionaries. "All we did was distribute barrels of food, clothing and medicine. There was never enough, but we kind of felt that we were doing good. Looking back, I would say that our visits were a distraction for the people... they had nothing to fear from us in that we were peacemakers. They also had nothing to gain from us. Our relationship to them was paternalistic." Mary Hartman, "Jailers with Compassion" in Ron Ridenour, *Yankee Sandinistas: Interviews with North Americans Living and Working in the New Nicaragua* (Willmantic, Connecticut: Curbstone Press, 1986), 34. This view was strongly contested by S. Raymond Grieble who wrote, "My experience as an early missionary was filled with constant visits, a week at a time, in the river villages. There we catechized, prepared many to receive the sacraments, had marriage encounters and visited all the houses. In between, we attended, as best we could, the sick. Our relationship to them was that of love, concern. What we shared with them was charity." Grieble, *Note,* 11 April 1999. Perhaps the evaluation of the sisters' work in Waspam by Bishop Salvador will shed light on the subject, "In the field of evangelization among the people of Waspam, Puerto Cabezas and Rosita, the Agnesians have left an indelible memory. Waspam is the cradle of their apostolate, and they worked among the indigenous Indians of the Miskito Race with great sacrifices ...." Salvador Schlaefer, bishop, and Paul Schmitz, auxiliary bishop, to the Agnesian Sisters, 6 June 1985.

45. S. María del Carmen Avendaño and Mrs. Mabel Rivera maintained the clinic in the interim.

46. S. Anne Jude wrote later, "We had each been performing 'in our slots', so to speak—the sisters were teaching in school, the priests were working in the framework of the preaching and sacramental ministry, and I was working in the medical field only. We came to a realization that our scope had to broaden; what the farmers were planting or *not* planting, resulted in nutritional problems for cattle and people. If people were ill this affected

family life, economics, education, and their relationship with God...." Anne Jude Van Lanen, *Health Care Systems for the Poor and Geographically Isolated: Health Care for the Peoples of the Río Coco Area—Atlantic Coast of Nicaragua— 1971*, unpublished paper, 31 May 1975.

47. Ibid.

48. S. Kenneth's arranging of the scheduling of classes for the elementary school, the high school, and the normal school in one building would eventually become the model for the whole country. The grade school children met from 7:00 a.m. to 12:00 noon, the high school students from 12:00 to 5:00 p.m., and the normal school from 5:00 p.m. to 10:00 p.m. The schedule had the further advantage of reducing absenteeism among the smaller children, who often couldn't get back to school in the afternoon because of the afternoon tropical downpours. S. Bertha Bumann, interview with author, 20 May 2000.

49. The plan began with missions that received a salary-covering approximately 660 sisters. The charge per sister per month was $6.50 for twelve months of the year. Health care for the remaining 145 sisters was carried in special expense accounts for infirmary services. Over a three-year period, results indicated that the Health Fund group effected substantial balances each year, with no restrictions placed upon expenses incurred. The opening of Nazareth Heights in September 1965 was expected to reduce or eliminate many costs. *Chronicles* 1966, 14.

50. "We all smiled at your comment that life in Sapos was so simple. Where there is a school, life usually tends to become complex, but I am sure you agree that without one, there is a certain instability very noticeable in the foundation. The Sisters from Puerto Cabezas are now writing that some of their former pupils are teaching in their school. This is the fruit of many years of spade work done by the sisters in the classroom. Now that these former pupils are adults, their contact with the sisters can still be an influence on their lives besides providing them with a profession which gives them dignity and status. The beginnings are slow, hard, and results, imperceptible, but I am still convinced that CCD work alone does not have the formative powers present in the classroom. That you can do both in Rosita is a consoling thought." Mother M. Rosita Handibode to Sister Peter (Dolores Taddy) 25 May 1967.

51. Giovanni Battista Montini, was born in northern Italy, the son of a prominent newspaper editor, studied in Rome and entered the Vatican Secretariat of State in 1922. During World War II he was able to get large sums of money to aid the Jews. In 1953 he was made archbishop of Milan. He declined the cardinalate offered to him by Pope Pius XII, but was made a cardinal by Pope John XXIII. He was an enthusiastic supporter of Vatican II and supervised the implementation of many reforms. He was

described as gentle, humble, and a man of "infinite courtesy." To the dismay of liberals, he reaffirmed the church's teaching on artificial contraception and priestly celibacy. He died on August 6, 1978. *Biography Pope Paul VI*, <www.vatican.va/holy father/paul vi/> Internet; accessed 20 March 2005.

52. The year 1963 was also marked by the controversial Supreme Court decision which ended Bible reading and prayer in the public schools. A declared atheist, Madalyn Murray O'Hair took credit for the suit which had been already filed and embarked on a career attacking religious schools, the phrase "under God" in the pledge of allegiance, tax exemptions from church property, etc. There were rumors that she intended to attack the public schools in Ellis County, Kansas, which employed habited Sisters of St. Agnes, had crucifixes and statues on the premises, etc. Catholics in Hays still remember their anger and fear that Ms. Murray would attack their schools when she visited Kansas in August 1963. Interviews in Kansas by S. Mary Catherine Grief, in March and April, 2004.

53. R.W. Gleason, S.J., *To Live Is Christ* (New York: Sheed and Ward, 1961.)

54. Leon-Joseph Cardinal Suenens, *The Nun in the World* (Westminster: Newman Press 1963). Suenens was born in Brussels on 16 July, 1904. Appointed cardinal by Pope John XXIII, he was one of the four moderators for the Second Vatican Council. During the Council, he called for dialogues with the faithful, with our separated brethren, and with the non-Christian world. He is remembered as an advocate of reform within the Church.

55. Suenens, 20.

56. Suenens, 173.

57. After the Cardinal presented the encyclical *Pacem in Terris* to the United Nations, he observed, "I'm preaching peace in the United Nations and preaching war in the convents." John W. Donohue, S J, "Of Many Things," *America*, 13 November 1999, 2.

58. Mother Rosita's determination to acquaint the sisters with the latest knowledge seems heroic when we place it beside a story told of her initial introduction to the changes that were expected to follow from the considerations of Vatican II. Following a meeting of the Conference of the Major Superiors of Women where the major superiors were told that the Holy See would ask for changes and modification in religious life, she delivered the message to the sisters in "a voice that sounded like a death knell." She spent the next several weeks in the infirmary, seriously ill from an insulin reaction. S. Miriam Therese Putzer, interview by author, 4 July 2002.

59. Mother M. Rosita Handibode, *Report of the Superior General of the Congregation of the Sisters of St. Agnes for the Six-Year Term, June 1968 to June 1969*, 2.

60. As early as 1910 society had begun to criticize orphanages as being psychologically inhumane. Eventually the states established foster care programs

and orphanages began to be phased out. As the abuses of the foster care system have become increasingly hard to ignore, the question of orphanages has been raised again.

61. Mother Rosita, *Sketch*,2.
62. S. Rosita Handibode, *Memoirs of Sister Rosita*, 1-2.
63. In point of fact, there were always sisters on missions who helped out their neighbor. S. Marie Wagner remembered S.Virginia Hickey sending sisters across the street with soup for a sick man. Wagner, *Notes*, January 2004. The decision also opened the opportunity for sisters to become prepared in public health nursing.
64. *General Chapter Proceedings, 1969.*

Chapter XI ~ Gathering Clouds

1. *Chronicles*, 1964, Foreword.
2. 60 percent of the sisters had relatives in religious life. There were three sets of five blood sisters in the congregation at one time.
3. Young Catholic girls were frequently intrigued by the sisters. One wrote: "I'd seen the nuns, of course, on my way to and from Main Street walking the circular drive on Second Street. They jingled when they walked around and around reading out of small black books.... When I started first grade...Mother must have been ready to strangle me... 'S'ter says, S'ter says.' Every pearl of wisdom was faithfully repeated at home. As the years went by, I found some of the sisters were easier to like than others. But we girls wanted to be sisters when we grew up. In fact, Kathleen, Jane, Nancy and I had a Sisters Club. Every Saturday we got dressed in our habits and played sister. I even had a habit for my Shirley Temple doll." Patricia Sage Hinn, letter to author, 4 May 1996.
4. Mother M. Rosita to S. Mary Donald (S. Mary Neff), 20 January 1964.
5. St. Agnes Convent, *To Be Used for Public Spiritual Reading*, n.d.
6. Ibid.
7. For example, the girls did not participate in extra-curricular activities.
8. The principal preparation for religious life had been in its living. An exception was Pierre Cotel's *Catechism of the Vows for the Use of Religious* (New York: Benziger Brothers, 1924) which provided a basic, if not extremely tedious, treatment of the subject.
9. Enrollment at the Springs rose from 633 students in the 1957-1958 school year to 717 students in the 1958-1959 school year. Students whose siblings had attended the Springs and who had assumed the Springs was *their* school were not necessarily accepted. As late as 2004, St. Mary's Springs had not yet recovered from the backlash.

10. The aspirancy in Puerto Cabezas for Nicaraguan women was also opened that year with nine young women.
11. *General Council Minutes*, 11 November 1966.
12. *Chronicles*, 1966, 36.
13. S. Mary Neff, interview with author, 10 June 2001.
14. *CSA Formation Handbook*.
15. *Chronicles*, 1965, 23.
16. The celebrated "baby boomers" are frequently described as challenging boundaries and conventions. It is indisputable that, as a group, their values differed in some respects from those of the preceding generations.
17. The congregation's retirement home.
18. Jeanne Kliejunas, e-mail to author, 4 April 2004.
19. S. Ruth Battaglia, letter to author, n.d. S. Ruth was a novice from 1968 to 1970.
20. *Chronicles*, 1968-1969, 34.
21. S. Marise Meis, *The Sisters of Saint Agnes in the Vicariate of Bluefields*, unpublished paper, n.d. [1998].
22. *Chronicles*, 1968-1969, 27.
23. *Chronicles*, 1965, 7.
24. Even so, money was far from plentiful. The sister faculty, novices, and candidates spent several weeks before the opening of the college putting desks together and cleaning the new buildings. The clean-up was completed early in the morning the day the first students arrived on campus.
25. Acts 9: 36-41. Father Blied's intent was to honor the women who served the church in domestic ways. The body of the church represents a sewing basket, the steeple is in the form of a needle. Blied arranged to have one hundred orphaned children in India baptized "Dorcas" when the chapel was dedicated.
26. The six-building Marian College campus was built at a total cost of four million dollars. *Chronicles* 1968-1969, Foreword.
27. Digging the well was far more complicated than had been anticipated. The drillers' tools were lost and that delayed the process for about six weeks. The completed well produced water at the rate of 135 gallons a minute. *Chronicles*, 1964, 22.
28. *Chronicles*, 1965, Foreword.
29. Mound Bayou, in northwestern Mississippi, was founded by an ex-slave in 1867. An all-black community with a population of less than 2000, the town was in great need of health care and educational facilities. S. Benedict Dorey went to Mound Bayou with Mother Rosita's permission but without her cooperation in the venture. Seven years later, Sister Benedict was joined by Sister Perpetua Michelin who taught at St. Gabriel's School there. S. Benedict Dorey, interview with author, 10 February 2003.

30. James Groppi, a civil rights activist in Milwaukee in the 1960s, gained national recognition for his leadership in open housing marches.

31. S. Judith Schmidt, quoted in Charles J. Wallman, *Built on Irish Faith: 150 Years at St. Bernard's* (Madison: Wisconsin: 17 Impressions, 1994), 452-453.

32. *General Council Minutes*, 22 November 1966.

33. *Norms for Implementing the Decree, On the Up-to-date Renewal of Religious Life Ecclesiae Sanctae II*, August 1966. Vatican Council II, 624-633.

34. S. Jean Steffes, *Apostolic Religious Life in the United States Since Vatican II: a Journey Leading from Transition to Transformation*, n.d., 3.

35. Ibid.

36. Sacred Congregation for Religious and Secular Institutes, "Instruction on the Renewal of Religious Life, 6 January 1969," *Vatican Council II*, 634-655.

37. Ibid.

38. The movement was the inspiration of the post-war Italian Jesuit, Ricardo Lombardi to deepen the spiritual life and promote peace. He worked with bishops at the Vatican Council stressing dialogue in prayer and communication along with personal and social integration and application. It was one of the first times for most Sisters of St. Agnes that dialogue and faith sharing with others were presented as a further means to reach God.

39. *Report of the Superior General of the Congregation of St. Agnes for the Six-Year Term, June 1963 to June 1969, 4.*

40. Reordering the archives was done as a result of the Quinquennial Reports submitted to Rome. When Albert Cardinal Meyer was Archbishop of Milwaukee, he had read the reports "As we found out when we received recommendations from Rome based on these reports. One was that our archives were not in order." S. Rosita, *Memoirs*, draft, 6.

41. Some observers held that the demise of the diploma program had led to a loss of role-modeling and the reinforcement of Catholic ideals.

42. S. Digna Desch traveled the United States to organize Alumnae Chapters of St. Agnes School of Nursing. From May 7 to October 29, 1961, she organized 25 chapters in ten states and Washington, D.C. There were representatives of every class since 1910. Emily Hadley, RN and S. Juliana Kohne, RN. *Supplement to the Golden Jubilee History, 1960-1966* (St. Agnes School of Nursing, 1966), 47-48.

43. Hadley, 13-14 .

44. Graduates of the St. Agnes School of Nursing would disagree with the terms of the argument. Graduates of the School of Nursing felt that the school provided an excellent theoretical base for a registered nurse. The bachelor's degree added liberal arts courses to nursing theory. S. Susan Stucki, e-mail, 13 August 2004.

45. The bus was donated by a benefactor and father of one of the students, Walter Lazynski of Milwaukee, Wisconsin.

46. St. Margaret Mary Parish in Milwaukee provides one such example of a parish determined to build a school. The parish began with eleven acres of land and two renovated houses, one for a rectory and one for a convent. Before the parish opened, the appointed pastor had begun contacting religious communities for sisters for a projected school. In July 1955, the parish opened with three hundred families. Mass was said in the basement of Divine Savior High School. More than six hundred of the parish children were bused to other parochial schools. The assistant pastor was one of the bus drivers. In 1957, when the new temporary church was dedicated, the parish had one thousand families. Meanwhile, over a period of three years the pastor visited twenty-five motherhouses. In February 1958, Mother Rosita agreed to provide three teachers. In 1959 the grade school, constructed with classrooms planned for a maximum of fifty or fifty-five students, opened with three sisters, thirteen lay teachers, and 720 children in grades 1 through 5. By 1962 the school had eight grades and an enrollment of approximately one thousand.

47. Between 1950 and 1961 the number of lay teachers teaching in elementary schools increased 23 percent and the number teaching in secondary schools increased 40 percent. James J. Vanecko and Maureen Gleason, "The American Catholic Educational Enterprise" in *Contemporary Catholicism in the United States*, Philip Gleason, ed. (Notre Dame, Indiana: University of Notre Dame Press, 1969). By 1965, religious sisters were educating only 12 percent of the students in this country. Tim Unsworth, "Nuns of Mythology, Reality and Legacy," *National Catholic Reporter Online.* <http://www.natcath.com/NCR_Online/archives/022103/022103x.htm>Internet; accessed 2 June 2004.

48. Steinfels, 219.

49. Steinfels, 220.

50. *Chronicles,* 1966, 17.

51. *Chronicles,* 1967, Foreword.

52. Ibid.

53. The principal was a priest. A number of sisters expressed the opinion that they were merely "work-horses." *Chronicles,* 1964, 14.

54. Fr. Finian Sullivan provides an example of a pastor much respected and appreciated by the sisters as well as by the parishioners. He demanded much of them as teachers but they always found him supportive. He made efforts to give the sisters recreational opportunities such as scenic trips to the neighboring states and Washington, D.C. There could have been few Sisters of St. Agnes unaware of and perhaps a little envious of the "perks" of teaching in Yonkers.

55. *Ibid.,* 18-19.

56. *Annals,* 2 February 1970.

57. In a pluralistic society, proponents of the argument claimed it is unfair to stress the values of some while ignoring the values of all. Therefore, society should agree to ignore all values.

58. John B. Watson (1878-1958) originated the school of psychology known as behaviorism, in which behavior is described in terms of physiological response to stimuli.

59. Hanlon owed much to Abraham Maslow (1908-1970) and his theory that as basic human needs are met humans strive to meet higher needs. Because humans have the ability to make choices and exercise free will they have the potential of becoming self-actualized and in control of their own destiny.

60. Christopher J. Kauffman, *Ministry and Meaning: A Religious History of Catholic Health Care in the United States* (New York: Crossroad, 1995), 276-278.

61. *Chronicles,* 1965, 10. The *Chronicles,* 1967-1968, noted with pride that the government inspector for Medicare stated that out of seventy Wisconsin hospitals visited (there were seventy in the state) that the sister staff in the accounting department of St. Agnes Hospital has the best setup in the state for handling Medicare, 23.

62. *Chronicles,* 1964, 24.

63. *Chronicles,* 1967-1968, 22.

64. *Chronicles,* 1968-1969, 25.

65. Two tragic events contributed to some of the problems. The chairman of the fund-raising drive met with a sudden death, while the acting chairman of the special gifts section drowned while vacationing. *Chronicles,* 1966, 12.

66. *Chronicles,* 1967-1968, 22.

67. Hadley Memorial Hospital, originally called The Protestant Hospital, was founded in 1925 and had its roots in the Methodist denomination.

68. St. Anthony Hospital was planning to apply for Hill-Burton funds to assist in the project. But both hospitals had to face the near certainty that the government would not provide funds for two hospitals in one small town.

69. *Chronicles,* 1964, 25.

70. *Chronicles,* 1966, 12.

71. *Chronicles,* 1968-1969, 25.

72. The Immigration Act of 1952 admitted only a certain number of persons of each nationality. In 1965 a new act gave preference to persons with skills needed in the United States and close relatives of U.S. citizens.

73. *Chronicles,* 1965, 10.

74. *Chronicles,* 1967-1968, 25.

75. Although St. John's Rest Home had been a member of the Catholic Hospital Association since its inception, in the eighties, when the CHA discovered that the home was neither a diocesan institution nor sponsored by a religious congregation, its membership was questioned.

76. Angelyn Dries, *The Missionary Movement in American Catholic History*, American Society of Missiology Series, No. 126, (Maryknoll, New York: Orbis Books, 1998), 181.

77. The congregation purchased a spacious two-family house at the cost of twenty-five thousand dollars.

78. Little boys, for example, would throw their books on the floor when the servants arrived to take them home. The servants were expected to pick the books up and carry them. One sister waged a campaign against the practice. She judged her efforts to teach the boys some respect and consideration were successful. S. Raymond Grieble, interview by author, 14 February 1999.

79. *Chronicles*, 1964, 37-38.

80. On one occasion S. Raymond went an entire week without water. Sister had one bottle of cola that she used to wash her eyes and finger tips. S. Raymond Grieble, interview by author, 14 February 1999.

81. In the interim between the arrival of the first sisters and this period, the habit of the missionaries was modified.

82. S. Paulette Shaw, interview by author, 17 November 1997.

83. There were no maternal or newborn deaths, which was extremely unusual for the area. *Chronicles*, 1966, 30.

84. One cooperative program provided a corn-soy mixture to be administered to the children to fight anemia. It was impossible to administer until the sisters persuaded the government to give the extra food to the whole family. Although the mixture did not seem to affect anemia, with the good breakfast the children's grades improved. S. Paulette Shaw, interview by author. Ibid.

85. S. Juana de la Cruz added, "There was no place to go to the bathroom so I tried not to eat much. I just took a little coffee in the morning to prevent a headache. I went to bed early because I was very tired. That year I lost twenty pounds .... The townspeople spoke of the 'Fathers de los Sapos' and the 'Sisters de los Sapos.' It made me think that there was a line of little toads following me."

86. *Chronicles*, 1966, 31-32.

87. *Chronicles*, 1966, 31.

88. *Chronicles*, 1972-1973, 21. Eventually, the native Daughters of Charity were able to accept the mission.

89. *Chronicles*, 1964, 38.

90. S. Anne Jude Van Lanen, *Health Care Systems for the Poor and Geographically Isolated: Health Care for the Peoples of the Río Coco Area—Atlantic Coast of Nicaragua—1971*, unpublished paper, 31 May 1975, 7.

91. Mary McDonough, DC. S. Mary's personnel needs assessment study was the basis of the decision to withdraw. Interview with S. Janet Ahler, 12 November 1998.

92. Although the hospital was still unopened upon her arrival, S. Paulette was able to help raise the standards for nurses in Quito during her relatively short time in the area. In addition, she helped improve the areas of clinical experience for the BSN students around the city of Quito. She collaborated with local and international representatives of the World Health Organization, and became the first foreigner to be elected to the Ecuadorian National Board of Nursing. Responsible for hiring professional nurses on the staff of the hospital, she insisted that the university agree to pay salaries at the level equivalent to that of an executive secretary, a major victory for the underpaid nursing profession. Before she returned to the United States, among the projects she initiated for updating professional nurses, Sister established a course for ward clerks, designed to keep nurses from doing clerks' duties. When the military hospital there adopted the program, it became mandatory for the entire country. After two years, illness forced her to return to the United States. S. Paulette Shaw, interview with author, 17 November 1997 and e-mail to author 23 February 2005.

93. *Chronicles,* 1967-1968, 25.

94. Mother M. Rosita, CSA, to "Dear Sister Peter (Dolores Taddy)" 4 March 1967.

95. "Rosita Mines," The work in the mines was so dangerous that when a man's teen-aged son went to work in the mines, the family had a big feast as the odds were that the young man would lose his health and possibly his life. *Sandal Prints,* September-October 1963, 40.

96. *Chronicles,* 1968-1969, 27.

97. Meis, 6.

98. Gregory Smutko, OFM Cap., gives special credit to S. Marcella Wasinger (Aquiline) and Sister Guadalupe Ortiz for their work with the women. *Santa Rosa Parish in Mina Rosita, Nicaragua,* draft of unpublished manuscript, n.d.

99. In July, only months after the sisters left, the so called "football war" broke out between Honduras and El Salvador. Salvador was small and over-populated; the Hondurans were convinced that the Salvadorans were trying to steal their land. When an altercation broke out over a soccer game and erupted into a war, Nuevo Ocotopeque was in its path. Father Roderick was not as fortunate. He "was taken prisoner and by the time the American embassy managed to win his freedom, walking over the hill from Guatemala, he came into Nuevo Ocotopeque, now a city of silence, death and destruction...the hatred for the God of this kingdom was spelled out in desecration of the sacred vestments and all things needed for the Holy

Sacrifice. The chalice was used for target practice, the arms of the wooden crucifix were cut off, and the corpus pierced with a bayonet. *Chronicles, 1968-1969*, 31.

Chapter XII ~ An Unknown Destination

1. The Cardinal-Archbishop of Los Angeles, James F. McIntyre, demanded that the sisters wear a habit, use a standardized form of prayer, remain in the schools, and be obedient to his wishes. As the sisters believed both in the validity of their own experience and accepted the message of Vatican II, they could not obey. McIntyre dismissed them from the schools in the Archdiocese. Eventually, the community split over the issue. A majority left and formed another community.

2. Mother Rosita, CSA, Sister M. John Baptist, CSA, Sister Evangeline, CSA, Sister Imogene, CSA, Sister Bonita, CSA. *Report of the Superior General of the Congregation of St. Agnes for the Six-Year Term, June 1963 to June 1969*, 3.

3. *CMSW Sisters Survey* "Current Conditions, Community and Communications (Assessment of Community Life in the Local Community)," 1966-1967.

4. The *Survey* would eventually become a source of controversy. S. Elizabeth McDonough, OP, has suggested that the survey went beyond its original purpose of assessing the readiness of American sisters for change and in effect became an instrument promoting change. Ann Carey, *Sisters in Crisis: The Tragic Unraveling of Women's Religious Communities* (Huntington, Indiana; Our Sunday Visitor Inc., 1997), 124.

5. *CSA Study Composite; Prepared from Proposals Submitted by the Sisters of the Congregation for the Delegates to the General Chapter of 1969 by the Self Study Committee.*

6. Ibid., 4.

7. After his death, one of the sisters wrote a letter quoted in the Capuchin necrology: "[He was] Always leaps ahead of most of us, he patiently presented the new and the challenging to us. Even preparing us for Vatican II. He helped to put on the new Christ in the modern church. His influence spread from the east coast to the west coast and beyond." David Belongea, OFM Cap., "Florian Ruskamp, 1918-2000," *The Minutes*, January, 2002, vol. V, no.1, 14-25.

8. *Chronicles*, 1963, 34.

9. de la Jara, a diocesan priest from Spain, was a liberation theologian active in the Christian base community movement in Nicaragua.

10. [Latin American Sisters] *Formation in Action*, 16 May 1969.

11. S. Paulette Shaw, interview by author, 17 November 1997.

12. S. Bertha Bumann, interview by author, 4 August 2002.

13. Larger houses had at least twenty-four members. The "groupings" were comprised of smaller houses, but they were not necessarily contiguous. For example, a house from Kansas could be included with houses from Pennsylvania. *Constitutions of the Congregation of the Sisters of Saint Agnes, Fond du Lac, Wisconsin* (Techny, Ill. Mission Press, 1928), 90.

14. Allowing all professed sisters active and passive voice was already a modification of the constitution which gave this privilege only to sisters who had been ten years professed. At this time, sisters were perpetually professed after six years in temporary vows.

15. Sisters were ranked according to the year of their profession group and within that group their chronological age.

16. Mother Rosita, *Circular Letter,* 21 March 1969.

17. *Chronicles,* 1968-1969, 27.

18. *CSA Constitutions,* part two, "The Government of the Congregation," chapter one, par. 210.

19. S. Julieta Portocarrero represented the native Nicaraguans; two junior sisters were elected and had active voice in the proceedings. A large majority of sisters favored open sessions with some restrictions. *Opinionnaire,* n.d. [1969.]

20. *Perfectae Caritatis* called for a revision of "constitutions, directories, books of customs, of prayers, and ceremonies" and that "obsolete prescriptions...[be] suppressed" and brought into line with conciliar documents.

21. *Report of the Superior General 1963,* 7.

22. *Guidelines for Living; Acts of the Renewal Chapter, 1969,* 1.

23. *Minutes,* Chapter of 1969.

24. Ibid., 10.

25. *The Decalog,* recommendations of the religious life commission.

26. *Guidelines,* 2.

27. *Minutes,* Special Chapter of Affairs, 3 July 1969, 5.

28. According to the *CSA Self Study,* two-thirds of the sisters in health care were not satisfied with the method of communication between personnel in health and allied services and the major superiors. Question A35.

29. Sisters in health care asked for a commission representing those in the field to serve as a consultative and in some instances as a decision-making body. Question A33.

30. *Guidelines,* 3.

31. Ibid., 13.

32. Ibid.

33. *Guidelines,* 15. The greatest dissatisfaction in the congregation appeared to be in regard to obedience. Only 120 sisters believed that obedience permits initiative, creativity, and mature judgment as opposed to the 546 sisters who did not. *CSA Study Composite,* 7.

34. *Guidelines*, 15.
35. *CSA Study Composite*, 7.
36. *Guidelines*, 18.
37. Marian joined other Catholic women's colleges in this venture. According to Thomas M. Landy, "1968 marked the beginning of a massive realignment of gender ideology in Catholic institutions ...." "The College in Context," in Tracy Schier and Cynthia Russet eds., *Catholic Women's Colleges in America* (Baltimore: The Johns Hopkins University Press, 2002), 94.
38. There were already plans to ask Dr. James Hanlon to accept the presidency.
39. *Guidelines*, 20.
40. *Ibid.*, 22.
41. *Chapter 1969 Health Care Report*, 4-5.
42. Ibid.
43. *Sisters Survey*, F 9.
44. *Guidelines*, 28.
45. Ibid.
46. Ibid. Beginning in 1969, sisters who had been professed three years were allowed, but not required, to make perpetual vows.
47. *Guidelines*, 30.
48. *Foreign Missionary Apostolate, Minutes and Follow Up.* 4.
49. *Formation in Action*, 2.
50. Ibid.
51. Although the statements were made in 1969, the difficulties had been long-standing.
52. *Formation in Action*, 3.
53. *Report*, 1-4.The document was signed by each Nicaraguan sister.
54. Ibid., 3.
55. *Foreign Missionary Apostolate*, 5.
56. Ibid., 6.
57. Segundo Galilea was one of Latin America's most respected theologians. A priest of the Archdiocese of Santiago in Chile, he emphasized the connection between faith, poverty, the gospel and social justice and urged personal engagement in the world.
58. *Foreign Missionary Apostolate*, 6.
59. Ibid., 7.
60. S. Mary Charlotte O'Neill, *Reply to Questionnaire Addressed to Former General Councilors,* January 1997.
61. On one memorable occasion, S. Mary Sheila Burns defused a particularly incendiary discussion by arriving at the session with a fire extinguisher.
62. *Perfectae Caritatis.*
63. Metanoia marks the moment of personal or historical repentance or change of mind.

64.   Mother Rosita, *Memoirs*, 7.
65.   "Obituary," n.d. S. Rosita died August 21, 1987.
66.   Ibid.
67.   S. Claude Feldner, interview by author, 10 February 1995.

Chapter XIII ~ Continuing in Faith

1.   S. Madonna Dionis, interview with author, 27 May 2004.
2.   S. Rachel Doerfler, *Qualities of a Transforming Experience*, unpublished paper, 1978.
3.   *Report of the Superior General of the Congregation of St. Agnes for the Four-Year term July 14, 1969-1973*. S. John Baptist described the entire document in those terms.
4.   At the beginning of her term in office, S. John Baptist took a Management Development and Training Workshop in which she created a set of personal objectives. She wrote: "1) to live a free person, dependent on God, sensitive to others, but never unduly limited or dominated by people's opinions or expectations of me, 2) to be prudently, consistently honest and straightforward in my dealing and relationships with my Sisters, 3) to be available, particularly in difficulties, not so much to answer questions and solve problems, but to share in doing so, 4) to make possible a comfortable, loving, trusting relationship between the community and its administration, 5) to be open to insights, suggestions, recommendations, observations from the community; to implement where and as reasonably possible, 6) to push, prod, inspire and hopefully share in a leap from the comfortably mediocre to the discomfort of radically living the Gospel, that is, from being to being holy, 7) to personally respect and encourage respect for the capabilities and talents and limitations of each Sister. Here lies our strength, 8) to break through the work syndrome 'my worth is in the work I do.' This isn't meant to discourage work or encourage indifferent performance. It simply means to place value on the person as person. She is not *being used*, 9) to urge, promote and provide the broadening of personal, community and local perspectives to global vision and concern." [1969].
5.   *Chronicles*, 1969-1970, 11.
6.   The 1969 Chapter had followed the Holy See's instruction on religious formation which permitted sisters to make perpetual vows any time, with the farthest limit of time-extension being nine years. *Chronicles* 1969-1970, 27.
7.   Innovations during this period were renewal week-ends for sisters in temporary vows and the Middle Years' Workshops. *Formation a Lifelong Process: a Report to the General Chapter*, 1977.
8.   The congregation made efforts to approach the issue gently. The first stage, pre-retirement, followed after the sister left her full-time job. Sisters did vol-

unteer work of all kinds, visiting the sick, helping out in the schools as tutor, librarian, or teacher's aid, or helping in parish ministries. These sisters did not like to think of themselves as "pre-retired" or "retired." Retirement would come later.

9.   The rationale for the program was given by S. Juliana Kohne: "Many a religious ... is plagued with the thought 'What am I going to do when I can no longer do the work I have been doing for many years?' Deeply imbedded in our nature are three desires: the desire to belong, the desire to contribute, the desire to be needed .... It is precisely an attempt to fulfill these desires, to dissipate fears, and to develop ...positive attitudes toward aging and retirement that the program was initiated." *History and Structure of Program for Pre-Retirement and Retirement Planning,* July 1976, 31.

10.   S. Francis Assisi Pielmeier, *Reply to Questionnaire Addressed to Former General Councilors,* January 1977.

11.   *Guidelines for Living for the Apostolate; Acts of the Renewal Chapter, 1969,* 10.

12.   They were Sisters Madonna Dionis and Judith Schmidt, elementary education; S. Bonita Willnecker, secondary education; S. Lucina Halbur, health and allied services, and S. Colette Hartman, the foreign missions.

13.   S. Madonna Dionis, *Reply to Questionnaire Addressed to the Apostolic Councilors,* January 1977.

14.   S. Carol Geels, *Reply to Questionnaire Addressed to the Apostolic Councilors,* January 1977.

15.   *Guidelines,* 3.

16.   *Ministry in CSA,* Chapter 1981, 3.

17.   *Chronicles,* 1969-1970, 10.

18.   S. Michaela O'Brien, *Reply to Questionnaire Addressed to the Apostolic Councilors,* January 1977.

19.   S. Lucina Halbur, interview with author, 20 November 1999.

20.   S. Michaela O'Brien, *Reply to Questionnaire Addressed to the Apostolic Councilors,* January 1977.

21.   S. Michaela O'Brien, Reply.

22.   The continuing negotiations in Hays between St. Anthony Hospital and Hadley Hospital is a case in point.

23.   *Guidelines,* 11.

24.   Ibid.

25.   *Guidelines,* Appendix, 6.

26.   *Guidelines,* 12.

27.   *Proceedings, CSA Renewal Chapter, 1969-70,* Vol. II, 2 June 1970, 3. At the end of the session, the chair of the commission on the apostolate gave the commission's answers to the questions. 1) Sisters should not go outside the community until they feel they are an integral part of the community. 2) We

should do so when the ecclesial request and the individual's expressed interest coincide. Essential priorities for education are: religious education, education of the poor, education that is innovative. 3) There is very little data on this project, and it deserves very serious study. 4) Cultivate many good friendships within CSA. Seek counseling where necessary. 5) Community responsibilities involve some attempts through the house chapter to create unity through acceptance of each other, a deep appreciation and understanding of diversity among us, and provision as well as such contacts as regional meetings, days of recollection and contacts with sisters in nearby houses. Alienations can take place within and without community apostolates, and responsibility to remedy such alienations rests both with the individual and the community.

28.   When the plan of government was accepted, it was also referred to the government commission for refinement of detail. *Guidelines*, 5.

29.   CSA, *Summons to Sanctity in Joyful Service Interim Constitution: Special Chapter Acts* (Fond du Lac Wisconsin: privately printed, 1970), 67. The first section of this chapter describes the congregation's struggle with its internal adaptations; the second, with the changes that took place in the ministries and the role of the sister within those ministries. Through it all the congregation held firm in its determination to foster the spirit of renewal that would shape the congregation for the twenty-first century.

30.   *Summons*, 63.

31.   Ladislas Örsy had suggested the institution of a tribunal with proper judicial power as a means to resolve doubts about the interpretation of the constitutions, correct faulty decisions or perceived injustices, etc. It proved to be a concept clearly contrary to the ethos of the congregation. Örsy, 205-207.

32.   Daniel Yankelovich, "How American Individualism is Evolving," *The Public Perspective* February/March 1998. <http://www.danyankelovich.com/howamerican.html> Internet; accessed 24 August 2004.

33.   The New Age is a heterogeneous movement of individuals. Among the fundamental beliefs held by many new age followers: pantheism, reincarnation, karma, personal transformation, ecological responsibility, universal religion, the unfolding of a new world order. *New Age Spirituality: a.k.a. Self-Spirituality, New Spirituality, Mind-body-spirit.* www.religioustolerance.org/newage.htm> Internet; accessed 28 August 2004.

34.   At the beginning of the sixties, the *Catholic Periodical Index* listed several hundred articles under the heading religious life—in 1970 there were fewer than fifteen.

35.   "Priests and spiritual directors were, often, just as ambivalent about change. One monsignor who addressed a large group of sisters told us that in five

years all of us would be married. (He said this in 1965)." S. Marie Wagner, *CSA Leadership in Relation to the Times,* unpublished paper, October 1996.

36. S. John Baptist, *Renewal: A Journey in Faith,* unpublished paper, n.d.
37. The Somoza family, however, was supportive of missionary endeavors. Bishop Niedhammer was able to get some economic concessions for missionary activities. In addition, President Somoza gained great credit with the people of the Río Coco region by building five brick school buildings. S. Francis Borgia Dreiling, letter to author, April 1998.
38. Tomás Borge, Carlos Fonseca, and Silvio Mayorga.
39. "Theological reflection means bringing a faith perspective to the realities we look at in order to work for social justice. Its goal is pastoral and practical: it aims at transformation of social structures and institutions and at fuller personal integration and conversion." *Jesuit Center for Theological Reflection Bulletin,* <www.jctr.org/bulletins> Internet, accessed 30 December 2004.
40. Liberation theology argues that the church should work actively to combat social, political, and economic oppression. The movement is international but especially active in Latin America and bases its case on Jesus Christ's ministry to the poor and outcasts of society.
41. Many Christian theologians used Marxism as a means of analyzing social forces, but held that their ultimate end differed. Richard H. Ullman, "At War with Nicaragua," *Foreign Affairs* 42 (Fall 1983): 1047.
42. Originally the National Liberation Front, FLN, the party paid tribute to Augusto Sandino by incorporating his name in their title.
43. The earthquake measured 6.2 on the Richter Magnitude Scale.
44. S. Bertha Bumann, *Account of Earthquake,* to the congregation, 6 January 1973.
45. *Proposals: Chapter 1973.*
46. S. Francis Assisi Pielmeier, to the congregation, 6 December 1972.
47. S. John Baptist, *Report of the Superior General of the Congregation of St. Agnes for the Four-Year Term, July 14, 1969 to July 14,1973,* 1-2.
48. Ibid.
49. *Minutes of the 1973 Chapter,* 9 July 1972, 22.
50. Ibid., 21.
51. Sacred Congregation of Religious, letter to CSA, 10 July 1972.
52. S. John Baptist, *Renewal: A Journey in Faith,* speech delivered at the Community of Our Lady, Oshkosh, Wisconsin, June 1974, 6.
53. A community composed of sisters in different ministries.
54. Extended apostolates was the term given to service other than that traditionally undertaken by the congregation.
55. *CSA Challenge,* No. 4, 6.
56. *Chapter Report, 1973,* No. 4, 3.

57. Raymond L. Fitz, SM, and Lawrence J. Cada, SM, saw religious orders historically experiencing cycles of breakdown and conflict, which led to darkness and exploration, and which eventually may lead, after personal transformation of members, into reintegration. "The Recovery of Religious Life," 34 (*Review for Religious*, 1975/76), 690-718.

58. It is difficult, of course, to see the old convent in its final hours, stripped of its antique Victorian innards, its chapel windows gone, the lightning rods removed from the roof, the latticed gazebo hauled away from the grounds, and with only the outer walls concealing the silent abandonment within. Even the last gentle ringing of the old convent bell seemed to sharpen an awareness of a painful parting with the past ... But no matter what the memory, the old convent soon will be gone. Yet this is merely an adjustment for the Sisters of St. Agnes who have moved into remodeled motherhouse quarters in the former nursing school building so that the health care needs of the Fond Lac area can be met with a modern, expanded hospital addition. *Chronicles*, 1975, 5.

59. S. Beatrice Grams, *CSA Finances*, n.d.

60. When Congress passed the Social Security Act in 1935, coverage did not include persons with a vow of poverty. The combination of a growing elderly population and skyrocketing hospital expenses led to the passage in 1965 of a bill designed to provide all older Americans with extensive health insurance—Medicare. According to Sister Margaret Kern, SP, General Treasurer for the Sisters of St. Mary of the Woods at the time of this legislation, religious institutes then became interested in acquiring coverage for their members. Congress did approve an act. After prolonged study and consultation, religious agreed on a method for determining the basis for the taxation. "The method was to compute the actual cost for the living expenses of the sister/brother such as food, clothing, medical, housing, personal supplies, etc. Each year the congregation ... would compute the actual average living expense and pay the combined rate (employee/employer) of tax on the average for each member covered by the program. This expense became the amount to be considered as income and so also the basis of the paid benefit when the individual reached sixty-two or sixty-five years of age. Each congregation determined the age of retirement. After review, Congress agreed and passed the bill in 1972 .... The legislation permitted an institute to enter the program retroactively five years by paying in the proper amount of tax for its eligible members over those five years." S. Margaret Kern, SP., e-mail to Regina Siegfried, ASC, 11 November 2004.

61. Two schools closed: St. Ignatius in Houghton, Michigan, and St. Joseph in Carnegie, Pennsylvania. Among the schools which experienced with-

drawals of sisters were: Canevin High School, Pittsburgh; Holy Trinity, Kewaskum, Wisconsin; St. Isidore, Cloverdale, Illinois; St. Jude, Wauwatosa, Wisconsin; St. Alphonsus, New Munster, Wisconsin; St. Lawrence, Muncie, Indiana; St. Louis, Fond du Lac, Wisconsin; St. Fidelis, Victoria, Kansas; St. Mark, Two Rivers, Wisconsin; St. Mary Help of Christians, West Allis, Wisconsin; St. Mary, Mayville, Wisconsin; St. Mary, Hays, Kansas, and St. Zachary, Des Plaines, Illinois.

62. *Harlem Sunday News*, 28 June 1970, sec. M, 18.

63. *Chronicles*, 1969-1970, 8.

64. S. Donna Innes, CSA. *The Philosophical and Psychological Perspectives of Instruction in Relation to Hanlon's Theory of Education.* (Master's thesis. School of Education, University of Dayton, 1976), 1.

65. The structure was severely criticized because school principals were not represented while Marian College was over-represented.

66. Dr. Kramer had previously been Dean of Mt. St. Paul College in Waukesha, Wisconsin. He had become acquainted with Dr. Hanlon at Marquette University.

67. The TV channel suspended operations on 19 November 1972. The faculty wrote and produced ten programs dealing with themes—the five dealing with practical applications of the theme were not completed. The expected grants to finance the production did not arrive.

68. During the first semester the faculty studied Dr. Hanlon's theories; beginning with the second semester, elementary school faculties were given released time to write curricula and syllabi for their programs.

69. S. Leanne Sitter, e-mail to author, 23 September 2004.

70. *Chronicles*, 1975-1976, 9.

71. Single-sex schools all but lost favor in the sixties, in part due to a developing feminist consciousness which turned against such institutions. Women's colleges driven by the need to retain students opened their doors to men. Thomas M. Landy, "The Colleges in Context," in Tracy Schier and Cynthia Russet, *Catholic Women's Colleges in America* (Baltimore: The Johns Hopkins University Press, 2002), 75.

72. [The plan] called for an articulated school system with self-actualization as the basic goal of education. Change would be initiated at the college level where all the components of education would be evaluated and modified in terms of the envisioned goal. According to Hanlon, "[The plan] would demand some drastic changes in the college climate, beginning with the curriculum. Separate subjects, as such, will need to be relinquished. Old methodologies need to be abandoned for those which accent insight, discovery, inquiry, evaluation."*Minutes of the General Council.* 27 September 1969.

73. The study was based on the recommendations of the leading expert in curriculum design in higher education, Paul Dressel from Michigan State. The

freshman year focused on man in himself, the sophomore, man in society, and the upper division, man in his profession. There were interdisciplinary elements in the plan as well as experiments in team teaching.

74. Ibid.

75. In 1973, the number rose from eighteen to thirty-five, which included the president, academic dean, secretaries, housekeeper, and additional faculty. Ibid., 2.

76. The nursing faculty applied Hanlon's principles when constructing their curriculum.

77. Lance J. Kramer, letter to author, 23 September 2004.

78. The computerization of the Marian campus began in 1973 with the purchase, by the Student Senate for the library, of one hand-held calculator for $143.00. Bruce Prall, interview by author, 6 October 2006.

79. Between 1940 and 1965, insurance plans grew from covering 9 percent of the population to 71.4 percent, leading to increased expenditures in facilities, medical, technology in research, in additional personnel, and increases in physicians' fees and hospital costs. The increased costs excluded millions of people, particularly the elderly. In 1950 the federal government established a program to allocate grants to states to pay hospitals and physicians' fees, but it was inadequate. In 1964, the Kerr-Mills bill was passed that provided Medicare coverage for hospitalization and physician's fees for the elderly and Medicaid coverage for the poor.

80. The hospitals had been separately incorporated in the 1960s.

81. Between 1965 and 1975 the number of Catholic hospitals dropped from 803 to 671 and the number of hospital sisters declined from 13,618 to 8,980, Kauffman, 283.

82. *Minutes of the General Council*, 12 May 1971.

83. Oren Windholz, e-mail to author, 21 July 2005. Windholz began his employment at St. Anthony in 1966, was appointed CEO in 1972, and retired in 1991.

84. *Minutes of the Annual Meeting of the Board of Directors of the Congregation of Sisters of St. Agnes of Fond du Lac, Wisconsin, Inc*, 29 November 1971, 6. The Medical Dental Association at this time was pressuring for one hospital to purchase the other, or both, either to become part of a new corporation, or sell to a third party.

85. *Chronicles*, 1971-1973, 17.

86. *Chronicles*, 1973-1974, 17.

87. *Chronicles*, 1974-1975, 13; *1976-1977*, 13.

88. *Minutes of the General Council*, 12 May 1971.

89. *Chronicles*, 1971-1973, 17.

90. The first laymen were elected to the Board of Directors at St. Thomas Hospital in the expectation that the election of local trustees would provide

a closer link for community involvement with the hospital. *Prairie Drummer*, 14 October 1972.

91. *Chronicles*, 1972-1973, 17-18.
92. *Chronicles*, 1969-1970, 22.
93. Ibid.
94. *Monroe Times*, 10 January 1974, 1.
95. *Chronicles*, 1974-1975, 14.
96. *Minutes of Board of Directors*, 17 December 1975, 6.
97. *Chronicles*, 1975-1976, 11.
98. *Chronicles*, 1976-1977, 13.
99. *Chronicles*, 1971-1973, 17.
100. *Chronicles*, 1973-1974, 16-17.
101. *Chronicles*, 1974-1975, 14-15.
102. S. Joan Wirz, interview by author, 12 October 2004.
103. *Annals*, 28 January 1976.
104. The unionization of health care professionals has always created a dilemma for Catholic hospitals. Catholic social teaching casts unions and collective bargaining not only as a human right but a positive good in the modern work place. But management has a natural reluctance to lose its flexibility by placing itself in a position where it must negotiate for wages, benefits, working conditions, and rights. In addition, the ultimate weapon of the labor union is the right to strike, and the majority of health care professionals have regarded withholding their services as the antithesis of the ethics of their profession.
105. *Annals*, 27 June 1978.
106. *Annals*, 13 March 1980.
107. *Minutes of Board of Directors*, 17-18 December 1973, 9.
108. *Minutes of Board of Directors*, 2 December 1974, 8.
109. *Chronicles*, 1975-1976, 12.
110. The original bequest stated that if the Home were used for a purpose other than the care of the elderly it would revert to the Boyle Family.
111. The first Agnesians to work at the Catholic Welfare Office were Sisters Agnes Rita Fisette, Francis Ann Karlin and Mary Mattern. In 1974 the office was renamed the Service Center of Catholic Social Services. At that time it was funded by Catholic Charities and Ladies of Charity.
112. The Italian sisters had been invited by the previous bishop during the 1950s when a major source of employment, Brookley Field, had been closed. Tension had developed between the Catholic Welfare Office and the Catholic Social Services staffed by clergy, laity, and the Trinitarian Sisters. "The latter is a very sophisticated office-based professional apostolate. Catholic Welfare is simple and direct service with a minimum of record-keeping. Bishop May favored the welfare approach and defended the

Verona sisters. The Vicar from Social Services in the diocese is lodged in the Social Service and embarrassed by the breach between the two services and is eager to integrate them." *Minutes of the Executive Board of the Congregation of the Sisters of St. Agnes,* 9 May 1973.

113. S. Jean Salchert, *The Story of the Sisters of St. Agnes in Mobile,* unpublished manuscript, 1995.

114. S. John Baptist, "Dear Sisters," 19 March 1977.

115. *General Chapter 1977,* 8 July 1977, No. 2, 1.

116. Ibid.

117. "Categorization of Community Values," *Bulletin,* No. 5, 1977, 5

118. They were: the horarium; house chapter; recreation; vacation; celebration of holidays and holy days; home visits; and life style. Ibid.

119. *General Chapter, 1977,* 8.

120. Ibid.

Chapter XIV ~ Hope in Our Hearts

1. S. Judith Schmidt, *Message to the Chapter of 1977.*

2. Rome had given congregations a limited time to experiment. At the end of that period, the constitutions were to be sent to Rome for review, and, it was hoped, approval. With the help of a canon lawyer, a committee would then write the document in language acceptable to Rome, return it to the congregation for suggestions, rewrite it, and submit it. The process would take at least six or seven years.

3. In addition to the formal council meetings, the general council met numerous times. A note after the conclusion of the March 20, 1978, meeting reads: "Sister Miriam Therese informed us that this was the 88th meeting since July 25 of more than one hour in duration which all four members of the Generalate attended."

4. The importance of meetings in the congregation was underlined by the decision, not a wholly popular one, to fill in the swimming pool in the motherhouse in order to provide a large meeting room.

5. The processes included private meditation, and small and large group sharing.

6. "A Community in Transition," *Corporate Renewal Program, Chapter '81,* 1.

7. Ibid., 1-2.

8. Ibid., 2.

9. "A Community in Transition," 3, 4.

10. *Accountability Session, June 25-2, 1979,* 1.

11. S. Judith Schmidt, *Reply to Questionnaire Addressed to Former General Superiors, January 1997.*

12. A tertianship provided further time of reflection, prayer and study for the younger professed sisters. It has often been called a second novitiate.

13. On December 27, 1974, Sandinistas seized the home of a former government official and took as hostages a group of leading Nicaraguans. They were able to force the government to pay 1,000,000 US dollars in ransom and release fourteen Sandinista prisoners.

14. One who lives in a rural area or works on a farm.

15. "These events [the tortures, imprisonments and killings] as well as sharing with fellow teachers and students in Rosita, the ideals of Liberation Theology, seeing the unjust structures that existed and the abuses of power...put me in an attitude of support for the Sandinistas who were operating clandestinely in the area of the mines. There came a moment where I was asked to collaborate actively in small ways with the 'guerrilleros' and I accepted." S. Marise Meis to author, 30 April 1998. S. Marise transported Seiko watches the men used to coordinate their activities.

16. The experience of the Capuchins illustrates the struggle that missionaries faced in their relations with their host country. At their annual retreat in June 1976 "Friars David Zywiec and Theodore Neihus brought with them the names of around 250 persons who had disappeared. What to do? We were split 50/50 ... If we denounced we could cause a blood bath in the country. If we did not, blood would continue to flow at any cost ... Something strange happened during these days of intense soul searching. We came to the last day of the retreat and still had not reached a decision. At the last session Reynold Rynda called for a moment of silent prayer to the Holy Spirit. We fell into a dead silence ... Suddenly we began singing *Come, Holy Ghost* ... Reynold now called for a vote of hands...We went around the room. Miracle of Miracles!! It was 100% that we denounce the disappearances." David Belongea, OFM, Cap., letter to author, 19 May 2004.

17. S. Marise Meis, 3.

18. S. Bertha Bumann to S. Rachel Doerfler, 22 September 1978.

19. Ibid.

20. The Sandinistas were receiving military supplies from Costa Rica and Cuba and had secret training camps in Costa Rica and Honduras.

21. In September 1980, Anastasio Somoza was assassinated in Paraguay.

22. S. Eileen Mahony, interview by author, 18 November 1997.

23. "We Believe," *Nicaraguan Agnesian Week, 1979*, November, 1979.

24. Ibid.

25. Ibid.

26. S. Raymond Grieble, interview by author, 14 February 1999.

27. The ruling Junta was composed of five top Sandinista officials.

28. Some of the missionaries hoped that the contact with religious Nicaraguans would benefit the young Cubans. S. Emily Schug wrote from Rosita: "We have contact with nineteen of the Cuban teachers working in Nicaragua. There are fine young people, all atheists, but from families where the oldsters are Catholic. Many are learning the bible. Hopefully before two years are up, they will know Christ." S. Emily Schug to family, 12 April 1980.

29. Compulsory party gatherings and festivities were scheduled during the usual times for religious services. Religion could not be taught during school hours in parochial schools. Sandinista posters replaced the pictures in the schools. Religious iconography was used for political purposes. Salaried personnel were required to attend "conscientization" classes.

30. The Reagan government, fearing the spread of communism and Nicaragua's connections with the USSR and Cuba, was inimical to the revolution.

31. The eleven Nicaraguan Agnesians saw their families affected by the new government in very different ways. While one Sister's family, owners of a coffee plantation, lost property, discrimination against the middle class and ethnic groups was experienced most severely by the Chow family. S. Nancy, whose Chinese father had been a successful merchant, saw her sister in prison for almost a month and the Chinese forced to leave the Atlantic Coast. S. Nancy Chow, interview by author, 17 November 1998.

32. *Los Cristianos Están con la Revolución*, Costa Rica: Departamenta Ecumentista de Investigaciones in Humberto Belli, *Breaking Faith: the Sandinista Revolution and Its Impact on Freedom and Christian Faith in Nicaragua* (Puebla Institute: Crossway Books, 1986), 3.

33. S. Eileen Mahony, letter to family and friends, 10 October 1979.

34. Eventually the Bishop's Conference asked those priests to step down. Some resisted and finally the bishops compromised by allowing them to remain provided they did not perform their priestly duties in public.

35. The term "popular Church" is generally taken to refer to those who embrace and practice liberation theology through "base communities" that serve for both Bible study and political action.

36. Peter Davis, *Where Is Nicaragua?* (New York: Simon and Schuster, 1987), 301.

37. S. Judith Schmidt, e-mail to author, 5 January 2005.

38. S. Judith Schmidt, *Circular Letter*, August 1980.

39. Because the nominal process squeezed out marginal opinions, sisters who wished could send separate cards or proposals to the committee.

40. There was continuing tension because of a perception that the same sisters were always elected as delegates and that the large number of delegates concentrated in Fond du Lac had too much weight. There was a proposal which would give active and passive voice in elections only to those active-

ly engaged in the apostolate as there was fear that the sisters in the retirement home would vote as a bloc. Others asked that the community provide statements on a nominee's views and positions prior to voting. This did not happen. In the long run, results seemed to have been most influenced by a sister's apostolate: eleven sisters were from elementary education; ten from secondary; seven from Marian College; six from Health and Allied Services; three from Nicaragua; nine were from the motherhouse. Thirty-two sisters resided in Wisconsin; the greatest number from any other geographic area was four. The delegates had an age range of forty years: one sister was seventy years old; ten Sisters were in their sixties; fifteen in their fifties; fifteen in their forties and eight in their thirties.

41. Members discerned their ministries as a matter of personal preference and call. At the same time, members were no longer guaranteed employment in congregation-sponsored ministries.

42. *CSA Needs Assessment, 1981.*

43. Other religious communities, grappling with emotion-laden issues such as the habit and government, had found outside facilitators useful. They have been used in CSA ever since.

44. *The Myers-Briggs Type Indicator (MBTI)*, based on Jungian psychology, was designed to measure characteristics described as energizing, attending, deciding, and living. The instrument classifies personalities according to the styles of understanding and interacting different people prefer to employ. It was hoped that committee work would be facilitated if the members had a better understanding of themselves and each other.<www.humanmetrics. com/cgi-win/JTypes.2.asp> Internet; accessed 24 July 2006.

45. *"Leadership Report '81,"* 1981. Members of the constitutions writing committee were: Sisters Mary Charlotte O'Neill, coordinator, Edith Brotz; Jean Hinderer, Joyann Repp, Patricia Hayes and Rita Little. S. Margaret Mary Modde, OSF, was engaged as a canon lawyer to guide and direct the committee.

46. S. Judith Schmidt, "Address to the Chapter Delegates," *CSA Report '81*, 6.

47. Ibid.

48. *Statement of Corporate Thrust—Chapter 1981.*

49. *CSA Report '81*, 4.

50 Ibid., 5.

51. Ibid., 6.

52. S. Judith Schmidt, *Address to the Chapter Delegates, 1981*, 7. The constitutions state only that "perpetually professed members wear a plain gold ring as a symbol of their religious profession."

53. *To the Delegates of the General Chapter of 1977, Government Decentralization*, signed paper distributed to Chapter delegates.

54. *Constitutions and Directives*, 1985, 47.
55. Ibid., 41-51.
56. The *Minutes* of that day do not record the vote.
57. Not without some unhappiness. "I feel as though I have been manipulated .... It also disturbs me very much that there is no choice in the matter .... As I understand it, the last chapter did vote for a revision of the present structure. Why all the effort into a new model, and no effort in the revision of a structure that has facilitated us for the past twelve years?" S. Kathleen Ries to the council. 12 April 1981.
58. *Constitutions and Directives*, 1985, 38.
59. *Government Structure for the Congregation of Sisters of St. Agnes: Approved by the General Chapter, 1981.*
60. S. Carol Geels, *Reply.*
61. The first regional coordinators were: Sisters Alice Marie Skiko, Esther Hicks, Jean Steffes, Joyann Repp, Rachel Doerfler, and Raymond Grieble.
62. *Contrarevolucionarios.* The core members of this group was composed mainly of members of the old *Guardia.*
63. Protestants were harassed and Catholics saw their bishop, Salvador Schlaefer, OFM Cap., subjected to a hundred petty harassments as he attempted to protect and remain with his people.
64. One unforgettable day an armed Sandinista marched into the convent in Waspam and demanded that one of the sisters whom he found attractive be handed over to him. In spite of his rifle, he was no match for S. Raymond Grieble, a woman not to be intimidated, who simply said, "You are going no further." But it was impossible not to wonder, "Would we be as lucky next time?" S. Eileen Mahony, interview by author, 18 November 1998.
65. S. Maureen Courtney to S. Judith Schmidt, 26 September 1982.
66. S. Bertha Bumann, interview by author, 15 February 1999.
67. Ibid.
68. One of the changes that came with the revision of the constitutions was the ability to share the convent. It was used for courses, meetings, Vicariate Assemblies, piano concerts, etc. Marise Meis, *Changes in Latin America since Vatican Council II*, presented 13 January 2000 at the CSA Regional Assembly, 2.
69. S. Kenneth Struckhoff, *Only He Has the Answer*, unpublished paper, 30 April 1982.
70. S. Bertha Bumann, interview by author, 15 February 1999.
71. S. Raymond Grieble, interview by author. 15 February 1999.
72. S. Judith Schmidt had also planned to visit houses in Rosita, Waspam, and Puerto Cabezas but was refused permission.
73. S. Judith Schmidt, *Circular Letter*, 16 February 1982.

74. Christian, 263.
75. S. Raymond Grieble, Ibid.
76. S. Eileen Mahony, Ibid.
77. "No single decision the commandantes ever made was as permanently dev-astating to their worldwide prestige." Stephen Kinzer, *The Blood of Brothers* (New York: G. P. Putnam's Sons, 1991), 204.
78. Years later S. Raymond learned that Don Luce who had driven them back was imprisoned by the Sandinistas for three years for his kindness to the sisters.
79. S. Patricia Hayes, interview by author, 24 March 2005.
80. S. Patricia Hayes quoted in the *Nanty-Glo* [Pennsylvania] *Journal*, 5 October 1983.
81. S. Anne Jude Van Lanen, *Notes*, February 2004.
82. S. Colette Hartman, interview by author, 28 June 1997.
83. The Peace Commissions, the result of the Esquipulas II, attempted to secure the release of prisoners, sought to facilitate dialogues between the Sandinistas and the Contras and set up contacts for family members who had escaped to other countries.
84. Bishop Salvador Schlaefer to the Sisters of St. Agnes, 16 April 1983.
85. S. Eileen Mahony, interview by author, 15 September 1999.
86. A large donation was given to Hazotte ministries to be used by St. Francis Home for projects of service. A house adjacent to the Home was purchased for $100,000 to serve as a residential option for elderly non-dependent persons. The house, named St. Clare Terrace, was remodeled and the first persons took up residence there in fall 1984. Federal subsidies were obtained for this facility.
87. Grants were given to some of the institutions where the sisters minister. The intent was that the money be invested and the interest used by the institution for tuition assistance or aiding the needy. The 1985 *Leadership Report* shows grants given to Beloit Catholic High School, Marian College, St. Agnes Hospital, St. Francis Home, and St. Mary's Springs High School.
88. The program lends money at lower interest rates than normally procured from other investments.
89. *Leadership Report, 1985*, 13.
90. *Congregation of St. Agnes Long Range Planning Report*, September 1984.
91. Ibid., 7-8.
92. Ibid., 10-20.
93. The affiliate period is a time of decision-making in which both the interested woman and the community examine her possible call to religious life.
94. The woman lives in a CSA local community and experiences CSA values, spirit, tradition, and spirituality, while participating in community events and daily living activities.

95. The novice continues discerning her call to live as a Sister of St. Agnes. The novitiate extends over a two-year period.

96. Following the novitiate, the woman is a temporarily professed sister for three to six years.

97. "Pre-retirement" was a term with which the community has never felt comfortable.

98. "CSA Sponsorship Statement," *Leadership Report, 1985,* 21.

99. Thirty-three proposals, some covering much of the same ground, were also submitted. Expressive of conservative values, one asked that sisters always be called "Sister," that they return to convents at an early hour, and raised the possibility of returning to a uniform habit.

100. *Chronicles,* 1983-84, 16.

101. The belief that leadership in the military should not be left entirely to products of a military education provided one argument for joining the program as well as the opportunity given to students to help provide for their education. The majority of students in the ROTC were nursing students.

102. *Chronicles,* 1984-1985, 11.

103. *Leadership Report 1985,* 22-23.

104. *Chronicles,* 1979-1980, 23.

105. *Chronicles,* 1980-1981, 28.

106. *Chronicles,* 1984-1985, 14.

107. S. Anne Jude Van Lanen, *Notes,* February 2004.

108. *Chronicles,* 1980-1981, 27.

109. *Annals,* 9 January 1985.

110. *Chronicles,* 1978-1979, 20.

111. "I did often refer to his [Hanlon's] ideas in my graduate course work and in my teaching later. I appreciated the frame he provided for teaching and curriculum development, and was truly disappointed his work did not continue—with some practical refinements the "in-the-trenches teachers could have made …. I am sure his philosophy infiltrated most of my educational works even today …." S. Julie Ann Krahl, e-mail to author, 10 November 2005.

112. They were influenced by the principles of Shalom Ministries: described as "mission in reverse, bridge-building and contextualization." Sharon Baudry, letter to author, 4 April 2005.

113. Ibid.

114. *CSA Leadership Report, 1985,* 51.

115. Ibid., 43.

116. S. Judith Schmidt, interview by author, 28 October 2002.

117. *CSA Report 1985,* 3.

118. According to Robert Hoover, who developed an analysis of social change, organizations grow, decline [breakdown], and if they resist change,

inevitably disappear. S. Mary Maher, SSND, sees in religious life since Vatican II the concurrence of both renewal and decline—with the result that congregations are faced with the decision between re-foundation and death. Mary Maher, SSND, *Between Imagination and Doubt; Religious Life in Postmodern Culture*. Lecture given at the Washington Theological Union, http://www.wtu.edu/news/lectures/rel-life-symp-maher.htm>Internet; accessed 15 December 2004.

Chapter XV ~ Commitment to Transformation

1. According to Walter Brueggemann, "The prophetic task is to get people to have a perceptive consciousness that will stand against the dehumanizing and death dealing aspects of our culture." Quoted in Elizabeth A. Dreyer, "Prophetic Voice in Religious Life," *Review for Religious*, 62 (May-June), 254." The official identification of religious with the prophetic role found its first significant mention in the year 1978 in the church document "Religious Life and Human Promotion," quoted in Michael H. Crosby, OFM Cap., *Can Religious Life Be Prophetic?* (New York; The Crossroad Publishing Company, 2005), 11.
2. S. Judith Schmidt, *CSA Report 1985*, 3.
3. The 1976 goals of the LCWR included articulating a contemporary theology of religious life, education for justice, prayer, action, and study on women's issues; collaboration with others to the maximum extent possible. *LCWR Subpages* <http://www.lcwr.org/lcwraboutus/history.htm>Internet; accessed 17 May 2006.
4. Some sisters would have agreed with Ann Carey who wrote: "The writers in *The Changing Sister*, ed. S. M. Charles Borromeo Muckenhirn, (Notre Dame, Indiana: Fides Publishers) deviated from the ... principle that the traditional primary value of Religious men and women is who they *are* –consecrated persons who witness to the transcendent—and instead placed nearly the entire emphasis on what Religious *do*. And they introduced a new primary mission for Religious—social justice—which they claimed had superiority over the traditional apostolates of Religious, even though those traditional apostolates have consistently encompassed social justice issues." *Sisters in Crisis: The Tragic Unraveling of Women's Religious Communities* (Huntington, Indiana; Our Sunday Visitor. Inc), 1997, 112.
5. Ronald Rolheiser, *Against an Infinite Horizon: the Finger of God in Our Every Day Lives, rev. ed., (New York: Crossroad Publishing Company)*, 2001.
6. Nor was it. In his encyclicals, Pope Leo XIII had linked social justice with the natural-law tradition. Fr. John Ryan linked Catholic social thought with the American progressive movement, "and gave to American Catholics the

578   **Endnotes for Chapter XV**

foundation of a social gospel." Jay P. Dolan, *The American Catholic Experience: A History from Colonial Times to the Present* (Garden City, New York: Doubleday & Co., 1985), 343.

7.   "Action on behalf of justice and participation in the transformation of the world fully appear to us as a constitutive dimension of the preaching of the Gospel, or, in other words, of the Church's mission for the redemption of the human race and its liberation from every oppressive situation." World Synod of Catholic Bishops, 1971, *Justice in the World*, <www.osjspm.org/cst/jw.htm.> Internet; accessed 30 June 2005.

8.   Michael Crosby, "Justice," *The New Dictionary of Catholic Spirituality*, ed. Michael Downey (Collegeville, Minnesota: The Liturgical Press, 1993), 578.

9.   *Constitutions and Directives, 1987*, 104.

10.   *CSA Report, 1985*, 27.

11.   *CSA Report, 1985*, 7-23.

12.   *Minutes of the General Council*, 18 August 1985.

13.   For example, the council discussed a policy regarding civil disobedience as early as November. It established the principle that the individual exercises her freedom of conscience in relation to her responsibility as a member of CSA. Ibid., 21 November 1985.

14.   *CSA Report, 1985*, 4-5.

15.   *Minutes of the Joint Session*, August 1987, 3.

16.   *Discernment Process for Ministry and Community*, 10 September 1988.

17.   S. Jean Steffes, *Twists and Turns a Memoir of My Life*, draft, n.d.[2005], 5.

18.   *Minutes of the Meeting of the Ministry Planning Committee*, 2 December 1989.

19.   S. Jean Steffes, "Probing Our Call," *CSA Leadership Report, 1993*, 5.

20.   S. Mary Daniel Turner, "Hold Fast the Dreams," 5 *New Theology Review* (November 1992): 30-44, quoted in Steffes, *The Challenge of Religious Life Today: Putting Out Into the Deep*, 12 February 1993, 25.

21.   S. Jean Steffes, *Advent Letter, 1986*.

22.   CSA, *Statement of Mission*, 1986.

23.   *Chronicles*, 1996-1987, 2.

24.   Sacred Congregation for Religious and for Secular Institutes, *Essential Elements in the Church's Teaching on Religious Life As Applied to Institutes Dedicated to Works of the Apostolate*. <www.ewtn.com/library/papaidoc/eselem.htm> Internet; accessed 8 August 2005.

25.   Lora Ann Quiñonez, CDP, and Mary Daniel Turner, SNDdeN, *The Transformation of American Catholic Sisters*, (Philadelphia: Temple University Press, 1992), 2.

26.   *Constitutions and Directives: Congregation of The Sisters of St. Agnes 1987*, 7.

27.   Ibid., 3.

28.   *Annals*, 4 December 1990.

29. S. Sandra Schneiders explores different perspectives on the issue in "Selling All: Commitment, Consecrated Celibacy, and Community in Catholic Religious Life," *Religious Life in a New Millennium*, vol. 2, (New York: Paulist Press, 2001), 330-352.

30. *Leadership, 1989*, 27-31.

31. Ibid.

32. Ibid.

33. S. Marie Scott, e-mail to author, 4 May 2006.

34. S. Jean Steffes, e-mail to author, 18 May 2006.

35. *CSA Board Minutes*, 15 March 1986.

36. *CSA Board Minutes*, 7 March 1987.

37. Ibid.

38. S. Jean Steffes, *The Challenge of Religious Life Today: Putting Out into the Deep*, 12 February 1993, 15.

39. The program is based on the conversion model used in *The Rite of Christian Initiation of Adults (RCIA)*. The RCIA program is modeled on the catechumenate of the ancient church.

40. *Bringing Forth the Vision: Leadership Report, '89*, 45.

41. Ibid., 13.

42. Sisters who had experienced the poverty of the depression years or grew up hearing stories of their grandparent's struggles believed they understood the meaning of poverty. They soon discovered that the poverty of people oppressed because of differences of race, by inhuman living conditions, by violence and abuse, and by ignorance was of a far different nature.

43. *CSA Leadership Report, 1985*, 1-3.

44. *Chronicles* 1986-1987, 28.

45. *CSA Leadership Report*, 1989, S-2.

46. S. Raymond Grieble, "Notes," in Words of Madre Maureen Courtney, CSA, in *The Weak of the World Confound the Strong*. (Fond du Lac, Wisconsin: Congregation of St. Agnes), 1990.

47. Vehicles were ordinarily not allowed on roads after dusk during the hostilities.

48. *The New York Times*, January 3, 1990, A11.

49. *1989 Assembly Joint Resolution of the State of Wisconsin, Enrolled Joint Resolution Relating to the Life and Public Service of Sister Maureen Courtney*, 4 April 1990.

50. On February 29, 1990, the congregation had a call from the State Department. *Annals*, 29 February 1990.

51. Paul Furiga, Washington News Bureau. *Fond du Lac Reporter*, 3 February 1991, 5.

52. Fr. David Belongea, OFM Cap., pastor in Puerto Cabezas at the time of the ambush, was asked by Bishop Salvador Schlaefer to find out what he could about the attack and who was responsible. A former officer in the

Contras told him that a certain Stedman Faggot, originally a Sandinista but later a Contra, was the target. Neither group trusted him and, it seemed, both had made plans to assassinate him. The Contras' intelligence informed them that Faggot and his sister would be traveling from Managua to Puerto Cabezas in a white pickup. They planned to kill him somewhere along the road. When a white pickup was seen with a man and woman in the front seat, they supposed it was Stedman and his sister. When a group of trigger-happy young Contras patrolling the area saw the white pickup they thought they had their target and began an attack. When they heard Bishop Paul Schmitz shout that they were Catholic missionaries, the young men disappeared. It seemed that the attack was a case of mistaken identity on the part of the Contras and not an attack against the Catholic Church or the North American missionaries. David Belongea, OFM, Cap., e-mail to author, 21 July 2004.

53.   Meis, 4.
54.   A corporate stance is a public statement and/or action agreed upon by a predetermined percentage of the body of members of the organization. Religious congregations commonly take a position in regard to Gospel concerns, human issues, or societal concerns.
55.   This was not accomplished readily, e.g., the Marian College faculty was among those who rejected the proposal the first time on the grounds that a nuclear free zone was an impossibility. It was only with some minor modifications and the fact that CSA again requested an assent that the faculty agreed to accept the proposition.
56.   Feminist theology is described by Peter Steinfels as "a critique of the patriarchal bias built into all sacred texts and traditional teachings, a struggle to recover women's voices in religious history that have been suppressed or marginalized and an effort to employ the previously neglected or excluded insights and experiences of women in rethinking the church's whole range of doctrines, symbols, and rituals." Steinfels, 280.
57.   S. Jean Steffes, *Reply to Questionnaire Addressed to Former General Superiors*, January 1997.
58.   According to church directives, The homily "should ordinarily be given by the celebrant himself. He may entrust it to a concelebrating Priest, or occasionally … to a Deacon, but never to a layperson." Congregation for Divine Worship and Discipline of the Sacraments, *Instruction on the Eucharist*, Liturgy Documentary Series 15 (Washington D. C. : United States Conference of Catholic Bishops, May 2004), 34.
59.   S. Jean Steffes, *Reply*.
60.   At the same time, the Catholic Hospital Association helped the hospitals study the status and options of lay sponsorship under canon law; establish

proper relationships among the local bishop, the sponsoring group and the health-care facility; and set up a process for the annual review of the sponsor's stewardship. Kaufmann, 303.

61. Sponsored Institutions were St. Agnes Hospital, St. Francis Home, and Marian College in Fond du Lac, Wisconsin; St. Anthony Hospital in Hays, Kansas; St. Clare Hospital, Monroe, Wisconsin. Unity House in Chicago was a division of Hazotte Ministry which was sponsored by CSA.

62. Each hospital sponsored by the congregation is dedicated to the promotion of health in all areas of human concern including the physical, spiritual, emotional, and psychological well-being of the patient, family, community, and economically poor. Their mission also includes fostering a sincere spirit of caring service, maintaining and evaluating personnel policies and benefits which reflect human concern for the dignity as well as the physical, spiritual, and emotional needs of all employees. As a Catholic hospital, it is obliged to reflect and promote the teaching of Christ in all relationships and activities. *Chronicles* 1987-1988, 14.

63. *Leadership Report*, 1989, 41.

64. *Chronicles*, 1987-1988, 19.

65. The signing of the federal budget reconciliation package by President Reagan on December 22, 1987, had a particularly traumatic effect. One CEO of an Agnesian hospital said, "If any one significant factor will jeopardize our institutions it is the inadequacy of reimbursement from Federal programs." *Chronicles*, 1987-1988, 15

66. *Chronicles*, 1986-1987, 17.

67. Ibid.

68. *Chronicles*, 1986-1987, 19.

69. *Sisters of St. Agnes Governance Updates 1960-2002*, [2002], 4.

70. "Hospitals Have New Name, New Chief," *The Hays Daily News*, editorial, 9 April 1991.

71. S. Mary Mollison, interview by author, 11 November 2005.

72. Neither hospital had allowed abortions. Sterilizations would be offered by the Hadley Foundation in facilities that would not be leased to the new hospital.

73. Both the congregation and representatives of Hadley Memorial Hospital placed three members on the corporate board. This board appointed the board of directors. The arrangement endured for ten years.

74. The new administration almost immediately authorized $250,000 for marketing and other research to stabilize and advance the college. *Chronicles*, 1985-1986, 31. The following year the congregation guaranteed a $1.2 million dollar loan. *Chronicles*, 1986-1987, 12.

75. Dr. Edward Henry had been professor and chair of the department of government at St. John's University in Minnesota, president of both St. Mary's

College in Notre Dame, Indiana, and St. Michael's College in Vermont. Dr. Henry was also, for seven years, mayor of St. Cloud, Minnesota. In an interview by the local newspaper, Dr. Henry said: "I took on Marian College because I saw great potential here. I like coming back to a small college because I savor the educational advantages—every student gets to develop face-to-face relationships with the faculty. If you want to develop human virtue, it's best done one-to-one." *Fond du Lac Reporter*, 28 August 1986, A5. After leaving Marian, Dr. Henry served as interim president of Belmont Abbey College in Charlotte, North Carolina.

76.   *Chronicles*, 1986-1987, 11. Much of Dr. Henry's success came from his conviction that "The nation needs small colleges like Marian .... They are the overlooked treasuries of American higher education! We need them because they still preserve a sense of direction about the educational process and a certain cohesion in reaching for proper goals. We need them because students learn best when they enjoy a sense of personal security that comes from belonging to a close community .... And what is more conducive to developing a profound respect for our own humanity and that of others than the theological undergirding which characterizes the Marians of our time? And which in their concept of the total person strike the delicate balance between the material and the spiritual; between the secular and the sacred; and between the human and the divine?" Dr. Edward L. Henry, *Why I Came to Marian College*, n.d. Marian College Archives.

77.   During the summer of 1988, Marian College purchased the assets of a for-profit corporation and established an International Values Institute for the College as well as establishing the American Center for Quality and Productivity. These ventures proved less successful.

78.   Ibid., 12.

79.   Ibid., 3.

80.   Ibid.

81.   Ibid., 1.

82.   *CSA Mission Statement*, 1990.

83.   Ibid.

INDEX